Student Teaching: Early Childhood

Practicum Guide
5th Edition

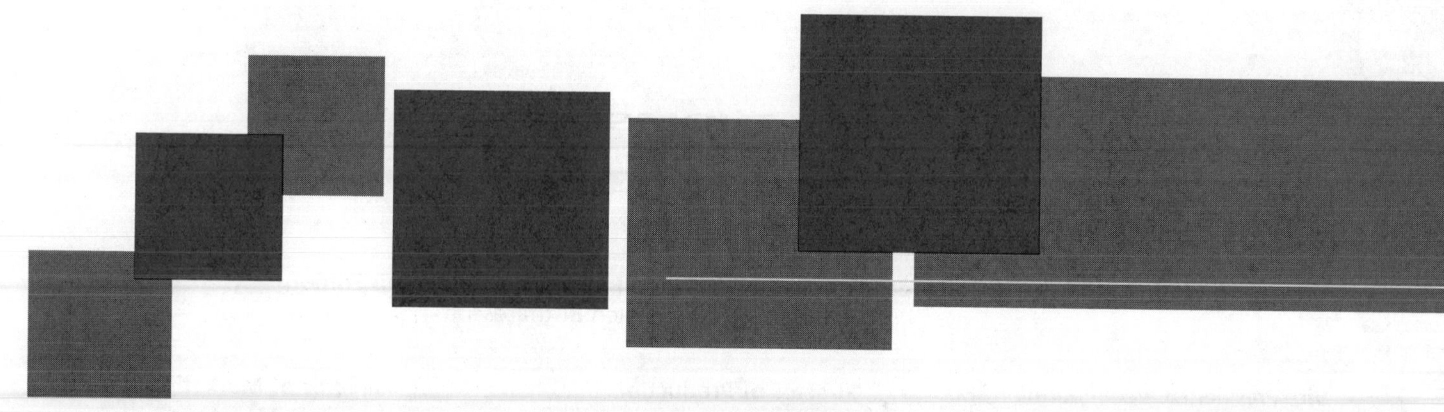

Student Teaching: Early Childhood

Practicum Guide 5th Edition

JEANNE M. MACHADO, EMERITA
San Jose City College

HELEN MEYER-BOTNARESCUE, Ph.D.
California State University—Hayward

THOMSON
DELMAR LEARNING

Australia Canada Mexico Singapore Spain United Kingdom United States

Student Teaching: Early Childhood Practicum Guide, Fifth Edition
Jeanne Machado Helen Botnarescue

Vice President, Career Education SBU:
Dawn Gerrain

Director of Editorial:
Sherry Gomoll

Acquisitions Editor:
Erin O'Connor

Developmental Editor:
Alexis Breen Ferraro

Editorial Assistant:
Ivy Ip

Director of Production:
Wendy A. Troeger

Production Editor:
Joy Kocsis

Technology Project Manager:
Joseph Saba

Director of Marketing
Wendy E. Mapstone

Channel Manager:
Donna J. Lewis

Cover Design:
Andrew Wright

Composition:
Type Shoppe II Productions, Ltd.

Printed in the United States of America
1 2 3 4 5 XXX 08 07 06 05 04

For more information contact Thomson Delmar Learning, Executive Woods, 5 Maxwell Drive, Clifton Park, NY 12065-2919.

Or find us on the World Wide Web at www.thomsonlearning.com, www.delmarlearning.com, or www.earlychilded.delmar.com

Library of Congress Cataloging-in-Publication Data

Machado, Jeanne M.
Student teaching : early childhood practicum guide / Jeanne M. Machado, Helen Meyer-Botnarescue.-- 5th ed.
p. cm.
Includes biliographical references and index.
ISBN 1-4018-4853-2
1. Student teaching--Handbooks, manuals, etc. 2. Early childhood education--Curricula. 3. Lesson planning. I. Meyer-Botnarescue, Helen. II. Title.

LB2157.A3M28 2004
380'.71--dc22

2003068764

NOTICE TO THE READER

Contents

SECTION V The Child

SECTION VI Parents

SECTION VII Professional Concerns

Preface

Student Teaching: Early Childhood Practicum Guide is designed for students who are assuming teaching responsibilities under guided supervision. Student teaching is a memorable, individual struggle to put theory into practice. It is a synthesizing experience from which each student emerges with a unique professional style. This text attempts to help each student teacher reach that goal.

It is the authors' wish that this text guide student teachers in their studies and in the practical application of the knowledge acquired. *Student Teaching: Early Childhood Practicum Guide, 5E* will serve as a useful reference tool for teaching tips and problem-solving techniques as the student enters the professional world.

Many aspects of teaching that affect the student teacher, both now as a student and later as a professional, are discussed. The topics are diverse, including, among others, teaching the "special" child, infants, and toddlers; working with parents; principles of classroom management; interpersonal communication skills; observation and assessment (of both children and student teachers); values identification; and trends and issues in early childhood education. Each topic is discussed in detail, often using case studies and applying current and classic theories.

As the authors watched student teachers struggle with such aspects as wondering what to do during the initial days of student teaching, wanting ideas about classroom management and the special needs children in their classroom, assessment, and how to relate to parents, we were inspired to write this text. As it has gone through first one, then another, and now a fifth revision, we feel that each has been better able to meet the needs of both student teachers and their instructors.

ORGANIZATION OF THE TEXT

All chapters offer learning objectives, chapter summaries, suggested activities, review questions, and lists of references. Comments of former student teachers begin the chapters. These personal revelations may provide insight and reading enjoyment. A short student teacher and/or child scenario at each chapter's end presents a narrative that focuses readers' attention on chapter content. Each case scenario deals with issues, problems, and dilemmas student teachers might encounter. Questions following each scenario promote contemplative and reflective thought, and can be used for class discussion.

Chapter 1, "Introduction to Student Teaching Practicum," includes many different topics such as training guidelines, initial feelings, key participants, the currently employed student teacher, samples of a variety of forms student teachers might have to complete, and an introduction to the National Association for the Education of Young Children's *Code of Ethical Conduct*. Differences between student teaching at the preschool and elementary level are covered, as are topics related to health. Descriptions of the variation that may exist in cooperating teachers' supervision styles offer students insight into how quickly or slowly they might assume full teaching responsibilities and duties. Maintaining records, writing in a journal, and preparing for the first days of student teaching are explained in depth with such topics as previsit preparations, introducing yourself to the administrator in charge and your cooperating teacher, staff behavior, and portfolio development.

Chapter 2, "A Student Teacher's Values and Developing Teaching Style," introduces student teachers to the subject of how their values impact their teaching style. Your authors firmly believe that teaching style evolves from our values. Thus, student teachers are presented with exercises designed to help them define their values and how these translate into classroom activities. The acquisition of values is mentioned, as are professional ethics and the development of teaching style. Examples of authoritative and authoritarian styles are given, along with precautions related to stereotyping and the need for flexibility.

Chapter 3, "Being Observed: Discovering Your Competencies," includes such topics as the goals and methods of observation, and provides several examples of observation forms college supervisors and/or cooperating teachers might use, and a few self-rating sheets that student teachers could implement. Competency-based training, critical thinking, and reflective behaviors are introduced because the authors believe that self-analysis is critical to becoming an effective teacher. The concept of NAEYC's developmentally appropriate practice is also introduced but is covered in greater depth in Chapter 5.

Chapter 4, "Review of Child Development and Learning Theory" has been updated to include recent discoveries related to memory, critical thinking, and multiple intelligences. Also included is research on brain development and emotional intelligence.

Chapter 5, "Instructional Planning," is introduced as student teachers are asked to look at the need to identify child interests and ways to look at early childhood curriculum. Accepted standards are discussed. Authentic assessment is introduced; activity resources and other curriculum approaches are mentioned, along with the implications of the federal "No child left behind" legislation. The effect of a student teacher's attitudes and beliefs on expectations for children in the classroom is covered briefly, as is NAEYC's ethical responsibility as it relates to curriculum. Play and how it affects learning and the need to be sensitive when instructing non-English speaking children and the anti-bias curriculum are mentioned.

Written activity plans for preschool and child care center settings and lesson plans for elementary settings are presented in detail. Sample plans and forms a student teacher might use are presented. Topics such as promoting cognitive skills, using community resources, teaching tips, and room environments are found.

Chapter 6, "Classroom Management Goals and Techniques," includes information on conflict resolution in addition to looking at the five areas of management: physical arrangement of the classroom, curriculum choices, time management, managing classroom routines, and the guidance function. New research on guidance as social development and several management techniques are suggested.

Chapter 7, "Analyzing Behavior to Promote Self-Control," highlights information related to Erikson, Gardner, and other developmental theorists. The relationship between Erikson's psychosocial theory and the professional development of student teachers has been clarified.

Chapter 8, "Common Problems of Student Teachers," focuses on the topic of stress. Both its causes and effects on student teachers are discussed, and ideas for students to implement to reduce stress are suggested. Conferencing, preparing one-day wonders, utilizing conflict resolution, and developing communication skills all serve to reduce stress and solve problems encountered..

Chapter 9, "Case Studies, Analyses, and Applications," includes examples of several observation forms together with their applications in looking at specific children. The forms are then analyzed to demonstrate how learning plans for these children can be developed, based on the observations and analyses.

Chapter 10, "Working with Special Needs Children," introduces the student to federal laws that mandate special education and related services to all identified special needs children. Ideas for how a student teacher might be involved in a preliminary diagnosis and strategies for working with children having specific disabilities have been expanded. Team efforts have been emphasized.

Chapter 11, "The Changing American Family," includes the latest available information and statistics on families. Included is material on welfare reform (TANF) and its effects on families. The section on the changing family briefly mentions what one researcher believes is our greatest concern regarding children today: the lack of nurturance and protection by the children's families.

Chapter 12, "Parents and Student Teachers," discusses the importance of parent-teacher partnerships and the role of the student teacher. Models of communication allow the student teacher to analyze the narrative of a conference between a parent and a preschool teacher and a home visit. Ideas for conferencing are included, as are several examples of other home-school interactions.

Chapter 13, "Quality Programs," discusses programs in relationship to whether they meet children's needs, provide a balanced program, and meet other standards of quality programs. The relationship between different types of accreditation and quality are discussed, along with findings of several studies that have looked at quality in preschool and child care programs and quality in elementary school programs.

Chapter 14, "Professional Commitment and Growth," looks at the student teacher's (and, indeed, all teachers') growth as a professional. Concerns in the profession, professional behavior and commitment, advocacy, individual learning cycles, NAEYC's professional development position statement, and several professional growth opportunities are included.

Chapter 15, "Trends and Issues," addresses some of the major trends in early childhood education and education in general: child abuse, standards in teacher preparation, growing private investment in preschool programs, the shortage of teachers in kindergarten through Grade 12, charter schools, parent choice, and school-age programs. Universal and state-sponsored prekindergarten program growth is added, as is federal legislation.

Chapter 16, "Student Teaching with Infants and Toddlers," includes updated material on quality indicators and studies related to quality. Special issues such as separation from parents, infant/toddler child care and identity formation, infants born to teenage parents, toilet learning, biting, and several ideas for activities are included. The use of signing is described and discussed as a technique to enhance infant communication.

FEATURES OF THE FIFTH EDITION

New additions to the fifth edition include a list of Web sites in each chapter that are pertinent to the students' further study and research. Case scenarios, also a new feature, describe situations encountered by former student teachers or of interest to student teachers, and specifically relate to chapter subject matter. Questions following the narrative promote discussion, reflection, and contemplation.

The authors and Thomson Delmar Learning make every effort to ensure that all Internet resources are accurate at the time of printing. However, due to the fluid, time-sensitive nature of the Internet, we cannot guarantee that all URLs and Web site addresses will remain current for the duration of this edition.

Photographs have been updated and new figures appear. Current research citations have replaced former references where possible. Activities that promote in class discussion and the sharing of individual student teacher discoveries, insights, and happenings have been added.

Retained from the fourth edition are features current users of the text have found valuable. These include:

- Quotes from former student teachers
- Reading objectives stated at each chapter's beginning
- Chapter summaries
- A suggested activities section
- Chapter review questions to allow feedback on the students' grasp of content

The text also continues to encourage journaling and the development of a professional student teacher's portfolio.

ANCILLARIES

The following ancillaries are available to accompany the fifth edition of *Student Teaching: Early Childhood Practicum Guide.*

Instructor's Manual

The Instructor's Manual provides general instructional activities with student teachers, suggested instructional activities by chapter, answers to Chapter review questions, and teaching resources.

Computerized Test Bank

The computerized test bank (CTB) comprises true/false, multiple-choice, short-answer, and completion questions for each chapter. Instructors can use the computerized test bank software to create sample quizzes for students. Refer to the CTB User's Guide for more information on how to create and post quizzes to your school's Internet or Intranet.

Online Companion™

The Online Companion™ that accompanies the fifth edition of *Student Teaching: Early Childhood Practicum Guide* is your link to early childhood education on the Internet. The Online Companion™ provides evaluation forms from the text that students can download and use in their student teaching experiences. Forms that appear in the Online Companion™ are identified by an Online Companion™ icon in the text. New to this edition of the Online Companion™ are additional Web sites for each chapter that promote further student research and study.

Reflective Questions for each chapter that can be used for class or student-to-student online discussion have been added.

A new chapter dealing with employment particulars, entitled "The Search: Resumes, Interviews, and Legal Issues," has been developed for instructors who have requested this material and deemed it applicable to their particular training program and student group. It is available as a component of the Online Companion™ and includes the following topics:

- The job market
- Long- and short-range goals
- Ladder and lateral mobility
- Accredited programs
- Public or private employment
- Direct or indirect services
- Fact-finding
- Certification
- Male job seekers
- Seeking kindergarten/primary positions
- Resume preparation and cover letters
- Interviewing
- Law and the early childhood worker

This online chapter has been designed to enable the instructor to aid students' search for fulfilling and satisfying employment. It also sensitizes students to worker laws.

The Online Companion™ can be found at:
http://www.earlychilded.delmar.com

USING THE TEXT

Instructors are urged to select those chapters most relevant to the needs of their students. The authors recognize that many associate degree programs have required courses in child development and home, school, and community. They may choose to omit Chapters 4 and 11, or ask students simply to skim quickly through them for any possibly new material. Instructors at the baccalaureate level may also choose to omit Chapters 4 and 11 if they know their students have already studied the topics in previous courses. In addition, baccalaureate degree programs may not find Chapter 16 pertinent and are advised to omit it.

Instructors in both associate and baccalaureate degree programs may want to pick and choose the trends and issues presented in Chapter 15 that they feel are most relevant for their respective students. Another way to work with the topics in Chapter 15 would be to have students choose and discuss one or two facts that hold interest for them in particular.

Instructors may find the comprehensive test questions of value and are urged to choose those they feel are most appropriate for their students.

Your authors feel that the key to using the fifth edition of *Student Teaching: Early Childhood Practicum Guide* is, first and foremost, flexibility.

About the Authors

The authors of this text, Jeanne M. Machado and Helen Meyer-Botnarescue, are actively involved in child care and teacher training programs. Jeanne received her M.A. degree from San Jose State University and a Vocational Life Credential from the University of California, Berkeley. She has experience as an early childhood education instructor and department chairperson at San Jose City College and Evergreen Valley College. As a past president of two professional associations— Northern California Association for the Education of Young Children (Peninsula Chapter) and California Community College Early Childhood Educators—Jeanne is deeply involved in early childhood teaching issues. Her text, *Early Childhood Experiences in the Language Arts*, is currently in its seventh edition.

Helen Meyer-Botnarescue received her Ph.D. from the University of Alabama. She also received a Life Credential in Psychology. Currently, Helen is a professor of education emerita from the Department of Teacher Education at California State University, Hayward. In addition, she has served as graduate coordinator of the Early Childhood Education master's program. She has been an advisor to the campus Early Childhood Center. Helen is an active member of four professional organizations: California Association of Early Childhood Teacher Educators, an affiliate group of the National Association of Early Childhood Teacher Educators; the California Association for the Education of Young Children, a branch of the National Association for the Education of Young Children; the World Organization for Preschool Education (OMEP); and the Association for Childhood Education International (ACEI), and its state and local affiliates. She has served on the governing board of the National Association of Early Childhood Teacher Educators, has been an active member of and presenter at congresses sponsored by the Organisation Modiale pour l'Éducation Préscolaire (OMEP), and is past president of the California Association for Childhood Education.

Acknowledgments

The authors wish to express their appreciation to the following individuals and institutions for their contributions to this text.

Reviewers

Linda Aulgur, Ph.D.
Westminister College
Fulton, Maryland

Lynn Baynum, Ph.D.
Shippensburg University
Shippensburg, Pennsylvania

Audrey Beard, Ed.D.
Albany State University
Albany, Georgia

Sylvia Brooks, Ed.D.
University of Delaware
Newark, Delaware

May Lou Brotherson, Ed.D.
Nova Southeastern University
Miami, Florida

Debra G. Murphy
Cape Cod Community College
W. Barnstable, Massachusetts

Illustrations and Photos

Mary Stieglitz, Ph.D.
Jody Boyd
The parents of photographed children

Individual Assistance

The directors and staff of the San Jose City College and Evergreen Valley College Child Development Centers, and enrolled student teachers.

Barbara Kraybill, Director, Afterschool Programs, Livermore, California

Cheryl Needle-Cohn, Instructor, Borough of Manhattan Community College, New York, New York

Preschools, Centers, and Elementary Schools

San Jose City College Child Development Center

Evergreen Valley College Child Development Center

Young Families Program, San Jose, California

California State University Associated Students' Child Care Center

Pexioto Children's Center, Hayward, California

Parent-Child Education Center, Hayward, California

Festival Children's Center, Hayward, California

Jackson Avenue School, Livermore, California

Harder School, Hayward, California

St. Elizabeth's Day Home, San Jose, California

Donnelly Headstart, Donnelly, Idaho

Cascade Elementary School, Cascade, Idaho

Redeemer Lutheran Church Child Development Center, Redwood City, California

We also wish to express our appreciation to We Care Day Treatment Center, Concord, California, for permission to photograph attending children.

Students, Instructors, and Professors

San Jose City College

Evergreen Valley College

California State University, Hayward

Intern Students and Taiwanese preschool teachers attending National Hispanic University

SECTION 1

Orientation to Student Teaching

CHAPTER 1

Introduction to Student Teaching Practicum

Objectives After studying this chapter, the student should be able to:

1. Identify some important goals of a student teaching experience.
2. Describe the relationships and responsibilities of student teacher, cooperating teachers, and supervisors.
3. List three professional conduct considerations for student teachers.
4. Describe preplacement activities and considerations.
5. Identify pertinent information to be obtained on a student teacher's first day.
6. Pinpoint three activities a student teacher can use as an introduction, to learn the children's names, or develop rapport with the children.
7. Identify three valuable skills for staff meetings.

Comments of student teachers after their first week in the classroom:

On the first day of student teaching I was very excited. I felt nervous and tried my best to fit in as though I had been there many times. I memorized all the children's names before the day was over.

—May Valentino

I worked hard to get into this final class in the training program. I did it part-time going evenings after a full day of work with young children. My college supervisor insisted I student teach at a center away from my job. I resented it but found I was able to grow, gain new skills, see quality I'd never experienced.

—Janice Washington

On my first day of student teaching I was scared and nervous . . . shaking in my boots. Not knowing where things were made me feel unsure. It was a good thing that I had a compassionate cooperating teacher; she put me at ease and directed me so I could begin to find my own way.

—Felicia Martinez

Student teaching is both a beginning and an end. It begins a training experience that offers the student a supervised laboratory in which to learn. New skills will develop, and the student will polish professional skills already acquired. Student teaching is usually the final step in a formal training program offering a certificate, degree, license, or credential. It completes a period during which exposure to theory and practical application have occurred. It requires the synthesizing of all previous coursework, training, workshops, and background experience.

Congratulations! You have satisfied all the prerequisites for student teaching. Now you will assume teacher responsibilities and duties with young children and become a member of a professional teaching team.

One of the culminating phases of your professional preparation for teaching, your student teaching provides opportunities to try your wings if you are not presently employed. If employed, the student teaching experience will sharpen and expand already acquired competencies. Hollingsworth (1998) reports former student teachers judge student teaching to be the most valuable experience in preservice training.

TRAINING GUIDELINES

The National Association for the Education of Young Children (NAEYC) in consultation with other professional groups has taken the lead in advocating training guidelines for the preparation of teacher education programs in both associate of arts degree programs and in four- and five-year bachelor's and advanced degree programs. NAEYC's *Guidelines for Preparation of Early Childhood Professionals* (1996) suggests that training programs provide opportunities to apply knowledge and skills in working with children in a variety of field experiences with increasing levels of interaction with children. The importance of supervised practice teaching has not been overlooked. The Child Development Associate (CDA) program demands that 50 percent or more of a trainee's total training be spent in supervised field work, and NAEYC's guidelines propose a minimum number of practicum hours be spent in each of two settings. Many states have developed state training guidelines, which dictate a specific number of student teaching hours and cite approved or suggested placement settings. Each graduating student is expected to have successfully completed a supervised practicum experience or alternative equivalent during which the student assumes major responsibility for a full range of teaching and caregiving duties for a group of young children. Skills, knowledge, and attitudes gained prepare the student to demonstrate the knowledge and competencies required to meet state licensing requirements and/or permits, certificates. and/or credentials.

National Association for the Education of Young Children (NAEYC)—largest American early childhood professional organization, which deals with issues of children from birth to age eight and those who work with young children.

Child Development Associate (CDA)—an early childhood teacher who has been assessed and successfully proven competent through the national CDA credentialling program.

INITIAL FEELINGS

Many students approach student teaching with mixed feelings of trepidation and exhilaration. The challenge presents risks and unknowns, as well as opportunities for growth, insights, and increased self-awareness. Student teaching will be memorable. You will cherish and share with others this "growing stage" of your development as a person and teacher.

Everyone who comes to the field of early childhood brings some kind of relevant experiences with young children, experiences that form a foundation on which to construct teaching theory and practice (Jones, 1994).

THE MECHANICS OF STUDENT TEACHING

Student teaching (sometimes called practicum, field experience or internship) in an early childhood program involves three key people: the student teacher, the cooperating teacher who is responsible for a group of young children, and a supervisor who is a college instructor or teacher trainer. The cooperating teacher models teaching techniques and practices, and the supervisor observes and analyzes the development of the student teacher's skills. Both also serve as consultants and advisors. These three key people are defined as follows:

Student Teacher: A student experiencing a period of guided teaching during which the student takes increasing responsibility for the work with a given group of learners over a period of consecutive weeks. (Other terms used: apprentice, intern.)

Cooperating Teacher: One who teaches young children, models techniques and practices, and supervises student teaching and/or other professional laboratory experiences. (Other terms used: supervising teacher, laboratory school teacher, critic teacher, master teacher, directing teacher, resident teacher.)

College/University Supervisor: The college representative responsible for supervising a student teacher or a group of student teachers. (Other terms used: off-campus supervisor, resident supervisor, clinical teacher, teacher trainer.) In some college training programs, two or more instructors are responsible for a student teacher group.

KEY PARTICIPANTS PLAY A ROLE IN STUDENT TEACHER DEVELOPMENT

Personality, settings, child groupings, the commitment and professionalism of individuals, and many other factors contribute and influence the quality and variety of training opportunities. Key participants (student teacher, cooperating teachers, college and university supervisors) each play a role in student teacher development.

Each student teacher is responsible for serious effort. We have all met people who have a desire and knack for getting everything possible from a given situation. Their human "antennae" are actively searching, receiving, and evaluating! As a student teacher, you will guide much of your own growth. Your cooperating teacher and college or university supervisor will support and reinforce your commitment to learn. Your increasing skill will depend, in part, on you.

Cooperating teachers, as a first duty, must fulfill the requirements of their positions. Child instruction is paramount. Student teacher direction and guidance are additional tasks for which they may or may not be compensated. Even in laboratory school settings, educating and caring for children supercedes the training of student teachers, which is seen as an auxiliary function.

Cooperating teachers differ. One might place cooperating teachers on a degree of control continuum between directive (high structure) to collaborative (unstructured) style. Cooperating teachers falling on the unstructured end believe student teachers should be given considerable latitude as emerging professionals learning to make decisions on their own. They would promote collaboration and student ownership of problem-solving. Glickman et al. (1998) note directive style cooperating teachers often shift to a more unstructured mode as their student teacher becomes more competent in handling classroom responsibilities. They believe this may not happen at all, depending on the student teacher's rate of development and/or the cooperating teacher's dedication to a directive style.

Justen and McJunkin (1999) describe effective cooperating teachers as monitors who urge student teachers to suggest alternative solutions to classroom problems. Cooperating teachers who explain teaching techniques, and what was done and why, aid student teacher growth. A student teacher who closely observes and takes part in discussion and collaboration about classroom practice gains increased insight (Schriver, 1999).

The college or university supervisor's role includes being responsive to a student's concerns, encouraging, understanding, being sensitive and supportive, as well as being serious and rigorous in promoting each student teacher's attention to professional high standards of performance and timely completion of responsibilities. Your supervisor will take an active interest in your career development and in your existing and growing skills and competence.

Jones (1986), speaking about the role of a campus laboratory instructor who supervises student teachers, suggests:

> If I were a preschool lab instructor supervising students' work with children, I'd challenge more, because the student in that setting has responsibilities as a teacher as well as learner. . . .
>
> To be a learner, I think, is to have a chance to mess about, try things out, make mistakes. Practice and self-correction go a long way.

BEFORE PLACEMENTS

College and university departments and individual college instructors (supervisors) have developed guidelines for selecting placement sites long before the first days of student teaching practicum classes. Some colleges and universities endeavor to canvas widely their community preschools and centers to recognize those meeting their training standards as certified student practicum placement sites. Decisions involve selection of the best training site(s) for students, considering the constraints of their particular situations. Selection criteria may depend on location, placement staff experience and training, licensing and accreditation of a placement school or center, law, state guidelines, willingness and ability of administrators and staff to carry out procedures and responsibilities, as well as other factors.

A number of group and individual consultations have taken place as supervising college and university instructors set the scene for student teacher experiences, activities, assignments, and evaluation procedures. Informational written material, including a student teacher and cooperating teacher handbook, may have been designed and produced. The handbooks attempt to cover all facets of training and need to be read carefully and kept handy.

The student teacher should recognize that decisions concerning the number of classroom or center placements per semester (quarter or training period) have already been established. In some communities, a wide variety of child classrooms are available and possible. In other areas, placement classrooms are few or limited.

Colleges and universities may offer early childhood education training programs that can include preparation for diverse teaching specialties. Infant–toddler teacher and school-age teacher (before and after primary school) are two areas provided within traditional early childhood or child development training programs. Some colleges and universities make student teacher placements in both private and public kindergartens or elementary school classrooms where students assume assistant teacher or aide duties.

Student teaching classes are offered at baccalaureate degree-granting colleges and universities (both private and public). Students enrolled in these classes are completing coursework to fulfill state credentialing requirements, and possibly, an advanced degree such as a master of arts degree in education that includes teacher certification. Student teachers at primary grade level usually function as practicing teachers with full responsibility for their assigned classrooms while under the supervision of their assigned cooperating teachers. Rarely do student teachers at prekindergarten level immediately assume full teaching responsibilities. More commonly, they gradually perform an increasing amount of duties, program planning, and instruction, and work their way up to total teacher responsibilities while still under their cooperating teacher's supervision.

The Currently Employed Student Teacher

In some instances, currently employed student teachers may be required to student teach in one or two different child facilities or classrooms. For the currently employed student teacher, the logistics of putting in unpaid hours at another child center may seem an undue hardship, yet many will welcome the opportunity to gain insight into another teacher's competencies and profit from the professional consultation that occurs. In some training programs, one may have to become a day student instead of a night student to enroll in a student teaching class. College and university supervisors are sometimes able to work out placements that allow a student to student teach at a place of employment by placing a special student teacher mentor in the classroom. This arrangement does not deprive the student of the chance to work and view a quality early childhood model, for the mentor is felt to provide and model excellent practice.

Increasingly, students entering early childhood work start classes after employment.

Learning and Growth

Being a unique individual, each student teacher has developed her own learning style. Life and school experience has molded how you see yourself and how you proceed toward knowing and accomplishing new knowledge or skill. Hopefully, your student teaching class will offer diverse ways to learn and also give structured aid in the form of clear guidelines, directions, and suggestions by both your instructor and your cooperating teacher. You will no doubt work alone at times and also in small and large groups.

A portion of your time will be spent in pondering what you have read and experienced. You will closely observe other adults in child classrooms and try to gauge the outcomes of their behaviors. You will also become an avid watcher of yourself and the reactions of others to you. As Carter and Curtis (1994) explain, effective teaching requires continual analysis, adjustment, reflecting, and refocusing. Growth will build and proceed on what you already know as you take tentative and then firm steps in new directions.

Part of the joy of teaching is experimenting, innovating, and inventing new approaches. These new ways will always be offered after judging whether they mesh with your basic conclusions considering what is safe and developmentally appropriate for young children.

Empathy

Most cooperating teachers and college supervisors have themselves been student teachers at the beginning of their own careers. Their feelings tend to be empathetic and supportive, while at the same time, they expect a serious student attempt to develop competency. They provide counseling and assistance.

The whole student teaching experience can be viewed as a miniature world, a slice of life, a human laboratory that will be full of memorable events including the ups and downs all student teachers experience. Every student ideally comes to a clarification of self in relation to people and situations designed to provide quality care and educationally sound environments for young children. New insights concerning values, goals, cultures, self-realization, and other important life issues are attained.

Student Teacher Progress. If the student completes student teaching duties and responsibilities successfully, the student receives recognition of teaching competency. Observation and analysis of the student's performance, followed by consultation with the teaching team, is an integral part of student teaching (see Figure 1–1).

How should the student teachers view their progress and learning in a student teaching class? Rasinski (1989) observes:

> Students can no longer be viewed as passive recipients of knowledge dispensed by teachers; rather, students need to be perceived as active and responsible participants in their own education, relying on their own knowledge and experience to contextualize the educational process.

A child care center is seen as a growing place for everyone, not only for the student teacher. Every human who enters the class can grow from each experience. It is presumed that all adults—even the cooperating teacher and supervisor—are unfinished products. Each participant is viewed as a combination of strengths and talents, with the possibility of expanding.

ORIENTATION

Introductions, tours, oral and written guidelines, instructions and informational data, and completing forms are all part of student teaching orientation meetings.

Figure 1–1 Your cooperating teacher may work beside you on your first days in the classroom.

Remembering names and taking notes are advisable. First impressions are important, and "body language" will send many messages to others.

Introductions and tours enable the student teacher to become familiar with people and settings and help reduce anxieties (see Figure 1–2). Anxieties may increase when responsibilities and requirements are described. Supervisors and cooperating teachers may require the completion of various assignments. Keeping each in order may mean coding or keeping different folders or binders. A datebook or daily appointment calendar is also recommended because many important meetings, appointments, and deadlines will occur. As always, the newness, the attention required for details, and the amount of information to remember and read may temporarily produce stress. Creating a buddy system with other student teachers can be helpful.

Forms, Forms, Forms

Various informational written materials provide helpful guidelines for orientations. They are categorized as follows:

Supervisor

- Supervisor's course guide sheet
- Supervisor's list of student teacher placement responsibilities (see Figure 1–3)
- Supervisor's tips, aids (see Figure 1–4)
- Supervisor's assessment forms
- Supervisor's forms for cooperating teachers (see Figure 1–5)

Center

- Parents' guide and policy statement
- Center newsletter
- Policy for visitors and observers
- Children's records
- Center handbook

Figure 1–2 The school receptionist/secretary is an important staff member.

1. Be prompt and prepared.
2. If you are ill on your assigned days, call your supervisor and cooperating teacher as close to 8 A.M. as possible.
3. If you must be absent, phone ahead and let your school know you are unable to be there that day. Preferably, let the school know ahead of time if there will be an unavoidable absence during your student teaching assignment.
4. Remember, the cooperating teacher depends on your services as a fellow teacher.
5. Sign in and out if required.
6. Consult with your supervisor on lesson planning when help is needed.
7. Make an appointment with your supervisor to discuss class-related questions or problems.
8. Remember to avoid conversations that label children or deal with confidential information.
9. Sign in the lesson plan book at least one week in advance if your cooperating teacher or supervisor requests it.
10. Complete assignments.
11. Complete your student teacher file, and take it to the director's office as soon as possible. (Included in this file are TB clearance, personal data sheet, rating sheets, return envelope.)
12. Be sure to have your fingerprint card and background check completed prior to beginning your first observation and/or student teaching assignment.
13. Please see and do what needs to be done without direction. Ask questions. Assume as much teaching responsibility as you can handle.

Figure 1–3 Sample of student teacher responsibilities

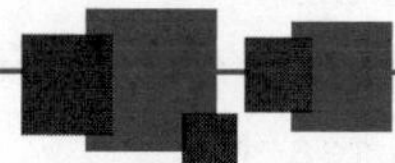

1. Get your TB and criminal background clearances to your center's director as soon as possible. (Note: This is not required in some states.)
2. Leave your belongings in the place provided.
3. Sign in.
4. Enter the children's room quietly, wearing your name tag.
5. Look for emergency room evacuation plans (posted on wall).
6. Consider child safety. Watch and listen for rules and expectations.
7. Actively involve yourself helping staff and children. See what needs to be done. Ask only what is necessary of staff after saying hello or introducing yourself. (Do not interrupt an activity. Wait until the cooperating teacher is free.)
8. Let the staff handle child behaviors that are puzzling on first days.
9. Write down any questions concerning children, programs, and routines that baffle you, and discuss them with your supervisor.
10. If you are sick on your scheduled day, call both your supervisor and your cooperating teacher.
11. Keep a brief diary of your activities, feelings, perceptions, and the like. You may want to buy a pocket-sized notebook.

Figure 1–4 Sample of trainer's tips for student teachers' first days

1. Let your student take as much responsibility as possible.
2. Give feedback on progress if possible.
3. Written tips, hints, and suggestions on lesson plans are helpful.
4. Let your student teacher work out the "tight" spots when possible. You may want to set up a signal to indicate when the student wishes you to step in and remedy the situation.
5. Gauge your student's ability. (Some student teachers may be able to handle a full morning's program from the beginning.) Each student needs the experience of handling the group.
6. Discuss the student teacher's performance in confidence after the activity. Some suggestions while an activity is occurring may be necessary for child or equipment safety.
7. Your student teacher may ask you for a letter of reference.
8. Peer evaluations have been assigned. This means perhaps that another student teacher may observe and rate the student assigned to you. This may happen twice during the semester.
9. Please call the student's supervisor if a difficulty or question arises.
10. Rate the student on the last week of participation. A rating sheet is part of your student teacher's folder. The student will remind you a week in advance.
11. The student teacher has been instructed to consult with you on lesson plan activities. If you want the activities to deal with particular curriculum areas or themes, this is your choice. The student has been told to abide by your wishes.
12. Your student's personal data sheet has information concerning special interests, background, and so on.
13. The student's supervisor will visit periodically to give the student feedback on competencies and possible growth areas.
14. Frequent conferences help the student obtain a clear picture of skill progress.
15. Near the end of the student teacher's assignment, the college/university will schedule a three-way conference with you, your student teacher, and the supervisor for the closing student teacher evaluation.

Thank you for taking on the extra work involved in having a student in your classroom.

Figure 1–5 Sample of supervisor's written instructions to cooperating teachers

Cooperating Teacher

- Student teacher assignments, responsibilities rating sheet
- Children's daily schedule
- Children's names (with pronunciation guides if necessary)
- Student teacher rating sheets
- Staff meeting dates and times (optional)
- Placement classroom guidelines for student teachers (see Figure 1–6)

The following forms are common to student teaching. Many must be on file before the student's first working day.

- Class schedule (location, rooms, and times of any additional courses)
- Student teacher sign-in sheets (to keep track of arrival, departure, and volunteer and assigned work hours)
- Tuberculin (TB) clearance (mandatory in many states)
- Staff information form, personnel record
- Personal background form (see Figure 1–7)
- Physical examination, physician's report
- Criminal background clearance

Suggestions for guiding behavior:

1. Redirect behavior in a positive way whenever possible (e.g., feet belong on the floor).
2. Do not give a choice when one does not exist.
3. Give help only when it is needed.
4. Do not be afraid to limit or channel destructive behavior.
5. Help the children understand by explaining.
6. Encourage children to use their words during peer disagreements.
7. Inform the children a few minutes ahead of the next activity to come. ("It's three minutes until cleanup/snack.")
8. Watch for situations that may be explosive, and step in. Try to let the children settle problems themselves. If they cannot, redirect them.
9. Remember, an ounce of prevention is worth a pound of cure.

Inside:

1. Modeling dough stays in the creative activities room.
2. Parents have been asked not to send their children with toys, except on sharing days.
3. Running is for outside; walking is for inside.
4. Encourage children to pour their own drinks from the pitchers provided. This will probably mean frequent spills so sponges should be available on all tables. Have children pass things to each other.

Outside:

1. Adults need to distribute themselves throughout the center and the playground rather than grouping together. Your attention should be on the children, observing them so you can be ready to step in when guidance is needed.
2. Children are to climb up the ladder and slide down on their bottoms when using the slide.
3. All sand play and sand toys must be in the designated area.
4. Remind the children that water from the fountain is for drinking. Sand and cornmeal should be kept away from the water fountain to avoid clogging.
5. Help children park wheeled toys along the fence before going in. Please keep the gate area clear.
6. All wheeled toys have a specific use and should be used properly.

Figure 1-6 Sample of child center guidelines for student teachers

Criminal History and Background Check

An increasing number of states are requiring a criminal history and background inquiry prior to a student teacher field placement. All paid and volunteer staff are required to comply and receive clearance, which then is placed in the child care facility or school's personnel files.

PROFESSIONALISM

Extra attention to teacher conduct is required because of the age and vulnerability of young children and the influence a teacher may have with parents. Katz and Ward (1978) reminds us:

> In any profession, the more powerless the client is in relation to the practitioner, the more important the practitioner's ethics become. That is to say, the greater the necessity for internalized restraints against abusing that power.

PERSONAL DATA SHEET

NAME ____________________

ADDRESS ____________________ CITY ____________

PHONE ____________ MESSAGE PHONE # ____________ EMERGENCY PHONE # ____________

CAR yes ____________ no ____________

E-MAIL ____________

FAMILY DATA (optional) ____________________

HEALTH (Concerns you wish to share affecting your work) ____________________

____

EXPERIENCES WITH CHILDREN (past employment, volunteer, family, etc.)

____

____

____

COLLEGE year ________ major ____________________

COURSES in early childhood major not presently completed

____

____

Previous college work related to student teaching

____

____

Presently Employed ________ Where (optional) ____________________

Hours ____________ Duties (optional) ____________________

____

SPECIAL INTERESTS ____________________

____

WHAT WOULD YOU LIKE YOUR COOPERATING TEACHER TO KNOW ABOUT YOU? ____________

____

HOBBIES AND SPECIAL TALENTS OR SKILLS ____________________

____

CAREER GOALS ____________________

____

____

Figure 1-7 Sample of personal background information

> Early childhood practitioners have great power over young children, especially in child care centers. Practitioners' superior physical power over young children is obvious. In addition, practitioners have virtually total power over the psychological goods and resources of value to the young in their care.

practitioners—persons engaged in the practice of a profession or occupation, in this case, early childhood education. Other terms used: educator, teacher, assistant teacher, aide, student teacher.

When you reach the level of student teaching, others presume you have a certain amount of educational background and some degree of professional skill. Some parents may feel you are an expert in child-rearing and may try to seek your opinion(s) on a wide variety of developmental issues. You will need to direct these parents to your cooperating teacher, who may refer them to the director or other staff, who, in turn, may refer them to professionally trained individuals or community resources.

As a student teacher, you represent a profession. As a professional, you are asked to abide by certain regulations, including a professional conduct code (see Figure 1–8). Confidentiality is an integral part of this code as it protects children and families, and should be maintained at all times. Staff meetings and individual conferences are conducted in a spirit of mutual interest and concern for the children and adults' welfare, and the center's high standards. At such conferences, student teachers are privy to personal information that should not be discussed elsewhere.

professional—individual engaged in an occupation considered a learned profession such as law or medicine. In this text, the field of education.

confidentiality—requirement that results of evaluations and assessments be shared with only the parents and appropriate school personnel.

This point needs to be stressed. Student teachers can become so involved with classroom happenings and individual children that they inadvertently discuss privileged information with a fellow student teacher or friend, or within the center in earshot of a parent or another individual. One can easily see how this might happen and cause irreparable damage.

Classes of student teachers are frequently reminded by their instructors/supervisors that real child and family names cannot be used in seminar/class discussions.

The student teacher's appearance, clothing, and grooming contribute to a professional image. Fortunately, comfortable, functional clothing, which allows a student teacher to perform duties without worrying about mobility or messy activity supervision, is relatively inexpensive (see Figure 1–9). Many supervisors suggest a pocketed smock or apron and a change of shoes.

Responsibilities

A clear picture of the responsibilities of the student teacher, cooperating teacher, and supervisor will help students make decisions about handling specific incidences as professionals. As a general rule, it is better to ask for help than to proceed in any questionable situation that goes beyond one's responsibilities and duties (barring emergency situations that call for immediate action) (see Figures 1–10 and 1–11).

Exposure to Bloodborne Pathogens

You will be instructed at your placement site about exposure to children's blood, skin, eye, and mucous membrane secretions, and other potentially infectious materials, and will be provided with protective gloves and equipment. Should a classroom situation occur, cooperating teachers will prefer to handle the incident. Discuss this with your cooperating teacher. Privacy laws protect parents who do not wish to disclose child conditions; therefore, it is wise to follow exposure guidelines strictly. The Occupational Safety and Health Administration, by means

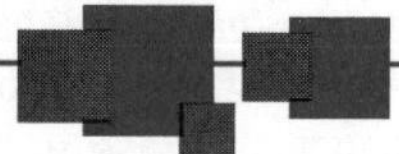

Section 1: Ethical responsibilities to children

Childhood is a unique and valuable stage in the life cycle. Our paramount responsibility is to provide safe, healthy, nurturing, and responsive settings for children. We are committed to supporting children's development, respecting individual differences, helping children learn to live and work cooperatively, and promoting health, self-awareness, competence, self-worth, and resiliency.

Ideals:

I-1.1—To be familiar with the knowledge base of early childhood care and education and to keep current through continuing education and in-service training.

I-1.2—To base program practices upon current knowledge in the field of child development and related disciplines and upon particular knowledge of each child.

I-1.3—To recognize and respect the uniqueness and the potential of each child.

I-1.4—To appreciate the special vulnerability of children.

I-1.5—To create and maintain safe and healthy settings that foster children's social, emotional, intellectual, and physical development and that respect their dignity and their contributions.

I-1.6—To support the right of each child to play and learn in inclusive early childhood programs to the fullest extent consistent with the best interests of all involved. As with adults who are disabled in the larger community, children with disabilities are ideally served in the same settings in which they would participate if they did not have a disability.

I-1.7—To ensure that children with disabilities have access to appropriate and convenient support services and to advocate for the resources necessary to provide the most appropriate settings for all children.

Principles:

P-1.1—Above all, we shall not harm children. We shall not participate in practices that are disrespectful, degrading, dangerous, exploitative, intimidating, emotionally damaging, or physically harmful to children. This principle has precedence over all others in this Code.

P-1.2—We shall not participate in practices that discriminate against children by denying benefits, giving special advantages, or excluding them from programs or activities on the basis of their race, ethnicity, religion, sex, national origin, language, ability, or the status, behavior, or beliefs of their parents. (This principle does not apply to programs that have a lawful mandate to provide services to a particular population of children.)

P-1.3—We shall involve all of those with relevant knowledge (including staff and parents) in decisions concerning a child.

P-1.4—For every child we shall implement adaptations in teaching strategies, learning environment, and curricula, consult with the family, and seek recommendations from appropriate specialists to maximize the potential of the child to benefit from the program. If, after these efforts have been made to work with a child and family, the child does not appear to be benefiting from a program, or the child is seriously jeopardizing the ability of other children to benefit from the program, we shall communicate with the family and appropriate specialists to determine the child's current needs, identify the setting and services most suited to meeting these needs, and assist the family in placing the child in an appropriate setting.

P-1.5—We shall be familiar with the symptoms of child abuse, including physical, sexual, verbal, and emotional abuse, and neglect. We shall know and follow state laws and community procedures that protect children against abuse and neglect.

P-1.6—When we have reasonable cause to suspect child abuse or neglect, we shall report it to the appropriate community agency and follow up to ensure that appropriate action has been taken. When appropriate, parents or guardians will be informed that the referral has been made.

P-1.7—When another person tells us of a suspicion that a child is being abused or neglected, we shall assist that person in taking appropriate action to protect the child.

P-1.8—When a child protective agency fails to provide adequate protection for abused or neglected children, we acknowledge a collective ethical responsibility to work toward improvement of these services.

P-1.9—When we become aware of a practice or situation that endangers the health or safety of children, but has not been previously known to do so, we have an ethical responsibility to inform those who can remedy the situation and who can protect children from similar danger.

Figure 1-8 Selected section of NAEYC's Code of Ethical Conduct. Reprinted with permission from the National Association for the Education of Young Children. NAEYC, ©Copyright 1998.

Figure 1--9 A student teacher assists this cooperating teacher in a group activity.

of the Occupational Safety and Health Acts of 1970 and 1992, recognizes the need for child care worker training and protections. Each center (there are a few exceptions) by law must develop a written exposure control plan, provide protective clothing and equipment, give employees information and training, and provide vaccine and medical help to exposed employees. Centers will instruct student teachers concerning who gives first aid.

It is suggested that each student teacher consult his private physician regarding the advisability of hepatitis B vaccination.

Student Teaching in a Kindergarten or Primary Grade in a Public or Private Elementary School. When you are assigned to student teach in a kindergarten or primary grade classroom, your first days will involve you in many of the same activities as when you were assigned to student teach in a prekindergarten.

Most elementary schools have staff handbooks. You will be given a copy and be expected to read it. A handbook will contain vital information such as the school calendar, a list of the school board members, and the dates their terms end. The names of the school principal, secretary, nurse, librarian, head maintenance person, community liaison person, and so on, will be listed. School rules and regulations will be presented. In reading the handbook, you will have a firm idea of policies you will be expected to follow during your student teaching period.

Different colleges and universities have different ways in which student teaching is arranged. In some states which have certification for nursery/kindergarten/primary (NKP) teaching, you may have three different placements: one at a preschool, another at the kindergarten level, a third in a primary grade. Other states require only two experiences: one at preschool and a second at either

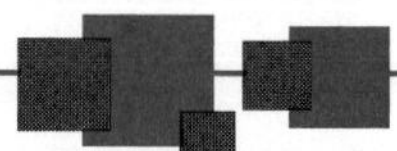

Student's Responsibilities
- Attendance and promptness
- Performance and completion of all assignments and duties
- Working with a minimum of direction
- Translating theory into performance

College/University Supervisor's Responsibilities
- Conducting orientations
- Clearly outlining duties, responsibilities, and class assignments
- Arranging and monitoring placements
- Observing progress and confirming strengths and talents
- Providing feedback
- Helping students develop individual plans for future growth
- Working as a liaison between cooperating teacher and student, consulting frequently as a team member
- Becoming aware of cooperating teacher's assigned tasks for student teacher
- Serving as a resource and modeling when possible
- Evaluating student's competencies

Cooperating Teacher's Responsibilities
- Orienting student teacher to room environment, schedules, class rules, and children
- Serving as a model of philosophy, teaching style, and teaching technique
- Clearly outlining student teacher expectations, duties, and assigned work
- Answering questions
- Giving feedback on observations when possible
- Providing ideas for child activities and materials
- Increasing the student teacher's opportunity to gain and sharpen skills by giving increased responsibilities when appropriate
- Following agreed-upon tasks

Responsibilities of All
- Maintaining professional conduct
- Communicating ideas and concerns; seeking aid when in doubt
- Gaining new skills and sharpening existing skills
- Working as supportive, caring team members

Figure 1–10 Responsibilities

kindergarten or primary level. In some certification programs, all theory and methods classes precede a one-semester, 12-week, all-day student teaching experience. Other programs integrate some of the theory and methods courses with short observation assignments lasting for approximately four weeks. Again, these precede a major student teaching assignment that most typically covers one academic semester. In California, early childhood education is an "emphasis" appended to the multiple subject (elementary) credential; colleges and universities with similar state-approved programs must provide student experiences at both primary and intermediate grade levels in addition to an experience in a preschool. Assignments, then, often involve a short practicum-observation in a preschool, often only in the mornings (sometimes paid experience may be substituted), another assignment in the intermediate grades (usually grade four), and a final longer assignment of approximately 12 to 15 weeks, all day, in a kindergarten or primary grade.

In student teaching assignments that cover only one semester, you probably will have only one college/university supervisor. Most supervisors are cho-

In accepting the role of a cooperating teacher to ______________________________
(student's name)

I agree to perform the following:

1. Orient the student to all school child safety procedures, school policies, staff handbook, and other pertinent particulars concerning the operation of school or classroom.
2. Read all written material and become acquainted with all facets of the student teaching situation including time lines, deadlines, training objectives and goals, tasks, and responsibilities of both the student and myself.
3. Meet with the student teacher at least weekly at regular times for consultation, progress evaluation, and planning.
4. Schedule periodic meetings with the student's college supervisor, and immediately contact college supervisor as the need arises.
5. Observe and offer clear, honest opinions of student strengths and training needs to promote student's growth in teaching and human interaction skills and competency.
6. Be open to questions, provide a professional example, and communicate directly to student concerning daily problems, matters, and concerns.
7. Develop procedures that record student's actual attendance hours in classroom.
8. Complete the formal exit evaluation of the student that details student's level of competence and suggests future growth areas.

As a training model, you directly contribute to teaching excellence and professional recognition of our career field.

Please sign below and return to the College Supervisor before ______________________

Cooperating teacher ______________________________ Date __________

School ____

Address ____

Phone # ______________________ Message phone # ______________________

Fax # ______________________ E-mail # ______________________

Figure 1–11 Example of contract listing cooperating teacher training tasks, procedures, and responsibilities.

sen for their expertise; most are former primary grade teachers themselves. In colleges and universities with programs that include short practica or observation periods prior to student teaching, you may well have more than one college/university supervisor. (Some of these practica or short observation periods may not be directly supervised; the college may rely on the cooperating teacher or principal for any supervision that is needed.) Having different supervisors can provide you with the benefit of exposure to more than one type of supervision technique. One supervisor may stress the need to see lesson plans as you are teaching. Another, schooled in clinical supervision techniques, may focus on the communication and questioning strategies you use. A third may watch your interactions with your pupils.

Student teaching assignments are usually made very carefully. Cooperating teachers are chosen for their expertise as well as for their willingness to help train a student teacher. Many states require any cooperating teacher to have had at least three years of experience prior to being considered; most principals will choose their most competent teachers for this role.

Distance Learning

A few colleges offer student teaching practica using satellite locations and electronically monitored classroom placements. Packaged course content may be provided and accessed through the Internet, by interactive television, audio cassettes, or some other technological vehicle. Students may conference with their college supervisor by phone lines, e-mail, periodic face-to-face meetings, or by other means and arrangements. Some distance learning classes have evolved with unique features that attempt to promote a quality student teaching experience in rural settings. Distance learning often makes study available at any hour of the day or night and at nontraditional campus locations. It is becoming commonplace to keep in touch with one's college supervisor by computer or through video conferencing.

Student Teaching Class Hours

Whitmire (2000) reviewed surveys of new and practicing teachers conducted by Public Agenda and the U. S. Department of Education. He suggests that although new teachers are dedicated and enthusiastic about their jobs, some felt unprepared for the realities of classroom teaching and craved additional hands-on experience. Some also felt past college student teaching coursework inadequate. Colleges, professional associations, standards committees, and training programs have debated the ideal number of required student teaching course hours with 300 hours being the number most frequently recommended.

STUDENT TEACHING GOALS

The most important goal of student teaching is to gain adequate (or better) teaching competence. The acquisition of skills allows the completion of training and new or continued employment.

Specific objectives vary, but they generally are concerned with understanding children, planning and providing quality programs for children and families, acquiring technical teaching skills, and personal and professional development. A list of common student teacher objectives follows:

- Knowing and accepting themselves (Sudzina, Giebelhaus, & Coolican, 1997)
- Increasing awareness of a child and family's individuality
- Building rapport with children, staff, and parents
- Understanding ethnicity, neighborhood values, and individual group cultural values
- Identifying a child's needs
- Creating a climate that helps child expression instead of child fear of making mistakes (Sudzina, et al., 1997)
- Promoting child growth and development
- Identifying the goals of instruction
- Acquiring an individual teaching style
- Offering a child activities and opportunities
- Applying theory and past experiences to present situations

- Preparing interesting classroom environments
- Assuming a teacher's duties and responsibilities
- Learning school routines
- Developing self-confidence
- Evaluating effectiveness
- Growing personally and professionally
- Acquiring communication skills
- Taking advice and acting on it (Sudzina, et al., 1997)
- Experimenting and creating
- Using creative problem-solving techniques
- Guiding child behavior appropriately
- Establishing and maintaining working relationships
- Assessing strength and endurance
- Understanding supportive family services
- Developing a personal philosophy of early childhood education
- Participating in advocacy efforts
- Learning state guidelines, standards, and laws

Individual **goals** reflect each student teacher's idea of professional conduct and skill, and how each feels about the kind of teacher and person she would like to become. Teachers constantly make choices in agreement with their values and goals.

goals—overall, general overviews of what student teachers expect to gain from the practicum experience.

Student Teacher Observational Record-Keeping

Before your student teaching class, you completed coursework covering methods, techniques, and observational strategies. It is time to review that material now because you will be watching and listening to children closely. You will be especially focused on how your behavior and actions affect individual children or the total child group. Remember that children's nonverbal messages are as important as their verbal ones; you will be constantly alert to new and repeated behaviors as well as puzzling ones.

Busy cooperating teachers are usually quite interested in daily observations and student teacher written accounts of child incidents and happenings. It gives cooperating teachers an "outside opinion." This may be the first perception by another adult that they have heard concerning child behavior they are trying to trace or evaluate themselves.

It takes only a few minutes a day for student teacher record-keeping, unless a cooperating teacher has assigned more lengthy observation exercises. Any notes are confidential and should be guarded closely. One can easily understand the apparent danger if a student teacher leaves observational notes lying around! Anecdotes are jotted down quickly with the date and time, and they differ from records of accidents, injuries, or illnesses noted during the day. The latter are detailed and necessary for school record-keeping; each school or center has its own specific form or format.

journal—a written and/or pictorial or audio record of experiences, occurrences, observations, feelings, questions, work actions, reflective thoughts, and other happenings during student teaching.

Student Journals (Logs)

Many training programs require the student teacher to begin a **journal** (log) of experiences and feelings during student teaching. Supervisors periodically monitor journal entries (or student tape recordings) to keep on top of student growth, work actions, concerns, feelings, questions, and needs. It is suggested that student teachers make at least one five-minute daily entry (written or typed) on participation days while impressions are fresh. Some college supervisors give suggestions for recorded topics:

- personal views, insights, and expressions
- classroom dilemmas
- feelings about all aspects of the classroom
- insights concerning the philosophy of the cooperating teacher
- relationships with particular children
- perceptions of student teacher skills
- what is going well; what is not
- staff relationships
- areas student pinpoints for self-growth
- ways the student has overcome a problem
- new ideas to improve instruction and how they worked
- why it would be great (or not) to be a child in this classroom
- special children's needs
- children's interests
- planned activities
- unscheduled activities
- favorite spots in the classroom
- difficult times of day

The goal of journaling is not to have students display knowledge but rather to jot down reflections on their classroom experiences, perceptions, and opinions. Its purpose includes having student teachers focus on themselves as learners. In journaling, student teachers can wonder, question, celebrate insights, describe setbacks, generate ideas, and in general reflect on their growth as teachers. Instructors may suggest students write in their journals on the right two-thirds of the page so others can dialogue with them in the left-hand space.

Reading assignment reactions may also be recorded if supervisors so request. The time required either to write or react to journal entries may be built into training class time.

Journal entries are dated in left-hand margins.

Some college supervisors write in the student's journal, giving supportive assistance or encouragement. A journal is really used as a communication device and promotes shared understandings and intimacy. Follow-up conferences may concentrate on student progress. Log entries are sometimes included when student teachers develop professional career portfolios and will be mentioned later in this chapter.

PREPARING FOR YOUR FIRST DAYS

Before your first day of student teaching, you have been given your cooperating teacher's name and the school's address, and you may have attended orientation meetings for student teaching at your placement site. Your first working day is near. You have either an "on campus" or "off campus" child center or school assignment.

If your soon-to-be students live in the vicinity, a stroll through the neighborhood will help you discover something about them. Observe the community, its businesses, its recreation, its uniqueness. Do not overlook the opportunity to observe this community's resources for planning child activities. Perhaps a construction site is an interesting possibility for a field trip, or an orchard or park holds treasures to be discovered.

With an on-campus laboratory school placement, you may have previously participated in the children's program and perhaps completed observation assignments. The center and its staff and children may be familiar. You will now assume the role of student teacher. Take a new look at the campus and the resources of the campus community.

If you have been told to meet with the director or principal of the school, call to make an appointment. Plan to have the meeting at least fifteen minutes before you are scheduled to be in the classroom. Ask about available staff parking. Remember to avoid parent parking spots or drop-off areas.

It is time to dust off the resource idea files and books you have collected during your training because you may be using them to plan activities. Choose a short activity to offer on your first day, even if it has not been assigned. Brush up on fingerplays or short songs to be used as "fill-ins" or transitions. If they are not memorized, put them on cards that slip into a pocket. It is important for you to be prepared to step in with an activity if you are asked to do so (see Figure 1–12).

Some good ideas for first-day activities that have worked well for other student teachers are as follows:

- A name tag–making activity
- A puppet who tells a short story about his name, introduces the student teacher, and wants to know the children's names
- A favorite book or tape recording to discuss
- A simple food preparation activity
- An art or craft activity that uses children's names
- A collage or chart that shows interesting things about a student teacher's life
- A collection of photographs that are important to the student teacher
- A game made by the student teacher that involves children's names and places in their community
- A beanbag activity that uses children's names
- A flannelboard story
- A new song or movement activity
- A "my favorite" chart on which the student teacher shows three favorite objects, then writes the children's favorite things next to their names
- A storytelling experience
- An activity involving a particular student teacher skill (e.g., musical instrument, dance, carpentry)
- A tape recording of school or neighborhood sounds to guess and discuss

Figure 1–12 A spur-of-the-moment play dough activity with accessories was a hit for this student teacher.

Last-Minute Preparations

Activities that can be easily carried and quickly set up work best. Get the necessary materials together the night before your class. If you received a set of classroom rules and a schedule of routines and planned activities, study it beforehand.

Think about clothing. Make sure it will be comfortable and appropriate. A smock, shirt, or apron with a pocket will hold a small notebook, pen, tissues, and other small necessities. You should wear shoes that will protect your toes and help keep your balance and speed on the playground.

MEETING WITH THE ADMINISTRATOR

It is customary to meet with the administrator before going to the classroom. At that time, the student teacher's records will be added to the personnel file. The file usually includes a TB clearance, a physical examination form, an emergency form, a personal background form, cooperating teacher guidelines (hints), and rating sheets from the supervisor.

Some topics you might discuss are the procedures for storing your coat and personal items, sign-in and sign-out requirements, and miscellaneous details. The following are also possible subjects for this first meeting with the administrator.

- The general plan of classes under the administrator's domain
- Staff members and their special skills
- The children attending the school
- The degree of parent participation
- The center's community involvement
- The administrator's expectations of a student teacher

Most centers have a written plan for new staff orientation and/or a handbook of school operation and policies that can include the following written materials:

- Mission statement
- Philosophy statement
- Program goals
- Curriculum description
- Personnel policies (see Figure 1–13)

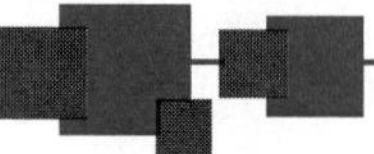

- Organizational chart
- Job titles and description of duties and responsibilities
- Salary schedule
- Benefits
- Yearly calender including events, meetings, holidays, in-service, and the like
- Code of ethics or conduct
- Dress code
- Professional growth and development, career lattice particulars
- Job performance procedures and assessment criteria
- Absences and substitute policy
- Grievance procedure
- Resignation, termination procedures
- Licensing or other state or local regulation particulars
- Parent involvement or other parent procedures
- Child and staff health policies
- Center and/or employee record forms

Figure 1–13 A listing of common personnel handbook features

code of ethics—agreed-upon professional standards that guide behavior and facilitate decision making in working situations.

- Parent handbook or guide
- Lists of names and ages of attending children
- List of parent names and addresses

If a calendar or schedule of school happenings and events is available, it will contain valuable information for the student teacher.

Student teachers usually make a good impression with an administrator (and staff) when they look a person directly in the eyes, speak clearly with confidence, and smile.

YOUR CLASSROOM

There probably will be time for a smile and a few quick words with your cooperating teacher. Your introduction to the children can wait until a planned group time. Introduce yourself briefly to other classroom adults when you are in close proximity. Your cooperating teacher may ask that you observe instead of participate. Otherwise, actively participate in supervising and interacting with the children. Pitch in with any tasks that need to be done. Wear a provided or self-made name tag.

Ask questions only when necessary; jot down others on a pad of paper, which you should carry with you. Use your judgment as to where you are needed most. Do not worry about assuming too much responsibility; your cooperating teacher will let you know if you are overstepping your duties. New student teachers tend to hold back and wait to be directed. Put yourself in the teacher's place. Where would the teacher direct you to supervise or assist children when the teacher is busy with other work? Periodically scan the room to determine whether you are needed elsewhere.

Class Computers

Many classrooms have child-use computers and available software programs. Usually, these areas have rules and require adult supervision. Prepare yourself by learning operational procedures and previewing child programs before or after class sessions after consulting with your cooperating teacher.

Supplies

Familiarize yourself with storage areas to minimize the need to ask questions about the location of equipment and supplies. Check with your cooperating teacher when he is not involved with children or parents. Make your inspection when you are free from room supervision (see Figure 1–14). Become familiar with yard storage also. During team meetings, you should inquire about your use of supplies for planned activities.

Child Records

Some early childhood centers will allow student teachers access to child and family records; others will not. Knowing as much as possible about each child increases the quality of your interaction. Remember that confidentiality should be maintained at all times if permission to review the records is granted. During this review, you may wish to make note of any allergies, specific interests, and special needs of each child. For example:

allergies—physiological reactions to environmental or food substances that can affect or alter behavior.

Figure 1–14 Storage space is never quite large enough in most centers.

Roberto eats no milk, cheese, or dairy products

Clorinda needs pink nap blanket

Jake likes horses

Pierre occasionally gets leg cramps

Lei Thien uses toothbrush with own special paste

Elan parent requests no photographs

Each child's file may contain the following:

- Emergency information
- Health history and record
- Physical examination form
- Application form and family or child history
- Attendance data
- Anecdotal records, specimen records, timed observation records, assessments, and conference notes
- Requests for excluding children from class photos
- Court orders such as restraining orders
- Individual Educational Plans (IEP) and Individual Family Service Plans (IFSP)

anecdotal records—methods of observation involving written "word pictures" of an event or behavior.

More commonly, cooperating teachers or directors will informally alert you to the special needs or circumstances, prohibitions, health-related conditions, and the individual particulars of attending children; in other words, everything you need to know.

Emergency Procedures

Acquaint yourself with the location and use of first aid supplies. For emergencies such as fire, earthquake, and storms, become familiar with evacuation plans showing exit routes. Most states require that these plans be posted. Enforce all health and safety rules. If you have any questions regarding health and safety, be sure to note them so they can be discussed.

Opening

Be aware of how children and parents are greeted on arrival. What activities or choices are available for child exploration? A keen observer will notice which children separate and make the transition from parent to center with ease, and which classroom adults contribute to the classroom's atmosphere or tone.

Dismissal Procedures

Be aware that each center or school has a policy regarding adults who can remove a child from the classroom at a session's close or any other time. You should not release children to arriving adults. This is your cooperating teacher's responsibility. Make sure adults coming to pick up children are directed to talk with the child's teacher before exiting.

In today's society, some families may consist of a variety of related or unrelated adults and children. Because of problems that exist between single or divorced parents or other family factors, court-issued restraining orders can affect who is authorized to pick up a child.

Seeing Where You Are Needed

Cooperating teachers overwhelmingly state they appreciate student teachers who are watchful and notice where they are most needed. This is difficult for new student teachers unless they consciously endeavor to know "the lay of the land." Figure 1–15 attempts to help you focus on aspects of the classroom program and its enrolled children, procedures, and interactions.

Observing at Your Placement Site

During your first days and weeks, you will learn a lot about your placement school. Answering the questions in Figure 1–15 will make you aware of the factors or features that make your placement unique. Discuss any concerns with your college supervisor. Your supervisor may advise you to consult with your cooperating teacher or urge you to keep your conclusions and judgments to yourself.

Pitfalls

During the first days of work, it is not unusual for the student teacher to acquire some bad habits unconsciously. It helps to be aware of these pitfalls in advance.

During class time, avoid having extended social conversations or small talk with other adults, and seeking the company of other adults as a source of support. Use your breaks for this purpose if necessary.

Refrain from talking about children to another adult in their presence. Avoid the tendency to label a child. Keep your judgments and/or evaluations to yourself, and save questions for staff meetings.

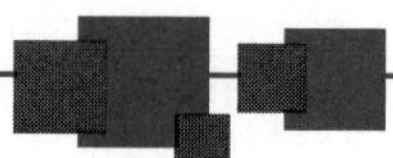

Facilities

Where are materials and supplies stored?
Are storage areas organized?
Where are exits? How do windows open, lights work, temperature controls operate?
How do doors open?
What is the classroom layout? Traffic patterns?
What school area or rooms have specific functions? House particular staff?
What is the play yard's appearance, equipment, built-ins?
Where are the safety controls, fire extinguisher, alarm, etc.?
Is any safety hazard apparent?
Are there special building features for individuals with special needs?
Where are emergency health supplies? Who is authorized to administer first aid?

Children

What individual physical characteristics are apparent?
What is the multicultural composition of the group?
What activities are popular?
Can all children in the room be viewed from one spot in the room?
Do all children seem to lose themselves in play?
What kinds of play exist? Solitary? Cooperative? Other?
What languages are spoken?
Does any child seem uncomfortable with adults?
What seems to be the group's general interest, general behavior?
Are there any children who need an abundance of teacher attention?
Are there any children with special needs?

Teaching Behaviors and Interactions

Are children "with" teachers?
How is guidance of child behavior undertaken?
Are all children supervised?
What style of teaching seems apparent?
Are feelings of warmth and acceptance of individuality shown?
If you were a child in this room, how might you feel?
Do teachers show enthusiasm?

Program

Does an atmosphere exist where children and teachers share decision-making and show respect for individual differences?
Are children exploring with teachers more often than being directed by them?
What are the planned activities?
Is there small group or large group instruction?
Is it a developmentally appropriate program?
How do activities begin and end?
Is the program based on child interest?
Does lots of dialogue exist among children? Among children and adults?
Are the children "tuned in" or "out"?
How are children moved from one activity to the next?

Overall First Impressions

What immediate questions would you like answered about the classroom?
What emotions have occurred as you observed?
What were your first impressions of the classroom?

Figure 1–15 Knowing your classroom

Introductions

Group time is introduction time. Your cooperating teacher may ask you to introduce yourself. You might start by saying, "My name is Sonia Smith." Note that some schools prefer Miss, Mrs., or Mr. instead of first names. "I'm a teacher, and I'm going to be here every day until December." Your face and body language should express acceptance and warmth. Alternatively, you might do a short "hello" activity that emphasizes your name.

—says hello with a finger . . .

—says hello with a hand . . .

Continue the activity using your elbow, arm, and other body parts, and finish by using your whole body to say hello. Then invite the children to repeat the entire activity with you.

If you have prepared an activity, briefly describe and check with the cooperating teacher regarding the best time to offer it.

BEGINNING DAYS

Your first few working days are going to be both exciting and exhausting. Many factors contribute to the situation. The Kraft and Casey (1967) comments that follow, although dated, are still relevant today!

> The induction of the student into actual teaching is a delicate and critical process. Unfortunately, no procedure exists that would guarantee universal success because many uncontrollable factors must be considered. The attitude of the student, the classroom climate, the inclination of the cooperating teacher, and the time of year are but a few of the many factors.

First impressions are important. Show initiative, be alert to the total classroom, listen closely, and try to be as self-directed as the situation calls for. Warner (1995) suggests your natural enthusiasm and "life is an adventure attitude" will be catching. Display your caring nature and positive attitude toward child accomplishment. Smile and make eye contact.

After-Session Conferencing

At team meetings, after important issues are discussed, your cooperating teacher and other staff adults will be interested in the questions and impressions you have developed after the first sessions. Be prepared to rely on your notes or journal. They are useful in refreshing your memory. Think of team conferences as debriefings when participants compare ideas, hypothesize, and make assumptions calling for the cognitive processing of information.

This meeting is also an appropriate time to clarify your cooperating teacher's expectations during your next few work days. If a class calendar (see Figure 1–16) is available, it will aid your activity planning. Most schools have their own system of planning activities. You may be asked to schedule your own activities at least one week in advance on a written plan.

The cooperating teacher may want you to stay within the planned subject areas or may give you a wide choice. Copies of a student teacher weekly activity sheet (see Figure 1–17) can be made and given weekly to the cooperating teacher. Ask about the best time to consult with your cooperating teacher.

MAY

SUNDAY	MONDAY	TUESDAY	WEDNESDAY	THURSDAY	FRIDAY	SATURDAY
						1 JAPANESE AM. WEEK
2	3	4 Megan's Birthday	5 BIRDS (MOTHER'S DAY GIFTS)	6	7 WORLD HEALTH DAY	8
9	10	11	12 PLANTING SEEDS	13	14	15
16	17 Paul's Birthday	18	19 BUGS AND INSECTS	20	21	22
23	24	25	26 ANIMALS OF THE WOODS	27 SECRETARIES DAY	28 ARBOR DAY	29

Figure 1–16 Sample of a class calendar (preschool level); theme instruction approach

BECOMING A TEAM MEMBER

You will become aware of each staff member's function and contribution to the operation of your assigned classroom. Nonteaching staff support educational efforts and realization of the center's goals (see Figure 1–18).

In addition to your own growth and development, one of your major goals as a team member is to add to the quality of young children's experiences. This involves teamwork. Teamwork takes understanding, dedication, and skill. Your status and acceptance as a member of the team will be gained through your own efforts.

For purposes of this field of study, team teaching involves and includes those people employed or connected with the daily operation of an early childhood center who work to achieve the goals of that center. They include paid and volunteer staff and parents. Understanding the duties and responsibilities of each team member will help you function in your role.

team teaching—an approach that involves coteaching in which status and responsibility are equal rather than having a pyramid structure of authority, with one person in charge and others subordinate.

Student Teacher ______________________________ Week ______________

Cooperating Teacher ____________________ Conference Time with Cooperating Teacher ________

STUDENT TEACHER RESPONSIBILITIES

Time	Monday	Tuesday	Wednesday	Thursday	Friday

Figure 1–17 Sample of a student teacher weekly activity sheet

Do the following staff members exist at your placement center?

	Yes	No	Names
1. Clerical staff	______	______	______________________
			______________________
2. Food service personnel	______	______	______________________
			______________________
3. Maintenance staff	______	______	______________________
			______________________
4. Bus drivers	______	______	______________________
			______________________
5. Community liaisons	______	______	______________________
			______________________
6. Health or nutrition staff	______	______	______________________
			______________________
7. Consultants or specialists	______	______	______________________
			______________________
8. Classroom aides	______	______	______________________
			______________________
9. Volunteers	______	______	______________________
			______________________
10. Others	______	______	______________________
			______________________

In what capacity? ____

Figure 1–18 Checklist of nonteaching support staff

GOALS OF THE TEAM AND PROGRAM

The importance of joint planning with your cooperating teacher is crucial to your success and competency growth. The feeling of team spirit is enhanced when your efforts reinforce or strengthen the efforts of other members.

Inadvertently, and unfortunately, some student teachers may tend to emphasize what they feel is the superiority of their college's training and its laboratory center. Teaching methods, materials, furnishings, supplies, staffing patterns, or just about every school feature may differ from what they have experienced in the college's training program. It may take a while to realize community programs have fewer resources, tighter budgets, and perhaps less expertise. Sensitivity is necessary along with an open mind. It is commendable to be enthusiastic and idealistic, but also to appreciate the cleverness and ingenuity many developmentally appropriate centers display while operating on limited funding and resources.

Team Meetings

Team meetings often include only the staff members associated with child instruction. Because staff meetings are new to student teachers, they are full of learning opportunities. Attend staff meetings if your student teaching schedule permits. The extra time involved will be well spent. To make these meetings as successful as possible, and to make them work for you, there are several things you can do before, during, and after the meeting.

Before

- Mark the time, date, and place of the meeting on your calendar.
- Clarify your role. Are you a guest, an observer, or an active participant?
- Get a copy of the meeting agenda and study it. Jot down notes to yourself.
- Make sure you understand the purpose of the meeting.
- Bring your notes and notebook.
- Review your notes from the last meeting you attended.
- Arrive on time.
- Prepare to stay for the entire meeting.

During

- Take notes, particularly when the discussion concerns student teachers.
- Participate and contribute when appropriate.
- Help staff members reach their objectives.
- Watch interactions between individuals.
- Look for preferences in teaching tasks expressed by others.

The more understanding you possess concerning individuals and group dynamics, the better prepared you will be to function as an effective team member. As you become "one of them," it is highly likely you will modify and change your initial thoughts and feelings.

After

- Mark the date of the next meeting.
- Complete your responsibilities.
- Prepare to report back at the next meeting.

Ask yourself the following questions:

- Do common bonds exist?
- Was satisfaction of individual needs apparent?
- Is there shared responsibility in achieving group goals?
- Was group problem-solving working?
- Are members open and trusting?
- Are individual roles clear?
- Did you notice cooperation?
- Do members know each others' strengths?
- Was the meeting dominated by one or a few?

Staff Behaviors

A number of behaviors may be exhibited during staff interactions. Some of these can be evaluated as positive team behaviors because they move a team toward the completion of tasks and handling of responsibilities. The following is a summary of supportive and positive staff behaviors.

- Giving or seeking information; asking for or providing factual or substantiated data
- Contributing new ideas, solutions, or alternatives
- Seeking or offering opinions to solve the task or problem
- "Piggybacking," elaborating, or stretching another's idea or suggestion; combining ideas
- Coordinating activities
- Emphasizing or reminding the group of the task at hand
- Evaluating by using professional standards
- Motivating staff to reach decisions
- Bringing meeting to a close and reviewing goals; making sure everyone understands the expected outcome
- Recording group ideas and progress

During staff meetings, individual staff members sometimes exhibit attitudes and sensitivities that soothe and mediate opposing points of view. Some examples follow:

- Encouraging, praising, respecting, and accepting diverse ideas or viewpoints
- Reconciling disagreements and offering "a light touch" of humor to help relieve tension
- Compromising
- Establishing open lines of communication
- Drawing input from silent members
- Monitoring dominance of discussion

Student teachers increasingly find that teaching teams contain differing cultural viewpoints. In situations when communicating across cultures takes place, Delpit (1995) suggests careful listening to alternative viewpoints:

> To do so takes a very special kind of listening, listening that requires not only open eyes and ears, but open hearts and minds.

> We really do not see through our eyes or hear through our ears, but through our beliefs. To put our beliefs on hold is to cease to exist as ourselves for a moment—and that is not easy, but it is the only way to learn what it might feel like to be someone else and the only way to start the dialogue.

NAEYC (1998) suggests the following staff relationship criteria:

- Staff interactions reflect mutual trust, respect, and support for each other
- Staff members seek out and acknowledge each other's ideas and opinions; staff gives positive recognition to each other's skills and accomplishments
- Staff provides appropriate supports for each other when dealing with stress
- Staff respects each other's rights to confidentiality
- Staff communicates with each other to ensure smooth operations

As a student teacher, you may have a clearer picture of the student teacher/cooperating teacher relationship than you do of the relationships among the assistant teacher, aide, parent, and student teacher. Usually, student teachers, aides, and volunteers work under the cooperating teacher who makes the ultimate decisions regarding the workings of the classroom. Moving from assistant to coteacher, a student teacher is the closest to the status of assistant or volunteer and assumes greater responsibility as time passes. Because of the changing role and increasing responsibilities, clear communication is a necessity.

Continuing to Observe

You will observe the unique characteristics of enrolled children and constantly monitor behaviors and conjecture causes for behaviors and underlying needs (see Figure 1–19). Unconsciously or consciously, you will begin to sort children into loose groupings that change daily in an almost unlimited number of ways. More noticeable characteristics will be the first to be recognized, and as you gain additional experience, subtle differences and similarities.

You will experience differing emotions with each child as you observe and interact. Many of the children will become memorable as children in your first class, as ones who taught you something about all children, or something about yourself.

Figure 1–19 You will come to know each child as an individual.

Parent Contacts

On your first meeting with parents, they may wonder who you are or immediately accept you as another classroom adult worker. Read their faces and introduce yourself if they seem interested. Be friendly and open rather than talkative. Mention your student teacher status and your training program. Remember, in this meeting as in all others you are representing the early childhood teaching profession.

Every classroom has a "feeling tone;" that is, it projects a certain atmosphere that creates feelings and perceptions in the minds and hearts of those who enter. Your classroom, no doubt, was designed and furnished with children in mind, but possibly includes a parent corner or an area making parents also feel at home or welcome.

Parents may see you as an expert and ask advice. You should refer these parents to your cooperating teacher.

In today's busy world, some parents will look rushed and anxious to get their child out the door. Others you observe will take time to touch base with their child and teachers before leaving. All parents will appreciate your knowing the location of their child's belongings and what needs to be taken home, and also your aid in promoting the child's transition back into parental care. Activities planned for parent pick-up times should allow children to easily stop and finish.

professional portfolio—a representative collection of your student teacher accomplishments.

Professional Portfolio Development

You may be required to put together a representative collection of your training accomplishments. Wolf and Dietz (1998) define a teaching portfolio as follows:

> A teaching portfolio is a structured collection of teacher and student work created across diverse contexts over time, framed by reflection and enriched through collaboration, that has as its ultimate aim the advancement of teacher and student learning.

A student teacher portfolio is not a miscellaneous collection but rather selected items and records of student teacher growth, progress toward goals, and attainment of professional standards. It best represents a student teacher's accomplishments and assessment information about teaching effectiveness. Wade and Yarbrough (1996) note training programs hope student teachers' development of a portfolio helps them become more reflective and improves their classroom practices. Other advantages can be the recognition of a student teacher's past performance compared to present skills and identified future growth areas. Input and interaction with college supervisors and cooperating teachers is included.

The portfolio represents who you are, what skills and competencies you possess, and what experiences have been part of your training. Because CDA training, a national training program, includes portfolio development, the collection of such materials has become increasingly required.

Caruso and Fawcett (1999) advise that an examination of portfolio materials should enable a supervisor, staff member, or peers to raise questions and to draw inferences about the owner's assumptions of how young children learn, what the educator values, how children should spend their time, and the ways in which the educator and children should interact. They point out that bulky, unwieldy portfolios can become very time-consuming if a reader tries to evaluate their contents, so select and organize material to emphasize quality, not quantity.

Your portfolio may also include "befores" and "afters" or specialized student talents and abilities. It can include a vast number of diverse visual, audio, and written materials including:

- An autobiography
- Supervisory comments
- Rating sheets and evaluations
- Letters of recommendation
- Projects
- Thematic units of study
- Examples of child work
- Child case studies
- Class papers
- Photographs
- Sample lesson plans
- Activities offered

- Discovery center creations
- Classroom schedules
- Examples of developing student teacher specializations
- Certificates such as CPR or first aid, awards, and other commendations
- Examples of individualized instruction
- A statement of personal educational philosophy or mission statement
- Parent letters or comments
- Designed room arrangements
- Conference attendance or other professional activities
- Accreditation involvement
- Videotapes
- Examples of classroom instructional materials created
- Any other items that display teaching ability or competency

The formatting of portfolios differs from one institution to another, but written materials usually include articulation of learning outcomes, reflections or related experience, and documentation.

The state of New Mexico has developed portfolio guidelines for certificate, associate, and bachelor's degree programs. Guidelines specify elements to be included and completed. These elements are reviewed by peers, faculty, and community representatives at the time of the student's exit from a training program (Turner, 2002). This type of portfolio may differ from the one your state, training institution, or supervisor requires. To review characteristics of a sample portfolio according to New Mexico's guidelines, see the appendix. Note that training instructors can attempt to evaluate the efficacy of instruction in offered courses, and the training program as a whole, using New Mexico's student portfolio elements.

Getting Organized

Suggestions for managing the multiple tasks and projects assigned in student teaching follow:

- Plan one week in advance
- Color-code project folders
- Decide what is (1) important and urgent, (2) important but not urgent, (3) not important but necessary, and (4) not important and not urgent
- Work on only one thing at a time. (1) Narrow focus by working on parts of a task. (2) Gather resources. (3) Bring tasks to closure

SUMMARY

The student teaching experience is the last step in a training sequence for early childhood teachers. Three key participants—the student teacher, the cooperating teacher, and the supervisor—form a team enabling the student teacher to gain new skills and sharpen previously acquired teaching techniques.

Student teaching involves the integration of all former training and experience. The cooperating teacher and supervisor guide, model, observe, and analyze the student teacher's progress in an assigned classroom as the student teacher assumes greater responsibilities with children and their families. Initial orientation meetings and written requirements and guidelines acquaint the student teacher with expectations and requirements. The student teaching experience is unique to each training institution, yet placement in a children's classroom with a supervisor's analysis of competency is common to all.

A caring, supportive atmosphere helps each student teacher attain established goals, and helps develop the student teacher's personal style and philosophy.

Before your first day of student teaching, it is a good idea to get an understanding of the children's environment by acquainting yourself with the children's home neighborhood and community. Also, you may wish to plan an activity to introduce yourself on the first day.

Active classroom interaction, as well as asking questions, should typify your first days. You can obtain necessary information concerning your work from the cooperating teacher when both you and the cooperating teacher have no supervision responsibilities.

In time, you will develop smooth working relationships and earn team status and acceptance with other staff members. Meetings are important vehicles for learning, and they will be a part of your future employment. You will be able to understand how each staff or team member contributes to the goals of a particular child center through observation and interaction.

HELPFUL WEB SITES

http://www.childrensfoundation.net

The Children's Foundation. Offers publications including the *2001 Child Care Licensing Study.*

http://nccic.org

National Child Care Information Center. A resource that provides links to other Web sites and information promoting high-quality care.

http://nccic.org

Lists available publications and full-text documents.

http://www.nncc.org

National Network for Child Care. Search for items of interest.

http://ericeece.org/

ERIC Clearinghouse on Elementary and Early Childhood Education. The best known Web site for information, research, and publications.

SUGGESTED ACTIVITIES

A. Read the following essay by Patricia Pruden Mohr (from California Child Development Centers' Administrators Association Newsletter). Which ideas and/or phrases do you feel are important? Discuss with the class how this description relates to centers or schools where you have observed or have been employed.

Philosophy for a Children's Center

A philosophy statement for a children's center is a critical starting point. It presents the ideal toward which a staff and parents strive. It establishes a basic premise from which all activities of the center emanate. It's a returning point, a centering, in time of crisis.

Here then is a philosophy adhered to by one center. Perhaps it will facilitate you in the development or reassessment of yours.

The Children's Center is designed to create an environment of trust where people can grow emotionally, intellectually, socially, and physically. The people of the Center are those children and adults who participate in its program. Each person is a learner, each a teacher, each a valued individual.

What a young child experiences is what s/he will learn. There is that of the young child in all of us. The Center is a learning place, a place to experience oneself in relationship to others and to the environment. The Center is a place of feeling, a place where the individual and his or her feelings are accepted and valued. The Center is a place of wonder that provides the opportunity to question, to explore, to succeed, to celebrate. It is a sharing environment based on the premise that each of us has a unique gift to share—the gift of self. The Center is a pluralistic environment that has a commitment to support ethnic, economic, and social similarities and differences.

Each of us is here together to experience, to learn, to support one another in the experience that is life. Each person has a right to experience him/herself as a person of worth who participates in determining his/her own destiny as much as s/he is able without causing harm to self or others. Each person has the obligation to recognize, respect, and support the rights of others. Each person has the right to move at his or her own pace honoring his/her individual development rate. The Children's Center is designed to support the search for direction of children and adults who participate in the program and to permit each person to set the design of his/her own becoming.

B. Cut a large gingerbread figure out of paper. With crayons, illustrate your feelings toward student teaching at this point of the experience, the first days. Pin the figure to your blouse or shirt, and silently walk around the room studying others' gingerbread figures. In groups of two, discuss your interpretations of each gingerbread figure. Discuss similarities and differences between your gingerbread figure and others. Briefly discuss your discoveries with the class. (Figures can be pasted to a large chart, then posted.)

C. If you were to describe yourself using a self-designed logo or a popular song title, what would it be? As you enter this student teaching experience, try to describe briefly who you are, what you do, and any individual unique teaching perspectives or life experiences you might hold. Share with a classmate.

D. Read and discuss the following with a group of classmates. Report the group's reactions to the whole class.

   There was a world of difference between student teaching and daily work environments (employment site). The lab school was rich in staff role models and materials. The community (employment site) program was ill-equipped with both. At the lab school, there was [sic] almost enough wheel toys for each child to have one, while at the child care center, about a dozen children vied for the opportunity to ride one working vehicle. It was almost impossible to translate what I was learning at the university into practice at my job because the basic ingredients were so different. Discouragement and frustration were the result. (Whitebook, 1994)

E. Complete the requests in Figure 1–20 and prepare a daily teaching responsibilities list similar to Figure 1–21.

F. Obtain a copy of your placement school's disaster plan. Bring to class to discuss.

G. Rate each of the items in Figure 1–22 on a scale of 1 to 5. Discuss the results as a group.

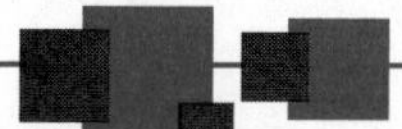

1. Make a rough map of your classroom and yard.
2. Briefly describe the child group. Identify children about whom you would like additional information.
3. List names of staff members.
4. Describe your relationship with your cooperating teacher during your first days.
5. Describe available materials and equipment. Do you feel they are adequate and satisfactory in all aspects?
6. What are some memorable experiences of your first days?

Figure 1–20 Placement observation form.

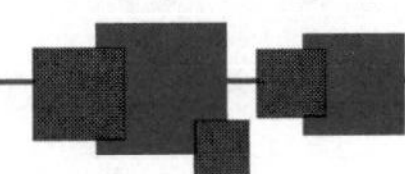

Three-year-olds—Morning program

8:00–8:30	Check to see that room is in order and materials are on proper shelves. Check snack supplies. Check day's curriculum. Know what materials are needed.
8:30–8:45	**Arrival of Children** • Greet each child and parent. • Help children locate their lockers. • Help children with name tags. • Help children initiate an activity.
8:30–9:20	**Free-play Time Inside**—Art, block play, dramatic play, manipulative materials, science, math, housekeeping area, language arts. • Supervise assigned area. Proceed to another area if there is no child in your area. • Interact with children if you can. Be careful not to interfere in their play. • Encourage children to clean up after they finish playing with materials. • Manipulative materials, including modeling dough and scissors, stay on the table. • Be on the child's level. Sit on the floor or on a chair, or kneel. • Children wear smocks when using paint or chalk. Print children's names on their art work in upper left corner. • Give five-minute warning before clean-up time.
9:20–9:30	**Transition Time**—Clean up, wash hands, use bathrooms. Help with clean-up. Guide children to bathroom before coming to group. All children should use the bathroom to wash hands and be encouraged to use the toilet. • Place soiled clothes/underpants in plastic baggies and place them in children's cubbies. • Children flush the toilet. • Let them wash hands, using soap. • Bathroom accidents should be treated matter-of-factly. • Use word "toilet." • Help children with their clothes but remember to encourage self-help skills.
9:30–9:45	**Large Group**—Assist restless children. Leave to set up snack if it is your responsibility. Put cups and napkins around table. Make sure there are sufficient chairs and snack places. • Teacher of the week leads group time. • Show enthusiasm in participating with the activities.
9:45–10:00	**Snack** • There should be one teacher at each table. • Engage in conversation. • Encourage self-help skills. Provide assistance if needed. • Encourage children to taste food. • Demonstrate good manners such as saying please and thank you. • Help children observe table manners. • Children should throw napkins in trash can. • If spills occur, offer a sponge. Help only if necessary. • Quickly sponge down tables.
10:00–10:45	**Outside Play**—Check children and cubbies to make sure children are wearing outside clothing if the weather is cold. If a child does not have sufficient clothing, check the school supply of extra clothing. **Outside Activities**—Tricycles, sand toys, climbing equipment, balls, and so on. • Supervise all areas. Spread out.

continues

Figure 1–21 Guide to daily teaching responsibilities.

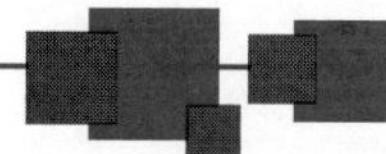

- Help children share toys and take care of the equipment.
- Always be alert to the physical safety of the children.
- When necessary, remind them that sand is to be kept in the sandbox.
- Water faucet is operated only by adults or when there is adult supervision.
- Children may remove shoes during warm weather only.
- If raining, children stay under shelter.
- Teachers should refrain from having long conversations with each other. Attention should be on the children all the time.
- Bring tissue outside to wipe noses if needed.
- Give five-minute warning to clean up and go inside.
- Children must help return toys to the storage room.

10:45–11:00 **Clean up, Use Bathroom, Prepare for Small Group**

- Children go to assigned small groups.
- Each child sits on a carpet square.

11:00–11:20 **Small Group**—Transitional activities include flannelboard stories, discussion with visual aids, games, filmstrip if applicable, songs, and fingerplays. Teacher puts children's rest mats out.

11:20–11:30 **Rest Time**

- Children lie on mats.
- Quiet music is played.
- Children do not bother other children. Whisper to restless children and tell them it is a quiet time.
- Children fold blankets, rugs, or mats and put them in their cubbies.

11:30 **Departure**

- Get children's artwork to take home and put in their cubbies.
- Help children with coats, shoes, etc.
- See children off.

11:30–12:00 **End-of-Morning Session**—Help with clean-up. Double check that all areas are clean and all materials are in their correct places. Share any observations with teachers, and solicit their observations and feelings during your team meeting.

NOTE: This daily guide is typical of guides used in a morning prekindergarten laboratory school placement for student teachers. A similar guide can be developed for any placement site by a student teacher once room schedules are known.

Figure 1-21 Continued

1 strongly agree	2 mildly agree	3 cannot decide	4 mildly disagree	5 strongly disagree

Staff status is not earned. There is always a pecking order.	Food service people are usually held in high regard by early childhood teachers.	Ethnic and cultural differences are the cause of most staff disagreements.	Children are affected by staff spirit.
One staff member may be responsible for enthusiastic staff meetings.	Giving dignity and respect to each job is the key to positive staff relationships.	Maintenance staff and teaching staff have few interactions at most early childhood centers.	It would be a good idea for staff members to trade positions for one day.
Meetings should be evaluated.	Aides and assistants in the classroom regard student teachers as threatening.	Cooperating teachers do not see students teachers as co-teachers.	The students teacher is the only one who is observed and evaluated.
Its is easy to get along with staff.	Speaking up in staff meetings can be scary.	Most student teachers are used to participating in meetings and group efforts.	It would be a good idea to post a student teacher's photograph in the lobby of a preschool.
There are some people who just will not talk at meetings.	A golden rule in staff relationships is to leave an area as orderly as you found it.	All staff members should be on a first name basis.	Food and coffee can help break barriers at staff or other meetings.
Meeting notes should be taken by a student teacher.	Everything that is said in a meeting is confidential.	The children's progress is the subject of most meetings.	Individuals should rate them-selves on both the quantity and quality of their input at meetings.

Figure 1-22

REVIEW

A. Choose the statements that describe what you feel are important goals of a student teaching experience.

1. The student teacher increases the quality of the children's daily program.
2. The student teacher evaluates the cooperating teacher's style.
3. The student teacher becomes aware of vocational skill and strengths and weaknesses.
4. The student teacher develops unique capabilities.
5. The student teacher gains practical experience.
6. The three key members stimulate each other's growth through supportive, caring interactions.
7. The centers reduce costs by working with training programs.
8. The student teacher is another expert with whom parents can consult regarding their child's progress.
9. Communities benefit when early childhood teacher training produces well-trained, competent teachers.

B. Select the answer that best completes each statement.

1. Student teaching practices and procedures are:
   a. very similar when one compares different teacher training programs.
   b. as different as pebbles in a pile.
   c. uniform and dictated by state law.
   d. different at training institutions and agencies but always involve five key individuals.

2. The individual who is supposed to gain the most new skills through student teaching is:
   a. the student teacher, but the cooperating teacher's and supervisor's new skills may surpass the student's skills.
   b. the child.
   c. the supervisor, who has learned each student teacher's unique way of performing duties.
   d. the reader of this text.
   e. impossible to determine.
3. Being observed and analyzed during student teaching means:
   a. being watched and criticized.
   b. self-evaluation and evaluation of others will take place.
   c. others will try to pinpoint the areas where the student teacher needs to sharpen skills.
   d. parents, directors, and all members of the adult team will evaluate student competency.
   e. children's behavior will determine ratings of student teacher competency.
4. In most states, the record that must be completed before the student teacher works with children is the student teacher's:
   a. health history.
   b. personal history.
   c. bonding agreement.
   d. insurance clearance.
   e. TB clearance.
5. Professional conduct can mean:
   a. insisting that a child say please and thank you.
   b. dressing appropriately with attention to personal hygiene.
   c. speaking candidly to a parent about the limitations of a cooperating teacher's method.
   d. none of these.

C. List four considerations in preparing for your first day as a student teacher.

D. Describe two activities you might plan for your first day as a student teacher. List two reasons you selected these activities.

E. Read "Getting the Most out of Student Teaching Depends on You" (see Figure 1–23). Write a one-minute summary of the items that you feel will be the most difficult and also the easiest to follow.

F. Rate the following student teacher meeting skills in order of priority from 1 to 10, number 10 being the highest. You may give equal points to items if necessary.

- Speaking one's mind
- Listening
- Being prepared
- Following through
- Asking questions
- Staying the whole meeting
- Not interrupting
- Bringing notes
- Giving solutions
- Suggesting innovations
- Giving data
- Taking notes

1. Examine your attitude and decide you are going to expend every effort to learn new skills. Risk trying new ways and making mistakes. Communicate your desire to be given added and more challenging responsibilities. Welcome and encourage feedback from those supervising you.
2. When in doubt, ask questions. Select the time and place most convenient for your supervisors or write questions down for them if conferencing is immediately impossible. Be willing to come early or stay late if necessary.
3. Being professional involves a timely arrival and telephone calls when you need to be late or absent. Inform your college supervisor of field trips, testing, or special events when her observation of your work would not be possible. Your dress, personal appearance, and manner represent your professional image.
4. Make decisions using your best judgment. Seek clarification if you are uncertain of rules or expectations.
5. Realize the cooperating teacher's first priority is the needs, safety, and welfare of children. You are an added responsibility. Be aware there are times when the cooperating teacher cannot focus on you or your concerns.
6. See what needs to be done and do it without waiting for directions. Observe and study the children, program, and environment. Familiarize yourself with all aspects of the situation. Know where equipment and materials are stored. Be alert to daily schedules and routines.
7. See yourself as a needed assistant being increasingly responsible and alert to where you are most necessary.
8. Be friendly, learn names, and fit into classroom life quickly by being helpful and sensitive to school staff members.
9. Watch teacher skills, techniques, and behaviors with children and parents. Try to identify the goals of instruction behind words and actions.
10. Avoid socializing with other adults during work periods and instead be watchful, observant, and ready to learn from children and classroom situations. Scan the area, develop "eyes in the back of your head." When sitting, choose positions that allow the best classroom views.
11. Remain nonjudgmental when site politics are present. Try to inwardly evaluate staff conflicts. Discuss with your college supervisor your position as a "fence sitter" who avoids taking sides if a difficult situation or power struggles between adults arise.
12. When viewing new techniques or methods, remain open-minded and reflective. If ethics are involved, ask for a college supervisor consultation quickly.
13. Receive input from supervisors with the belief that both compliments and suggestions for growth will enable you to become a more skilled and valuable early childhood educator.

Figure 1-23 Getting the most out of student teaching depends on you.

G. Identify some of your placement site's program goals in the following child development areas.
   - Academic—intellectual—cognitive
   - Social—emotional development and behaviors
   - Physical development and skill
   - Creative potential development
   - Language development
   - Multicultural understanding
   - Self-help skills

H. Develop a freehand line chart that represents levels of responsibility at your placement center. Begin with person(s) who directs, owns, or administers at the top level, and work down to yourself. Add this to your journal.

CASE SCENARIO

Setting: Tyra's Placement Classroom

Tyra's worst fears faced her on the first day in her student teacher placement classroom! Talk about feeling like an outsider, there wasn't one child who spoke English well. The children were friendly enough, and only a few children stared at the color of her skin. Tyra understood about half of what the children said to her. A few children seemed really out of control and ignored what she said to guide them. The cooperating teacher was welcoming but so busy she had little time to interact with Tyra. Things improved slightly as the school day progressed because Mrs. Solorozano, the teacher's aide, interpreted what the children said and explained classroom routines and procedures when Tyra had a question. Tyra felt this classroom would be a great learning opportunity, even if she felt uncomfortable at times.

Questions for Discussion:

1. According to the chapter, something evidently did not take place or did not prepare Tyra for her first day. What could have helped prepare her?
2. Should Tyra consult her college supervisor quickly or perhaps wait and see if things improve?
3. Could seeking her college supervisor's help make her supervisor suspect Tyra was not ready for student teaching?

REFERENCES

Carter, M., & Curtis, D. (1994). *Training teachers: A harvest of theory and practice.* St. Paul, MN: Redleaf Press.

Caruso, J. J., & Fawcett, M. T. (1999). *Supervision in early education: A developmental perspective.* New York: Teachers College Press.

Delpit, L. (1995). *Other people's children: Cultural conflict in the classroom.* New York: The New Press.

Feeney, S., & Kipnis, K. (1998). *Code of ethical conduct* [Brochure]. Washington, DC: National Association for the Education of Young Children.

Feeney, S., & Freeman, N. (1999). *Ethics and the early childhood educator: Using the NAEYC code.* Washington, DC: National Association for the Education of Young Children.

Glickman, C., Gordon, S., & Ross-Gordon, J. (1998). *Supervision of instruction: A developmental approach.* Boston: Allyn and Bacon.

Hollingsworth, S. (1998, Fall). Making field based programs work: A three level approach to reading education. *Journal of Teacher Education*, 39.

Jones, E. (1986). *Teaching adults*. Washington, DC: National Association for the Education of Young Children.

Jones, E. (1994). Constructing professional knowledge by telling our stories. In J. Johnson & J. McCracken (Eds.). *The early childhood career lattice: Perspectives on professional development*. Washington, DC: National Association for the Education of Young Children.

Justen, J. E., & McJunkin, M. (1999). Supervisory beliefs of cooperating teachers. In M. Scherer (Ed.). *A better beginning: Supporting and mentoring new teachers* (173–180). Alexandria, VA: Association for Supervision and Curriculum.

Katz, L., & Ward, E. (1978). *Ethical behavior in early childhood education*. Washington, DC: National Association for the Education of Young Children.

Kraft, L., & Casey, J. R. (1967). Roles in off-campus student teaching. Champaign, IL: Stipes.

National Association for the Education of Young Children (1998). *Accreditation criteria and procedures of the National Association for the Education of Young Children*. Washington, DC: Author.

National Association for the Education of Young Children. (1996). *Guidelines for preparation of early childhood professionals*. Washington, DC: Author.

Rasinski, T. V. (1989). Reading and the empowerment of parents. *The Reading Teacher, 43*(3).

Schriver, A. K. (1999). "I am so excited!" Mentoring the student teacher. In M. Scherer (Ed.). *A better beginning: Supporting and mentoring new teachers* (77–84). Alexandria, VA: Association for Supervision and Curriculum.

Sudzina, M., Giebelhaus, C., & Coolican, M. (1997, Winter). Mentor or tormentor: The role of the cooperating teacher in student teacher success or failure. *Action in Teacher Education, XVIII*(4).

Turner, P. (Ed.). (2002). *La ristra: New Mexico's comprehensive professional development system in early care, education and family support*. Santa Fe, NM: Office of Child Development, Youth and Families Department.

Wade, R., & Yarbrough, D. (1996, Spring). Portfolios: A tool for reflective thinking in teacher education? *Teaching and Teacher Education, 12*.

Warner, J. (1995). *The unauthorized TEACHER'S survival guide*. Indianapolis, IN: Park Avenue Publications.

Whitebook, M. (1994). At the core: Advocacy to challenge the status quo. In J. Johnson & J. McCracken (Eds.). *The early childhood career lattice: Perspectives on professional development*. Washington, DC: National Association for the Education of Young Children.

Whitmire, R. (2000, May). Survey: New teachers love jobs, feel unprepared, *The Idaho Statesman*, 10A.

Wolf, K., & Dietz, M. (1998, Winter). Teaching portfolios: Purpose and possibilities. *Teachers Education Quarterly, 25*(1).

CHAPTER 2

A Student Teacher's Values and Developing Teaching Style

Objectives **After studying this chapter, the student should be able to:**

1 Define the role of personal values in teaching.

2 Describe how values influence what happens in the classroom.

3 Describe how the activities the student teacher enjoys reflect personal values.

4 List at least five values that guide the student teacher's lessons and activities.

5 Identify at least three different teaching styles.

6 Define and describe his or her own teaching style.

7 Discuss the relationship between a philosophy of education and a teaching style.

I've learned that I am a rather biased person rather than the enlightened minority group member I thought I was. Understanding and accepting this was my first step toward change. I've had to analyze the origins of my attitudes.

—Felecia Arii

I like a well-organized, tidy classroom. My cooperating teacher likes the three-ring circus approach to classroom activity which offers plenty of child choices. I suspect my supervisor chose to place me here to broaden my horizons, to "loosen me up" so to speak, and it's happening. I can tolerate clutter and minor confusion better.

—Bobbette Ryan

My cooperating teacher had very definite attitudes concerning the celebration of Halloween. When she explained how she felt, I had a new view. Now I'm feeling it's good to question if some traditional celebrations add to the quality of children's lives.

—Mannington Lee

I was intimidated watching my cooperating teacher. She was so professional. After a while I realized I had teaching strengths she admired and appreciated. We made a great team. She "zigged," I "zagged" but we pulled together. Our different approaches to the same goals made the classroom livelier. Oh what discussions we had!

—Maeve Critchfield

KNOWING YOURSELF AND YOUR VALUES

We will begin this chapter with an exercise. On a separate sheet of folded paper, number the spaces from 1 to 20. Then list, as quickly as possible, your favorite activities. Do this spontaneously; do not pause to think.

Now go back and code your listed activities as follows.

- Mark those activities you do alone with an *A*.
- Mark those activities that involve at least one more person with a *P*.
- Mark with an *R* those activities that may involve risk.
- Mark those in which you are actively doing something with a *D*.
- Mark with an *S* those activities at which you are a spectator.
- Mark activities that cost money with an *M*.
- Mark activities that are free with an *F*.
- Mark with a *Y* any activity you have not done for one year.

Now that you have coded your activities, what have you learned about yourself? Are you more a spectator than a doer? Do you seldom take risks? Did you list more than one activity in which you have not participated for more than one year? Do you frequently spend money on your activities, or do most of your activities cost little or nothing? Were any of your answers a surprise? We hope you learned something new about yourself.

Let us try another exercise. Complete the following sentences as quickly as possible.

1. School is . . .
2. I like . . .
3. Children are . . .
4. Teaching is . . .
5. Little girls are . . .
6. I want . . .
7. Children should . . .
8. Little boys are . . .
9. Parents are . . .
10. Teachers should . . .
11. I am . . .
12. Fathers are . . .
13. I should . . .
14. Mothers are . . .
15. Teachers are . . .
16. Parents ought to . . .
17. School ought to . . .
18. Aggressive children make me . . .
19. Shy children make me . . .
20. Whiny children make me . . .

Did you find this activity easier or more difficult than the first? This exercise is less structured than the first. You had to shift your thinking from statement to statement. We hope it made you take a thoughtful pause as you were forced to shift your thinking as verbs changed from simple or declarative to the more complex conditional or obligatory forms. Present-tense forms such as "is" or "are" encourage concrete, factual responses. With the conditional "should" or obligatory "ought," your response may have become more a reflection of what you feel an ideal should be. In addition, with the present tense, a response is usually short whereas with the conditional "should" or obligatory "ought," you may have used more words to explain your response.

Look at your answers. Do you find you have different responses depending on whether the present tense, the conditional tense, or the obligatory form of the verb was used? What do these differences tell you about yourself? Van Leuvan (1997) believes an initial step and essential component in the development of reflective processes in teaching is the examination and clarification of one's belief about what constitutes and contributes to effective teaching.

THE ACQUISITION OF VALUES

Let us reflect on how we acquire our values. Logically, many of our values reflect those of our parents. As children, we naturally absorbed our first values through observing our parents and family members, and direct parental teaching (see Figure 2–1). Few children are even aware that they are being influenced by their parents; they take in parental attitudes and values through the processes of observation and imitation. We want to be like our fathers and mothers, especially because they appear to have the power over the rewards we receive. Smiles when we do something of which they approve, hugs, and "that's right" said over and over shape our behavior so that we begin to accept what our parents accept. Wedman, Espinosa, and Laffey (1998) point out a person's beliefs about teaching are well established before entering college.

Figure 2–1 Family teachings and traditions influence children who absorb values through observation and imitation.

Why are you attracted to the profession of teaching? Is there a teacher in your family? Does your family place a value on learning? Did you enjoy school yourself? Were your parents supportive of school when you were young? The chances are that you answered positively to at least one of these questions. One reason many people teach professionally is that they truly enjoyed being a student themselves. Learning has been fun and often easy. As a result, an education is highly valued. Teachers frequently come from families in which the profession was valued, not because it pays well but, more likely, for the pleasure received in working with young children and the intangible experience of influencing young lives (see Figure 2–2).

Grant and Murray (1999) suggest:

> Teachers of both genders choose teaching for the intrinsic satisfactions and joy of the work. They feel whole and connected and engaged in meaningful work in a way that many in modern society do not. The leading reasons teachers say they chose the profession are that they like to work with children (66 percent), that they like the inherent meaning and value of the job (38 percent), and that they are interested in a specific subject-matter field (36 percent).
>
> Other surveys show that most teachers (87 percent) find their greatest satisfaction in reaching students and knowing they have learned.

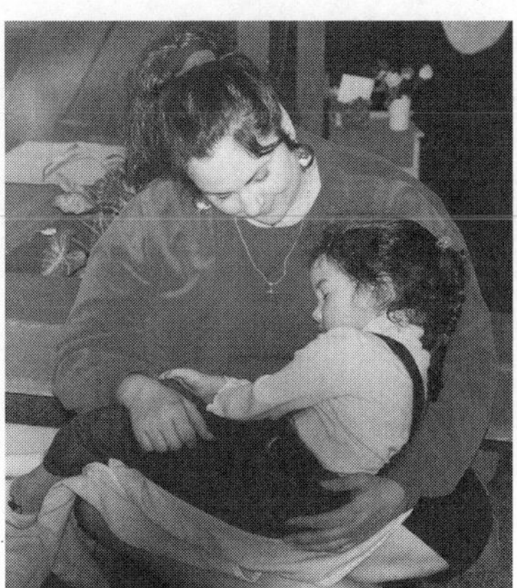

Figure 2–2 Nurturing young children is one of the appealing aspects of a teaching career.

One problem many teachers face is accepting negative attitudes from parents or caregivers who do not place similar values on education. It is difficult to relate to them. You need to remember that some parents may come from cultures where educational opportunities were denied. In addition, some parents may feel that an education never did them any good; they may be products of education systems that failed them. These parents have different values than you. What can you do? Always show, through your actions (they speak louder than words), that you care for their children and that you want to help their children. Assuming that the parents want their children to have better opportunities, that they want the best for their children, you can earn the parents' respect and cooperation.

On a separate sheet of paper, judge the following as true or false.

1. Your ethnic background was not an issue when you were a child.
2. Your neighborhood was multicultural.
3. People treated you differently because of your ethnic heritage.
4. You were financially secure most of your childhood.
5. Religion is important in your life.
6. You're proud of your racial group.
7. Life was full of hope rather than despair in childhood.
8. You have been the object of discrimination.
9. Your ethnic group is minimally understood by most Americans.
10. Your identity, sense of self, is well formed.

Many of our most enduring values were formed through contact with our family when we were too young to remember. Others were acquired through repeated experience. Let us use an example. Assume that you were raised in the city and lived in apartment houses your entire life. Because you never had a yard of your own, you have had little experience with plants beyond the potted variety. You are now renting a house with a yard, and you enjoy puttering around in the garden. Because your experiences with gardening have been pleasurable, you have acquired a positive value for it. If your experiences had been bad, you could have acquired a negative value just as easily.

Krathwohl's Hierarchy

One way of looking at the acquisition of values is to look at Krathwohl's taxonomy (1984). Krathwohl and his associates were interested in looking at the "affective domain," or the field of knowledge associated with feelings and values. Krathwohl arranged the affective domain into a hierarchy as follows:

1. Receiving (attending)
2. Responding
3. Valuing
4. Organization
5. Characterization by a value or value complex.

For you, as a teacher of young children, the first three levels are the most important. Suppose you had not been willing to receive the stimulus of potted plants being a pleasure to see? Being aware of the aesthetics of having plants and enjoying their presence is the first sublevel of receiving; that is, becoming sensitive. Becoming interested in them and enjoying their beauty moves one beyond mere awareness to the next sublevel: willingness to receive. There is a third sublevel of receiving: controlled or selected attention. What does this mean? How is this demonstrated? Looking at potted plants and remarking on their growth, need for water, and flowers are all examples of selected attention.

If you saw that the plant needed water and proceeded to water it, you have moved to the second level of the hierarchy; responding. If you water the plant after being asked to do so, you have reached the first sublevel; acquiescence in responding. If you do it without being asked, you are at the second sublevel; willingness to respond. Noting satisfaction in the growth of the plant because you have been a part of its care moves you into the third sublevel of responding; satisfaction in response.

Valuing, the third level, also has sublevels. The first is acceptance of a value. When you buy your own potted plants, for example, you are revealing a value. You like potted plants enough to buy and care for them. The second sublevel is showing a preference for a value. For example, if you chose to rent a house with a yard instead of an apartment because of the opportunity to work in the yard, you have shown preference for a value. Taking care of the yard then moves you into the third sublevel; commitment. (From Awareness to Action, Project Wild, 1986, Western Regional Environmental Education Council.)

Let us now study these three levels of value in more specific terms. Try the following exercise (adapted from Biehler & Snowman, 1990). Write your answers on a separate sheet of paper.

Receiving (Attending). The learner becomes sensitized to the existence of certain phenomena and stimuli.

1. Awareness: What types of awareness do you want your students to have? For example, do you want them to be aware of the books in the classroom? List those things you want the children to become aware of.
2. Willingness to receive: What types of tolerance do you want your students to develop? For example, do you want your students to sit quietly and listen when you read a book to them? Describe the behavior you hope to see from your students regarding their willingness to receive.
3. Controlled or selected attention: List the things you want the students to recognize that are frequently ignored by trained observers. For instance, do you want your students to recognize the predictability or pattern of repetition in a story?

Responding. The learner does something with the phenomena.

1. Acquiescence in responding: What habits of responses do you want to encourage? Do you want your students to respond to your questions about the story you just read?
2. Willingness to respond: List the voluntary responses you want to encourage. Do you want the students to ask their own questions about a story as you read it?
3. Satisfaction in response: List the habits of satisfaction you want your students to develop. Do you want them to respond with smiles, excitement, or laughter to the story? Do you want them to listen with anticipation, predicting the outcome with pleasure and enthusiasm?

Valuing. The learner displays consistent behavior reflecting a general attitude.

1. Acceptance of a value: List the types of emotional acceptance you want your students to develop. Do you want your students to go voluntarily to the book corner to "read" the same book you just read to them?
2. Preference for a value: What values do you want your students to develop to the point of actively identifying with the stimulus? Do you want them to urge other children in the class to "read" the story? Do you

want to see them choose this book to "read" while role-playing school and you as teacher?

3. Commitment: List the behaviors you want your students to develop that will enable you to decide whether they are committed to the stimulus. Do you want them to check out the book from the class to take home? Do you want them to take out the book from the local library? Do you want them to go to the book corner at least three times each week? What evidence of commitment to your stimulus are you looking for?

We will not continue further with this exercise because you may not know if the students have absorbed your stimulus into their value systems until after they move on from your class. For yourself, however, go back over this exercise and ask yourself the following:

1. Why did I choose that particular example as the stimulus I wanted my students to receive and respond to?
2. What does this reveal about my own value system?
3. Is this value a part of *me*, a part of my character?

If you cannot answer these questions, we suggest that you go back and repeat the exercise with another stimulus. For example, your choices may range from some facet of the curriculum—story time and books—to some facet of behavior—paying attention, sharing toys, not fighting—among other possibilities.

YOUR VALUES

Why is it important for you as a student teacher to be aware of your values? We hope that you already know the answer. In many ways, the answer lies in what Rogers (1966) calls congruence. Self-knowledge should precede trying to impart knowledge to others. By looking closely at your values, you will be able to develop a philosophy of teaching more easily. Your particular life stories can be the starting point for reflection and dialogue (Jones, 1994).

Let us move on to another exercise. On a separate sheet of paper, trace the figure on page 51. In the top left-hand section, draw a picture of what you believe is your best asset. Next to it in the top right-hand section, draw a picture of something you do well. In the middle left-hand section, draw a picture of something you would like to do better. In the middle right-hand section, draw a picture of something you want to change about yourself. In the bottom left-hand section, draw a picture of something that frightens you. In the bottom right-hand section, write five adjectives that you would like other people to use to describe you. Look at your drawings and think about what your **affective** responses were to this exercise. Did you find it easier to draw a picture of something that frightens you? Was it easier to draw than to list five adjectives? Did you feel more comfortable drawing or writing your responses? What does this say about you? Were you able to write the first two or three adjectives quickly and then forced to give some thought to the remaining two?

affective—caused by or expressing emotion or feeling.

Some of us have more difficulty handling compliments than negative criticism; thus, we find it easier to draw a picture of something we do well. Some of us have negative feelings about our ability to draw anything; being asked to do an exercise that asks for a drawn response is a real chore. Did you silently breathe a sigh of relief when you came to the last part of the exercise and were asked for a written response? Does this suggest that you are more comfortable with words than with nonverbal expressions?

If you are more at ease with words, what are the implications regarding any curriculum decisions you might make? Would you be inclined to place a greater emphasis on language activities than on art activities, especially those involving drawing? If you can deal more easily with the negative aspects of yourself than with the positive aspects, what are the implications for your curriculum decisions? Is it possible that you would find it easier to criticize rather than compliment a student? Is it possible that you are inclined to see mistakes rather than improvements? Think about this. How do the activities you enjoy reflect your personal values and thus influence your classroom curriculum? Go back to the first exercise you completed in this chapter. What were the first five activities you listed? List them on a separate piece of paper. Next to this column, write five related classroom activities. Does your list look something like this?

Activity	**Related Curriculum Activity**
Playing the piano	Teaching simple songs with piano accompaniment
Jogging	Allowing active children to run around the playground
Skiing	Climbing, jumping, gross motor activities

PERSONAL VALUES AND ACTIVITIES

What is the relationship between activities and personal values? Van Leuvan (1997) believes that teachers who aim to improve their professional practice must recognize not only what they are doing but also must understand the origins and effects of their actions. In this way, they might consider alternative approaches to teaching and learning. It seems obvious that we would not become involved in an activity that did not bring us some reward or pleasure; we have to be motivated (see Figure 2–3). Usually, that motivation becomes intrinsic because significant people in our lives provided an extrinsic reward, usually a smile or compliment. Given enough feedback in the form of compliments, we learn to accept and even prize the activity.

feedback—information given and deemed to be a true and accurate account of what happened. May be evaluated as positive, negative, or otherwise by the informant or listener.

Figure 2–3 Will you feel that displaying the flag is appropriate for early childhood classrooms?

Many of us want to teach young children because we genuinely like them. When did we learn this? Some teachers, as the oldest of many siblings, learned to care for and enjoy being with younger brothers and sisters. Others had positive experiences from baby-sitting.

Perhaps we want to teach young children because they are less threatening than older children. In addition, young children are often more motivated to please the adults in their lives than teenagers.

Attitudes toward or against something are often formed when we are so young that we do not know their origin. We only know that we have a tendency to like or dislike something or someone. Because these attitudes arouse a strong *affect*, or feeling for or against, they can influence our values. People of different backgrounds who do not share similar ideals often find their values being challenged.

reflective teaching—a serious effort to thoughtfully question teaching practices, perceptions, actions, feelings, values, cultural biases, and other features associated with the care and education of young children.

ethics—a set of moral principles or values that serves as the basis for conscientious, sound, professional decision-making or judgments.

Other student teachers in your class (group) will demonstrate individual degrees of teaching experience, background knowledge, teaching skill, and technique. You are urged not to compare what you have to offer children with what you perceive others possess, but rather that you stretch and advance in your own directions.

We urge you to be thoughtful, open-minded, and reflective concerning your training experiences, stepping back at times to think about your conclusions and experiences in child classrooms, and to participate in discussions that clarify and enlighten. This is called reflective teaching.

Some college supervisors require student teachers to write personal or life histories and mission statements. They recommend including sections describing experiences as pupils, as scholars preparing for teaching, as members of ethnic and cultural groups, and as members of unique and diverse families.

PROFESSIONAL ETHICS

Katz (1992) defines ethics as a set of statements that helps us deal with the temptations inherent in our occupations. Ethics may also help us act in concert with what we believe to be right rather than what is expedient. Making decisions in the best interests of children and their families may take courage and commitment to professional excellence. One may risk losing a job or license, or risk other serious consequences by sticking to one's ethical standards.

Educators have considerable power over children's daily lives and general welfare, and often are seen as experts by parents. This occupational situation enables them to impact and influence lives, self-esteem, and so on. They also can possibly cause short- and long-term damage.

So many situations may test ethics in student teaching. Cecile, a student teacher, faced a situation that unfortunately may not be unique. Cecile's cooperating teacher often made comments about the occupation and community status of children's parents. It seemed to Cecile that some children received special and more attentive teacher treatment if the cooperating teacher was awed by parents with perceived high status and income. Cecile thought "Who cares if children's parents are doctors, mayors, lawyers, etc!" After discussing the situation with her college supervisor, she was able tactfully to approach the subject with the cooperating teacher. Cecile decided to risk a retaliatory cooperating teacher evaluation, but as it turned out, that fear wasn't realized during or at the close of her placement.

Other examples of student teacher dilemmas encountered by the author's student teachers include student teachers who:

- saw other student teachers cheating on exams.
- noticed licensing law violations at their placement site.
- accidentally broke, damaged, or lost some type of classroom equipment.
- saw others in an act of theft.
- overheard a teacher lying to a parent.
- received expensive gifts from parents.
- received sexist advances from a fellow teacher.
- heard discriminatory classroom comments.

When faced with some dilemmas, one may be able to make an argument for both opposing sides. In other cases, ones initial position may be clear, but when further explanation and information occurs, one may mediate or change a beginning stance.

Speaking of the power a teacher exerts over children in care, Stephens (1999) notes the following:

> I possess tremendous power to make a child's life miserable or joyous. I can be a tool of torture or an instrument of inspiration. I can humiliate or humor, hurt or heal. In all situations it is my response that decides whether a crisis will be escalated or de-escalated, a child humanized or de-humanized.

Ward (1992) notes:

> The members of a profession monitor themselves from within. They take appropriate steps to ensure the ethical basis of programs, goals, and directions. They critique themselves and their field.

Figure 2–4 lists a segment of NAEYC's Code of Ethics concerned with ethical responsibilities to colleagues. Stephanie Feeney and Kenneth Kipnis (1989) are recognized as the extensive researchers and developers of the "Code of Ethics and Statement of Commitment" which evolved into NAEYC's *Code of Ethical Conduct and Statement of Commitment: Guidelines for Responsible Behavior in Early Childhood Education* (1998).

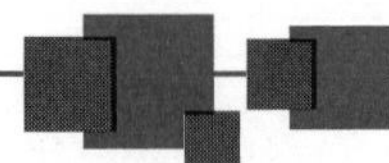

Section III: Ethical Responsibilities to Colleagues
In a caring, cooperative workplace, human dignity is respected, professional satisfaction is promoted, and positive relationships are modeled. Based upon our core values, our primary responsibility in this arena is to establish and maintain settings and relationships that support productive work and meet professional needs. The same ideals that apply to children are inherent in our responsibilities to adults.

A—RESPONSIBILITIES TO CO-WORKERS

Ideals:

I-3A.1—To establish and maintain relationships of respect, trust, and cooperation with co-workers.

I-3A.2—To share resources and information with co-workers.

I-3A.3—To support co-workers in meeting their professional needs and in their professional development.

I-3A.4—To accord co-workers due recognition of professional achievement.

Principles:

P-3A.1—When we have a concern about the professional behavior of a co-worker, we shall first let that person know of our concern, in a way that shows respect for personal dignity and for the diversity to be found among staff members, and then attempt to resolve the matter collegially.

P-3A.2—We shall exercise care in expressing views regarding the personal attributes or professional conduct of co-workers. Statements should be based on firsthand knowledge and relevant to the interests of children and programs.

Figure 2–4 Reprinted with permission from the National Association for the Education of Young Children. ©Copyright 1998.

When Values Clash

In our diverse society, individual values are bound to clash. Some parents may advocate spanking, others may feel their daughters should not participate in active sports, and a staff member may feel it appropriate to accept an expensive personal gift from a parent. The I-2.4 section of NAEYC's code bids teachers to respect families' child-rearing values and their right to make decisions for their children. The P-1.1 code section states:

> Above all, we shall not harm children. We shall not participate in practices that are disrespectful, degrading, dangerous, exploitive, intimidating, emotionally damaging, or physically harmful to children (1998).

The code notes "this principle has precedence over all others in the code." It is clear that when ethical dilemmas arise, teachers are first to consider what is best for the child. If parental values are inflexible, parents can choose to terminate a child's attendance. Centers may be able to propose other, less final, solutions. The center or school has the responsibility to communicate clearly its ethical and professional position to parents and to try, *if possible*, to problem-solve difficulties.

curriculum—overall master plan of the early childhood program reflecting its philosophy, into which specific activities are fit.

TEACHING STYLE

What is meant by teaching style? It is the vehicle through which a teacher contributes his or her unique quality to the curriculum. Much has been written about teaching style, in particular, the phenomenon of teachers modeling themselves after the teachers who influenced them in the past.

Placing a student teacher with a "master" or cooperating teacher has its disadvantages as well as advantages. Most college supervisors try to place student teachers with those cooperating teachers who will provide a positive model and are willing to allow the student teacher to practice. However, there are many excellent teachers who are unwilling to work with student teachers. This is because it takes much energy and time to work with student teachers; they have to be watched, referred to resources, conferenced, and encouraged. In addition, most colleges and universities do not compensate cooperating teachers in any tangible form for their time and energy. As a result, some student teaching placements may be less than desirable.

Of course, this situation sometimes works out well. A student teacher with experience as a teacher aide may do quite well in a classroom where the cooperating teacher is less than an excellent model and provides little supervision or guidance. In some cases, the student teacher may even act as a *positive role model* for the mediocre cooperating teacher.

Good cooperating teachers will offer suggestions about different lessons to try. They will introduce the student teachers to all areas of the curriculum, usually one area at a time (see Figure 2–5). Most cooperating teachers will allow a certain amount of time for student teachers to observe and become acquainted with the children. Before the end of the student teaching experience, however, most strong cooperating teachers will expect a student teacher to handle the whole day and all parts of the curriculum. All student teachers will inevitably "borrow" or copy their cooperating teachers' styles; this results from having worked so closely together.

Figure 2–5 At first, student teachers will work in areas where they are most comfortable. Later, they will be expected to handle all parts of the curriculum.

Sometimes, though, a cooperating teacher's style is so unique, so much a part of herself, that it is too difficult to copy. We are reminded of a male cooperating teacher who stood 6 feet, 4 inches tall and weighed around 240 pounds. Female student teachers had problems using his behavior control techniques; the difference in their sizes precluded the use of physical presence as a guidance technique. One complaint the college supervisor heard regularly was, "Of course Mr. Smith has no problems of control! Look at him!" What many student teachers failed to recognize initially was that Mr. Smith used other techniques as well such as close **observation** of the classroom, moving toward the source of potential trouble before it erupted, quietly removing a child from a frustrating activity, and firm and consistent application of classroom rules.

observation—the process of learning that comes from watching, noting the behavior of, and imitating models.

A cooperating teacher may be so gifted that a student teacher feels overwhelmed. In this situation, the student teacher should be directed to look at only one facet of the cooperating teacher's expertise at a time. For example, in focusing on how the teacher begins each day, the student teacher may find a model that is not quite so difficult as the total model appears. It may be that the cooperating teacher takes time each morning to greet each child with a smile and a personal comment.

There are also situations where the cooperating teacher is unable to explain how something is done, like the mathematician who can solve a complex problem without knowing how. Intuitive teachers and those who are very involved have this difficulty; they are unable to explain why they do one thing and not another.

Teaching styles are also an extension of the teacher's self. Rogers and Freiberg (1994) contend that the teacher must know the self before effectively teaching another. This means that you have enough self-knowledge to judge from observing your cooperating teacher what activities and techniques will work for you, which ones you may have to modify, and which ones are best not used. Techniques with which you are truly uncomfortable are best put aside until you can become comfortable with them.

congruent—refers to the similarity of what a person (the sender) is thinking and feeling, and what that person communicates; behaving/acting in a state of agreement with or reflection of inner feelings and/or values.

Rogers and Freiberg (1994) emphasize the need for teachers to be congruent, acceptant, and empathic. To be **congruent** means that your actions should be a reflection of who you are as a person (see Figure 2–6). To be acceptant means that you accept or "prize" (to use another term Rogers and Freiberg employ) each and every one of your students. Every child deserves to be accepted, but it is important to differentiate between acceptance of a child's value as a fellow human being and his behavior, which you may or may not accept. Empathy means that you are able to put yourself in the child's place, to understand why she is acting as she is. The Native American expression of withholding judgment until you have walked in another's moccasins relates to having empathy. Another way of remembering these characteristics is to use the acronym CARE. To congruence, acceptance, and empathy is added reliability; children need to know that their teachers are reliable, that boundaries exist, and that certain behaviors are acceptable and others are not. Remember, safety for your students rests in your ability to CARE.

Figure 2–6 The display of photographs and dolls in this toddler classroom reflects this teacher's attempts to provide diverse models of ethnic backgrounds.

Specific Models of Teaching Style

kindergarten—German word, literally meaning "garden for children," coined by Friedrich Froebel for his program for young children.

Mr. Smith is a true master teacher. After having taught every grade in elementary school and because he believes there are too few male teachers in the lower primary grades, he has chosen to teach **kindergarten**. Choosing kindergarten also reflects Mr. Smith's beliefs in the importance of having children begin elementary school with a positive step and in the importance of the family. He plans to involve the parents in the learning processes of their children and extends an open invitation to parents to visit in his room any time they wish. At Back-to-School Night, Mr. Smith is prepared with a Parent Handbook he has developed and elicits from his parents promises to assist at classroom learning centers, to be available as chaperones on field trips, to bake cookies or cupcakes for classroom celebrations, and to help in other appropriate ways such as sharing on "International Day," teaching the children a folk song in their native language, demonstrating a special art technique typical of their respective culture, and so on.

On entering Mr. Smith's room, a visitor can immediately see that it is arranged into several areas. An entrance area is formed by a desk to the left of the door and the children's cubbies on the right. A parent bulletin board is mounted on the wall by the desk. A large area with shelves housing large blocks, trucks, cars, and other items, is found behind the cubbies. An inside climbing structure, built by the parents, is located in the corner. Underneath, there is a housekeeping area complete with stove, sink, cupboards, table, and chairs. In the opposite corner is a quiet area protected by a large, comfortable couch. This area is further defined by its carpet, floor pillows, and bookshelves. On the shelves, there are many picture and storybooks that Mr. Smith periodically changes for added interest. Three tables with chairs are to the left of the quiet area and straight ahead from the door. Shelves and cupboards along the wall can easily be reached by the children and contain art materials and small manipulatives including puzzles, Legos, unifix cubes, Cuisinaire rods, geoboards, and so on. The window wall opposite the door is the math and science center. In addition, a water play area is found here as well as a terrarium and a large magnifying glass with objects to investigate in a nearby box.

The first impression most visitors have is how busy and happy everyone appears to be. A parent may be found supervising at the language center, writing down a story dictated by one of the children (to be illustrated later); another parent may be supervising at the workbench outside the door, watching as four or five children saw, hammer, and nail a wood sculpture. Mr. Smith may be located at the science center directing two children's attention to their bean plants.

One way of studying Mr. Smith's classroom is to look at his teaching style. It seems very student-centered, which it is. It is highly flexible, changing as student interests change. For example, one day, a child brought a chrysalis to school. Mr. Smith immediately asked the children to guess what they thought it might be. He listened intently to every guess, even the wild ones. He asked the child who brought it if she knew what she had found. When the child indicated that she did not, Mr. Smith proceeded to tell the students that they should watch the chrysalis every day to see what was going to happen. He resisted the urge to tell them anything more other than they would receive a big surprise. He placed the chrysalis in a large jar, placed cheesecloth over the opening, and secured it with a rubber band. Fortunately, the butterfly emerged from the chrysalis on a school day, and the children had the excitement of watching it. Mr. Smith allowed the children to watch despite the fact that science had not been scheduled for that particular time. Indeed, the children were so interested that no one wanted to go out to recess when the bell rang!

One might ask whether Mr. Smith's teaching style is congruent with one's perception of him as a person. In talking to him and becoming better acquainted with him, one might find that Mr. Smith sees himself more as a learner than as a teacher. He attends teacher conferences regularly to learn new techniques and presents workshops himself in his areas of expertise: how to plan and implement a "developmentally appropriate" kindergarten curriculum; using science to stimulate the kindergarten child's interest; managing the center-based kindergarten; and so forth. He was one of the first teachers in his school to ask that special needs children be placed in his classroom, even before federal and state laws were enacted. His bias that all students are special and his student-centered classroom make it easy to integrate children with special problems.

Further exploration reveals that he is an avid gardener, likes to fish, enjoys woodwork, and would like to enroll in a workshop on stained glass. Mr. Smith appears as gifted outside of the classroom as he is within it.

It is easy to see that Mr. Smith values all the children in his class. It is one of the reasons he is so effective, especially in regard to working with special needs children. It is also apparent that Mr. Smith is able to empathize with his children. He is gentle with those who have experienced a serious loss; he refuses to allow an angry child to bait him, and quietly speaks to the child one-to-one; he shares in the excitement of a child who has taken a first train trip and may urge this child to share the experience with the others. The only times anyone has seen him angry involved a suspected case of child abuse.

If a student teacher was to ask Mr. Smith about his teaching style, he would answer that it is based on his philosophy of education. This, he would continue, is the belief in the inherent goodness of all children and in their innate need to explore the world. He would be able to provide a written statement of his beliefs and curriculum goals for the year.

Mr. Smith's teaching is very much a part of himself: steady and imaginative with a desire to create a total learning environment for his students. In looking at Rogers and Freiberg's criteria, it is clear that Mr. Smith is congruent, acceptant, reliable, and empathetic, and that his students perceive these characteristics in him as well. One can tell that each child is as important as the next. He uses many nonverbal responses, touching one child on the shoulder as a reminder to settle down and get to work, giving another a sympathetic hug, and getting down on his knees to speak directly and firmly to an angry child. From all of his words and actions, it is obvious that Mr. Smith teaches children much more than just subject matter.

Let us now look at another teacher, Mrs. Lehrer, a teacher of an alternative "school within a school," an ungraded primary class of 24 children in grades one through three. Mrs. Lehrer starts each day by having the children line up outside the door, walk quietly into the classroom, and form a semicircle around her by the chalkboard. The children sit down and Mrs. Lehrer takes the roll. Next, a child announces the day of the week and the date and places the date on a cardboard calendar beside the chalkboard. Children frequently share the books they have written and illustrated at the writing center. Mrs. Lehrer teaches the children bookbinding so that all of the children's own books may become a part of the class library. Checking out and reading each other's books is one of the children's favorite activities during Sustained Silent Reading (SSR).

After sharing, the children are then assigned different tasks. One group of four may be assigned the writing center where a parent eagerly awaits to assist. Another group of three may be asked to work at the art center, illustrating the stories they have written the day before. Two children may be assigned to paint at the easels and to design pictures for the next bulletin board. A group of six may be assigned to work with the bilingual aide on a social studies report they will present later to the class. Six more may go to one of the shelves containing the pattern blocks and wait for Mrs. Lehrer to give them directions on what to do with the Math Their Way task they are to complete. Six of the remaining children may go to the science center to record the results of an experiment begun the day before that involves the diffusion of food coloring in water. Once finished with their recording, they look in the folder placed in the center for the next experiment to complete. A parent oversees the center to help when needed. Of the remaining six, Mrs. Lehrer has arranged them in cross-age pairs; three third graders are helping first and second grade "buddies," one who is possibly learning disabled and two others who seem to be "slow learners" with their reading.

A strict disciplinarian, Mrs. Lehrer does not allow any aggressive acting-out behavior. If a child becomes involved in a fight, that child is quickly reminded that such behavior is not allowed and is sent to the principal. Mrs. Lehrer does not allow a child to interrupt when someone is speaking. Mrs. Lehrer has the classroom rules posted prominently in the front of the room beside one of the chalkboards. If asked, she will explain that the class cooperatively decided on the rules. Interestingly, there are only three: "I have the right to express myself in my classroom" (a picture illustrates a raised hand and is placed next to the words); "I have the right to be heard in my classroom" (the picture illustrates several children's heads listening to a child standing and speaking); and "I have the right to feel safe in my classroom" (the picture with the international sign for "No" illustrates two children fighting).

On entering Mrs. Lehrer's classroom, the visitor is impressed by how noisy it is. All of the children seem to be busy at the assignments they have been given. Two parents are busy assisting, one at the writing center, the other at the art center where children are busy constructing papier-mâché figures for a puppet show they will present that will introduce their peers to a story one of them has written. The bilingual aide is assisting two Hispanic children with their Spanish reading, and Mrs. Lehrer is circulating throughout the room, checking on the progress of the others. Two special needs children are in the Resource Center at the time of observation and four soon-to-be-identified Gifted and Talented third graders are engrossed in practicing a play to be presented initially to the class and then at the upcoming PTA meeting.

What kind of teacher does Mrs. Lehrer appear to be? Is she congruent, acceptant, and empathetic? In talking with Mrs. Lehrer, it is obvious that she sees herself as a good teacher. After all, her children do well on the end-of-year tests. Many of them, in particular, are above grade level in reading and math. Her children also obey class rules and respect each other. As one listens to Mrs. Lehrer and observes more closely what is happening in her classroom, it becomes more apparent that, in spite of the seeming freedom and flexibility of the centers and the learning assistance of parents and aide, Mrs. Lehrer's classroom is more teacher-oriented than student-oriented. Children are assigned to centers; they do not have any choice. Although most of them appear contented and actively involved, during the time of observation, an incident has occurred that has made the visitor uncomfortable—one of the first-grade boys argued with his third-grade "buddy" and called him a name. Mrs. Lehrer's face became angry-looking and she said sharply, "We work cooperatively in our classroom. If you can't cooperate with Justin, David, go to the 'time out' chair until I tell you you may return." David replied that he thought the "time out" chair was "stupid," and Mrs. Lehrer immediately sent the boy, accompanied by the "buddy," to the principal's office. Later, she explains to the visitor, "I simply won't tolerate that talking back from any of my children, especially from those 'fresh-mouthed' boys!"

Is Mrs. Lehrer a congruent teacher? Is her teaching a reflection of herself? If we become friends with Mrs. Lehrer, we would discover that her small house is immaculate, with everything in its place. She is a person of habit; rising, eating, and going to bed at the same time every day whether it is a school day or not. When meeting for an evening out, her friends know she will be punctual, almost to the minute. They know that she will have only one cocktail before dinner, order a fish special from the menu, and fall asleep at a musical performance because she usually goes to bed at 10:00 p.m. Because her schedule is just as rigid and exact as her teaching, Mrs. Lehrer is a congruent teacher.

Mrs. Lehrer is respected by many parents, especially those who have chosen to have their children placed in her room. They are pleased that many of the children are reading above grade level; they like the cross-age "buddy" system; however, they are somewhat in awe of Mrs. Lehrer because of her reputation as a strict, although "good," teacher.

If one inquired about Mrs. Lehrer's philosophy of education and curriculum goals, she would most likely answer, "It's simply to direct each of the children, to teach them to behave, read, write, and learn their mathematics." In terms of curriculum goals, Mrs. Lehrer would state, "I always follow district guidelines. In fact, I served on the curriculum committee the year the goals were revised." If questioned further, Mrs. Lehrer would again talk about the importance of reading, writing, and mathematics. Most likely, she will point out that some parents approve of her emphasis on the basics. (One, of course, will wonder why Mrs. Lehrer has said nothing about the children!)

Another way of studying these two teachers is to look beyond their teaching styles to their leadership styles. As we know, Mr. Smith runs a student-centered classroom and has a flexible curriculum that changes with student interest and enthusiasm. We also know that the students' needs come first. What is his leadership style? One might say that it is **authoritative**. The students all have a say as to what will happen from day to day. Mr. Smith respects all opinions and ideas, and he teaches this to his students.

authoritative—substantiated, supported, and accepted by most professionals in the field of early childhood education or having an air of authority.

Mrs. Lehrer, in contrast, runs a teacher-centered classroom and has a fixed, somewhat rigid curriculum. In terms of her leadership style, one would have to admit that it is authoritarian. She is the final authority in her room.

OTHER TEACHING STYLES

We presented extreme examples of two teaching and two leadership styles. With most teachers, however, you will find variants of these extremes. Between these two contrasting styles—student-centered and teacher-centered or authoritative and authoritarian—lie others. The style of most teachers lies somewhere between Mr. Smith's and Mrs. Lehrer's, and a few may even lie at a further extreme. Many teachers follow a more or less set schedule from day to day. Free play usually starts the day in preschool; a "sponge" activity, such as journal writing or a few simple math problems, frequently starts the day in grade school. Sharing activities and attendance follow. Outdoor play and recess follow indoor activities. Quiet play alternates with active, noisy play. Rest follows lunch. Free play and less structured activities such as art, music, or physical education occur before dismissal time.

Many teachers follow a more or less rigid schedule with such curricula as reading and math. These disciplines are sequential; children must know A before they can proceed to B. Many teachers allow more flexibility with activities such as the fine arts. Thus, many curriculum choices may be a reflection of student and/or teacher interest (see Figure 2–7). A teacher who is proficient in art will provide many art activities; a teacher with interests in music will provide many musical experiences for the students.

Figure 2–7 This area was developed as a result of the teacher and children's interests.

While observing as a student teacher, you will find there are almost as many different teaching styles as there are teachers. Teachers tend to emphasize those areas of the curriculum that they feel are more important; they also tend to emphasize those areas in which they have greater expertise. The major characteristic of all truly great teachers, though, is their ability to empathize with their students. Look closely; does the teacher show evidence of really liking the students? Does that teacher CARE? CAREing is the secret to good teaching.

No matter what teaching style your cooperating teacher displays, you will want to display student teacher behaviors that will be valued (see Figure 2–8).

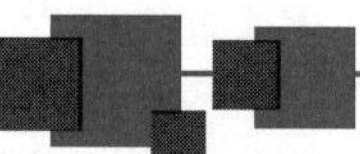

Cooperating teachers value student teachers who:

- remember staff names and their pronunciation.
- introduce themselves to center support staff.
- share lunch time with staff in staff rooms or with children if on duty.
- make phone calls when ill or late.
- clean up after themselves.
- return or replace supplies and/or equipment.
- ask before using supplies.
- respond when asked for comments and contribute to discussions when appropriate.
- are watchful for needed assistance and pitch in.
- live up to student teacher responsibilities.
- are prepared and timely.
- treat other's opinions with respect; are open-minded and reflective.
- refrain from interrupting.
- ask questions when unsure.
- are friendly and communicative.

Figure 2–8 What most cooperative teachers value.

Stereotyping Good and Bad

In order to understand fully a teacher's style, one has to understand the teacher's philosophy and underlying attitude toward the students. Does this teacher accept the children? Does this teacher feel that children are inherently good? Some teachers believe that all children are essentially bad and have to be taught to be good. Their teaching style reflects this attitude. Usually authoritarian, they have rigid classroom rules. Children are told that they will behave in a particular way; any infringement on the rules will usually bring swift punishment.

Does the teacher feel that children can be trusted? The teacher's style will reflect this belief. Classroom rules will be elicited from the children, with the teacher reminding them of a rule they may have overlooked. Children who misbehave are not considered bad but as needing more socialization time in which to learn. Punishment often takes the form of physical removal from the situation and isolation until the child feels ready to rejoin the class.

Does Mr. Smith believe children are good or bad? Does Mrs. Lehrer? From the information presented so far, you can only guess that Mr. Smith believes children are inherently good and that Mrs. Lehrer may not.

A teacher may believe that most children are good and then have an experience with a psychologically damaged child who challenges this belief. At this point, the teacher may accept the fact that most, but not all, children are good. The danger is that the experience with the psychologically damaged child can lead the teacher to formulate a stereotype about all children who look like this child, who come from the same socioeconomic background, who belong to the same racial or ethnic group, or who are of the same sex. Of Mr. Smith and Mrs. Lehrer, which is most likely to use stereotypic thinking? Stereotypic thinking occurs more often in rigid people than in flexible people.

Flexibility

Let us also look at another factor: curriculum planning. The amount of planning needed is often overlooked in a classroom like Mr. Smith's. The visitor does not realize how much work goes into the arrangement of the learning centers. The classroom looks open, free, and flexible. Indeed, it is all of these. None of it is possible, however, without a great deal of careful planning. Ask Mr. Smith how many years it has taken to develop his classroom and how much work he still does during free time to maintain the atmosphere. You will find that Mr. Smith is continually revising, updating, and trying out new things. Much careful planning goes into any successful open and free environment.

flexibile—willing to yield, modify, or adapt; change or create in a positive, productive manner.

In contrast, observe Mrs. Lehrer. During questioning, you will discover that she is still using many of the materials she developed during her student teaching years and first years of teaching. If she makes a change, it is usually at the request of her principal or at the suggestion of the parent of a child she likes. She seldom makes changes on her own and is quite comfortable with what she has always done. Some of her critics have suggested, "Mrs. Lehrer claims to have twelve years of experience; I maintain she has one year of experience repeated eleven times!" There is, unfortunately, much truth to the statement.

SUMMARY

In this chapter, we discussed the relationships among our attitudes and values, the curriculum choices that might be made as a result, and how these could reflect our developing teaching style. Several learning exercises were included to help you define more clearly some of your personal values and the curriculum choices to which these might lead.

We observed Mr. Smith, a model authoritative master teacher with a clearly stated (and written) curriculum philosophy and goals of education. We have also looked at what is perhaps a typical teacher, Mrs. Lehrer. Although more authoritarian than Mr. Smith and less acceptant of all children, Mrs. Lehrer's teaching style with its emphasis on the basics is admired by many parents. We also suggested that there is a relationship between a teacher's ability to CARE and her philosophy of education, which leads her to establish clear curriculum goals for the students.

Of the two teachers described, Mr. Smith obviously CAREs; Mrs. Lehrer would protest that she does CARE, but in reality, she lacks empathy for the more assertive boys in her room.

What should you, as a student teacher, do? Perhaps of greatest importance is to discover your own teaching style. With what areas of the curriculum are you most comfortable? Why? Do you see yourself as a CAREing person? Do you have a philosophy of education? In our two examples, do you see the relationship between each teacher's beliefs and curriculum practices? Think about your curriculum goals; consider how your feelings about working with young children influence these goals. Remember, especially, the positive model of Mr. Smith. Think of how he looks upon himself as a learner, how he looks at each child, how he listens to them, how flexible his curriculum is, how student-centered his curriculum style, and how authoratative his leadership style.

HELPFUL WEB SITES

http://www.nl.edu

The Center for Early Childhood Leadership (National-Louis University). Publishes *Research Notes* on critical issues facing early childhood practitioners.

http://www.selectsmart.com

Values Assessment. Presents tests and assessments to help one "know thyself." Dozens of multiple-choice exercises.

http://www.zerotothree.org

Zero to Three. Investigate a publication entitled *What Grown-ups Understand about Child Development.*

SUGGESTED ACTIVITIES

A. Complete the following exercises in small groups of three to five. Discuss the processes involved in making any decisions. What did you learn about your self and your peers as a result?

   1. Draw a picture of what you collectively believe to be an effective teacher. Label each part of the drawing to indicate what characteristics is being exemplified. For example, a picture of an extremely large ear might indicate a willingness to listen to the children in your care; an apron with many pockets (including several labeled objects) might indicate the many different items an effective teacher needs at his fingertips. Use your collective imaginations; nothing is too extreme, but you must justify why the item is included.

2. Draw a picture of your collective vision of an ideal child/student. As in the above exercise, label each part of the drawing that exemplifies a desired characteristic.
3. Referring to the first exercise in this chapter, discuss among yourselves any insights learned.
4. Look at your responses to the exercise that involved listing activities you enjoy and the related curriculum activities. What does this tell you about your developing teaching style?

B. Write your developing philosophy of education. Describe it in relation to your curriculum style. Discuss it with your peers and supervisor.

C. In small groups, discuss the following:

1. Following your cooperating teacher's directions, you have always placed your purse and coat in the teachers' closet. The closet is locked after the teacher, aide, and any parent volunteers have arrived in the child center or primary grade classroom. Only the teacher and aide have keys. One day after you have left the center/school and stop at a store to buy a few groceries before going home, you discover that $10.00 is missing from your wallet; only a five and a one dollar bill remain. Your immediate reaction is . . .
2. You are a student teacher in a preschool classroom for four-year-old children. One day, Mike arrives with a black eye and wearing a long-sleeved sweater in spite of the pleasant weather. He winces when you approach him to give him a good morning hug. When you ask him what's wrong, Mike shakes his head "no" and doesn't answer.

   Later in the day, as the weather has turned sunny and warmer, you are able to persuade Mike to remove his sweater. Almost immediately, you notice bruises on his left arm. Quickly, you report to your cooperating teacher. "Sarah, would you come and look at Mike? I think he's been abused. What are the procedures we should follow?"

   Sarah replies, "Leave it to me; I'll talk to Mrs. R. (the director). She needs to know about possible child abuse and she'll take care of it."

   By the time the children are being picked up by their parents, no one from either Child Protective Services or from the police have arrived to look at Mike or interview you.

   What should you do?
3. You have recently been hired as the afternoon kindergarten teacher at the ABC School. The DEF District policy stipulates that the morning teacher assists the afternoon teacher and vice versa. You feel that this will provide you with wonderful support from the older, more experienced morning teacher, Mrs. Sexton.

   On your first day of work in late August, you are surprised to see that there are no interest centers arranged in the kindergarten room. There are only five tables with six chairs at each, a book shelf and two desks for the teachers.

   "Mrs. Sexton," you inquire, "don't we have blocks, easels, or play house materials?"

   "We have the reading workbooks on the shelf over here," she responds, "and the math workbooks on the shelf by the desk. DEF District has a curriculum for kindergarten that we follow; haven't you read it?"

You confess that although you received the district guidelines two days before when you were hired, you had not had enough time to read through them.

"Well," Mrs. Sexton says, "you'll see that there are specific goals in reading and math that we must reach this year. The children all have their workbooks and we use direct teaching to achieve the goals. By the way, you do know that Mrs. Maier (the principal) expects you to have your lesson plans ready for her perusal on Friday of each week and you do understand that DEF District uses the five-step lesson plan format?"

You begin to have doubts about having accepted the position, but you need a job to pay off the student loans you had acquired while going through college. You know that this classroom is not "developmentally appropriate" according to NAEYC guidelines. You hope, however, that maybe you can at least do more developmentally appropriate activities in your afternoon class. You decide to spend some money borrowed from your parents to buy some unit blocks, and you visit the local public library for some picture books for an in-class library. You also visit the local teacher supply house to price items like unifix cubes, play house materials, and an easel and paint. You estimate that you may be able to afford different items with each month's paycheck.

You remain in the classroom late on the day before school opens to arrange a "reading corner" with the books from the library, and you shift the bookshelf to form a protected corner. You place two large beanbag chairs you used at college in the "reading center." Then you bring in the blocks and place them in the opposite corner of the room on a shelf you also had in college. A carpet you retrieved from the city's once-a-month clean-up day is placed in the block area to reduce noise.

When school opens the next day, Mrs. Sexton exclaims, "What have you done to my room? You had no right to change anything!"

What do you do now?

4. A parent of one of the three-year-olds in the parent participatory preschool where you are student teaching has formed a close relationship with you; you are both about the same age; you both have experienced financial stresses you've shared. One day, Ms. Sharif confesses that she's just discovered she's pregnant again (she has a baby as well as the three-year-old in your class) and that she's thinking of having an abortion. What is your reaction?

D. Role-play the following situations.

1. As the parent (grandparent, foster parent, significant adult) of a child attending the school, identify the concerns you may have and any possible curriculum changes you would like to see. Note this is the first parent meeting of the school year.

   You may choose to be any of the following:

   a. Mother of attending child who is from an inner-city housing project.
   b. Mother of attending child who is ethnically different from most of the other children enrolled in the school.
   c. Grandmother of attending child who cares for child evenings while mother works a night-shift job.
   d. Mother, recovering alcoholic, who is afraid social workers may be spying on her child at school in order to decide whether the child belongs in the father's custody.
   e. Newly arrived immigrant father who speaks limited English.

2. As the teacher (aide, volunteer), describe and briefly outline a handout you would distribute to the above parents to help them become more involved in the curriculum.

   You may choose to be:

   a. Teacher of the class.
   b. Teacher's paid aide who lives in the children's neighborhood.
   c. Senior citizen who volunteers at the school and who also lives in the neighborhood.

E. Answer the following with a group of peers.

1. Do people often mispronounce your name?
2. Do you sometimes feel pressure to dress differently to fit in?
3. Have you had past teachers from your ethnic group?
4. Have you been told you can not do something because of your gender?
5. Have you felt uncomfortable because of your perceived difference in a social group?
6. Have you been asked to speak about or present an opinion you feel is held by the majority of individuals in your cultural or ethnic group?

REVIEW

A. List five personal values.

B. Write an essay describing how the values you listed in Review Question A influence what you do in the classroom.

C. Read the following descriptions of classroom interaction. Identify each teaching behavior as student-centered or teacher-centered. If a behavior is neither, identify it as such.

1. Teacher A is standing to one side of the playground during outdoor free play. She is busy talking to her aide. One child approaches another who is riding a tricycle. The first child wants to ride the tricycle and attempts to push the rider off. "How many times do I have to tell you you have to wait until I blow the whistle? You won't get your turn until you learn to wait!"
2. Teacher B is busy assisting four children on a cooking project. The bilingual aide is working with six children on a reading ditto. A parent volunteer is working with five others on an art project, and the student teacher is overseeing the remaining children with their unfinished reading assignments. A child with the student teacher complains in a loud voice, "This is a dumb assignment! I want to cook! Why can't I?" Teacher B looks at and signals the student teacher to try and resolve the problem alone.
3. Two boys are arguing loudly as they enter the preschool. Teacher C, who is standing by the door greeting each child, quickly takes a boy in each hand. She quietly asks, "What's the matter with you two today?" After listening to each boy and insisting that each listen to the other, she suggests a separate active play, based on the knowledge of what each enjoys doing. They comply, and minutes later they and another child are spotted playing cooperatively with the large blocks.
4. Teacher D is standing in front of her class. The children are watching as she explains the activity: making pumpkins out of orange and black paper. After the children go to their assigned tables, it is apparent that at

least two children do not know what to do. They sit glumly with their hands in their laps. Teacher D comes over and says, "Don't you two ever listen to directions?"

5. During roll, one of the boys in Teacher E's room begins to cry. Another child yells, "Cry-baby." Teacher E quietly speaks, "Sean, remember that we agreed we wouldn't call each other by names that can hurt. Stevie, come up here by me so we can talk. The rest of you can choose what activities you want to do. Mrs. Castilla, will you take over so I can talk to Stevie?"
6. The children are all sitting on the floor in a semicircle facing Teacher F. Teacher F asks, "Who has something they want to share today?" Several hands go up. "Let's have George, Ana, Mike, and Jan share today." Noting a look of disappointment on Mary's face, he says, "Mary, I know you're disappointed but remember, you shared something with us yesterday. Don't you think we ought to give someone else a chance today?" Mary nods in agreement, and George begins to speak.
7. Deerat is standing at the front of the class reading a story from the basic reader. The other children are following along, reading silently. It is obvious that Deerat is a good reader and tries to vary her tone of voice. The child fluently reads the paragraph, but something is wrong. Teacher G interrupts her. "You are reading carelessly. It's not 'the coat', it's 'a coat.' Now, start over again, and read every word correctly."
8. Ron is a new child in preschool. After greeting him and walking with him to the table with crayons and paper, Teacher H goes back to the door to greet more children. When Teacher H thinks to look back at Ron, he notices Ron is busy drawing all over the top of the table. He goes quickly over to Ron, hands him another piece of paper, and says quietly, "Ron, use paper for drawing." He later comes back with a wet sponge and shows the child how to clean up the marks.

CASE SCENARIO

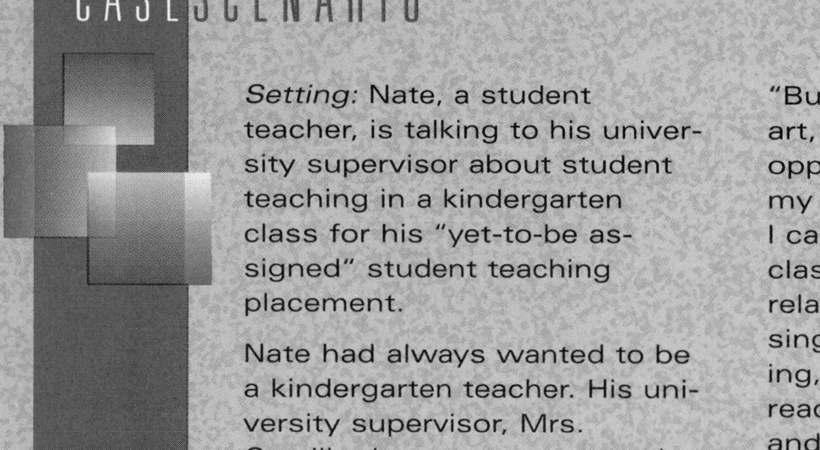

Setting: Nate, a student teacher, is talking to his university supervisor about student teaching in a kindergarten class for his "yet-to-be assigned" student teaching placement.

Nate had always wanted to be a kindergarten teacher. His university supervisor, Mrs. Castillo, however, suggested that he might discover that he would be more employable in an upper grade.

"But I really enjoy music and art, and I think I'd have more opportunity to infuse them into my lessons in a kindergarten. I can bring my guitar into the classroom, teach some songs, relate what the children are singing to art, language, reading, and even dance. I've already collected several picture and story books with themes that involve music and other fine arts."

"I understand why you feel the kindergarten placement would

continues . . .

. . . continued

be better than the primary grade one, but I'm still concerned about whether a school district would hire you for a kindergarten class. Think your options over, okay?"

Nate thought about what Mrs. Castillo had said over the next few days. He then sought her out for further discussion.

"Mrs. Castillo, I've given a lot of thought to what you said about my student teaching placements and I still want to student teach in a kindergarten for the next assignment."

"I'll try to accommodate your desires as I check with the schools I know and see if there is a principal and supervising teacher who would accept you," Mrs. Castillo answered.

Questions for Discussion:

1. Are you as in touch with your values as they relate to your future teaching as Nate?
2. Could Mrs. Castillo be somewhat "gender blind" regarding kindergarten teachers or was she just being realistic about males being hired for upper grades?
3. If you could advise your supervisor concerning a second student teaching placement, what would you request? Why?

REFERENCES

Biehler, R. F., & Snowman, J. (1990). *Psychology applied to teaching* (6th ed.). Boston: Houghton Mifflin.

Feeney, S., & Kipnis, K. (1989, January). Code of ethical conduct. *Young Children, 45*(1), 15–22.

Grant, C., & Murray, C. (1999). *Teaching in America: The slow revolution*. Cambridge, MA: Harvard University Press.

Jones, E. (1994). Constructing professional knowledge by telling our stories. In J. Johnson & J. McCracken (Eds.). *The early childhood career lattice: Perspectives on professional development*. Washington, DC: National Association for the Education of Young Children.

Katz, L. G. (1992). Ethical issues in working with young children. In *Ethical behavior in early childhood education*. Washington, DC: National Association for the Education of Young Children.

Krathwohl, D. R., Bloom, B. S., & Masia, B. B. (1984). *Taxonomy of educational objectives: The classification of educational goals. Handbook II: Affective domain*. New York: David McKay.

Rogers, C. R. (1966). To facilitate learning. In M. Provus (Ed.). *Innovations for time to teach*. Washington, DC: National Education Association.

Rogers, C. R., & Freiberg, H. J. (1994). *Freedom to learn* (3rd ed.). New York: Merrill/Macmillan.

Stephens, K. (1999, January). Bringing light to darkness: A tribute to teachers. *Young Children*, *49*(2).

Van Leuvan, P. (1997, Summer). Using concept maps of effective teaching as a tool in supervision. *Journal of Research and Development in Teacher Education*, *30*(4).

Ward, E. H. (1992). A code of ethics: The hallmark of a profession. In *Ethical Behavior in Early Childhood Education*. Washington, DC: National Association for the Education of Young Children.

Wedman, J. M., Espinosa, L. W., & Laffey, J. M. (1998, Winter). A process for understanding how a field-based course influences teacher's beliefs and practices. *The Teacher Educator*, *34*(3), 189–214

Being Observed: Discovering Your Competencies

Objectives **After studying this chapter, the student should be able to:**

1. List important goals of observation, evaluation, and discussion.
2. Describe five observation techniques.
3. Identify five possible student teacher observers who are able to evaluate competencies.
4. Describe the major areas of teacher competency.
5. Complete a self-assessment process.
6. List desirable personal characteristics and abilities of teachers.
7. Develop a plan that arranges, in order of priority, the student's future competency development.

Peer evaluations were valuable and eye-opening. The skills fellow student teachers displayed and the way the room looked and the on-going activities gave me lots of ideas. I think I obtained more insight into the role of a supervisor.

—Joan Chang

I never did get used to being watched!

—B. K. Sutton

I could have kissed my college supervisor! She noticed my cooperating teacher really wasn't letting me teach. So she asked her to join her in the teacher's lounge for a mid-morning cup of coffee. Finally I was teaching!

—Legretta Banks

Why is it I do poorly when I'm watched? Things ran smoothly as long as I didn't know I was being observed. Fortunately both my strong points and growth areas were talked about in daily evaluations. The problem finally disappeared except for the tiny knot I get now. Maybe I'll always have it.

—Casey Morgan

assessment—the act of appraising, judging or evaluating another's efforts, performance, or actions.

A process combining observation, feedback, and discussion is often necessary to acquire new skills or expand existing skills. Methods of observation vary with each training program, but they all are basically a record of what was seen and heard. An analysis of this record is called an assessment or evaluation. Observation, analysis, evaluation, and discussion can be described as a continuous cycle. It starts during student teaching and ends at retirement.

Professional teaching involves lifelong learning and continuous efforts to improve.

As more discoveries are made about the process of human learning and as our society changes, teachers assess existing teaching methods, try new ones, and sometimes combine elements of both new and old methods. Observation is important to this process. The student teacher begins by being watched and ends up watching herself as a practicing teacher!

Teaching competency can be viewed as a continuum—you can have a little of it, some of it, or a lot of it—and there's always room for more competency growth.

As student teachers gain experience, they may feel teaching is more of an art and craft than a science. Grant and Murray (1999) point out beginning teaching involves trying first one piece of the puzzle and then another, learning from mistakes, and overcoming embarrassments. They suggest there are many things that can be taught and *learned* by practitioners of any craft along with experiencing intuitive insights. The act of teaching involves the heart and the mind.

It's important to realize you will probably doubt your ability at times, especially on "bad days," which are bound to happen:

> It is human to have bad days—days when I just don't like putting a lot of effort into my school plans, days when I seem short-tempered and nothing seems to go right, days when I feel discouraged and question my effectiveness as a teacher, and even days when I feel overwhelmed rather than excited by all there is to learn about teaching, and children (Humphrey, 1989).73

The National Association for the Education of Young Children (NAEYC) *Standards for Early Childhood Professional Preparation: Baccalaureate or Initial License Level* are found in Figure 3–1. These are the recommended skills and abilities successful candidates are to display before graduating.

GOALS OF OBSERVATION, EVALUATION, AND DISCUSSION

Important goals of the observation/evaluation/discussion process for student teachers follow:

- To give student teachers valid assessments of their level of performance through specific, descriptive feedback
- To allow suggestions and helpful ideas, which aid students' acquisition of skills to flow between participants
- To create a positive attitude toward self-improvement and self-knowledge
- To establish the habit of assessing performance
- To maintain the standards of the teaching profession, and promote student teacher attainment of core competencies

1. Promoting child development and learning
   Candidates use their understanding of young children's characteristics and needs, and of multiple interacting influences on children's development and learning, to create environments that are healthy, respectful, supportive, and challenging for all children.
2. Building family and community relationships
   Candidates know about, understand, and value the importance and complex characteristics of children's families and communities. They use this understanding to create respectful, reciprocal relationships that support and empower families, and to involve all families in their children's development and learning.
3. Observing, documenting, and assessing to support young children and families
   Candidates know about and understand the goals, benefits and uses of assessment. They know about and use systematic observations, documentation, and other effective assessment strategies in a responsible way, in partnership with families and other professionals, to support children's development and learning.
4. Teaching and learning
   Candidates integrate their understanding of and relationships with children and families; their understanding of developmentally effective approaches to teaching and learning; and their knowledge of academic disciplines, to design, implement, and evaluate experiences that promote positive development and learning for all children.
   - 4a. Connecting with children and families
     Candidates know, understand, and use positive relationships and supportive interactions as the foundation for their work with young children.
   - 4b. Using developmentally effective approaches
     Candidates know, understand, and use a wide array of effective approaches, strategies, and tools to support young children's development and learning.
   - 4c. Understanding content knowledge in early education
     Candidates understand the importance of each content area in young children's learning. They know the essential concepts, inquiry tools, and structure of content areas including academic subjects and can identify resources to deepen their understanding.
   - 4d. Building meaningful curriculum
     Candidates use their own knowledge and other resources to design, implement, and evaluate meaningful, challenging curriculum that promotes comprehensive developmental and learning outcomes for all young children.
5. Becoming a professional
   Candidates identify and conduct themselves as members of the early childhood profession. They know and use ethical guidelines and other professional standards related to early childhood practice. They are continuous, collaborative learners who demonstrate knowledgeable, reflective, and critical perspectives on their work, making informed decisions that integrate knowledge from a variety of sources. They are informed advocates for sound educational practices and policies.

Figure 3–1 From NAEYC Guidelines Revision, *NAEYC Standards for Early Childhood Professional Preparation: Baccalaureate or Initial Licensure Level* (2001, July). Washington, DC: NAEYC. Reprinted with permission from the National Association for the Education of Young Children.

Through observation and evaluative feedback, the student teacher receives objective data that by herself she cannot collect. Evaluation may sound ominous to the student teacher because it is usually connected to a grade or passing a class or training program. A breakdown in trust may occur. Actually, evaluation is a chance for improvement, a time to realize that all teachers are a combination of strengths and weaknesses.

Figure 3–2 You will be observed working with children.

The quality of the feedback given to a student teacher is an important factor, and feedback needs to be consistent and constructive throughout a student teacher's placement.

Observational feedback may pinpoint behavior the student can then examine while teaching (see Figure 3–2). Feedback is information, which the reporter believes to be true and accurate, on an individual happening or interaction. Discussions following observations include identifying what went well, descriptive analysis, examination of situational factors, the creation of action plans, further analysis of written records, child behavior particulars, action/reaction relationships, and any other feature of the observation that is important.

Ideally, when supervisors build trust, student teachers can be:

- clear about the supervisor–student teacher evaluation relationship.
- supervised by people who listen well, clarify ideas, encourage specificity, and take time to understand what the student is trying to present to the children.
- free to request value judgments.
- convinced their supervisor is an advocate for their success in the classroom.

However, time can be a limiting factor. Colleges and other training programs vary greatly in both the expected number of visits to observe student teachers in action and the amount of time available for consultation. Whereas one supervisor may have the luxury of being assigned only a few student teachers, another may have a large number. One of your authors, for example, was privileged to be able to supervise only six student teachers one quarter, and all were placed in one school. College and training program decisions are influenced by budgets, state supervision formulas, politics, philosophy, and other factors.

METHODS OF OBSERVATION

Observations can be categorized into three types: informal, co-educator, and formal.

1. An informal visit is described as the casual, unfocused visit of a supervisor in which a general overall picture of the classroom emerges. The student teacher's style, the cooperating teacher's style, staff interactions, room organization, children's behavior, classroom routines, the learning environment, and so on is observed. The supervisor may pitch in or not. Notes may be written later and can include a supervisor's questions about room particulars, unique child behaviors, or features that are uncommon, unusual, or unexpected.
2. In a *co-educator* observation, the supervisor, like the cooperating teacher, is an active participant in the classroom sharing teaching responsibilities. Together, they spend enough time in the classroom to determine its dynamics. They focus on the children, program, and the student teacher's involvement in child learning. Supervisors gain experience with the diversities and problems that exist, and may be able to understand the classroom from the student teacher's point of view. They are also able to model techniques and step in during student teacher difficulties. Many college supervisors cannot spend this kind of time with their individual student teachers. In some placement classrooms college supervisors prefer formal observation.

3. *Formal* observation is defined as the observation of a student teacher that happens when a supervisor slips in noticed or unnoticed and remains unconnected to classroom action. Some type of recording takes place whether it be a narrative, a checklist, tally, or another type described later in the chapter. Many training programs feel this type of observation is more reliable and accurate because the observer is exempt from teaching responsibility and able to catch details and see events unfold from beginning to end. Often, a supervisor focuses on a different dimension of student teaching during subsequent observations.

checklist—a method of evaluating children or teachers that consists of a list of behaviors, skills, concepts, or attributes that the observer checks off as a child or teacher is observed to have mastered the item.

Training programs collect data on student teachers' performances in many different ways. The most common collection techniques follow.

Direct Observation

Direct observation is usually accomplished by means of a recorded specimen description, time sampling, and/or event sampling. This can be either obtrusive (the observed individual is aware of the process) or unobtrusive (collecting data without the subject's knowledge, perhaps from an observation room) (see Figure 3–3 and 3–4).

- Time sampling: An observer watches and codes a set of specific behaviors within a certain time frame.
- Specimen description or narrative: A "stream of consciousness" report that attempts to record all that occurs.
- Specimen description involves recording everything that the individual does or says with as much information about the context (people involved, circumstances that might be influencing the behavior, and so on) as possible.
- Event sampling: A detailed record of significant incidents or events.

time sampling—a quantitative measure or count of how often a specific behavior occurs within a given amount of time.

Figure 3–3 Viewing from an overhead loft works well in some programs.

Figure 3–4 College supervisors often take notes while observing to help their memory of factors affecting the teacher situation.

Criterion-referenced Instrument

An analysis of whether the subject can perform a given task or set of tasks. (An example can be found in the Appendix.)

Interview

Usually, a specific set of questions asked in a standard manner (see Figure 3–5).

Area	Percentage				
	Almost always	Usually	Undecided	Sometimes	Seldom
1. Does the student teacher plan adequately for classroom experience?					
2. Does your student teacher utilize up-to-date teaching methods effectively?					
3. Does your present student teacher provide adequately for individual differences?					
4. Is your student teacher able to manage the behavior of children?					
5. Does your student teacher meet class responsibilities on time?					
6. Is your student teacher able to evaluate children adequately?					
7. Does your student teacher cooperate with you?					
8. Is your student teacher willing to do more than minimum requirements?					
9. Does your student teacher attend extra classroom-related social and professional functions?					
10. Does your student teacher seem ethical in his relationships with staff, children, and parents?					
11. Is your student teacher able to motivate children?					
12. Does your student teacher demonstrate facility in oral communication?					
13. Is your student teacher able to organize?					
14. Does the student teacher seem to believe in developmentally appropriate practice?					
15. Does your student teacher demonstrate an adequate background in early childhood education?					

Figure 3–5 Sample of interview instrument used for cooperating teachers' evaluation of student teachers.

Rating Scale

The observer sets a point value on a continuum in order to evaluate a characteristic or skill (see Figure 3–6).

NAME ______________________________

The professional qualities of each student teacher will be evaluated on the following criteria:

A four-point scale is used:
(1) needs improvement
(2) satisfactory
(3) above average
(4) outstanding

PERSONAL QUALITIES	1	2	3	4
1. Attendance and punctuality	___	___	___	___
2. Dependability	___	___	___	___
3. Flexibility	___	___	___	___
4. Resourcefulness	___	___	___	___
5. Self-direction, sees what needs to be done	___	___	___	___
6. Sensitive to other people's needs and feelings	___	___	___	___
7. Tact, patience, and cooperation with others	___	___	___	___
8. Sense of humor	___	___	___	___
9. Attitude toward children	___	___	___	___
10. Attitude toward adults	___	___	___	___
11. Attitude toward administrators	___	___	___	___
12. Well-modulated voice, use of language	___	___	___	___
13. Ability to evaluate self and benefit from experiences	___	___	___	___
14. Dressed appropriately	___	___	___	___
Comments: ______________________________				

WORKING WITH CHILDREN	1	2	3	4
1. Aware of safety factors	___	___	___	___
2. Understands children at their own levels	___	___	___	___
3. Finds ways to give individual help without sacrificing group needs	___	___	___	___
4. Skill in group guidance	___	___	___	___
5. Skill in individual guidance	___	___	___	___
6. Listens to children and answers their questions	___	___	___	___
7. Consistent and effective in setting and maintaining limits	___	___	___	___
8. Encourages self-help and independence in children	___	___	___	___
9. Sensitive to children's cues in terms of adding to their knowledge or encouraging verbal skills	___	___	___	___
10. Aware of total situation, even when working with one child	___	___	___	___
11. Sensitivity to a developing situation in terms of prevention rather than cure	___	___	___	___
12. Sense of professional ethics	___	___	___	___
Comments: ______________________________				

WORKING WITH OTHER TEACHERS, PARENTS, AND VOLUNTEERS	1	2	3	4
1. Willingness to accept direction and suggestions	___	___	___	___
2. Is friendly and cooperative with staff members	___	___	___	___
3. Observes appropriate channels when reporting on school matters	___	___	___	___
4. Respects confidential information	___	___	___	___
5. Establishes good working relationships	___	___	___	___

Figure 3–6 Student teacher responsibilities and evaluation form (rating scale)

continues

6. Does not interfere in a situation another teacher is handling ____ ____ ____ ____
7. Shows good judgment in terms of knowing when to step into a situation ____ ____ ____ ____

Comments: ______________________________
____

PROGRAMMING

1. Provides for teacher-directed and child-initiated activities ____ ____ ____ ____
2. Plans in advance and prepares adequately ____ ____ ____ ____
3. Makes routines and transitions valuable and interesting ____ ____ ____ ____
4. Plans and implements age-appropriate, attractive activities and materials in the following areas:
   - Self-Esteem/Self-Help ____ ____ ____ ____
   - Music/Movement ____ ____ ____ ____
   - Health/Safety ____ ____ ____ ____
   - Science/Discovery ____ ____ ____ ____
   - Cooking/Nutrition ____ ____ ____ ____
   - Art/Creative ____ ____ ____ ____
   - Outside Environment/Play ____ ____ ____ ____
   - Cultural Awareness/Antibias ____ ____ ____ ____
   - Language/Literature ____ ____ ____ ____
   - Dramatic Play ____ ____ ____ ____
   - Math/Measurement ____ ____ ____ ____
   - Other Areas ____ ____ ____ ____
5. Creative and problem-solving activities are interesting and appropriate ____ ____ ____ ____
6. Plans developmentally appropriate activities ____ ____ ____ ____

Comments: ______________________________
____

Figure 3-6 (continued)

VIDEOTAPING

A video camera records a student teaching sequence.

Tape Recording

Only sound is recorded.

Filming

A sound or silent record.

Combinations of these methods are frequently used. Some cooperating teachers work alongside their student teachers and take mental notes rather than written ones.

CLINICAL SUPERVISION

Clinical supervision was initially promoted as a method to improve instructional practices by providing supervisors with a structured and cooperative approach to teacher supervision and accountability. Developed by Cogan and his associates in the 1950s while working with student teachers in Harvard University's Master of

Arts in Teaching program, clinical supervision, "in contrast to other supervisory efforts, [was] designed as a professional response to a specific problem. . . . Cogan and his colleagues decided that their supervisory practices of observing a lesson and then conferring with the [student] teacher were inadequate." (Sullivan, 1980). Clinical supervision was quickly adopted by other universities in their teacher education programs and by school district personnel in supervising experienced teachers.

Underlying clinical supervision is the assumption that if the student teacher and his supervisor cooperatively define the focus of each supervision visit, the student teacher has the opportunity to address specific problems rather than global ones. A supervisory visit might focus, for example, on the student teacher's questioning strategies or on the responses the teacher makes to student questions. It might also focus on interactions among specific students in the class or on management techniques used by the student teacher. The advantage of using clinical supervision was thought to lie in the reduction of stress for the student teacher and increased ability to address specific, mutually agreed upon problems.

The steps in clinical supervision are as follows:

1. The preobservation conference where the focus for the upcoming observation is decided.
2. The observation itself.
3. Analysis by the supervisor with consideration of possible strategies for improvement.
4. The postobservation conference.
5. The postconference analysis by the student teacher and the supervisor, at which time strategies for improvement are elicited from the student teacher and confirmed or counseled for change by the supervisor.

In reality, clinical supervision has been reported to have had varying degrees of success. Some supervisors saw extensive possibilities in the use of clinical supervision. On the other hand, others cited three specific reasons why clinical supervision was not more widely used: (1) the complexity of the process, (2) the lack of clearly identified competencies for performance, and (3) the lack of research. Additional reasons are the need for training and practice in the process and the pressures of time on many supervisors.

Lacey, Guffey, & Rampp (2000) describe clinical supervision as a goal-oriented model that assumes a professional relationship exists between a student teacher and a supervisor in an environment characterized by a high degree of mutual trust, understanding, support, and commitment. There is also an assumption that the supervisor is knowledgeable with regard to the analysis of instruction and learning and productive human interaction.

Reflective Supervision

Reflective supervision is a refinement and outgrowth of clinical supervision. It attempts to bring the student teacher and college supervisor together in a collaborative way to help the student teacher develop a disposition and ability to construct knowledge (Titone, Sherman, & Palmer, 1998). It is characterized by supervisor–student teacher interactions that practice collegiality and that demonstrate teaching as a reflective, inquiry-based, and knowledge-producing activity. The method assumes the following to be the basic needs and rights of the student teacher:

1. to be treated professionally
2. to have an opportunity to develop self-understanding in a nonthreatening atmosphere

3. to learn to analyze curriculum
4. to learn to understand the sociocultural dynamics present in every classroom
5. to work in an intentionally collegial relationship with an experienced teacher and full-time faculty member (Titone, et al., 1998)

Because trust is essential, McBride and Skau (1995) point out that limited meeting time during field placements makes this supervision model a challenge for some college programs.

The ultimate goal of the relationship between the student teacher and supervisor is to enable the student teacher to develop the disposition and ability to self-assess accurately in every context in which she works (Titone, et al., 1998).

Cognitive Coaching

Cognitive coaching is a process involving (student) teachers exploring the thinking behind their practices (Garmston, Linder, & Whitaker, 1993). This type of evaluation process helps student teachers talk about their thinking and also become aware of teaching decisions. It does not require following a specific model of instruction but instead supports the student teacher's acquired skills and strengths while also promoting growth in unexpected teaching areas. A cognitive coach (in this case, a student teacher's supervisor) asks questions about skills to be honed and improved, and possible new ventures in growth areas.

Cognitive coaching is similar to clinical supervision in its use of the preconference, observation, and postconference format. It emphasizes to a greater degree teacher improvement of instructional effectiveness by becoming more reflective about teaching and informed teacher decision-making. (Garmston, et al., 1993).

The ultimate goal of using this evaluatory process is enhancing the student teacher's ability to self-monitor, self-analyze, and self-evaluate.

Preconference discussion concentrates on four basic questions:

1. What are your objectives?
2. How will you know when you have reached them?
3. What is your plan?
4. On what other aspects of your teaching do you want information? (Garmston, et al., 1993)

A supervisor skilled in cognitive coaching asks probing questions. Student teachers may feel uncomfortable working out questions for themselves rather than being given immediate answers. When faced with self-analysis, teachers, experiencing a cognitive coaching evaluation, search their own minds, unlocking ideas that might not have presented themselves. Garmston, et al. (1993) believe the reflection learned through this method of evaluation helps develop problem-solving skills as teachers examine, experience, generate alternatives, and evaluate actions.

RELIABILITY

Observations must serve as a reliable and accurate source of information. In student teaching, the participants understand that each observation record covers only a short space of time compared to the length of the student teacher's placement. Areas of competence that receive similar interpretations from different observers over a period of time should be of special interest to student teachers.

While all observers have different points of reference depending on their individual life experiences in the student teaching situation, their goals are similiar. They honestly attempt to examine, interpret, and reflect on what they have seen and possibly recorded to improve student performance through follow-up dialogue.

Any attempt to interpret meaning brings with it the possibility of misinterpretation based on the limits of what one can perceive and the observer's biases stemming from his existing values and preconceptions (Caruso & Fawcett, 1999). Observers may have a "mind set" that predisposes them to look at particular teaching skills and overlook others. Using a variety of observation tools and forms can help remedy the situation.

biases—particular tendencies or inclinations, especially ones that prevent impartial consideration; prejudices.

Reliability refers to the extent to which observations are consistent over time and "the extent to which a test is consistent in measuring over time what it is designed to measure" (Wortham, 1995). The similarity of information in data gathered in different observations confirms the reliability of the measurement. For example, if both a videotaped observation and a time sampling seem to point to the same measurement of skill or teaching behavior, the reliability of the data will increase.

reliability—a measure or a test indicating that the test is stable and consistent, to ensure that changes in score are due to the child, not the test.

The degree of obviousness of the collection method also merits consideration. Videotaping may produce unnatural behavior. Hidden cameras and tape recorders raise ethical questions. Observation rooms and one-way screens are familiar and unobtrusive methods commonly used in laboratory training centers. Objective recording of teaching behavior is a difficult task. Observations can be subjective and reflect the observer's special point of view.

Supervisors and cooperating teachers try to keep all observations objective during student teaching. Discussions between the observed and observer can add additional factors for consideration before analyses and evaluations occur.

To remove subjective comments from teacher observation, observers should attempt to describe precise teaching episodes, using extensive note-taking that leaves little doubt. Observers can use the following steps as observation guidelines.

1. Noting the physical layout of the class by observing such items as the arrangement of tables, learning aides (bulletin boards, resource centers, and other places/items of interest), and storage areas for child and adult materials.
2. Observing the cordiality of verbal greetings between teacher and children. Data on the number of children present, sex of the children, and diversity of group add further information.
3. Noting the patterns of action in the classroom. How children move about the room (getting water, for example) provides information regarding both organization and management.
4. The verbal and nonverbal interactions between teacher-child and child-child are a crucial part of the supervision-observation process. How does the teacher approach children? What tone of voice and choice of words does the teacher use? What is the reaction of the children? Are teacher comments distributed equally to children?
5. How are rules established and adhered to? How does the teacher respond to disruptive behavior? What preceded the behavior? How do students respond to the teacher's actions?
6. One important aspect of classroom life that appears crucial to teacher performance is that of tracking time and the sequencing of activities (see Figure 3–7). What do teachers use as transitions? What are the frequency and smoothness of transitions?

Figure 3–7 Posted schedules help observers to see student teacher actions during transitions.

7. As in most supervisory settings, the importance of the postobservation conference cannot be overstated. The student teacher should present her personal impressions of activities viewed prior to discussing the supervisor's observation. This facilitates self-evaluation and recall of the salient aspects. The additional information provided by the supervisor's narrative aids the student teacher in clarifying and understanding the antecedents and the consequences of classroom events.

Ongoing and cumulative evaluations of students' performances are designed to verify students' competencies. In student teaching, they allow students to discover, plan, and ponder. Without outside assessment and evaluation, assessment is limited to self-assessment.

Observers and Evaluators

It is possible to be observed and assessed by many people during your student teaching experience. Some students prefer only the supervisor's and cooperating teacher's assessments (see Figure 3–8). Others actively seek feedback from all possible sources. A wide base of observational data on competency seems best. Other possible observers in most student teaching placements are:

- self (see Figures 3–9 and 3–10)
- classroom assistants, aides, and volunteers
- other student teachers
- the center or school's support staff (cooks, nurse, secretary, and so on.)
- children
- parents
- community liaison staff
- administrative staff or consulting specialists (see Figure 3–11)

Student Name ______________________ Evaluator Name ______________________
Date ______________________ Center ______________________
Time of Observation ______________________ Activity Planned ______________________
Rating Scale: 1 = Unsatisfactory 2 = Needs Improvement 3 = Satisfactory 4 = Good 5 = Excellent

Principle	Possible Evidence—Teaching Behaviors	Rating
The student teacher can create learning experiences that make subject matter meaningful for children. Further evidence:	Explains skills or concepts accurately. Engages children in discovery opportunities. Relates skills or concepts to students' lives. Links skills or concepts to children's prior knowledge. Integrates various fields of knowledge. Prepares hands-on activities and opportunities.	
The student teacher understands how children learn and develop, and can provide learning opportunities that support their intellectual, social, and personal development. Further evidence:	Converses with individual children effectively. Identifies and uses learning strategies that are developmentally appropriate for children. Uses a variety of approaches to aid child's discovery and experimentation. Monitors and adjusts activities to fit students' needs. Follows and supports children's self-initiated activities.	
The student teacher understands student uniqueness and plans opportunities that are adapted to diverse learners. Further evidence:	Uses various and multiple strategies that are matched to learners. Determines how individual children learn best. Uses information from students' families, cultures, and communities to make activities suit child group. Monitors child feedback and is responsive to necessity to change. Creates techniques adjusted to learner needs and interests.	
The student teacher encourages children's development of critical thinking, problem-solving, and child solutions. Further evidence:	Uses techniques that encourage children: • to assume responsibility for themselves and each other • to participate in decision-making • to do independent and collaborative work • to engage children in meaningful and purposeful activity Asks questions that promote higher-level thinking. Asks open-ended questions.	

continues

Figure 3–8 Student teacher evaluation form

ONLINE COMPANION

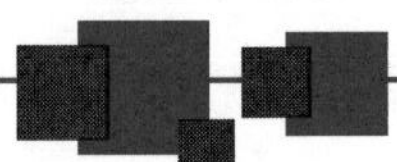

Principle	Possible Evidence—Teaching Behaviors	Rating
The student teacher uses an understanding of individual and group motivation and behavior to create a learning environment that encourages positive social interaction, active engagement in learning, and self-motivation. Further evidence:	Engages students actively in hands-on learning activities. Provides attention and feedback. Promotes problem-solving. Provides model for positive interactions with others. Treats children as unique individuals within context of large group. Provides opportunities for group interaction.	
The student teacher uses effective verbal, nonverbal, and communication techniques to foster active inquiry, collaboration, and supportive interaction in the classroom. Further evidence:	Provides opportunities for group activities and learning experiences. Models positive and active listening skills. Asks questions to stimulate discussion, probe for understanding, help students articulate ideas, promote risk-taking and problem-solving, facilitate recall, stimulate curiosity, and encourage convergent and divergent thinking. Uses standard English, both written and oral.	
The student teacher uses classroom equipment and materials (both commercial and teacher-made) to aid child discovery and learning. Attention is given to proper use and maintenance. Further evidence:	Understands how materials can enhance learning. Returns to storage areas. Is careful in usage. Consults with cooperative teacher on usage and care. Creates teacher-made materials. Understands safety considerations.	
The student teacher fosters relationships with school colleagues, parents, and community to support children's learning and well-being. Further evidence:	Works with colleagues in curriculum-planning activities. Participates in team-teaching activities. Communicates with parents effectively. Understands community diversity.	

continues

Figure 3–8 (continued)

Principle	Possible Evidence—Teaching Behaviors	Rating
The student teacher creates a classroom environment suited to the needs and diversity of children. Further evidence:	Room areas are developmentally appropriate, offering an adequate variety of play choices, and reflect the diverse backgrounds of children. Considers and monitors child safety. Offers appropriate written and pictorial materials. Considers aesthetics.	
The student teacher is a skilled communicator and promotes smooth human relationships with fellow staff, parents, community representatives, and the general public. Further evidence:	Interacts with others effectively. Assumes responsibility for actions and behavior. Treats others with respect and dignity. Works in collaboration with others. Sensitive to cultural diversity.	
Child guidance and classroom management are undertaken in accordance with accepted early childhood strategies and techniques. Further evidence:	Clear statement of class rules and expectations are apparent. Visual supervision of all children is continual. Strategies used are developmentally appropriate. Works toward child self-control.	
Student teacher views his work as a professional and understands work responsibilities. Further evidence:	Is timely and dependable. Assignments are completed. Clothing and grooming reflect professionalism yet are appropriate and comfortable. Able to develop and maintain professional relationships.	

Summary of Teaching Behaviors

Strengths	Areas of Improvement

Signature of Student / Date	Signature of Evaluator / Date

Figure 3-8 (continued)

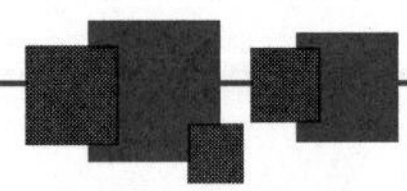

Instructions:
Evaluate your own performance on this form. To the left of each characteristic listed below, write a W if you are working on it, M if it happens most of the time, or an A if it happens always.

Relationships

___ 1. I share my positive feelings by arriving with an appropriate attitude.
___ 2. I greet children, parents, and staff in a friendly and pleasant manner.
___ 3. I accept suggestions and criticism gracefully from my coworkers.
___ 4. I can handle tense situations and retain my composure.
___ 5. I make an effort to be sensitive to the needs of the children and their parents.
___ 6. I am willing to share my ideas and plans so that I can contribute to the total program.

Goals

___ 1. The classroom is organized to promote a quality child development program.
___ 2. I constantly review the developmental stage of each child so that my expectations are reasonable.
___ 3. I set classroom and individual goals and then evaluate regularly.
___ 4. I have fostered independence and responsibility in children.

Classroom Skills

___ 1. I arrive on time.
___ 2. I face each day as a new experience.
___ 3. I can plan a balanced program for the children in all skill areas.
___ 4. I am organized and have a plan for the day.
___ 5. I help each child recognize the role of being part of a group.
___ 6. I help children develop friendships.
___ 7. I maintain a child-oriented classroom, and the bulletin boards enhance the room.

Professionalism

___ 1. I understand the school philosophy.
___ 2. I maintain professional attitudes in my demeanor and in my personal relationships while on the job.
___ 3. I assume my share of joint responsibility.

Personal Qualities

___ 1. I have basic emotional stability.
___ 2. My general health is good and does not interfere with my responsibilities.
___ 3. My personal appearance is suitable for my job.
___ 4. I evaluate my effectiveness as a member of my teaching team in the following manner:

– 0 1 2 3 4 5 +
(Low) (High)

My Teaching Team

___ 1. I've earned the respect and acceptance of team members.

Figure 3–9 Student teaching self-evaluation form

STUDENT SELF-EVALUATION

Put a check on the number in each line which best describes your performance.

1	2	3	4	5	
I often think critically about how my behavior affects children and other adults.	Sometimes I try to analyze classroom interactions.	From time to time I think about how I affect others in the classroom.	I rarely rehash what happened during the day in the classroom.	I give little thought to classroom interactions.	REFLECTION
I have a clear idea of important goals with children and work daily to accomplish them.	Some of my goals are clear; others are still being formed.	My goals are not always clear, but at times I think about them.	I use my center's goals for planning and have a few of my own.	I mainly handle each day by providing activities that teach specific concepts and making sure children behave.	CLARITY OF GOALS
I'm always responsible for what I do and say.	Most of the time I take responsibility for what happens.	At times I feel responsible for my actions.	I can't control all that happens—that's my attitude.	What goes wrong is mostly others' fault.	RESPONSIBILITY
I do what's assigned and needed before deadlines, and check to see it's completed on time.	I usually complete jobs in a timely manner.	I finish jobs that I choose to finish mostly on time.	I start, but often something happens before I finish assignments.	I'm late, and often don't finish what's expected of me.	DEPENDABILITY
I always find what I need and create when necessary in activity planning.	I'm pretty good at getting what needs to be secured.	I sometimes can find or create what is necessary.	I rarely know how to go about getting things I need for the classroom.	I expend little effort at locating hard-to-find items or materials for child instruction.	RESOURCEFULNESS
I rarely need others to direct my work.	Most of the time I don't need the help of my supervisor.	I ask for help when the going gets rough and that's not often.	I need advice frequently and depend on others to solve my problem.	Lots of help and supervision are necessary.	INDEPENDENCE
I'm active in teacher associations and attend nearby conferences.	Sometimes I attend professional association meetings and training opportunities.	I go to the library occasionally to consult the experts.	Haven't the time now to join or attend professional group doings but plan to in the near future.	I don't wish to become a member of a professional group.	PROFESSIONAL GROWTH
I change and create new happenings in my classroom and try new ways joyfully.	I will try some new ways and strategies.	If it's suggested, I try new ways to do things.	I'm pretty stressed about trying something I've not done before.	The old routines and ways are comfortable. Why change them?	CREATIVITY
I respect and enjoy being a helpful team player.	I do help others on my team.	I will share ideas and give time to other team members.	I don't really function well with others; I'd rather do it myself.	Teams don't accomplish much and waste time. Not helpful at all.	TEAM MEMBERSHIP
I'm aware of children's cultural backgrounds.	I'm sensitive to the cultural learning styles of attending children.	I've developed the skill to promote multicultural respect and dignity.	My students' cultural diversity is reflected in classroom displays and materials	I've expended time and effort to become knowledgeable concerning the culture of attending children.	CULTURAL SENSITIVITY

Figure 3–10 Rate yourself

Emotionally mature and well-adjusted personality
Alert and enthusiastic
Professional competency
Genuine interest in people, children, teaching
Professional attitude
Good appearance and grooming
Above-average scholastically
Wide interests and cultural backgrounds
Leadership qualities
Sense of humor
Willingness to learn and desire to grow professionally
Success in directed teaching
Creativeness
Understanding of children
Interest in community participation
Moral character
Cooperative
Good health
Ability to communicate effectively
Good penmanship
Interest in curriculum development
Flexibility
Sincerity
Appropriate humility
Ability to organize

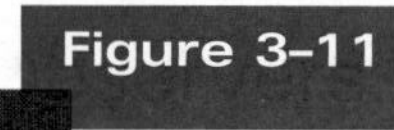

Figure 3–11 Administrators' responses to the question, "What would you like to know about student teachers?"

Student teachers can develop their own rating systems based on teaching characteristics that are important to them. Simple tallies are helpful in recording changes in behavior.

Discussion

Discussions held after data are collected are keys to growth. The meeting's feeling, tone, its format, location, time of day, and degree of comfort can be critical. The communication skills of both participants contribute to success in promoting student teacher skill development.

Two types of discussions, formative and summative, occur during student teaching. An initial formative discussion sets the stage for later discussions. Goals, time lines, and evaluative procedures are explained. Additional formative discussions will follow placement observations. A summative conference finalizes your total placement experience and scrutinizes both the placement site and your competencies.

During discussions, you will examine the collected data, add comments about extenuating circumstances, form plans to collect additional information, and consider initiating new actions that could strengthen your existing skills through change or modification. Suggestions for improvement are self-discovered and formed jointly with the cooperating teacher or supervisor.

Child behavior resulting from student teacher behavior is a focal point for discussions. Influencing factors such as room settings, routines, child uniqueness, and the student teacher's techniques, methods, and behaviors are examined closely.

Discussions that are descriptive and interpretative and involve value judgments about child education and professional teaching are common.

Giving criticism is as much a skill as receiving it. Instructional criticism is given with the intent to improve, and usually specific ideas are offered for the listener's consideration. Evaluation sessions need to be viewed by student teachers as opportunities for growth and with a "I'm going to get as much as I can from this person supervising me" attitude. It is a time to listen to understand rather than with an intent to respond.

Ideally, when you know and value yourself and have a strong sense of your individual identity and self-worth, criticism can be taken at face value, in stride, and can be seen as providing helpful suggestions that can lead to reflection concerning new ideas, changes, and professional growth possibilities. You may hear yourself saying "I'll take that into consideration. Thanks for sharing it with me," Teachers are committed to lifelong learning, and student teachers begin to gauge the complexities inherent in working in the career field. During formative evaluation discussions, student teachers can discover career skills they want to investigate, try out, or polish.

formative evaluation—ongoing assessment to ensure that planned activities and methods accomplish what the teacher intended.

The authors have met student teachers who have become angry and aggressive and taken suggestions as personal attacks, others who have melted in tears, and still others skilled enough to walk away when strong emotions overcome them, saying "I need to think about what you've said, and I'll get back to you." Asking questions to better understand, paraphrasing to clarify points, taking notes, and adding unknown information about a viewed situation were also common student techniques to help us—their college supervisors—see things in a more complete light.

Pre- and Postconferences—Supervisor Evaluations. More and more supervisors are conducting preobservation conferences so student teachers can brief them about classroom details and the activities or lesson plan the supervisor will observe. Postconferences after supervisor observation are a standard procedure, and the review of observation notes helps student teachers reflect on their skills. Tips, resource ideas, and possible areas for growth are discussed. Sometimes, discussions and summative evaluation meetings lead naturally to preconference ones. "What happens next week?"

summative evaluation—an assessment that follows a specific lesson or unit to evaluate whether the children have met the objectives.

Dealing with Evaluations

Student teachers should try to develop a positive attitude about what may appear to be an emphasis on their weaknesses. However, this attitude may come slowly for some student teachers. Conferencing covers student teachers' strengths but sometimes promotes a "report card" feeling that is hard to shake.

As a preparation for discussion, it is a good habit to get into self-evaluation early in your student teaching assignment. The following weekly questions are helpful:

- What did I learn this week?
- Have I identified goals for myself?
- Are my goals realistic or do they need modification?

- Am I expecting perfection, or am I satisfied with an honest attempt?
- Am I communicating effectively?
- Do I seek help when I need it?
- Am I falling behind or keeping up?
- What improvements or adjustment do I need to make?

Skillpath (1997) offers additional pointers in Figure 3–12.

One strategy a student teacher will find useful when handling evaluator comments is saying, "Yes, I understand your concern. I had concern as well. Let me tell you about the circumstances that occurred. Tell me what you would have suggested in that case."

Discussions can describe a wide range of student and teacher behaviors. Clarification of terms can be helpful to student teachers. Keeping records of discussions will aid your planning. They can be reviewed prior to follow-up conferences. Action plans resulting from previous discussions are usually the primary focus of later ones.

College supervisors have the ultimate and final burden of approving a candidate for graduation from training programs. If one questions a gathering of supervisors, one hears both anguish and elation, elation that they have had a small part in an individual teacher's development; anguish because they are forced to make decisions. Their goal as supervisors is to assure that each candidate possesses the knowledge, skill, and competency necessary to interact sensitively, creatively, and successfully with both children and adults. The task of assessing individual students involves observing human relations. Some student teachers of diverse cultural and language backgrounds may be tremendously talented and insightful with children, but they may find readings and academic testing in student teaching classes particularly difficult, therefore needing tutoring assistance.

- Be your own best critic
- Know your strengths and weaknesses
- Predict what the person might say before the person says it
- Rehearse your responses to anticipated feedback
- Assume the best intentions
- Recognize that everyone needs feedback to grow
- Separate yourself from the criticism
- It's OK to dislike your behavior and still like yourself
- Think about improving, not labeling yourself
- Deal with the issue, forget personalities
- You are the only person responsible for your behavior, not others
- When the intention to learn from our mistakes overcomes our fear of failure, we're less likely to view criticism as a personal put-down

Figure 3–12 Receiving criticism. Used by permission of Skillpath Seminars.

PEER EVALUATIONS

Many graduated student teachers feel peer evaluations were tremendously helpful for a number of reasons.

1. They are nonthreatening because a "grade" is not at issue.
2. A peer may have greater empathy or understanding because they are experiencing many of the same or similar problems.
3. Peers know how it feels to be observed and evaluated, so "tread softly."
4. Suggestions offered may have recently been field tested. A student teacher's successes are passed on to another student teacher for consideration.
5. When one becomes the evaluator, one experiences increased insight into the role of the college supervisor and cooperating teacher.
6. Seeing a peer's assigned classroom and cooperating teacher offers new data, new techniques.
7. Additional teaching methods, activities, and so on, are observed and possibly considered and tried in their own classroom.
8. There is something in assuming the role of an observer-evaluator that makes one feel competent and professional.

All the positive aspects of peer evaluations have not been mentioned in this discussion, and there have been unfortunate instances of friction between peers.

It is wise to follow college instructor guidelines closely. Often, peer evaluators are asked to stick to the positive aspects of a peer's behavior and carefully suggest growth areas. A rating form used by a peer can focus on a variety of teaching skills (see Figure 3–13). Postevaluation discussions center on the observed explaining to the observer what was happening during the observation and what student teacher intentions were present. The assignment may involve turning in both peers' notes of the evaluation discussion rather than observational particulars.

Increasingly, peer evaluations are seen as aiding student teachers' reflective thinking and their analysis of skills. Student teachers observing others often ask themselves important questions about their own teaching styles (see Figure 3–14).

Constructive Evaluation

Evaluation should be viewed as a critique promoting positive change. The following are suggestions designed to provide maximum evaluating benefits:

- Start your debriefing by asking the evaluator (cooperating teacher, college/university supervisor, director/principal) to identify what she thought were the best parts of the lesson/activity and what parts needed improvement.
- Ask for specific examples to clarify what the evaluator means.
- An "I hear what you're saying" response is better than a defense or argument.
- Separate specific comments from other teaching areas where you are functioning well; try to remember that it is the lesson being critiqued, not you as a person.
- Think of suggestions as being constructive, not as being negative criticisms.

Student teacher's name ______________________ Peer's name ______________________

Date ______________

STUDENT TEACHER EFFECTIVENESS SCALE

Excellent	Above Average	Average or Adequate	Needs Improvement	Unacceptable	Unable to Determine
1	2	3	4	5	6

Place rating on continuum line.

A. Feeling Tone

Warm	______________________	Cool
Friendly	______________________	Withdrawn
Supportive	______________________	Authoritarian
Interacts often	______________________	Interacts rarely
Accepts dependency behavior	______________________	Does not accept dependency behavior
Physical contact often	______________________	Rare physical contact
Open to suggestion	______________________	Rigid

B. Quality of Presentation and/or Interactions

Organized	______________________	Seems disorganized
Enthusiastic	______________________	Neutral
Flexible	______________________	Rigid
Clear	______________________	Vague
Reasonable age level	______________________	Unreasonable age level
Appropriate child expectations	______________________	Inappropriate expectations
Promotes problem-solving	______________________	Furnishes all answers
Motivates	______________________	Turns off
Rewards attention to tasks	______________________	Ignores or negatively reinforces attending behaviors
Sensitive to Cultural diversity	______________________	Ignores
Expands interests	______________________	Ignores expanding opportunities
Provides developmentally appropriate activities	______________________	Activities limited by lack of understanding of appropriateness
Manages time well	______________________	Poor time management
Discovery centers planned and prepared	______________________	Poor or little planning/preparation
Child-initiated activities	______________________	Teacher-dominated activities
Plans outdoor activities	______________________	Ignores outdoor planning
Activity smoothness	______________________	Poorly sequenced
Activity cleanup	______________________	Little or no cleanup

C. Child Behavior Management Techniques

Positive	______________________	Seems negative
Firm	______________________	Lax
Supervises all	______________________	Supervises only a few
Uses modeling	______________________	Few models provided
Notices accomplishments	______________________	Ignores accomplishments
Restates rules	______________________	Rarely restates rules
Uses redirection	______________________	Rarely uses redirection
Uses many methods to change behavior	______________________	Limited strategies used
Promotes child resolution	______________________	Teacher resolution frequent

D. Verbal Interaction

Enjoys child conversation	______________________	Ignores
Clear	______________________	Unclear
Receives children's nonverbal communication	______________________	Ignores
Specific directions	______________________	Vague directions

continues

Figure 3–13 Peer rating sheet

Appropriate questioning techniques	________	Inappropriate questions
Encourages concept formation	________	Limits concept formatiov
Voice volume appropriate	________	Inappropriate volume
Frequent eye contact	________	Limited eye contact
Negotiates	________	Rigid
Promotes child discovery	________	Stifles discovery
E. Housekeeping		
Promotes child clean-up	________	Ignores child ability to clean up
Replaces	________	Leaves out
Sees housekeeping tasks	________	Needs to be directed
Spends appropriate time	________	Seems to spend more time than necessary
F. General		
Good attendance	________	Poor attendance
Well-groomed	________	Questionable grooming
Dependable	________	Unreliable
Total area supervision	________	Close focus
Flexibility	________	Rigid
Takes constructive suggestions	________	Ignores suggestions
Could easily recommend as early childhood education teacher	________	Limited recommendation possible

Greatest Strengths:

Areas for Future Growth:

Additional Comments:

____

____

____

Figure 3–13 (continued)

Figure 3–14 Would I climb this structure to speak to a child who is blocking the slide entrance?

COMPETENCY-BASED TRAINING

Teacher education has experienced a movement toward competency-based training (sometimes called performance-based) as an outgrowth of the application of behavioristic psychology, economic conditions, and major teacher education evaluation studies. Federal funds promoted the identification of the Child Development Associate (CDA) competencies. A CDA is a person who is able to meet the physical, social, emotional, and intellectual growth needs of a group of children in a child development setting. These needs are met by establishing and maintaining a proper child care environment and by promoting good relations between parents and the center.

competencies—the knowledge and skills desirable in education professionals working in various staffing positions in early childhood care.

CDA competencies are a widely distributed and accepted listing of early childhood teacher competency goals (see Figure 3–15).

The Council for Early Childhood Professional Recognition administers the CDA credentialing program. Figure 3–16 displays the number of CDA credentials awarded in the years between 1975 and 2002.

If your placement is a Head Start classroom, *Head Start Program Performance Standards* clearly define expectations for all Head Start programs. The standards are a built-in system for ensuring Head Start goals are attained (Caruso & Fawcett, 1999). They reflect sound practice, research, and a focus on quality (U.S. Department of Health and Human Services, 1996).

What are Core Knowledge and Competencies?

In order to promote quality early childhood teacher training programs that subsequently affect the quality of child care in their state, many states legislatures have adopted state child care career development systems and have established articulation agreements between two- and four-year colleges. Core knowledge areas are identified and specify which knowledge and what skills are to be accomplished in which college or training courses. This includes student teaching coursework. In 1998, 28 states had implemented core knowledge and competencies for early childhood teachers (Stoney, 2001).

THE WHOLE TEACHER

Teaching competency growth can be compared to child growth. Teachers develop intellectually, socially-emotionally, physically, and creatively, as do children. Skills often omitted on competency listings, yet becoming more and more important to early childhood teachers in our society, are stress reduction and stress management techniques, holistic health awareness and practice, moral and ethical strength, researching skill, parenting education and family guidance counseling, public relations, and political "know-how." Job situations can create the need for skills not covered in your teacher training. As society changes, the early childhood teacher's role as a partner to parents in child education changes.

Personal Abilities and Characteristics

What personal characteristics, dispositions, traits, abilities, or "gifts" are described in early childhood teachers? According to Hamachek (1992), effective teachers who have few discipline problems possess a sense of humor; are fair, empathetic; more democratic than autocratic; and are able to relate easily and naturally to pupils on any basis, group or one to one. Teacher behaviors that exemplify the "effective teacher" include:

discipline—generally considered a response to children's misbehavior.

CDA Competency Goals	Functional Areas	Definitions
I To establish and maintain a safe, healthy learning environment	1. Safe	Candidate provides a safe environment to prevent and reduce injuries.
	2. Healthy	Candidate promotes good health and nutrition and provides an environment that contributes to the prevention of illness.
	3. Learning Environment	Candidate uses space, relationships, materials, and routines as resources for constructing an interesting, secure, and enjoyable environment that encourages play, exploration, and learning.
II To advance physical and intellectual competence	4. Physical	Candidate provides a variety of equipment, and intellectual competence activities, and opportunities to promote the physical development of children.
	5. Cognitive	Candidate provides activities and opportunities that encourage curiosity, exploration, and problem solving appropriate to the developmental levels and learning styles of children.
	6. Communication	Candidate actively communicates with children and provides opportunities and support for children to understand, acquire, and use verbal and nonverbal means of communicating thoughts and feelings.
	7. Creative	Candidate provides opportunities that stimulate children to play with sound, rhythm, language, materials, space, and ideas in individual ways and to express their creative abilities.
III To support social and emotional development and provide positive guidance	8. Self	Candidate provides physical and emotional security for each child and helps each child to know, accept, and take pride in himself or herself and to develop a sense of independence.
	9. Social	Candidate helps each child feel accepted in the group, helps children learn to communicate and get along with others, and encourages feelings of empathy and mutual respect among children and adults.
	10. Guidance	Candidate provides a supportive environment in which children can begin to learn and practice appropriate and acceptable behaviors as individuals and as a group member.
IV To establish positive and productive relationships with families	11. Families	Candidate maintains an open, friendly, and cooperative relationship with each child's family, encourages their involvement in the program, and supports the child's relationship with his or her family.
V To ensure a well-run, purposeful program responsive to participant needs	12. Program Management	Candidate is a manager who uses all available resources to ensure an effective operation. The Candidate is a competent organizer, planner, record keeper, communicator, and a cooperative co-worker.
VI To maintain a commitment to professionalism	13. Professionalism	Candidate makes decisions based on knowledge of early childhood theories and practices, promotes quality in child care services, and takes advantage of opportunities to improve competence, both for personal and professional growth and for the benefit of children and families.

Figure 3–15 CDA competency goals and functional areas. Reproduced from *Essentials for Child Development Associates Working with Young Children* by permission of Carol Brunson Day, Ph.D.

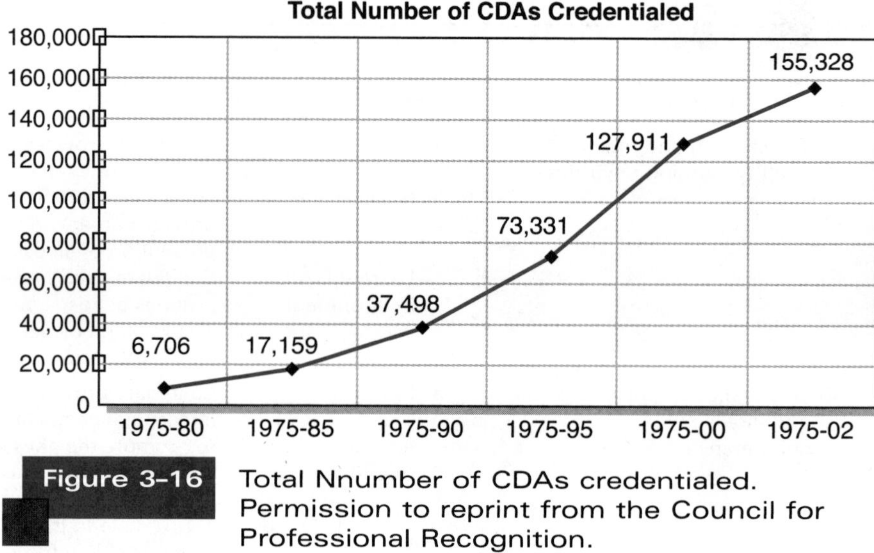

Figure 3–16 Total Nnumber of CDAs credentialed. Permission to reprint from the Council for Professional Recognition.

- Willingness to be flexible, to be direct or indirect as the situation demands.
- Ability to perceive the world from the child's point of view.
- Ability to personalize their teaching.
- Willingness to experiment, to try new things.
- Skill in asking questions (as opposed to seeing selves as a kind of answering service).
- Knowledge of subject matter and related areas.
- Ability to assess child growth and development.
- Reflection of an appreciative attitude (evidenced by nods, comments, smiles, and the like).
- Use of conversational manner in teaching; informal, easy styles (see Figure 3–17).

CDA training materials specify the following personal capacities as essential for CDAs:

- To be sensitive to children's feelings and the qualities of their thinking.
- To be ready to listen to children in order to understand them.
- To use nonverbal forms and adapt adult verbal language and style to maximize communication with the children.
- To be able to protect orderliness without sacrificing spontaneity and childlike exuberance.
- To be perceptive to individuality and make positive use of individual differences within the group.
- To be able to exercise control without being threatening.
- To be emotionally responsive, taking pleasure in children's successes and being supportive in their troubles and failures.
- To bring humor and imagination into the group situation.
- To feel committed to maximizing the child and family's strengths and potentials.

Cartwright's (1999) description of the characteristics and qualities displayed by a good early childhood practitioner includes inner security; maturity; self-awareness; integrity; a theoretical background, a general knowledge with an emphasis on environmental science, community, and young children' books; warmth and respect for children; trust in children; intuition; professional detachment; laughter; and the ability to model emotion, thought and behaviors.

Sullo (1999) suggests individuality is an essential attribute of an "inspiring" teacher. He also believes nearly all gifted teachers share certain qualities. They:

- Have the ability to develop positive relationships
- Have a passion for learning
- Are lifelong learners
- Display actions that match their words
- Have a love and appreciation of children
- Are open-minded

Behaviors teachers should avoid include:

- Repeating ideas beyond the point of usefulness
- Talking in a monotone voice and teaching lethargically
- Talking "at" or "down to" children
- Disengaging from children (Sullo, 1999)

Figure 3–17 Using a conversational manner is a competency.

REFLECTIVE BEHAVIORS IN STUDENT TEACHERS

reflective teaching—a serious effort to thoughtfully question teaching practices, perceptions, actions, feelings, values, cultural biases, and other features associated with the care and education of young children.

Not all educators agree exactly on what constitutes **reflective teaching**; it is still under study. Three elements are usually discussed in the current writings:

1. Cognitive functioning, which includes information processing and teaching decisions.
2. Background, which includes individual past experiences, goals, values, and social interactions.
3. Individual perceptions, feelings, and interpretations of classroom events and happenings (Schoonmaker, 1998).

Teacher training programs emphasizing reflective teaching are based on a desire to help student teachers move toward serious and thoughtful questioning, and provide an understanding of their own and others' teaching practices, perceptions, actions, feelings, values, and cultural biases (Schoonmaker, 1998). The Association for Childhood Education International (ACEI) (1997) in its "Position Paper on the Preparation of Elementary Teachers" stressed the need throughout the training program for student teachers to have the opportunity to reflect in order to analyze their own practice. In this way, the association believes that once graduated, student teachers would continue to reflect on their teaching and be open to acquiring new knowledge.

A myth common to some student teachers promotes the idea that teaching success can happen if someone would only tell them "how to do it" or would point them to a book containing all the answers. Reflective teaching behaviors, on the other hand, lead student teachers to construct their own personal theory of teaching and learning through hands-on classroom experiences, careful and keen observation, and social interaction with children and other adults. Loranger (1997) lists and describes these reflective teacher behaviors (see Figure 3–18).

Behaviors	Descriptors
Risk-taker.	Open to change; willingness to try new approaches to learning; willing to change direction in the middle of a lesson; willing to consider new evidence; invites evaluation of teaching.
Flexible/thinks on feet.	Knows when to change direction during a lesson; seizes "teachable moments."
Willingness to confront	Willing to explore conceptions of self as a teacher, not so secure as to not want to learn and grow; willing to confront conceptions of self squarely and openly.
Considers context when making decisions.	Carefully examines context when making decisions; understands that contexts either enable or limit educational activity.
Accepts multiple perspectives.	Views an issue simultaneously from the perspective of several people (teacher, student, researcher, parent).
Accepts responsibility for success/failure of lesson.	Recognizes decisions she makes; looks to herself for explanations when something goes awry; accepts responsibility for choices.
Ability to recognize dilemmas and make rational choices.	Ability to use practical, pedagogical, and ethical criteria when making choices; ability to assess consequence of choices.
Links theory and practice/makes connections.	Knows how to use research and integrate it into instruction; comes to value theory as a means for expanding understanding.

Figure 3–18 List of reflective behaviors with descriptors. Originally published in Ann L. Loranger's article titled "Exploring Reflective Behaviors with Preservice Teachers" in the fall 1997 issue of *Teaching and Learning: The Journal of Natural Inquiry*, Vol. 12, No. 1. It is reprinted here with permission from the publisher.

Whatever preparatory classes have been completed prior to the student teaching assignment will influence teaching behavior as the student teacher weaves this knowledge into practice. Beginning teachers are also influenced by their concepts of what an effective or "good" teacher is and does. These perceptions are frequently based on our own remembered experiences of teachers we had when we were students ourselves.

Schoonmaker (1998) believes that learning to deal with the wide range of emotions that children can evoke in student teachers and the thought of being in charge are so overwhelming that "it colors almost everything they do."

Dispositions

A relatively new term is used by Katz (1993) to describe desirable teaching behaviors: "dispositions." Various attempts to define dispositions include the words "inclinations," "traits," "tendencies," "propensities," "proclivities," and "predilections." Katz believes usage of the term "dispositions" is ambiguous and inconsistent. She believes dispositions are habits of mind or tendencies to act or react to events, people, situations, or happenings in certain ways unique to the individual. Descriptors, such as kind, friendly, assertive, thoughtful, curious, and so on might apply rather than descriptors associated with skill or specific knowledge.

A student teacher can have as a goal to strengthen certain desirable teaching dispositions and weaken undesirable ones. Having a skill and knowledge of professional practices may not mean one actually uses them. Katz (1993) uses the example of a children's curriculum that presents early formal instruction in reading skills during preschool that may undermine children's dispositions to be readers.

What teaching dispositions do you as a teacher wish to strengthen? Probably:

- a curiosity and wonderment about classroom happenings and experiences.
- an enthusiasm concerning the challenges of teaching.
- a desire to observe and uncover children's needs and interests.
- a realization that one can continually learn, develop, and sharpen teaching skills and abilities.
- working to gain children's trust and confidence and promote each child's self-realization.

Perhaps you can think of many others.

CRITICAL THINKING

Kress (1992) designed a course of study and subsequent class activities to help early childhood college majors become aware of and use critical thinking skills. Kress' study concluded that critical thinking skills or use of them could be increased through training exercises. Ennis (1985) identified thirteen dispositions (defined as attitudes and motivations) of critical thinkers; they follow.

The ability to:

1. Be open-minded.
2. Take a position (and change a position when the evidence and reasons are sufficient to do so).
3. Take into account the total situation.
4. Try to be well informed.
5. Seek as much precision as the subject permits.
6. Deal in an orderly manner with the parts of a complex whole.
7. Look for alternatives.
8. Seek reasons.
9. Seek a clear statement of the issue.
10. Keep in mind the original and/or basic concern.
11. Use credible sources and mention them.
12. Remain relevant to the main point.
13. Be sensitive to the feelings, level of knowledge, and degree of sophistication of others.

Let us look at a couple of classroom situations and decide what critical thinking skills could be modeled by this teacher.

Situation 1. A posted chart keeps slipping off the wall. Children bring it to the teacher's attention, and Jamie asks, "Why won't it stay? What can we do to fix it?"

Situation 2. Large wooden blocks are being carried outside for play on a cement patio. Children are busily making structures. Teacher knows these blocks were donated by the parent group and now are being scratched and damaged. She decides to discuss the problem with the class.

Situation 3. Everyone wants a turn looking at a new book read at story time. The waiting list is long, and some children are anxious that they won't have a turn before having to leave for home.

Manley-Casimer and Wasserman (1989) point out that many classroom environments encourage teacher action "without thinking" or taking the time to process a decision. They feel teacher preparation often ignores the decision-making responsibilities of teachers. As a student teacher, you will take on an increasing amount of daily decisions. Would you use the thoughtful, reflective approach of a critical thinker in situations 1, 2, and 3 above?

In situation 1, a critical thinking approach to the wall chart problem would begin with the teacher recognizing the alertness and helpfulness of the children. Jamie might be answered with "Let's find that out, Jamie. Why might the chart keep slipping?" If nothing is offered by the child, the teacher could think out loud, giving a few possible reasons (#8 above, and also might involve #3, #5, and #12).

Developmentall Appropriate Practice in Early Childhood Programs (DAP)—guidelines developed by the National Association for the Education of Young Children as a response to the growing trend toward more formal, academic instruction of young children. The primary position of the guidelines is that programs designed for young children should be based on what is known about young children's development. DAP also reflects a clear commitment regarding the rights of young children to respectful and supportive learning environments and to education preparing them for participation in a free and democratic society.

The teacher's behavior suggests he enjoys the quest for answers. If children do offer ideas such as "The tacks fell out," "The glue came off," or "Johnny did it," each idea is accepted and investigated. Analyze situations #2 and #3 to determine how many critical thinking skills might be modeled by the teacher or promoted in children.

How does a student teacher become proficient in critical thinking skills? By participating in a training program, Carter and Jones (1990) point out, adults learn complex teaching tasks in much the same way as young children learn: through experimenting, problem-solving, talking with peers, asking questions, and making mistakes and reflecting on them.

National Association for the Education of Young Children's Developmentally Appropriate Practice

NAEYC's Developmentally Appropriate Practice in Early Childhood Programs (DAP) (Bredekamp & Copple, 1997) is a tremendous accomplishment. Identifying competent teacher behaviors in a detailed fashion, it serves as a guidebook for early childhood educators. Excerpts from the volume are found in Figure 3–19. The authors suggest student teachers become familiar with the total volume.

SELF-PERCEPTION

Researchers have attempted to probe how "effective" or "good" teachers view their abilities and the abilities of others. If a teacher likes and trusts himself, that teacher is more likely to perceive others the same way. According to Hamachek, (1992),

> They seem to have generally more positive views of others—students, colleagues, and administrators. They do not seem to be as prone to view others as critical, attacking people with ulterior motives: rather they are seen as potentially friendly and worthy in their own right. They have a more favorable view of democratic classroom procedures. They seem to have the ability to see things as they seem to others—from the other's point of view. They do not seem to see students as children "you do things to" but rather as individuals capable of doing for themselves once they feel trusted, respected, and valued.

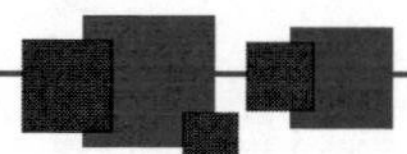

A. Teachers respect, value, and accept children and treat them with dignity at all times.

B. Teachers make it a priority to know each child well.

(1) Teachers establish positive, personal relationships with children to foster the child's development and keep informed about the child's needs and potentials. Teachers listen to children and adapt their responses to children's differing needs, interests, styles, and abilities.

(2) Teachers continually observe children's spontaneous play and interaction with the physical environment and with other children to learn about their interests, abilities, and developmental progress. On the basis of this information, teachers plan experiences that enhance children's learning and developmental.

(3) Understanding that children develop and learn in the context of their families and communities, teachers establish relationships with families that increase their knowledge of children's lives outside the classroom and their awareness of the perspectives and priorities of those individuals most significant in the child's life.

(4) Teachers are alert to signs of undue stress and traumatic events in children's lives and aware of effective strategies to reduce stress and support the development of resilience.

(5) Teachers are responsible at all times for all children under their supervision and plan for children's increasing development of self-regulation abilities.

C. Teachers create an intellectually engaging, responsive environment to promote each child's learning and development.

(1) Teachers use their knowledge about children in general and the particular children in the group as well as their familiarity with what children need to learn and develop in each curriculum area to organize the environment and plan curriculum and teaching strategies.

(2) Teachers provide children with a rich variety of experiences, projects, materials, problems, and ideas to explore and investigate, ensuring that these are worthy of children's attention.

(3) Teachers provide children with opportunities to make meaningful choices and time to explore through active involvement. Teachers offer children the choice to participate in a small-group or a solitary activity, assist and guide children who are not yet able to use and enjoy child-choice activity periods, and provide opportunities for practice of skills as a self-chosen activity.

(4) Teachers organize the daily and weekly schedule and allocate time so as to provide children with extended blocks of time in which to engage in play, projects, and/or study in integrated curriculum.

D. Teachers make plans to enable children to attain key curriculum goals across various disciplines, such as language arts, mathematics, social studies, science, art, music, physical education, and health.

(1) Teachers incorporate a wide variety of experiences, materials and equipment, and teaching strategies in constructing curriculum to accommodate a broad range of children's individual differences in prior experiences, maturation rates, styles of learning, needs, and interests.

(2) Teachers bring each child's home culture and language into the shared culture of the school so that the unique contributions of each group are recognized and valued by others.

(3) Teachers are prepared to meet identified special needs of individual children, including children with disabilities and those who exhibit unusual interests and skills. Teachers use all the strategies identified here, consult with appropriate specialists, and see that the child gets the specialized services he or she requires.

continues

Figure 3-19 Competencies in developmentally appropriate practice. Reprinted with permission from the National Association for the Education of Young Children.

E. Teachers foster children's collaboration with on interesting, important enterprises.
   (1) Teachers promote children's productive collaboration without taking over to the extent that children lose interest.
   (2) Teachers use a variety of ways of flexibly grouping children for the purposes of instruction, supporting collaboration among children, and building a sense of community. At various times, children have opportunities to work individually, in small groups, and with the whole group.

F. Teachers develop, refine and use a wide repertoire of teaching strategies to enhance children's learning and development.
   (1) To help children develop their initiative, teachers encourage them to choose and plan their own learning activities.
   (2) Teachers pose problems, ask questions, and make comments and suggestions that stimulate children's thinking and extend their learning.
   (3) Teachers extend the range of children's interests and the scope of their thought through presenting novel experiences and introducing stimulating ideas, problems, experiences, or hypotheses.
   (4) To sustain an individual child's effort or engagement in purposeful activities, teachers select from a range of strategies, including but not limited to modeling, demonstrating specific skills, and providing information, focused attention, physical proximity, verbal encouragement, reinforcement and other behavioral procedures, as well as additional structure and modification of equipment or schedules as needed.
   (5) Teachers coach and/or directly guide children in the acquisition of specific skills as needed.
   (6) Teachers calibrate the complexity and challenge of activities to suit children's level of skill and knowledge, increasing the challenge as children gain competence and understanding.
   (7) Teachers provide cues and other forms of "scaffolding" that enable the child to succeed in a task that is just beyond his or her ability to complete alone.
   (8) To strengthen children's sense of competence and confidence as learners, motivation to persist, and willingness to take risks, teachers provide experiences for children to be genuinely successful and to be challenged.
   (9) To enhance children's conceptual understanding, teachers use various strategies that encourage children to reflect on and "revisit" their learning experiences.

G. Teachers facilitate the development of responsibility and self-regulation in children.
   (1) Teachers set clear, consistent, and fair limits for children's behavior and hold children accountable to standards of acceptable behavior. To the extent that children are able, teachers engage them in developing rules and procedures for behavior of class members.
   (2) Teachers redirect children to more acceptable behavior or activity or use children's mistakes as learning opportunities, patiently reminding children of rules and their rationale as needed.
   (3) Teachers listen and acknowledge children's feelings and frustrations, respond with respect, guide children to resolve conflicts, and model skills that help children to solve their own problems.

Figure 3–19 (continued)

The results of several studies dealing with the way "good" teachers typically see themselves follow:

- Good teachers see themselves as identified with people rather than withdrawn, removed, apart from, or alienated from others.
- Good teachers feel basically adequate rather than inadequate. They do not see themselves as generally unable to cope with problems.

- Good teachers feel trustworthy rather than untrustworthy. They see themselves as reliable, dependable individuals with the potential for coping with events as they happen.
- Good teachers see themselves as wanted rather than unwanted. They see themselves as likable and attractive (in a personal, not a physical sense) as opposed to feeling ignored and rejected.
- Good teachers see themselves as worthy rather than unworthy. They see themselves as people of consequence, dignity, and integrity as opposed to feeling they matter little or can be overlooked and discounted.

Students entering the field of teaching have their own ideas regarding qualities important for success. Most include being able to communicate ideas, having interest in people, having a thorough knowledge of teaching skills, having a pleasing manner and creative ability, and being able to get along well with colleagues.

You have received feedback from your cooperating teacher, your supervisor, and perhaps others. This input is the basis of your understanding of how your competencies are viewed by others. Your perception of your teaching competencies is formed based on your own self-analysis and others' feedback.

SELF-ANALYSIS

Self-analysis will increase your awareness of discrepancies and inconsistencies between your competency goals and your present teaching behavior. As you become more accurate in self-perception, your professional identity and confidence will grow. You may even be able to predict how others will react to your teaching behaviors. You will resolve the tendency to center on yourself (a common tendency of beginning teachers), and develop the ability to focus more on children's learning and teacher/child interactions.

Numerous self-rating scales exist; Figures 3–20, and 3–21 are examples.

After assessment, you can decide what additional skills you would like to acquire. Put these skills in order of their importance to you. You are the director of your learning and the designer of your plan for future accomplishment.

When trying to assess your progress, it may be difficult to isolate how you feel about yourself from how you feel about how others view you.

ADDING TO YOUR PROFESSIONAL PORTFOLIO

A portfolio is a "container" for documenting one's learning over time (Turner, 2002). Today's world requires that teachers adapt to change as they become conscious of their ability to address the evolving needs of children (Davis, 2000). You will reflect on your student teaching happenings and the resulting changes you have considered and acted on, and add this to your portfolio.

Assessments by others will focus attention on teaching strengths and areas of possible development. Former student teachers evaluating portfolios usefulness make comments like the following:

"... forced me to evaluate my strengths and weaknesses"

"... showed me what to work on"

"... a complete record of my growth."

"... writing daily critiques of my day helped me recognize priorities."

1. Do I work within the policies and procedures established by the placement site?
2. Do I make use of knowledge and understanding of child development and curriculum in early childhood education?
3. What are my relationships with each child?
4. How do I manage small and large groups?
5. Do I use good judgment in situations?
6. Do I plan for appropriate blocks of time indoors and outdoors?
7. Do I make good use of indoor and outdoor space?
8. Do I provide for transitions and routines?
9. Do I add to the attractiveness of the playroom?
10. Do I take care of equipment?
11. Do I consider health and safety factors in planning my activities?
12. Do I offer a wide range of experiences so that children can make choices according to their interests and needs?
13. Do I allow for various levels of ability among children?
14. Do I know how and when to ask questions?
15. Do I talk too much?
16. Do I make adequate provisions for variety in planned activities?
17. Do I see myself as a member of a team?
18. Do I coordinate my efforts with those of my coworkers?
19. Am I able to assume full responsibility in the absence of coworkers?
20. Do I participate in staff meetings?
21. Am I able to transfer concepts from theoretical discussions at staff meetings and workshops to action in my own program?
22. Do I find ways to help children understand the roles of other adults at school?
23. Do I maintain good professional relationships with parents?
24. Do I recognize the importance of seeing the child as a member of the family?
25. Do I share a child's experiences with the parents?
26. Do I know when to refer parents' or a child's problems to an appropriate person?
27. Do I experiment with note-taking systems to assist in planning, to evaluate growth, and to form the basis for written records?
28. Do I use the information in records appropriately?
29. Am I a member of at least one professional organization in the field?
30. Do I attend meetings conducted by professional groups?

Figure 3-20 Student teachers' self-evaluation guide

Davis (2000) suggests student teachers need to peer through the looking glass in order to evaluate what they want to accomplish in their careers as did Alice in Wonderland.

> "Would you tell me, please, which way I ought to walk from here?"
> "That depends a good deal on where you want to get to," said the Cat.
> " I don't much care where. . . ." said Alice.
> "Then it doesn't matter which way you walk," said the Cat.
> ". . . so long as I get somewhere," Alice added as an explanation.
> (Carroll, 1923)

An additional end-of-the-year (end-of-the semester) self-evaluation is found in the Appendix.

Using a 1–5 rating scale—1 meaning possesses much skill in this area to 5 meaning little skill displayed. Rate both yourself and how you feel others rate you.

	Self	Others
1. Clear explanations	_____	_____
2. Leads children to self-conclusions and discoveries	_____	_____
3. Verbal interaction	_____	_____
4. Gives reasons	_____	_____
5. Motivates children's desire to find out	_____	_____
6. Demonstrations	_____	_____
7. Promotes comparisons	_____	_____
8. Enthusiastic encounters	_____	_____
9. Accepts children's limitations	_____	_____
10. Plans effectively	_____	_____
11. Guidance techniques	_____	_____
12. Organizes time	_____	_____
13. Developmentally appropriate activities offered	_____	_____
14. Parent interactions	_____	_____
15. Directing work of others	_____	_____
16. Keeping records	_____	_____
17. Observing children	_____	_____
18. Awareness of child needs	_____	_____
19. Awareness of adult needs	_____	_____
20. Cultural sensitivity	_____	_____
21. Accepts responsibility	_____	_____
22. Knows routines	_____	_____
23. Builds effective relationships with children	_____	_____
24. Attracts children's interests	_____	_____
25. Liked by children	_____	_____
26. Liked by adults	_____	_____

Figure 3-21 Rate yourself

SUMMARY

Observation, evaluation, and discussion are integral parts of student teaching. Different methods are used to observe the student's progress. The realization of professional growth through the use of an evaluative method and subsequent discussion depends on a number of different factors, including the process and method of measurement and the people involved. It is important for the student teacher to maintain a positive attitude and consider self-evaluation a vehicle for improvement. Both formative and summative discussions are part of an analysis of the student teacher and the placement experience. Planning to enhance strengths and overcome weaknesses takes place during discussions and is a growth-promoting part of student teaching.

"The whole teacher" is made of a vast array of possible teaching skills and abilities. Teaching competencies (performance objectives) have been identified by individuals and groups based on value judgments concerning appropriate or desirable teaching behaviors. There are many teaching competency lists in circulation; the CDA list is widely accepted.

Each student teacher gathers feedback on teaching skills from others and from self-analysis. Examples of self-rating scales were presented to aid the student's development of a plan of priorities for future competency growth.

HELPFUL WEB SITES

http://www.cdacouncil.org

Council for Professional Recognition. Information about Child Development Associate (CDA) credentialing.

http://www.ncate.org

National Council for Accreditation of Teacher Education. Search for information concerning national standards and acccreditation particulars.

http://www.ascd.org

Association for Supervision Curriculum Development (ASCD). Easy-to-use, organized listing of Web sites is available.

SUGGESTED ACTIVITIES

A. Form groups of four. On slips of paper, write down your fears about being observed and evaluated. Put the slips in a container. Each student takes a turn drawing a slip of paper and describing the fear and the possible cause.

B. Complete the following statements.
   1. My present strengths (teaching competencies) include . . .
   2. My plan for developing more competencies includes working on . . .

C. Where do you belong on the line between each extreme? Draw a stick person at that spot.

Talkative ______________________ Quiet
Eager to please ______________________ Self-assured
Outgoing ______________________ Shy
Punctual ______________________ Late
Accepting ______________________ Rejecting
Leader ______________________ Follower
Flexible ______________________ Rigid
Sense of humor ______________________ Serious
Organized ______________________ Disorganized
Academic ______________________ Nonstudious
Patient ______________________ Impatient
Warm ______________________ Cool
Enthusiastic ______________________ Apathetic
Active ______________________ Passive
Open ______________________ Secretive
Direct ______________________ Indirect
Good communicator ______________________ Poor communicator
Autonomous ______________________ Conformist
Creative ______________________ Noncreative
Animated ______________________ Reserved
Talented ______________________ Average

Sexist ________________________________ Nonsexist
Specialist _____________________________ Generalist

D. As a class, vote on the validity of the following statements. Use a "thumbs up" signal if the statement is true; remain still if you believe the statement is false or if you can not decide. When voting on the more controversial statements, ask your instructor to turn from the class, elect a student to count the votes, and record the final tally.

1. It is unfair to compare one student teacher to another.
2. It is a good idea to have one student teacher tutor another.
3. Peer evaluations should be part of everyone's student teaching experience.
4. Confidentiality in rating student teachers is imperative.
5. Sharing discussion notes with other student teachers may be helpful to both students.
6. Evaluations by supervisors or cooperating teachers should never be shown to employers of student teachers.
7. A student teacher's placement could inhibit the growth of professional teaching competencies.
8. One can experience considerable growth without evaluative feedback.
9. Criticism is threatening.
10. Being observed and evaluated is really a game. Self-discovery and being motivated to do your best are more important.
11. An individual's manner of dress, hair style, and the like should not be included in an evaluation because this has nothing to do with effective teaching.
12. Observation and evaluation can increase professional excellence.
13. Every student should receive a copy of all written evaluations of her performance.
14. There is no such thing as constructive criticism!
15. Evaluators tend to see their own teaching weaknesses and inadequacies in the student teachers they observe.

E. Read a. and b. following and briefly describe your reactions and make comments. Share your ideas with the class.

a. There is no perfect early childhood teacher, rather only individual teachers with varying degrees of competence exist. Teacher training should magnify strengths and produce teachers who differ greatly.

b. Celebrate your "uniqueness!" You may offer children what others cannot. Your weakness may be another's strength, their weakness your strength. Feel middle of the road in everything? Middle of the road may provide stability, safety, familiarity, and at "homeness."

F. Reactions to criticism in performance evaluation discussions. Rate the following using M = most often, S = sometimes, and R = rarely. Discuss with a small group of peers.

_____ 1. I'm quiet while supervisors talk about my performance.
_____ 2. I refrain from defending myself.
_____ 3. I'm aware of messages I'm sending with facial expression and body language.
_____ 4. I ask for feedback frequently.
_____ 5. I discuss my evaluations with peers.
_____ 6. I feel "unliked" when criticized, as if something about me makes others act unfavorably.
_____ 7. I tend to think things over before reacting.

_____ 8. I tend to gage whether criticism is well-intentioned and has some basis in truth.

_____ 9. Inside, I'm immediately angry when criticized.

_____ 10. Inside, I'm immediately hurt and crestfallen when my weaknesses are pointed out.

_____ 11. I feel criticism is a personal attack.

_____ 12. I ask for suggestions to improve.

_____ 13. If I'm not sure what's meant, I ask for clarification.

_____ 14. Examples of my behavior help me see myself through supervisors' eyes.

_____ 15. I'd rather have honest feedback than none at all.

_____ 16. I can say "thank you" after a less than excellent rating by a supervisor.

_____ 17. I look at evaluation discussions as necessary and helpful but still unpleasant.

_____ 18. I feel that there is no such thing as constructive criticism.

_____ 19. I'm motivated to improve my professional skills.

_____ 20. I'll never like criticism but when it's honest and well intended, it's really an opportunity.

_____ 21. I can tactfully add information that may give supervisors additional insight into my behavior.

_____ 22. I can talk my way out of most situations.

G. Read and discuss the following. Give examples from your own life and mention some of your teaching "joys."

"A man rarely succeeds at anything unless he has fun doing it. I've known men who succeeded because they had a rip-roaring good time conducting their business" (Carnegie, 1936).

H. Read Vivian Paley (1994). Princess Annabella and the black girls. In A. H. Dyson and C. Genishi (Eds.). *The need for story: Cultural diversity in classroom and community* (pp.145–154). Urbana, IL: National Council Teachers of English.

Form groups of four to five classmates. Role-play by assigning the following roles:

1. *Paley's supervisor.* Pretend Paley is a student teacher who has been observed and is now having a follow-up conference.
2. *Paley as a student teacher.*
3. *An African American parent* who has volunteered in the classroom and has questions about the intent of Paley's storytelling.
4. *Paley's cooperating teacher* who wonders why Paley (her student teacher) persists in telling daily stories.

REVIEW

A. Name three methods of observational data collection. Give examples.

B. Select the answer that best completes each statement.

1. The process of observation, evaluation, and discussion:
   a. includes observations from supervisors and employers.
   b. usually ends when the student teaching experience ends.

c. continues after the student teacher graduates and is valued by teachers and employers.
d. ends when improvement occurs.
e. can be best performed by the student teacher alone.

2. One of the primary goals of observation, evaluation, and discussion is to:
   a. stress the student teacher's weaknesses through peer evaluation.
   b. increase control.
   c. judge how quickly a student can respond to suggestions.
   d. criticize student teachers.
   e. None of these.
   f. All of these.
3. Feedback can be defined as data that:
   a. are collected through observations and are to be evaluated and communicated to the one being observed.
   b. are recorded by a student teacher during discussion.
   c. include a free lunch.
   d. are withheld from a student teacher.
   e. None of these.
4. If interviews are used to collect data on student teaching, each interviewee should:
   a. answer only the questions he wishes to answer.
   b. always be asked the same questions in the same manner.
   c. be asked for factual data only.
   d. be asked for opinions only.
   e. be given a specified length of time to answer each question.
5. One benefit of videotaping for the purpose of observation is:
   a. the student teacher and supervisor can evaluate the tape together.
   b. it is less frightening than other methods.
   c. a camera captures a more natural view of a student teacher.
   d. it saves time.
   e. All of these.
6. If a student teaching skill is evaluated using three different observational methods and each confirms the same level of competency, the three tests would probably be:
   a. rated as reliable.
   b. rated as highly valid.
   c. rated as accurate.
   d. standardized.
7. The collection technique that records a series of significant incidents is called a(n):
   a. time sampling.
   b. rating sheet.
   c. specimen description.
   d. event sampling.
   e. questionnaire.
8. An unobtrusive method of observation might involve:
   a. hidden microphones.
   b. an observer with a tape recorder.
   c. an observer viewing from a loft.

d. an observer in an observation room.
e. All of these.

9. If one was trying to assess the rapport that a student teacher developed with a group of children, one could:
   a. observe how many children initiated conversation with the student teacher during a given time period.
   b. record and analyze what the children say.
   c. count how many times a child touched the student teacher during a given time period.
   d. observe how many times a child shares an interest or concern with a student teacher.
   e. All of these.
10. A final discussion that informs the student teacher about his teaching skills is a(n):
   a. formative discussion.
   b. initial discussion.
   c. summative discussion.
   d. incidental discussion.
   e. alternate discussion.

C. Complete the following statement.
The five individuals who could probably provide the most reliable and valid data concerning my teaching competency are . . .

D. Five individuals observed the same traffic accident. Match the person in Column I to the feature in Column II that he or she would be most likely to observe.

I	II
1. Car salesperson	a. driver's license and/or license plate numbers
2. Police officer	b. children involved in the accident
3. Doctor	c. damage to the automobiles
4. Teacher	d. make and model of the automobiles involved
5. Insurance adjuster	e. injuries of those involved

E. What adjusted five skills would most cooperating teachers observe before a summative discussion?

F. Write three pieces of advice to student teachers to help them accept constructive criticism.

G. Choose the answer that best completes each statement.
1. A student teacher:
   a. needs to develop all the competencies that experts recognize.
   b. should strive to display all competencies.
   c. should develop an individualized plan for competency development.
   d. should rely completely on feedback gained through the comments of others when developing a professional growth plan.
   e. can ignore competencies others consider important.
2. Lists of teacher competencies are based on:
   a. research studies that correlate teacher behaviors and child accomplishment.
   b. value judgments of individuals and/or groups.
   c. recognized teacher abilities and skills.
   d. the qualities parents feel are desirable in teachers.
   e. what teacher training programs produce in student teachers.

3. The most widely accepted list of teacher competencies for teachers of children under age five is:
   a. Head Start teacher competencies.
   b. graduating level competencies.
   c. NAEYC competencies.
   d. early childhood education competencies.
   e. CDA competencies.
4. A student teacher's view of competency best forms when:
   a. others comment on student teaching episodes.
   b. children are watched for growth through the student teacher's planned activities or behavior.
   c. self-evaluation and feedback are combined.
   d. parents assess the student teacher's effectiveness.
   e. feedback includes comments from the entire staff.
5. The main purpose of developing plans to acquire other teaching skills is to:
   a. facilitate growth.
   b. have student teachers learn all listed competencies.
   c. make student teachers realize their limitations.
   d. make student teachers realize their strengths.
   e. make sure the profession maintains quality performance.

CASE SCENARIO

Setting: Morgan is a student teacher in a four-year-olds' classroom. Her college supervisor has just arrived to observe.

Morgan's cooperating teacher suggested she take a quick look at her activity plan which had involved collecting leaves in the play yard and returning and sorting them.

Unfortunately, rain has made the plan unusable. Remembering that physical activity seemed necessary at this time of day for the group she had planned to handle, Morgan started a substitute activity. She gathered the group and initiated a discussion of children's names. Morgan drew the letter "B" on a chart-sized piece of newsprint and a child offered that his name was a "B" name. "'B' is the first letter of your name, Brent. I see the 'B' on your name tag." Morgan then asked the group to watch where she was putting the "B" chart. She quickly crossed the room and taped the chart on a wall and returned. She then discussed how she could go and touch the chart using "baby steps" then return and sit down. She demonstrated. "Could anyone think of

continues . . .

. . . continued

another way?" Morgan queried. A child suggested "elephant steps" which he then demonstrated. The whole group moved in elephant steps to the chart and back. The game proceeded with other first letters of children's names and children's suggestions about different ways to cross the room.

The activity held children's interest and the children created clever ways to cross the room.

Questions for Discussion:

1. What do you think of Morgan's alternate activity?
2. Do you feel the alternate activity was planned as a back-up or created on the spot? Why?
3. Acting as the college supervisor, what teaching skills would you commend? Why?

REFERENCES

Association for Childhood Education International. (1997, Spring). Position paper on the preparation of elementary teachers. *Childhood Education, 73*(3).

Bredekamp, S., & Copple, C. (Eds.). (1997). *Developmentally appropriate practice in early childhood programs* (rev. ed.). Washington, DC: National Association for the Education of Young Children.

Carnegie, D. (1936). *How to win friends and influence people.* New York: Simon and Schuster.

Carroll, L. (1923). *Alice's adventures in wonderland and through the looking glass.* New York: Winston.

Cartwright, S. (1999, July), What makes good early childhood teachers? *Young Children, 54*(4), 4–7.

Carter, M., & Jones, E. (1990, October). The teacher as observer: The director as role model. *Child Care Information Exchange, 100.*

Caruso, J. J., & Fawcett, M. T. (1999). *Supervision in early childhood education.* New York: Teachers College Press.

Davis, M. A. (2000, Summer). Through the looking glass—Pre-service professional portfolios. *The Teacher Educator, 37*(1), 27–36.

Ennis, R. H. (1985). A logical basis for measuring critical thinking skills. *Educational Leadership, 43*(2).

Garmston, R., Linder, C., & Whitaker, J. (1993, October). Reflections on cognitive coaching. *Educational Leadership, 51*(2).

Glickman, C. C., Gordon, S. P., & Ross-Gordon, J. M. (1998). *Supervision of instruction: A developmental approach.* Boston: Allyn and Bacon.

Grant, G., & Murray, C. (1999). *Teaching in America: The slow revolution.* Cambridge, MA: Harvard University Press

Hamachek, D. (1992). *Encounters with the self* (4th ed.). New York: Harcourt Brace.

Humphrey, S. (1989, November). The case of myself. *Young Children, 45.*

Katz, L. C. (1993). *Dispositions, definitions, and implications for early childhood practice.* Champaign, IL: ERIC Clearinghouse on Elementary and Early Childhood Education.

Katz, L. G. (1993, September). Dispositions as educational goals. *ERIC Digest*, EPO-PS-93-10.

Kress, A. (1992). Infusing thinking skills in early childhood education: Coursework to facilitate decision making by community college students. *Practicum Report*, Nova University, ED 350078.

Lacey, C. H., Guffey, J. S., & Rampp, L.C. (2000, Spring). Clinical supervision using interactive compressed television. *The Teacher Educator, 35*(4), 97–107.

Loranger, A. (1997, Fall). Exploring reflective behaviors with pre-service teachers. *Teaching and Learning, 12*(1).

Manley-Casimir, N., & Wasserman, S. (1989). The teacher as decision maker: Connecting self with the practice of teaching. *Childhood Education*, Annual Theme Issue, *65*(5).

McBride, M., & Skau, K. (1995). Trust, empowerment, and reflection: Essentials of supervision. *Journal of Curriculum and Supervision, 10*(3).

National Association for the Education of Young Children, (2001). *NAEYC Standards for Early Childhood Professional Preparation: Baccalaureate or Initial Licensure Level.* Washington, DC: Author.

Paley, V. G. (1994). Princess Annabella and the black girls. In A. H. Dyson and C. Genishi (Eds.). *The need for story: Cultural diversity in classroom and community* (pp. 145–154). Urbana, IL: National Council of Teachers of English.

Schoonmaker, F. (1998, Spring). Promise and possibility: Learn to teach. *Teacher's College Record, 99*(3).

Skillpath Seminars. (1997). *Conflict management skills for women.* Mission, KS: Skillpath.

Stoney, L. (1997). *Common threads: Weaving a training and career development system for 21st century Pennsylvania.* Boston: The Center for Career Development in Early Care and Education, Wheelock College.

Stoney, L. (2001, Summer). Financing early care and education: Key issues. *State Education Leader, 19*(2) 3–4.

Sullo, R. A. (1999). *The inspiring teacher: New beginnings for the 21st century.* Annapolis Junction, MD: National Education Association of the United States.

Sullivan, C. G. (1980). *Clinical supervision: A state of the art review.* Washington, DC: Association for Supervision and Curriculum Development.

Titone, C., Sherman, S., & Palmer, R. (1998, Winter). Cultivating student teachers' disposition and ability to construct knowledge. *Action in Teacher Education, XIX*(4).

Turner, P. (Ed.) (2002). *La ristra: New Mexico's comprehensive professional development system in early care, education and family support.* Santa Fe, NM: Office of Child Development, Youth and Families Department.

U.S. Department of Health and Human Services. (1996). Head Start program performance standards. Washington, DC: Author.

Wedman, J. M., Espinosa, L. M., & Laffey, J. M. (1998, Winter). A process for understanding how a field-based course influences teachers' beliefs and practices. *The Teacher Educator, 34*(3), 189–214.

Whitmire, R. (2000, May). Survey: New teachers love jobs, feel unprepared. *The Idaho Statesman*, 10A.

Wortham, S. C. (1995). *Measurement and evaluation in early childhood education* (2nd ed.). Englewood Cliffs, NJ: Prentice-Hall.

CHAPTER 4

Review of Child Development and Learning Theory

Objectives

After studying this chapter, the student should be able to:

1 Identify four major child development theories that influence early childhood education.

2 Describe how children learn.

3 List five ways in which the student teacher can help a child learn.

I'm attracted to some children more than to others. I purposely try to spend equal time with and give equal attention. The active child's the hardest.

—Mia Mendonca

One of my instructors said "the hardest thing about being a teacher is figuring out how individual children learn." During student teaching I found many learn quickly from other children, some learn by doing something over and over again, and some learn by observing and asking questions. I found if I wanted to teach something, I definitely had to capture their attention first. I often did this by being enthusiastic.

—Doreen Liu

Play really is the work of the young child. They become so focused, so serious, so excited at times. It's great fun to accompany them, to watch their enthusiasm and sense of wonder.

—Shelby Ochoa

THEORIES OF CHILD DEVELOPMENT

Historical Background

Historically, three theories of child development have been prevalent in developing educational programs for young children: the *nativist*, the *nurturist*, and the *interactionist*.

The **nativist** tradition, based on the philosophy of Rousseau (1742/1947), takes the view that children are like flowers, unfolding in a natural way. Out of the nativist tradition has developed the concept of children's natural development or maturation as the determinant of their ability to learn with little direction from adults (parents or teachers). Gesell, Ilg, and Ames (1974), as proponents of the maturational theory, best exemplify the nativistic point of view. The traditional nursery school of the 1920s, 1930s, and 1940s, and still seen today in some programs, is based on this nativistic philosophy.

Another variant of the nativist tradition can be seen in the psychoanalytic theories of Freud and Erikson (1963). Erikson's **psychosocial theory** stressed eight stages of human development and posited a specific task to be resolved at each stage. For example, the task of infancy is the resolution of basic trust versus mistrust; for toddlers, the task of autonomy versus shame and doubt. During the preschool years, the task is initiative versus guilt; and for elementary school-age children, industry versus inferiority. The concepts that the major tasks of toddlers and preschoolers are autonomy and initiative have evolved into the philosophy of child-directed learning seen in such programs as some of the traditional preschools and Montessori programs.

The **nurturist** tradition, based on the philosophy of Locke, looks at development from the point of view that the minds of children are a *tabula rasa* or blank slate. From the nurturist tradition have evolved programs based on the theory of **behaviorism**. The concept that children are much like Locke's "blank slate" on which adults "write" or "impress" learnings, started models such as DARCEE and DISTAR, which best exemplify this model in practice. Both of these programs have received considerable reaction and disagreement. Some traditional teacher-directed elementary school programs also exemplify the nurturist or behaviorism philosophy.

Interactionists view development and learning as taking place in the interactions between children and their respective environments. Programs exemplifying this point of view are those of the **constructivist theory**. Jean Piaget (1952), although influenced by Rousseau's concept of children as active explorers of their respective environments, extended the concept of natural unfolding by maintaining that children create their own knowledge as they interact with their social and physical environments. "Piaget calls this interaction **assimilation** and **accommodation**, and **equilibration**" (Seefeldt & Barbour, 1998). Programs based on the Piagetian point of view are best exemplified by Lavatelli (1973), High/Scope (Hohmann, Banet, & Weikart, 1979), and Kamii and DeVries (1978). In each of these programs, Piaget's theory is translated in somewhat different ways: Lavatelli tends to emphasize the structural aspects; High/Scope, the relationship between the theory and children's spontaneous activities; and Kamii and DeVries, the constructivist aspects.

The National Research Council (2000) points out that although theories differ in important ways, they share an emphasis on considering children as active learners who are able to set goals and to plan and revise. They recognize children's **cognitive** development evolves gradually as they acquire strategies for remembering, understanding, and problem-solving.

nativist—one who adheres to the theory that children are born with biological dispositions for learning that unfold or mature in a natural way.

psychosocial theory—the branch of psychology founded by Erik Erikson, in which development is described in terms of eight stages that span childhood and adulthood.

nurturist—one who adheres to the theory that the minds of children are blank or unformed, and need educational input or direct instruction in order to develop and "output" knowledge and appropriate behavior.

behaviorism—the theoretical viewpoint, espoused by theorists such as B. F. Skinner, that behavior is shaped by environmental forces, specifically in response to reward and punishment.

interactionists—those who adhere to the theory that language develops through a combination of inborn factors and environmental influences.

constructivist theory—a theory, such as that of Jean Piaget, based on the belief that children construct knowledge for themselves rather than having it conveyed to them by some external source.

assimilation—according to Jean Piaget, one form of adaptation, which takes place when the person tries to make new information or a new experience fit into an existing concept.

accommodation—according to Jean Piaget, one form of adaptation, which takes place when an existing concept is modified or a new concept is formed to incorporate new information or a new experience.

equilibration—according to Jean Piaget, the state of balance each person seeks between existing mental structures and new experiences.

cognitive—pertaining to the mental processes of perception, memory, judgment, and reasoning.

What Student Teachers Should Know

It has been said that a teacher training program is successful if its graduates know just one thing well: how children learn. Feiman-Nemser, Carver, Schwille, & Yusko (1999) believe beginning teachers have two jobs: they have to teach and they have to learn to teach. Current learning theory is based on views of human development that differ among experts. The concept that each child is a unique individual who learns in his or her own way further complicates the issue. How does a beginning teacher begin to understand how children learn?

There is a basic knowledge about children's learning that forms the base on which theories have been built. Hendrick (1985, 1993) has identified the following:

- Children pass through a series of stages as they grow.
- Children learn things a step at a time.
- Children learn best through actual experiences.
- Children utilize play to translate experience into understanding.
- Parents are the most important influence in the development of the child.
- The teacher must present learning within a climate of caring.

The traditional approach by maturationists as nativists emphasizes discovery by the child. This approach is the basis of learning at the traditional nursery school and play school. The approach of **cognitive developmental theory**, notably by Piaget and Montessori, has led to programs such as the Weikart cognitively oriented curriculum. The studies of Erikson, a psychosexual interactionist, are less concerned with cognitive development and more concerned with social-emotional development. Emphasis is placed on social interaction and discovery (Stevens & King, 1976). In view of these different approaches to child development, it is obvious that no one theorist has the final word on how children learn.

cognitive developmental theory—the theory formulated by Jean Piaget that focuses on how children's intelligence and thinking abilities emerge through distinct stages.

HOW DO CHILDREN LEARN?

Learning occurs as a child interacts with the environment using the five senses: seeing, hearing, touching, tasting, and smelling. Some theorists say there is a sixth sense, the kinesthetic, or the sense of where the body is in relation to space. The human child is a goal-directed individual who actively seeks information (National Research Council, 2000).

Look at a baby; offer a new toy. What does the baby do? The baby looks it over carefully, shakes it to see if it makes any noise, puts it in the mouth, and turns it over and over in the hands. It seems that the baby uses all of the senses to discover all there is to know about the toy. Look at a young child. Look at how the child is concentrating (see Figure 4–1); the child stares intently and grasps the boat carefully. We may assume the child is listening closely, with the mouth open and tongue pressed against the teeth to help concentration. All of these actions show us that the child is learning. A learning sequence may proceed as follows:

- The child attends and records.
- The child experiences and explores.
- The child imitates actions, sounds, words, and so on. The child becomes aware of similarities and differences and/or matching events.
- The child responds appropriately to actions and words; discusses and questions.

- The child talks about what has been learned or discovered.
- The child remembers and uses knowledge.

When something is learned, the child may respond with appropriate nonverbal behavior. The child may point to, show, or do what has been discovered (see Figure 4–2). In addition, the child may name or talk about what has been learned and may apply the knowledge.

Discussions of child learning usually include the following:

reinforcement—in behavioral theory, any response that follows a behavior that encourages repetition of that behavior

- If a child's action receives positive reinforcement immediately, there is a strong possibility that the act will recur.
- If a child's action receives negative feedback or is ignored, repetition of the act will be discouraged.
- Habit behavior is difficult to change.
- Periodic positive reinforcement is necessary to maintain children's favorable actions.
- The motivation level may increase persistence in learning tasks.
- For each child, all classroom experiences have a "feeling tone," ranging from pleasant to neutral to unpleasant.
- Motivation may contain a degree of tension, which may aid or inhibit success.
- There are two types of motivation: intrinsic and extrinsic motivation. Intrinsic motivation comes from within. Children act in a certain way

Figure 4–1 Nonverbal behavior tells us this child is concentrating and learning.

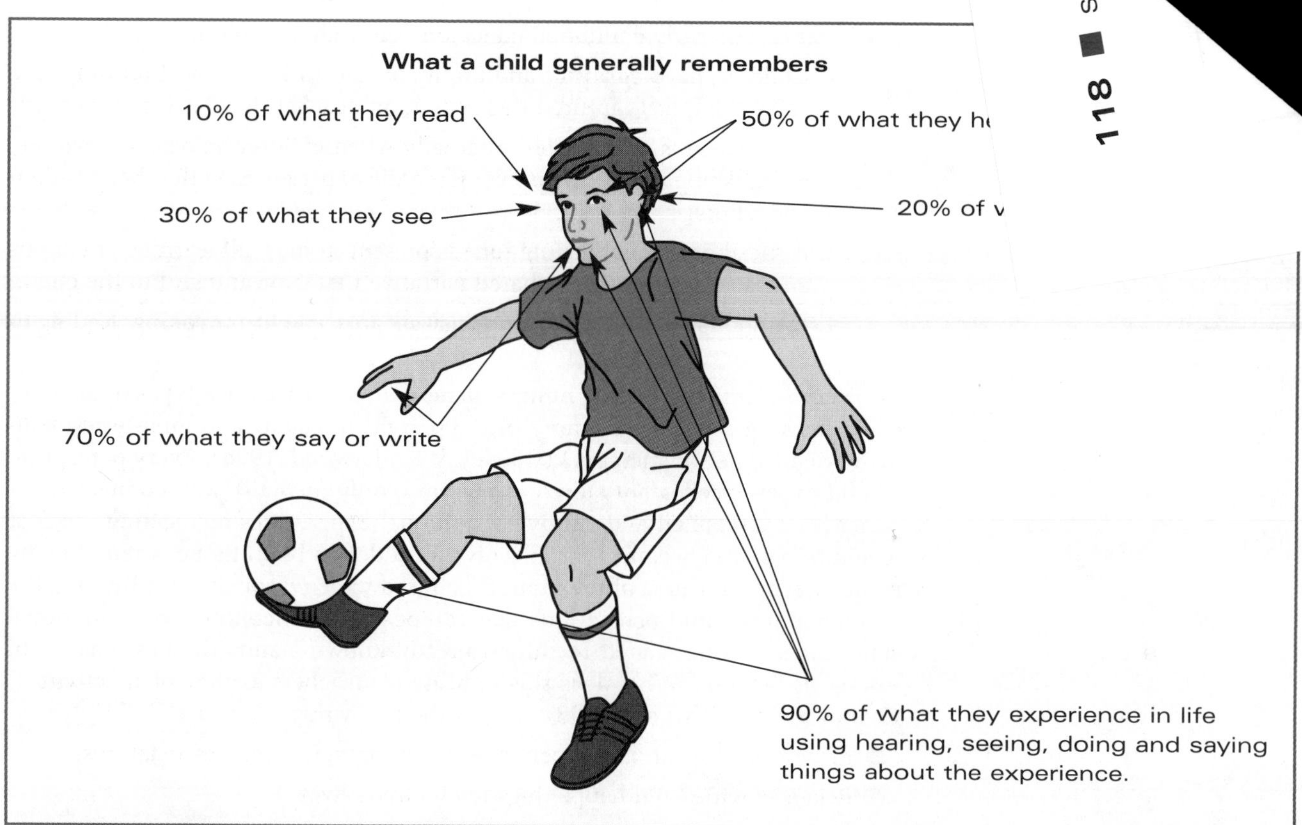

Figure 4–2 Adapted from Dale, E. A. (1969). *Audiovisual Methods in Teaching* (3rd ed.). New York: Holt, Rinehart, and Winston.

because of their interest in any given activity. Extrinsic motivation is imposed from without. Children act because of a perceived reward or punishment. For example, a child may play with puzzles simply because he enjoys the activity (intrinsic motivation), but may resist coming to circle time when asked because he then cannot continue with what he's been doing (a punishment in his eyes and, therefore, coming to circle time is due to extrinsic motivation).

The emotions that exist within individuals during experiences may enhance or retard how much learning takes place. Infants and children have anxiety levels ranging from overload (extreme agitation or excitement) to underload (boredom) in life situations. If overwhelmed, the infant will tune out and turn away. Learning is best accomplished when anxiety is low and the excitement about finding out and knowing is high, but not too high.

A teacher's technique or way of interacting, which includes pressuring, embarrassment, or increasing a child's self-doubt or feeling of inadequacy, can limit child learning. Student teachers unfortunately may only need to look back into their own schooling experiences to find examples they do not want to repeat.

On the other hand, we all remember teachers who accepted our ideas as important contributions, smiled when they were with us, appreciated our perhaps feeble attempts, noticed our efforts, and made us feel unique and special.

What else do early childhood educators know about child learning?

1. Children have curiosity and are motivated to know and find out more about what has captured their attention or what they have experienced.
2. Knowledge is constructed internally when children move, act, explore, and talk about the environment and life experiences with other children and adults.
3. A social-emotional feeling tone is present in most all learning situations and is accompanied by shared narrative that is meaningful to the child.
4. Questions are welcomed, and answers are thought-provoking, leading to discovery.

Neuroscientists studying human memory theorize that two types of memory exist: working memory (memory of the present moment) and long-term memory (extended period memory) (Cowley & Underwood, 1998). Every perception a child experiences is not stored as memory; only mentally well-connected experiences are retained and survive. Additional experiences connecting the first to additional ones become more deeply embedded in brain tissue, strengthening memory. A specific area of the brain is believed to be responsible for filtering the vast amount of child perceptions that can occur. An encounter with emotional significance or one related to things already known stands the best chance of storage as memory. What does this indicate for teachers as they plan activities? Cowley and Underwood (1998) suggest the following:

- Review and repeat past experiences to strengthen mental associations.
- Relate activities and happenings to children's lives.
- Provide opportunity for the practice of skills.
- Aid children's ability to put their discoveries into words.
- Verbally repeat what's discovered.
- Relate present ideas to what children already know.
- Create an emotionally significant relationship with each learner.

Those student teachers using theme (unit) planning (discussed in chapter 5) will appreciate the idea that **thematic teaching and instruction** gives children multiple and connected opportunities to experience new material through a variety of associated and related activities.

thematic teaching and instruction—a theme approach to child program planning including theme identification, environmental needs, activities, presentation, and evaluation, usually designed for a selected period of study. It can encompass a wide range of curriculum areas including art, music, mathematics, language, science, motor, social and other development opportunities.

A critical feature of effective teaching involves eliciting from young children their existing understanding of a subject at hand. This knowledge provides possible curriculum planning opportunities (National Research Council, 2000). When a child says "Milk comes from the store," teachers know a trip to a dairy farm or another type of planned activity concerning cows would be expanding. Teachers pay close attention to the knowledge, skills, and attitudes possessed, plus how children are affected by their cultural backgrounds.

Problem-Solving

In a rapidly changing world, the ability to solve problems becomes a survival skill. Problem-solving involves and includes convergent and divergent thinking skills, classification, patterning, and evaluation skills (see Figure 4–3). To become a more effective problem-solver, the child must:

1. have a general knowledge of the properties of objects
2. have the ability to notice incongruities or inconsistencies, and define the problem (the "what is wrong here")

3. have the ability to think of new and unconventional functions for familiar objects
4. have the ability to generate many possible solutions
5. have the ability to evaluate various solutions
6. have the ability to implement a solution she thinks will best fulfill the requirements of solving the problem.

Early childhood student teachers need to analyze whether problem-solving is a priority in their planning and daily interactions with young children.

Elder and Paul (1998) suggest critical thinking is enhanced when one develops a questioning inner voice that routinely asks such questions as:

- "In this situation, what do I really know? What do I think I know but am not completely sure of? What do I need to learn? What do I still need to figure out?" (intellectual humility)
- "Am I uncritically accepting what I have learned, or do I have the courage to question what I have learned? Am I afraid to question certain beliefs or practices because I may be rejected for questioning them?" (intellectual courage)
- "Am I honestly trying to imagine this situation from this other person's point of view? Can I accurately state another person's point of view that is in conflict with my own?" (intellectual empathy)
- "Am I thinking through this issue in a way that does justice to its complexity, or do I come to a conclusion too quickly? Do I give up when figuring things out becomes frustrating?" (intellectual perseverance)

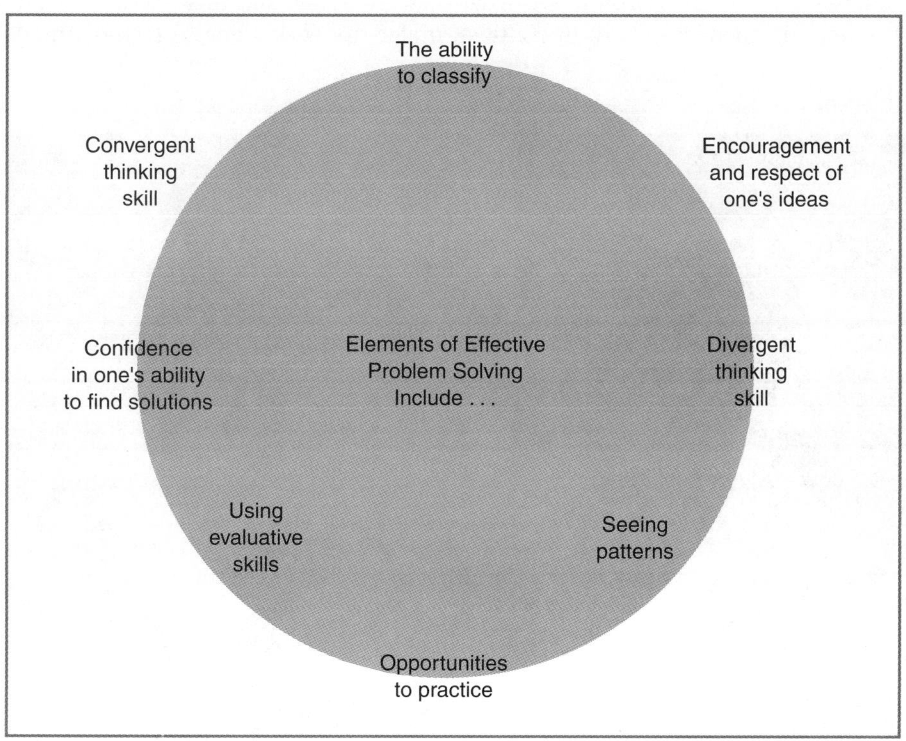

Figure 4-3 Solving problems

Learning Modalities

materials—the smaller, often expendable items used in early childhood programs that are replaced and replenished requently.

Recent studies have tried to identify children who learn more efficiently through one sense or modality than through others. A child who enjoys looking at books and notices your new clothes may be a visual learner as opposed to the child who listens intently during storytime and is the first to hear a bird chirping outside the window. The latter child may be an auditory learner (see Figure 4–4). The child who enjoys playing with **materials** of different textures—for example, finger paint, clay, feelie-box games—may be a kinesthetic learner, one who learns best through touch and body motion (see Figure 4–5). Many children are visual learners, but most, especially preschoolers, use a combination of all the senses to gather impressions. A teacher can expect greater retention of knowledge if all senses are involved. See the Appendix for a learning modalities exercise attempting to assess elementary school students.

Learning Styles

field sensitive—a child who needs encouragement from the teacher and peers for motivation, who does not trust himself, and who looks for reassurance from others.

field independent—a child who works independent of distractions in the surrounding environment; a child who is self-motivated and self-monitoring.

In addition to learning from the use of their senses, or learning modalities, children also learn from the adults in their lives. Traditionally, some children learn as apprentices to their parents. The Native American child's parents may model a particular type of learning mode, as do parents of many other cultures.

Some children, however, demand more attention as they learn than others. The terms **"field sensitive"** and **"field independent"** can be used to describe certain types of children. Field-sensitive children like to work with others and ask for guidance from the teacher. They have difficulty completing an open-ended assignment without a model to follow. The field-sensitive child waits until the other children begin an art lesson to see what they are doing, and then starts to paint. The field-independent child, in contrast, prefers to work alone, is task-oriented,

Figure 4–4 Children who enjoy listening activities may be auditory learners.

Figure 4–5 Children who enjoy playing with materials of different textures may be kinesthetic learners.

rarely seeks guidance from the teacher, and prefers open-ended projects. The field-independent child will try new activities without being urged to do so. In terms of learning, this child enjoys the discovery approach best. Study the rating forms (see Figures 4–6 and 4–7) for each type of child. Which children at your center or school are field sensitive or field independent?

FIELD-SENSITIVE OBSERVABLE BEHAVIORS

Instructions: Evaluate the child for each behavior listed below by placing a check in the appropriate column.

__________ Child's Name   _____ Grade   __________ School   _____ Date

__________ Observer's Name

__________ Situation (e.g., art, block play, etc.)

Field-sensitive observable behaviors	Frequency: Not True	Seldom True	Sometimes True	Often True	Almost Always True
RELATIONSHIP TO PEERS 1. Likes to work with others to achieve a common goal 2. Likes to assist others 3. Is sensitive to feelings and opinions of others					
PERSONAL RELATIONSHIP TO TEACHER 1. Openly expresses positive feelings for teacher 2. Asks questions about teacher's tastes and personal experiences; seeks to become like teacher					
INSTRUCTIONAL RELATIONSHIP TO TEACHER 1. Seeks guidance and demonstration from teacher 2. Seeks rewards which strengthen relationship with teacher 3. Is highly motivated when working individually with teacher					
CHARACTERISTICS OF CURRICULUM THAT FACILITATE LEARNING 1. Performance objectives and global aspects of curriculum are carefully explained 2. Concepts are presented in story format 3. Concepts are related to personal interests and experiences of the child					

Developed by H. Krueger and M. Tenenberg for Instructional Strategies Class, California State University, Hayward, 1985.

Figure 4–6 Field-sensitive child rating form

FIELD-INDEPENDENT OBSERVABLE BEHAVIORS

Instructions: Evaluate the child for each behavior listed below by placing a check in the appropriate column.

Child's Name ______ Grade ______ School ______ Date ______

Observer's Name ______

Situation (e.g., art, block play, etc.) ______

Field-independent observable behaviors	Frequency: Not True	Seldom True	Sometimes True	Often True	Almost Always True
RELATIONSHIP TO PEERS 1. Prefers to work independently 2. Likes to compete and gain individual recognition 3. Task oriented; is inattentive to social environment when working					
PERSONAL RELATIONSHIP TO TEACHER 1. Rarely seeks physical contact with teacher 2. Formal; interactions with teacher are restricted to tasks at hand					
INSTRUCTIONAL RELATIONSHIP TO TEACHER 1. Likes to try new tasks without teacher's help 2. Impatient to begin tasks; likes to finish first 3. Seeks nonsocial rewards					
CHARACTERISTICS OF CURRICULUM THAT FACILITATE LEARNING 1. Details of concepts are emphasized; parts have meaning of their own 2. Deals with math and science concepts 3. Based on discovery approach					

Developed by H. Krueger and M. Tenenberg for Instructional Strategies Class, California State University, Hayward, 1985.

Figure 4–7 Field-independent child rating form

Learning Styles and Learning

Since the publication of H. Gardner's book, *Frames of Mind*, in 1983, there has been a new look at the influence of learning style on how children learn. Gardner posited seven types of intelligences: linguistic, logicomathematical, spatial, bodily-kinesthetic, musical, interpersonal, and intrapersonal. Gardner (1988), rightfully perhaps, accuses schools of teaching only to those children with linguistic and logicomathematical intelligence, and largely ignoring the other five types.

It is interesting to note that Gardner now believes that there is an eighth type of intelligence: naturalist intelligence or the capacity to recognize patterns in nature and classify objects. In an interview with Checkly (1997), he states that the naturalist ability is one "we need to survive as human beings" and that all of the great biologists—past and present—could be said to possess it. Gardner then suggests that further research may show that there are also other intelligences (for example, existential intelligence) but that we do not as yet have any indication that existential intelligence exists in the nervous system, "one of the criteria for an intelligence" (Checkly, 1997; Gardner, 1999; Meyer, 1997).

Using Gardner's theory, early childhood educators are able to look at children in a new and yet already recognized way; in a *global* fashion. Intelligence, or human cognitive competence, Gardner believes, can be described in terms of sets of abilities, talents, or mental skills called intelligences with all normal individuals possessing each of these skills to some extent, degree, and/or combination (Gardner, 1993).

As we age, most of us become aware that there are some learning areas where learning is easy and others where one may struggle to comprehend what others grasp rapidly. Areas of human growth encountered in life can be described as being multiple, diverse, unknown, perhaps limitless, and as yet untested because one has not been introduced to or encountered them. People often discuss having received "gifts" that enable them to do, or learn easily, some "intelligence-connected" life pursuit. People also speak of the "gift" of opportunity in their lives that resulted in a positive outcome allowing them to grow or excel.

Educators trying to put into daily practice the theory of multiple intelligences would look closely at each child, seeing that child as unique, complex, perhaps gifted, or with strengths not easily discovered. Educators would then encourage, appreciate, accommodate, promote, enjoy, develop, and offer help and opportunity. They would understand a child observed with skill in one area may not have skill in another. They would not let a child's culture, physical appearance, economic circumstance, color, or any other external factor cloud their observations.

Early childhood program planning and environmental design and furnishings would be given greater consideration. Under Gardner's tutelage, educators become particularly aware that a multitude of approaches and avenues to the same learning may be possible, and some may suit some children more than others. They would plan and offer activities that involve not only linguistic or logicomathematic features, but spatial, kinesthetic, musical, individual, and group components as well.

Educators should worry as Gardner worried:

> I am not worried about those occasional youngsters who are good in everything. They're going to do just fine. I'm concerned about those who don't shine in standardized tests, and who, therefore, tend to be written off as not having any gifts of any kind (Gardner, 1993).

Gardner envisions a new set of roles for educators in his design of an ideal school:

- *Assessment specialist* whose job entails trying to understand the abilities and interests of children.
- *Student-curriculum broker* whose job would be matching children's profiles, goals, and interests to particular curricula and particular styles of learning.
- *School-community broker* who would match children to learning opportunities in the wider community. This might include apprenticeships, mentorships, and vocational and avocational opportunities.

Gardner notes some talented young children may experience "crystallizing experiences" (Walters & Gardner, 1986) and overtly react to some attractive quality or feature of a domain indicating, perhaps, an innate talent. Early childhood teachers often see a child who produces a great volume of rainbows or other paintings using vivid colors at the paint easel typically focusing totally and excluding all other choices of activity. Early childhood educators, following Gardner, hopefully will be instrumental in providing opportunities in all identified, and perhaps yet to be identified, domains of intelligence.

Some of us were fortunate enough to have had parents, teachers, or others who recognized our interest and/or ability, and "fanned the flame."

The Key School is a public elementary school in the inner city of Indianapolis. Initially stimulated by their reading of *Frames of Mind*, eight teachers from Indianapolis approached Gardner for training on how to implement his theory in their school. After two years of work, the Indianapolis school district allowed the teachers to open Key as a public "options" school. Patricia Bolanos, one of the original teachers, is now principal. The success of the school can be seen in action on "The Creative Spirit," Part I, which was shown on the Public Broadcasting System in 1993, and in the enthusiasm of the teachers, students, and parents who vie for the opportunity to place their children at Key.

Two schools cited in Gardner's *Multiple Intellingences: The Theory in Practice* (1993) have encouraged many other schools to implement techniques that teach to all of the seven (now eight) multiple intelligences.

Perhaps one of the more thorough looks at learning style, especially in relation to providing teachers with ideas for how to teach to children with different styles or ways of processing information in the classroom, has been the work of McCarthy (1987). In establishing her 4MAT system, she provides the reader with a succinct, easy to read and understand summary of many of the ways of looking at learning style, including research on the Myers-Briggs Inventory, the Gregorc Student Learning Styles, Kolb's Experiential Learning, and others. Many of these are based on the work of Carl Jung (1976), who suggested that there were four ways in which people perceive and process information: feeling, thinking, sensing, and intuiting.

In an extensive article, published in 1997, McCarthy illustrates how the 4MAT theory works in practice. She writes about four children, each of whom exemplifies one of the four types of learners. Type 1 is "the highly imaginative learner who favors *feeling and reflecting;*" Type 2 is "the analytic student who favors *reflecting and thinking;*" Type 3 is "the common sense learner who favors *thinking and doing;*" and Type 4, "The dynamic learner who favors *creating and acting.*"

In a related article, Sternberg (1997) states that there are four abilities children use in learning: the ability to memorize, the ability to analyze, the ability to be creative, and an ability to be practical. In most preschools, we do well on all four, but once children begin elementary school, we tend only to teach to those with the first two abilities. Sternberg cites a program that took place in the New Haven, Connecticut, public schools to demonstrate how providing experiences that used all four abilities improved the students' grades, especially those students from ethnic and racial minorities.

One of the reasons that some methods of teaching to learning styles have not been addressed in schools is because they are difficult to evaluate, and too much emphasis has been placed on discrete, item-to-item, day-to-day evaluation. Another reason is related to our own biases as teachers; we teach in the way we learn best. Many teachers are strong visual, experiential learners.

Frederick J. Moffett's poem "Thus A Child Learns" gives additional advice for dealing with the process of learning:

> Thus a child learns; by wiggling skills through his fingers and toes
> into himself; by soaking up habits and attitudes of those around
> him, by pushing and pulling his own world.

> Thus a child learns; more through trial than error, more through pleasure than pain, more through experience than suggestion, more through suggestion than direction.
>
> Thus a child learns; through affection, through love, through patience, through understanding, through belonging, through doing, through being.
>
> Day by day the child comes to know a little bit of what you know; to think a little bit of what you think; to understand your understanding.
>
> As you perceive dully or clearly; as you think fuzzily or sharply; as you believe foolishly or wisely; as you dream drably or goldenly; as you bear false witness or tell the truth—thus a child learns.

Preschool, kindergarten, and primary grade teachers, using the statements in Figure 4–8, can observe their respective students and learn more about their children's preferred learning styles. (For other learning style questionnaires, see the Appendix.)

	Yes	No
In the classroom the child:		
1. Usually chooses to play/work in a quiet area.		
2. Usually chooses to play/work in the noisier areas.		
3. Prefers to work/play with music in the background.		
4. Becomes distracted if music is played in the background.		
5. Is able to concentrate, even if others are talking or are noisy.		
6. Prefers to work/play near window areas or in brightly lighted ones.		
7. Usually chooses to play/work at a table or desk.		
8. Usually chooses to play/work on the floor, or a chair.		
9. Concentrates for longer periods of time in the morning.		
10. Often appears more tired in the morning than in the afternoon.		
In relating to adults and other children, the child:		
1. Prefers to work/play alone.		
2. Prefers to play/work with only one friend.		
3. Works/plays better if the teacher/peer helps.		
4. Likes clear directions regarding how to complete any specific task.		
5. Prefers to play/work with several friends.		
6. Looks to teacher/peers to reinforce directions as a task is being completed.		
7. Frequently starts an activity but seldom finishes.		
8. Has difficulty following spoken directions unless a demonstration, with an example, is given.		
9. Notices whenever teacher or playmates have a new hair style, glasses, or are wearing new clothing.		
10. Follows spoken directions easily.		

Figure 4–8 Observation checklist to assess child's preferred learning style

Multiple Intelligence in the Classroom

Preschools involve children's abilities to use multiple intelligences. Playing with blocks, both large and small, involves spatial, bodily-kinesthetic, linguistic, and sometimes logicomathematical intelligences. Learning associated with height, length, weight, number, inclines, size relationships, and other concepts, which are difficult to grasp without first hand experience, can be understood in the course of play. Big, bigger, biggest is often discussed by block-play children. During dramatic play, by using linguistic and interpersonal intelligences, children learn momma, daddy, and baby role-playing skills. Art activities can focus children's attention on color and the properties of different media while children explore using spatial, linguistic, and bodily-kinesthetic intelligences. At circle times, linguistic and interpersonal intelligences come into play when young preschoolers learn appropriate "student behaviors" such as raising one's hand to speak in a group.

In elementary schools, more focus may be placed on linguistic and logicomathematical intelligences. However, in the Key School, for example, children may learn new vocabulary words by composing a "rap" song (linguistic and musical intelligences), and they can be seen dissecting owl pellets in small groups, trying to match pieces of bone found to a chart of mice bones, all the time talking to each other and using linguistic, interpersonal, spatial, naturalist, and bodily-kineshetic intelligences at the same time. This activity could also involve logicomathematical intelligence if students are directed to chart the number of bones found in different pellets and to hypothesize how many mice the owls have eaten. Even a lesson that involves only reading and writing uses linguistic and bodily-kinesthetic intelligences.

Strongly influenced by his reading of Gardner's *Frames of Mind* and research into how the brain works when children learn to read and write, Thomas Armstrong gained insight into why he considered himself aliterate. In other words, he knew how to read but often chose not to. Because he felt that there seems to be a "basic contradiction when it comes to the actual practice of the theory of multiple intelligences," Armstrong (2003) has looked more closely at the use of the theory with many of his publications such as *Multiple Intelligences in the Classroom* (2nd ed.), published in 2000, and *The Multiple Intelligences of Reading and Writing* (2003).

Temperament

temperaments—children's inborn characteristics such as regularity, adaptability, and other dispositions that affect behavior.

Children also reveal different temperaments. These can also determine how a child relates to the environment. Examine Figure 4–9, which lists the characteristics of temperament. Where do you fit on the lines between the extremes? Are you more or less active? Are your body rhythms regular or irregular? Do you tend to be impulsive or cautious in making decisions? Do you see yourself as an adaptable person? Do you have a quick or slow temper? Are you generally an optimist or a pessimist? Are you easily distracted, or could the house burn down around you when you are reading a good book? Your answers to these questions describe your temperament.

Chess and Thomas (1986, 1995) have undertaken longitudinal studies looking at nine characteristics of temperament identified by Thomas, Chess, Birch, Hertzig, and Korn (1963) and further investigated by Soderman (1981). Their studies suggest that there are three general types of children, depending on where they fall on the nine characteristics: the easy-to-get-along-with child; the feisty one; and the slow-to-warm-up child. Children who are easy to get along with

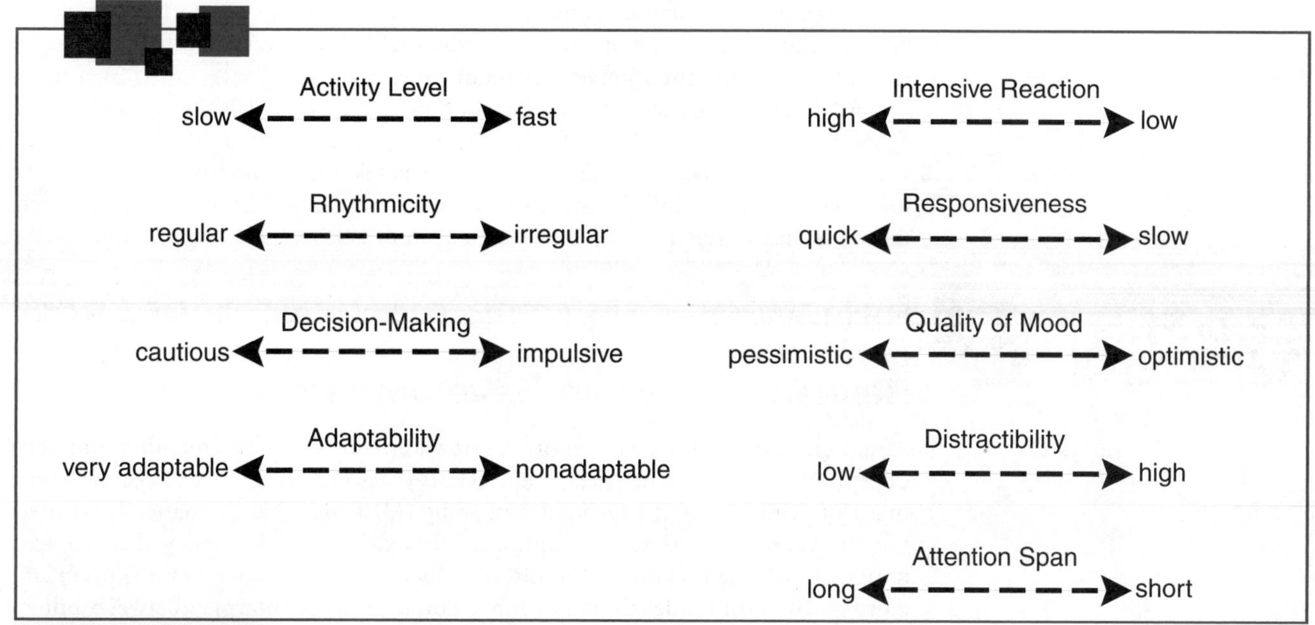

Figure 4–9 The nine characteristics of temperament

have moderate activity levels and regular rhythmicity. They are moderate in decision-making, adaptable, slow to anger (without being so slow that they do not assert themselves when appropriate), both quick and slow to respond depending on the situation, and more optimistic than pessimistic. They tend to have low levels of distractibility and lengthy attention spans. These children may also be more field independent than field sensitive. The behavior of children who are feisty goes to extremes. The children have fast activity levels and irregular rhythmicity. They are cautious, nonadaptable, quick to anger (temper tantrums), generally negative, and easily distracted. They have short attention spans. Children who are slow to warm up tend to be so cautious in making a decision that they will often wait for a decision to present itself before they move. They are slow to respond, have low adaptability levels, and are generally more pessimistic.

You should be aware that there are no good or bad temperaments; there are only different ones (see Figure 4–10). Take another look at where you fall on the line between the extremes. Generally, you will have difficulty relating to children at opposite extremes from yourself. For example, if your body rhythms are very regular, you may have less patience toilet training a child who does not have regular body rhythms. This can happen because you may not understand why the child is not regular like yourself. If you are a trusting, optimistic person, it may be difficult to relate to the suspicious, cautious child. The teacher with a lengthy attention span and low level of distractibility may have less patience with the child who is easily distracted and has a short attention span. In planning, the teacher may feel that an activity will take fifteen minutes only to discover that this child flits through it in three minutes.

Figure 4–10 This child reveals a low level of distractibility and lengthy attention span.

What is the teacher's role in working with children of different temperaments? First, be careful not to label a child with a different temperament as good or bad. Second, take a cue from the characteristics and plan the lessons accordingly. The child with a short attention span can learn to lengthen it. Give the child activities that can be completed quickly at first. Look to see what activities the child prefers. Then plan an activity that will take a little longer to finish and encourage the child to remain with it. Gradually, you can persuade the child to attend to the activity for a longer period of time.

All teachers soon realize that children do not accomplish the lesson or skill at the same speed, and they differ in the amount of time and attention they devote to activities. The number of repetitions needed for children to memorize or know varies. In general, the memory of an experience will become stronger each time it is encountered.

REVIEW OF SELECTED CURRENT RESEARCH

Research on Brain Development

Although much of the research on the development of the brain and its implication for caregivers and teachers is almost 30 years old, the ability to see the brain in action with a magnetic resonance imaging (MRI) scan has dramatically pointed out the validity of the earlier findings. Life experiences are believed to control both how the infant's brain is "architecturally formed" and how intricate brain circuity is wired. Brain development hinges on a complex interplay between inherited genes and life experiences (Shore, 1997). Prenatal conditions, as most of you already know, also affect brain development.

Shortly after birth, a growth spurt in the brain occurs as the axons (which send signals) and dendrites (which receive them) explode with new connections (synapses). The number of brain cells is not as important as the number of connections these cells can make (Sullo, 1999). Electrical activity, triggered by a flood of sensory experiences, fine-tunes the brain's circuity, determining which connections will be retained and which will be pruned (Nash, 1998).

Sensitive periods or "windows" are felt to exist (for example, the learning of language). At these times, certain types of input create or stabilize long-lasting structures. As Kantrowitz (1997) states:

> Every lullaby, every giggle and peek-a-boo, triggers a crackling along his neural pathways, laying the groundwork for what could someday be a love of art or a talent for soccer or a gift for making and keeping friends.

Most cognitive science researchers accept the following as key findings:

1. Learning changes the physical structure of the brain.
2. These structural changes alter the functional organization of the brain: in other words, learning organizes and reorganizes the brain.
3. Different parts of the brain may be ready to learn at different times. (National Research Council, 2000).

The world is in the midst of an extraordinary outpouring of scientific work on brain function, on the processes of thinking and learning, on the neural processes that occur during thought and learning, and on the development of competence (National Research Council, 2000).

Open-ended art and musical experiences in early childhood are believed to facilitate the later learning of concepts in math, science, language, and reading. Activities that prompt mental imaging such as family storytelling, art, and music are deemed developmentally important to the brain's ongoing development of mental connections (learning). They are also crucial to the child's development of self-confidence and aid in the development of social relationships, personality adjustment, and the child's natural creative ability (Archilles, 1999; Sylwester, 1998; Szyba, 1999; Weinberger, 1998).

Just as the above-mentioned authors believe that brain research shows how very early experiences influence brain development, Bruer (1998) argues that overstatement and—at times—distortion and hyperbole have led parents and educators scurrying to ensure that children receive the "right" types of enrichment before age three. Bruer also suggests that the same misinformation has led legislators to develop educational policy based on misinterpretation and "hype."

A difference of opinion exists concerning deterministic and lifelong effects of early nurturing by parents and care providers (Harris, 1998). Harris, heavily criticized by well-respected child development scientists for the "extreme position" she holds, bases her assumptions on a behavioral genetics viewpoint (Begley, 1998). She believes that parenting has been oversold and that parents have been led to believe they have more influence on their child's personality than they do in actuality (Begley, 1998).

A second difference of opinion exists between Bruer's (1998) contention that "the specifics of home or preschool environments matter little, if at all, to how children's sensory and motor systems develop" and Lowery's (1998) belief that they do. Lowery presents examples from the research of how the brain constructs knowledge, perceives relationships, and how carefully planned sequential activities and curriculums allow children to explore and thus facilitate brain connections. Whether Lowery's analysis is correct or not, what is true is state lawmakers are connecting recent research that emphasizes the early and rapid development of infants' brains with the need for good quality programs for young children. Over a dozen state legislatures have passed early childhood initiatives that directly reference brain development. Other state initiatives were approved after legislators were specifically informed about brain research (Groginsky, Robison, & Smith, 1999).

Brain-Based Learning

All learning is brain-based, and teachers can become more effective with some knowledge of how the brain senses, processes, stores, and retrieves information (Perry, 2000). Perry believes the following is necessary teacher knowledge, especially for *elementary grades*, when teachers attempt lecture presentations:

1. Learning requires attention and neural systems fatigue quickly. In three to five minutes of sustained brain activity, neurons become less responsive and need to rest.
2. Neurons respond to patterned and repetitive events rather than sustained, continuous stimulation.
3. In familiar and safe environments, children's brains will seek novelty.
4. A factual lecture can be tolerated four to eight minutes before the brain wanders. If a teacher is not providing novelty, the brain focuses elsewhere.
5. When concepts are presented in isolation and are unrelated to what the child knows, a fatiguing effect ensues.
6. Information is easiest to digest when there is emotional "seasoning." Humor, empathy, and other emotions, coupled with factual concepts, make them easier to digest.
7. Linking related concepts helps the formation of brain connections.
8. A presentation that bobs and weaves between facts, concepts, and narrative in a lecture presentation is a prudent approach.

9. Human beings are storytelling primates, both curious and fond of learning (Perry, 2000).

Early childhood educators can use the above information when giving directions and explanations, when leading discussions, when trying to develop emotional rapport, and when planning activities. Perhaps you have had college lecturers who were unfamiliar with the above!

The teacher who wishes to end an activity on a satisfying "high note" before children's lack of ability to attend sets in will watch the timing of activities, consider the novelty factor, and consider repetition useful. She also will notice children's highly enjoyed activities. These are ones children request and say "Do it again." When reading certain picture books, they will know words, actions, or the story well. Repeated favorite book readings are commonplace in prekindergarten classrooms. Children's genuine feelings of pleasure and accomplishment can be displayed in both indoor and outdoor curriculum activities.

Research on Emotional Intelligence

Since the publication of Goleman's *Emotional Intelligence* in 1995, there has been a renewed interest in how children's emotions impact on their learning. Greenspan (1997) emphasizes that certain kinds of emotional nurturing propel infants and young children to intellectual and emotional health, and suggests that affective experiences help them master a variety of cognitive tasks. Early childhood educators, alert to new research-based data on emotional intelligence, are provided with additional fuel to advocate for the importance of and need for quality child care.

Public school teachers and administrators, recognizing the impact of emotional and social well-being on their students' abilities to learn, have begun to develop programs to help (Cummings & Haggerty, 1997; Elias, Bruene-Butler, Blum, & Schuyler, 1997; Weissberg, Shriver, Bose, & DeFalco, 1997). Although some criticism has been provoked by the thought of teaching a social-emotional program, Elias and his associates contend that social-emotional learning ties several areas of the curriculum together (for example, AIDS education, drug-abuse education, stress prevention, and so on) (Elias, et al., 1999).

Pool (1997) cites Goleman as positing five dimensions of emotional intelligence: (1) self-awareness, (2) the ability to handle emotions (impulse control, for example), (3) motivation, (4) empathy, and (5) social skills. As you can see, Goleman believes that social skills are a component of emotional intelligence. How can a child with little self-awareness or self-control—even if motivated—develop social relationships without empathy? Is emotional intelligence related to IQ? Goleman (1995) provides several examples from the research to demonstrate how emotional skills are essential, not only for school achievement but also for success in life.

Research on Self-Esteem and Learning

self-esteem—children's evaluation of their worth in positive or negative terms.

After much research in the 1960s and 1970s on the relationship of self-esteem to learning, the 1980s saw little being done. A new interest emerged in the 1990s, however, and researchers were again impressed with the interrelationships between how children view themselves and their abilities to learn. Initial work by Coopersmith (1967) and others has shown that children who perceive of themselves as capable and competent, and who have a feeling of belongingness (in terms of the classroom atmosphere), are more likely to do well in school than those who do not. For teachers, then, the task is clear: we need to help children feel that they are competent and valued as persons, have control over their own behavior, can make valid choices within the classroom structure, and with the development of self-respect can learn to respect others. We must be aware of any hidden biases we might hold, and learn to treat all of our children fairly and honestly and to encourage individual responsibility (Curry & Johnson, 1990). Our curricular goals must value the thinking processes children use as well as any product; we need to emphasize what Katz and Chard (1989) call dispositions such as "curiosity, resourcefulness, independence, initiative, responsibility, and other positive dispositions."

Some self-esteem curricula have been developed such as Magic Circle, Quest, and Tribes. Preschools, child care programs, and elementary schools using these programs have reported increased interest in cooperation and learning among their children.

Teachers familiar with the need for children to see themselves as capable and belonging to their classroom group often provide opportunities within the curriculum as a whole for building self-esteem. These teachers offer children viable choices, utilize cooperative learning groups, and modeling, among other techniques, to boost children's self-esteem (see Figure 4–11).

Figure 4–11 Children are allowed to choose child-authored books during silent reading (first grade classroom).

Research on Levels of Representation

According to Piagetian theory, children go through four stages of cognitive development. Gonzalez-Mena (2001) reviewed these stages in her textbook, *Foundations: Early Childhood Education in a Diverse Society* (2nd ed.). Piaget posited the four stages as follows:

1. **Sensorimotor stage** (birth to age two or three)—Starting at birth, infants and toddlers during the sensorimotor stage learn primarily through their senses: seeing, hearing, touching (manipulating), smelling, and tasting. Remember the example of the baby with the new toy?

2. **Preoperational stage** (age two or three to eight or nine)—At this stage, beginning with the development of language approximately at age two, the preschooler develops what Piaget terms "preconcepts" and learns by using his intuition. Thus, a three-year-old child makes typical mistakes in conceptual learning and may call a cow, seen for the first time, by the name of the only large animal with which he has knowledge, "horsie."

   Adults can see the children's intuition at work as they make grammatical errors in overgeneralizing plurals. For example, "mouse" becomes "mouses," just as "house" becomes "houses." "Foot" becomes "foots" or "feets." "I don't have no more cookies" becomes standard emphasis for the three-year-old, the use of the double negative being normal usage.

   Piaget often called children in the preoperational stage "perception bound," meaning that they are limited by what they can see, hear, touch, manipulate, and so on, and that they have difficulty seeing comparisons when differences are dramatic. A child at this stage may not understand that a Chihuahua and a Great Dane are both dogs. One two-year-old, for example, called a Scottie dog a "funny cat" because her only acquaintance with small furry black animals had been her own large female Persian cat.

3. **Concrete operational stage** (ages six to eight to age eleven and even to adulthood)—At this stage, the child begins to be able to form classifications

sensorimotor stage—Piaget's period covering infancy.

preoperational stage—Piaget's period covering the preschool years.

concrete operational stage—Piaget's period covering the elementary school years.

and to see the similarities among categories despite their differences. All dogs and all cats, for example, become "animals." Birds that fly, such as sparrows and cardinals, can be grouped with chickens and, sometimes with difficulty, ducks and geese.

Also during the concrete operational stage, the child begins to understand the principles of conservation, essential to the understanding of mathematics. These are the development of understanding that the mass of clay does not change even if it is rolled into an elongated shape or left in a ball; that the liquid in a tall, thin glass is the same as that in a short, fat glass; that area does not change if there are the same number of objects placed on a field, even though one field looks more crowded because the objects are scattered and the other field seems to have more area because the objects are aligned along one side.

conservation—ability to recognize that objects remain the same in amount despite perceptual changes, usually acquired during the period of concrete operations.

4. Formal operational stage (age eleven to adulthood)—According to Piaget, during this final stage in intellectual development, the child begins to be capable of abstract thinking. At this stage, the child can formulate hypotheses and learns to monitor his own thinking (metacognition).

formal operational stage—Piaget's period covering adolescence.

Much of the research developed by Vygotsky (Berk & Winsler, 1995), a contemporary of Piaget, was kept unknown to Western psychologists and educators by the USSR. After *perestroika* and the breakup of the USSR, many of the former Soviet researchers came to the United States, and a wide distribution of Vygotsky's research has become available.

Considered a sociocultural theorist, Vygotsky saw learning as taking place through social contact and the development of what he termed "private speech." Children talk to themselves, either silently or vocally, in the attempt to internalize learning, monitor themselves, and solve problems. Vygotsky emphasized the importance of language in the development of socially shared cognition in which adults, or peers, assisted the child to move ahead in development by noticing what the next logical step might be. The term zone of proximal development (ZPD) was applied to the adult's or peer's recognition of when the child needed assistance and when the child did not. This assisted learning is called scaffolding.

zone of proximal development (ZPD)—in Vygotsky's theory, this zone represents tasks a child cannot yet do by herself but that she can accomplish with the support of an older child or adult.

scaffolding—a teaching technique helpful in promoting language, understanding, and child solutions, that may include supportive and responsive teacher conversation and actions following child-initiated behavior.

Understanding Vygotsky's theory in teaching has led to the emphasis on cooperative learning, scaffolding or assisted learning, and teaching children to use private speech to help in their problem-solving. A teacher might notice that a child is having difficulty placing one piece of a puzzle in the right place and suggest that the piece be rotated. A peer familiar with the same puzzle might do the same. Likewise, a teacher might suggest that the child verbalize as she is putting the pieces into the puzzle, saying such words as, "I see the yellow piece here and I see more yellow there; maybe the piece fits in here."

Translating Theory into Practice

Beliefs about educational practice are shaped both by training coursework and personal experiences working with children (Brown & Rose, 1995). Discrepancies between theory and practice may exist in workplaces and in the placement classroom of a student teacher. Overreliance on experience may not lead to the best practice (Cassidy & Lawrence, 2000). Student teaching requires *sustained examination* of classroom practice, and *reflection* if a student teacher hopes to understand or articulate the relationship between theory and practice (Kvernbekk, 1997). Over time, it is believed the ability to explain a rationale for a teacher's classroom behaviors may represent a form of "grounded theories" in which the theories to which teachers have been exposed are supported through experience become the bedrock of their teaching philosophy and beliefs (Cassidy & Lawrence, 2000).

STUDENT TEACHER INTELLIGENT BEHAVIOR

Costa (1991) suggests that there are several characteristics of intelligent behavior displayed by children. These behaviors apply to adults as well. In this case, student teachers can gain insight into their own behaviors. Costa notes that these are suggested intelligence characteristics and are not meant to represent a complete listing. He urges teachers to discover additional indicators through "kid-watching and self-analysis."

Costa's characteristics of intelligent behavior follow:

1. Persistence or persevering when the solution to a problem is not immediately apparent
2. Decreasing impulsivity
3. Listening to others with understanding and empathy
4. Using flexibility in thinking
5. Metacognition, defined as awareness of one's own thinking
6. Checking for accuracy and precision
7. Questioning and problem-posing
8. Drawing on past knowledge and applying it to new situations
9. Using precision in language and thought rather than confused, vague, and imprecise language to express ideas (this includes using complete sentences, providing supportive evidence for ideas, elaborating, clarifying, and defining terminology in written and oral expression)
10. Using all the senses
11. Displaying ingenuity, originality, insightfulness, and creativity
12. Displaying wonderment, inquisitiveness, curiosity, and the enjoyment of problem-solving; displaying a sense of efficacy as a thinker

Other indicators of intelligent behaviors Costa mentions that are not found in the above listing are a sense of humor and ethical/moral reasoning.

SUMMARY

Several identified theories currently influence decisions and views about child learning. Individuality in learning is apparent; children learn at different rates and learn from different techniques. The teacher's understanding of child development and learning theory, and the idea of how children will learn best, should serve as the basis for the children's guidance and growth.

The senses gather information that is stored mentally and is under continual revision as new situations are met. There is a definite sequence to the learning processes, and teachers need to be aware of individual styles and preferred learning modality to make the experience easier for each child. Many learning behaviors seen in early childhood remain our preferred learning styles throughout our lives.

HELPFUL WEB SITES

http://www.ed.gov

National Institute on Early Childhood Development. Sponsors comprehensive and challenging research.

http://www.fpg.unc.edu

National Center for Early Development and Learning. Search research and select on-page summaries of the latest research.

http://ericae.net

ERIC Assessment and Evaluation Clearinghouse. Look for readings.

http://www.sred.org/

Society for Research on Child Development. Excellent source of newest research on child development. Publishes journal, *Child Development.*

SUGGESTED ACTIVITIES

A. After reviewing Costa's (1991) 12 characteristics and then envisioning the kind of preschool environment that would promote or even allow children's intelligent behavior, it is easy to see that lots of time for child-initiated activities, child discovery, child experimentation, and child time for free choice within a dynamic and interesting classroom suit Costa's characteristics. What opportunities for intellectual behavior and growth are possible in adult-child situations when "listen and learn" group instruction dominates? Discuss with a few classmates.

B. Rate the following situations as A (appropriate; justified by current learning theory) or I (inappropriate). If appropriate, cite the theory that supports the answer. Discuss your choices with four or five others in a class group meeting.

1. Marilee, a student teacher, encounters two children who want to learn to tie their shoes. Because she realizes shoe tying is a complex skill, she says, "When you're a little bigger, you'll be able to do it."
2. Thien, a student teacher, would like to tell a group of three-year-olds about the country of his birth, Vietnam. However, Thien realizes they probably would not be able to grasp the concept of a foreign country, so he presents a simple Vietnamese song he learned as a child instead.
3. A cooperating teacher presents an activity in which she names and appreciates children who give correct answers.
4. Toni, a student teacher, notices Mike and Eduardo are using the toy razors to shave their legs. She redirects their play, asking them to shave their faces like their fathers do.
5. Elena (student teacher) notices that Tilly, an independent child, always hides when inside time is announced. She decides to interest Tilly in an indoor activity before inside time is called to avoid having to find Tilly and coax her in.
6. Johnny refuses to attend any group activities. Laura, a teacher, suspects that he has had negative experiences at previous group times, and decides to make group time so attractive Johnny will want to join in. Laura has planned an activity with large balloons that children sit on and pop.
7. Lisa, Garrett, and Thad often gather at the reading corner and read new books. Stephanie Lynn, the student teacher, sees this as an example of intrinsic motivation.

8. Bud notices that his cooperating teacher always calls on each child by name in any conversation at group or discussion times.
9. Carolyn, a student teacher, feels she needs only to set out activities for the children and they will select the ones they need for their intellectual growth.
10. Gregorio, age three, has just poured water on the floor. The student teacher approaches, saying, "You need to tell me why you poured water on the floor."
11. Carlos says he hates carrots. Susan, the student teacher, tells him she likes them.
12. A child whines, "You know, so tell me!" Joanne, the student teacher, is reluctant to give a direct answer because she feels the child should explore the toy and find out for himself which puzzle piece fits. "Try turning the piece," she suggests.
13. On driving to her assigned preschool, Margo notices a street barricade. When the first parent arrives, she asks what is happening.
14. There is a new child in the classroom. This child has a tattoo, which fascinates other children. The cooperating teacher feels it is best not to ask the child about it at group time because it might embarrass the newcomer. When a child asks about it, she answers, "I can see you're really interested in the mark you see on our new friend's arm."
15. In Mrs. Clements' preschool, the children select activities, and they have the choice of attending group times or engaging in other quiet activities.

C. In groups of three, act out a teaching/learning situation (two children, one teacher) based on any of the major theories discussed in this chapter. Have other groups guess which theory you chose to role-play.

D. Read the following quote. Then in groups of four, discuss what interests, passions, and "wants-to-do's" you think might exist in a class of four-year-olds living in (1) an innercity, (2) in a rural area, and (3) in a small town near the Mexican border. List your ideas and share with the total training group.

> If teaching is conceived as constructing a bridge between the subject matter and the student, learner-centered teachers keep a constant eye on both ends of the bridge. The teachers attempt to get a sense of what each student knows, cares about, is able to do, and wants to do (The National Research Council, 2000).

What did you discover from this exercise?

E. Think back to your first days in your assigned classroom. What elements made the classroom feel safe and comfortable for you, the adult? What cooperating teacher actions made you feel "at home," capable, and encouraged? Did you feel that you would learn something and do well in student teaching? Were there situations in which you felt like an outsider? What events and features would you replicate in your future classrooms to have children feel part of the group, capable, and at ease? Discuss with your training class.

F. With a small group of fellow student teachers, discuss student teaching situations that have called for intelligent action, and how you or others in your student teaching assignment proceeded or behaved. Share significant conclusions with the total class.

REVIEW

A. Choose the best answer to complete each statement.

1. Beginning teachers should:
   a. have a clear idea of how children learn best because research has discovered the learning process.
   b. realize that there are a number of learning theories.
   c. expect children to learn in their own unique ways, making similarities between the children's learning patterns insignificant.
   d. look to their own experiences for clues on child learning.
   e. None of these.
2. A theory is someone's attempt to:
   a. gain fame.
   b. help instructors teach.
   c. make sense of a vast series of events.
   d. control others.
   e. make others think like the theorist.
3. It is generally accepted that children should:
   a. be grouped according to ability.
   b. be grouped according to age.
   c. be asked to practice and recite learnings.
   d. play because it promotes learning.
   e. be exposed to planned group times that teach survival skills.
4. When one hears that children pass through stages in their development, it means that:
   a. all the children pass through stages in an orderly, predictable way.
   b. children should tour buses and theaters.
   c. there seem to be phases in growth that teachers and parents can expect.
   d. most children will return to previous stages at times.
   e. All of these.
5. Children generally remember a concept best when:
   a. they see a picture of the concept.
   b. they watch a demonstration of the concept by the teacher.
   c. they hear the teacher describe the concept.
   d. they use the concept in the discovery center.
   e. All of these.
6. Gardner (1988) believes that in elementary schools, teachers too often teach only to children with:
   a. logicomathematical and intrapersonal intelligences.
   b. logicomathematical and spatial intelligences.
   c. logicomathematical and linguistic intelligences.
   d. logicomathematical and bodily-kinesthetic intelligences.
   e. logicomathematical and interpersonal intelligences.
7. According to research into temperament, the easy-to-get-along-with child has the following characteristics:
   a. a regular rhythmicity, an easy adaptability, a positive quality of mood, a low distractibility, and a long attention span.
   b. a regular rhythmicity, an easy adaptability, intense reactions to environmental stimuli, and a negative quality of mood.
   c. an irregular rhythmicity, a fast activity level, an easy adaptability, a negative quality of mood, and a long attention span.
   d. a regular rhythmicity, a negative quality of mood, high distractibility, a long attention span, and intense reactions to stimuli.

e. a regular rhythmicity, a cautious approach to decision-making, adaptability, a negative quality of mood, and a long attention span.

8. Field-sensitive children tend to:
   a. want to work and play alone.
   b. seek reinforcement frequently from the teacher.
   c. like to work and play in small groups.
   d. tend to like math and science better than concepts related to personal interests.
   e. b and c.
   f. a and d.
9. Costa (1991) suggests that among the intelligent behaviors displayed by children (and adults) are any of the following:
   a. persistence.
   b. impulsivity.
   c. questioning and problem-posing.
   d. flexibility in thinking.
   e. a, b, and c.
   f. a, c, and d.
10. Children with a strong sense of self-esteem generally:
    a. do poorly in school.
    b. do well in school.
    c. are resourceful.
    d. are dependable.
    e. a and b.
    f. c and d.

B. List any accepted learning theories you feel were excluded from this chapter. Cite your source (text, individual, etc.).

C. Define convergent thinking and divergent thinking.

CASE SCENARIO

Setting: In a first grade classroom, the student teacher, Leah, is observing the children during the first week of her assignment. After the children leave, she talks with her cooperating teacher, Ms. Hails.

Leah wondered about the behavior of the little boy who was sitting under the table when children were doing table work, and whether he should be allowed to sit there while the other children were doing their assigned work.

Ms. Hails explains that Carlos is new to the classroom and comes from a Spanish-speaking family. She is not sure if his grasp of English is strong enough for planned activities. She suggests Leah choose Carlos for her case study assignment.

A week later, Ms. Hails asks Leah what she has learned from observing Carlos. Leah says she feels Carlos knows little English. She explains that even when she spoke a few

continues . . .

. . . continued

Spanish phrases, she got a weak response. Carlos just ducked his head. Leah thinks he is shy or has another problem.

"Based on your understanding of child development, what are the possible difficulties with Carlos?" Ms. Hails asks.

Leah mentions Carlos has not connected with any of the other children who are Spanish-speaking. Leah believes he goes under the table to hide whenever he's faced with something he doesn't understand.

Ms. Hails responds. "I'm going to call for an evaluation by the school psychologist. Until we have further information we'll have to work with Carlos as best we can. I'm going to ask you to check on how Carlos seems to learn best. What does he do on the play yard at recess?"

Leah responds, "Most of the time, he tries to kick the soccer ball. She relates that she asked him once, mostly using body language, if he wouldn't like to climb on the climbing structure, but he shook his head, "no." But then when the other children had gone on and left the structure empty, Carlos did climb up on it and seemed to enjoy going as high as he could, even balancing dangerously on the top bars. So he obviously enjoys physical activities using his whole body. And she noticed he has good eye-foot coordination; he kicks the soccer ball well and seems to have past experience. Leah believes if Carlos has a preferred way of learning, it may be bodily-kinesthetic, thinking of Gardner's multiple intelligences. His behavior on the climbing structure would also suggest spatial intelligence.

She also remembered he liked playing with the pattern blocks and one day, arranged them in the pattern shown on the card.

Ms. Hails suggests that as Carlos becomes more familiar with the classroom and the children, he will open up. She tells Leah she has scheduled a parent conference. "I want you to work with him on a one-to-one basis whenever you can," she instructs.

Questions for Discussion:

1. What do you think might be some of the problems Carlos is experiencing?
2. If you were his student teacher, what activities might you try?
3. Does language appear to be Carlos' principal difficulty? What indications in the scenario would suggest this?

REFERENCES

Achilles, E. (1999, January). Creating music environments in early childhood programs. *Young Children, 54*(1).

Armstrong, T. (2000). *Multiple intelligences in the classroom* (2nd ed.). Alexandria, VA: Association for Supervision and Curriculum Development.

Armstrong, T. (2003). *The multiple intelligences of reading and writing: Making the words come alive.* Alexandria, VA: Association for Supervision and Curriculum Development.

Begley, S. (1998, September 7). The parent trap. *Newsweek.*

Berk, L. E., & Winsler, A. (1995). *Scaffolding children's learning: Vygotsky and early childhood education.* Washington, DC: National Association for the Education of Young Children.

Brown, D., & Rose, T. (1995). Self-reported classroom impact of teachers' theories about learning and obstacles to implementation. *Action in Teacher Education, 17*(1), 20–29.

Bruer, J. T. (1998, November). Brain science: Brain fiction. *Educational Leadership, 56*(3).

Bruer, J. T. (1998). *The myth of the first three years.* New York: Free Press.

Cassidy, D. J., & Lawrence, J. M. (2000). Teachers' beliefs: The "whys" behind the "how to's" in child care classrooms. *Journal of Research in Childhood Education, 14*(2), 193–204.

Checkly, K. (1997, September). The first seven . . . and the eighth: A conversation with Howard Gardner. *Educational Leadership, 55*(1).

Chess, S., & Thomas, A. (1986, 1995). *Temperament in clinical practice.* New York: Guilford.

Coopersmith, S. (1967). *The antecedents of self-esteem.* San Francisco: Freeman.

Costa, A. L. (1991). The search for intelligent life. In *Developing minds: A resource book for teaching thinking.* Alexandria, VA: Association for Supervision and Curriculum Development.

Cowley, G., & Underwood, A. (1998, June 15). Memory. *Newsweek.*

Cummings, C., & Haggerty, K. P. (1997, May). Raising healthy children. *Educational Leadership, 54*(8).

Curry, N. E., & Johnson, C. N. (1990). *Beyond self-esteem: Developing a genuine sense of human value.* Washington, DC: National Association for the Education of Young Children.

Elder, L., & Paul, R. (1998, Spring). Critical thinking: Developing intellectual traits. *Journal of Developmental Education, 21*(3).

Elias, M. J., Bruene-Butler, L., Blum, L., & Schuyler, T. (1997, May). How to launch a social and emotional learning program. *Educational Leadership, 54*(8).

Elias, M. J., Zins, J. E., Weisberg, R. P., Frey, K. S., Greenberg, M. T., Haynes, N. M., Kessler K., Schwab-Stone, M. E., & Shriver, T. P. (1997). *Promoting social and emotional learning: Guidelines for educators.* Alexandria, VA. Association for Supervision and Curriculum Development.

Erikson, E. (1963, 1993). *Childhood and society.* New York: Norton.

Feiman-Nemser, S., Carver, C., Schwille, S., & Yusko, B. (1999). Beyond support: Taking new teachers seriously as learners. In M. Scherer (Ed.). *A better beginning: Supporting and mentoring new teachers* (pp. 3–12). Alexandria, VA: Association for Supervision and Curriculum Development.

Gardner, H. (1983). *Frames of mind: The theory of multiple intelligences.* New York: Basic Books.

Gardner, H. (1988). *Beyond the IQ: Education and human development.* National Forum, 68(27).

Gardner, H. (1993). *Multiple intelligences: The theory in practice.* New York: Basic Books.

Gardner, H. (1999). *Intelligence reframed: Multiple intelligences for the 21st century.* New York: Basic Books

Gesell, A., Ilg, F. L., & Ames, L. B. (1974). *The child from five to ten.* New York: Harper & Row.

Goleman, D. (1995). *Emotional intelligence: Why it can matter more than IQ.* New York: Bantam Books.

Gonzalez-Mena, J. (2001). *Foundations: Early childhood education in a diverse society* (2nd ed.). Mountain View, CA: Mayfield.

Greenspan, S. I. (1997). *The growth of the mind and the endangered origins of intelligence.* Reading, MA: Addison-Wesley.

Groginsky, S., Robison S., & Smith, S. (1999). *Making child care better: State initiatives.* Washington, DC: National Conference of State Legislators.

Harris, J. R. (1998). *The nurture assumption: Why children turn out the way they do.* New York: Free Press.

Hendrick, J. (1985, 1993). *Total learning for the whole child.* Columbus, OH: Merrill/Macmillan; New York: Merrill/Macmillan.

Hohmann, M., Banet, B., & Weikart, D. (1979). *Young children in action.* Ypsilanti, MI: High/Scope Press.

Jung, C. G. (1976). *Psychological types.* Princeton, NJ: Princeton University Press.

Kamii, C., & DeVries, R. (1978). *Physical knowledge in preschool education: Implications of Piaget's theory.* Englewood Cliffs, NJ: Prentice-Hall.

Kantrowitz, B. (1997, Spring/Summer). Piaget for early education. In M. Day & R. Parker (Eds.). *Preschool in action.* Boston: Allyn & Bacon.

Katz, L. G., & Chard, S. C. (1989). *Engaging children's minds: The project approach.* Norwood, NJ: Ablex.

Kvernbekk, T. (1997, May). What can we learn from experience? Paper presented at the California Association of Philosophers of Education, Stanford, CA.

Lavatelli, C. (1973). *Piaget's theory applied to an early childhood curriculum.* Boston: American Science and Engineering.

Lowery, L. (1998, November). How new science curriculums reflect brain research. *Educational Leadership, 56*(3).

McCarthy, B. (1987). *The 4MAT system: Teaching to learning styles with right/left mode techniques.* Barrington, IL: Excel.

McCarthy, B. (1997, March). A tale of four learners: 4MAT's learning styles. *Educational Leadership, 54*(6).

Meyer, M. (1997, September). The GREENing of learning: Using the eighth intelligence. *Educational Leadership, 55*(1).

Moffett, F. J. (1984). *Learning and schools.* San Francisco: Acme-Sherwood.

Nash, J. (1998, February 3). Fertile minds. *Time, 149*(5).

National Research Council (2000). *How people learn: Brain, mind, experience and school.* Washington, DC: National Academy Press.

Perry, B. D. (2000, November/December). How the brain learns best: Easy ways to gain optimal learning in the classroom by activating different parts of the brain. *Instructor, 110*(4), 34–35.

Piaget, J. (1952). *The origins of intelligence.* New York: International Universities Press.

Pool, C. R. (1997, May). Up with emotional health. *Educational Leadership, 55*(1).

Rousseau, J. J. (1947). L'Emile ou l'education. In O. E. Tellows and N. R. Tarrey (Eds.). *The age of enlightenment.* New York: F. S. Croft (First published, 1742).

Seefeldt, C., & Barbour, N. (1998). *Early childhood education: An introduction* (4th ed.). New York: Merrill/Macmillan.

Shore, R. (1997). *Rethinking the brain.* New York: Families and Work Institute.

Soderman, A. K. (1981, November). *Marching to a different drummer: A look at temperament in the development of personality.* Presentation at the annual conference of the National Association for the Education of Young Children.

Sternberg, R. J. (1997, March). What does it mean to be smart? *Educational Leadership, 54*(6).

Stevens, J. H., Jr., & King, E. W. (1976). *Administering early childhood programs.* Boston: Little, Brown.

Sullo, R. A. (1999). *The inspiring teacher.* Annapolis Junction, MD: National Education Association of the United States.

Sylwester, R. (1998, November). Art for the brain's sake. *Educational Leadership, 56*(3).

Szyba, C. M. (1999, January). Why do some teachers resist offering appropriate, open-ended art activities for young children? *Young Children, 54*(1).

Thomas, A., Chess, S., Birch, H. G., Hertzig, M. E., & Korn, S. (1963). *Behavioral individuality in early childhood.* New York: New York University Press.

Walters, J., & Gardner, H. (1986). The crystallizing experience: Discovering an intellectual gift. In R. Sternberg & J. Davidson (Eds.). *Conception of giftedness.* New York: Cambridge University Press.

Weinberger, N. M. (1998, November). The music in our minds. *Educational Leadership, 56*(3).

Weissberg, R. P., Shriver, T. P., Bose, S., & DeFalco, K. (1997, May). Creating a districtwide social development project. *Educational Leadership, 54*(8).

SECTION II

Programming

CHAPTER 5

Instructional Planning

Objectives **After studying this chapter, the student should be able to:**

1 Complete a written activity or lesson plan form.
2 Identify three ways of assessing child interest.
3 Describe three different approaches to curriculum development.
4 Describe the benefits of written activity/lesson plans.
5 Identify factors to consider when planning settings for teacher-guided activities.
6 Plan a group activity.
7 Discuss factors that promote group-time success.
8 Describe a teaching unit (theme) approach to early childhood instruction.
9 Cite two possible benefits and limitations of theme-centered curriculums.
10 Outline preparation steps in theme construction.

The most memorable part of student teaching has been the daily experience in my placement classroom. The lessons I have learned and the information shared has been a storehouse that will take years to exhaust.

Being forced to write lesson plans has helped me with my planned classroom activities. It has also widened the activities I present in my employment classroom. I'm more aware of my own capabilities and knowledge.

—Judy Mabie

My first day of student teaching was easy. My cooperating teacher didn't ask much of me, so I made a point of being helpful, handing out papers so she could continue talking, etc. Later she said, "If you have any ideas of things you'd like to do, feel free. . . ." That filled me with dread. I didn't know what to do with first graders, and I was hoping she'd clue me into the sorts of things we'd be doing the next few weeks so I'd be able to figure out how to fit in. I remember thinking that the kids seemed older, bigger than I expected, but I was soon reminded of their age when they were trying to do any reading or writing.

—Fononga Pahula

My supervisor suggested I plan activities in areas of my own personal interests. Since I'm an avid needlework enthusiast, I planned an activity in which I taught simple stitchery. The children (even the boys) loved doing sewing. Some went on to do long-term projects.

—Amanda St. Clair

I can remember by the end of the day I was completely exhausted. I remember how surprised I was when we did a week's worth of carefully planned ideas (activities) in the first day. I remember feeling panic-stricken; what am I going to do tomorrow?

Calli Collins

LOOKING AT ACCEPTED CURRICULUM STANDARDS

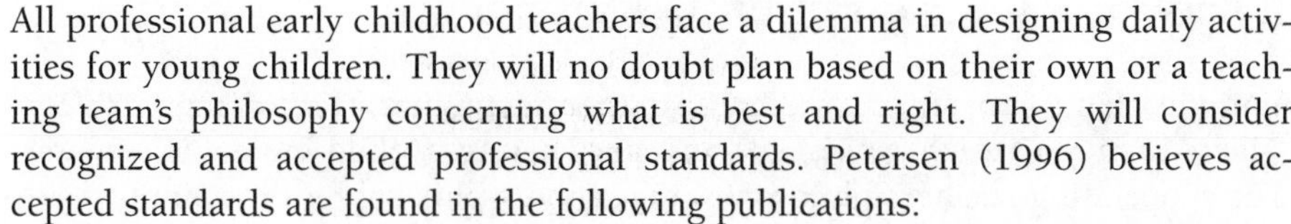

All professional early childhood teachers face a dilemma in designing daily activities for young children. They will no doubt plan based on their own or a teaching team's philosophy concerning what is best and right. They will consider recognized and accepted professional standards. Petersen (1996) believes accepted standards are found in the following publications:

Association for Childhood Education International. (1997). Position papers on the preparation of early childhood and elementary teachers. *Childhood Education 73*(3).

Bredekamp, S., & Copple, C. (Eds.). (1997). *Developmentally appropriate practice in early childhood programs* (rev. ed.). Washington, DC: National Association for the Education of Young Children.

Head Start Bureau, Administration for Children and Families, Department of Health and Human Services. (1975). *Head Start performance standards.* Washington, DC: Department of Health and Human Services.

National Academy of Early Childhood Programs. (1991). *Accreditation criteria and procedures of the National Academy of Early Childhood Programs* (rev. ed.). Washington, DC: National Association for the Education of Young Children.

National Association of Elementary School Principals. (1990). *Standards for quality programs for young children: Early childhood education and the elementary school principal.* Alexandria, VA: Author.

National Association for the Education of Young Children and National Association of Early Childhood Specialists in State Departments of Education. (2002). *Early learning standards: Creating the conditions for success (joint position statement).* Washington, DC: Author.

National Center on Education and the Economy. (2001). *New standards/speaking and listening for preschool through third grade.* Washington, DC: Author

U.S. Department of Health and Human Services. (1996). *Head Start program performance standards.* Washington, DC: Author.

In addition to those listed above, state legislators and policymakers have established *voluntary* standards that exceed their state's licensing regulations in an effort to improve the quality of their state's early childhood programs (Groginsky, Robison, & Smith, 1999).

Some of these may have been encountered in your training, others perhaps not.

The dilemma is to put philosophy and standards to work in curriculum design and daily lesson planning, and further, to weigh or insert parental and perhaps community concerns and input into that curriculum. An additional task is to decide the *what* and *how* of teaching. The *what* can be defined as the scope of information, experiences, and skills to be presented, promoted, and provided. The *how* is defined as the teaching techniques and teaching vehicles to be used.

Wolverton (2000) describes Head Start and Early Head Start curriculum development:

> No two curricula in Head Start and Early Head Start look exactly the same. There are two basic approach programs used to determine the curriculum. Staff and parents may base a curriculum on an already developed model, and adapt or "tailor" it for the group of children being served. Or staff and parents may develop a local curriculum. Either way, the curriculum must be in keeping with all the requirements of the Head Start Performance Standards and based on sound child development principles.

IDENTIFYING CHILD INTERESTS

You will plan, prepare, and present classroom activities. The teaching day contains structured (teacher-planned) and unstructured (child-initiated) activities. The cooperating teacher's philosophy, the school's philosophy, the identified program goals, and classroom setting determine the balance between child-initiated activities and teacher-planned activities. In activity-centered classrooms, or those with a Piagetian view, student teachers arrange room centers to invite and promote child discovery and learning. "Every time we teach a child something, we keep him from reinventing it. On the other hand, every time a child discovers it himself, it remains with him for the rest of his life" (Piaget, in the film Patron: Piaget in New Perspective).

Using Child Interest and Improvising

Teaching is a complex task requiring continual on-the-spot decision making (Carter & Curtis, 1994). Carter and Curtis believe master teachers have certain qualities that distinguish them from teachers who depend on curriculum activity books, follow the same theme plans year after year, or struggle daily to get the children involved in anything productive. Master teachers possess a set of attitudes and habits of mind to respond to classroom dynamics and multiple needs of children with the readiness of an improvisational artist.

An example of the above master teacher mind-set can be seen in the actions of one student teacher (Fredrica) in the following:

> A book about cats was brought to school by a child. After being previewed, Fredrica shared the book with a group of the child's friends. Susan, a four-year-old, went to the scrap paper and craft table later in the afternoon and cut long paper nails for one hand. She then asked Fredrica for tape to secure them to her fingers. They again looked at the book's illustrations to see if long cat nails were visible. Susan enjoyed meowing, pretending to scratch a tree trunk, and climbing the outdoor structure. Other children wished to cut and color cat nails of their own. Fredrica supplied materials. Soon a number of children were pretending to be cats! Fredrica was prepared to intervene if nails were used aggressively. The following day Fredrica set up a discovery area which included taped domestic animal sounds, cat figures to manipulate, and pictures of different house cat varieties. Poems about cats were part of story times. A cat visited school and cat care particulars were listed by the children on a wall chart printed with child ideas.

Fredrica and the children explored how the cats' sharp nails helped cats climb trees in one activity, and how cats use their nails to protect themselves in another.

You will be searching for activity ideas that will interest and challenge the group of children to which you are assigned. Observing children's play choices and favorite activities will give you ideas (see Figure 5–1). Children's conversations provide clues as to what has captured their attention. (You can make comments in your pocket notebook concerning individual and group curiosity and play selections.) Watch for excitement among the children. What were they eager to try? Was considerable time spent exploring or concentrating on an experience (see Figure 5–2)?

Figure 5–1 Children discuss ways classroom materials might be used.

Living in the Pacific Northwest, teacher Maggie Meyer (1997) noticed that her students were interested in water quality monitoring. Her school is involved in an "integrated watershed curriculum [which] is a part of a larger national effort—the Global Rivers Education Network (GREEN)." Based on the children's interests in what was happening around them in their home environment on the Budd/Deschutes Watershed in south Puget Sound, Meyer had her students "take samples of aquatic organisms on the Deschutes River" and submit them to chemical analysis.

Although Meyer's students were in a sixth-grade classroom, any preschool or primary grade teacher, fortunate to have a creek or pond in the environs of the school and noticing that children are interested in looking at the water, could have children collect samples of the water and look at them under a microscope the teacher has set up and focused.

All you need to do is be observant of your children's interests in their environment, and use your own interests and enthusiasm to excite and motivate them.

After the children's interest is identified, educators can use a three "W" strategy: What's known, What's unknown but wants to be known, and a What's been learned format.

Figure 5–2 Discovering together is an enjoyable aspect of teaching.

Many times, a teacher piques children's interests by focusing their attention on a new feature, event, object, or something that arises in the course of the day. What is unknown serves as the basis for teacher activity planning and the teacher's supportive assistance. The creative or spontaneous planning ability of an educator striving to adjust classroom circumstances that lead children to answers with or without teacher's help is part of the joy of teaching. The third "W" aims to promote putting what's learned into words, acts, or representations. It is a kind of recap or solidifying activity that reinforces what has been discovered or experienced.

CONSTRUCTIVISM AND DEVELOPMENTALLY APPROPRIATE PRACTICE

It is difficult to read any written material dealing with early childhood curriculum development and pedagogy that does not mention:

- child-centered
- child-initiated
- active learning
- constructivist
- developmentally appropriate

The first two terms are self-explanatory. Constructivism, a cognitive-developmental notion, has direct roots within the structuralism that underlies Piaget's theory of intellectual development (O'Loughlin, 1991). A constructivist takes the position that learners must have experiences with hypothesizing and predicting, manipulating objects, posing questions, researching answers, imagining, investigating, and inventing for new constructions to be developed (Fosnot, 1989).

What distinguishes the constructivist approach is the mental action that takes place as children infer from what they are experiencing and create a system of knowledge from the activity (Epstein, Schweinhart, & McAdoo, 1996). A secure, noncoercive classroom environment is believed to allow children to cooperate, develop respect for one another, exercise their curiosity, and gain confidence in their ability to figure things out on their own and become autonomous. Kamii and DeVries (1975/1977) describe the teacher's role as having four components.

1. Creating an environment and an atmosphere in which the child is independent, uses his own initiative in pursuing his interests, says exactly what he thinks, asks questions, experiments, and comes up with a variety of ideas.
2. Providing materials, suggesting activities, and assessing what is going on inside the child's head from moment to moment; the teacher proposes ideas rather than imposes.
3. Responding to children in terms of the kind of knowledge involved; the teacher shares a child's pleasure, frustration, and disappointments when the child seeks her company, and encourages the child's construction of logical knowledge; social knowledge is stated and reinforced.
4. Helping children extend their ideas without intruding or interrupting.

Early childhood educators realize the importance of teacher interaction in classrooms. Child-initiated activities and social communication take place in many learning situations, particularly with three-, four-, and five-year-olds. O'Loughlin

(1991) hopes the present emphasis on constructivism will consider and incorporate children's culture, race, class, learning histories, gender backgrounds, language, and the reality of teacher as power figure into the early childhood field's recommended teaching model.

The National Association for the Education of Young Children's (NAEYC's) Developmentally Appropriate Practice in Early Childhood Programs (BredeKamp & Copple, 1997) has been highly praised and acclaimed as the field's most respected guide to child activity planning. Revised and expanded, DAP (Bredekamp & Copple, 1997) is a "must-read and study" for all planning curriculums for young children. Vander Wilt and Monroe (1998) believe DAP is neither a curriculum nor method, but rather a way of thinking and working with children, and they have outlined what they feel are DAP's central principles and practices. They suggest these are easily implemented:

1. *Wholeness of the child.* Children are whole persons in whom physical, social, emotional, and cognitive development are integrated. Each area of development is important and affects every other area of development.
2. *Active involvement.* Children must be active participants in their own learning. Manipulation of real, concrete, and relevant materials contributes to children's understandings.
3. *Interaction with adults and peers.* Learning occurs when children interact with people in their environments. Interactions with both adults and other children facilitate the mental manipulation and ownership of ideas.
4. *Authentic experiences.* Children learn best from personally meaningful experiences that flow from the reality of their lives. When school experiences reflect the reality of life beyond the school, learning is more purposeful and relevant.
5. *Appropriate learning activities.* Appropriate learning activities include projects, learning centers, and such activities as building, drawing, writing, discussing, and reading. Research, exploration, discovery, problem-solving, and excursions are examples of recommended educational experiences.
6. *Integrated curriculum.* Integrated thematic units form the foundation for an appropriate curriculum, enabling children to make connections among and between ideas and knowledge. Distinctions among the various traditional subject areas are arbitrary and not very meaningful for children.
7. *Intrinsic motivation.* Fostering intrinsic motivation has the potential to support the development of responsible and autonomous learners—that is, learners who develop a passion and love for a lifetime of learning. When learners are reliant on extrinsic motivators, they become distracted and experience reduced interest in their learning.
8. *Authentic assessment.* Evaluation of children's progress should flow directly from the tasks and experiences in which they have been engaged. Evaluation and instruction must be integrally related so that each informs the other.
9. *Inappropriateness of grade retention.* Grade retention is inappropriate. The assumption in developmentally appropriate practice is that each child grows and develops at his or her own pace. And because children do not grow at the same pace, the classroom is expected to meet and accommodate the unique learning needs of each child, making retention inappropriate except in rare cases.

A commitment to DAP's pedagogy, teacher enthusiasm, and administrative support are important factors as teachers try to introduce DAP in their classrooms. Dunn and Kontos (1998) suggest teachers often struggle with implementation.

Developed through the efforts of many individuals and groups under NAEYC's leadership, DAP has been widely accepted although it is not without its critics. O'Loughlin (1991) believes that although developmentally appropriate practice, as described in NAEYC's 1988 publication, envisions the curriculum to be built around items of child interest, he questions whether children always know what interests them or whether teachers can teach something initially uninteresting but deemed important by the teacher.

Progress in Adopting Developmentally Appropriate Practice

Have early childhood educators adopted DAP in their classrooms?

NAEYC's National Academy of Early Childhood Programs has denied accreditation to programs in which the curriculum does not meet the criteria for DAP. A DAP approach to early childhood curriculum planning runs into difficulty when staffing, facility, material resources, and preparation time are far from ideal.

Interacting as a partner as DAP suggests rather than as a presenter means someone else is available in the classroom to supervise the total group. Providing a continually interesting opportunity-rich classroom environment demands storage space, equipment, and materials; and time to plan, collect, and set up the room and yard activities for child-initiated play and exploration.

Zahorik (1997) states that in addition to problems of storage, material resources, and preparation time, there are two other dilemmas faced by elementary school teachers when they attempt to implement DAP. The first is to err on the side of the students. By that, Zahorik suggests that allowing students to develop their own understandings from their personal constructions may lead them to overlook what research might add to their conceptual understanding. The second error, of course, is to design the curriculum around what "experts" have already discovered. After student's have devised their own constructions and arrived at what they may feel is the "correct" concept being taught, teachers may be all too quick to present knowledge from the discipline. For example, if the teacher brings in a variety of different types of leaves (such as oak, maple, palm, pine, cedar, and so on) and asks students, working in small groups, to classify them, it is not important that each group classify the leaves in exactly the same way or in a way that is biologically correct. It is more important that the children justify their classifications. As children grow older, then scientific **classifications** can be introduced.

classifications—according to Piaget, the child's ability to arrange similar and dissimilar objects into complex hierarchies.

eclectic—describing an approach in which various desirable features from different theories or methods are selected; drawing elements from different sources.

Schools and teachers who believe traditional education has proved its merits over the years, parents who want traditional teacher-planned and directed learning activities and curriculum, educators who feel their group of young children is far from mainstream and require specific experiences before first grade, and centers offering unique or **eclectic** (combined) educational approaches are faced with a dilemma. Their center's or school's curriculum is not based only on child interests.

This text includes a section on student teacher–written activity plans to aid students whose training program mandates this requirement. We believe that in trying to expand already noted child or group interest, written lesson planning, skill, and practice are useful and necessary. Also, we think most teachers often wish to attempt teaching something they believe educationally sound and valuable because of some school or societal happening important to children's growth.

In general, it is easier at the prekindergarten level, kindergarten, and lower primary grades to teach with **learning center** activities. Most states limit the number of children per teacher in early childhood centers to 10 to 15. Many private schools limit the number of children in kindergarten and primary classrooms to 20 to 25. In public school kindergarten and primary grade classrooms where the number of children can be as high as 30 to 35, DAP can be difficult, and the teacher-centered, more **authoritarian** approach often becomes necessary.

learning centers—also called activity or interest areas; where materials and equipment are combined around common activities (for instance, art, science, or language art).

authoritarian—requiring obedience and exercising control over others.

Wein (1995) describes the "contrasting reality" early childhood college supervisors can sometimes find when a training program encourages DAP and student teachers work in field placements:

> I could frequently see that carrying out this practice [DAP] was very difficult for teachers. Rather than providing situations where children could engage in child-initiated activity, play freely with friends, and try out absorbing activities in an atmosphere of exploration and a climate of social responsibility (as the ideology suggests), day care centers more frequently operated like miniature factories, with fixed time periods for activities and children moving through them as if they were in an assembly line.

developmentally appropriate instruction—educational practice that reflects the importance of meaningful and contextually relevant experiences for children that are based on a knowledge of attending children, their social and cultural context, and how children develop and learn.

She also discusses the location of power in contrasting **developmentally appropriate instruction** and **teacher dominion (directed) instruction**:

> In teacher dominion instruction, the location of power is in the adult. The child is viewed as a container to be filled with knowledge: the adult transmits knowledge through direct instruction. . . .
>
> In developmental appropriateness, the location of power alternates between adult and children, with power shared. Both adults and children are believed to be active agents who seek out and construct knowledge through active interaction with others.

teacher dominion (directed) instruction—educational practice that is characterized by teacher-dominated lessons or activities that the teacher decides are necessary for child growth or learning, as opposed to child discovery experiences or methods.

One definition of DAP is that it provides "learning activities suitable for a child's age, stage of development, and interests," and is appropriate for the group's age as a whole (Seefeldt & Barbour, 1998). Another consideration in defining the term is that the "curriculum is designed to develop children's knowledge in all developmental areas—physical, social, emotional, and intellectual—and to help children learn how to learn—to establish a foundation for life-long learning" (Bredekamp & Copple, 1997).

OTHER CURRICULUM APPROACHES

Programs may plan activities based on an **emergent model**, with activities developed out of child, parent, teacher, and community interests and focuses. One activity may meld into a logical sequence of others. It can be described as a teacher weaving a web of interconnected activities to follow children's emerging queries for further information, solutions, or skills. The emergent curriculum model is sometimes connected or associated in early childhood literature with the terms child-centered and reflective (Curtis & Carter, 1996), responsive, and child-initiated (Edwards, Gandini, & Forman, 1993), project approach (Helm & Katz, 2001) (Katz & Chard, 1993), and creative curriculum (Dodge & Colker, 1992).

emergent model—a program of instruction, based on child, parent, teacher, or community interests or concerns, in which there is a logical sequence of study using interconnected activities and experiences.

A teacher's (staff's) ability to listen continuously, observe children's chosen course of study, gain insights, and transfer these into daily activities and needed classroom media or materials is viewed as crucial. Behind-the-scenes staff collaboration and identification of ways to enrich, extend, and promote children's discovery or experience and also assess or document child growth, makes using this curriculum model a professionally challenging and time-consuming task.

Advocates mention the possible "staleness" and the teacher-centered nature of traditionally preplanned and prepackaged curriculums. They feel these may squelch child curiosity, initiative, and enthusiasm for learning.

The Reggio Emilia model, an emergent curriculum model, has captured the attention of a sizable group of early childhood educators.

Therefore, many of the well-documented aspects of Reggio Emilia programs appeal to American educators, including:

- the aesthetic, artistic child art
- in-depth child project work
- skilled teachers dedicated to observing, guiding, collaborating, and supporting children's quests for knowledge
- documentation of child progress
- parent involvement
- community support
- dedication to the value and worth of each child

Rinaldi (2001) describes Reggio Emila as a combination of social services and education: a kind of education that focuses on the child in relationship to the family, the teacher, other children, and the broader cultural context of the society. She states one of the fundamental points of the Reggio philosophy is an image of the child who experiences the world, who feels a part of the world from birth; a child who is full of curiosities, full of desire to live; a child who is full of desire and ability to communicate from the start of his life; a child who is fully able to create maps for his personal, social, cognitive, affective, and symbolic orientation. School environments following the Italian model should offer a sense of security that comes from feelings of acceptance and welcome (Rinaldi, 2001).

Curriculum emerges as the teacher, who acts as a participant-observer, closely monitors children's ideas and interests and then shapes what the teacher thinks will contribute to children's growth (Gandini & Goldhaber, 2001). Documentation of children's activities and learning furthers a teacher's understanding of the concepts children are building, the theories they are constructing, and the questions they are posing (Gandini & Goldhaber, 2001) (see Figure 5–3).

As Montessori has captured and held many early childhood teachers' attention, Reggio Emilia also seems to have generated enthusiasm, and may become a special unique segment or widely imitated model of early education in the United States.

A skill-based model suits the philosophy of other early childhood curriculum designers. Activity planning starts with the identification of specific physical, social, or intellectual knowledge, or goals or objectives. Activities focus on a planned attempt to help children attain expected behavior or action through teacher co-exploration, guidance, or instruction.

skill-based model—refers to a curriculum model that identifies specific physical, social, or intellectual knowledge, skills, goals, or objectives, and then plans learning activities that promote the attainment of expected child behavior, information, or action.

balanced curriculum—a curriculum that takes into consideration and reflects a broad spectrum of cognitive, physical, socioemotional, linguistic, and creative development opportunities for young children. It attempts to neither slight nor sacrifice one developmental area for another.

Balanced and Integrated Program Planning

A balanced curriculum approach to program planning assures all possible child growth areas are fully promoted. Cognitive, physical, social-emotional, linguistic, and creative development opportunities are included, and individual areas are not slighted or sacrificed but given appropriate program-planning attention. Advocates believe demands to increase program planning to enhance children's intellectual abilities should not crowd out other planning areas. Balance is also planned in

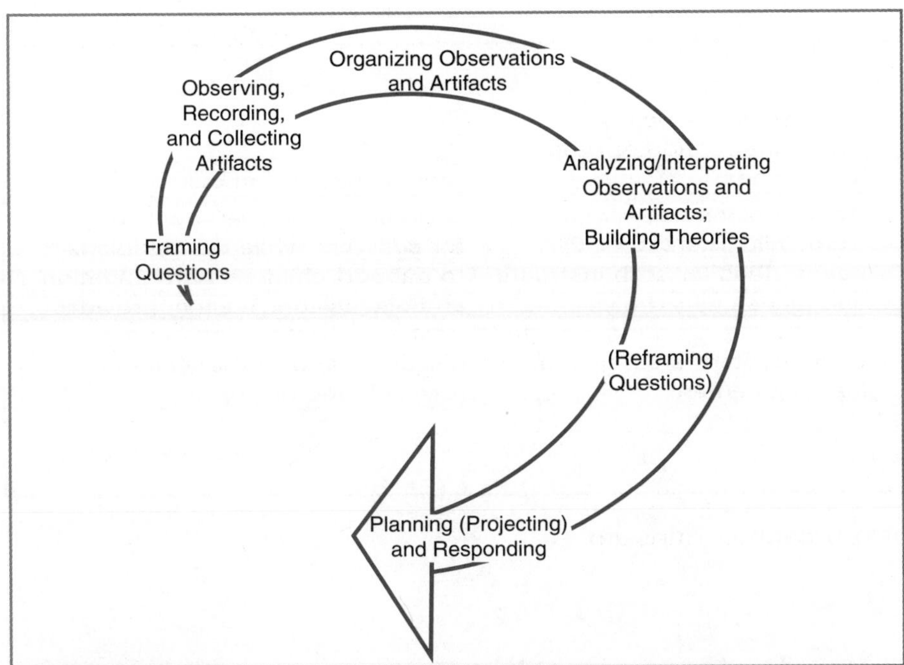

Figure 5-3 The documentation process as a cycle of inquiry. Reprinted by permission of the publisher from Gandini, L., & Goldhaber, J. (Eds.). *The Italian Approach to Infant/Toddler Care,* (New York: Teachers College Press, ©2001 by Teachers College, Columbia University. All rights reserved.) p. 136.

small and large motor skill activities, active and quiet offerings, individual and group experiences, child-initiated and adult-led activities, indoor and outdoor experiences, and approaches to learning using different learning modalities such as linguistic, kinesthetic, visual, auditory, and spatial experiences.

An integrated curriculum's goal is to create a planned program that focuses on more than one ability, developmental skill, or subject matter area at the same time or in the same activity. Recognition is given to the idea that development in cognitive, physical, social-emotional, linguistic, and creative abilities can be interconnected and integrated in both planned and spontaneous activities. An integrated learning approach is believed to aid children's problem-solving skills and their ability to see relationships between a variety of ideas and events.

integrated curriculum—a curriculum in which concurrent learning is possible by focusing on more than one ability, developmental skill, or subject matter area at the same time in the same activity. It is believed to promote children's problem solving and aid the children's ability to see relationships among a variety of ideas or events.

A theme or project organization of planned activities can include and promote both a balanced and integrated approach to child discoveries and learnings.

A Curriculum Continuum

Educators tend to envision curriculum approaches and practice along a continuum between child-centered or child-based to traditional teacher-decided ones (see Figure 5–4). An instructional approach not mentioned so far in this discussion but popular with many early childhood teachers is a discovery center-based curriculum. Classroom areas (centers), table tops, and other areas are set up daily or weekly for children to choose to explore and consequently discover concepts and experience skill growth. The practice of skills and the extension of understanding is also promoted.

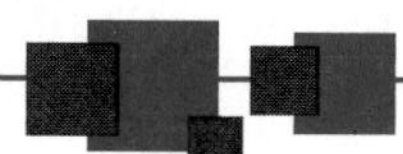

Teacher Controlled Curriculum	Instruction (including theme instruction or other approaches)	Child-Initiated Curriculum
Activity plans primarily grow out of teacher decisions concerning the appropriate content of activities based on the teacher's idea of children's educational, social, and physical needs and interests.	Activity plans usually grow from child interests and needs. Teacher both instructs and plans child-choice opportunities around a central topic, content area, theme, or learning center.	Children follow their own search for answers while teacher plans to support children's investigation and discussion. Teacher provides materials and settings to aid discovery and further child research and discussion.

Figure 5–4 Instructional approach continuum

Many states, like Texas, have developed their own set of prekindergarten curriculum guidelines to help Texas educators identify curriculum content. These guides describe specific goals for prekindergarten children. Use is voluntary and programs can adopt, add, or amend sections depending on their particular circumstances. Texas guidelines can be viewed online. See the helpful Web sites section at the end of this chapter.

Teacher Attitudes and Beliefs

You will be trying to match your planned activities to what your child group and individual children can profit from physically, socially, and educationally. Lumsden (1998) urges teachers to realize that teacher decisions are based on assumptions of child potential and have a tangible effect on child achievement. Children tend to internalize the beliefs teachers have about their ability, and they generally rise or fall to the level of expectation of their teachers.

Effective teachers can be described as planning activities that exhibit both high and appropriate expectations of child performance for all children. Studies of teacher behaviors tend to confirm that teachers engage in affirming nonverbal behaviors such as smiling, leaning toward, and making eye contact with students more frequently when they believe they are dealing with high-ability students.

Treating children in ways that imply children share the teacher's enthusiasm for "wanting to know" and "wanting to find out" is more than an admirable teaching skill. Lumsden (1998) points out that to the extent that one treats young children as if they are eager learners, they will be more likely to become eager learners.

ACTIVITY RESOURCES

Files, resource books, and activity ideas you collected during training will now come in handy such as research books that describe child activity ideas. You will have to discern whether the ideas fit your group. Teachers' and children's magazines often have timely seasonal activity planning ideas.

Draw on your own creative abilities. All too often, student teachers feel that tried-and-true ideas are superior to what they invent. The new and novel activities you create will add sparkle and uniqueness to your teaching. Do not be afraid to draw from and improve a good idea or change successful activities your children have already enjoyed. Some classroom activities are designed because of an overabundance of scrap or donated material. Take another look at materials in storage that are not receiving much attention or have been forgotten. Perhaps these can be reintroduced in a clever, new way.

CURRICULUM

Most prekindergarten curriculums include arts and crafts, music and movement, language, science, large and small motor skill development, cooking and nutrition activities, numbers and measurement, perceptual motor activities, health and safety activities, social learnings, multicultural awareness activities, and plant and animal study. Primary classrooms often follow district-approved guidelines.

Areas of study with different degrees of acceptance include anti-bias; conflict resolution; economics and consumer awareness; ecology and energy study; moral and ethical values; the study of changing sex role responsibilities; the study of changing family patterns; introduction to photography; introduction to computers; tolerance, nonviolence and peaceful solution training; and structured games. These may or may not be integrated and combined in a single planned activity, but usually areas overlap. Gardening, for instance, may involve counting plants, small motor skills, science, and language.

Academic programming at prekindergarten and kindergarten levels is programming that seems pushed down from above and is of great concern to the field of early childhood education. This type of programming usually requires young children to sit passively for long periods of listening or requires learning by rote memorization, and is consequently inappropriate. Research studies have confirmed early childhood educator's long-held belief concerning more stress and anxiety being evident in children in didactic environments rather than child-initiated ones (Dunn & Kontos, 1998). Marcon (1999) suggests formal academics are less effective with boys than girls during early years. Brent (1996) believes it also creates long-term negative effects in later schooling. Children's cognitive development, creativity, language development, and views of themselves as cognitive learners were also enhanced when classrooms were described as child-initiated rather than academically oriented.

Parental opposition to DAP can exist if parents prefer academically oriented programs. Dunn and Kontos (1998) note low-income parents whose children may profit most from developmentally appropriate practice may prefer other types of programs, particularly academic ones.

In planning activities, you will be striving to provide for active exploration integrated with each child's previous out-of-the-classroom experiences. You will attempt to match age-appropriate developmental needs and characteristics of the group with activities. Children will explore, manipulate, converse, move about, play, and freely talk about what is happening and what it means to them. Activities will provide for heterogeneous child abilities. NAEYC's Code of Ethical Conduct (1999) cites educators' ethical responsibilities and further guides curriculum development (see Figure 5–5).

Your placement classroom will already have planned activities and you may be asked to start planning and presenting activities.

1-1.2—To base program practices upon current knowledge in the field of child development and related disciplines and upon particular knowledge of each child.
1-1.5—To create and maintain safe and healthy settings that foster children's social, emotional, intellectual, and physical development and that respect their dignity and their contributions.

Figure 5-5 Ethical responsibility and curriculum development. Reprinted with permission from the National Association for the Education of Young Children. Washington, DC: Copyright 1998.

Your planned activities may attempt to meet the special needs of culturally and linguistically diverse students as well as those of other students with special needs. At prekindergarten level, you will plan for abundant child play.

Your previous early childhood education training courses have promoted your sensitivity to and awareness of cultural pluralism. Activities and interactions with children are designed to eliminate practices and materials that discriminate on the basis of race, sex, age, ethnic origin, language, religion, or handicapping conditions.

Oyemade and Washington (1989) point out the fact that some families have barriers to economic security, good health, good education, a nice home, and a safe neighborhood:

> Some families have more barriers to overcome to achieve these dreams than others. Some have to fight poverty, crowded housing, inadequate health care, crime, illiteracy, unemployment, and/or ethnic stereotypes as they struggle to achieve their dreams of self-sufficiency.

The social-emotional emphasis in activity planning has gained additional status. The social skills involve cooperation, assertion, responsibility, empathy, and self-control, and are viewed as keys both to acceptable behavior and academic achievement.

In developing curriculum, remember that each class is unique and that each child is an individual. What is or is not learned depends on classroom materials and interactions between adults and children and/or children and other children as they attempt to understand what is experienced and how it relates to them and others.

Look at your placement classroom in a different way. What do children seem to be learning? What have they already mastered? What line of learning could be extended by provision of materials or a planned activity? The answers to these questions may help your ability to customize your activities.

Assessment and Curriculum Planning

There are broad categories that constitute the major functions of assessment in the early years: assessment to inform instruction, assessment for diagnostic and selection purposes, and assessment for accountability and program evaluation. When assessment is used carefully and appropriately, it is used to adjust instruction and promote educational benefits.

With increased state and federal legislation affecting the early childhood years, there appears to be more pressure on educators to use standardized tests.

The issue of using standardized testing is a controversial subject. Advocates believe this type of assessment identifies atypical developmental patterns, determines whether children are reaching program goals, and makes instructional programs accountable.

Others with opposing views such as Kohn (2001) suggest young children are rarely able to communicate their understanding when standardized assessments are used. He points out tests often create stress. Wesson (2001) notes limited English speaking children invariably score lower in language fluency areas when testing is conducted in English. Most educators acknowledge the "younger the child, the more likely they are to be incorrectly labeled."

In early childhood, strategies other than standardized testing are often preferred, professionally accepted, and widely used. These include observation, child portfolio development, and the documentation of children's accomplishments. These approaches can allow instructional planners to tailor curriculum to individual children's needs and do so without labeling children unfairly.

Gable (2002) recognizes child assessment is a continual teacher task.

> A teacher's ability to continuously gather information about children and to transfer these insights to routine interactions and weekly planning is critical to healthy relationships.

Meisels and Jewkes (2001) offer a position statement on testing endorsed by many early childhood educators:

> Despite the lack of agreement about how to define readiness, tests often are used to decide whether a child is "ready" or not. Many problems are associated with such tests. To begin with, one must consider the appropriateness of formal testing for young children under any conditions. Testing situations may produce anxiety, especially if children do not understand what is occurring, and can simply be so confusing that some children will be unable to perform optimally. In particular, on-demand, time tests are weak indicators of a child's overall ability because they do not account for normal developmental variations. A better solution is continuous, observational curriculum-embedded assessment that enhances teachers' instruction while improving children's learning.

New State Standards for Public School Kindergarten. Kindergarten teachers in many states are under pressure to prepare children for testing. Children's test scores have been used to rank schools, judge individual teacher performance, and reward or withhold funding. Educators fear developmentally appropriate practices and classes offering hands-on flexible curriculums are being sacrificed or compromised for "drill and skill" approaches and structured academic content (Harrington-Lueker, 2000).

Spotting reading readiness and reading problems early is being given top priority. A number of school districts have adopted kindergarten workbooks that require kindergartners to complete "tear out" page exercises. Child-centered practices are in conflict with school district policy that mandates showing students' progress toward specific goals. In North Carolina, a few public schools have initiated pre-K programs for at-risk four-year-olds. These schools have discovered that 20 percent of attending kindergartners entered school unprepared to learn. These new programs have attempted to combine developmentally appropriate practice with a focus on language and literacy. Pre-K children participated in four literacy circles each lasting between 10 and 30 minutes each day (Harrington-Lueker, 2000).

Early childhood educators intent on preparing children to meet the challenges of kindergarten realize social skill is a critical factor in child success. Gamel-McCormick (2000) surveyed kindergarten teachers regarding what they felt were the most important skills entering kindergartners could possess and found teachers' top skill choices were exhibits self control, interacts cooperatively, communicates needs and preferences, cares for own bathroom needs, and attends to peer or adult talking. Kindergarten teachers in this study were also asked for a written definition of readiness. Gamel-McCormick summarized their "readiness definitions" as follows:

- Except for physical skills, most teachers included components of all domains in their definitions.
- Almost all definitions addressed social and behavioral skills, and skills that would allow students to be independent.
- A significant minority of teachers included pre-academic and academic skills in their definitions.
- For most teachers, the definitions focused on children's abilities to interact with peers and adults.

Being Aware

On any given day, certain classroom events and happenings evolve naturally as children react to the weather, the setting, the choices set out, activities, people encountered, and so on. The dynamics and personalities present influence children. Student teachers need to be curious, watchful, and ready to support child discoveries rather than closely focus on planned, teacher-directed efforts.

Some early childhood programs are "mapping" their communities for possible child learning opportunities. Figure 5–6 cites examples of sources of community-based natural learning opportunities.

GOAL STATEMENTS

In the first chapter, you were asked to secure and read your center's handbook. Handbooks include goal statements or curriculum objectives. Study these if available.

Goal statements or curriculum guidelines can be general or specific. They often are written by a group of people including staff, administrators, parents, community representatives, and at times, accrediting or licensing personnel. The proposed outcomes of a center's planned instruction are stated, and goal statements may spell out not only children's fields of study but also cultivation of children's talents and dispositions such as perseverance in tasks, responsibility, self-control, self-esteem, empathy, honesty, problem-solving, cooperation, inventiveness, kindness, friendliness, social connectedness, creativity, and so on. A new area of early childhood study, technology awareness and skill, may also be included.

The procedures to assess how well center instruction has attained its goals may also be included along with timelines.

Daily Schedules

Daily time schedules alert teachers to that day's planned happenings. Children's needs dictate what takes place. Food, rest, and toileting times are inserted in time slots. Active periods alternate with quiet ones. Group times include announcements of that day's particular events and activities, and recognize and welcome each child's presence.

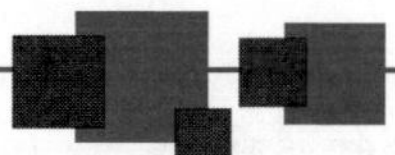

Natural Land and Water Features.

Mountains	Desert Areas	Rivers
Forests	Lakes, Ponds, and Other Water Bodies	Oceans
Farmland		Sand Areas

Outdoor Activities

Swimming	Farming	Jogging
Boating	Hiking	Walking
Biking	Riding	Skiing
Camping	Horseback Riding	Local Walks and Races
Fishing	Skating	Kite Flying
Gardening		

Parks and Recreational Activities—Federal, State, County, City, and Community Attractions and Amusement Facilities

Public and Commercial Enterprises	Monuments	Zoos
	Planetariums	Historical Sites
Aquariums	Museums	Cultural Happenings
Bird Sanctuaries	Science Centers	Plays, Ballets, and Concerts
Displays	Trains	

Club and Organization Sponsored Events, Community and City Celebrations Learning and Educational Activities

Art Classes	Dance Classes	Nature Center Activities
Book Store Story Hours	Drama Classes	Parent Education Classes
Bookmobile	Enrichment Classes	Petting Zoos
Ceramics Classes	Gymnastics/Tumbling	Puppet Shows
Children's Museum Activities	Library Story Times, Movies, and Activities	Religious Education
		Science Center Activities
Creative Movement Classes	Magic Shows	Storytellers
	Music Classes	

Sports Activities

Baseball/T-Ball	Ice Skating/Sledding	Softball
Basketball	Karate	Swimming
Bowling	Roller Skating	Tennis
Football	Soccer	Track and Field
Golf/Miniature Golf		

Note: Each geographic location is unique. You may find your locale offers opportunities not listed above. This figure does not attempt to list all possibilities.

Figure 5-6 Community learning opportunities

With a schedule, teachers and children know what comes next. Teachers plan in advance for necessary room settings, materials, equipment, furniture, and staffing needs. Each center and school decides on the flexibility of its daily schedule, and most deviate often when the unexpected occurs and children can profit from a newly created activity. Schools are rarely slaves to schedules, but rather capitalize on unplanned learning opportunities or immediately revise a schedule when planned activities in some way fizzle or fail to capture interest.

Play and Learning

A commonly heard saying in early childhood literature, "Play is the work of the young child," should be coupled with "Play is learning." Children use play to translate experience to understanding. Teachers often see in the child's play the reenactment of behaviors the child has viewed in others. Behaviors that may be puzzling or significant in their lives are "tried on for size." They step inside the other person's shoes and seemingly gain insight through the reliving.

In children's random and investigative play, discoveries are made. Happenings are tested, retested, varied, and extended. Focus may be keen, and at times, they are eager to talk about what they understand and experience.

Peers often function as tutors or providers of information. Adults observe, supply, talk about, encourage, and appreciate without interfering except when safety is a factor. Adults do ask provocative questions and give suggestions but guard against inflicting their own directions or intentions concerning the child's choice of play.

All of the following may be part of play episodes:

- exploring
- experimenting
- comparing
- ordering
- classifying
- imitating
- verbalizing
- organizing
- discovering
- questioning
- creating
- problem-solving and other thinking skills

Reynolds and Jones (1997) use the term "master player" to describe the young child who plays well. They note that experiences and feelings represented in child's play involve "symbol making in order to know." They see master players as both master dramatists and master artist-builders, and note that children's play includes many forms, styles, and types of expressions. For a long while, educators have been concerned about young children who are unable to play or who play poorly. Play, a developmental task of preschool years, is accomplished when young children become "players" who are able to lose themselves spontaneously and enjoyably with and without peers.

Reynolds and Jones (1997) have also coined the term "response-ability" and defined it as a teaching skill possessed when an adult notices and responds to an initiative a child shows in play. They point out:

> Most teachers will admit that the times when children are asked to accommodate to schedules, and routines, and to teacher's agendas, are not the times of the day when children thrive. Children are at their best when creating their own reality.

Teachers are searching for ways to support and sustain children's self-selected and/or self-initiated play themes. Besides watching closely for safety, the teacher considers what teacher interventions might support a child's needs, interests, inquiry, or discovery, and at the same time, encourage classroom goals such as nonviolence, negotiation, cooperation, and individual rights. It is not an easy job. Many times, teacher "response-ability" involves helping a child's entry into an existing play group, helping a group get along by making concessions, starting negotiations, or promoting other social play skills. Helping children discover or creatively search for information is another common teacher undertaking.

Through closely watching child's play, future possible activity ideas may be identified. Reynolds and Jones (1997) advise the following:

> Except for imminence of the next transition in the schedule or for authentic threats to safety, the only reason for an adult to intervene in children's play is to sustain or enrich the play. Play that is in danger of breaking down through conflict or failure of good ideas needs an adult to mediate conflict resolution or to add a prop or an idea.

Planning for Play

You will most likely be asked to plan and set up varied play opportunities, including providing well-equipped play areas with abundant materials for props. The importance of child make-believe play is not overlooked in child-appropriate curriculums. At times, you will join child play with small groups and individual children and make-believe yourself, carefully avoiding directing, overpowering, or stifling child initiative and control. Most often, you will zip in and out, providing additional materials, redirecting damage or aggression, asking leading questions that might add depth while still being interested, enthusiastic, supportive, communicative, responsive, warm, and understanding. Not an easy teaching task!

HOW LANGUAGE INSTRUCTION FITS INTO ALL ACTIVITY PLANNING

In 2002, President George W. Bush announced his early-childhood education plan. It proposed teacher retraining to facilitate explicit early-reading instruction involving alphabet knowledge, letter sounds, early emergent writing experiences, and carefully designed group projects (Kantrowitz & Wingert, 2002). Early childhood educators have mixed feelings about how to incorporate literacy activities into diverse curriculums and developmentally appropriate practice. Some educators fear children will be pushed into early reading exercises. Others fear not enough will be done for preschoolers living in poverty, those just learning English, and those with special needs.

The Bush administration understands the critical and important role care providers and early childhood educators play in ensuring that young children enter school equipped with the necessary literacy, cognitive, social, and emotional foundations that they will need for success.

One of the goals of the administration's initiative *Ready to Read, Ready to Learn* focuses on preparing all young children to learn to read with ease when formal reading instruction begins (Ohl, 2002). Research undertaken after 2002 questions the meager research data underpinning this federal early literacy effort (Coles, 2004).

Federal funds are helping all states develop state guidelines that identify language and literacy criteria and prereading skills, and then align these with K-12 standards. States are urged to recognize that this does not mean simply pushing kindergarten and first grade instruction, methods, and materials to preschool level.

Early childhood educators who work with infants and toddlers understand early language development involves their promotion of infants' language knowledge and oral use, and that quality programs offer activities focusing on language sounds and the tempo and rhythm of words and phrases. As Ohl (2002) points out:

> The better babies are at distinguishing the building blocks of speech at six months of age, the better they will be at other more complex language skills at two and three years of age, and the easier it will be for them at four and five to grasp the idea of how sounds link to letters.

Prekindergartners' teachers will continue to plan, present, and promote a developmentally appropriate language arts curriculum including listening, speaking, printing, and reading components. They attempt to ensure a love of books by reading aloud a wide range of quality literature using techniques that make the experience pleasurable to each child. Classrooms that are conversational and print-rich with alphabet activities, child dictation, and word labels are now commonplace. A new inclusion of activities involving oral letter sounds is occurring promoted by current research. The challenge for early childhood educators is how to make these activities interesting, engaging, interactive, fun, and useful to preschoolers.

Gundling (2002) believes:

> A high-quality program includes effective early literacy teaching practices and reflects knowledge of the continuum of children's early development in reading and writing.
>
> and
>
> Programs should include research-based effective practices, well-planned activities, and use of curricula. Well-designed, ongoing classroom-based assessment of children's developing language and literacy skills can help teachers learn more about how to build success.

Further suggestions developed to help young children become successful readers and writers urge teachers to:

- Support oral language and vocabulary development
- Expand children's background knowledge
- Promote phonemic awareness
- Build beginning knowledge of letters, letter sounds, and words
- Build supportive relationships within social interactions
- Give attention to all aspects of children's development including cognitive, language, social-emotional, and physical growth areas
- Focus on program quality

At the elementary school level, unique programs to increase reading and literacy skills are appearing. California's Scott Lane Elementary School made a public promise to beginning kindergartners' parents by stating that their children would read fluently by the end of second grade (*San Jose Mercury News*, 2000). Forty percent of Scott Lane's enrolled children are from immigrant families whose home language is not English.

Gable (2002) reminds teachers of young children to be aware of the importance of teacher-child relationships if they wish to attain quality instruction:

> When children experience the security of supportive teacher-child relationships, they know that their basic needs will be met; are confident about their thoughts, feelings, and ideas; and have a foundation from which to explore and develop their own relationships with other children.

No matter what the educational level, most of us have experienced at one point in our educational career that kind of school practice. In the current push to ensure children's emerging communicative skill, planners should consider the foundations necessary for quality instruction: the climate in the classroom.

If one examines America's schooling historically, they might find it was not the general rule to educate students to think and read critically, to express themselves clearly and persuasively, and to solve complex problems in science and mathematics (National Research Council, 2000). Today, these literacy skills are necessary to participate successfully in contemporary life pursuits.

Language learning is a natural part of young children's play and exploration. Listening, speaking, and becoming aware of print and books happens throughout a preschool day. Teachers are urged to help young children discover the functional use of language and the integrated nature of the language arts in meaningful settings.

Language will be involved with whatever you plan for young children. Teaching strategies can facilitate emerging literacy, both functional and literary.

An early childhood program involves continual child interactions with pleasurable, quality picture books read by enthusiastic adults skilled in discussing and expanding child interest and enjoyment. With familiarity and repetition and access to a book collection, children explore, notice book features, start to pretend to read, join in the reading, predict outcomes, look for picture clues, feel at home with print, read to themselves, and usually glide naturally into reading on their own. This sounds easy but takes time and planned actions on the adult's part. Many homes offer this type of literary background to young children and couple book reading with pencil (crayon) and paper home activities. These homes are usually verbal environments where conversations about joint parent-child happenings abound. All preschoolers do not experience this backdrop for literacy development. Some have experienced a similar home environment in a language other than English and can be very literate in that language and culture. English literacy development at school is usually designed along the same lines described in the enriching homes above.

Other children have arrived at school with limited or spotty experiences with books, print, or conversationally interested adults. The center or school attempts to supply a rich language and literature program that not only introduces picture books but also print and its functional use, nursery rhymes, classic word and movement activities (finger and body play), music with words, listening experiences and games, poetry, puppetry, storytelling, mechanical language aids (computers, books with tapes, language master, projectors, among others), and additional language activities, all offered with supportive, skilled, word-providing teachers. Most schools believe language pervades all school happenings and take clues from child preferences, interests, and pursuits in developing their curriculum. Teachers become subtle opportunists who engage in daily conversations, question and provide suggestions, and provide materials and environments that lead to child discovery and further exploration and activity (see Figure 5–7).

Instructing Non-English-Speaking Children

Projections based on mid-1990s census figures predict that by the year 2025, more than half of the children enrolled in U.S. schools will be members of minority

Figure 5–7 Staff members, consultants, parents, and community representatives all may be involved in program planning and development.

groups, not of European American origin (U.S. Bureau of the Census, 1995). The new immigrants arriving are expected to primarily be from Asia and Latin America.

Early childhood teachers, regardless of their preparation or background, will have the task of helping children learn English and make it a successful experience (Genishi, 2002).

Plutro (2000) describes Head Start's multilingual and multicultural programming:

> Four elements of Head Start's overall philosophy are particularly relevant to the task of developing and implementing multilingual and multicultural programming: building trusting relationships, being sensitive to cultural preferences of families, building bridges between cultures for both children and adults, and acknowledging that staff and parents are in a true partnership.

She notes a study of the diversity of Head Start families found that enrolled families spoke more than 150 languages and dialects. In nearly 20 percent of children's homes, a language other than English was spoken, the most common being Spanish, followed by Chinese, Hmong, and Vietnamese.

There are two opposing positions concerning a teacher's need to be fluent in a child's home language to be able to plan an effective curriculum for a particular child. Kuster (1994) advocates that teachers become fluent in the attending children's language and knowledgeable about their culture. Others cite what has been traditional and historic in education in the United States: a standard English-speaking teacher using standard English. Each early childhood program will plan instruction based on its own opinion.

Types of Activities

Planned activities can promote child growth through child/teacher discussion and interaction. Important factors that need consideration in the planning and preparation of any activity are:

- Child safety
- The goal or objective of the activity
- Appropriateness to children's ages, experiences, and skill levels

- Setting environment and its comfort, lighting, and sound level
- Number of children and adults
- Duration and time of day
- Materials, furnishings, objects to be used
- Expense
- Cleanup provisions
- Transition to next activity
- Nonsexist and nonracist language; appropriate values

It is generally agreed that activities for young children should:

- Capture and hold their attention
- Provide opportunities for active involvement with minimal time spent waiting
- Provide firsthand sensory experiences and explanations when necessary
- Allow for discovery and pursuit of interests
- Give children a sense of confidence in themselves and their learning competence
- Be connected to past experiences so they can bridge the gap between what they already know and the new experience. However, activities should not be too closely related so as to slow down the child's learning due to boredom. Also, activities should not stretch beyond the child's capacity for learning; this could result in feelings of frustration.
- Add to the quality of their lives
- Be of a reasonable duration
- Fit into quiet and active periods, and be planned according to noisy or quiet locations
- Provide for individual differences
- Have clearly stated directions and expectations if necessary
- Be flexible enough to provide for unexpected child interests
- Be intellectually stimulating

Multicultural and Anti-Bias Curriculum

In student teaching classes, the student teachers may well represent a wide spectrum of different, diverse values and cultural outlooks, or a relatively narrow, limited perspective. Child classrooms are increasingly multicultural in most parts of the United States whereas some remain only barely ethnically and culturally diverse. In both cases, your assumptions about adults and enrolled children will need careful examination as you strive to embrace, appreciate, and respect cultural and ethnic similarities and differences. Offering a child a curriculum that ensures dignity to diverse groups and individuals will be a challenging teaching task and requires a conscious effort.

Delpit (1995) suggests teachers appreciate the "wonders of the cultures" represented in their classrooms.

> If we are to successfully educate all of our children, we must work to remove the blinders built of stereotypes, monocultural instructional methodologies, ignorance, social distance, biased research, and racism. We must work to destroy those blinders so that it is possible to really see, to really know the students we must

> teach. Yes, if we are to be successful at educating diverse children, we must accomplish the Herculean feat of developing this clear-sightedness, for in the words of a wonderful Native Alaskan educator: "In order to teach you, I must know you." I pray for all of us the strength to teach our children what they must learn, and the humility and wisdom to learn from them so that we might better teach.

You will want to make sure appropriate anti-bias activities and diverse visual model representation are planned for child activities. An anti-bias curriculum is described as follows:

> Anti-bias curriculum incorporates the positive intent of multicultural curriculum and uses some similar activities, while seeking to avoid the danger of a tourist approach. At the same time, anti-bias curriculum provides a more inclusive education: (a) it addresses more than cultural diversity by including gender and differences in physical abilities; (b) it is based on children's development tasks as they construct identity and attitudes; and (c) it directly addresses the impact of stereotyping, bias, and discriminatory behavior in young children's development and interactions (Derman-Sparks and A.B.C. Task Force, 1989, 1998).

Written Activity (Lesson) Plans

Activity plans are useful devices that encourage student teachers to think thoroughly through the different parts of their planned activities. They help beginning teachers foresee possible problems and find solutions. With adequate preparation through written planning, the student teacher can approach each planned activity with a degree of confidence and security. Cooperating teachers and supervisors often contribute ideas on the student's written plans or consult with the student, making plans a team effort. Written plans are a starting point from which actual activity flows, depending on the children's reception and feedback. Monitoring the children's interest is a teaching task (see Figure 5–8), and will often re-

Figure 5–8 Monitoring children's interest is one of the teacher's tasks.

sult in improvising and revising the activities to suit their needs. Written **lesson plans** proceed one step farther and isolate a teacher's or student teacher's plan for what will happen during a specific time block and in a specific location.

A weekly classroom plan (or **schedule**) is usually developed to pinpoint specially planned activities that will take place in different learning centers or room areas. The plan includes which classroom adult has responsibility for preparation, providing necessary materials and equipment, supervision, and cleanup.

The activity plan guide in Figure 5–9 is one of many possible forms that can be used by student teachers. It is appropriate for most, but not all, planned

lesson plans—the working documents from which the daily program is run, specifying directions for activities.

schedule—a planned series of happenings for a specific time period, to accommodate needs and goals.

1. Activity title ______
2. Curriculum area ______
3. Materials needed ______
4. Location and setup of activity ______
5. Number of children and adults ______
6. Preparation ______
7. Specific behavioral objective ______
8. Developmental skills necessary for success ______
9. Getting started ______
10. Procedure (step by step) ______
11. Discussion (key concepts, attitudes, facts, skills, vocabulary, etc.) ______
12. Apply (or additional practice of skill or learning) ______
13. Cleanup ______
14. Terminating statement ______
15. Transition ______
16. Evaluation: activity, teacher, child ______

Figure 5–9 Activity plan guide

activities. Story times, fingerplays, flannel-board stories, songs, and short-duration activities usually are not written in activity plan form. Activity plan titles are descriptive, such as Sink and Float, Making Farmers' Cheese, or Tie Dyeing. They quickly clarify the subject of the planned experience.

Filling in the curriculum area space sometimes leads to indecision. Many early childhood activities are hard to categorize. Subjects seem to fall into more than one area. Use your own judgment and designation; it is your plan!

Identification of materials, supplies, and tools comes next. Some activities require visual aids and equipment for teachers as well as those materials used by children. Make sure you, as the student teacher, know how to use visual aids and operate the equipment. Estimating exact amounts of necessary materials helps calculate expenses and aids preparation. You will simply count out the desired quantities. Student teachers generally know what classroom supplies are available to them and what they will have to supply themselves.

The location of a planned activity has much to do with its success. The following questions can help decide the best location.

- What amount of space will children need?
- What room or outdoor features (for example, windows, water, flat floor, storage or drying areas, rug, lighting, grass, shade) are necessary?
- Will electrical outlets be necessary?
- Will noise or traffic from adjacent areas cause interference?
- Will one adult be able to supervise the location?

Figure 5–10 The trays used in this activity set-up invite exploration and delineate child space.

Self-help and child participation in cleanup, if necessary, need consideration. Cleanup might involve a sorting game with teacher and children working together, or a teacher might provide containers strategically placed for small item storage or throw away. Adjacent soapy water and sponges help take care of messes. Cleanup often will not proceed smoothly if a student teacher does not prepare beforehand. Seeing cleanup as an integral part of the ending process of a planned activity is the key. Activities that actively engage children and invite exploration suit young children's needs. Random setups can lead to confusion and conflict over work space and supply use. A good setup helps a child work without help, and promotes proper respect for classroom supplies and equipment and consideration for the work of others (see Figure 5–9). Each setup reflects a teacher's goals and philosophy of how children best learn.

Figure 5–11 This student teacher of toddlers has prepared for easy clean-up and is deciding on the best arrangement of materials to promote self-help.

Student teachers usually begin planning for small groups and then tackle larger groups and the total-room activity plans. A number of fascinating early childhood activities call for close adult supervision and can happen safely or successfully only with a few children at a time. Instant replays or ongoing activities may be necessary to accommodate all interested children. Waiting lists are useful in these cases, and children quickly realize they will be called when it is their turn. The number of children on activity plan forms could read, "Two groups of four children," for example.

Preparation sections on lesson plans alert the student teacher to tasks to be completed prior to actual presentation. This could include making a number of individual portions of paste, moving furniture, mixing paint, making a recipe chart, or a number of other similar teacher activities. Preparation includes attention to features that minimize child waiting and decrease the need for help from the teacher (see Figures 5–10 and 5–11).

Writing Lesson Plans for Elementary Schools. There are several ways, each based on a different theoretical model, to approach a lesson plan.

One of the more popular models, and one based on behavioristic theory, is the six-step lesson plan, a direct instruction model. Popularized by Hunter (1984) and used in many elementary schools, the six-step plan consists of:

1. Review of previously learned material.
2. Statement of objectives for the lesson.
3. Presentation of new material.
4. Guided practice with corrective feedback.
5. Independent practice with corrective feedback.
6. Periodic review, with corrective feedback if necessary (Gunter, Estes, & Schwab, 1990).

As teachers of young children, however, the Hunter model is not necessarily the "developmentally appropriate" one. More applicable to our students is the cooperative learning model. Slavin (1987, 1988) has looked extensively at cooperative learning and has conducted research that indicates its efficacy. Some of the steps included in this model will look familiar. As in any lesson plan, a cooperative learning lesson begins with

> A statement of the "performance objective" (written in terms of observable behaviors such as, "Students will explore in cooperative learning groups a lesson on health and safety. As they participate in the activity, they will discover why cooperative learning groups are helpful. We will allow 30 minutes for group time.").

Step 1. Anticipatory set: A motivational question or statement, intended to pique student interest such as, "Wouldn't it be neat if someone else helped you with your homework?"

Step 2. Instruction: Generally, beginning with a follow-up question or statement to the "anticipatory set" one and intending to motivate further student curiosity, the instruction step involves listing any materials needed and the procedures to be followed.

Example (following from the above question):

Materials needed: Health texts and additional related reference materials from in-classroom library.

Motivation statement: "Today we are going to look at a way that you can help each other get ready for your health and safety test. I know you'd rather do this by yourselves . . . No? . . . Okay, Let's try this then . . ."

Procedures: A step-by-step look at what happens next. "Please do not move until I ask you to. The first thing I'm going to do is to put you into six groups with five people in each group. Each group will study one of the parts you need to know for our health test tomorrow. This way no one group has to do it all. How does this sound? Each group will report its findings to the class as a whole, and I'll write down all the important facts you'll need for the test on the board." (The student teacher arranges the groups heterogeneously with a leader being designated for each group. Other roles, such as recorder [appointed for his handwriting ability], researchers [usually more than one who look up in books, notes, encyclopedias, and so on, any material relating to the subject they are to present to their peers], may be designated by the student teacher or, in groups accustomed to the process of cooperative learning, chosen by the students in the group. The critical difference in cooperative learning as opposed to what has often been called a group project is that each student in the group has a clearly defined role; no one student has to feel responsible for doing all the work of the group to receive the approval of his peers or a group grade. In the example illustrated here, students would not be receiving a grade; however, it is possible that some reward would be given to the best group report by the rest of the students in the class. In another example, each member of the group might grade both herself and also each other member of the group. In this way, the student teacher is able then to arbitrate in cases of disagreement.)

Step 3. Guided practice: At this point, the student teacher circulates from group to group and checks to see that each group has the materials it needs and that each student in the group is working. She may have to intervene in a group having difficulty, praise a group working smoothly, assist a student researcher with an idea of how to obtain more information about the topic under study, and so on. In this example, each group studies one aspect of the material to be learned for the test rather than all of the material. When the groups report back to the class, notes on all important concepts will be written on the chalkboard and copied by each individual student for further study at home. (If the class has had practice in taking part in a jigsaw lesson, studying for the test could also be handled as a jigsaw.)

Step 4. Closure: As the time for the lesson draws to a close, the student teacher alerts the groups to the end of the group study period and the need to prepare for their reports to the class as a whole. If the reports are to be presented on the same day, as in this example they should be, the student teacher possibly needs to have the groups make their respective presentations after a recess. So closure might consist of the following reminder: "In 10 minutes it'll be time for recess. When we come back, we'll have our oral reports from each group. Recorders, make sure your notes are legible. Reporters, be sure to read the recorder's notes so you can ask for clarification on any words you're unsure about."

Step 5. Independent practice: After recess ends and the oral reports have been given, the student teacher will need to remind the class that they are responsible for information in the reports from each group. (The student teacher should carefully print all essential information on the board as the reports are presented and have the cooperating teacher circulate to make sure that each student copies them down.) At the end of the oral reports, the student teacher should then remind the class, "For homework tonight, I want you to study the notes you took during the group reports. Remember, we're going to have a test on the information tomorrow." Homework, in this example, is independent practice.

Step 6. The test on the following day.

(Thank you to Colleen Sequeira, student teacher at California State University, Hayward, for this third-grade lesson plan. Colleen's initial lesson plan might have used the format in Figure 5–12).

In our lesson plan above, the cooperative learning model is an example from the social learning theory and recognizes that children often learn best from one another, especially in some cultures.

Other models for lesson planning include concept attainment, concept development, synectics, and inquiry, among others. A student teacher should keep in mind that sometimes the purpose of a lesson will dictate what type of plan she will use. In many mathematics lessons, for example, the student teacher may want to use the social learning model as students frequently can better explain a process to a peer than can an adult. Paired learning teams are another variant of the social learning model. Inquiry lends itself well to science, especially when the student teacher wants his class to explore a scientific phenomenon.

For example, fall and why it is called fall might be introduced to first graders by a walk through the school grounds with each student having a paper bag to collect interesting objects they observe. After a return to the classroom, the student teacher might ask students to cover their desks with newspaper and place on the desk the items they have collected. Using brainstorming as a technique, the

Name: ______________________ Date: ________

School: ______________________ Grade: ________

Objectives: ______________________

____

Materials needed: ______________________

Teacher Activities	Student Activites	Time

Anticipatory set

1.

2.

3.

4.

5.

6.

7.

8.

9.

10. Use fewer steps or add more, if needed.

Independent Practice

Evaluation: ______________________

____

____

____

____

____

____

Figure 5–12 Lesson plan format

student teacher might then ask students to tell what they have collected. After writing and sketching each named item on the board, the student teacher could ask student pairs to try, in a five-minute period, to group or classify the listed objects. Then after listing (and drawing) examples of the classifications on the board, the student teacher might want to ask students what any two or more groups might have in common in an attempt to enable students to develop hierarchical categories, a difficult task for primary grade children. This sort of lesson models concept development as a part of the inquiry process. One typical answer in one first-grade class has been, "We found all these things on the ground." The conclusion that fall is named because items have fallen on the ground is fairly obvious. A follow-up art lesson involves the children making fall "sculptures" with their materials by inserting various pieces into a clay base.

LESSON PLAN GOALS AND OBJECTIVES

objectives—aims; specific interpretation of general goals, providing practical and directive tools for day-to-day program planning.

instructional objectives—aims or goals, usually set for an individual child, that describe in very specific and observable terms what the child is expected to master.

specific behavioral objectives—clearly describes observable behavior, the situation in which it will occur, and the exact outcome or the criteria of successful performance.

observable behavior—actions that can be seen rather than those that are inferred.

Planned and unplanned activities and experiences have some type of outcome. Written student teaching plans include a section where objectives are identified. This serves as the basis for planning and presentation and all other form sections.

Cooperating teachers and supervisors differ in requiring activity plans with specific behavioral or instructional objectives. Instructional objectives are more general in nature and may defy measurement. Examples of specific behavioral objectives (SBO) and instructional objectives (IO) follow:

SBO: When given four cubes of different colors (red, blue, green, and purple), the child will point to each color correctly on the first try when asked.

IO: The child will know four colors: red, blue, green, and purple.

SBO: When given a cut potato, paper, and three small trays of paint, the child will make at least one mark on the paper using a printing motion.

IO: The child will explore a printing process.

SBO: After seeing the teacher demonstrate cutting on a penciled line and being helped to hold scissors with the thumb and index finger, the child will cut apart a two-inch strip of pencil-lined paper in two out of five attempts.

IO: The child will learn how to cut on a line.

Note: Written specific behavioral objectives use verbs that clearly describe observable behavior (see Figure 5–13). They consist of three

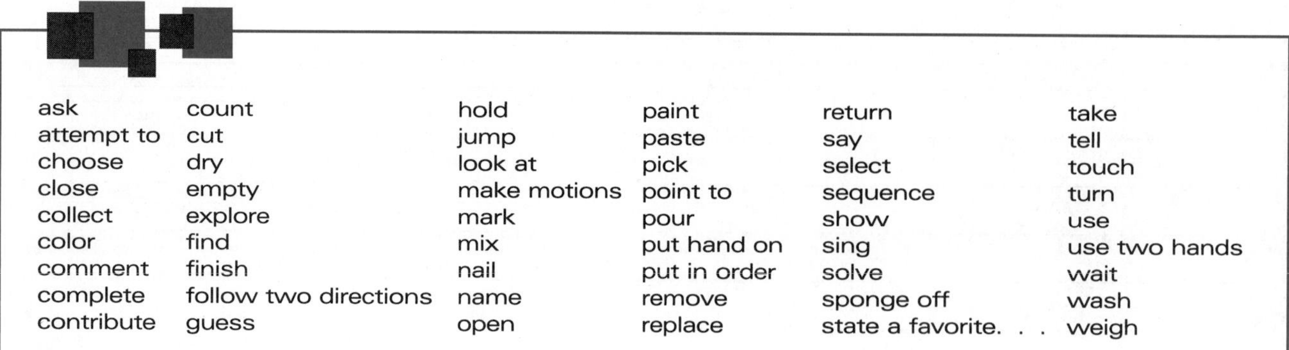

ask	count	hold	paint	return	take
attempt to	cut	jump	paste	say	tell
choose	dry	look at	pick	select	touch
close	empty	make motions	point to	sequence	turn
collect	explore	mark	pour	show	use
color	find	mix	put hand on	sing	use two hands
comment	finish	nail	put in order	solve	wait
complete	follow two directions	name	remove	sponge off	wash
contribute	guess	open	replace	state a favorite. . .	weigh

Figure 5–13 Verbs used in writing specific behavioral objectives

parts: (1) conditions and circumstances in which learning takes place; (2) the child's observable behavior; and (3) acceptable performance or criteria for success.

It is best for beginning teachers to accomplish one objective per activity, do it thoroughly and well, and keep the activity short and lively. Student teachers tend to plan activities involving multiple concepts or skills. Usually, none of these skills is accomplished because of the amount and diversity of learning. Objectives of any kind may or may not always be realized. Evaluation sections analyze whether the student teacher achieved what he set out to do. Centers with clearly defined objectives, combining their teaching team's efforts, have a greater chance of realizing their objectives.

DEVELOPMENTAL SKILLS

Each activity builds on another. A child's skill and knowledge expands through increased opportunity and experience. Knowing the children's developmental skills makes student teachers aware of their capacities and levels. The ability to sit and focus for a period of minutes can be the requirements in a planned preschool activity, and having the ability to pick up small objects can be part of another. Planning beyond children's capacities may occur because of the student teacher's eagerness to enrich the children's lives and try out different ideas. A close look at the children's achievements and abilities will help the student teacher plan activities that are successful for both the children and the student teacher. Levin and Long (1981) comment on prerequisite skills in relation to new learning.

> Each new learning task requires some cognitive prerequisites on the part of the student. These prerequisites help students relate new ideas, skills, or procedures to what they already know, and better understand the instruction.

Planning for Skill Attainment

Petersen (1996) points out some activity planning involves skill-focused activities. She states:

> There are certain skills that every teacher wants children to master before they leave the program. These are skills agreed on in the early childhood field as appropriate to the development, limitations, and capabilities of children with whom the teacher is working. They are probably skills that the early childhood program and the children's parents believe are important for teachers to teach. These skill-focused activities should consistently appear in daily lesson plans.

Skills can be divided into intellectual, social-emotional, and motor skills, and some skills seem to overlap and fit more than one category. Intellectual skills are skills such as memory, problem-solving, sorting, ordering, categorizing, predicting, hypothesizing, and so on. Motor skills may deal with eye-hand coordination, balance, and strength in both small and large body muscles. There is an individual timetable and a natural sequence in the appearance of children's motor skills. Muscle systems develop and become controllable with use, practice, proper nutrition, and, at times, adult guidance. Take riding a tricycle as an example. It is a definite motor skill that many but not all children master during preschool years depending on their life circumstances and their individual physical developmental capability.

Social-emotional skills deal with interaction with others, sharing, group living, playing, impulse control, negotiation, self-regulation, cultural and accepted manners, and so on, and cannot be ignored when lesson planning.

Getting Started

Some student teachers find a lesson plan outlined on a 3 x 5 card and kept on the lap or in a pocket acts as a cue card, reminding them step by step how the activity unfolds. Planning a first statement that motivates children by creating a desire to know or do increases their attention. Motivational statements need to be studied for appropriateness. Statements that create competition ("The first one who . . . ") or are threatening ("If you don't try it, then . . .") cause unnecessary tensions. Appropriate motivational statements strike a child's curiosity and often stimulate the child to action or exploration. They capture attention, and hopefully, engage the child's mind.

> John brought a special pet. I think you'll want to see him.
>
> There are some new items in the collage box for pasting today. Where have you seen a shiny paper like this?
>
> Today you'll be cooking your own snack. Raise your hand if you've seen your mom or dad make pancakes.
>
> Do you remember the sound our coffee can drums made yesterday? There's a bigger drum with a different sound here today. Let's listen.

Focusing activities such as fingerplays, body movement actions, or songs are often used as a "getting started" routine. If planned, this is written in the "getting started" section of the lesson plan. Many teachers find helpful the practice of pausing briefly for silence that signals that children are ready to find out what will happen next. The following types of statements are frequently used.

> When I hear the clock ticking, I'll know you're listening. . . .
>
> If I see your eyes, I can tell you're ready to find out what we're going to do in the art center today. Martin is ready, Sherry is ready. . . .

Lowering the volume of one's voice motivates children to change their behaviors so they can hear. This creates a hushed silence, which is successful for some teachers. Enthusiasm in a teacher's voice and manner is a great attention-getter. Children are quick to notice the sparkle in the teacher's eyes or the excitement in the voice tone, stress, and/or pitch.

During an activity's first few minutes, expectations, safety precautions, and reminders concerning class or activity rules should be covered if necessary. Doing so will avoid potential activity problems.

Procedure

If an initial demonstration or specific instruction needs expressing, this can be noted and written briefly in a step-by-step fashion. Because involvement is such an important aspect for the young child's learning, active, rather than passive, participation is part of most planned activities.

This section of the plan outlines sequential happenings during the activity. Student teachers identify important subcomponents chronologically. The student teacher mentally visualizes each step and its particular needs and actions.

Discussion

Although teacher discussion and questioning is appropriate for many child activities, it can be intrusive in others. When deeply involved, children do not usually benefit from a break in their concentration. Other activities lead to a vigorous give-and-take, question-and-feedback format that helps children's discovery and understanding.

The following questions clarify the written comments that may be included in this lesson plan section.

1. What key points, concepts, ideas, or words do you intend to cover during conversation?
2. What types of questions, inquiries, or voluntary comments might come from the children?
3. Are you going to relate new material to that which was learned previously?

Application

Sometimes, an activity leads to an immediate application of a new knowledge or skill. If the idea of a circle was introduced or discovered, finding circular images or objects in the classroom can immediately reinforce the learning. Repetition and practice are key instruments in learning.

Evaluation after Presentation

Hindsight is a valuable teaching skill. One can evaluate many aspects of a planned and conducted activity. Goal realization, a close look at instructional techniques or methods, and student teacher actions usually come under scrutiny. The following questions can aid activity and self-evaluation:

1. Was the activity location and setup appropriate?
2. Would you rate the activity as high, middle, or low in interest value and goal realization?
3. What could improve this plan?
4. Should a follow-up activity be planned?
5. Was enough attention given to small details?
6. Did the activity attempt to reach the instructional objectives?
7. Was the activity too long or too short?
8. If you planned to repeat the activity, how would you change it?
9. Were you prepared?
10. Which teacher/child interactions went well? Which ones went poorly?
11. Was the size of the group appropriate?
12. Was the activity a success with the children?
13. Were my reactions to boys and girls nonsexist?
14. Was the activity above, at, or below the group's developmental level?
15. What did I learn from the experience?
16. What seemed to be the best parts of the activity?
17. Did I learn anything about myself?
18. How good was I at helping children put into words what they experienced or discovered?

19. In what way(s) do I now know more about the children involved in the activity?

Evaluation and comments from others will add another dimension. Team meetings usually concentrate on a total day's happenings but may zero in on the student teacher's supervision and planned activities.

OTHER ACTIVITY PLAN AREAS

Many activity plans pay close attention to cleanup. Usually, both children and adults clean up their shared environment. Drying areas, housecleaning equipment, and hand washing can be important features of a plan (see Figure 5–14).

terminating statements—an ending summary or recap of what has been discovered, discussed, experienced, enjoyed, and so on, after a learning activity.

In terminating statements, a teacher may summarize what has been discovered and enjoyed, and tie loose activity ends together, bringing activities to a satisfying group conclusion.

> After watching Roddie, the hamster, eat today, Leticia noticed Roddie's two large teeth. Sam plans to bring some peanut butter on toast for Roddie tomorrow to see if he likes it. Ting wants to telephone the pet store to ask the storekeeper what hamsters eat. We decided to get a library book about hamsters to find out. Our list shows Roddie nibbled on celery and lettuce today.

Figure 5–14 A drying line with clothespins next to easels facilitates child cleanup.

Unforeseen Distractions

The best prepared activities can often go awry because of events beyond the teacher's control. Although the true life example given below is humorous, the educator's quick thinking and open-ended questioning is to be commended.

> A kindergarten teacher thought it a good idea to have a live mouse visit the classroom. The children's favorite storybook that year involved a small boy's pet mouse and the reactions of family members. The teacher secured a mouse from the sixth grade science teacher. He assured her the mouse was tame and friendly. She introduced the mouse to her class by gathering the children in a circle with children's legs outstretched touching the feet of a peer.The mouse was in a cage at the circle's center. She unlatched the cage door and the mouse immediately ran up her leg. She stifled a scream, clamped down, and caught the mouse through her pant's leg about knee high. In a barely controlled voice she asked, "Can anyone think of a way we can get the mouse back in the cage?"

Skilled teachers often creatively draw child attention back to focus with a statement when interruptions occur. They also decide to follow group interest with discussion or unplanned actions, determining on the spot when to pursue an educational opportunity.

TRANSITIONS

transition statement—planned verbalization that moves young children from one activity to another.

Transitions are defined as statements that move children in an orderly fashion from one activity to the next. To end group times, a transition statement or transition activity is used. The transition statement should create an orderly departure rather than a thundering herd or questionable ending. There are thousands of possibilities for disbanding the group members one by one. Some examples are:

"Raise your hand if your favorite ice cream is chocolate. Alfredo and Monica, you may choose which area in the room you are going to now."

"People with curly hair stand up."

"Put your hand on your stomach if you had cornflakes for breakfast. If your hand is on your stomach, walk to . . ."

"Peter, Dana, and Kingston, pretend you are mice and quietly sneak out the door to the yard."

"After you've placed your clay pot on the drying rack, you can choose to play in the block area or the yard."

"Raise your hand if you're wearing long pants that touch your shoes. If your hand is up, get your jacket and meet Carol near the door. Raise your hand if you're wearing a belt today."

"Suzette, I can see you're finished. If you look around the room, you'll see something else you may want to do. Bill is in the loft reading to Petra and Alphonso."

In the preschool and lower primary grades, a teacher may ring a bell five minutes before recess. A teacher may also remind children of what is expected, as in, "Be sure to put away your math manipulatives; try to finish your stories with Mrs. Chandler in the writing center. The rest of you need to shelve your books and get ready." Another teacher may blink the classroom lights; still another may play a few chords on the piano. You will want to try different techniques to decide what works best for you.

manipulatives—toys and materials that require the use of the fingers and hands, for instance, puzzles, beads, and pegboards.

Warnings or alerting bells or whistles are used with large groupings of older children. Teachers of young children use softer signals sufficient to gain the attention of small groups.

Promoting Cognitive Skills

You know from child development classes that young children often rely heavily on what they see. As Jones (1986) explains:

> If a line is longer, there must be more. Young children think differently than they will when they are older. That's important to remember if you're working with them. Observe, ask questions, get a sense of what this child understands and when he's ready to move to a new level of understanding. But if you try to *make* him understand, he may learn your words, but he won't *know* what they mean. Teaching requires patience.

When you interact, you can expect some children will begin to pause, reflect, consider and try out more than one idea, and will begin to attend to more than one factor. The National Research Council notes children are problem-solvers by nature, and through curiosity, generate questions and pursue answers. They attempt to solve problems and also seek novel challenges, and persist because success and understanding are motivating in their own right (National Research Council, 2000). Many tasks or experiences presented to young children are purposely open-ended, with different ways available to proceed. Many activities promote diverse and individual courses of action or ways of using, or thinking about, or creating. These types of activities promote reflective thinking and child planning.

The dialogues teachers have with young children often involve imagining, observing, predicting, brainstorming, and creative problem-solving. Discussions can be lively. Child answers are accepted and further discussions welcomed and promoted. Child comments are based on child experience, consequently correct in light of what the child knows.

Educators intent on promoting children's thinking should listen closely, and interact with pertinent comments, acknowledgments, and questions following children's line of thinking and focus. Question types that only test the children's memories rarely ask for higher thought processes. Thinking-promoting teacher questions call for children's mental choices, opinions, judgments, cause-and-effect relationships, predicting, conjecture, solutions, reasoning, hypothesizing, and creative expression. These types of questions take teacher effort to formulate and teacher control of her urges to jump ahead in conversations rather than allowing conversational silences and pauses as the child mulls over mentally, cogitates, and processes the question toward a response. Rephrasing or paraphrasing by the teacher may help clarify child meanings and alert one child to another child's ideas on any given subject, and are additional techniques.

Representing ideas in words is not an easy task for young children. Vygotsky (1986) emphasizes that meaningful social exchanges prepare children for uniting thought and speech into "verbal thought."

Using Community Resources

The whole community is a learning resource for young children's activities. Each neighborhood has unique features and people with special talents and collections. Industries, businesses, and job sites may provide field trip opportunities, resource speakers, or activity material "giveaways." Cultural events and celebrations, ethnic holidays, parks and recreation areas, and buildings easily integrate into the school's activities and promote a "reality-based" children's program.

Pitfalls

The biggest pitfall for the student teacher is the tendency to stick to the plan when children's feedback during the activity does not warrant it. Teachers should take their cues from the children's interests and encourage their growth. Expanding the children's interests can mean spending additional time providing additional opportunities and materials. In some cases, it can mean just talking if the children want to know and do more.

If children's interests cut into other activities, some activities can be postponed. Others may be revised to fit into the schedule. The unforeseen is always happening. It sometimes captures and holds the children's attention. Getting the children to refocus on a planned activity may mean having to clear the children's minds of something more important to them.

Teachers usually try to relate unexpected occurrences to the planned activity. For example, "That was a loud booming noise. We can listen for another while we finish shaping our bread before it goes into the oven." If efforts to refocus fail, a teacher knows the written plan has been preempted.

A real teaching skill involves using unplanned events to promote identified specific curriculum objectives, or objectives that were not even considered but are currently timely and important.

One of the difficulties in using Hunter's (1984) six-step lesson plan is its inflexibility. In working with young children, a teacher must, above all, be flexible.

Going out on a Limb

In planning activities and reviewing results, expect successes and failures. You may well experience more growth from your "duds!" They will need analyzing and could stimulate your creativity. Don't forget that taking risks (within safety limits, of course) and trying new ideas and new ways of doing things may temporarily create uncertainty, but also may offer challenge, excitement, and growth. Approaching child curriculum in unique ways is part of the fun of teaching. When college and university supervisors and cooperating teachers see students branching out in new directions, they see serious effort. To grow, adults, like children, explore, experiment, fail, create, invent, talk about, and follow their own curiosities.

Teaching Tips

As mentioned before, your enthusiasm while presenting the lesson plan must be emphasized. When your eyes sparkle and your voice sounds excited about what you and the children are accomplishing, the children will probably remain interested and focused. Your level of enthusiasm needs to be genuine and appropriate. Langness (1998) believes one of the most powerful services a teacher can deliver is to help children anticipate each day as an exciting learning opportunity. She states that an educators' enthusiasm promotes children's seeing the pursuit of knowledge as a gift that they open with pleasure.

You will be eager to start the activities you have designed. You will be anxious to see whether you have captured the children's attention and stimulated their developmental growth. When you feel that the group joins in your excitement and discovery, no other reward is necessary.

Look for the unexpected to happen during your activities. Children will see things that you do not, ask unexpected questions, and make statements you will find a challenge to understand. Listen closely to the children's responses. If you cannot understand them, probe further. More often than not, you will understand the wisdom of their thoughts that are based on their unique past experiences.

Do not panic when a child corrects you or you do not have an answer. Develop a "we'll find out together" attitude. A teacher who has all the answers often fails to notice the brilliance, charm, and honesty of children.

Room Environments

Looking closely at room environments will be a challenging aspect of student teaching. You may be asked to "take over" a particular area, redesign, restructure it, or create a new interest or discovery area. In other classrooms, the cooperating teacher may not wish anything moved or "improved." In this case, you cannot help but evaluate its arrangement.

You will be looking at child behaviors affected by physical surroundings and notice popular and unpopular room areas. Problem room areas may be immediately apparent. Some room spaces will appear designed for special purposes, accommodating the need(s) of one or many children.

Experimentation in placement of furniture, equipment, and supplies is an ongoing teacher task in most classrooms (see Figure 5–15). Prekindergarten classrooms may change dramatically from week to week, depending on a course of study. Many pieces of preschool furniture have been designed for multi-use flexibility and utmost mobility.

Effective classroom arrangements do not just happen. They are a result of much hard work and planning. Considerable thought and observation of child play pursuits is involved. Because of budget (usually lack of it), creative solutions to classroom environments abound.

Figure 5-15 This furniture and equipment arrangement was designed to encourage familiarity with writing activities and the alphabet.

Student teachers will find some room areas need their constant attention! Analyzing the possible provoking factors may lead to one reason or many, including the room arrangement itself, furnishings, activities, setups (the way individual activity materials are arranged), storage, supplies or lack of them, and cleanup provisions.

Greenman (1989) suggests "a rich, responsive learning environment" or room areas that allow children to plan and explore independently, and can allow staff to focus on "prime times," which he defines as one-to-one caring and learning moments that lie at the heart of healthy development. Room arrangements, he feels, regulate behavior(s) and, by dividing space into clear boundaries and traffic patterns, help to control child crowding and wandering.

Greenman also promotes sensory and motor aspects of room environments:

> Build sensory learning into the environment. Within a coordinated tasteful aesthetic, use different textures, lighting; colors, temperatures or breezes, views or angles of visions. . . . Build motor learning into the environment. Furniture and equipment that encourage or allow climbing up or over, moving around, through, over, under, etc.

In some placement classrooms, student teachers may notice and recognize the cooperating teacher's priorities and individuality. A musically inclined teacher's room might have considerable space devoted to children's experiences and exploration of music-related activities. Another child center or classroom may emphasize gardening activities both indoors and outdoors, and so on. You are probably already aware of your own favorite instructional areas, and envision your own future classroom that will incorporate your own creative ideas.

Chapter 6 will expand on the effect that classroom arrangements may have on management issues.

WORKING WITH GROUPS

Group times are covered in detail in this chapter because student teachers frequently need help in planning and conducting them. The authors do not intend to suggest planned group gatherings are the best or most efficient vehicles for child learning. Play and spontaneous child activity offer equally excellent opportunities.

group times—also called circle or story times; time blocks during the day when all of the children and teachers join together in a common activity.

Group Size

More and more early childhood teachers prefer planning and working with small groups of young children within their classrooms. Consequently, large groups consisting of the total class may only happen when a group is formed early in the morning or at closing. These larger child groups tend to facilitate information passing rather than instruction. Think about your former training classes and classroom discussions, and your feelings about group meetings and consultations in your own training classes. Most teachers admit they were comfortable offering their ideas and felt "listened to" when groups were kept small.

Successful Group Times

It pays to think about and analyze elements that promote success. Student teachers will tend to imitate their cooperating teachers' group times and carry techniques into their own future classrooms.

Identifying the purpose of group times precedes their planning. During these times, the children not only learn but draw conclusions about themselves as learners. The following teacher skills during planned group times are considered important:

- Preserving each child's feeling of personal competence as a learner, speaker, and group member
- Strengthening each child's idea of self-worth and uniqueness
- Promoting a sense of comfort with peers and the teaching team
- Helping children gain group attendance skills such as listening to others, offering ideas, taking turns, and so on.
- Helping children to want to find out about the world, its creatures, and diversity; helping children to preserve their sense of wonder and discovery
- Promoting children helping others

Child Characteristics and Group Times

How can group time become what you would like it to be? Go back in your memory to age and stage characteristics. Group times are based on what a teacher knows about the children for whom activities are planned. The children's endurance, need for movement, need to touch, enjoyment of singing, chanting, ability to attend, and other factors are all taken into consideration. The dynamics of the group setting and the children affect outcomes. Two children seated together could mean horsing around. Maybe some children have sight or hearing problems. Perhaps there is a child who talks on and on at group times. All situations of this nature should be given planning consideration.

Planning

The following are guideline questions you might ask yourself when planning a small-group activity:

- How will I promote child self-help and independence?
- Why will or how will children be motivated to want to know, discover, and/or find out about planned group subject matter?
- How will I minimize waiting?
- Will my materials attract them?
- Are materials or tools to be shared? How will children know?
- If a demonstration is necessary before children proceed, will materials be temptingly close to children during the demonstration?
- How does my setting provide for active participation?
- Cleanup? Who? How?
- How will children know what's to happen next or where to go?

Whether it is group time or any other time during the day, you will want to promote discussion and elicit children's ideas. Lively interchanges promote comprehension and clarify what everyone is experiencing. Most often, discussions pursue what is of interest to children, and teachers find that one topic leads to another.

Student teachers often plan their group times with other adults. The following planning decisions are usually discussed:

- Which adults will lead? Which adults will be aides?
- When and where? How long? How will the children be seated?
- What will be the instructional topics, activities, and goals?
- How many adults and children will attend?
- Will there be one presentation or instant replays?
- What materials or audiovisuals will be needed?
- Who will prepare needed materials?
- How will children be gathered?
- Will children be asked to raise hands before contributing?
- In what order will events happen?
- Can the children actively participate?
- Will a vigorous activity be followed with a slow one?
- Will children share in leading?
- How will the results of group time be reviewed or tied together if necessary?
- How will children leave at the conclusion?

There seem to be distinct stages in group times. For example, there is the gathering of children and adults. This then leads to a focusing of the children's attention. There is a joint recognition of the persons present at group time. At that point, someone begins to lead and present the activity. This is followed by the children participating and reacting. In the final stage of group time, there can be a brief summary and then a disbanding.

Building Attention and Interest

Teachers use various methods to gather the children and get their attention.

- A signal like a bell or cleanup song helps to build anticipation: "When you hear the xylophone, it's time to . . ."
- A verbal reminder to individual children lets them know that group time is starting soon: "In five minutes we'll be starting group time in the loft, Tina. You need to finish your block building."

In order to help the children focus, the teacher might initiate a song, fingerplay, chant, or dance in which all perform a similar act. Many group leaders then build a sense of enthusiasm by recognizing each child and adult. An interesting roll call, a "selecting name tags" activity, or a simple statement like "Who is with us today?" are good techniques. Children enjoy being identified.

> "Bill is wearing his red shirt, red shirt, red shirt . . . Bill is wearing his red shirt at group time today. Katrina has her hair cut, hair cut . . ."

To build motivation or enthusiasm, some teachers drop their voice volume to a whisper. Others "light up" facially or bodily, showing their enthusiasm. The object is to capture interest and build a desire in the children to want to know or find out. Statements like: "We're now going to read a story about . . ." or "You're going to learn to count to six today . . ." do not excite children. In contrast, statements like: "There's something in my pocket I brought to show you . . ." or "Raise your hand if you can hear this tiny bell . . ." build the children's interest and curiosity. Tone of voice and manner will be a dead giveaway as to whether wonder and discovery are alive in the teacher. Teachers use natural conversation. Presenting materials or topics (of an appropriate age level) close to the heart of the presenter is a key element. Experiences from one's own love of life can be a necessary ingredient. New teachers and student teachers should rely on their own creativity and use group times to share themselves.

Sheinman (2000) describes one teacher's method of gaining attention so directions are clear and better understood. It follows:

> When I need to gain children's attention, I ask them to stop and give me "five." They have to do five things for me to give out my directions: (1) look at me, (2) close their mouths, (3) stop what they are doing, (4) open their ears, and (5) raise their hands. They are to indicate they have done all five by raising all five fingers showing that they completed what they are expected to do. When all hands are up, I give my directions (Sheinman, 2000).

Practice

If memorized songs, fingerplays, or chants are part of the group time, practice is necessary. Time spent preparing and practicing will promote a relaxed presenter (see Figure 5–16). Lap cards may be used as insurance if the student teacher forgets under pressure.

Practice sessions often alert the student teacher to whether most of the group time activity is led by the teacher and children do little more than listen. If so, there is time to redesign the activity.

Feedback

A student teacher's group time awareness and verbalizations promote goal realization and success. Feedback from children and adults needs to be monitored

Figure 5-16 The children's attention is focused on this Valentine's Day activity.

while presenting. For example, seeing a child hesitate may cue the presenter to repeat and emphasize words. It is worthwhile to see what really interests the children and spend additional time with that activity. Sometimes, even the best group time plans are discarded, revised, and another created based on feedback.

Recognition

One technique that helps recognize individuality is giving credit to each child's idea. "John says he saw a fox in the woods, Mike thinks it was a wolf, and Debbie says it looked like a cat." Bringing a child back to focus by naming him or asking a question is common. "Todd, this dog looks like your dog, Ranger," or "Todd, can you show us . . . ?"

Guidance

Handling child behaviors during group time can distract a student teacher and upset the sequence of thought. Quick statements such as "If everyone is sitting down, you will be able to see" or "Mei-Lee and Josh are waiting for a turn," help curb distracting behaviors. A group leader can be very grateful for an alert aide or assistant teacher to handle group or individual behaviors so the group time can proceed.

Evaluation

If time and supervision permit, you should analyze your group activity after you have relaxed and reflected on its particulars. Hindsight is valuable now. If possible, you might consider videotaping your group time. This offers tremendous growth opportunities. Listen closely to the supervisor's and cooperating teacher's objective comments and suggested improvements.

THEMATIC TEACHING

theme approach—a popular child program planning approach that involves a course of study with identified child activities focused on one subject, idea, or skill such as butterflies, friendship, biking, or a picture book.

The theme approach to child program planning is popular in many early childhood centers and classrooms. A theme includes a written collection of activity ideas on one subject, idea, or skill such as a picture book, butterflies, homes, neighborhood, kindness, friendship, biking, swimming, or jogging, among others. Activities within the theme encompass a wide range of curriculum areas including art, music, numbers, science, small and large motor development, and so on. A theme's course of study involves a day, week, or longer period; one week is typical. Though usually preplanned, themes can be developed after a child's or group's interest is recognized. Curtis and Carter (1996) make a clear distinction between traditional and developmental themes. *Traditional theme topics* are teacher-chosen rather than those selected after uncovering topics of child interest a teacher observes in child play and exploration. In *developmental theme* planning, the teacher bases her approach on inquiry and learning, which focuses on the realities of children's lives, relationships, and issues. Materials and planned activities are designed to provoke child curiosity and promote the exploration of the new ideas and pursue the questions children generate. Themes differ from teacher to teacher and school to school; each offers a unique collection and presentation of activities.

Possible Instructional Benefits

There are a number of reasons for using the theme approach in young children's instruction. Some major ideas are as follows.

- A theme tackles instruction through a wide variety of activities that reinforce child learning as the same new ideas, facts, skills, and attitudes are encountered through different routes. Discovery and deductions happen in varied activities, keeping classrooms enthusiastic and alive.
- The classroom environment can be "saturated" with activities and materials on the same subject.
- A theme approach lets children gather, explore, and experience the theme at their own pace and level of understanding because of the number of choices in room activities and materials.
- Planned group times offer shared experiences and knowledge.
- Teachers can identify and gather theme materials for future use, saving time and energy.
- Teachers can best guide child discovery through knowledge gained from their own research during theme preparation and construction.
- Community resources become classroom materials, and community uniqueness is incorporated into instruction.
- The teacher collects and develops audiovisuals and "real objects."
- A theme can evolve from the unplanned and unexpected, giving curriculum flexibility.
- The teacher's and children's creativity and resourcefulness are encouraged and challenged.
- Once the environment is set, the teacher is free to help uninvolved individuals and interact intimately with the highly focused children.
- The classroom environment becomes a dynamic, changing, exciting place for both children and adults.

- A theme can provide a security blanket for new teachers outlining a plan for one week's activities or longer.

Elementary Grades

An integrated curriculum's goals for language and literacy programming are for children to expand their ability to communicate orally, and through reading and writing and to enjoy these activities. The teacher might read part of a stimulating story to the class and ask the children what they think will come next. After listening to several examples of what might come and writing them on the chalkboard, the teacher might then assign the students to cooperative groups to write their own endings. Children who may have difficulty reading or writing because of a learning disability may be good at generating ideas or illustrating the final product. As briefly explained in the previous section, it is also important to understand that cooperative groups have been shown to be remarkably effective for children of all ability levels.

Another way to integrate across the curriculum is to use a theme approach. Such topics as dinosaurs or the family are immensely popular, and can be introduced with a book where children are asked to write their own version or to write a sequel. An in-class library can house several books about dinosaurs or families that children can use for reference and for enjoyment. The books should encompass several different grade levels so each student can have the opportunity to read independently. In listening and writing and reading activities, "whole language" again is used. Spelling and mechanics are an integrated part of the final stories the children write and illustrate. (Each cooperative group needs to have a good editor, maybe two creative thinkers, at least one logical sequential thinker to keep his peers on target, and a good illustrator.) After groups have created book covers and flyleaf synopses, the creative teacher will then teach students bookbinding. Finally, card pockets can be affixed to the inside covers, and students can check out the efforts of their peers. Students can also be invited to go to another class and share their stories, a very real self-esteem booster. This process is the essence of "whole language."

How would the theme of "family" relate to the other curricular areas. Let us look at a first-grade social studies example, "We Are All Unique and Special":

> *Reading, including language arts:* Reading and writing about the children's own families. Telling stories about family traditions, special events, favorite foods, and so on.
>
> *Art:* Illustrating their stories about their families.
>
> *Math:* Counting the number of girls and boys in the class; graphing the results. Counting the number with various different characteristics: eye color, hair color, wearing something red, and so forth; graphing the results; and posting them on the bulletin board. Counting the number of siblings in each student's family; preparing a graph of the results. Predicting the number of siblings a new child coming to the class would most likely have.
>
> *Science:* As an extension of eye color, hair color, and skin color, have students talk to parents and grandparents, if available, about where their ancestors lived. (Be sensitive about the child who is living in a foster family. Perhaps you would want to contact the foster mother and father initially before beginning this assignment.) Bring a globe into the classroom and post a world map for children to use. Have them point out where their grandparents and great-grandparents lived. Use colored thread and map pins for each child to place on the map to indicate where her grandparents or ancestors came from. Have the children stretch

a thread from one area of the map to the area where your school is located. Talk about the weather where they live. Talk about what the weather must be like where their grandparents and great-grandparents lived. Have books available in your in-class library that illustrate life in several different parts of the world. Have the children look at styles of dress, housing, or foods being sold in markets. Have them compare these to their lifestyles. Do not expect first graders to be able to understand concepts related to cultural anthropology; you could expect them to understand that those families who lived near the equator had darker skin, eyes, and hair than those who lived near the Arctic areas. It may then be possible to talk about how we are all unique, and at the same time, we are all alike. (Based on materials and suggestions in Project Reach.)

One way of planning a thematic unit is to use a process called "webbing." Figure 5–17 presents a web based on an unplanned event which evoked considerable child interest. The teacher then developed a "question and comment web" based on children's queries and comments as an initial step to developing a subsequent web to reflect children's specific areas of interest. In making a web, the student teacher is laying out the central theme of the plan and illustrating how

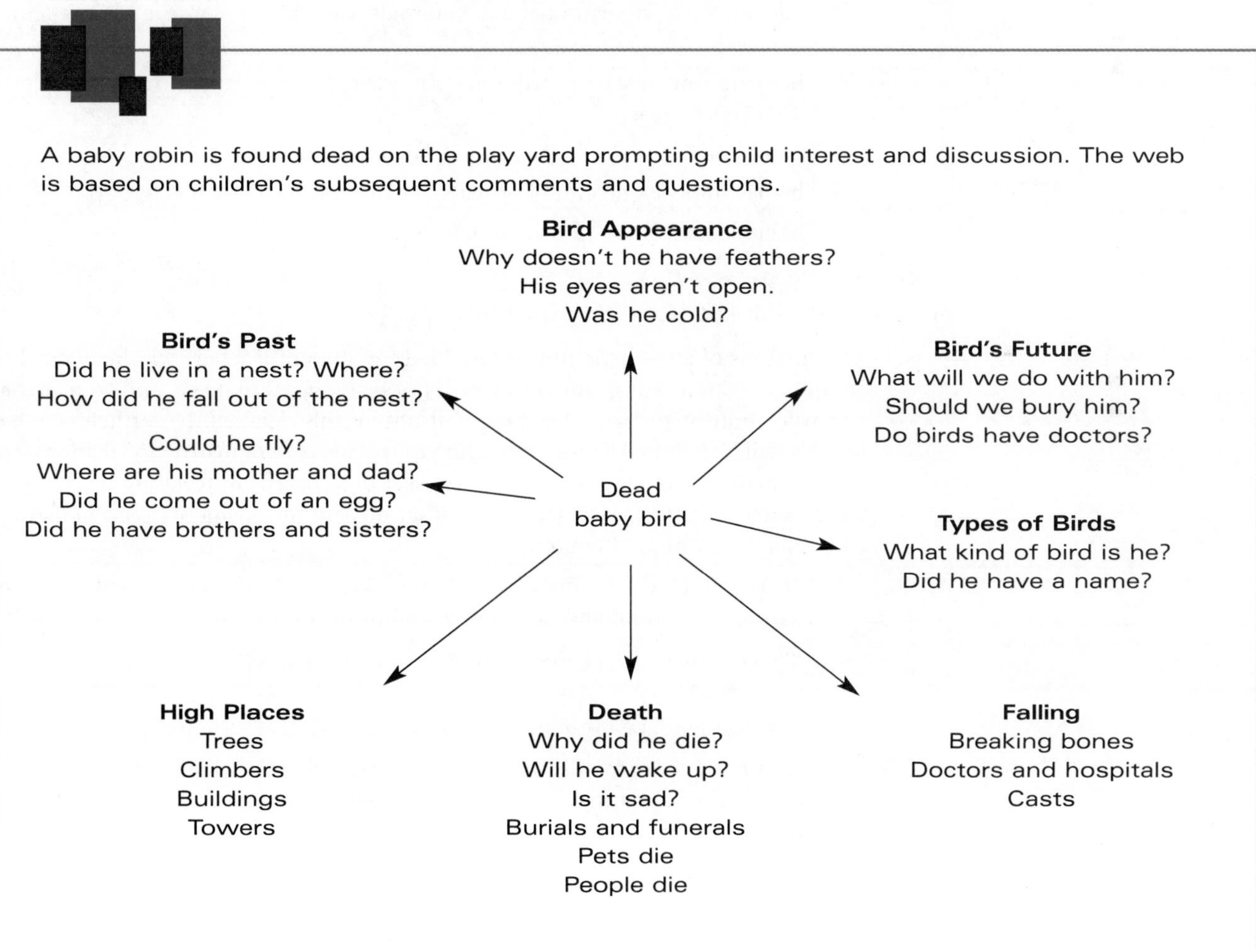

Figure 5-17 Unplanned event web—initial planning

the pieces fit together in a diagram that might resemble a spider web, thus the name. Webbing may provide the student teacher with a picture of how one topic integrates across curricular areas (see Figure 5–18). An early childhood educator could use the same webbing techniques with a picture book or topic of interest using other early childhood curricular areas or categories.

Possible Limitations or Weaknesses

Critics of thematic teaching mention several limitations of this type of programming for both preschool and elementary school.

- Once developed, thematic units tend to become a teacher-dictated curriculum.
- A reliance on this crutch produces dated programs.
- Themes may not be closely evaluated or critically analyzed for appropriateness during construction.
- Theme teaching promotes the copying of teaching techniques rather than the developing of individual styles.
- A dependence on commercial materials can add expense and lose child interest.
- Thematic unit teaching promotes the idea that preplanned units are a preferred way to teach.
- Themes often overlook geographic, socioeconomic, and cultural factors.
- Themes impose one child's or teacher's interest on the whole group.
- Thematic units may be used to compare teachers.

Thematic Subsections

This analysis of a thematic unit is provided for student teachers who may need to compile a written unit. Some of you will not be required to do so, and your preparation for unit or thematic teaching will not be this detailed. Nevertheless, what follows will be helpful to those intending to try this type of instructional approach.

Thematic units may have many subsections. Based on teaching preferences and teacher decisions, each section is either present or absent. Subsection listings contain a description of contents:

- *Title page* includes theme identification, writer's credit line, ages of children, classroom location, and descriptive and/or decorative art.
- *Table of contents* lists subsections and beginning pages.
- *Instructional goals description* contains writer's identification of concepts, ideas, factual data, vocabulary, attitudes, and skills in the unit.
- *Background data* are researched background information with theme particulars useful in updating adults on the subject. Technical drawings and photos can be included.
- *Resource list* includes teacher-made and commercial materials (names and addresses) and/or supplies. Also contains audiovisuals, community resources, consultants, speakers, field trip possibilities, and inexpensive sources of materials.
- *Weekly time schedule* pinpoints times and activities, supervising adults, and duration of activity.
- *Suggested activities* uses activity plans, procedure descriptions, and/or plans for room settings, centers, and environments.

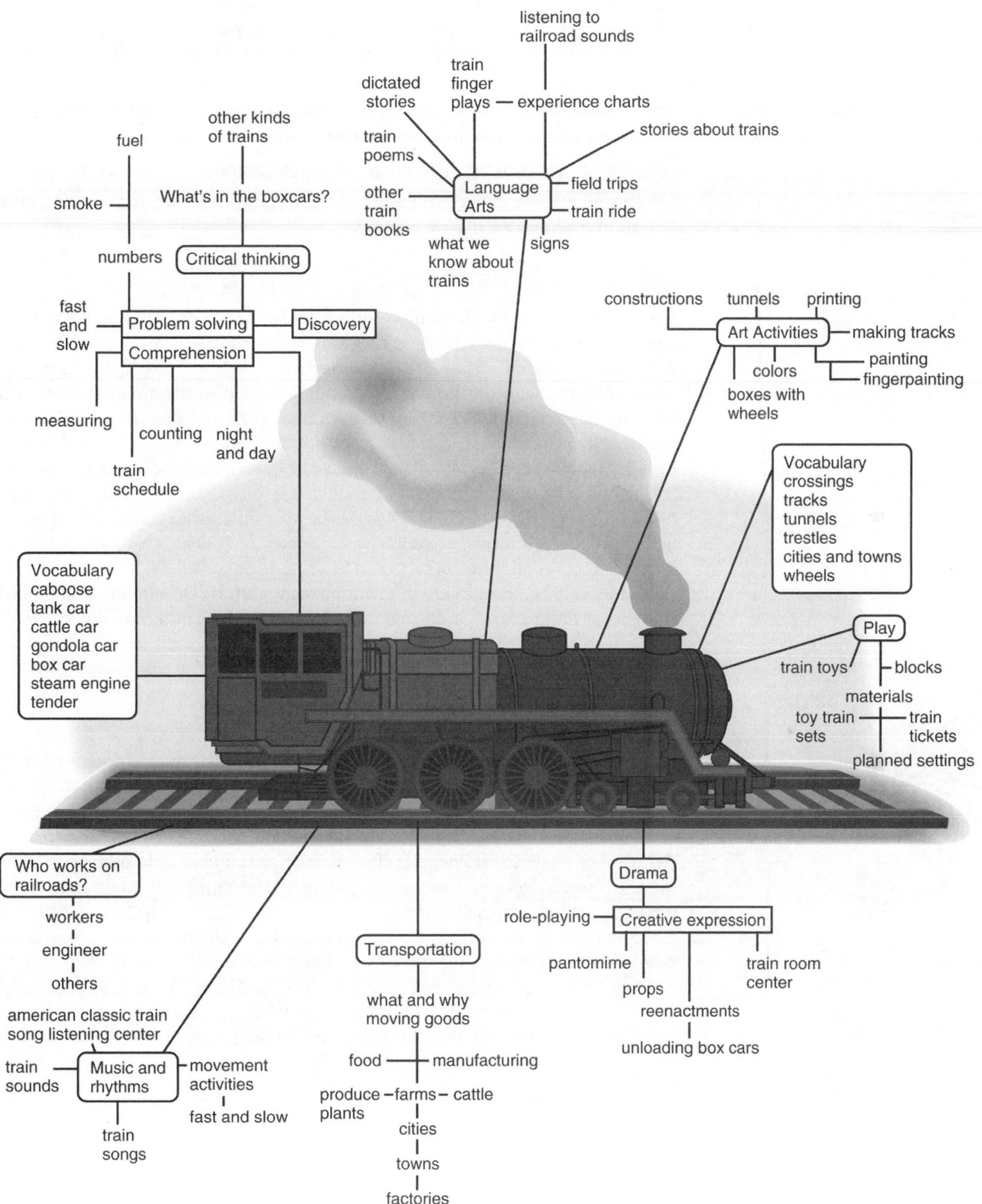

Figure 5-18 This webbing example suits a theme based on a picture book about trains such as Donald Crew's book, *Freight Train*.

- *Children's book lists* identify children's books related to the theme.
- *Activity aids* describe patterns, fingerplays, poems, storytelling ideas, recipes, chart ideas, teacher-made aids and equipment, ideas and directions, and bulletin board diagrams.
- *Culminating activities* offer suggestions for final celebrations or events that have summarizing, unifying, and reviewing features.
- *Bibliography* lists adult resource books on theme.
- *Evaluation* contains comments concerning instructional value, unit conduct, and revisional needs.

How to Construct a Thematic Unit

Initial work begins by choosing a subject and possibly webbing it. Then data are collected and researched. Next, brainstorming (mental generating of ideas) and envisioning "saturated" classroom environments take place. Instructional decisions concerning the scope of the proposed child course of study are made. The search for materials and resources starts. Instructional goals and objectives are identified, and activities are created. A tentative plan of activities is compiled and analyzed. After materials, supplies, and visual aids have been made or obtained, a final written plan is completed. The unit is conducted, concluded, and evaluated. Each aspect of instruction is assessed. Notes concerning unit particulars are reviewed, and unit revisions, additions, or omissions are recorded. The unit's written materials are stored in a binder for protection. Other items may be boxed.

Units can be an individual, team, or group effort. Developing a unit during student teaching creates a desired job skill and may aid in preparing for the first job. A written theme, finished during student teaching, can display competency and become a valuable visual aid for job interviews.

Saturated Environment

Thinking of ways to incorporate a unit's theme into the routine, room, yard, food service, wall space, and so on means using your creativity. Background music, room color, the teacher's clothing, and lighting can reflect a theme. The environment becomes transformed. Butterfly-shaped crackers, green cream of wheat, special teacher-made theme puzzles, face painting, and countless other possibilities exist. Do not forget child motor involvement and child and adult enactment of theme-related concepts and skills.

A moderate amount of activity choices on a theme at any given hour is deemed best rather than a large or overwhelming array of activities (Stipek, 1996). Because themes are spread out over time, this can be decided, depending on the teacher's logical sequencing of activities, on what activities seem to grow out of stimulated child interest and questions, or what activities complement each other.

Project Approach

Katz and Chard's (1993) text, *Engaging Children's Minds: The Project Approach*, sensitized teachers to the idea that children in most early childhood classrooms had no active role in deciding what they wanted to learn. Activity planning can include both teacher- and child-generated activities if teachers listen and provide ways for children to follow their own line of inquiry. Elliott (1998) starts with an introduction to a theme and works with kindergarten children to develop a related-to-theme child interest project. She states that during project work, children ask thoughtful questions, engage in focused investigation, use problem-solving skills effectively, discover the power of teamwork, and take ownership of what they are learning. Katz (1994) defines a project as an in-depth investigation of a topic worth learning more about. The investigation is usually undertaken by a small group of children within a class, sometimes by a whole class, and occasionally by an individual child. Examine Figure 5–19 for an example of a daily time schedule

Typical Time Blocks	Project Activities that May Occur at this Time
Greetings Gathering Time	Viewing of displays on tables regarding topic Browsing of books/resources on rug Reviewing and discussion of photos of previous work
Circle or Meeting Time	Exploration and discussion of new topics Sharing of group investigations Review of work Introduction of resources such as books, new artifacts Presentations by visiting experts
Work (or Center) Time (not less than 45 minutes)	Investigations by individuals or groups Meetings of small groups Opportunities for representation such as drawing, painting, working with clay Creating play environments Construction and building of models
Review Time	Reports by groups of progress Introduction of new ideas Sharing of representations Developing questions for further investigation
Outdoor Time	Project investigations and observations if relevant to topic Role-play related to project
Small-group Activities	Focusing of small groups on project work Demonstration or practice of related content or skills Continuation of work begun in work time Adults sharing resources in small groups Presentations or demonstrations by experts Project activities needing more teacher guidance (detailed construction, modeling, reviewing, and discussing with groups)
Story or Book Time	Sharing of expository books on project topic Sharing of project history books Sharing of storybooks that relate to the topic and are realistic Journal writing
Music Time	Sharing of music related to topic
Language/Literacy or Math Workshop Times (first grade)	Introduction of content skills useful for project work such as graphing, charting, counting, measuring, problem-solving, reviewing and adding to the word wall, making items for communication needs of project (signs, invitations, brochures, thank you notes), writing in journals, writing narratives for display, and project history books

Figure 5–19 Scheduled time blocks and project activities. Reprinted by permission of the publisher from Helm, J. H., and Katz, L. G., *Young Investigators: The Project Approach in the Early Years*. New York: Teachers College Press, (c) 2001 by Teachers College, Columbia University. All rights reserved p. 25.

for a project approach to instruction. The key feature of a project is that it is a research effort deliberately focused on finding answers to questions about a topic posed either by the children, the teacher, or the teacher working with the children. The goal of a project is to learn more about the topic rather than to seek right answers to questions posed by the teacher.

Projects evolve out of child curiosity and questions. The teacher supports the children's activities and helps children proceed in their investigations and problem-solving while keeping them safe. Answers are not supplied by the teacher; he only suggests avenues toward answers. Children's hypotheses may not turn out as expected, and they learn from their mistakes. In presenting a discussion on a unit (theme) about birds to preschoolers and probing what they are curious about or what they may want to find out, many possible child investigative projects can be discovered.

Teachers who strongly believe in young children's innate ability to pursue information, solutions, and answers, given adult assistance, will find this educational approach attractive. Children will no doubt learn many things the teacher had not planned!

Discovery (Learning) Centers

discovery centers—classroom areas specifically designed and equipped for child exploration, discovery, play, creativity or another educational opportunity.

Room areas that suggest specific types of play and exploration are sometimes called **discovery centers**. A theme or topic connected to the room area may identify a discovery center as the insect corner, train station, weighing and measuring place, or tortilla factory.

Student teachers are often given the assignment of developing a new room area or changing an existing one. Again, children's interests will provide clues to the possible popularity of a proposed teacher-developed discovery center. An increasing number of programs are recognizing the value and worth of children's self-selected pursuits. The teacher's role is changing from initiator to facilitator with themes more frequently emerging from the children's own play and interests. Teachers design and supply classroom areas with materials and space for child exploration and experimentation. Once child interest in a particular area is achieved, the teacher's new role includes being both a provider of additional and supplemental materials and also a thoughtful co-explorer who promotes discovery, obstacle resolution, and problem-solving as a facilitor rather than a leader. The teacher may weave in and out of the picture as in his judgment he feels it is appropriate. One might also think of the teacher as a watchful opportunist who realizes there is a fragile line between invading child play and helping children sustain interest and gain additional information. During this type of child-teacher interaction, the teacher encourages children's verbalizing and representing their ideas and experiences with other media, thereby further "cementing and reinforcing" new ideas and learning.

Usually, discovery centers are a self-selected child activity. They can be designed to be open only at specific times when an adult helper is available.

Instructional goal-setting precedes discovery center planning, and child discovery is enhanced through thoughtful teacher analysis of possible materials and child exploration.

There is considerable teacher time and activity (usually unpaid) spent collecting items for classroom centers. Many times, teachers are delighted with the receptiveness they find in securing donated items from parents and community. After the teacher explains that it is for child classroom use, many individuals willingly help.

Some discovery centers seem to be immediately popular with children. Interest may wane or continue, so monitoring of centers and possibly adding new features is a part of the teaching task.

Planning Outdoor Activities

Student teachers are expected to use all existing child space for the children's play, discovery, and learning opportunities.

Each yard area has a number of "givens," which could include:

- Boundaries (for example, fences, walls, and so on)
- Space for child use
- Built-ins or existing features (examples may be elevations, vegetation, and other features)
- Traffic patterns
- Ground surfaces
- Movable equipment and supplies
- Storage
- Water access
- Shade and/or sunny areas
- Maintenance personnel
- Additional features

One can think of each given as an instructional asset. Take each of the listings above and briefly, mentally list ways fences and/or walls could be used for the children's activity. Did you include child water painting? Displaying child work or using a fence as a base for child easels? Or as a base to tie on ropes that could, with old blankets, enclose an area for a playhouse, stage, or special activity area?

Your creativity in using givens for the children's activities always must consider child safety and supervision first.

If natural areas exist, children can develop a sense of wonder for the world around them and an awareness of growth, change, and natural resources (Wilson, Kilmer, & Knauerhase, 1996).

Think about what play areas add beauty and create a state of "relaxed alertness," or else can be classified as warm, cozy, child-friendly places. Look at what yard features have a significant affect on the children's behavior. Can music be introduced?

Movable and mobile furnishing and equipment will have a lot of possible uses. Adding tires, boxes, signs, and donated items to the yard should be explored.

Weather and climate will determine what's possible and not possible during the year's seasons.

For many reasons, outside activities may take additional staffing. Outdoor projects can be ongoing or theme-related activities.

Animal and insect study takes place in many centers. A great number of science discoveries can happen that are not possible in indoor settings.

When planning outside activities, Greenman (1989) advises:

> Children, like bag ladies, take seriously the maximum: materials placed close together will be used together. Thus, if construction projects can be painted, adjoin the construction area and the art area. Unless the guinea pig can swim, keep animals away from the water play area. . . . Conflict, accidents, and messes follow cramped space.

Other considerations for yard activities include:

- shade and sun
- traffic flow

- necessary water access
- ground surfaces

Make sure to consult with your cooperating teacher concerning your plan(s) for outside activities.

Griffin and Rinn (1998) encourage teachers to add obstacle courses to play yards for variety, developmental value, spatial awareness, adventure, cooperative and gross-motor skill development, creative expression, dramatic play, self-esteem, and challenge (see Figure 5–20). They believe the possibilities for obstacle course ideas are limited only by safety considerations and imagination. Obstacle course items suggested by Griffin and Rinn (1998) include:

- tires
- plastic cubes
- milk crates
- plastic hoops and bottles
- cable spools
- appliance boxes
- plastic trash cans
- cushioned tumbling wedge and mats
- carpet remnants
- child's plastic swimming pool
- trampoline
- planks, balance beam, and teeter-totter, and
- pillows

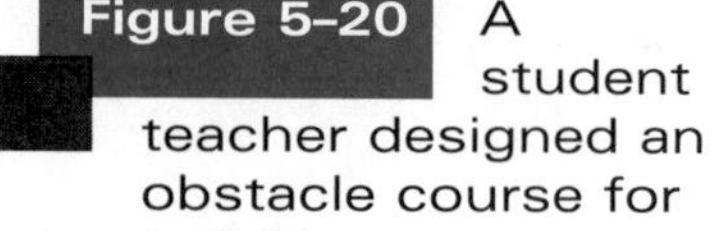

Figure 5–20 A student teacher designed an obstacle course for toddlers.

The Teacher's Role in Outdoor Settings

Most early childhood educators would agree that it is a teacher's responsibility to "set the stage" for learning, monitor safety, encourage exploration and social interaction, respond to the children's actions, mediate, or promote the children's own solutions and social negotiations during outside free-choice play. Observation of child development, interests, feelings, and individual capabilities is also accepted practice. Some disagreement exists as to whether teachers should also participate in the children's chosen play themes. Most professionals agree teachers can frequently question with the aim to promote growth, verbally add to children's concept development, clarify incidental learning, or promote dialogue, as long as these teacher actions are not overly intrusive. The issue rests on ideas concerning children's freedom without adult intervention except in unsafe play.

Your cooperating teacher may function somewhere between occasional interventions in the children's free play to considerable adult-child interaction, or you may find outside teacher supervision is seen as a time to be alert but also to rest if possible.

McGinnis (2002) suggests outside play may need "an outdoor transition area." This area could include passive play pursuits where seating or observation areas with binoculars, periscopes, or telescopes for children are placed to ease the shift from indoor less vigorous movement to outdoor freedom. The area could also facilitate moving inside work to an outside location with tables and seating for art project completion, snacks or other unfinished classroom work.

McGinnis encourages teachers to plan observing, experimenting, and discussion activities that involve birds, insects, plants, the weather, dirt, water, or other available natural environmental materials. Painting cement with water and watching it disappear is an example of this kind of activity or watching ice cubes melt.

Work Ethic Activities

Remember the status that went along with being selected as the waste basket dumper or human chalkboard eraser? Cleaning, cooking, room maintenance, material repair, and similar activities are planned regularly in some classrooms. These work-related activities can offer opportunities for children to develop work skills and attitudes, a sense of accomplishment, independence, and feeling of competency. Working alone or in groups is possible. Polishing shoes, cleaning silverware, and shelling peas falls into this work category. Often, these activities are a popular choice. Curtis and Carter (1996) suggest developing clean up kits using a window cleaning theme. Kits may include spray bottle, sponges, squeegees, paper towels, window cleaning fluid, tubs, and buckets.

Monthly Plans

Petersen (1996) offers 10 steps for developing a monthly curriculum plan and advises identifying individual and group skill area needs and interests of attending children beforehand. As a student teacher, you most likely will not need to develop a monthly plan. Petersen's 10 steps are mentioned here to equip you for your future work and to help you see how your planned daily activities fit into the monthly plans of your cooperating teacher.

The 10 steps follow:

1. Check your monthly calendar to see what may affect your plan.
2. Review and/or think about your own program's goals and strategies. If one is available at your assigned school or center, study it.
3. Review the developmental milestones of the age group with whom you work.
4. Choose and enter the basic activities that children will always do on a daily basis.
5. Review a summary of the individual needs of attending children. Choose and enter today's (first day) individualized activities.
6. Choose and enter a variety of sequenced skill-focused activities that are developmentally appropriate for your group.
7. Choose and enter activity ideas that mesh with your current theme or unit.
8. Choose and enter the activities required or suggested by your program that must occur regularly.
9. Check anecdotal records and individual education plans for special needs children, and enter appropriate notes if necessary.
10. Gather any special materials you need.

This 10-step guide would follow dividing days into blocks of time allowing for child food service, bathroom use, nap or rest periods, outdoor and free play periods, and transition times if necessary because of unique facility characteristics.

SUMMARY

Planning, presenting, and evaluating activities are a part of student teaching. Written activity plans are usually required and encourage student teachers to examine closely all aspects of their curriculum. Guidelines and criteria for planning activities promote overall success. Consultation with teachers often aids in the development of written plans. Learning objectives can be written as instructional objectives or in measurable specific behavioral objective terms.

A number of lesson plan forms exist; this text provides two suggested forms (see Figures 5–9 and 5–12). Preparing a written plan allows for greater student teacher confidence and less stress, and it averts potential problems. A lesson plan is only a starting point and has the flexibility to change or be discontinued during its presentation, depending on interest and need among the children.

Many planned activities are not to be put into lesson plan form because of their simplicity or their focus on creative expression. Lesson plans are a beginning teacher's attempt to be thoroughly prepared.

Each classroom's group times differ in intent and purpose. Student teachers plan and present group instruction after carefully analyzing goals and the group's particular dynamics, needs, and learning level. Many decisions affect the smooth, successful flow as different stages evolve. Technique, preparation, presentation, and goal realization are all factors that should be evaluated.

Thematic unit teaching is a popular instructional approach. However, there are different views of the benefits and limitations of unit teaching. Construction of a teaching unit includes theme identification, research, decisions concerning instructional objectives, activity development in a wide range of curriculum areas, and gathering of materials, supplies, and teaching aids. Each thematic unit is a unique collection of activities planned for a specific group of young children, and it should take into consideration their particular geographic, socioeconomic, and cultural setting. The choice of unit sequence and subsectioning is up to the individual. After a thematic unit is presented, it should be evaluated by the writer for improvement.

HELPFUL WEB SITES

http://www.cpsc.gov/

Consumer Products Safety Commission. Check safe products.

http://www.boundlessplaygrounds.org

This site assists communities in the creation of playgrounds.

http://www.naeyc.org/

National Association for the Education of Young Children (NAEYC). Search for a position statement on school readiness.

http://www.naeyc.org/

NAEYC/SDE. Presents an executive summary outlining the essential elements of early learning standards.

http://www.ecs.org/

Education Commission of the States (ECS). Offers an outline of a long-range approach to improving early care and education.

http://www/fpg.unc.edu/

National Center for Early Development and Learning (NCEDL). Investigate links to research reports. Click "index."

http://members.aol.com

Reggio Emilia. Bibliography of reading material is available.

http://www.acf.hhs.gov/

Head Start. Search for Part 1304, Subpart B, Early Childhood Development and Health Services.

http://www.whitehouse.gov/
United States Government.Read more about the Good Start, Grow Smart initiative.

SUGGESTED ACTIVITIES

A. In groups of two to four, identify which activity plan section needs greater attention by the student teacher in the following situations.
   1. Danielle is presenting an activity with her collection of seashells. She has repeatedly requested that children look while she explains the details of the shells. Most of the children who started the activity are showing signs of disinterest.
   2. Francisco introduced a boat-floating activity that has children excited to try it. The children start pushing, shoving, and crowding.
   3. Dean prepared an activity with airplanes landing on a tabletop landing strip. Children are zooming loudly and running about the room, interfering with the work of others. The situation is getting out of hand.
   4. Claire's activity involves making a greeting card. Many children are disappointed because Claire has run out of the metallic paper used for her sample card. Others are requesting help because their fingers are sticky with glue.
   5. Kate's activity making cinnamon toast works well until Joey burns his finger on the toaster oven.
   6. Spencer has given a detailed verbal explanation of how the children should finish the weaving project he has introduced. However, the children seem to have lost interest.
   7. During Jackie Ann's project, paint gets on the door handles, and the children are unable to turn on the faucets because of slippery hands.
   8. Boris and Katrina have combined efforts during an activity. They have spent 10 minutes returning the area to usable condition for the next activity.

B. In groups of two to three, write up a plan using a form similar to one presented in this chapter. Fill in lesson plan sections that seem to fit your idea. Give it to your instructor for comments.

C. In groups of five or six, discuss why many activities are not prepared in written lesson plan form. Share key ideas with the total group.

D. Plan and present a group-time activity.

E. List the advantages in conducting a group time with seven to 10 children rather than 15 to 20 children.

F. After the class has been divided in half, select either the "pro" or "con" views of theme teaching as an instructional approach. Use 20 minutes to plan for a debate in a future class.

G. Develop a web or outline on the concept of "houses," or on a subject of your own choosing.

H. Read, then react to the following. Share your reaction with others.

   There is a new teaching fad every week or at least every few years! Today, it is teaching preschoolers early reading skills.

I. Examine your assigned classroom's curriculum. Try to cite specific incidences of the following. How do children:
   1. Anticipate consequences of their actions or elements in instructional activities?

2. Gather information for themselves?
3. Recognize and pinpoint problems?
4. Generate theories or ideas that might solve problems?
5. Gain control over strong emotions?
6. Make choices between different courses of action?
7. Evaluate the outcomes of their choices?
8. Participate in problem-solving discussions?

REVIEW

A. List two ways to identify children's interests.

B. Write three examples of motivational statements for activities you plan to present or could present.

C. Match items in Column I with those in Column II.

I	II
1. curriculum area	a. ethnic dance group
2. specific behavioral objective	b. "Those with red socks can wash their hands before lunch."
3. transitional statement	c. four out of five times
	d. "Snails have one foot, which slides along on a slippery liquid that comes fromthe snail."
4. motivational statement	
5. an activity plan criterion	e. nutrition
6. setup	f. has three parts
7. community resource	g. "Have you ever touched a bird's feather?"
8. performance criterion	h. too many concepts attempted
9. summary statement	i. paper left, then patterns, crayons, scissors at far right on table
10. pitfall in student teacher lesson planning	j. child safety

D. List considerations for group instruction planning.

E. Describe five important considerations when a student teacher is planning to conduct a 20-minute group time with 15 four-year-olds.

F. Complete the following statements.
   1. Two ways to improve a teacher's skills in conducting groups are . . .
   2. Activities that approach the same knowledge through art, music, science, cooking, measurement activities, and language activities can reinforce . . .
   3. A "saturated" environment might be described as . . .
   4. Using a thematic unit developed in another section of the country is probably . . .

G. List possible thematic unit subsections.

H. Identify the items listed below as a theme unit subsection (S) or part of a subsection (P).
   1. child activities
   2. child skill level

3. adult/child ratio
4. teacher evaluation
5. weekly time schedule
6. furniture and comfort
7. child safety
8. index
9. culminating activity
10. table of contents
11. artistic decoration
12. description of instructional goals
13. resource list
14. cultural values
15. background data
16. audiovisuals and real objects
17. title page
18. balance of curriculum areas
19. book lists
20. bibliography

I. List what you believe are two benefits and two limitations of theme teaching.

CASE SCENARIO

Setting: Outdoor play area. Inge, a student teacher in an urban cooperative preschool, is about to present an outdoor science activity.

Inge has planned an exciting outdoor science activity. After turning in her lesson plan, securing her cooperating teacher's approval, and collecting her visuals at a local creek, she takes a group of three-and-a-half-year-olds to a shaded grassy area outdoors.

She has prepared a small table and a covered tub with air holes. Children's paint aprons are waiting on a chair. At this time of day, other mixed-age classes are using the play yard.

Inge gathers her group of seven children, and tells them she has a surprise in the tub but they are to put on paint aprons first. The group stands around the tub. Inge has children guess what is in the tub. Then with a flourishing "Ta Ta" she removes the cover. Small creek frogs start to jump from the tub. Pandemonium, panic, and fear break out immediately. Some children run away screaming. Other children in the yard approach and crowd around the tub, delighted with the frogs. Inge tries to assure the children left in her group that the small frogs will not hurt them. Other teachers in the yard come to help.

continues . . .

. . . continued

Questions for Discussion:

1. What step or steps on Inge's lesson plan form were poorly conceived (see Figure 5–8)?
2. Think about Inge's educational intent. What would you say to Inge if you were her cooperating teacher?
3. Can anything positive be salvaged from Inge's disaster?
4. Does Inge's cooperating teacher share some responsibility for the lesson's outcome?

REFERENCES

Brent, D. (1996). The incidence of delayed school entry: A twelve year review. *Early Education and Development, 7*(2), 121–135.

Bredekamp, S., & Copple, C. (Eds.). (1997). *Developmentally appropriate practice in early childhood programs* (rev. ed.). Washington, DC: National Association for the Education of Young Children.

California Department of Education. (1991). *Exemplary program standards.* Sacramento, CA: Author.

Carter, M., & Curtis, D. (1994). *Training teachers: A harvest of theory and practice.* St. Paul, MN: Redleaf Press.

Coles, G. (2004, January). Danger in the classroom: "Brain glitch" research and learning to read. *Phi Delta Kappan*, 344–351.

Curtis, D., & Carter, M. (1996). *Reflecting children's lives: A handbook for planning a child-centered curriculum.* St. Paul, MN: Redleaf Press.

Derman-Sparks, L., & The A.B.C. Task Force. (1989, 1998). *Anti-bias curriculum.* Washington, DC: National Association for the Education of Young Children.

Delpit, L. (1995). *Other people's children: Cultural conflict in the classroom.* New York: The New Press.

Dodge, D. T., & Colker, L. (1992). *Creative curriculum for early childhood.* Washington, DC: Teaching Strategies.

Dunn, L., & Kontos, S. (1998, March/April). Developmentally appropriate practice: What does research tell us? *Journal of Early Education and Family Review, 5*(4).

Edwards, C., Gandini, L., & Forman, G. (Eds.). (1993). *The hundred languages of children: The Reggio approach.* Stamford, CT: Ablex Publishing.

Elliott, M. (1998, July). Great moments of learning in project work. *Young Children, 53*(4).

Epstein, A., Schweinhart, L., & McAdoo, L. (1996). *Models of early childhood education.* Ypsilanti, MI: High/Scope Press.

Fosnot, C. T. (1989). *Inquiring teachers, inquiring learners: A constructive approach for teaching.* New York: Teachers College Press.

Gable, S. (2002, July). Teacher-child relationships throughout the day. *Young Children, 57*(4), 42–47.

Gamel-McCormick, M. (2000). Exploring teachers' expectations for children entering kindergarten and procedures for sharing information between Pre-K and K programs. Conference Presentation. The National Association for the Education of Young Children Annual Conference, Atlanta, GA.

Gandini, L., & Goldhaber, J. (2001). Two reflections about documentation. In E. Gandini & C. P. Edwards (Eds.). *Bambini: The Italian approach to infant/toddler care* (pp. 124–145). New York: Teachers College Press.

Genishi, C. (2002, July). Young English language learners: Resourceful in the classroom. *Young Children, 57*(4), 66–72.

Greenman, J. (1989). Living in the real world. *Child Care Information Exchange, 67.*

Griffin, C., & Rinn, B. (1998, May). Enhancing outdoor play with an obstacle course. *Young Children, 53*(3).

Groginsky, S., Robison, S., & Smith, S. (1999). *Making child care better. State initiatives.* Washington, DC: National Conference of State Legislatures.

Gundling, R. (2002, Fall). Promoting early literacy in early childhood programs. *Child Care Bulletin, 27,* 7.

Gunter, M. A., Estes, T. H., & Schwab, J. H. (1990). *Instruction: A models approach.* Boston: Allyn & Bacon.

Harrington-Lueker, D. (2000, January). High stakes or developmental practice? MAYBE BOTH! *The School Administrator, 57,* 6–11.

Helm, J. H., & Katz, L. C. (2001). *Young investigators: The project approach in the early years.* New York: Teachers College Press.

Hunter, M. (1984). Knowing, teaching, and supervising. In P. L. Hosford (Ed.). *Using what we know about teaching.* Alexandria, VA: Association for Supervision & Curriculum Development.

Jones, E. (1986). Teaching adults. Washington, DC: National Association for the Education of Young Children.

Kamii, C., & De Vries, R. (1975/1977). Piaget for early education. In M. Day & R. Parker (Eds.). *Preschool in action.* Boston: Allyn & Bacon.

Kantrowitz, B., & Wingert, P. (2002, April 29). The right way to read. *Newsweek,* Vol. CXXXIX (17), 6–66.

Katz, L. (1994, April). *The project approach* (ERIC Digest, EDO-PS-94-6).

Katz, L., & Chard, S. (1993). *Engaging children's minds: The Project Approach.* Norwood, NJ: Ablex.

Kohn, A. (2001, March). Fighting the tests: Turning frustration into action. *Young Children, 56*(2), 19–24.

Kuster, C. A. (1994). At the core: Language and cultural competence. In J. Johnson & J. McCracken (Eds.). *The early childhood career lattice: Perspectives on professional development.* Washington, DC: National Association for the Education of Young Children.

Langness, T. (1998). *First-class teacher: Successful strategies for new teachers.* Santa Monica, CA: Canter and Associates, Inc.

Levin, T., & Long, R. (1981). *Effective instruction.* Alexandria, VA: The Association for Supervision and Curriculum Development.

Lumsden, L. (1998, Jan./Feb.). Teacher expectations: What is professed is not always practiced. *The Journal of Early Childhood and Family Review, 5*(3).

Marcon, R. A. (1999). Differential impact of preschool models on development and early learning of inner-city children: A three-cohort study. *Developmental Psychology, 35*(2), 358–375.

McGinnis, J. R. (2002, May). Enriching the outdoor environment. *Young Children, 57*(3), 28–29.

Meisels, S. J., & Jewkes, A. M. (2001, Summer). "School readiness" not easy to determine. *State Education Reader.* Education Commission of the States (ECS), *19*(2), 15.

Meyer, M. (1997, September). The GREENing of learning: Using the eighth intelligence. *Educational Leadership, 55*(1).

NAEYC Code of Ethical Conduct (1999). In S. Feeney and N. Freeman, (Eds). *Ethics and the early childhood educator: Using the NAEYC code.* Washington, DC: National Association for the Education of Young Children.

National Research Council. (2000). *How people learn: Brain, mind, experience and school.* Washington, DC: National Academy Press.

National Research Council. (2000). *How people learn: Brain, mind, experience and school.* Washington, DC: National Academy Press.

Ohl, J. (2002, Fall). Linking child care and early literacy: Building the foundation for success. *Child Care Bulletin, 27*, 1–4.

O'Loughlin, M. (1991, April 3–7). *Beyond constructivism: Toward a dialectical model of the problematics of teacher socialization.* Paper presented at the Annual Meeting of the American Educational Research Association, Chicago.

Oyemade, U. J., & Washington, V. (July 1989). Drug abuse prevention begins in early childhood. *Young Children, 44*(5).

Patron: Piaget in new perspective. New York: Parents Magazine Films, Inc.

Petersen, E. (1996). *A practical guide to early childhood planning methods and materials.* Boston: Allyn and Bacon.

Plutro, M. (2000, March). Planning for linguistic and cultural diversity—We must continue to respond. *Head Start Bulletin, 67*, 19.

Reynolds, G., & Jones, E. (1997). *Master players: Learning from children at play.* New York: Teachers College Press.

Rinaldi, C. (2001). Reggio Emilia: The image of the child and the child's environment as a fundamental principle. In E. Gandini & C.P. Edwards (Eds). *Bambini: The Italian approach to infant /toddler care* (pp. 55-56). New York: Teachers College Press.

San Jose Mercury News. (2000, December). Spelling out commitment: Scott Lane School's reading promise should be the norm, not a news story. 6B, Author

Seefeldt, C., & Barbour, N. (1998). *Early childhood education: An introduction.* Columbus, OH: Merrill.

Sheinman, A. J. (2000, August). Six behavior tips that really work. *Instructor, 110*(1), 24.

Slavin, R. E. (1987). Cooperative learning and the cooperative school. *Educational Leadership, 47.*

Slavin, R. E. (1988). The cooperative revolution catches fire. *The School Administrator, 44.*

Stipek, D. (1996). Motivation and instruction .In D. Berliner & R. Calfee (Eds.). *Handbook of educational psychology.* New York: Macmillan.

United States Bureau of the Census. (1995). *The foreign-born population: 1994.* Current Population Reports. Washington, DC: Government Printing Office.

Vander Wilt, J., & Monroe, V. (1998, July). Successfully moving toward developmentally appropriate practice: It takes time and effort! *Young Children, 53*(4).

Vygotsky, L. (1986). *Thought and language.* Cambridge, MA: MIT Press.

Wein, C. A. (1995). Developmentally appropriate practice in "real life." New York: Teachers College Press.

Wesson, K. A. (2001, March). The "Volvo Effect"—Questioning standardized tests. *Young Children, 56*(2), 16–18.

Wilson, R., Kilmer, S., & Knauerhase, V. (1996, September). Developing an environmental outdoor play space. *Young Children, 51*(6).

Wolverton, E. D. (2000, March). The curriculum: A written plan for action. *Head Start Bulletin, 67*, 4–5.

Zahorik, J. A. (1997, March). Encouraging and challenging student's understanding. *Educational Leadership, 54*(6).

SECTION III

Classroom Management Revisited

Classroom Management Goals and Techniques

Objectives

After studying this chapter, the student should be able to:

1 List the five major management areas.

2 Discuss the effects of the classroom environment on children's behaviors.

3 Define the role of the guidance function in the management of the classroom.

4 List and describe five common guidance techniques.

5 Identify the different behaviors children display when resisting adult authority.

6 Analyze what guidance techniques work best and state why.

I once heard in a beginning class what one teacher tried when a child picked up a large tree branch and brandished it threateningly at other children. The teacher went to the child and said "What a marvelous branch, could I hold it?" That led into a discussion about the branch hurting someone, and the child's deciding it needed to be given to the custodian. The teacher later had the custodian carry it in at a small group time for discussion. The child received attention and status for considering the safety of others.

I tried this technique with a child who'd picked up a playground rock. It worked well for me, too. I'm sure it won't always work but it might work most of the time.

—Peter Mills

CLASSROOM MANAGEMENT

What comes to your mind when you hear the words "classroom management"? Many student teachers, and many teachers themselves, associate the phrase with another word: discipline. Classroom management goes far beyond discipline, although the guidance function is certainly a part of what is involved in managing the classroom. Classroom management, in the fullest sense of the meaning of the phrase, involves five separate prongs: (1) the physical arrangement of the classroom(s), (2) curriculum choices, (3) time management, (4) managing classroom routines, and (5) the guidance function. Guidance, in turn, has two facets: (1) managing routine behavior problems and (2) managing serious behavior problems.

classroom management—consists of supervising, planning, and directing classroom activities and the room environment. It also involves making time length decisions, providing appropriate direction, and guiding child behavior to enable children to live and work effectively with others.

The Physical Arrangement of the Classroom

What is the "best" arrangement for a preschool classroom? Curtis and Carter (1996) remind teachers that environments have a great influence on how people feel and behave. Put yourself at children's eye level when evaluating a classroom. Questions such as the following should be considered:

- Where should blocks be located? Are they easy to reach?
- Where should an art area be located? On a easy-to-clean floor area? Near a water supply?
- Should there be a clothesline on which to hang paintings?
- Is the dramatic play area attractive? Are there enough changes of clothing to simulate a variety of roles?
- Is there a quiet corner where children can look at books (see Figure 6–1)?
- Is there plenty of space, especially outside, for active play?

Figure 6–1 Notice the abundant pillows immediately in front of the book display.

- Do children have an opportunity to climb, run, and ride wheeled toys without endangering each other's safety?
- Given an empty room of 20 feet by 30 feet, where should different areas be located? How can the teacher define each?
- Are children's physical needs and safety considered?
- Is there a sense of order?
- Would the room promote child curiosity, wonder, intrigue, or beg to be physically explored?
- Is the room aesthetically pleasing and does it offer elements of natural beauty?
- Are room retreats designed to offer feelings of soft, cuddly, calming textures, seating, and privacy (see Figure 6–2)?
- Is the room set up for child self-help?
- Do thought-out storage areas exist?
- Do classroom furniture or equipment arrangements promote crowded conditions in some classroom areas?
- Is child comfort a priority?
- Are creative materials and toys open-ended?
- Is there a secluded "escape hatch" area?
- Are room arrangements and areas flexible, and can they expand if need be?
- Are there smooth, flowing pathways in and out of room areas?
- Do visual displays reflect children's lives, interests, and cultural experiences?

Room features sometimes overlooked include background noise level, smells, temperature, and lighting.

Figure 6–2 A climb-into hideaway

Look at Figure 6–3. Is this the best possible arrangement this first-grade teacher could have made? What flaws can you see? Was the teacher wise in placing the reading area next to the water fountain? Where should the math manipulatives be stored? Given the configuration of the desks, what circulation problems might you anticipate? Can you think of what you might do should your cooperating teacher allow you to rearrange this classroom? You may want to discuss this with your fellow student teachers.

Now look at Figure 6–4. Is this the best possible arrangement for this preschool play yard for three- and four-year-olds? Can you point out any possible areas of difficulty related to the placement of the play equipment in the yard? Was

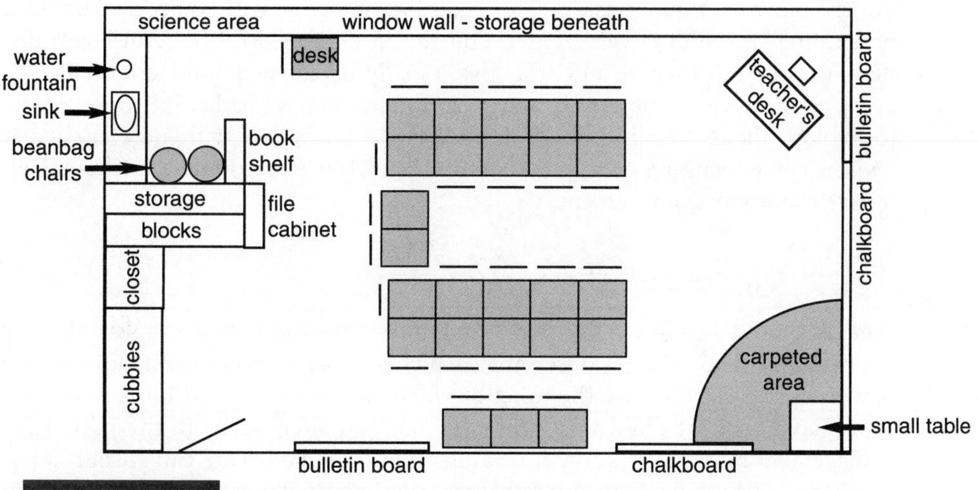

Figure 6–3 Why might the arrangement of this first-grade classroom lead to management problems?

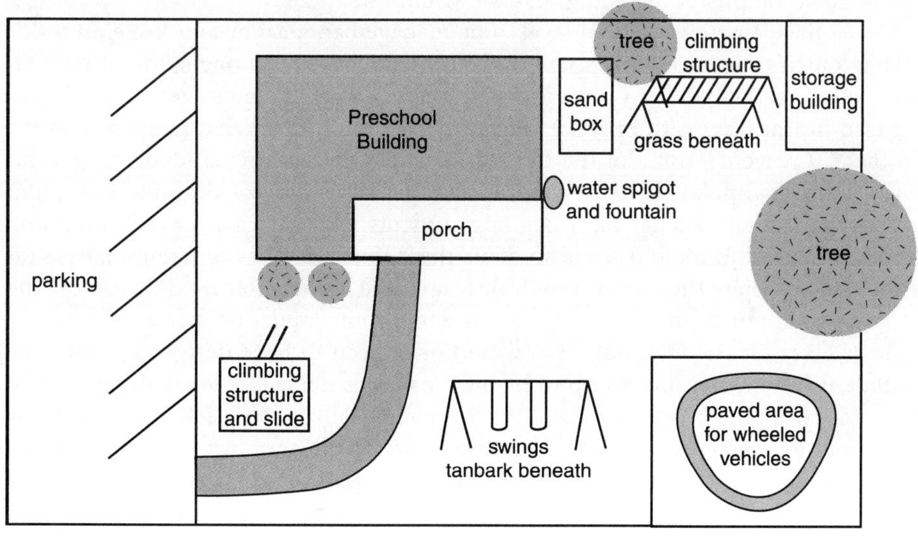

Figure 6–4 What might be the possible problems with the arrangement of this preschool play yard?

it wise of the person who designed the yard to have placed the sand area by the water spigot and fountain? Should the storage shed be located where it is? Is the paved area for wheeled vehicles large enough and stimulating enough? Again, you may want to discuss this play yard arrangement with your peers and describe any changes you may feel would be justified and why.

Curriculum Choices

Each choice you make regarding curriculum is another part of classroom management. First, choose the materials you will set out for children to explore. Second, decide which materials, such as scissors and glue sticks, can be used only under your direct supervision. Third, decide how you will equip the dramatic play center or the discovery center. Fourth, develop colorful bulletin board displays that are informative and attractive. Finally, decide which materials are used every day and which materials change after children have had ample opportunity to explore them. Keeping children adequately motivated with new curricular choices while retaining those materials children clearly love both contribute to effective classroom management.

Time Management

Time is a limited source. Time management involves more than simply following a schedule. It also involves observing each child closely and understanding when one child may need to use the toilet or when another may need to be redirected from playing with a child with whom he has had altercations in the past. Time management means you know how long children in your care can sustain interest. Choose books for story time that not only pique the children's interests but also are short enough to sustain their attention. Time management means planning activities that are neither too long nor too short, and giving children more opportunities to engage in activities. Sometimes, there never seems to be enough time to accomplish everything that we would like to do.

At the elementary school level, time management also means "time on task." How much time is actually spent on learning activities? In one study of time allotted to mathematics in a second-grade classroom, students were actively engaged in learning math only 30 percent of the total time. What happened to the other 70 percent? Some of the time was spent in reminding students to get out the math manipulatives they were to use that day. Some of the time was spent with the student teacher reprimanding students who were not paying attention. In fact, he had to remind some students three times to take the manipulatives off the shelves where they were stored. How might he have better used the time? One simple solution to the loss of attention while some students were slow to go to the shelves for the manipulatives would have been to have designated only one student from each table group to be the "materials manager" for that day.

A word of caution: not all of the 70 percent of time off-task that seemed to be "wasted" actually was. Students used part of the time when they appeared to be off-task or day dreaming to think, a critical part of problem-solving and unlocking their creative potential. Can you remember the times when you might have taken time to withdraw, in a sense, from active participation in a classroom just to think? Your children or students do likewise.

As mentioned in Chapter 4, recent research on the activities of the brain, together with the burgeoning influence of schools that have implemented brain-based learning, has shown what happens in the brains of people when they think. When the material to learn is new, children (adults also) need more time to reflect or think about what it is they are learning. Young children need to be taught how to talk about what they are doing because that helps them develop the capacity to reflect. Later, they can be encouraged to speak silently to themselves as a part of developing the ability to think about thinking (metacognition) (Abbott, 1997).

A further note of caution: McCarthy (1997) cautions us to remember that thinking involves both reflection and action. Although some children will sit quietly and "process" newly presented material, others will want almost immediately to act on the material or experiment with it. Our classroom needs to support both types of children. Classroom experiences with teaching to children's multiple intelligences also supports brain-based learning (Caine & Caine, 1997).

Time management also means wise use of your own time: try to balance your work, preparation, home and family, relaxation, and recreation times. Set priorities and try not to become so overwhelmed with preparation for school that you have no time for other things.

Managing Classroom Routines

For student teachers, it is essential to your success that you carefully observe your cooperating teacher's routines. Should you want to introduce a change in routine, clear it with your college supervisor first; then check with your cooperating teacher. One may say no, but another may suggest that you try but that you be aware of what a change in the routine may do to two or three of the children. Always remember, that for some children, routines offer predictability and, therefore, safety.

THE GUIDANCE FUNCTION IN CLASSROOM MANAGEMENT

When we think of the guidance function and its role in classroom management, what do we mean? **Guidance** can be the act of guiding; it can mean leadership or directing someone to a destination or goal. In the classroom, guidance is the teacher's function in providing leadership. In particular, it is the act of assisting the child to grow toward maturity. This is the major goal.

guidance—ongoing process of directing children's behavior based on the types of adults children are expected to become.

Guidance can also be looked at as a

> system, one in which people are interdependent and each action taken by one person influences the others. What is expected of children, the schedule and routines of the adults, all contribute to the system of discipline (Boulden, Hiester, & Walti, 1998).

To Boulden, et al. (1998), it often seems that some people are born with a natural talent for being able to set appropriate guidelines for children, whereas others have to work at it, learn by trial and error—and a few hard knocks—and only gradually improve.

Yet Boulden admits that when she asks these naturally talented people how they do what they do, they invariably admit that they, too, struggled with learning what worked for them and what did not. Walti (Boulden, et al., 1998) states that one of the problems she sees today is that "we are exposed to literally dozens of options and hundreds of articles on the subject," all of which make it sometimes difficult to know what to choose at any one time. Schoonmaker (1998) agrees and suggests that until student teachers feel confident that they can control or manage children's behaviors, they may be preoccupied by issues of discipline (management).

Conflicts Arise

Conflict among preschoolers is an expected part of social development (Killen & Turiel, 1991). When children's different needs and wishes collide, feelings erupt. Play partner selection can be a factor. Transitions from one activity to another may provoke problems if transitions are abrupt. Anger, frustration, and disappointment may trigger child outbreaks. Violence may have become a learned behavior. Browning, Davis, and Resta (2000) remind teachers that children may frequently witness verbal and physical aggression in their homes or neighborhoods, and emulate that model.

Outcomes.

Educators who study children's conflicts observe four common outcomes:

1. *Lack of resolution*, which happens if the issue is dropped, children leave the area, select different toys or different activities, or seek other play partners
2. *A mutual solution* is achieved through discussion, bargaining, compromising, settling on a creative alternative, or making the conflict into a game
3. *Submission* happens if a child or children "give in" and willingly or unwillingly yield
4. *Adult intervention* imposes, settles, or suggests a solution

As Gillespie and Chick (2001) point out, submission is an undesirable outcome because a clear winner and loser is established, creating or promoting bullying and victimization. Adult intervention, though sometimes necessary, is not the educators' primary goal, which is to minimize the need for adult intervention. When this happens, children negotiate and resolve conflicts themselves. Practice of problem-solving skills may be necessary and educators take the time to offer practice opportunities by providing supportive assistance (Nelsen, Lott, & Glenn, 1997).

Managing Routine Behavior Problems

What is meant by "routine behavior problems?" Can any misbehavior be considered routine? Obviously, two-year-old children may present several "routine behavior problems" as they struggle with trying to establish their autonomy. But it isn't just two-year-olds who struggle with autonomy. To a certain extent, all children struggle with it. What do you see then? You see children who push against the limits, the boundaries. When you first take over the class from your cooperating teacher, you will often see children who seem to misbehave deliberately. You ask them to come to the circle time area and some children say "No." You ask others to pick up the blocks and replace them on the shelves prior to snack time; again, you hear, "No" and/or, "Why should I?" and/or, "I don't want any snack today."

So what is the student teacher to do? One set of guidelines is the four Cs: consistency, consideration, confidence, and candor. What is meant by consistency? Consistency of adult behavior, consistency of expectations, consistency of limits and rules. Consistency means that you understand yourself well enough that you can respond to children in a fair and impartial manner. It also means reliability; your behavior does not change from day to day and remains reasonably predictable to the children. For children, there is safety in knowing that the adults in their lives are predictable. Such reliability gives children feelings of security and safety. This becomes especially important when you, as a student teacher, are responsible for children who may be inconsistent and unpredictable.

The second C is consideration. This means that you are considerate of the children you teach and of the adults with whom you work. You respect the children and are aware of their needs, their likes, and dislikes. You are considerate by taking time to listen, even to the child who talks constantly. It means watching all of the children closely and noting which child needs an extra hug and which one needs to be removed from a group before a temper tantrum erupts. All of these actions show children that you care and will help you establish a warm relationship with them. Consideration helps to build rapport.

The third C is confidence. You need confidence to make decisions that reflect careful thought on your part, decisions that are free of bias and based on all evidence. Confidence implies that you realize you like some children better than others, and you know why you react differently to identical actions involving different children. Confidence is knowing when to stand up for your opinions and decisions and when to compromise. It means understanding when to be silent, knowing that waiting is the more mature action to take.

Candor, the fourth C, means that you are open and honest in your actions with the children, your fellow workers, and yourself. It means being frank and fair; you may inevitably "put your foot in your mouth," but you will gain a reputation for being honest in your relations with others. Candor is the ability to admit a mistake and being unafraid to apologize.

The four Cs can, perhaps, be spelled CARE. As Rogers and Freiberg (1994) wrote, good teachers possess three qualities: congruence, acceptance of others, and empathy. As mentioned in Chapter 2, these can easily be expanded to four: congruence, acceptance, reliability, and empathy (see Figure 6–5).

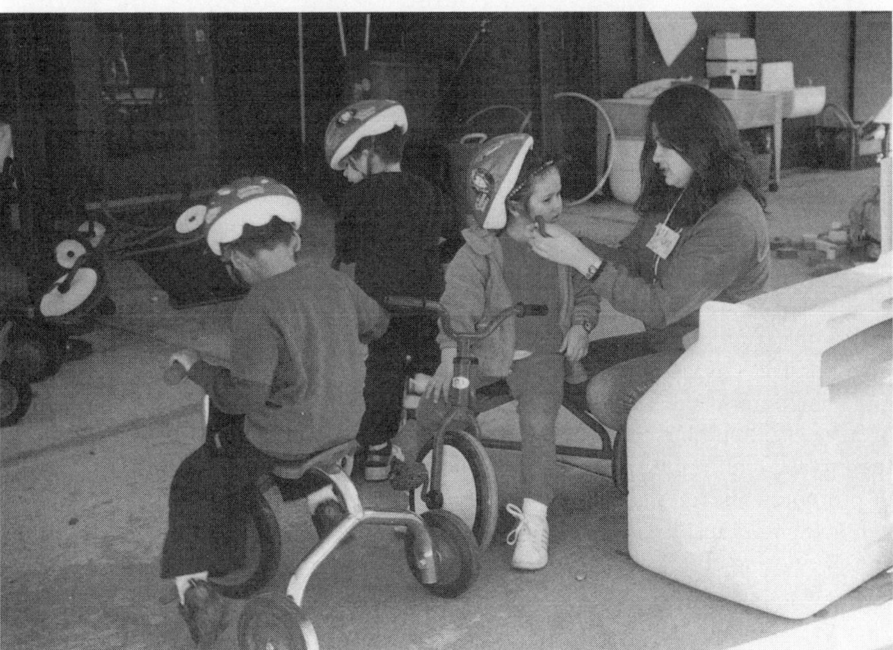

Figure 6–5 Student teaching offers many opportunities to show children you CARE.

Congruence, as Chapter 2 states, is Rogers' term for understanding yourself. Always remember that with truly great teachers, their teaching is such an extension of themselves that you see the same person whether that person is in the classroom, the office, the home, or the supermarket. These people radiate self-confidence in knowing who they are and what they want from life. It is sometimes difficult for the student teacher to copy the congruent teacher because the methods the teacher uses are so much a part of that person that the student teacher may not be able to emulate. This is related to the second goal of guidance: knowing yourself.

What you as a student teacher must learn is what methods are congruent with your inner self. The best methods are always those that seem natural to use, those that are an extension of how you feel about yourself.

Remember, acceptance in the Rogerian sense means truly caring about each child you teach. It means all children deserve your respect regardless of how they act. The aggressive, "acting-out" child is just as deserving of your acceptance as the star pupil of the class.

As mentioned before, reliability means that your children know you and the routine for the class. Being reliable also implies fairness.

According to Rogers, empathy implies being able to place yourself in the child's shoes, of seeing from that perspective. It is the ability to see that the hostile, aggressive child may need love and acceptance more than the happy, easygoing child. Empathy also means knowing that the happy child needs attention, even though it is not demanded. Learn to be empathetic; it is worth the effort.

Let us assume that you have learned how to CARE. Does that mean you will not have any behavior problems? Does that mean you will automatically have rapport with all your children? Of course not. It means only that you can, perhaps, understand children's behavior more easily and plan to teach self-discipline to those who need to learn.

CHILD EMPOWERMENT

empowering—helping parents and children gain a sense of control over events in their lives.

Your previous classes no doubt dealt with the issue of child choice and responsibility for behavioral actions. Empowering children in classrooms can mean giving them the opportunity to think about and guide their own actions, thereby allowing them to choose between possible actions in any given situation. Naturally, all child group living arrangements have rules to guard the safety of children and limit behaviors unpleasant to others.

It may be all too easy for a student teacher to "do everything" for children. It makes the student teacher appear busy and productive, in control, active rather than passive. Giving choices within limits takes time and is usually more work, and sometimes it creates room disorder. Is it easier to pass out paper at art times or have children help themselves? Easier to write names on the children's papers than to ask children if they want to write their own names on their work? Easier to promote children's taking turns as group leaders or helpers or doing the task yourself? Most teachers answer it is easier to do it themselves, but sharing tasks and promoting children's experiences and self-esteem are the preferred and most educative practices.

Hiester (Boulden, et al., 1998) would agree and states, "children's self-esteem is centered around how they were disciplined, the things that do or do not happen to children." She writes about the need for us to "face our monsters," those actions by children that most annoy and upset us. To Hiester, communication was the key: communicating both with the children (and being aware of how much is communicated through nonverbal behaviors) and the other adults in the room associated with the program. Allowing the children to take part in the management process (when it was concerned with nutrition breaks and cleanup times, for example) and asking them to help in deciding how to store materials in the classroom proved to reduce the times Hiester needed to intervene or be concerned.

Teachers strive to make rules consistent and clear. There are times during classroom life when a child cannot choose. These times are not presented as choices. As adults, we usually abhor, avoid, and sometime rebel in situations in which we lose our autonomy; so do young children.

The authors felt an update and review at this point in your student teaching would be useful. Unfortunately, there is no magic formula. This text aims to provide you with both the possible "whys" (Chapter 7) of children's behavior and the techniques used successfully by professional early childhood teachers.

Character Guidance

Ryan (1993) points out that schools and teachers unconsciously and consciously attempt to educate children:

- To be concerned about the weak and those who need help
- To help others
- To work hard and complete tasks as well as they are able, and promptly
- To control violent tempers
- To work cooperatively
- To practice good manners
- To respect authority
- To respect the rights of others
- To help resolve conflicts
- To understand honesty, responsibility, and friendship
- To balance pleasure and responsibilities
- To ask themselves and decide what is the right thing to do

Student teachers may experience many classroom adult-child learning situations that are also guidance situations, and may be concerned with one or more of the above-listed goals of the guidance function in classroom management.

Guidance as Social Development

Social behaviors are sometimes seen as difficult to teach because they so often involve the absence of doing rather than doing. In other words, we teach prosocial behavior by *not* doing. We choose not to grab; we choose not to spank; we try to model, in our own behaviors how we would like the children to behave. But what can we do actively? Honig and Wittmer (1996) suggest the following:

- Provide an environment sensitive to the needs of the children.
- Emphasize cooperation rather than competition. Teach cooperative and conflict-resolution games and sports.
- Set up classroom spaces and play materials to facilitate cooperative play.
- Use bibliotheraphy: incorporate children's literature to enhance empathy and caring in daily reading activities.
- Actively lead group discussions on prosocial interactions.

bibliotherapy—the use of books that deal with emotionally sensitive topics in a developmentally appropriate way to help children gain accurate information and learn coping strategies.

- Encourage social interaction between normally developing children and children with special needs.
- Develop class and school projects that foster altruism.
- Move very young children with peers to the next age group.
- Arrange regular viewing of prosocial media and video games.
- Invite moral mentors to visit the class.
- Work closely with families for prosocial programming.
- Establish a parent resource lending library.
- Establish a bias-free curriculum.
- Require responsibility: encourage children to care for younger children and classmates who need extra help.
- Become familiar with structured curriculum packages that promote prosocial development.
- Implement a comprehensive school-based prosocial program that emphasizes ethical teaching.
- Train older children as peer mediators.
- Cherish the children: create an atmosphere of affirmation through family/classroom/community rituals.

Gartrell (1997) emphasizes that

> [T]he objective is to teach children to solve problems rather than to punish children for having problems they cannot solve. The outcomes of guidance—the ability to get along with others, solve problems using words, express strong feelings in acceptable ways—are the goals for citizens of a democratic society.

To achieve this objective, Gartrell reminds teachers, first of all, that social skills are complex and take into adulthood to learn. Second, he stresses the need for the teacher to reduce the children's needs for what he terms "mistaken behavior." Third, he states that teachers themselves must practice positive teacher-child and teacher-adult relations. Whether we recognize it or not, we are role models of behavior for our children. How we handle anger, distress, frustration, fear, sadness, and so on does have an effect on the children in our charge. Fourth, it is important to remember that any intervention method chosen should be solution-oriented. Fifth, and you have heard this before: We need to build partnerships with parents. Last, teachers should use teamwork with adults. Gartrell states that it is a myth to think we can handle all situations alone.

Helping Children Understand and Express Emotions and Feelings. Researchers have attempted to identify stages in children's understandings of their own emotions, and the language and actions children use to express emotions. One major conclusion derived from these studies is that conversations about feelings provide an important context for learning about emotions and how to manage them (Kuebli, 1994). In everyday interactions, teachers have the opportunity to help children gain insight into emotions, their own and those of others, and develop socially acceptable expressions.

Kuebli suggests:

- Evaluating the classroom climate for staff acceptance of children's expressions of feelings and also the appropriate adult responses.
- Considering classroom features and settings where emotions and children's reflections on feelings can be experienced. Well-stocked play centers and

adults who prompt vicarious exploration can be part of the dramatic play area.

- Providing art materials conducive to emotional response, where adults promote "talking about," and child reflections concerning emotional happenings.
- Using storybooks dealing with emotions, asking children how they would feel in a similar situation, and discussing causes and consequences.
- Using audiovisual equipment. Children can recreate emotions they have seen. Then, they can dramatize a situation for themselves and discuss the choices children have made in responding to their own and others' emotions.
- Dealing with children's quarrels and disputes in a way that develops child understanding, and giving children time to tell their respective sides without interruption. Teachers can reflect back and ask for clarification while also urging each child to examine his personal contribution to the conflict. Talking about how they feel and what could be done differently next time helps children manage feelings rather than suppress or deny them.

Staffing almost always determines how much time individual teachers have to spend on children's disputes. Student teachers may play a special preventive and interactional role in social-emotional development and supplement the cooperating teacher's efforts.

Rules

Wherever you work with children, there will be rules. Some will be unique because schools and centers vary immensely in physical structures and staffing patterns. Even economics can influence rules for children. In an earlier chapter, you were asked to read any written rule statement in existence at your placement site. By now, you have probably discovered rule revisions and rules unique to your classroom that were not included, so-called unwritten rules. Rules are not secret! To be effective, each child needs a clear picture of the teacher's expectations of classroom behavior. Any new rules need to be discussed with the children.

All rules in an early childhood center, kindergarten, or primary classroom are related to four basic categories of actions:

1. Children will not be allowed to hurt themselves.
2. Children will not be allowed to hurt others.
3. Children will not be allowed to destroy the environment.
4. Everyone helps with the cleanup tasks.

   Another category also enters the picture when group instruction begins.

5. Children will not be able to impact other children's access to instruction.

In other words, they cannot interrupt, hamper, impede, or delay the smoothness or flow of the educational program by disruptive actions(s).

Student teachers need to examine rules closely (see Figure 6–6). If rules become picky or ultraspecific, it often indicates an overuse of teacher power. One student teacher shared with her student teaching class an incident where a child was admonished for eating his "pusher" first at lunchtime. The student teacher could not understand what a "pusher" was, or second, why the adult was interfering with the child's choice of what he wished to consume first. She found a "pusher" was the adult's word for a piece of bread. Another student teacher shared another unbelievable center mealtime rule. She observed children were not to eat just the frosting off their cupcakes. You will need to keep tabs on whether rules are reasonable and/or too numerous as you student teach.

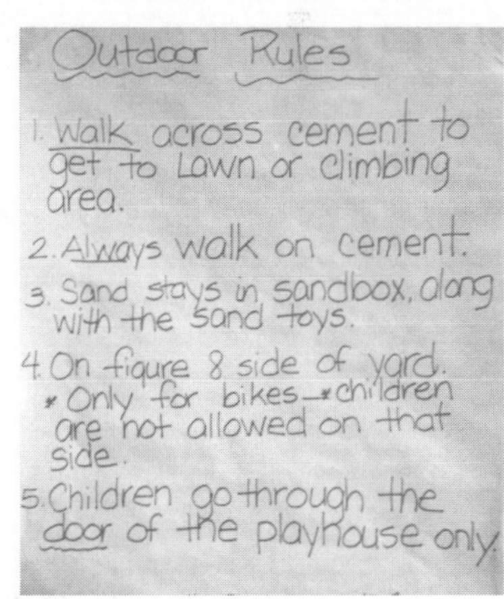

Figure 6–6 The rules posted on the door to the yard in this classroom helped the many adults who worked there to know what was expected.

A student teacher is an authority figure, one who assures rules are followed for the safety and welfare of all concerned. Authority figures expect that there may be occasions of child anger because the teacher's action(s) can block a child from her desire or goal. It is not realistic to expect enrolled children will always be happy with you. Do remember though, children will "test" you to see whether rules established by your cooperating teacher still apply when you are in charge.

Age of Child

Some loose guidelines will be discussed next concerning guidance techniques for children of different ages. Teachers of infants and toddlers find that techniques that require the physical removal of objects or the child from a given situation are used more frequently, although words always accompany teacher action. During preschool years, teachers often focus on changing environmental settings, or their instructional (planned) program, or the way they interact or speak, in order to help preschoolers with rule compliance. It is common in preschool, kindergarten, and lower elementary school grades to have teacher-child and teacher-group discussion about classroom rules, and the reason(s) behind rules, then classroom "trouble spots" or difficulties are solved together. Teachers are still the ultimate authority, but children have a greater feeling and understanding that rules protect everyone. Rules become "our rules" rather than "the teacher's rules."

CLASSROOM MANAGEMENT TECHNIQUES

Now let us look at specific techniques you might use to manage some of the problems you will encounter in any classroom. At the same time, do not forget the broader meaning of the term "guidance."

In its narrower sense of classroom or behavior management, guidance refers to those things you do to teach or persuade the children to behave in a manner of which you approve. There are many ways to manage behavior, but there are six that have proven to be more effective than others:

1. Behavior modification (applying principles of reinforcement to change a child's behavior)
2. Setting limits and insisting they be kept
3. Labeling the behavior instead of the child
4. Using the concept of logical consequences
5. Teacher anticipation and intervention
6. Conflict resolution

behavior management—behavioral approach to guidance holding that the child's behavior is under the control of the environment, which includes space, objects, and people.

behavior modification—the systematic application of principles of reinforcement to modify behavior.

Behavior Modification

In terms of behavior modification, it is important to be objective. The term has acquired a negative connotation that is unfounded. Everyone uses behavior modification, whether it is recognized or not, from turning off the lights when children are to be quiet to planning and implementing a behavior modification plan. See the Appendix for a behavior modification plan.

Setting Limits

Rules must be stated, repeated, and applied consistently (see Figure 6–7). The aggressive, acting-out child must often be reminded of these rules over and over again. You may have to repeatedly remove the acting-out child from the room or to a quiet area in the room. You may have to insist firmly and caringly that the child change the negative behavior. A technique that works one day, such as removing the child to a quiet corner, may not work the next. A technique that works on one child may not work on another.

There are several difficulties facing the student teacher regarding behavior management. One of the difficulties is the problem of developing a repertoire of techniques with which you are comfortable. A second difficulty is developing an awareness or sensitivity to children so that you can almost instinctively know what technique to use on which child. The third difficulty is understanding, usually through the process of trial and error, what techniques are congruent with your self-image. If you see yourself as a warm and loving person, do not pretend to be a strict disciplinarian. The children will sense your pretense and will not behave.

Figure 6–7 This school has an area where bikes are to be returned and parked when not in use.

Perhaps the most critical error made by many student teachers is confusing the need to be liked by the children and the fear of rejection with their need for limits. As a result, the student teacher may fail to set limits or interfere in situations, often allowing the situation to get out of hand. When the student teacher must finally intervene, the student teacher may forget to CARE; he may fail to be congruent and not accept the child causing the problem. The student teacher may not be consistent from day to day or child to child, and may not take the time to develop empathy.

The children, in contrast, know perfectly well the student teacher's need to be liked, but they do not know whether the student teacher can be trusted. Trust is acquired only when the children discover that the student teacher CAREs. It is more important that the children respect, rather than love, the student teacher. In fact, no child can begin to love without having respect first.

It is easier to explain your limits at the beginning of your student teaching experience than to make any assumptions that the children know them. They know what limits your cooperating teacher has established, but they do not know that you expect the same. In order to reassure themselves that the limits are the same, they test them. This is when you must insist that your rules are the same as the cooperating teacher's. You will have to repeat them often. Most children will learn rapidly that your expectations are the same. Others will have to be reminded constantly before they accept the rules.

Labeling the Behavior

What is meant by the phrase "labeling the behavior, not the child?" Essentially, we are referring to what Gordon (1974) calls "I" messages in contrast to "you" messages. In an "I" message, you recognize that it is your problem rather than the child's. For example, if one of your three-year-olds accidentally spills the paint, you are angry, not because the child spilled the paint, but because you do not want to clean up the mess. Unfortunately, you may lash out at the child and say something like "For goodness sake! Don't you ever look at what you're doing?" or "Why are you so clumsy?" The result is that the child feels that spilling the paint is the child's fault when it is possible that it is your fault. The paint may have been placed too close to the child's elbow. The spilled paint is your problem, not the child's. How much better to say something like, "I really hate to clean up spilled paint!" This is what is truly annoying you, not the child. Even children can understand a reluctance to clean up a spill. How much better it would have been to label the behavior, not the child.

There are times, of course, when you will honestly feel you do not like the child, and it is especially important then to let the child know that it is the behavior you do not like, rather than the child. Continue to look for other times when you can give an honest compliment. Do not try to use positive reinforcement unless the child's behavior warrants it. All children know whether they deserve a compliment; do not try to fool them.

Sending "I" messages is a technique that even young children can learn. As the teacher, you can ask children to say "I don't like it when you do that!" to other children instead of shouting "I don't like you!" By labeling the action that is disliked, the child who is being corrected learns what is acceptable behavior without being made to feel bad. The children who are doing the correcting also learn what is acceptable. Eventually, they also learn how to differentiate between who a child is and how the child behaves. It is a lesson even adults need to practice.

Logical Consequences

logical consequences—Rudolf Dreikurs' technique of specific outcomes that follow certain behaviors and are mutually agreed upon by teacher and children/students.

Developed by psychiatrist Rudolf Dreikurs, the concept of logical consequences is based on his long association with family and child counseling. Eventually relating his theories of family-child discipline to the classroom, his landmark books, *Psychology in the Classroom* (1968), *Discipline without Tears* (co-authored with P. Cassel, 1972), and *Maintaining Sanity in the Classroom* (co-authored with B. Grunewald & F. Pepper, 1982) introduced teachers and administrators to his concepts of natural and logical consequences.

For example, a natural consequence of not coming to dinner when called might be the possibility of eating a cold meal. In the classroom setting, however, natural consequences are not easily derived, so logical consequences are generally used instead.

Dreikurs' key ideas relate to his beliefs that all students want recognition, and if unable to attain it in ways teachers would call "socially acceptable," children will resort to four possible "mistaken goals:" attention getting, power seeking, revenge seeking, and displaying inadequacy. To change the behavior, then, teachers need first to identify the student's mistaken goal. This is accomplished by recognizing student reaction to being corrected.

time-out—technique in which the child is removed from the reinforcement and stimulation of the classroom.

If the student is seeking attention, she may stop the behavior but then repeat it until she receives the desired attention. If seeking power, she may refuse to stop or even may escalate the behavior. In this case, a teacher may want, in as much as possible, to ignore the behavior in order not to provoke a power struggle with the student. Or the teacher may want to provide the student with clear-cut choices, "You may choose to go to the time-out area until you feel able to rejoin the group, or you may go to the math center and work on the tangrams." A student wanting revenge may become hostile or even violent; a teacher may have no recourse but to isolate the student or send her to the office. A student displaying inadequacy may refuse to cooperate, participate, or interact unless working one-to-one with the teacher.

To change student behavior, Dreikurs has several suggestions, some that reinforce what has already been said: provide clear-cut directions of your expectations of the students, and develop classroom rules cooperatively with them, especially those related to the logical consequences for inappropriate behaviors. Logical consequences should relate as closely as possible to the misbehavior, so the students can see the connection between them (Charles, 1992).

> Demond, a second grade student, just sits in class when it's time for math. Given a set of problems to finish after a demonstration at the board, he lowers his head, refusing to look at you when you suggest that he should begin working. Fifteen minutes later, he

still has not begun to respond. What does Demond's mistaken goal appear to be? If you identify it as inadequacy, you might say, "Demond, I know you can do this lesson. Take a look at the first problem. What does it ask you to do?"

One way to avoid the problem altogether might be to ask your cooperating teacher if you might pair the students for learning tasks or group them in blocks of four where the primary rule is "Three before me," a technique that means that students are responsible for teaching each other before they raise their hands for help from you.

As Eaton (1997) points out, "[l]ogical consequences are more complicated [than natural ones], yet they are still effective." She cites the need for the teacher to give the child the choice of following a rule ("We put on our coats before we go to play outside") or accepting its logical consequence ("If you don't put on your coat, you'll have to remain inside. You decide what you want to do."). In another example of a child, who continually interrupts during story time, the logical consequence of not listening might be to give the child the choice of going to a time-out area of the room or of going to a table where he could become involved in some quiet behavior such as drawing a picture. Again, the child is given choices of what he may do. Eaton stresses that the reason for suggesting to the child that he could go to a time-out area is not to punish the child but rather to provide the child with an opportunity to change his behavior. She continues, "A logical consequence makes clear the connection between the child's behavior and the resulting disciplinary action." It is too late if not attended to immediately.

Eaton also states that adult follow-through is another essential step in what she calls "positive discipline." She cautions teachers to remember that guiding a child's behavior "is a process, a developing skill." Critical to the child's learning are three behaviors a teacher needs to model in following through:

1. The teacher should get down to the child's level when speaking to the child.
2. The teacher should always use the child's name to attract and hold her attention.
3. The teacher should remain focused on the child when speaking to him and encourage "the child to learn that he is responsible for the choices he makes."

Eaton (1997) concludes by reminding us how important it is "for children to develop clear values that enable them to grow up being fair and considerate of others." To this end, a part of what children need to learn is to understand their own feelings and how to express these in what we would call "socially acceptable" ways. Another part of the process is learning how to make choices and to understand the natural and logical consequences of them because these will continue throughout adult life.

Marion (1995) stresses four points if the use of logical consequences is to be successful: "the adult has delivered an I-message; the consequence is 'logically' related to the unsafe or inappropriate behavior; the consequence is one the adult can readily accept and that the child would likely view as fair; the consequence is well timed." She illustrates each point with concrete examples that are easy to follow and understand. For example, if a child has repeatedly left toys and a bicycle in the driveway and the parent has had to move them to park or bring the car into the garage, the parent first would state an I-message followed by the logical consequence should the behavior repeat itself. "I can't park the car with all the toys lying around. So I'll put them in the shed if you decide not to pick them up tomorrow." In this situation, the parent has stated her point of view and a logical consequence should the child repeat the behavior; the child would probably view the consequence as fair, certainly more fair than if the parent had said, "If you can't pick up your toys from the driveway, I may run over them another time."

Gartrell (2003) suggests three levels of mistaken behavior instead of Dreikurs' four. Gartrell urges teachers to drop ideas about "misbehavior," which connotes willful wrongdoing, and look at inappropriate child behavior as "mistaken." In the process of learning such complex life skills as cooperation, conflict resolution, and acceptable expression of strong feelings, children, like all of us, make mistakes. Taking this view helps teachers see their role as mediators, problem-solvers, and guides.

Gartrell (2003) offers three levels of mistaken behavior (see Figure 6–8). Level-three behavior, survival behavior, is difficult for the teacher to accept because of its nonsocial, and at times, antisocial aspect. Strong needs result from psychological and/or physical pain beyond the child's ability to cope and should be interpreted as a cry for help. At level three would be the one or two or three children who misbehave because they have a need to exert power or are expressing hostility; these children typically would be misbehaving with the cooperating teacher as well as with you as their student teacher.

Suggested level-three techniques include:

- Nonpunitive intervention
- Building a positive child-teacher relationship
- Gathering more information by observing
- Seeking additional information through conversations with the child, parents, and caregivers
- Creating a coordinated individual guidance plan with other adults through consultation
- Implementing, reviewing, and modifying the plan as necessary

Motivational source	Relational pattern	Level of mistaken behavior
Desire to explore the environment and engage in relationships	Encountering	One: Experimentation
Desire to please and identify with significant others	Adjustment	Two: Socially influenced
Inability to cope with problems resulting from health conditions or the school or home environment	Survival	Three: Strong needs

Figure 6–8 Common sources of motivation, relational patterns, and levels of mistaken behavior (Gartrell, 2003)

Gartrell (2003) believes that level two, socially influenced mistaken behavior, is based in pleasing others, peers and/or adults. Children exhibiting this behavior seek high levels of teacher or peer approval; they seem to lack self-esteem and the strength to use their own judgment. The teacher's task is to nudge the child toward autonomy and observe whether one child or a group is involved in the mistaken behavior. As previously mentioned, a common problem for many student teachers is such a strong desire to be liked by the children that classroom rules are assumed and/or relaxed. The result is children's misbehavior because they have not yet learned to respect the student teacher and the student teacher's failure to understand that respect has to precede liking. At level two, then, the behavior becomes intentional.

Gartrell (1995) suggests that class meetings are a useful technique in handling level-two behaviors. The children are asked for their suggestions about how any given problem might be resolved. The teacher then monitors progress and, if needed, calls additional meetings. Teacher follow-up is necessary to acknowledge progress and new appropriate behavior, and to provide reminders concerning agreed-upon guidelines.

At level one, Gartrell (1995) suggests that young children may misbehave simply to experiment. The children who, unintentionally, are testing the limits of classroom rules when the student teacher takes over from the cooperating teacher are displaying level-one mistaken behaviors: they are experimenting to see whether the student teacher has the same rules as the cooperating teacher. Disagreements over toys also fall into this category. Gartrell (1995) states:

> [T]he teacher responds in different ways to different situations. Sometimes he may step back and allow a child to learn from experience; other times he will reiterate a guideline and, in a friendly tone, teach a more appropriate alternative behavior.

Depending on the situation, Gartrell (1995) offers the following suggestions to teachers:

- Increased levels of teacher firmness are necessary with level-two and level-three mistaken behaviors, with the element of friendliness retained.
- Serious mistaken behaviors occur when life circumstances make children victims.
- Aggression is a nonverbal request for help.
- In guidance situations, the victim (wronged child) gets attention first and the teachers assist calming down.
- Empathy-building is done by pointing out the victim's hurt.
- Stating that the teacher won't let anyone be hurt at school is necessary.
- Child-teacher discussions about how the problem could be avoided in the future take place.
- Asking how the aggressor could help the hurt child feel better is an appropriate technique.
- Assisting the aggressor to choose a positive activity is another teacher endeavor.

See Figure 6–9 for additional information showing how similar behaviors could be classified at different levels.

Important to remember is that the goal of discipline is to help children learn to assume greater responsibility for their own behavior. This is best accomplished by treating them with respect; distinguishing between what students do and who

Incident of mistaken behavior	Motivational source	Level of mistaken behavior
Child uses expletive	Wants to see the teacher's reaction	One
	Wants to emulate important others	Two
	Expresses deeply felt hostility	Three
Child pushes another off the trike	Wants trike; has not learned to ask in words	One
	Follows aggrandizement practices modeled by other children	Two
	Feels the need to act out against the world by asserting power	Three
Child refuses to join in group activity	Does not understand teacher's expectations	One
	Has "gotten away" with not joining in	Two
	Is not feeling well or feels strong anxiety about participating	Three

Figure 6-9 Classifying similar mistaken behaviors by level (Gartrell, 2003)

they are as persons; setting limits from the very beginning and consistently applying them; keeping demands simple; responding to any problems quickly; letting students know that mistakes, once corrected, are forgotten; and CAREing. It is also important to remember that "[w]hen there is serious mistaken behavior, the teacher meets with parents and other adults to develop and use a coordinated plan. Through coordinated assistance, children can be helped to overcome serious problems and build self-esteem and social skills" (Gartrell, 1997).

Anticipating Behavior or "with-it-ness"

The technique that takes time and experience to learn is anticipating aggressive behavior and intervening before the situation erupts (see Figure 6–10). By studying patterns in the child's behavior, you can learn to anticipate certain situations. Many children are quite predictable. Some children can be in a social atmosphere for only a short time before being overwhelmed by the amount of stimuli (sights, sounds, and actions) and may react in a negative way. If you conclude, from observing a child, that the child can play with only one other child before becoming aggressive, you can take care to allow that child to play with only one child at a time. If you know that another child really needs time alone before lunch, you can arrange it. Likewise, if you know a third child becomes tired and cross just before it is time to go home, you can provide some extra rest time for that child.

Learning to anticipate behavior is not easy. You will require much practice. Keep trying; it is worth the effort, and the children will be happier.

Conflict Resolution

As Wheeler (1994) points out, past pedagogy has viewed child-child conflicts and confrontations as undesirable, and has urged teachers to intervene or use preventive measures. Newer theory supported by current research suggests growth in social skill is acquired when peer conflict resolution strategies enable children to solve problems without adult help.

Conflict resolution involves teaching children positive alternative and socially acceptable ways to solve problems. It includes physical and verbal tactics that can be both aggressive and nonaggressive (Wheeler, 1994). Verbal interactions to resolve a conflict may be child statements opposing the other child's actions or verbalization, such as saying, "No! Don't," "I had it first," "My turn" or "My toy!" "Stop that," or similar statements, or can be forms of verbal negotiation, clever reasons to support one child's position and more mature and complex reasoning attempts to solve the problem. Children can agree on their own to seek teacher help.

Figure 6–10 Intervening is sometimes necessary to promote sharing and prevent aggression.

A student teacher will also notice that a teacher still needs to monitor and step in to encourage and support conflict resolution, especially with younger preschoolers who use physical **aggression** in disagreements. Teacher-generated solutions simply are held off to give children the opportunity to gain skill in using verbal conciliatory behavior that can lead to nonviolent, satisfying, cooperative play, peaceful conflict resolution, and the resumption of child-child play or partnership.

Wheeler (1994) offers these suggestions to teachers:

- Teachers need to be aware of children's intentions. Is this conflict one that the children are truly trying to resolve, or is it verbal play? Teachers should help children make clear their own understanding of the conflict.
- Children's ability to resolve conflicts increases as their verbal competence and ability to take other perspectives grow. If the children involved in a dispute are verbal and empathic, teachers should let them try to work things out themselves.
- Teachers' decisions to intervene should be made after they observe the issues of children's conflicts. Possession issues and name-calling generate less discussion than issues about facts or play decisions.
- Children who explain their actions to each other are likely to create their own solutions. In conflicts characterized by physical strategies and simple verbal oppositions, teachers should help children find more words to use.
- Teachers should note whether the children were playing together before the conflict. Prior interaction and friendship motivate children to resolve disputes on their own.
- Teachers can reduce the frustration of constant conflict by making play spaces accessible and providing ample materials for sharing.
- Children often rely on adults who are frequently happy to supply a "fair" solution. Teachers should give children time to develop their own resolutions and allow them the choice of negotiating, changing the activity, dropping the issue, or creating new rules.
- Many conflicts do not involve aggression, and children are frequently able to resolve their disputes. Teachers should provide appropriate guidance, yet allow children to manage their own conflicts and resolutions.

Gartrell (2003) also urges early childhood teachers to use conflict resolution as a guidance technique. Many of the suggestions Gartrell mentions are covered

conflict resolution—promoting child-child, or child-adult problem-solving through verbal interactions, negotiation, compromise, and use of acceptable physical tactics. It may include teacher support and assistance.

aggression—behavior deliberately intended to hurt others.

in the previous discussion of Gartrell's views on logical consequences and need not be repeated here.

Holden (1997) cautions us as that once we understand conflict resolution techniques, we should also realize that:

- *Teachers can't do it all.* There may be one or two children you really cannot reach. You may have to seek the help of others.
- *It takes time for behavior to change; learning takes place only through repetition.* In fact, changes you may begin when the child is in preschool may not be realized fully until kindergarten.
- *The difficulty to see the other person's point of view is difficult for adults as well as children.*
- *Violent behavior may have any of a number of causes, and in a specific incident, we may not know what the student is thinking.* However, our ability to CARE can alleviate stress and may help establish rapport with the student.
- *Conflict is unavoidable.* As much as we would like for our classrooms to be happy and positive all the time, it simply is not realistic. Children become angry, frustrated, and unhappy just as we adults do.
- *Remember that every conflict is not serious, so don't overreact.*
- *Adults must model ways of handling conflicts peacefully and compliment children who are doing so as well.*

Holden (1997) is a firm believer that young children can learn conflict resolution techniques, that they need adult supervision to learn how, and that they need to practice. As a result of her inability to find materials appropriate for the elementary grades, Holden has written her own program, "Students Against Violence" (Holden, 1997), which is geared for grades one through five.

ADDITIONAL MANAGEMENT STRATEGIES

Child behavior may always remain puzzling and challenge your efforts to help each child learn socially acceptable behaviors. A review of common strategies used by other teachers may be helpful. Naming strategies, describing them, and discussing when they are most appropriate and effective will sharpen your professional guidance skills.

In this chapter thus far, you have studied goals and techniques, the origins of behavior, and ways to promote self-control in children. One goal in guiding child behavior is the idea that the child will learn to act appropriately in similar situations in the future. This can be a slow process with some behaviors, speedy with others. There is a change from external "handling" of the child, to the child monitoring her own progress, and then acting and feeling that it is the right thing to do.

Environmental Factors

It is easy to conclude that it is the child who needs changing. A number of classroom environmental factors can promote inappropriate child behaviors in group situations. A dull variety of activities, an "above comprehension" program, meager and/or frustrating equipment, and a "defense-producing" teacher elicit behavior reactions to unmet needs. Close examination of the classroom environment may lead to changing causative factors rather than changing child behavior. School programs, room environments, and teaching methods can fail the children rather than the children failing the program.

As a student teacher, you should carefully examine the relationship between the classroom environment, the daily program, your teaching style, and children's reactions. Fortunately, your training program has developed your teaching skill as well as an understanding of quality environments. An analysis of your placement may lead you to discover that child appeal is lacking. Rearranging and/or creating new areas may add interest. Remember, however, that any changes need the cooperating teacher's approval.

Rapport

This is an important element of guidance. Trying to develop rapport, trust, or a feeling relationship with each child can be tricky. Mitchell, the active, vigorous explorer, may be hard to keep up with, even talk with! He may prefer the company of his peers, so how can one establish rapport? When it does happen, you will be aware of the "you're okay, I'm okay" feeling, and experience pleasure when he says "I enjoy being with you" with his eyes. Children respond to straightforward "honest talking" teachers in a positive way.

How important is child-teacher rapport during prekindergarten years? Data collected from Howes (2000) suggests children with close child-teacher relationships are also socially competent with their peers. Children perceived as difficult four-year-olds tended to build child-teacher relationships that were high in conflict through the second grade in elementary school. They also tended to be less able to establish social closeness. Academic content mastery through the use of a close child-teacher relationship was also more difficult for these children.

Same Behavior, Different Strategy

Child individuality can still result in unexpected reactions. The boy who finally swings at another child after letting others grab his toys and the child who slugs at every opportunity are performing the same act. You will decide to treat each incident differently. The age of children, their stage of growth, and the particulars of the situation will be considered. You have already learned that what works with one will not necessarily work with another. You will develop a variety of strategies, focus often on the child's intent, and hypothesize underlying causes.

You will be able to live with child rejection, come to expect it, and realize it is short-lived. Act you will, and react the child will. Sometimes, you will choose to ignore behavior and hope it goes away. You will find ignoring is appropriate under certain conditions.

Using Proximity

Many times, the teachers' physical presence will change a child's behavior. When the teacher becomes interested in a child's activity and asks questions concerning what the child is trying to accomplish, it may head off undesirable child behavior.

Other Common Strategies

Stating rules in a positive way serves two purposes. It is a helpful reminder and states what is appropriate and expected. "Feet walk inside, run outside" is a common positive rule statement. Statements such as "Remember, after snack you place your cup on the tray and any garbage in the waste basket" or "books are stored in your desk before we go to lunch." These clearly indicate the students' tasks.

Cause-and-effect and *factual statements* are common ways to promote behavior change. "If you pick off all the leaves, the plant will die." "Sand thrown in the eyes hurts." "Here's the waiting list; you'll have a turn soon, Mark." Each of these statements gives information and helps children decide the appropriateness or realize the consequences of their current actions.

modeling—in social learning theory, the process of imitating a model.

Using **modeling** to change behavior entails pointing out a child or teacher example:

"The paint stays on the paper. That's the way, Kolima."
"See how slowly I'm pouring the milk so it doesn't spill?"
"Nicholas is ready, his eyes are open, and he is listening."

These are all modeling statements see (Figure 6–11).

Always using the same child as a model can create a "teacher's pet." Most teachers try to use every child as a model. When children hear a modeling statement, they may chime in "me, too," which opens the opportunity for recognition and reinforcement of another positive model. "Yes, Carrie Ann, you are showing me you know how to put the blocks in their place on the shelf."

Redirection is a behavioral strategy that works by redirecting a child to another activity, object, or area.

"Here's a big, blue truck for you to ride, Sherilyn."

"While you're waiting for your turn, Kathleen, you can choose the puzzle with the airplane landing at the airport or the puzzle with the tow truck."

"I know you would have liked to have read one of the dinosaur books, Bokko, during SSR [sustained silent reading period], but they're all taken. Since you like trains and airplanes, why don't you read one of these two books instead?"

"Mieko, while you're waiting for Tina and Maria to finish the Spill 'n Spell game, why don't you and Jennifer look at some of the other games we have on the shelf and choose another one?"

Figure 6–11 When lunching with children, teachers model appropriate behavior.

These are additional redirection statements.

Statements like "Let's take giant steps to the door." "Can you stretch and make giant steps like this?" and "We're tiptoeing into snack today; we won't hear anyone's footsteps" may capture the imagination and help overcome resistance. The key to redirection is to make the substitute activity or object desirable. A possible pitfall is that every time the child cannot have her way, she may get the idea that something better will be offered. Offering a pleasurable alternative each time a difficulty arises may teach the child that being difficult and uncooperative leads to teacher attention and provision of a desirable activity or object.

Younger preschoolers (two- and three-year-olds) intent on possessing toys and objects usually accept substitutions, and their classrooms are equipped with duplicate toys to accommodate their "I want what he has" tendency.

In kindergarten and the primary grades, however, the use of redirection can indicate to children that they have an opportunity to make a second or third choice when blocked on their first.

Giving a choice of things you would like the child to do appeals to the child's sense of independence. Some examples are:

> "Are you going to put your used napkin in the trash or on the tray?"
>
> "Can you walk to the gate yourself or are we going to hold hands and walk together?"
>
> "You can choose to rest quietly next to your friend or on a cot somewhere else in the room."
>
> "Remember, Matti, we agreed that class would line up promptly when the bell rang. You have a choice now either to line up quickly or to be the last student to leave for recess."

Setting up direct communication between two arguing children works as shown in the following:

> "Use your words, Xitlali. 'Please pass the crackers.'"
>
> "Look at his face; he's very unhappy. It hurts to be hit with a flying hoop. Listen, he wants to tell you."

Taking a child by the hand and helping confront another to express the child's wishes or feelings lets the child know you will defend his rights. It also lets the child know that you care that rules are observed by all.

Marshall (1995) cautions teachers to remove "I like the way. . . ." statements in teacher attempts to praise or reinforce child behavior. She points out that using "I like" focuses the child on whether the teacher likes them rather than the learning task. As examples of more appropriately worded teacher statements, Marshall suggests the following:

> "Let's see who is ready to listen to the story."
>
> "Latasha is ready to learn about frogs."
>
> "Remember to find a place where you can be comfortable, where no one will disturb you."
>
> "You've made a 4. What do you think of it? Compare it with the 4 on the wall."
>
> "Let's sing our Good Morning song while Erlinda and Duane finish putting their things away so we can start sharing."

Kohn (2001) explains the unfortunate outcome that may occur when teachers overuse praise.

> In short, "Good job" doesn't reassure children; ultimately, it makes them feel less secure. It may even create a vicious circle such that

> the more we slather on the praise, the more kids seem to need it, so we praise them some more. Sadly, some of these kids will grow into adults who continue to need someone else to pat them on the head and tell them that what they did was okay..
>
> and
>
> The most notable feature of a positive judgment isn't that it's positive, but that it's a judgment.

It is sometimes difficult to change "good job" to more specificity because it may have been used extensively in one's own upbringing. Saying "Look at how that table shines! You scrubbed every spot. Now it is clean and ready for the next person, Willy" gives the child specific knowledge concerning his well-done job.

Self-fulfilling statements such as "You can share, Molly. Megan is waiting for a turn" and "In two minutes, it will be Morris' turn" intimate it will happen. Hopefully, you will be nearby with positive reinforcement statements, helping the child decide the right behavior and feel good about it. Positive reinforcement of newly evolving behavior is an important part of guidance. It strengthens the chances that a child will repeat the behavior. Most adults will admit that, as children, they knew when they were doing wrong, but the right and good went unnoticed. The positive reinforcement step in the behavior change process cannot be ignored if new behavior is to last. Positive attention can be a look of appreciation, words, a touch, or a smile. Often, a message such as "You did it" and "I know it wasn't easy" is sent.

Calming-down periods for an out-of-control child may be necessary before communication is possible. Rocking and holding help after a violent outburst or tantrum. When the child is not angry anymore, you will want to stay close until the child is able to become totally involved in play or a task.

ignoring—a principle of behavior management that involves removing all reinforcement for a given behavior to eliminate that behavior.

Ignoring is a usable technique with new behaviors that are annoying or irritating but of minor consequence. Catching the adult's attention or testing the adult's reaction may motivate the behavior. One can ignore a child who sticks out his tongue or says "you're ugly." Treating the action or comment matter-of-factly is ignoring. Answering "I look ugly first thing in the morning" usually ends the conversation. You are attempting to withhold any reaction that might reinforce the behavior. If there is definite emotion in the child's comment, you will want to talk about it rather than ignore it. Children can be taught the ignoring technique as well when they find someone annoying them.

When all else fails, the use of *negative consequences* may be appropriate. Habit behavior can be most stubborn and may have been reinforced over a long period. Taking away a privilege or physically removing a child from the group is professionally recognized as a last-resort strategy.

Isolation involves the common practice of "benching" an aggressive elementary-age student, sending her to a desk segregated from the rest of the class at the extreme front or back of the classroom, or short periods of supervised chair-sitting for a preschooler. Many educators use this technique only when a child is wildly out of control or is an imminent threat to others.

Teachers refer to this practice as time-out. Zabel (1986) notes that if applied immediately and consistently, time-out has been determined to be useful in the reduction of both verbal and physical aggressive behavior. Critics of the practice acknowledge it can reduce undesirable behavior but it fails to teach desirable behavior (Betz, 1994). Because of its effectiveness, the technique may be overused when relatively trivial child behaviors occur. Some children in a study by Readdick and Chapman (2000) who perceived themselves to be in time-out often, felt isolated, sad, scared, and thought they were disliked by their peers. Fewer than half of the preschoolers questioned could accurately recall what they had done before time-out occurred (Readdick & Chapman, 2000).

Teachers need to be careful not to shame or humiliate the child in the process. Statements such as "You need to sit for a few minutes until you're ready to . . ." allow the child an open invitation to rejoin the group and live up to rules and expectations. The isolation area needs to be supervised, safe, and unrewarding. Teachers quickly reinforce the returning child's positive, socially acceptable new actions.

Removal of privilege can restrict the child's use of a piece of play equipment or use of a play area for a short period. After the "off-limits" time, the child is encouraged to try again, with a brief positive rule statement to remind the child of limits.

Using statements that accept the child's reasons for actions show the child you recognize his need or desire. "You want to play with the puzzle." This is followed by "*but* Brianna is using the horse puzzle now." The comment helps the child realize others' rights. Saying "Soon it will be your turn" or "I'll tell you when it's your turn" can encourage children to wait and delay gratification. A teacher might add "You can wait while Brianna finishes or choose another puzzle to work while you're waiting." This indicates your confidence in the child's ability to wait. You will constantly try to increase each child's independence and growing decision-making ability, and must stay close enough to the situation to assure that what you stated will happen.

Your goal is promoting each child's self-controlled behavior, behavior that satisfies his unique personal needs and yet allows membership and inclusion into today's society. Encourage the development of the child's self-concept as a valued, worthwhile, capable and responsible person.

Out-of-Control Children

Student teachers often say the worst part of a day happens when an out-of-control child starts their stomach churning and creates feelings of inadequacy. Bakley (2000) suggests the following techniques:

- *Resist telling an upset child to calm down.* Because the lack of control occurs below the level of consciousness, the child with sensory integration problems cannot willingly calm himself down.
- *Redirect an escalating child to a sensory activity* such as play dough, water play, or bins of sensory materials. More vigorous physical activities such as digging, jumping, and running can also help. Some children will naturally gravitate to the calming motion of a swing or rocking chair. Others may want to retreat to a safe, quiet place away from busy activities.
- *Offer a firm hug or a lap to curl up in.* When a child is agitated, the external control provided by your enveloping physical presence can help restore inner control. Some experts believe a firm hug reaches deeply into the subcortical level of the brain, overriding reactions of rage and aggression.
- *Wait for the child to calm down before talking about what happened.* When a child is agitated, your physical approach may trigger a fight-or-flight reaction (striking out or running away). Wait for the child to regain composure. The calmer the child is, the more likely the child will learn from the experience.
- *Maintain a calm, cool demeanor when discussing misbehaviors.* Avoid no-win confrontations. Your composure sets the tone for the child's success in learning from his mistakes. Remember, although this is a child who will surely test your patience, the child desperately needs your help to learn acceptable behaviors.
- *Allow children to avert their gaze when you talk about their behavior.* Because so much effort is required to make and sustain eye contact, there is little energy

left for listening. Children with sensory integration problems are likely to listen better if allowed to avert their gaze.

- *Use simple, direct language.* Give brief, specific directions. Say "Put your hands in your lap" instead of "Keep your hands to yourself." Help the child remember what you've said by asking the child to repeat it.

Violent Play

Television, current events, young children's observations of older children, and community occurrences often influence the initiation of violent, aggressive play actions. The student teacher is faced with an immediate decision concerning children's safety and the prudence of allowing (which can be seen as approving) this type of play. Most teachers feel deeply about peaceful solutions to individual and world problems. New curriculums have been purposely designed by some early childhood professionals to promote peace and acquaint young children with the brotherhood of humanity concept.

Experienced teachers know that even if guns and other play weapons are not allowed at school, some children will still fashion play guns from blocks or other objects and engage in mock battles or confrontations.

Schools and centers make individual decisions concerning guns, superhero, and war play. It is best for student teachers to question their cooperating teacher if such play develops. Of course, an unsafe situation is stopped immediately and talked about later.

In looking at violence in the elementary school, Johnson, Johnson, Stevahn, and Hodne (1997) suggest that we can make our school safe by using the three Cs: cooperation, conflict resolution, and community values. To encourage cooperation, teachers should have students work in cooperative learning groups and plan cooperative activities. In addition, they stress the need for schools to work cooperatively with parents to establish mutual goals, participation in a division of labor, and shared resources.

Conflict resolution empowers students to learn how to resolve their own conflicts, reestablishes cooperation when the conflict appears within the group, and, according to Johnson, et al. (1997), "provides a source of creativity, excitement, motivation, energy, insight, synergy, synthesis, fun, and renewed support and caring for both teachers and students."

By using the term "community" or "civic values," Johnson and his co-authors stress that "A community cannot exist if its members have a variety of different value systems, believe in only their own self-interests, or have no values at all." The writers firmly believe that values such as caring, respect, responsibility, and other core values such as integrity, compassion, commitment, and appreciation of diversity, must pervade the classroom, that "civic values are the glue that hold the school together."

Superhero Play

In conducting research on the incidence of superhero (violent) play in preschoolers, Boyd (1997) discovered that "superhero play accounted for less than 1 percent of the 300 minutes of play observed." She suggests that teachers look at the developmental function of such play before banning it. She further believes that superhero play may offer children an opportunity to have power, which may help them to overcome feelings of powerlessness in an adult-dominated world. In addition, it involves children in "good guy" versus "bad guy" scenarios. Boyd concludes by stating that "educators should consider the best means for making positive use of this play . . . and decide . . . on the basis of information about their students and their needs, whether this sort of play is acceptable."

Child Strategies

Child strategies to remain in control are natural and normal. Rules can be limiting. Crying, whining, pleading, screaming, and arguing are common. Anger, outrage, and aggression may occur. Suddenly going deaf, not meeting adults' eyes, running away, holding hands over ears or eyes, becoming stiff, or falling to the ground may help the child get what is wanted. The child may also use silence, tantrums, changing the subject, bargaining, name-calling, threats to tell someone, or threats to remove affection. Even "talking them to death" or ignoring rules are not uncommon strategies. Much of the time, young children function in groups, showing consideration for others. Empathic and cooperative interaction of preschoolers within classrooms leads adults to admire both their straightforward relationships and their growing sensitive concern for others.

Managing Serious Behavior Problems

Many of the techniques and strategies already described may help you with children who display serious behavior problems. What do we mean by the phrase "serious behavior problems?" Depending on the age of the child, serious problems range from biting and hitting by a two-year-old to superhero play that is physically aggressive or destroying another child's work, and other aggressive behaviors such as fighting on the play yard by four- to eight-year-olds. And please do not overlook the overly quiet child who tries to disappear into the background of the classroom and/or play yard. She may need as much help as the overly aggressive child. What should you try to do?

First of all, you want to defer to your cooperating teacher; she may have already developed plans to help the child develop more socially appropriate behaviors. Additionally, the cooperating teacher may ask you to speak to the school psychologist, who may be seeing the child once or twice a week; or talk to the PIP (Primary Intervention Program) consultant working with the child; or even sit in on a parent conference with the school's student study team. All of these resource people may give you some more ideas of how to work more effectively with the child in question.

> Sandor, a student teacher in a third-grade classroom, was faced with a male child, Rory, who was getting into fights during the first recess of every day. Upon his return to the classroom, the principal would call over the intercom, "Rory, please come to the office at once!" The result of this behavior was that Rory inevitably missed at least half of the mathematics lessons that were taking place after the first recess. Sandor discussed the problem with Ms. Olivados, his cooperating teacher. She reassured him that Rory's behavior was not new and suggested that Sandor might observe Rory during the next morning's recess and try to determine why Rory got into fights with the other children.
>
> Following Ms. Olivados' suggestion, Sandor accompanied the class to the first recess the next day. Rory went with two or three other boys from his class to a corner of the play yard; Sandor discretely followed. Suddenly, Rory yelled, "You can't call my

mother that!" and hit Derek, the boy standing next to him. Sandor intervened by placing himself between the two and asked, "What did you say, Derek?"

The boy answered, "Oh, we were just playing the dozens; Rory knows that! And besides his mother is a ______!"

"How do you know that?" Sandor asked Derek.

"Oh, everybody knows," replied Derek, who attempted to kick Rory from under Sandor's arm.

"What do you think you might do instead of calling each other names or calling your mothers names?" Sandor asked both boys.

Neither boy replied, and the bell announcing the end of recess sounded before Sandor was able to take the discussion any further. Both Derek and Rory continued to yell at each other as they lined up to go back to the classroom.

Sandor again placed himself between the two boys in the line to prevent any further hitting or kicking. Upon reentering the classroom, Ms. Olivados noticed the angry faces of Rory and Derek and Sandor's distraught one. Before she could ask what had happened, the intercom clicked on and the principal said, "I want Rory C. and Derek K. in my office immediately!"

What might Ms. Olivados and Sandor try tomorrow to prevent further altercations between Rory and Derek?

How might we look at Rory's misbehavior? What might be his mistaken goal, according to Dreikurs? Does Rory seem to be vying for attention? For power? For revenge? It seems clear that he's not acting from a sense of inadequacy. Looking at Gartrell's levels of mistaken behavior, at what level of mistaken behavior does Rory's behavior appear to be?

Should you conclude that Rory's mistaken goal is revenge and/or power in his relationship with Derek, what intervention might be the best one to try? Should Sandor keep the boys separated during recess? Should Rory and Derek be involved in a role-reversal exercise? Should Mrs. Olivados involve the principal? The school's PIP professionals? What might be most appropriate?

Introducing "Harmony Models" in Literary Activities

Many picture books offer peaceful solutions to human conflict. Kreidler (1994) suggests using the following techniques:

- Read the book up to the point of conflict
- Ask children how they think the book's characters are feeling.
- Have children identify the conflict.
- Brainstorm ways characters could solve the conflict. Discuss which one the children think the characters in the story will use.
- Read the rest of the story. Discuss the characters' solution to their conflict. "Was it a good solution? Why? How do the characters feel now?"

  A few picture book titles follow:

  Clements, A. (1997). *Big Al.* New York: Aladdin.

  Cole, K. (2001). *No bad news.* Morton Grove, IL: Albert Whitman.

  Madrigal, A. (1999). *Erandi's braids.* New York: Puffin.

  Parakevas, B. (1999). *Hoppy and Joe.* New York: Simon & Schuster.

Thomas, S. M. (1998). *Somewhere today: A book of peace.* Morton Grove, IL: Albert Whitman

Lionni, L. (1996). *It's mine.* New York: Random House.

Using pictures and problem-solving posters (see Figure 6–12), and acting out "make-believe role-plays" in which children practice conflict resolution is suggested by Adams and Wittmer (2001).

GUIDANCE TECHNIQUES USED IN ELEMENTARY SCHOOLS

Assertive Discipline

Many elementary schools use a form of behavior management called **assertive discipline** (Canter, 1976; Davidman & Davidman, 1994). While an inappropriate technique for preschools, assertive discipline has been widely used in elementary school settings. Assertive discipline has been shown to work best when an entire school staff is committed to using the technique. In assertive discipline, teachers must initially set their classroom rules (best done at the beginning of the year, elicited from the children themselves, and posted prominently in the classroom). Teachers must consistently apply the rules and learn to use "I" messages indicating their displeasure or pleasure. "I don't like it when someone interrupts another student, Aisha." "I like the way you are all listening politely to Mustapha." Consequences of misbehavior must be clearly understood and consistently applied. At the first incidence, the teacher places the child's initials on the board in a place reserved and consistently used for assertive discipline markings. At the second incidence of misbehavior, a check mark goes by the child's name, and a specific and reasonable consequence is related to it. This may be having to remain in the room during a recess or having to move to an isolated area of the classroom. After a second check, the consequence may be a phone call to the

assertive discipline—a form of behavior management used primarily in elementary schools. The consequences of behavior are clearly stated, understood by children, and consistently applied.

Five Steps to Problem-Solving

1. What is the problem?
2. What can I do?
3. What might happen if...?
4. Choose a solution.
5. Is it working? If not, what can I do now?

Figure 6–12 A teacher-made problem-solving poster. Reprinted by permission of S. K. Adams & D. S. Whittmer, and the Association for Childhood Education International, Olney, MD. Copyright © 2001 by the Association.

student's parent(s) and a request for a conference. After the third check, the child is generally sent to the office, and the parent(s) is/are called and notified that the child must serve detention the next day or that the child must serve an in-house suspension. (This may involve assigning the child to another classroom, attended only by other in-school suspension students. The students are expected to complete assignments their teachers send with them, and the classroom is monitored by either a special teacher or a teacher assistant.) The child is usually assigned to the in-house suspension class until the parent(s) makes an appointment for a conference with the teacher and principal.

Crucial to the success of assertive discipline is following through with the predetermined consequences; empty threats cannot exist.

Although assertive discipline has been highly successful, it has also been criticized. Canter, however, maintains that the "assertive teacher is one who clearly and firmly communicates needs and requirements to students, follows those words with appropriate actions, responds to students in ways that maximize compliance, but in no way violates the best interests of the students" (Charles, 1992).

Glasser's Model

Another classroom management model commonly used in elementary schools is the Glasser model (1985). Glasser strongly believes that students have unmet needs that lead to their behavior difficulties, and that if teachers can arrange their classes in such a way that these needs are met, there will be fewer control problems. Student needs are identified as (1) the need to belong, (2) the need for power, (3) the need for freedom, and (4) the need for fun. By breaking the class into small learning teams, the teacher is able to provide students with a sense of belonging, with motivation to work on behalf of the group, with power to have stronger students help weaker ones, with freedom from overreliance on the teacher for both weaker and stronger ones, and with friends for all students, shy and outspoken. Two precautions: groups should be heterogeneously arranged, and groups should be changed at regular or irregular intervals. (Changes might occur as units or themes change, or they might change every six weeks. The teachers should decide for themselves which tactic works best in their respective classrooms.)

SUMMARY

Throughout this chapter, you have been able to formulate an idea of the scope of the classroom management function. Remember that in actuality, everything you do—planning activities, arranging the environment, planning the length of activities, planning how much direction you will provide—is part of the management function.

Another part is managing behavior. In this chapter, you were given two cues to use in managing behavior: the four Cs (consistency, consideration, confidence, and candor) and CARE (be congruent, acceptable, reliable, and empathetic). In addition, six specific techniques were explained: behavior modification, limit setting, "I" messages, logical consequences, anticipating behavior, and conflict resolution. Try them; experiment with others of your own. Discover which techniques work best for you and analyze why they work best.

Helping children satisfy needs in a socially acceptable way and helping them feel good about doing so is a guidance goal. Classroom environments can promote self-control, especially when rapport, caring, and trust are present. Examination of behavior—its intent and circumstances—may lead student teachers to different plans of action with different children. There is no "recipe" for handling guidance problems. A review of common strategies was contained in this chapter. They are as follows: positive rule statements, cause-and-effect and factual statements, modeling, redirection, giving a choice, setting up direct communication, self-fulfilling statements, positive reinforcement, calming-down periods, ignoring, and negative consequences.

Children's strategies to circumvent rules and limits cover a wide range of possible actions; yet, an obedience to rules and sensitivity to others is present most of the time. Check your responses to Figure 6–13, and you will be doing fine.

Students' Aptitudes	Instructional Treatments	Learning Outcomes
What do I know about the general developmental characteristics of the students I am teaching?	In what varieties of ways can I present instruction on a topic?	Do I consider both cognitive and affective learning outcomes for my students?
What cognitive development abilities can I expect them to exhibit?	What types of learning tactics and strategies can I teach?	Do the cognitive outcomes include higher-level thinking skills as well as basic knowledge?
Which learning style does each student seem to prefer?	What is the best way to organize and sequence the presentation of a lesson?	Do I explicitly share these learning outcomes and their purpose with students?
What social/emotional characteristics must I consider?	How can I present instruction at an appropriate ability level for students to achieve success with effort?	Do I connect these outcomes to students in meaningful ways?
What are the social behaviors that each student exhibits?	How can I present instruction that will be interesting and motivate students?	Do I specify how students will be assessed on their mastery of the outcomes?
What are the academic strengths and weaknesses that each student possesses?	What textbooks and other instructional materials best engage students in active learning?	Is my system of grading a valid evaluation of the content students have learned?
What are the special needs of students that I must take into account?	How can I help students better understand the connections between topics?	Do I provide nongraded formative evaluation to students to monitor their progress?
Who has influence on the students? Their peers? Their parents? Their teachers?	How can I help students develop problem-solving skills?	Do I allow multiple opportunities for students to achieve the learning outcomes?
What ethnic and cultural factors influence the way students communicate with others?	How can I instruct students at higher levels of cognition?	
What are the interests of each student?	How can I plan instruction that fosters creativity?	
What level or degree of prior knowledge does each student possess of a subject?	How can I maintain high expectations for all students?	
	How can I help students attribute their success to their abilities and efforts?	

Figure 6–13 Analysis checklist in establishing a well-managed elementary school classroom

HELPFUL WEB SITES

http://www.naeyc.org
National Association for the Education of Young Children. Search readings.

http://www.fpg.unc.edu
National Center for Early Development and Learning (NCEDL). Try child care designations.

http://www.nncc.org
National Network for Child Care. Search social and emotional development.

http://www.ascd.org/
Association for Supervision and Curriculum Development (ASCD). Readings on social and emotional growth. Click "reading room."

SUGGESTED ACTIVITIES

A. In a small group, read C. M. Charles' *Building Classroom Discipline*. Choose one of the techniques and present it to your peers, cooperating teacher, and supervisor for discussion.

B. Analyze your placement classroom's rules. Do many rules fall into the four basic areas mentioned in this chapter? Are there any rules that need a new category?

C. Write your own definition of aggression, assertion, and cooperation as they apply to child conflicts. Discuss your definitions with a small group of classmates. In your discussion, answer the following:
   - Is aggressive behavior normal behavior?
   - When does it emerge?
   - What socially productive alternatives do adults attempt to teach?
   - What anger management techniques are familiar to you?
   - How is cooperation fostered in young children?
   - When is assertion appropriate?

   Compare your definition with definitions found in the Glossary.

D. Go back to your own childhood. What techniques did you use to avoid punishment when you'd broken a family rule? What parental guidance techniques (or punishments) still remain vivid today? What guidance techniques used on others have you observed that created strong emotions in you? If you received but one unforgettable message from your parents concerning your behavior as a child, what was that message? Report the message to the total group.

E. Dewayne, a student in your kindergarten room, is in his usual negative mood. During morning planning time, he refuses to choose what interest center he will go to during the morning center choice period. Your reaction is to offer him a choice between the manipulatives center and the storytelling one. Dewayne tells you to f—— off. Your anger aroused, you are tempted to send him to the office immediately; instead you say quietly, "Dewayne, we don't use the "f" word at school." He glares at you defiantly, and you realize that the other students are looking expectantly at you to see what you'll do next.

   According to Dreikurs, what does Dewayne's mistaken goal appear to be? Discuss with your peers what responses might be most effective.

F. Read the following:

Mrs. X, the college supervisor, visited Miss Y at her preschool placement classroom, a church-related preschool program. The yard look spacious and well equipped. Miss Y was a paid employee doing her student teaching at her place of employment. She was also a member of the church that operated the program.

Mrs. X entered a small hallway with a desk and wall phone, then approached the doorway to the classroom and hesitated. Miss Y motioned her supervisor to enter.

A free play period was in progress. Children were busy at small desks or playing in groups. One child stood by the wall seemingly trying to push himself against it. Children looked at Miss Y frequently as if checking for some signal. Two small girls wanted to lean against Miss Y and followed her around the room. One patted Miss Y's arm periodically. The telephone in the hall rang. Miss Y went to answer, leaving Mrs. X in the room.

After a minute or so, a boy tried to grab a toy; another boy was running back and forth across the top of a small desk. The boy attempted to push the grabber away. He knocked over both the desk and the other child. Miss Y entered in time to see the child falling.

"We don't hit," she said sternly, "You know what happens now." The child who pushed said, "He did it," pointing to a third child. Other children seemed tense and frightened. The boy, hugging the wall, turned and faced it. Miss Y picked up the boy who had pushed the child, who tried to grab his toy, and headed toward the door. One girl put her head down on a desk and covered her eyes.

At this point, Mrs. X said, "It was an accident." Miss Y put the child down and said, "Mrs. X said it was an accident."

After watching another half hour, Mrs. X could finally consult with Miss Y on the play yard because another teacher had come on duty. Asking Miss Y to step to an area where they wouldn't be overheard, she said "I can see this school uses spanking. How do you feel about that policy?" Miss Y answered, "Oh it works very well. I don't have but rare acts of hitting now, and I've noticed the children are much more affectionate toward me." Mrs. X asked, "You've been present in classes where guidance techniques were studied. Was spanking a recommended technique?" "No, but it sure works well!" the student teacher answered. "You've seen no child behavior that bothers you?" Mrs. X asked. "No," Miss Y answered. "Have you noticed children accusing other children of things they might have done themselves?" (Mrs. X had seen this a number of times during her observation.) "Well, that always happens. I did it myself when I was a child." "Did you know spanking was against the law in preschools in this state?" Mrs. X asked. "Yes, but we have a form parents sign approving spanking," Miss Y answered. "My director and I think spanking works." "Can I give you permission to break the law and speed at 70 miles per hour?" asked Mrs. X. "No, I don't think that would work," answered Miss Y. "Can parents give you permission to break the law?" Mrs. X asked. "Well they have," retorted Miss Y.

After a discussion in which Mrs. X asked for another meeting, she left the school. Later in the day, Mrs. X telephoned the licensing agency responsible for licensing Miss Y's place of employment.

Discuss this story with three to four classmates. Report key ideas, observations, and conclusions to the total class.

G. Plan a discussion group with a small group of four-year-olds. (Have a picture of a child who might want to join these children's classroom handy.) Start your discussion with "We have a rule in our classroom. The rule is we ask for a turn if we want a toy someone else has chosen to use. Here's a picture of Suzy" (or any other appropriate name). "She wants to come to school with us. What will Suzy need to know about our classroom?" "If Suzy plays in the block center, what should we tell her?" "If Suzy wants to join us at snack time, what should we tell her?" Share the results of your discussion group with classmates.

H. Role-play the following situations with a small group of classmates. After each situation, have the student(s) playing the child explain any insights or feelings they discovered when stepping into the child's shoes. Critique the role-playing reaction according to the child's behavior and the guidance techniques used.

1. Tonette says Renata pushed her down. You've observed the incident, and Renata just happened to trip Tonette as she ran to pick up the ball.
2. Conner is large and muscular. He delights in terrifying other children by standing directly in their paths. He rarely physically hits, pushes, or touches the children he is frightening. You see Conner standing in front of the outside water faucet intimidating children who wish to drink.
3. Rogerio is telling your aide she's ugly and fat. The aide, being new, is distressed.
4. Scott cries every time he is not chosen to be first in line or when some other child gets a "handing out supplies" job he wants. You want Geoff to go to the aquarium to feed the fish. Scott's crying because Geoff got the job. Geoff turns to Scott and says, "Okay, stop it, you can do it."
5. Sierra's on a painting binge. It's time to clean up. You've told her it's cleanup time. "No way," says Sierra as she threatens you with a wet paintbrush.
6. Shania plays well with others until parent pickup time. As soon as she spots her parent(s) arriving, she will either throw a tantrum or cry. Her arriving parent is typically faced with an angry or an unhappy child.
7. Forrest, a four-year-old, disappears each time he has a bowel movement. Teachers try to monitor his problem and watch him closely, but are usually unsuccessful in steering him to the bathroom in time.
8. Stanton runs from one area to the next, dumping toys to the floor while smiling in satisfaction. So far, he has no pals who help him, but Lance seems to be on the verge of joining.

I. Now go back to the situations in H (1–8), but think about the child's needs, feelings, and point of view. Is there any way for the child to solve the inherent difficulty in the situation? Are there setting or time factors teachers could manipulate so the same problem doesn't happen again?
What are your inner feelings in each situation? Discuss with your group.

J. In a group of five others, vote individually and tally "yes" and "no" responses to the following. Then discuss.

1. Praise can't be overdone.
2. Whom a child chooses for a play partner can increase the child's physical aggression.
3. There are times when a child should submit to another child's bossy demands by just walking away.

4. If a child pushes another child in line, a teacher should try time-out.
5. Statements like "Well done," "That's good," and "I liked the way you hugged Marisa" are well-stated, positive reinforcement statements.

REVIEW

A. List four classroom factors that might promote inappropriate child behaviors.

B. Complete this statement.

The reason teachers may use different techniques in guiding aggression is . . .

C. 1. List four positive rule statements.
2. List four redirection statements.
3. List four modeling statements.

D. List six strategies a child may use to "get around" an adult who has just announced that it is time for all the children to come inside.

E. Select the answer that best completes each statement.

1. Roberta, a student teacher, feels sure a textbook or a practicing teacher will be able to describe guidance strategies that work. Roberta needs to know that:
   a. children are different but the same strategies work.
   b. teachers handle behaviors based on examples their parents and teachers modeled in their own childhood.
   c. there are no techniques that always work.
   d. books and practicing teachers agree on best methods.
   e. none of these.
2. Withholding of privilege is:
   a. a technique that may work.
   b. used before rule statements.
   c. not very effective.
   d. a rather cruel punishment.
   e. all of these.
3. When a teacher notices inappropriate child behavior, the teacher should immediately realize that:
   a. parents created the behavior.
   b. children may need to learn school rules.
   c. her teaching technique is ineffective.
   d. the director should be consulted.
   e. none of these.

F. Complete the following statements. Analyze your responses. What have you learned about yourself? Write a short paragraph.

1. The ideal classroom should . . .
2. When a fight breaks out, I want to . . .
3. As a teacher, I want to control . . .
4. Aggressive children make me . . .
5. Shy children make me . . .
6. Children who use bad language ought to be . . .
7. Little boys are . . .
8. Little girls are . . .
9. Whiny children make me . . .
10. Stubborn children make me . . .

G. Describe conflict resolution techniques.

CASE SCENARIO

Setting: A child care program for two-year-olds. Marcia is the student teacher, Mr. Rice is the cooperating teacher, Christina is the aide. It is late afternoon; most of the children have been picked up by their parents and Christina is watching the few who remain. Mr. Rice is talking to Marcia about an incident that happened during the morning activity period.

"Marcia, did you notice what Ramon and David were doing while you were working with the children at the crafts table?" asks Mr. Rice.

"I'm not sure I'm following you," Marcia responds.

"Had you noticed that David and Ramon were arguing about who was going to use the large red truck over by the block center and that David was biting Ramon?"

"Oh, yes, I turned to look when I heard Ramon scream," Marcia says, "but I have to admit that I didn't see what was happening because I was so busy with the craft table. Besides, I had my back to the block and truck area. Of course, I thought David was at fault; I missed Ramon's hitting him first and I didn't see the two of them tugging at the same truck."

"You know, we teachers have to place ourselves so we can get an overview of the entire classroom every time we plan an activity that has to be supervised. I don't mean this in a negative way, Marcia. Part of the reason you are a student teacher is to learn. Always place yourself so you can see the whole classroom or ask Christina or me to supervise where you can't see," Mr. Rice says gently. "Had you seen the two boys pulling at the same truck, you might have been able to leave the craft table and quickly intervene."

"I understand, Mr. Rice. I know I'm here to learn but it seems so hard at times," Marcia sighs. "I remember our college supervisor saying that we had to develop eyes in the back of our heads; now I understand why!"

Questions for Discussion:

1. How do you feel about what happened to Marcia? Has anything similar happened to you?
2. How might Marcia feel after her talk with Mr. Rice? How might you feel in her place?
3. Do you think Mr. Rice could have handled the situation differently? Why or why not?

REFERENCES

Adams, S. K., & Wittmer, D. S. (2001, Fall). "I had it first": Teaching young children to solve problems peacefully. *Childhood Education, 77*(5), 10–15.

Abbott, J. (1997, March). To be intelligent. *Educational Leadership, 54*(6).

Bakley, S. (2000, November). Through the lens of sensory integration: A different way of analyzing challenging behavior. *Young Children, 56*(6), 70–76.

Betz, C. (1994, March). Beyond time out: Tips from a teacher. *Young Children,49*(2), 10–14.

Boulden, K., Hiester, K., & Walti, B. (with Tertell, L.). (1998). *When teachers reflect: Journeys toward effective inclusive practice.* Washington, DC: National Association for the Education of Young Children.

Boyd, B. (1997, Fall). Teacher response to superhero play: To ban or not to ban? *Children Education, 74*(1).

Browning, L., Davis, B., & Resta, V. (2000, Summer). What do you mean "Think before I act"? Conflict resolution with choices. *Childhood Education, 14*(2), 232–238.

Caine, R. N., & Caine, G. (1997). *Education on the edge of possibility.* Alexandria, VA: Association for Supervision and Curriculum Development.

Canter, L. (1976). *Assertive discipline: A take-charge approach for today's educator.* Seal Beach, CA: Canter & Associates.

Curtis, D., & Carter, M. (1996). *Reflecting children's lives: A handbook for planning a child-centered curriculum.* St. Paul, MN: Redleaf Press.

Charles, C. M. (1992). *Building classroom discipline* (4th ed.). New York: Longman.

Davidman, L., & Davidman, P. (1994). *Teaching with a multi-cultural perspective: A practical guide.* New York: Longman.

Dreikurs, R. (1968). *Psychology in the classroom.* New York: Harper & Row.

Dreikurs, R., Grunewald, B., & Pepper, F. (1982). *Maintaining sanity in the classroom.* New York: Harper & Row.

Dreikurs, R., & Cassel, P. (1972). *Discipline without tears.* New York: Harper & Row.

Eaton, M. (1997, September). Positive discipline: Fostering the self-esteem of young children. *Young Children, 52*(6).

Gartrell, D. (1995, July). Misbehavior or mistaken behavior? *Young Children, 50*(5).

Gartrell, D. (1997, September). Beyond discipline to guidance. *Young Children, 52*(6).

Gartrell, D. (2003). *A guidance approach for the encouraging classroom* (2nd ed.). Clifton Park, NY: Thomson Delmar Learning.

Gillespie, C. W., & Chick, A. (2001, Summer). Fussbusters: Using peers to mediate conflict resolution in a Head Start classroom. *Childhood Education, 77*(4), 192–195.

Glasser, W. (1985). *Control theory in the classroom.* New York: Perennial Library.

Gordon, T. (1974). *T.E.T.: Teacher effectiveness training.* New York: David McKay.

Holden, G. (1997, May). Changing the way kids settle conflicts. *Educational Leadership, 54*(8).

Honig, A. S., & Wittmer, D. S. (1996, January). Helping children become more prosocial: Ideas for classrooms, families, schools, and communities. *Young Children, 51*(2).

Howes, C. (2000, Spring). Quoted in relationships child and teacher. *Early Development, 4*(1), 12–13.

Johnson, D. W., Johnson, R. T., Stevahn, L., & Hodne, P. (1997, October). The three Cs of safe schools. *Educational Leadership, 55*(2).

Killen, M., & Turiel, E. (1991). Conflict resolution in preschool social interactions. *Early Education and Development, 2*(3), 240–255.

Kohn, A. (2001, September). Five reasons to stop saying "Good job!" *Young Children, 56*(5), 24–28.

Kreidler, W. J. (1994). *Teaching conflict resolution through children's literature.* New York: Scholastic Professional Books.

Kuebli, J. (1994, March). Young children's understanding of everyday emotions. *Young Children, 49*(3).

Marion, M. (1995). *Guidance of young children* (4th ed.). Englewood Cliffs, NJ: Merrill/Prentice Hall.

Marshall, H. H. (1995, January). Beyond "I like the way . . ." *Young Children, 50*(2).

McCarthy, B. (1997, March). A tale of four learners: 4MAT's learning styles. *Educational Leadership, 54*(6).

Nelsen, J., Lott, L., & Glenn, H. S. (1997). *Positive discipline in the classroom.* Rocklin, CA: Prima Publishing.

Readdick, C. A., & Chapman, P. L. (2000, Fall/Winter). Young children's perception of time out. *Childhood Education, 15*(1), 81–87.

Rogers, C., & Freiberg, H. (1994). *Freedom to learn* (3rd ed.). New York: Merrill/Macmillan.

Ryan, K. (1993, November). Mining the values in the curriculum. *Educational Leadership, 51*(3).

Schoonmaker, F. (1998, Spring). Promise and possibility: Learn to teach. *Teachers College Record, 99*(3).

Wheeler, E. J. (1994, September). *Peer conflicts in the classroom.* ERIC Digest, EDO-PS-94-13.

Zabel, M. K. (1986). Time out with behaviorally disabled students. *Behavioral Disorders, 21*, 15–20.

CHAPTER 7

Analyzing Behavior to Promote Self-Control

Objectives

After studying this chapter, the student should be able to:

1 Identify what motivates children to act as they do.

2 Analyze behavior using Erikson's psychological theory of development and its relationship to the development of self-control.

3 Recognize the similarities as well as the differences among children of differing cultural backgrounds and how these relate to differences observed in their behaviors.

4 Identify two phases of development that are critical in terms of developing self-control according to Burton White.

5 Discuss the relationship between the guidance function and the ability of the child to learn self-control.

The hardest part of student teaching involved the children's understanding that I would enforce rules. I hated it when children cried or threw a wingding. A teacher is an authority figure. Children will not always like you.

—Ke-Chang Wang

I had been warned by the previous student teacher that a certain child would make my life miserable. I gleaned the best information on "power-seeking" children from a management book I knew. Lucky for me, I over-prepared because the child was not nearly as difficult as I anticipated.

—Catherine Millick

My placement classroom was a Montessori school. Each child automatically pushed his chair under the table when he got up. It was habit behavior. They also returned each child "game" activity to its own special place on shelves. It's the first classroom where I've worked where children picked up after themselves so effortlessly. I wish my placement had started in the fall so I could have seen how my cooperating teacher accomplished it.

—Marlis McCormick

To analyze the behavior of any child, you, as the student teacher, need to remember two important concepts:

1. All behavior is meaningful to the child, even that which an adult might call negative.
2. All behavior is reinforced by the environment (people, places, and things).

Let us begin this chapter by looking at some of the typical reinforcers of behavior. Perhaps the easiest ones to understand are physiological in nature: the need to eat when hungry, drink when thirsty, sleep when tired, dress warmly when cold, stay out of the sun when hot, and so forth. It is less easy to understand the psychological ones, although they control more of our actions.

ERIKSON'S THEORY OF PSYCHOSOCIAL DEVELOPMENT AND ITS RELATION TO SELF-CONTROL

Erikson's (1993) theory of psychosocial development is relevant to our understanding of behavior and self-control. According to Erikson, there are four different stages the child goes through from birth into elementary school age. Each stage has its developmental task to achieve (see Figure 7–1).

First Stage of Development

For the infant (birth to approximately one and one-half to two years), the task is to develop basic trust. If the infant is fed when hungry, changed when wet, dressed to suit the weather, and given much love and attention, the infant will learn that adults can be trusted. The infant who is not fed regularly and feels rejected or neglected may learn that adults cannot be trusted.

Look at a small baby. What do you see? If the child is younger than six months, you will notice almost immediately that this infant is constantly using the senses and the mouth. The presentation of a toy brings a multiple reaction. The child puts it into the mouth, tastes it, takes it out of the mouth, looks at it, turns it over in the hands, shakes the toy, listens to see if it will make a noise, and holds the toy to the nose to see if it smells. The child uses all of the senses to understand this toy that has become a part of the immediate environment (see Figure 7–2). Eyes (sight), mouth (taste), hands (touch), nose (smell), and ears (hearing) all come into action.

What does this have to do with learning self-control? Think about the interaction between the infant and the toy, and among the infant, toy, and significant adult, usually the mother. Think also about why the infant uses all of the senses to learn about a new toy or about anything in the environment. Why is learning about one's surroundings important? When one learns about the environment, one feels safe in that environment and learns to control it. Can you see why it is important for the infant to sense some control over the environment? How does the child feel when experiencing cause-and-effect relationships? What does the child learn from tasting, shaking, looking at, and manipulating an object? The child is learning that he has some influence on what is happening. It is this feeling of influence or control that is important to the child's learning of self-control.

Think about what can happen if the child feels no control over the environment. Suppose the significant adult in the infant's life holds out a new toy toward the child, shakes it in front of the eyes, and, as the infant reaches for it, takes it

Age	Task	Outcome ("Good Me")	Outcome ("Bad Me")
0–1 year	Acquiring a sense of BASIC TRUST	Child develops the ability to TRUST the significant adults in her life	Child develops a sense of MISTRUST in all adults and a sense of HOPELESSNESS
	PARENTAL/CAREGIVER ROLE:	Meeting physical needs, nurturing emotional and social needs; providing stimulation of intellectual and language needs; providing unconditional LOVE	
1–3 years	Acquiring a sense of AUTONOMY	Child develops SELF-CONTROL and willpower; learns give-and-take (leadership-follower roles)	Child develops SELF-DOUBT and a sense of SHAME
	PARENTAL/CAREGIVER ROLE:	Emotional support; firm, but gentle, limit setting; gradual granting of freedom; consistency in expectations and in establishing boundaries; providing simple choices	
3–5 years	Acquiring a sense of INITIATIVE	Child develops a sense of direction and purpose; is unafraid to explore new or changed settings	Child feels a sense of GUILT; becomes uneasy with new settings; only involves self in activities he knows well
	PARENTAL/TEACHER ROLE:	Communication; joint problem-solving; sharing of values and ideals; continued emotional support	
6–12 years	Acquiring a sense of INDUSTRY	Child learns that he is competent; experiments with methods to become competent; fully develops leadership-follower roles	Child develops feelings of incompetence and INFERIORITY; lacks understanding of leadership-follower roles
	TEACHER/PARENTAL ROLE:	Encouraging realistic goals; helping child become open to criticism; accepting criticism from child; answering child's questions; being open to all kinds of questions from child	

Figure 7–1 Erikson's developmental stages

Figure 7–2 The toddler "scientist" yearns to feel things firsthand.

away? Suppose the infant reaches for an object over and over, only to have it always withdrawn? How long do you think the child will continue to reach? The child will ultimately stop trying. The child will also learn to feel helpless and not in control over the environment. This child, then, will have difficulty in acquiring self-control. This is the child who becomes either underdisciplined or overdisciplined.

Experiencing some influence on the environment leads the child to understand that he affects the environment. An awareness of cause-and-effect relationships develops in this manner.

Figure 7–3 A little help is needed at first, but soon he will be zooming down the pathway.

autonomy—the second stage of development described by Erik Erikson, occurring during the second year of life, in which toddlers assert their growing motor, language, and cognitive abilities by trying to become more independent.

Second Stage of Development

As the child becomes mobile and begins to talk, the child enters the second stage of development. Erikson calls this the autonomy stage. Two-year-old children are motor individuals; they love to run, climb, ride, move, move, and move (see Figure 7–3). They are so active, they almost seem like perpetual motion machines! The developmental task of the two-year-old toddler is learning autonomy and self-discipline. It is this age in particular that is so trying for both the parents and preschool teachers.

Learning Autonomy.

(Its contrast is shame and doubt.) This stage coincides with two physiological events in the toddler's life: the ability to crawl and walk and learning how to use the toilet.

There has been much written about the problems of training a child to use the toilet. Many parents, child care workers, and family child care providers do not understand that most children will essentially train themselves, especially if given an appropriate model such as an older sibling who is toilet trained or a loving, caring parent who anticipates the child's need to use the toilet, and in an unthreatening way, sits the child on the seat and compliments the child on success. The adult needs to allow the child to look at, and even smell, what his body has produced. It is not uncommon for toddlers to play with their bowel movements, an action sure to bring down on them the wrath of the adult. What needs to be remembered is that the child is pleased and curious about what the body has done. Instead of becoming angry, adults should understand the child's interest, stating simply that the playing is not approved and direct attention to playing with clay, for example, as a substitute.

Problems arise when adults overreact to the child's playing with fecal matter. Many parents who try to toilet train what appears to be a stubborn, willful child fail to understand that the child is simply attempting to develop control, over the parent, in part, but over her own self as well.

At this time, the child reinforces the sense of having an effect on the environment. Assume that the toddler, as an infant, was allowed some degree of freedom in which to crawl and explore safely, that within this safe environment the infant had a variety of toys and objects with which to play and manipulate, and a loving adult to supervise. This infant then becomes an active, curious toddler, ready to expand her environment. Assume also that the parents, early childhood educators, and family child care providers with whom this toddler comes into contact continue to provide a safe environment in which the child can explore. What is the child then learning? At this particular age, the child is continually learning that she has control over the immediate environment. The child can learn only when given practice in self-control. In order to allow for practice, the environment must be physically safe, stimulating, and offer choices.

It is this third factor—offering choices—that is critical in terms of helping a child acquire self-control. Even an infant crawling around in a playroom can make choices about which toys he will play with and when (see Figure 7–4). As the child begins to feed himself, the child can make a choice between slices of apple or orange as a snack. The toddler can make the choice between two shirts that may be laid out. In the center setting, the toddler can easily make the choice between playing with clay or climbing on a play gym. As we talk about older infants and toddlers, we are also talking about allowing the child a choice between two alternatives chosen by the adult. The young child cannot handle a choice of six different activities; this is overwhelming. Too much choice is as bad as none. In either case, one child may become confused, anxious, and angry whereas another will withdraw and do nothing.

Figure 7–4 Toddlers frequently choose to play in inviting dramatic play areas.

But one concern we, the parents and teachers have, is that the young toddler often seems to be breaking limits deliberately. We fail to understand that one of the ways the child can be reassured that we care is repeatedly to test the limits to see if we really mean what we say. What sometimes happens is, that on days when we are rested and time is plentiful, we tolerate behavior that would not be tolerated under different circumstances.

If it is okay to throw a ball to another child, why is it wrong to throw a rock? If it is okay to run down the driveway in one instance, why is it wrong in another? (Boundaries are not understood very well, especially because the child can go somewhere with supervision but not without it.) In the toddler's mind, these are seen as inconsistencies regarding adult expectations. The child cannot differentiate safe from unsafe, so for parents and preschool teachers, it means repetition of rules and limits. Eventually, of course, the child does learn. "I don't go down the driveway without holding Mom's hand" or "I don't leave the yard unless Miss Jan holds my hand."

For some parents and teachers, the two-year-old child becomes too difficult to handle in a caring way. Two courses of action are frequently taken. Some parents confine the child rather than tolerate the need to explore. As a result, the child's basic motor needs are squelched, and the child becomes fearful and distrustful of her motor abilities. The child also learns to feel guilty about the anger felt toward the adults. Because these adults are still responsible for the child's primary care (food, water, love), the child feels that there must be something wrong with her if the adults inhibit the natural desire to explore. Thus, the child feels guilty, and learns to be ashamed of the anger and represses it. In the classroom, this child is the timid, shy, fearful one with poor motor abilities due to a lack of opportunities to practice them.

Other parents may refuse to assert their responsibilities and allow the child to do anything. (Think of how terrifying it is for the child to have such power over the parents!) As a result, the child's behavior becomes progressively worse until the parents finally have had enough and resort to punishment. A different result may be a child who fights against any kind of limits and becomes shameless in attempting to do the opposite of what an adult expects or wants, especially regarding motor restrictions. Just as the physically restrained child learns to feel ashamed and guilty, so does the unrestrained child. This child really wants to have reasonable limits set but cannot accept them without a struggle. This struggle of wills makes the unrestrained child feel just as guilty as the overly restrained child. Both children lack the inner controls that the emotionally healthy child has developed. Both lack self-discipline; the overly restrained child through a lack of opportunities to practice, the underrestrained child through a lack of learning any standards.

In the primary school setting, difficulties with autonomy can be seen in two very different types of behavior: overconfidence, willingness to try anything (the more outrageous, the better), frequently unrealistic expectations of physical prowess, students who appear to have leadership qualities but who become angry if thwarted in their attempts and who may then heap scorn on ideas that originally might even have been theirs; or a lack of confidence, students who continually ask if they are completing an assignment the way you want them to, students who seem to need additional cues before starting a creative writing or art project such as checking what their peers are doing before beginning their own work.

Third Stage of Development

initiative—the desire to do something by oneself. Identified as a developmental stage by Erik Erikson.

The next stage roughly approximates the usual preschool years of three to five. Erikson believes that the developmental task of the preschooler is to develop initiative, to learn when to do something by oneself and when to ask for help. The result of practice in asserting one's initiative results in a self-confident, cheerful child.

Again, as with the overly restrained toddler, the five-year-old who has been denied a chance to exert initiative learns instead to be ashamed. The child learns that any self-made decisions are of no importance; the adults in the child's life will make decisions. For example, if the child attempts to dress without help, the parents are likely to criticize the result. "Your shirt's on backwards. Don't you know front from back?" Sometimes, the correction is nonverbal; the parent or teacher will simply reach down toward the child, yank the T-shirt off the arms, turn it, and put the arms back through the sleeves. The child learns that he does not know how to dress and eventually may stop trying altogether. As the teacher, you then see a child of six or seven who cannot put on a jacket without help, who mixes left and right shoes, and who often asks, "Is this the way you want me to . . . ?" This child needs constant reassurance that the assigned task has been completed the way the adult wants it done. Given an unstructured assignment, such as a blank piece of paper on which to draw, this child looks first to see what the other children are doing. Because the child has no self-confidence, the child frequently comes to you for ideas.

The underrestrained toddler grows to be an underrestrained school-age child and becomes your most obvious classroom problem. This child enters preschool like a small hurricane, spilling blocks, throwing down a difficult puzzle, and tearing a neighbor's drawing because it is "not as good" as the child's own. This child is the one who pushes another off the tricycle to ride it and grabs the hammer from another when the child wants to use it.

The underrestrained child is also undersocialized. This child has never learned the normal give-and-take of interpersonal relationships, and does not know how to take turns or share (see Figure 7–5). This child has had few restrictions regarding what to do, when to do it, and where. At the same time, this

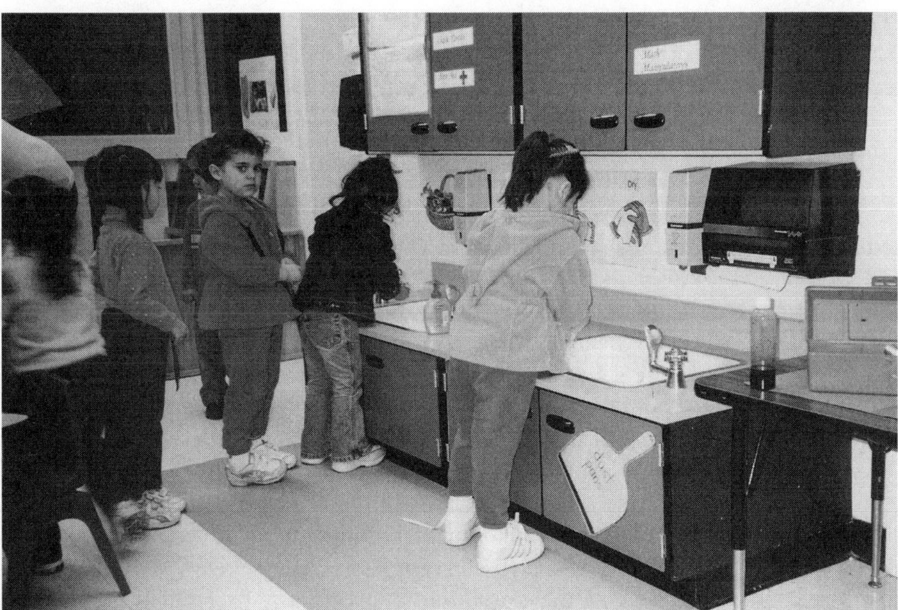

Figure 7–5 Learning to wait for her turn is not easy.

child often wanted the parents, caregivers, and teachers to tell her what to do and what not to do. A word of caution: some perfectly normal children who have little or no preschool experience will act like the undersocialized child simply because they lack experience. They learn rapidly, however, and some become quite acclimated to classroom procedures and rules. The underrestrained, undersocialized child does not learn rules and procedures easily, and continually pushes against any restrictions. At the same time, this child often wants parents, caregivers, and teachers to tell her what to do and what not to do.

Remember, the child who is most unloved is also the one most in need of your love. What are some of the ways you can help this child? Use the four Cs and CARE. It is difficult to accept this child; all children deserve your respect and acceptance regardless of how unlikable they may be. In fact, this particular child will probably sense your dislike; therefore, it is important to be scrupulously fair. Do not allow yourself to be caught in the trap of assuming that this child will always be the guilty party in every altercation. It does not take other children long to realize that they have the perfect scapegoat in their midst; it is too tempting for them to break a rule and blame it on the child who is expected to break rules. Remember to be firm. The underrestrained child needs the security of exact limits. They should be stated repeatedly and enforced. This is the child who will constantly need to be reminded of the rules and of his need to adhere to them as do the others in the class.

Ask your cooperating teacher about the child's family background. You are likely to discover there is little security. Bedtime may occur whenever the child finally falls asleep, whether it be on the floor in front of the television, on the couch, or in bed with an older brother, sister, or cousin. You may discover that mealtimes are just as haphazard. Breakfast may come at any time in the morning and only if there is food in the house. You may find out that family members eat as they each become hungry. This child may open a bag of potato chips for breakfast and eat whatever can be found in the refrigerator for dinner. Sometimes, the child's only meal is the one served at school. Life for this child is simply not very

trust—the first stage of development described by Erik Erikson, occurring during infancy, in which the child's needs should be met consistently and predictably.

safe or predictable. Mom may or may not be home when the child returns from school. Dad may come home and may work or not as the opportunity presents itself. There may be no one primary caregiver for this child. It is even possible that this child has always been an unwanted child and has been sent from relative to relative or from foster home to foster home.

In terms of Erikson's theory, this child, being unwanted, may never have learned to trust. This possibility is easy to check. As you try to be friendly, does this child's behavior worsen? As you reach out, does the child draw away and/or wince? Think of the consequences of not being wanted. If the child perceives that no one, especially the significant adults in the child's life, likes her, how can the child learn to like herself? How can the child learn to love without first receiving love from others, preferably from the significant adults in the child's life? The child cannot do these things. An unwanted, unloved child is a real challenge to any caring teacher. Because the child feels so little self-worth, attempts at friendliness on your part will be seen as weakness. To deal with this child, you first will have to acquire a tough skin. This child has learned how to "read" adult behavior. This is the child's form of protection. This child knows what you are going to do before you even do it. On the other hand, the child's behavior will seem less predictable to you. One day the child will obey the rules of the classroom; another day the child will not. This youngster will make friendly overtures to another child in the morning and kick that same child in the afternoon. The child will help a group of peers build a city with the blocks, only to knock them down when the project is finished.

You will have to repeat the limits and rules continuously. You continually will have to physically remove this child from the center of action to a quiet corner or room. There is no magic wand that can change this child overnight. In fact, you have to remember that it has taken two, three, or four years to shape the child into the person you are seeing. It make take weeks, even months to change the child. In rare cases, it may even take years.

Uncaring, neglectful families may have been warm and loving, and this child may have learned how to trust at least in part. Still, if this child has not resolved Erikson's second task of early childhood, learning autonomy, the child may frequently get into trouble. Never having learned how to set limits, this child is constantly going beyond the limits. The roof is off limits? This child finds a way to climb on the roof. The kitchen is off limits? This child continually goes to the kitchen. The child will continue the escapades even if an injury results. The child accepts a hurt as the correct punishment. In fact, this child seeks punishment. When you speak to the child's family, the answer often given is, "Just give him a good spanking. He'll behave then!"

Similar behaviors may be exhibited by the child who is overindulged at home and smothered with attention. This child expects to be the "center of action" at school.

Children with this type of behavior test every resource you have. Again, remember to use the four Cs and to CARE, even though it may be difficult. Repeat the limits and expectations over and over. Physically remove the child whenever necessary; isolation sometimes works best.

Another technique is to say what the child is thinking. "You want me to tell you that I hate you, but I'm not going to." Sometimes, the shock of hearing you put into words what the child is thinking is enough to change the behavior. It may work for a day, anyway. You will have to do this repeatedly. When the child hits another, you can say, "You expect me to yell at you for hitting Joey. Well, I'm not going to. I'm going to ask you to sit here with me until you think you can go back with the other children. You know we do not hit in this room." Insist again that limits be respected; the child must follow the rules just like everyone else.

Speak to the parents but be careful. Try not to speak down to them or in an accusing manner. Try to use the "I want to help your child" approach. Most parents want to help their children; however, some do not know how. You may have to explain why you have limits and rules, and suggest that the parents have some limits for the child at home. You may have to give many tips to some parents, and you will have to be tactful and show them that you care. If you sense a noncaring attitude, you can easily understand why the child has problems. In this case, you will have to work only with the child, but keep trying.

One technique that sometimes works with the aggressive, underdisciplined child is to "call" the child on the behavior. What is meant by "call?" One way to look at interactions between two or more children is to find the underlying motivators. Does this sound familiar? Some children are motivated by a desire to control because they have learned that their own safety lies in their ability to control their environment. This can provoke a tug of war between the child's need to control and yours. At this point, there is no sense in trying to reason, especially verbally. Simply isolate the child, repeat the rules or limits, and leave. Tell the child as you leave that you know what the child is doing and why. Be specific. "I'm not going to argue with you" or "Sit here until you feel ready to rejoin us."

Be prepared to understand that you will not be successful with every child. There will always be one or two children who will relate better to another teacher.

Once in a while you will see a child who is so psychologically damaged that the regular classroom may not be an appropriate setting. The child may be underfed, poorly clothed, uncared for, and unloved. Erikson would suggest that this child has never resolved the task of basic trust as an infant, much less having resolved the tasks of autonomy and initiative. Being unwanted and unloved makes it extremely difficult for a child to acquire any sense of self-worth.

As the teacher, your job is to provide the kind of environment in which the child is able to resolve these early developmental tasks, even if the child has not yet done so. It is never too late to learn to trust or to develop autonomy; it is never too late to fulfill earlier outcomes related to the "good me," even while working toward resolution of a different age-related positive outcome.

Fourth Stage of Development

For school-age children, there is probably no more important task than to learn that they are capable of learning. Erikson called this stage **industry** and its negative outcome, inferiority. Unfortunately, some children who have progressed through the earlier stages of development smoothly and who enter school trusting in others, knowing the give-and-take expected of group life, feeling confident in their own abilities, stumble when they reach kindergarten and first grade.

industry—the fourth stage of development described by Erik Erikson, starting at the end of the preschool years and lasting until puberty, in which the child focuses on the development of competence.

For some children, the fine motor tasks of writing manuscript, shaping numerals, and coloring within specified lines are difficult. They may then learn that they do not have the abilities rewarded by their preschool teachers (see Figure 7–6).

School, instead of being a place of joy and learning, may become a place where children fail. Inferiority is the obvious result. A secondary result can be that the child develops feelings of helplessness. Successful students generally believe that they are responsible for their successes and attribute any failures to lack of effort. Unsuccessful students, however, often attribute successes to luck and failures to factors beyond their control, or to lack of ability. The unfortunate consequence in students who feel helpless is that they often give up and stop trying. It then becomes extremely difficult for teachers to change the behavior.

In a classroom that offers developmentally appropriate materials for children to interact with actively, there is no difficulty with industry. A developmentally

Figure 7-6 Teacher attention and help is provided in developmental centers when children show an interest in learning to write.

appropriate classroom is likely to have centers to allow for active exploration and enough physical space to allow for movement opportunities at different times. For example, it may have a carpeted reading area with pillows where children can go to look at and "read" books; a science area with "attractive junk" to manipulate; floor space for the children who may wish to work on the floor; a math center with cuisinaire rods, unifix cubes, tangrams, and other manipulatives; a writing area, managed by an assistant teacher or parent volunteer where children can dictate stores or write and illustrate their own; and so on. In the classroom with many options for working alone, in pairs, or in cooperative groups, children discover that learning is enjoyable and industry is then the result.

assistant teacher—also called aide, helper, auxiliary teacher, associate teacher, or small group leader; works under the guidance of the head teacher in providing a quality program.

Erikson and the Professional Development of Student Teachers

Gratz and Boulton (1996) look at Erikson's stages of development as they might apply to you as student teachers, and to your futures as teachers and caregivers in general. At Stage 1, for example, *trust* develops as a student teacher feels prepared to handle the classroom and is confident in her abilities. At Stage 2, a student teacher develops *autonomy* as he successfully moves from teaching one small group of children to working with the entire class. At Stage 3, the student teacher develops *initiative* as she designs and implements her own activity or learning center. Stage 4 student teachers manifest *industry* by becoming involved in their professional organizations and attending conferences. Stage 5 student teachers develop an *identity* as a teacher "through the cumulative activities that have helped the teacher to achieve a sense of initiative and industry and eventually a sense of self as an early childhood educator." *Intimacy*, the developmental task of Stage 6, can be seen as the student teacher establishes relationships with his cooperating teacher, aides in the classroom, parents, and his college supervisor. At Stage 7, the student teacher, now actively working as a teacher, becomes what euphemistically can be called "a contributing member of society." In other words, she has become *generative* and may be asked to mentor to another student teacher or a beginning teacher. Or she may plan a presentation for a professional conference. Generativity can be seen in many ways. At Stage 8, the former student teacher, now a teacher for several years, feels a sense of *integrity* as a professional and "trusts in her own mature professional judgment." Where do you see yourself in relationship to Erikson's developmental stages as posed by Gratz and Boulton?

BURTON WHITE AND SELF-CONTROL

White (1975) divides the child's first three years into seven phases, each with its unique characteristics, needs, and preferred child-rearing practices.

Phase I: Birth to six weeks

Phase II: Six weeks to three and one-half months

Phase III: Three-and-one-half to five-and-one-half months

Phase IV: Five-and-one-half to eight months

Phase V: Eight to 14 months

Phase VI: 14 to 24 months

Phase VII: 24 to 36 months

According to White, during Phase I, the primary needs of the infant are to feel loved and cared for, and to have the opportunity to develop certain skills such as holding up the head while on the stomach and tracking objects held eight to 24 inches from the face. The newborn baby does not need much stimulation other than a change of position from back to stomach to the mother's arms.

During Phase II, helping the infant achieve certain skills such as holding up the head becomes more important than during Phase I. Phase II infants also need hand-eye activities such as crib devices.

Phase III infants have attained head control and are beginning to attain torso control. At this age, the child learns to turn from stomach to back and back to stomach. Also, the child's leg muscles are strengthened. Infants at Phase III enjoy being held so they can press their feet against a lap and practice standing. They are quite social and respond to tickling and smiling with their own coos and smiles. The infants "soak up" all the attention from family and strangers alike and respond easily.

Phase IV infants begin to show an understanding of language. "Mama," "daddy," "bottle," and "eat" may all be understood by the child. The child cannot say the words but can respond, indicating a knowledge of the words. Phase IV babies are beginning to develop real motor skills such as sitting independently, getting up on hands and knees, and rocking. A Phase IV child may even pull to a standing position. Phase IV babies need freedom in which to move and practice these growing skills. They can also grasp toys quite well and need suitable small objects with which they can practice picking up and holding. Toys such as crib devices to kick at, stacking toys, stuffed toys, balls to pick up, and objects that are two to five inches in size so they cannot be swallowed all help the Phase IV child learn about the world and gain mastery over the immediate environment.

During Phase V, the infant usually comes into direct conflict with significant adults for the first time. This is due to the child's growing mobility. Soon there is no area in the house or center that is safe from the child's active exploration. Knick-knacks, books, ashtrays, electric cords, pots and pans, utensils, and pet food dishes are stimuli to the active Phase V child, and bring the child into conflict with the parents or caregivers.

It is at this age that the child begins to develop self-control. It is important that the child has a child-proof area in which to play. Parents, early childhood teachers, and family child care providers need to know that the Phase V child can be safe from harm in that area.

If the Phase V child does not get into trouble, the Phase VI child will. At this point, mobility has been established. Phase VI children can walk and begin to run, climb, ride, push and pull objects, reach for and pull down, and talk. "No" becomes a favorite word, mostly because they hear it so often. "Mama," "daddy," "bye-bye," and "baby" are spoken. The Phase VI child begins to pay less attention to the people in the environment and to spend more time looking, listening, practicing simple skills, and exploring.

It is the exploring that causes difficulty for both the Phase V and the Phase VI child. Most houses and yards are not childproof. Children will pull flowers off stems, grab dirt pebbles and throw them, toddle down driveways and out into streets, climb up ladders, and push and pull at furniture. This struggle to experiment with growing motor skills comes into continued conflict with parental and center needs for the child's safety. Instead of complimenting the climber who has mastered the front steps and is now crying to be picked up so he can start over, we may scold the child, saying the steps are off limits. The Phase V and Phase VI child simply cannot comprehend this. It would be more beneficial to our peace of mind and the child's need to climb if a portable gate is placed across the third stair and the child is allowed to practice going up and down. If the child falls down the three steps, he will not be hurt and will approach the climb more carefully the next time.

Self-control grows from experiences like these. The Phase V and Phase VI child will become an autonomous, able Phase VII preschooler if allowed to experiment with what the body can do and is given opportunities to practice growing motor skills. As a Phase VII preschooler, the child will be able to:

- Get and hold the attention of adults
- Use adults as resources after first determining that a job is too difficult
- Express affection and mild annoyance
- Lead or follow peers
- Compete with peers
- Show pride in accomplishments
- Engage in role-playing activities
- Use language with increasing competence
- Notice small details or discrepancies
- Anticipate consequences
- Deal with abstractions
- See things from another person's viewpoint
- Make interesting associations
- Plan and carry out complicated activities
- Use resources effectively
- Maintain concentration on a task while simultaneously keeping track of what is going on (dual focusing)

According to Burton White, most babies grow at essentially the same rate until Phase V. Most family environments provide reasonable positive experiences for Phase I through Phase IV children. As mentioned, conflicts arise as the child's mobility increases. As a teacher of young children, you must provide the kind of environment in which the children have as much opportunity as possible to grow and learn about their environment and themselves.

Emotional Development of Infants and Toddlers

Greenspan (Lally, 1995) believes that there are six stages of emotional development:

1. *Regulation and interest in the world (birth +).* This stage lasts until infants are approximately four months of age. Infants take an interest in sights, sounds, smells, and other inputs from their environments, and attempt to understand these sensations. What the infant is learning is that he can regulate some of his needs: when he wants to sleep, for example, or nurse.
2. *Falling in love (four months +).* At this age, infants establish strong, loving relationships with their primary caregivers, usually the mother and father, and often do so with a secondary caregiver if the parents work. Stage 2 lasts until about eight months and the beginning of language skills. Infants between the ages of four and eight months are often seen as "euphoric;" they are generally happy, smile frequently, and coo at themselves and others. They begin to realize that they can affect their environment and are interested in their bodies. Some will watch their hands for several minutes.
3. *Purposeful communication (eight months +).* At this age, infants react to language, and parents and caregivers realize that the baby understands what is being communicated. Some infants will begin to repeat babbling sounds, and a few may even say a word such as "bu" for "book," "bottle," and "bu-bu" for "bye-bye." Infants now understand that the adults in their lives react to them and that they can cause a reaction with certain sounds, words, and activities.
4. *The beginning of a complex sense of self (10 months +).* "By 10 to 18 months babies need to be admired for all the new abilities they have mastered," to enable toddlers to begin to expand their sense of selves as competent individuals.
5. *Emotional ideas (18 months +).* Around the ages 18 to 24 months, toddlers begin to use fantasy play and to express emotions, sometimes intensely as with tantrums. It is important then to help toddlers put feelings into words and allow them to explore how they feel on any given day.
6. *Emotional thinking (30 months +).* "When children are about 30 months old, their emotional development involves shifting gears between make-believe and reality." It is important at this stage to set clear limits for children, yet allow them freedom to indulge in creative, dramatic play.

In contrast, Goleman (1995) and Mayer and Salovey (1995) address what they call *emotional intelligence* and the skills associated with it. The key skills include:

- *Self-awareness:* being able to recognize and name emotions, and understand why the child feels as she does.
- *Self-regulation of emotion:* being able to verbalize and cope with emotions such as anxiety, anger, and depression; being able to control impulses, aggression, and self-destructive and antisocial behavior; recognizing one's strengths in being able to handle emotions, both positive and negative.
- *Self-monitoring and performance:* being able to focus on the task at hand; ability to set short- and long-term goals; being able to modify one's performance

after feedback; ability to mobilize positive motivation and work toward optimal performance states.

- *Empathy and perspective taking:* becoming a good listener (see Figure 7–7); being able to empathize with others and to increase sensitivity to the feelings of others; the ability to understand another child's perspective, point of view, or feelings.
- *Social skills in handling relationships:* the ability to express emotions in relationships, harmonize diverse feelings and viewpoints; being able to express emotions effectively; ability to work as a member of a team/cooperative learning group; being able to exercise sensitivity to social cues; ability to respond constructively and in a problem-solving manner to interpersonal obstacles (Elias, et al., 1997).

Elias, et al. (1997) emphasize that "acquiring an integrated set of skills such as these often occurs in an experiential context, where the skills are learned through practice and role modeling." They further stress the developmental nature involved in the acquisition of emotional skills and the fact that emotional skills are best learned through experience and repetition during early childhood.

Goleman (1995) states that some of the key ingredients of effective programs to promote emotional intelligence include emotional, cognitive, and behavioral skills. As student teachers, you may be able to help children acquire these.

Figure 7–7 Listening to hear teacher directions is an important skill

1. Emotional Skills
   - Identifying and labeling feelings
   - Expressing feelings
   - Assessing the intensity of feelings
   - Managing feelings
   - Delaying gratification
   - Controlling impulses
   - Reducing stress
   - Knowing the difference between feelings and actions
2. Cognitive Skills
   - Self-talk—conducting an "inner dialog" as a way to cope with a topic or challenge, or reinforce one's own behavior
   - Reading and interpreting social cues—for example, recognizing social influences on behavior and seeing oneself as a part of a larger community
   - Using steps for problem-solving and decision-making—for instance, controlling impulses, setting goals, identifying alternative actions, anticipating consequences
   - Understanding the perspective of others
   - Understanding behavior norms (what is and is not acceptable behavior)
   - A positive attitude toward life
   - Self-awareness—for example, developing realistic expectations about oneself
3. Behavioral Skills
   - Nonverbal—communicating through eye contact, facial expressions, tone of voice, gestures, and so on
   - Verbal—making clear requests, responding effectively to criticism, resisting negative influences, listening to and helping others, participating in positive peer groups (Goleman, 1995)

Teacher Priorities

Teachers realize emotions and cognitive development are intertwined and inseparable. Hyson (2002) identifies six "priorities" in promoting emotional competence:

1. *Creating a secure emotional environment.* If teachers build close relationships and an emotionally secure climate, children are able to explore and learn.
2. *Helping children to understand emotions.* If teachers promote emotional understanding, children have insight into their own and others' feelings, thereby becoming more empathic and socially competent.
3. *Modeling genuine, appropriate emotional responses.* If teachers themselves show real emotions and if they are effective models, children are likely to adopt appropriate ways of showing their feelings.
4. *Supporting children's regulation of emotions.* If teachers gradually guide children toward expressing and regulating their emotions in appropriate ways, children will gain powerful tools that lead to healthy development in social, emotional, and academic areas.
5. *Recognizing and honoring children's expressive styles.* If teachers respect individual and cultural differences in how children express their feelings while promoting appropriate expressions, children feel affirmed and supported.
6. *Uniting children's learning with positive emotions.* If teachers give children many opportunities to experience the joys and to overcome the frustrations of new learning experiences, they become able to tackle hard work, persist at tasks, and seek out challenges.

Young children progressing toward the emotional growth and control, needed in kindergarten often display secure and trusting feelings for their teachers and peers. They are able to control, express, regulate, and understand a wide spectrum of their own feelings. They display curiosity, problem-solving abilities, persistence, positive relationships with others, and an eagerness to know and experience classroom activities. They are headed toward academic success.

Self-esteem and Self-control

Although much of the research on self-esteem was completed in the late 1960s and throughout the 1970s, the new millennium is bringing about a renewed interest. With the noticeable changes in families that have occurred in the past twenty years due to the problems of divorce and subsequent single-parenthood, mobility, the rise in the incidence of substance abuse, remarriage and "blended" families, teenage parenthood, smaller family size, homelessness, the two working-parent family, and difficulties with child care and/or after-school care, child caregivers and teachers are seeing more and more stressed and even "damaged" children. Characteristic of these children is low self-esteem. Children of divorced parents typically blame themselves for the divorce, a phenomenon that exists even in the most "friendly" of divorce cases. Children raised in single-parent homes, over 90 percent of them headed by a woman, often live in reduced circumstances. It is well known that most single-parent females are not able to command the salaries that the single-parent male can; the result has been the feminization of poverty and the consequent cost to children living in poverty: housing, if any, in less desirable and often more dangerous neighborhoods, little medical or dental care, insufficient clothing for the weather conditions, lack of proper nutrition, and just simply lack of care in too many instances. What you see in the classroom then is the damage to these children's self-esteem: parents too stressed, too busy, and too often suffering from low self-esteem themselves to parent their children properly or nourish their children's self-esteem. One word of caution: not all single parents are overstressed; some children are less stressed after a divorce between parents who constantly argued than before; some single-parent women do earn substantial salaries, are emotionally and psychologically healthy, and are able to build their children's self-esteem. As always, be careful of using stereotypes.

In his landmark research, Coopersmith (1967) cited three home factors that contribute to children's feelings of self-esteem: (1) unconditional acceptance of the child (although not necessarily accepting all of the child's behaviors), (2) setting clear expectations for behavior and consistently reinforcing the need for adherence to them, and (3) respecting the child's need for initiative within the set limits. Some children you see today in child care and school may have been accepted only when they did exactly what their parents demanded of them; tired from working, other parents may have abdicated their job as parents and allowed the children essentially to raise themselves or may have allowed the TV to raise them; still other parents may feel threatened by their children's desires for autonomy and initiative and may not respect the need to exert their wills.

For the caregiver and teacher working with "damaged" children with low self-esteem, the task is to attempt to provide the missing elements of acceptance, clearly defined limits, and respect for the child's need to assert autonomy and practice initiative within those limits. If this sounds like CAREing, it should.

self-control—restraint exercised over one's own impulses, emotions, or desires

Self-control can be defined as the ability to resist the inappropriate and act responsibly. Acting responsibly includes respecting the rights of others, showing compassion, being honest, and at times exhibiting courage. It entails dealing effectively with anger and other strong emotions, and having patience.

The suggestions for promoting children's social development and skill, cited by Honig and Wittmer (1996) (listed in Chapter 6), are still relevant here. You may want to refer to them.

MASLOW'S HIERARCHY OF NEEDS AND ITS RELATION TO SELF-CONTROL

Maslow (1968) attempted to develop a hierarchy of needs by which people are motivated (see Figure 7–8). Maslow grouped these needs according to whether they were "deficiency" needs or "growth" needs; whether or not the individual was growing in a positive direction. For anyone to grow positively, Maslow felt that the deficiency needs must be filled in order for the growth needs to be met.

The implications for the children you teach are multiple. The child who is hungry, cold, and more importantly, unloved, may not be able to grow and learn as we would wish. This child may be afraid to grow for fear of losing the known. Regardless of how inclement and/or unwholesome that child's current environment may be, there is a certain safety in the known. For this child, growth can be full of anxiety.

Maslow's hierarchy of needs—a theorical position which attempts to identify human needs and motivations. It describes the consequences of need fulfillment and the consequences of unmet needs on growth.

Anxiety and fear in the child are often seen in the classroom as opposites. One fearful, anxious child will withdraw physically from the environment. The child may cling to the mother or the teacher, refuse to try a new activity, and limit participation to what the child knows and can do best. Another fearful, anxious child will lash out verbally or physically, sometimes both.

Maslow's hierarchy of needs is another way of looking at what motivates behavior. The child who is hungry, poorly clothed, and unloved may have difficulty

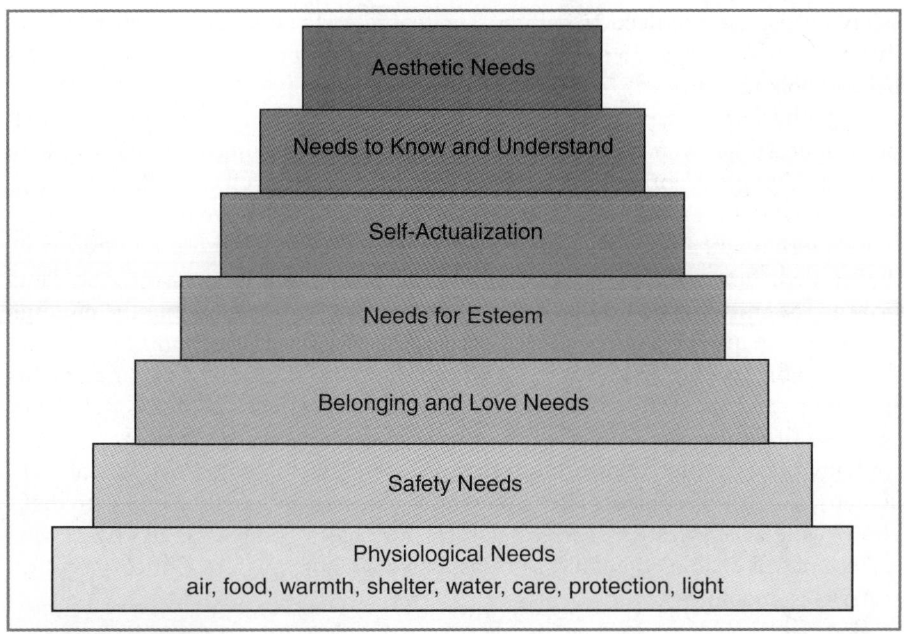

Figure 7–8 Adapted from Maslow, A. H. (1968). *Toward a Psychology of Being* (2nd ed.). Princeton, NJ: Van Nostrand Reinhold.

in becoming self-actualized. The same child may have difficulty in developing the natural desire to explore, know, and understand the environment. The overtly aggressive child and the fearful child are both underdisciplined or undisciplined.

In studying Maslow's hierarchy of needs, remember that if one goal is to help the child become self-actualizing, the child's deficiency needs must be met. The child's belongingness, love, and esteem needs must be met. Belongingness carries the implication of family identity, of belonging to a particular adult or group, and feeling that one is a part of this group. There is psychological safety in having a group to belong to. This group is the one that takes care of the physiological needs and makes sure that the environment is safe. This group also allows the growing child to develop self-esteem.

How is self-esteem developed? According to Maslow, it is developed in interaction with the important people in the environment. Look at the following sequence of events. It is morning. The infant cries; the mother goes to the crib, smiles, speaks softly to the baby, and picks up the baby. She changes the diaper, goes to the kitchen to warm a bottle or sits down in the rocking chair to nurse. As the infant feeds, she coos and speaks to the child and plays with her hand. What is the infant learning? Besides learning that this mother is reliable and loving, the baby is learning that he is important to the mother. Later, the child turns over from the stomach onto the back. The mother smiles, claps her hands, and says, "My, aren't you getting big! How smart you are to turn over!" The child is learning that he is physically competent. Self-esteem is developed through the continual interaction between the parent, child care workers, and child. Every time you give positive attention to the child, smile, and notice achievements, you are helping to build the child's self-esteem (see Figure 7–9).

Figure 7–9 A large part of teaching is giving attention to individual children.

The child from this type of environment will have no difficulty in becoming self-actualized. In contrast, the child whose home environment has not provided for these deficiency needs will have difficulty. For this child, you will need to provide those experiences that the child has missed: attention to physiological needs, safety needs, and the need to belong. The loving early childhood teacher or family child care provider can do much to help the child whose own family group has been unable to help.

Children are remarkably resilient; they can survive situations that seem almost impossible. Even given a poor beginning, if a child comes into contact with a warm, loving, accepting adult, the child will be able to self-actualize. Children who seem invulnerable or untouched by negative family environments (alcoholism, criminality, poverty, and/or mental illness) are also those children who, during their first year, had at least one significant adult in their lives who cared (Werner & Smith, 1982). This adult could be trusted, thus enabling the children to resolve the question of basic trust. According to Werner and Smith, these children are able to find other adults to whom they can relate in terms of resolving the other tasks of early childhood. These adults meet the children's deficiency needs so that they can self-actualize in spite of negative environments.

How does self-actualization relate to self-control? One aspect of self-actualization *is* self-control. The child who is able to self-actualize is able to make choices and accept leader or follower roles, and has a good sense of self. Having a sense of self enables the child to be assertive when appropriate or to accept directions from another.

Implications for Teachers

To summarize theorists' suggestions regarding the promotion of self-control, let us briefly look at each. Erikson relates self-control with resolving the question of autonomy, the task of toddlers. According to Maslow, self-control relates to the resolution of deficiency needs and the beginnings of self-actualization. Burton White's theory indicates that self-control develops as the child passes from Phase V to Phase VI in a healthy, positive environment with caring, loving parents. The child who has gained mastery over the environment gains self-control. Self-esteem theory would suggest that self-control is related to self-worth and that, when provided with acceptance, respect, and clearly stated classroom rules, the children who feel good about themselves will also exhibit self-control. Often, the parents of these children begin changing and showing interest when their children begin to feel good about themselves.

Sometimes words like "empower" and "belonging" are used to indicate that teachers who empower their students and provide them with a sense of belonging are also teaching students self-control. Empowerment means allowing children control over certain aspects of the classroom life (for example, choices of which learning center they want to study at or what the logical consequences might be for breaking certain classroom rules). And given an opportunity to feel a part of the classroom group satisfies the universal need to belong.

What does this mean to you as a teacher? First, you will need to provide the kind of environment where the children feel safe. Second, you must also provide the kind of personal environment where the children can grow positively. You must use guidance techniques and recognize, through keen observation, which children need more help than others to learn self-control.

What is meant by saying that you must provide for a safe environment? The physical arrangement of the rooms must be safe. It also means consistency of behavior expectations and predictability regarding the schedule and your own behavior. You must remember to use the four Cs of discipline. You must CARE so that the psychological climate is warm and loving. It means recognizing a child's developmental level in terms of self-control.

If the child has not learned to be autonomous, you will need to provide the kinds of opportunities that allow the child to practice. As mentioned, it means providing guided choices and allowing practice in decision-making. Does the child have a low self-image? Is the child's need to belong unfulfilled? You will need to provide success experiences for this child and a lot of tender, loving care (TLC, as it has been called). If this child has at least a sense of belonging in class, this is a start.

You may encounter a negative-acting child who appears to be at Burton White's Phase V and Phase VI stages. What has happened to this child? Most likely, if you check with the parents or other primary caregivers, you will find that the child's attempts to explore at Phase V were thwarted. This child was not encouraged to explore the physical environment and master newly emerging motor abilities. This is the child who becomes too fearful or shy or too aggressive. This child needs opportunities to explore and use motor abilities but needs to be told the limits over and over. This child must be urged ever so gently to try again.

Self-control, or self-discipline, is learned only through the initial imposition of controls from the significant adults in the child's life and the opportunity to practice the child's own controls secondarily.

Self-respect

Young children often want to share accomplishments with peers and caregivers. Requests to "Look at me, teacher!" pervade daily teacher-child interactions and help children respect themselves if given teacher attention. Many children take satisfaction in their appropriate behavior and accomplishments, and notice the inappropriate behavior of peers. Teachers deal with children's failures to act in line with their own developing good conscience as children move toward greater self-control. When classrooms model respect, compassion, and concern for others, children gain self-control and self-respect with greater ease. Teachers genuinely try to be the sort of people they hope children will become.

Talking through complications or problem situations with children is one way to help them understand the consequences of different choices. Story discussions also bring to light what choices and consequences occurred for story characters. Most teachers attempt to draw from children what choices existed in life situations and what consequences might follow. This promotes the child's own ability to reflect.

A CASE STUDY TO ANALYZE

Let us look at a sampling of behavior and see if you can apply any of the theories. More importantly, see whether knowing theory helps in teaching the child.

> Chris is a five-year-old whose mother brings him to school during the spring registration period. School policy invites spring registrants to attend class with the current children for a part of the morning session. You noted when he was enrolled that his mother looked much older than the others. Under "Reason for Enrollment," the mother wrote, "To give me a rest, and to give Chris a chance to be with children his own age."
>
> Later, in your initial conference with her, Chris' mother confessed, "You know, Chris was such a surprise to his father and me! After 20 years of being married, we never thought we'd ever have children. I thought I was going through the 'change,' you know, when I found out I was pregnant. What a shock! My husband and I lead such busy lives, you can imagine what having a baby did!"

On further investigation, you discover that Chris was carried full-term, the delivery was normal, and his arrival home was uneventful. Chris' mother assured you that her son had always been well cared for. "After all, my husband has a good income from his business (he's a CPA), and I used to run his office before Chris came. I'm a financial secretary, you know, and a good one."

When you asked about Chris' eating habits and sleeping patterns, she responded, "Well, of course, Chris doesn't have many regular habits. According to Mattie, our housekeeper, Chris eats when he wants to. Mattie takes care of Chris while my husband and I work. We don't see too much of him, you know, especially during tax season. But Mattie assures me Chris eats well, and I know he sleeps well when he finally goes to bed.

On further questioning, you find out that Chris "has a TV in his bedroom and usually falls asleep with it on. My husband or I turn it off when we go to bed."

Later, the mother volunteers, "Chris is such an active child that his father and I sometimes go nuts on the weekends. We tried locking Chris in his bedroom. That worked until he found out how to open his window screen and crawl out. Can you imagine that? And only three years old at the time. I can tell you we paddled him good for that!"

You wonder what Chris' behavior is going to be like when he comes for his scheduled visit. When Chris arrives with the housekeeper, unfortunately, your worst fears are realized. In less than 10 minutes, he has knocked down a castle Jaime and Roberto had been working on for more than 20 minutes, has run to the easels, grabbed the paintbrush from Anya's hand, and, to her cries of dismay, smeared her painting. Then, he has opened the hamster cage and none too carefully has searched through the wood shavings in the cage for the sleepy animal. At this point, you've had enough and intervene.

Why do you think Chris acts the way he does? What hypotheses or educated guesses can you make? Was he a wanted child? Do his basic physiological needs seem to be met? (The answer to that question is obvious. Chris is clean, well dressed, and large for his age. He shows no signs of malnutrition.) Moving to the next level on Maslow's hierarchy, safety needs, you can only guess at this point. Looking at his rather awkward large motor coordination and lack of ease in handling his body, it becomes apparent that Chris does not seem comfortable in the physical environment. Moving to the third level, the need to belong and be loved, you are no longer so sure. Chris parted from his housekeeper as soon as he came into the room.

However much he may have been used to being left with the housekeeper, it was obvious that she did nothing to restrain him. Her only remark was, "Good lord! Sometimes he used to act like that when I took him to visit at my friend's house. Now I don't even try to take him any more."

On intervening, you took Chris' arm firmly, closed the door to the hamster cage, and said, "You'll be able to play with Sebastian next fall. But, first, you will have to learn how. In our kindergarten, we respect each other's work, and we don't disturb others when they are busy. You have a choice of going to the clay table where you can pound on the clay and make something you'd like to make. Or, you can come to the workbench over by the door and drive some nails into some pieces of scrap wood and make a wood sculpture."

Looking at the fourth level of the Maslow hierarchy, do you think Chris has feelings of self-esteem? Is it likely that a child who destroys other children's work has good self-esteem? The answer is no. What are the chances, then, of Chris being able to self-actualize? At this point, they are probably not too good. Chris is a typical underdisciplined child, cared for in a material way but not in a loving way.

What would Erikson's theory reveal? Has Chris resolved the tasks of infancy, toddlerhood, and preschool? Is he ready to work on the tasks of school-aged children? It is possible that before Chris became an active crawler, his mother did love and accept him. She had reported a normal delivery and a healthy baby. In telling of his birth, she commented about what a pretty baby Chris was, and how she and her husband used to take him everywhere because he'd go to sleep anywhere as long as he was in his bassinet. You suspect that it was only after Chris began to crawl that he began to pose problems. You feel that Chris probably has some level of basic trust.

Autonomy, though, is another question. You already know that Chris was locked in his bedroom so his parents could rest. When asked, Chris' mother admitted that she generally kept him confined to the playpen while in the house or yard. "I couldn't have him get into my collection of miniatures or into his father's rose garden!" When asked if Chris had space in the yard for a swing set or other play equipment, Chris' mother said, "Heavens, no! My husband and I like to entertain in our yard in the summer; we can't have play equipment cluttering it up!"

It seems apparent that Chris has not had the kind of gross motor experiences of most preschoolers. In fact, you already noted during Chris' visit that he ran awkwardly as though he did not have much practice running in the past. Another observation was that Chris' mother took off his jacket for him; the boy did not do it for himself. When asked whether Chris dressed himself, his mother stated, "Oh, no. I always put his clothes on for him." When asked if Chris chose what to wear, she replied, "No. Chris wouldn't know what to choose! He'd end up with a blue plaid shirt and his green overalls when he ought to be wearing his gray pinstriped shirt and black jeans!"

You realize that Chris has had little experience in making the usual choices common to many kindergartners. Has he resolved the questions of autonomy or initiative? It seems unlikely. What does this mean for you in terms of having Chris in your kindergarten? First, it means a lot of close watching, restating rules, calm insistence of acceptable behavior, and gradual choices. You know it also means a lot of tactful, gentle education for Chris' parents.

CULTURAL DIFFERENCES

How do cultural differences reflect in analyzing student behaviors? The most important factor to remember is to avoid using **stereotypes**. All Asians are not quiet, nor are they all straight-A students, nor are Asians from one single cultural group. All African Americans are not inner-city dwellers nor do they all speak nonstandard English. All Hispanics are not Mexican or Puerto Rican or Cuban; they come from as many different separate Hispanic cultures as do Africans, Asians, or Europeans. Among Native Americans, you will note the same great variations depending on individual cultural backgrounds. It is important for you as future teachers to remain as open-minded as possible, not to use the kind of thinking that can ascribe to culturally different students behaviors that may not apply to them as individuals.

stereotype—a simplified conception or image of a person or group based on race, ethnicity, religion, gender or sexual orientation.

In observing children and families from cultures other than your own, the most important factor in establishing a good relationship with the family is to remain open-minded. Listen carefully to what a parent may say; even if you disagree, try to place yourself in the parent's shoes, to see from her perspective. Some parents from India typically greet another person with clasped hands and a bow of the head. To offer to shake hands is simply not appropriate. One teacher related that when she held a conference with one of her Afghan parents, the father had to be addressed through a male teacher: he made it clear that it was inappropriate for him to speak directly to his child's female teacher. A parent from Japan may often bow to his child's teacher; it is a sign of respect. A Latino mother may not look you straight in the eyes as she may feel that to do so connotes disrespect. Parents from Vietnam may have different names and legally be married (Berger, 1994).

Certainly one reason for the existence of stereotypes is that when we do not have the information, we rely on the news media, and typically television, for the "facts." But "bad" news sells more than "good," and stories of homicides, robberies, and assaults abound. Because many more of these occur in inner cities than in suburbs, the stereotype develops that because the inner city or barrio or wherever the violence is happening has more people of color living within its confines, all people of that particular race or ethnic group must be violent or prone to violence.

We need to remember that the first African Americans to come to what is now the United States came with Columbus and Coronado, and many more arrived, as did many whites, as indentured servants. It was only later historically that they were brought as slaves (Banks, 1984). We need also remember that Latinos had settled in the southwestern parts of the United States before the first Puritans settled in Massachusetts. If there is any one thing you should always remember about children from minority families in your classroom, it is to recognize their diversity (Berger, 1994). For some excellent ideas of how to avoid stereotyping and bias in your classroom, look at Derman-Sparks' (1989) book, *The Anti-Bias Curriculum: Tools for Empowering Young Children.*

SUMMARY

In this chapter, we have presented several different theories to help you analyze children's behaviors, together with suggestions to implement in your attempt to help children learn self-control. Among theorists mentioned were Erikson, Maslow, the self-concept theorists, and White.

In terms of the Erikson tasks, the one most closely related to self-control is autonomy. If resolved during toddlerhood, teachers see a child who knows how to play/work within the prescribed limits in any classroom, who understands both leadership and follower roles, who knows when to ask for help or when he can do a task by himself. Ideas for teachers to implement in the classroom for children who have incompletely resolved autonomy were also given: allowing choices, and reminding children of limits and rules are two.

Maslow believed that self-control evolved out of self-esteem (as do the self-concept theorists) and self-actualization. Thus, everything a teacher can do to build self-esteem and a feeling of belongingness in the classroom, and, again, to allow choices, all will lead to children with good self-control.

White focuses on infants during their first explorations with mobility, an event that usually comes between eight and 24 months. Given appropriate toys and the freedom to explore within safe limits, active babies and toddlers develop into healthy, happy preschoolers.

Finally, we presented you with the case study of a child, Chris, and gave some suggestions, related to the different theories, to analyze his behavior and develop and implement some management strategies.

HELPFUL WEB SITES

http://www.aecf.org/

Annie E. Casey Foundation—Kids Count. Search for KIDS COUNT Data Book: state profiles of child well-being are included.

http://nccic.org

National Child Care Information Center (NCCIC). Search infant and toddler topics.

http://www.apa.org

American Psychological Association. Look for readings in "early childhood."

http://zerotothree.org

Zero to Three: National Center for Infants, Toddlers, and Families. A wide range of material.

SUGGESTED ACTIVITIES

A. Read Burton L. White's *The First Three Years of Life.* Give close attention to Chapters 6 and 7. Discuss your readings with your peers, cooperating teacher, and supervisor.

B. Read Erik Erikson's *Childhood and Society.* In particular, read those chapters covering the first four stages of psychosocial development. Write a review of your reading and discuss it with your peers and supervisor.

C. You are concerned because Tahira, a student in your third-grade room, is frequently absent. A bright-eyed, eager-to-learn child, she does poorly on tests, and when she turns in her homework, it is often incomplete. Your co-operating teacher has also been concerned, and she suggests that you attend a conference she has arranged with Tahira's mother to help you understand. At the conference, you discover that Mrs. Bhas often keeps Tahira home to take care of her younger brothers and sister whenever one or more of them are ill. You explain that it is important for the child to be in school, but Mrs. Bhas demurs, "Tahira is my oldest girl; she knows she is supposed to help me. I work, and it's Tahira's duty to take care of her younger brothers and sister after school or when they are sick. Education is important for my boys but not for my girls. It is only important that they have a good marriage arranged for them."

In view of Mrs. Bhas' cultural expectations for her daughter, what might you do? How might you try to convince her that you think a third grader is too young to baby-sit or that a girl needs an education as much as a boy? Do any of the theories discussed in our chapter help you in understanding your dilemma about Tahira?

Applying Erikson's theory might indicate the satisfactory completion of basic trust, but is autonomy or initiative an expectation of Tahira by Mr. and Mrs. Bhas? It is more likely that being quiet and obedient (that is, doing as mother and father ask) are cultural practices more valued by her parents than are independence, exploration, and curiosity. One approach you might take is to ask Mrs. Bhas what her occupation is to determine whether or not an education is needed. Unfortunately, her response could be, "We own several motels in town and my job, and Tahira's and her sister's on the weekends, is to see that linens are changed, beds are made, and rooms are cleaned." It might be possible to find someone of the Bhas' own culture to explain the importance of education to them.

Using Maslow's hierarchy might point out the satisfactory completion of the deficiency needs, but interference with Tahira's "need to know and understand" by her culture.

D. Observe one child in your classroom closely and analyze the child's level of self-control. Discuss your observations regarding whether you feel the child has resolved the task of autonomy, feels competent, and is becoming self-actualized. State specific actions that reinforce your conclusions.

E. Close your eyes as a fellow student teacher reads the following:

A Visualization

Sometimes, visualizing what you're attempting to do in classroom management situations is helpful. Imagine a large metropolitan train station where at the moment, every child is happily playing. Imagine each child as a different kind of railroad car. All of a sudden, the box car and the coal car are becoming increasingly noisy and agitated, and rolling out of the station to a destination called Violence. The agitation can represent lots of different feelings including anger, frustration, fear, jealousy, anxiety, and other negative feelings. You, the railway security officer, aren't sure exactly how each car is feeling. You think it's best if the box car and coal car go to different destinations than Violence. Down in Violence, lots of hurtful things happen like hair pulling, biting, hitting and pushing, and so on. At times, you notice friends of box car or coal car want to ride down to Violence, too, ending up with many beaten up and crushed cars. Sometimes, a car comes out of Violence unscathed and rolls back into the station, ready to roll out to Violence with another car destined to become beaten or broken.

Your goal is to have cars in conflict buy tickets to Negotiation and/or Problem-Solving, a shorter trip and closer destination. You are willing to buy a ticket to either of these destinations and help the cars think of innovative solutions where both will ride back to the station with needs satisfied. You may be able to stop cars headed toward Violence before car feelings get heated up. You're ready to get them on the track to Negotiation and Problem-Solving quickly. You've found you are usually able to promote agreement in these destinations by:

- verbally stating that a problem exists
- stopping aggressive acts
- holding the conflict object if there is one
- drawing out in words the feeling of the nonaggressor and the aggressor
- reflecting back the expressed feelings to both parties
- describing and stating both sides of the conflict
- verbally drawing solution ideas from both sides until a satisfactory solution is discovered; offering a solution when a stalemate occurs

- promoting agreement on a solution
- congratulating parties on offering solution ideas
- monitoring both parties while they work through the agreed plan
- stating that the conflict solution has been accomplished

This process is also suggested for adult conflict situations in Chapter 8. How do the suggested techniques promote child self-control?

F. Read the following from Kathleen Grey (1995). Discuss with a group of classmates. Try to answer the questions posed in the second paragraph.

> A teacher is trying to reinforce the behavior of a child who has voluntarily carried out a classroom rule. She says to him, "Good job, Tom! You're doing just what you're supposed to do, aren't you? You're always such a good boy." The message to Tom is not about his intrinsic worth, but about his value when he does what his teacher wants him to. If Tom's teacher truly wants to affirm Tom's intrinsic worth, as he expressed it through his desire to participate competently in classroom culture, she might say, "I saw you carry all the dirty paintbrushes to the sink, Tom. You had to make three trips to get them all! I sure appreciate your help."

If Tom regularly hears the unspoken message in the first scenario, how is he likely to apply it to himself? How do you think this message will affect his ability to make judgments for himself? Would he have a different sense of his competence if he regularly received the message in the second sample?

G. Read the following and react: "Young children are often helped by a playful, imaginative approach when feelings are hard to face" (Zavitkovsky, Baker, Berlfein, & Almy, 1986).

Can you remember any life situations when a teacher or adult helped a child overcome or face fear using this approach?

REVIEW

A. According to Erikson, what are the first four stages of psychosocial development? What are the tasks associated with each?

B. Read the following description of behavior, then answer the questions at the end.

> Cindy, an only child, is a bright-eyed, small, three-and-a-half-year-old attending your child center for the first time. Her family recently moved to your community. Her mother and father are both teachers in local school districts. Her mother reported that Cindy's birth was normal, and she has had no major health problems. Coming to your child center will be her first experience with children her own age except for religious instruction school.
>
> Cindy appears to like child care very much. She is a dominant child despite her small size, and rapidly becomes one of the leaders. She plays with just about all of the toys and materials supplied at the center. Her favorite activities, however, appear to be the dramatic play center and easel painting when inside, and either the sandbox or swings when outside. She occasionally gets into arguments with her peers when they no longer accept her leadership. Cindy has difficulty resolving these conflicts and frequently has a tantrum when she is unable to have her own way.

1. Would you suggest that Cindy has basic trust? What evidence suggests this?
2. Do you think Cindy has resolved the task of autonomy? What evidence suggests that?
3. Erikson would suggest that Cindy's task at age three-and-a-half is to learn to use initiative. What evidence is there in the brief description of her behavior that suggests she is going through this phase of development in a positive or negative way?
4. Using Maslow's hierarchy of needs, at which level would you place Cindy? Why?

C. List the seven phases of development that occur during the child's first three years, according to Burton White.

D. List five characteristics of an autonomous, six-year-old child with positive self-esteem.

E. Rate each of the following teacher actions with a plus (+) if it would help a child develop self-control or a minus (–) if it would not. If the action would neither help nor hurt, rate it with an x.

1. Smiling each morning when the child enters.
2. Picking up and isolating the child who is fighting.
3. Spanking the child.
4. Setting strict limits and frequently reminding the child of them.
5. Asking the child who is fighting to please stop.
6. Moving toward a group of arguing children.
7. Complimenting the child when successful at a new task.
8. Applying the same standards to all the children.
9. Gently persuading the child.
10. Pairing a shy child with an outgoing one.
11. Ridiculing a naughty child.
12. Redirecting the attention of a child engaged in a potentially dangerous activity.

CASE SCENARIO

Setting: A private parochial school near a residential parochial college. Ron, a student teacher recently assigned to a second grade classroom, is complaining to his cooperating teacher, Mrs Kuefner.

"Mrs. Kuefner, I simply don't understand why the kids behave for you but won't for me." Ron says. "What am I doing wrong?"

"Some of the things you are doing are right; don't forget that!" Mrs. Kuefner replies encouragingly. "But, just reminding the children the first day you started to teach that you would abide by the same rules that I had established with them isn't enough. What do you think their talking, snickering, and lack of attention shows?"

"That they don't like me!" complains Ron.

continues . . .

. . . continued

"Didn't you learn about reasons students misbehave?" queries Mrs. Kuefner.

"The classroom management course was a year ago!" Ron states. "Now is the time I need it!"

"Do you know where the children come from?" Mrs. Kuefner asks.

"Aren't most of them local?" asks Ron. "I know we have children from various ethnic backgrounds and some whose families are immigrants, but I think most of them must be middle class, right?"

"To answer your questions, you might want to do a "Getting to Know You" activity. And, incidentally, you should answer the same questions you pose for the students so that they get to know you better," Mrs. Kuefner suggests. "And you should know that some of our students are here on a scholarship. Remember, too, I would need to see any proposed questionnaire prior to you implementing it.

"That still doesn't answer my question about what seems to be their disrespect of me," Ron says. "Before I started taking over for you, I was sure they liked me and thought of me as a friend.

"Mrs. Kuefner sighs. "You know the answer to that: before you can be a friend, you first have to be a teacher. And as a teacher, you need to establish your own authority; you can't just ride on mine. Think about that, please. And maybe talk to Dr. To, your university supervisor."

Questions for Discussion:

1. Have you ever had the same problem as Ron? Did you also want to be a friend, and as a result, were reluctant to make students adhere to classroom rules?
2. Is reminding students on your first day of teaching that your cooperating teacher's rules were the same as yours enough? Why?
3. What should Ron do now to establish discipline in his classroom?

REFERENCES

Banks, J. A. (1984). *Teaching strategies for ethnic studies.* Boston: Allyn & Bacon.

Berger, E. H. (1994). *Parents as partners in education: The school and home working together* (4th ed.). Columbus, OH: Merrill/Macmillan.

Coopersmith, S. (1967). *The antecedents of self-esteem.* New York: W. H. Freeman.

Derman-Sparks, L. D. (1989). *The anti-bias curriculum: Tools for empowering young children.* Washington, DC: National Association for the Education of Young Children.

Elias M. J., Zins, J. E., Weissberg, R. P., Frey, K. S., Greenberg, M. T., Haynes, N. M., Kessler, R., Schwab-Stone, M. E., & Shriver, T. P. (1997). *Promoting social and emotional learning: Guidelines for educators.* Alexandria, VA; Association for Supervision and Curriculum Development.

Erikson, E. H. (1993). *Childhood and society* (reprint of 2nd ed.). New York: Norton.

Goleman, D. (1995). *Emotional intelligence: Why it can matter more than IQ*. New York: Bantam.

Gratz, R. R., & Boulton, P. J. (1996, July). Erikson and early childhood educators: Looking at ourselves and our profession developmentally. *Young Children, 51*(5).

Grey, K. (1995, July/August). Not in praise of praise. *Child Care Information Exchange, 104*.

Honig, A. S., & Wittmer, D. S. (1996, January). Helping children become more prosocial: Ideas for classrooms, families, schools, and communities. *Young Children, 51*(2).

Hyson, M. (2002, November). Emotional development and school readiness. *Young Children, 57*(6), 76–78.

Lally, J. R. (1995, November). The impact of child care policies and practices on infant/toddler identity formation. *Young Children, 51*(1).

Maslow, A. H. (1968). *Toward a psychology of being* (2nd ed.). Princeton, NJ: Van Nostrand Reinhold.

Mayer, J., & Salovey, P. (1995). Emotional intelligence and the construction and regulation of feelings. *Applied and Preventive Psychology, 4*(2).

White, B. L. (1975). *The first three years of life*. Englewood Cliffs, NJ: Prentice-Hall.

Werner, E., & Smith, R. S. (1982). *Vulnerable but invincible: A longitudinal study of resilient children and youth*. New York: McGraw-Hill.

Zavitkovsky, D., Baker, K. R., Berlfein, J. R., & Almy, M. (1986). *Listen to the children*. Washington, DC: National Association for the Education of Young Children.

SECTION IV

Communication

CHAPTER 8

Common Problems of Student Teachers

After studying this chapter, the student should be able to:

Identify five common student teacher problems related to interpersonal communication.

List areas of possible conflict between student teachers, supervisors, and cooperating teachers, and their relationship to interpersonal communication.

Describe the goals of interpersonal communication during the student teaching experience.

Identify communication skills that aid in sending and receiving verbal and nonverbal messages.

Define "authenticity" of communication.

Identify a sequential approach to problem-solving.

Describe three alternatives when faced with problems.

Describe the goals of negotiation.

Explain the usefulness of an alternative solutions approach.

I was convinced my cooperating teacher didn't like me! I don't take criticism well. After hearing the same comment from different team members, I realized they were trying to help me.

—Jean Hamilton

Many of the parents of my placement classroom's children don't speak English. Some are new, struggling immigrants. My cooperating teacher makes all feel welcome. We've a classroom corner where tea and coffee is served and parents can sit and chat at pickup time on sunny days. It's a good idea.

—Margaret Hanneford

Something that threw me was the fact that the playground rules were different from the school where I work. When I saw a child standing on the big cement tunnel my first thought was "Oh my goodness he'll fall and kill himself!" Fortunately my cooperating teacher moved over to the tunnel and calmly asked the child to state how he could get down safely. This was a good lesson for the technique facilitated problem solving and used child ideas. My first day went faster than greased lightening, and I survived.

—Lois Akers

I'm working up the courage to tell a fellow student teacher she's not doing her share. My supervisor suggested I tell her how frustrated and angry I am before I explode. It's so easy to say "you" but I plan to stick to "I'm feeling. . . , I'm expecting . . . "

—Glo Hopkings

This chapter is not intended to solve all problems encountered during student teaching. It will probe possible reasons for difficulties, especially those related to communication, and help alert the student to possible courses of action. Knowing that problems are going to occur is stress reducing. You will relate more strongly to some ideas in this chapter than to others. Knowledge may help you escape some problems, confront others, and cope with ones that cannot be changed. Open communication with others—cooperating teacher, college supervisor, children—is often the key.

KINDS OF PROBLEMS

Do you know of any human relationship that is problem-free and always smooth sailing? Student teaching, involving close human interaction and communication, is no exception. Pressures, feelings, desires, needs, risks, and possible failures are inherent.

Stress

During the first days and weeks of student teaching, stress arises, usually from student teachers' desire to become good practicing teachers and feelings of self-doubt and lack of confidence. As you grasp the challenges through watching your cooperating teacher and attempt to put your own theory into practice, the task seems monumental. There is believed to be three sequential stages in teacher training: (1) focus on self or self-protection; (2) focus on pupils (children); and (3) focus on outcomes of teaching. Initial focus on self appears to be a necessary and crucial element in the first stage of teacher development.

stress—internal or external demand on a person's ability to adapt.

Another research study probing student teacher anxieties suggests supervisor's and cooperating teacher's evaluations of student teacher classroom competency was the most frequently mentioned contributing factor. Program planning and child discipline, class management, and staff relationships were other anxiety-producing factors (Morton, Vesco, Williams, & Awender, 1997).

Student teachers without past child care employment can feel overwhelmed by a beginning realization concerning teacher workloads. Brighton (1999) explains teaching is hard work requiring intelligence, preparation, creativity, determination, and perseverance.

Anxiety

An early focus on oneself may produce anxiety. A student teacher can feel uncomfortable until there is a clear feeling of exactly what is expected. One can react to stress in a number of ways. In student teaching, reactions could be:

anxiety—a general sense of uneasiness that cannot be traced to a specific cause.

- Becoming defensive
- Concentrating energies on passive, shy children

- Fear of being "unloved" if you discipline
- Illness
- Missing class sessions
- Sleeplessness
- Loss of hope
- Becoming extremely authoritarian; giving directions in every situation
- Looking for fault in others
- Becoming overly critical of the student teaching situation
- Withdrawing into busy work or room maintenance

Or, a more positive course of action is:

- Seeking additional written or oral guidelines (see Figure 8–1)
- Organizing tasks into time blocks
- Clearly outlining assignments on a calendar, file, or binder system
- Seeking the supervisor to communicate anxieties
- Using stress-reduction techniques

The first reactions can lead to immediate additional difficulties. The other reactions confront and possibly reduce tension. Anxiety may occur when there are changes in life. Change for student teachers occurs with their increasing responsibilities.

What can student teachers do to help themselves? Skillpath Seminars (1997) suggest the following:

- Talk to yourself, emphasizing positive thinking
- Visualize your happiness and success
- Reward yourself for a job or task well done
- Take on the responsibility to change situations that cause stress
- Exercise
- Learn to play as hard as you work

Figure 8–1 Are there guidelines concerning who can use the kitchen at your placement school?

- Take care of health concerns
- Reject perfectionism, yet strive for excellence
- Maintain optimism
- Develop a sense of humor
- Have fun at work
- Seek counseling if necessary

It will be helpful if you continue to pay attention to healthful living, use your sense of humor about the student teaching situation, develop or rely on a support system, obtain a positive outlook, exercise, and seek relaxation techniques if necessary. It's best to stay away from gossip if it exists, and eliminate or turn off destructive self-talk.

Canter (1998) suggests stressed teachers should look for opportunities to:

- Take a walk around the room or yard
- Do some deep breathing exercises to relax
- Identify the source of stress
- Talk to a colleague about it
- Surround themselves with positive-thinking people who appreciate the challenges of the teaching profession and the significance of a teacher's role in society

The negative comments of staff at a placement site and their complaining about lack of administrative support, work overload, parents, and so on, may affect a student teacher's stress level (Canter, 1998). Stress promotes a chemical change in the body creating tenseness and nervousness, and gears the body for action.

Clear, authentic communication of feelings, done with skill and sensitivity, is not often taught at either home or school. The student teaching experience puts student teachers, children, and other adults in close human contact, and adds the anxiety-producing procedure of observing and assessing the student teacher's competency development. If you have already acquired the abilities of speaking openly and frankly without alienating, being a skillful listener, and receiving and accepting suggestions, this chapter will serve as a review, perhaps giving additional insights and communication techniques.

Keirsey and Bates (1984) offer advice to individuals seeking to understand and communicate with others:

> If I do not want what you want, please try not to tell me that my want is wrong.
>
> Or if I believe other than you, at least pause before you correct my view.
>
> Or if my emotion is less than yours, or more, given the same circumstances, try not to ask me to feel more strongly or weakly.
>
> If you will allow me any of my own wants, or emotions, or beliefs, or actions, then you open yourself, so that some day these ways of mine might not seem so wrong, and might finally appear to you as right—for me.
>
> People are different in fundamental ways. They want different things.

The importance of relating and communicating with others in childhood work cannot be overestimated. Many early childhood teachers face cultural diversity daily. This necessitates increased awareness, sensitivity, and communication skill.

Sometimes, extreme reactions to student teaching happen.

> The situation is complicated by biases and stereotypes each of us may have about the teaching role. You may find yourself saying, "All teachers are bad . . . I will save these children and protect them from the teacher. I will do the opposite of what she does . . ." Or you may say, "All teachers are wonderful, superior people . . . I will copy the words, phrases, voice quality, and gestures of this teacher. Then I, too, will be marvelous" (Danoff, Breitbart, & Barr, 1977).

Even extreme feelings can be accepted as natural and to be expected. Once accepted, there is the chance to move on and get past them or at least cope.

> First of all, students can expect to feel inadequate when they begin participating in the school and probably for some time after that. They cannot possibly be prepared for all that may happen. No one can give instructions that will cover everything, certainly not in the time there may have been for preparation. Of course, students will not feel sure of what is expected of them or of what they are supposed to do. The teacher who is guiding them may not be sure of these things herself, as she does not know them yet or know what is possible for them. What we can do about the feeling of inadequacy at this point is to feel comfortable about having it (Read & Patterson, 1980).

You will find it is possible to be excited, eager to try your ideas and activities, eager to develop your own teaching style, and still be somewhat apprehensive. The caring and involvement student teachers bring to their work are commendable characteristics. These will promote their success in student teaching. Warner (1995) suggests "teachers should never feel guilty at the end of a teaching day, or think of themselves as a failure. If they have made a positive difference in just one child's life, they should view themselves as successful."

A contrast to the anxious approach to student teaching is the relaxed, confident one. This happens after your first successes. Self-confidence and self-esteem are important primary goals of student teaching. They evolve in student teachers as they do in children through actions resulting in success and through the feedback received from others. A strong feeling of success through child interactions is described by Read and Patterson (1980):

> A child's face lights up when he sees us come into the room, and we know that our relationship with him is a source of strength. He is seeing us as someone who cares, who can be depended on, and who has something significant to give him. It makes us feel good inside to be this kind of person for a child. It gives us confidence (see Figure 8-2).

Figure 8-2 "Look teacher, I can go really fast!"

Hints for dealing with anxiety suggest trying not to worry about being the teacher and, instead, reflect on teachers you liked when you were a child. Another method is to relax and treat children your own way, the way you really think about them. This will give you the confidence required to give more, try more, and be more effective.

Putting student teaching in perspective and being able to laugh at one's self help reduce anxiety. This is something each student teacher needs to consider.

Time Management

As mentioned in Chapter 6, time management is a part of total classroom management. For some student teachers, time management is a continual problem. A date book, file, or pocket and desk calendar help. Organization is a key element. Devise a system that puts what you need within reach; it will save time. Plan ahead and break large tasks into small, specific pieces. Use daily lists and give tasks priorities. Think of "must do first," medium priority, and "can wait" categories. Do not waste time feeling guilty. Working with a colleague or friend is a strategy that often gets difficult tasks accomplished.

Time and Energy

Time seems to be a problem for many students—enough time and organization of time. Cooperating teachers sometimes complain that students are not prepared, are tardy, or are unreliable. Working while student teaching limits the hours necessary for the preparation of activities. Student teachers must learn to manage their time. This involves planning ahead and analyzing task time lengths. Poor time management increases tension, destroys composure, and creates stress. Only the student teacher can make adjustments to provide enough time and rest necessary for student teaching. Standards of teacher training are rarely relaxed for just one individual.

SEEKING HELP

It is difficult for some student teachers to ask for help or suggestions. The risk involves having either the cooperating teacher or supervisor realize one's limitations. Therefore, student teachers sometimes turn to other student teachers. Trust is an important element in this dilemma. Fortunately, one builds trust through human reaction, and seeking help usually becomes easier as time passes. Self-doubt may cause a student teacher to resist asking questions for fear of looking dense, needy, or vulnerable. Leeds (2001) suggests asking "smart questions." She believes the following types of questions are effective problem-solvers:

- *Pose a question that lets the other person answer what you want to know.* "Would you like me to plan another physical development activity or branch out to another area?" If no, one can ask "Why not?" If yes, "Why?"
- *Begin conversations with open-ended questions.* "What kinds of words or actions might I use to calm down Rocky? Walk me through some."
- *End conversations with closed-ended questions.* "Am I making sense to you? Have I addressed everything?"
- *If you are dealing with a problem, explain what you have done so far, then pose your question.* "I read the label on the powdered paint can and mixed in more powder, but I'm wondering if it is still too runny. What do you think?"
- *Ask questions at a neutral time when the problem can be separated from strong emotions.*
- *Avoid asking negative questions.* For instance, instead of saying, "You didn't like the way my lesson went, did you?" ask questions such as "How could I have improved my planned activity?"

It is important to seek help quickly in many instances, and to use consultation times and meetings to pick the brains of others and seek assistance.

Figure 8–3 Seeking advice and assistance becomes easier as time passes.

The role of both the supervisor and cooperating teacher includes on-site support and advice (see Figure 8–3.) A beginning teacher needs encouragement, reassurance, comfort, guidance, instruction in specific skills, and insight into the complex causes of behavior. In the English primary school system, it is the usual practice that a beginning teacher receives advice and supportive assistance on a daily basis throughout the first full year of teaching. Some school districts in the United States provide mentors for beginning teachers.

The Half-a-Teacher Feeling

During their experiences, many student teachers are led to feel either by the children, cooperating teachers, or other staff members, that because of their position, they are not quite students and not quite teachers. Because of this "neither-here-nor-there" attitude, student teachers are not always treated as figures of authority. Read the poem in Figure 8–4. It may bring a knowing smile. Children in many instances may not recognize you as a teacher but refer to you as a student teacher. Some student teachers have had the experience of being treated as a "go-fer," and being asked to do what a teacher is not required to do.

Sometimes early in student teaching, a strong team feeling has not been developed. Its development is critical for all involved. It may be best to consult with one's supervisor first. Cooperating teachers have a number of factors to consider in relinquishing control of their classroom. Often, they feel uneasy about their routines and classroom behavior standards being threatened. They may also feel they are asking too much too soon of their student teachers and may be unclear of their role in giving assignments. It may be difficult for cooperating teachers to interchange their roles and become co-teachers instead of lead teachers. They can also be worried about child safety.

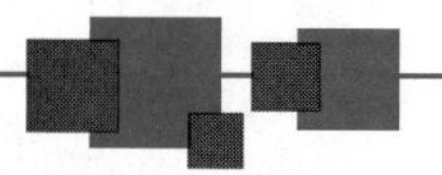

Not Quite

Her classroom
Her rules
Her kids
And ——
She's "the teacher" here.
I'm just an almost, a
"not quite"
Who's working hard to
get it right.
But wait and see
A real teacher I'm
beginning to be!

Figure 8–4 "Not Quite"

Most cooperating teachers get a real sense of teaming with student teachers as the semester progresses. One cooperating teacher describes her experience as follows:

> One student teacher was so perceptive that she would anticipate what I wanted or needed without my having to ask. As a result, we worked as a team and the children really accomplished a great deal (Sanders, 2002).

Student teachers may feel torn or frightened about taking risks. They may be eager to try new things but afraid of observer feedback if they differ significantly from their cooperating teacher's style (Brighton, 1999). They may decide to play it safe, not realizing they are losing opportunities for growth. New and beginning teachers are usually enthusiastic, optimistic, with a passion for teaching. Most hope to change children's lives and existing practice for the better (Hurst & Reding, 1999).

Guidance

Student teachers often find that the children will obey the rules when the cooperating teacher is present or asks but not when *they* ask them. Children test and question the authority of a new adult. Student teachers tend to force issues or completely ignore children when classroom rules are broken. These situations may be temporarily troublesome. In time, the children will realize that the student teacher means what is said. Consistency and firmness will win out.

When student teachers feel they cannot deal with these situations, they tend to stay close to self-controlled or affectionate children. This type of behavior indicates a possible withdrawal from the total room responsibility. If you are experiencing difficulty, look back at the ideas in Chapter 6.

Attachments

At times, a child may form a strong bond (or attachment) with a particular student teacher. The child may be inconsolable for a period after the student teacher's departure. Most students worry about this behavior and their supervisor's and cooperating teacher's reactions to it. It is an important topic for team meetings.

Male student teachers can have a unique experience during student teaching based on children's past experiences or lack of experiences with males. After a short period, the children will see the male student teacher as just another teacher with his own individuality. If not, further study of the child or children is in order.

Philosophic Differences

Sometimes, the cooperating teacher's view of child education and how children learn is quite similar to the student's; in other placements, it is not. An understanding of methods, techniques, curriculums, and goals and objectives of classrooms is the task of the student. When conflicting views are present in a supportive atmosphere, they are respected. Student teachers can gain a chance to clarify their own ideas when confronted with differing ones. New and diverse views result in the growth and clarification of a student's idea of what is best for children and families.

It is disconcerting and uncomfortable for both students and cooperating teachers when their teaching styles clash. Open discussion, particularly if it is done in a caring way that preserves the dignity of each teacher's opinions, is the best course of action.

Students should not surrender their philosophical values but tenaciously retain what they feel is best for children. Every wave of newly trained preschool and primary school teachers has its own contribution to make. The old or established way is always subject to questions in education. Practicing teachers continue to try innovative approaches; some are used in a complete or modified form, others once tried, are discarded. Thoughtfulness and open-mindedness help student teachers as does an "all win" attitude. Remember, everybody learns and grows!

Personality Conflicts

Whether or not you believe everyone has his own "vibes," you probably readily admit that you work much better with some people than with others.

Communication skill is critical in working relationships. Fortunately, student teaching is only a temporary assignment. Most difficult situations can at least become bearable through open communication.

Being Held Back

Very often, student teachers are not given the opportunity to work with children as much as they would like. As a result, they can become frustrated and feel that their potential for growth as teachers is being stifled. This can also happen when a cooperating teacher steps in during an activity or incident and assumes the student cannot handle the situation. These occurrences reduce the student's opportunity to work out of tight or uncomfortable spots. In the first example, the student is not allowed to start; in the second, to finish.

The student needs to know the "why's" behind the cooperating teacher's behavior; the cooperating teacher needs to grasp the student's feeling. Neither can happen without communicating.

> Your master teacher is not able to read your mind. The only way he is going to know the things you are worried about, any feeling of inadequacy or uncertainty you may have, as well as your positive feelings, is to tell him (Gordon-Nourok, 1979).

A special, agreed-upon signal can be used by the student teacher to alert the cooperating teacher to her need for help, immediate consultation, or suggestion.

One-Day Wonders

one-day wonders—preplanned and often prepackaged collections of materials that student teachers can easily set up or use on the spur of the moment to engage young children.

One way to avoid misunderstandings and difficulties with your cooperating teacher is to come prepared with a number of short activities that could be called "one-day wonders." These preplanned activities are a sort of insurance policy and relieve the panic of possibly being asked to do a last-minute activity. One can fit a number of them (stored separately) in a large tote bag or cardboard file that can be stowed somewhere in the classroom (see Figure 8–5).

A simple lesson, appropriate for fall, might be to come to class with the following materials for each child: a two-inch ball of clay (carefully wrapped in plastic so the clay won't dry out), paper plates to define work space, and lunch bags for gathering leaves and seeds lying on the ground. (This lesson has been successfully used with preschoolers and primary age children.) During free play or recess, the children can be directed to pick up and place in the bags items from the play yard that remind them of fall. Typically, students will gather all kinds of leaves, twigs, seed pods, dry weeds, and even stones and pebbles.

Figure 8–5 Student teachers may test activities with other student teachers watching. Courtesy of Iowa State University Child Development Laboratory School.

On returning to the classroom, the following directions can be given:

"At the science (or discovery) center, you will find a stack of paper plates and a large plastic bag with balls of clay. You may choose the science center as one of your options to explore this afternoon. Place one of the paper plates on the table; carefully take one of the balls of clay from the plastic bag and place it on your plate. Shape the ball of clay into any form you wish and use any of the materials you brought in from the play yard as decorations. When you finish, leave your sculpture on its paper plate and place it on the window sill."

(You will want to demonstrate the process as you give the directions, especially with preschoolers. With primary age children, drawings of each numbered step placed at the science/discovery center may be sufficient.)

Do you enjoy stories? Another example of a successful one-day wonder is the following first-grade language art lesson. Introduce as follows:

"I've brought you one of my favorite stories to share during story time today. It's called *Rosie's Walk*, by Pat Hutchins."

After you finish reading, you might tell the children, "Those children choosing to go to the writing center during our center activities may dictate to me or Mrs. Nguyen (or write) your own versions of *Rosie's Walk*. When you have finished, you may illustrate your story. Because only four students can come at once, remember that the rest of you will have a chance later in the week."

Other possibilities for one-day wonders are limited only by your imagination. Many cooperating teachers who may be reluctant to turn over large segments of time to a student teacher are willing to do so with one-day wonders that fit smoothly into the curriculum. Any area of the curriculum can work, but it is always best if you can agree with your cooperating teacher on one specific area, perhaps one that she does not particularly enjoy.

One-day wonders set up for on-the-spur-of-the-moment will most usually be used. Other one-day wonders designed by former student teachers follow:

- Colored gummed paper worker hats (precut chef, cowboy, firefighter, police officer, nurse, sailor, farmer, doorman, cab driver, and so on), art paper, crayons. Children lick and stick, add a face if they wish, and possibly share a story about their hat or give their created person a name.
- Tongs, tweezers (blunt), chopsticks, colored (three colors or more) cotton balls (shake powdered tempera and balls in *closed* plastic zipped bags), containers. Children sort colors by picking up with tools.
- Mounted photos of children snapped in action in the classroom. Lots of discussion and excitement. "Tell me about the photograph you've chosen." Works well if child stands in front of group giving all a good look first.
- Small plastic cars and roads drawn on shelf paper. The road is drawn by the student teacher beforehand with other features such as houses, stop signs, trees, dead-ends, railroad tracks, parking spots, and the like. Use your imagination. A roll of masking tape secures the road to table tops or floor. Good for outside as well as inside. Shelf paper can be rolled and ready. Many children will want to talk about what they are doing and where they are going.

One-day wonders for the elementary school can most easily focus on activities related to one of your favorite children's books. If you want a book that also ties into topics associated with the social studies curriculum, your cooperating teacher or college supervisor may have some suggestions. Your authors have found children's librarians to be of great help when they have asked for books on certain given topics such as families, pets and wild animals, and different countries. (Always make sure you have a range of books from one that can be read in one day to one that can be read in chapters.) Art and music are often "naturals," as is creative writing. Children can illustrate their own endings to any story, suggest a song to sing on the topic, or even create their own versions.

Some math one-day wonders can relate to such items as graphing months in which children have birthdays, and asking them to predict on the basis of which month has the most birthdays what your birthday or that of your cooperating teacher might be. Favorite foods, numbers of brothers and/or sisters, which student is wearing what colors: all of these lend themselves to graphing. How children get to school opens up the topic of modes of transportation, which is another graphing possibility.

Science activities can be as simple as having magnets and cartons (we personally like egg cartons) filled with all kinds of attractive "junk," ranging from paper clips, buttons, and other magnets to screws, nuts, bolts, and keys. (It is best if some of your paper clips, buttons, and keys are not magnetic whereas others are; this then lends itself to hypothesizing why similar objects are both magnetic and nonmagnetic.) Magnetism can extend to having children discover what items around the classroom are magnetic and what are not. Other science lessons can relate to classifying a variety of leaves and flowers and discussing their similarities and differences. (Do not expect children to classify in exactly the same way a botanist would, but do expect them to be able to justify why they have formed the classification they have.)

As with many things you might use as ideas for a lesson, you are limited only by your imaginations!

Site Politics

One of the most difficult placement situations is one that is consumed with conflicts. Power struggles between teachers, the director or principal, parents, community, or any other group makes the student feel as if he is being pressured to take sides. The student teacher is usually afraid to join either faction and tries to be a friend to all. This situation should be discussed with your supervisor quickly. Make sure to convey to the supervisor that you are willing to work through any difficult situation but that you want her to be aware of your perception of your placement site's political tensions.

Developing Supportive Staff Relationships

role model—a person whose behavior is imitated by others.

collaboration—parents and teachers working together for the ultimate good of the children or students.

Just as you **role model** behaviors for children, you consciously or unconsciously will model behaviors for colleagues. These actions may include empathy, friendliness, kindness, concern, **collaboration**, and other positive prosocial behaviors.

Professional conduct encompasses valuing staff diversity, staff special abilities, talents, and diverse staff educative ideas and approaches. Working together to accomplish goals may require:

- acceptance of differences
- careful listening and observation
- a personal resistance to feeling you need to change others or always defend your position
- an ability to communicate effectively
- honesty
- a thoughtful, reflective attitude
- an openness to the idea that there may be many avenues to reach program goals

- a genuine interest in staff growth
- an ability to collaborate
- an ability to work as a team member

Conflict Resolution

Conflict resolution usually refers to strategies that enable individuals to handle conflicts cooperatively, possibly attaining win-win situations. Mediation by a neutral third party can be part of the process. Skills enlisted by conflict resolution participants include, among others, communication, cooperation, tolerance, and positive expression of emotions (see Figure 8–6).

All conflicts, disputes, and so on may not be solvable when using the recommended conflict resolution techniques. Some problems do not have immediate fixes or short-term solutions, and it is unfortunate if student teachers hold that expectation.

Teacher training programs are introducing conflict resolution classes because the coursework is viewed as essential.

conflict resolution—a process to resolve disputes between people with different interests. This resolution process can have constructive consequences if the parties air their different interests, make trade-offs, and reach a settlement that satisifes the essential needs of each.

THE ROLE OF COMMUNICATION

Communication is a broad term, defined as giving and/or receiving information, signals, or messages. Human interactions and contacts are full of nonverbal signals accounting for 60 percent to 80 percent of most human encounters. Some of the more easily recognized nonverbal communications follow:

- facial expression (see Figure 8–7)
- body position (see Figure 8–8)
- muscle tone

communication—giving or receiving information, signals, and/or messages.

What may result in conflict resolution efforts is:

- the *recognition* that a problem exists, which focuses attention and motivates individuals to take action.
- a *clarification* of one's values, goals, wants, and ethics, and to what degree and intensity one cares.
- an *understanding* of others' goals, wants, values, and ethics.
- a *focus* on change.
- a *confidence* in oneself and the conflict resolution process when resolution is successful.
- a *feeling* that personal relationships with other staff can weather problems and disagreements.
- a *clearing of the air* and *reduction of stress*.
- an *emotional release*.
- a *new outlook* about conflict being a part of many working group situations.
- a *wake up call* regarding how one's actions and ideas can create problems with others.
- a *realization* that confrontational techniques can be scary, yet may lead to positive outcomes.
- a *realization* that boredom or staleness may be a problem in itself and a "ho-hum" attitude changes nothing.

Figure 8-6 Possible positive outcomes in conflict resolution attempts

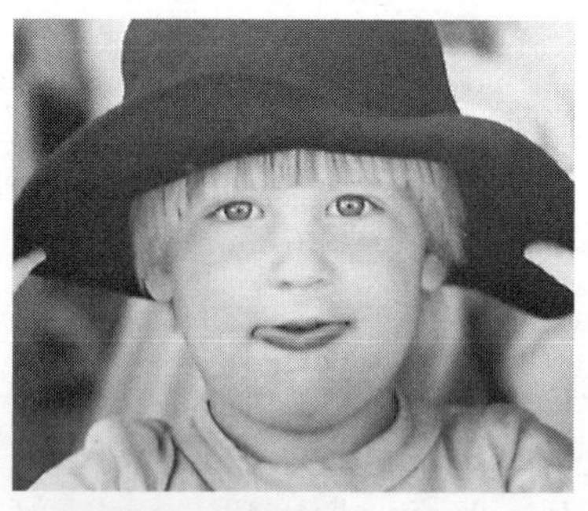

Figure 8–7 Reading the expressions in children's eyes and faces is a nonverbal communication skill.

- breathing tempo
- pitch of voice
- volume and inflection

A two-way process of sending and receiving (input and output) information occurs in true communication. Communication skills can be learned. Burke (1998) estimates only 7 percent of communication is actually influenced by the words of a communicator, with tone of voice and body language making the largest impact on the listener.

Being conscious of what messages people are conveying as they speak with body gestures and tone of voice is an important first step. The whole climate of interpersonal relationships in an education center can be affected by an individual's ability to communicate.

Figure 8–8 Silent messages: the above positions or gestures are some of the most common means of nonverbal communication.

Student teacher growth and self-realization can depend on the communication skills of the student teacher and others. According to Rogers and Freiberg (1994), it is through a mutually supporting, helping relationship that each individual can become better integrated and more able to function effectively. Student teachers can model appropriate communication behaviors, increasing effectiveness for other adults and children.

No doubt your student teaching group contains people with diverse opinions and backgrounds. Your placement site may also reflect our multiethnic and multicultural society.

Delpit (1995) believes we all carry worlds in our heads, and those worlds are decidedly different. She feels it is the responsibility of a dominant group member to attempt to hear the other side of an issue, and after hearing, to speak in a modified voice that does not exclude the concerns of minority colleagues.

Working productively with other staff members requires a mutual exchange that takes place in an atmosphere of openness, respect, and honesty (Caruso & Fawcett, 1999).

Communication: Reacting to Bias

With the multicultural representations in many early childhood classrooms and early childhood staff members, a teacher may encounter bias. What one adult deems appropriate and worthwhile another may see as inappropriate. Carter and Curtis (1994) point out that teachers have a set of seven choices in how to respond when adults express bias:

1. Attacking
2. Defending
3. Empathizing
4. Investigating
5. Reframing
6. Excusing
7. Ignoring

Some of a teacher's responding communication choices can be assaultive or defensive, whereas others may foster awareness and sensitivity (Carter & Curtis, 1994). Analyze the following teacher responses and decide which promote the early childhood goal of working as a supportive partner with parents.

Situation: Alfredo's mom tells you most of the activities planned at school and lots of the equipment don't allow Alfredo to be a real boy, and are more suited for attending girls.

Teacher's seven choices:

1. "Alfredo chooses his own activities, Mrs. Santos. You don't want us to force him to play more vigorous games, do you?"
2. "We're an accredited school; we've been approved by experts."
3. "You're distressed over Alfredo's behavior at school."
4. "You're concerned that Alfredo will not fit in with the other boys?"
5. "Alfredo chooses many sedentary activities over more vigorous play right now. He's really enjoying books and exploring writing tools. Your feeling is that this might not allow him to develop physical skill. Our program offers outdoor vigorous play, but at the moment, Alfredo is following his own interests."

6. "Well, Alfredo is just being Alfredo."
7. "Mrs. Santos, has this been a good day for you?"

Which choices would identify these problems appropriately? What bias is present? Could it be the parent's cultural expectations?

Caring and Sharing: A First Step in Communicating

What makes a person interesting or easy to talk with? Why do we discuss problems with some individuals and not with others? Perhaps it is because that person with whom we can talk freely loves and accepts us as we are at that moment. Love and acceptance can be demonstrated a number of ways. Saying it may be the easiest way; showing it through actions may be the toughest. With children, giving attention and not interfering with their freedom of choice helps develop their feelings of self-worth and value. Touching also usually reinforces rapport; a pat, hug, or open lap for young children expresses love and acceptance. A wink, a notice of accomplishment, or a sincere recognition of a special uniqueness in an individual helps feelings of caring and sharing grow. Setting the stage for easy approaching and interacting also helps.

Student teachers work and plan ways to establish rapport with children and adults during their first working days (see Figure 8–9). Communications depend on first contacts and interactions. There are definite skills, based on perseverance and know-how, beginning teachers can acquire to establish an easy flow of daily conversations with children. Some suggestions follow:

- Offer a personal greeting to each child.
- Take time to listen and respond to the child who is bursting to tell a story.
- Make a point of giving a special greeting to the shy child; verbalize the child's actions.
- Introduce new vocabulary.
- Help children plan for the day, building on prior experiences and introducing new ones.

Figure 8–9 Student teachers establish rapport on their first working days.

- Permit children to solve their own problems through language.
- Find time to talk personally with each child during the day about important events or experiences in their lives.
- Find opportunities to elaborate and expand children's language.
- Explain requests to children so that they will understand. Avoid repeating what children already know.
- Avoid expressing shock when children ask questions about physical functions.
- Talk to the children more than to classroom adults.

Children's communication skill and degree of cooperation may affect how a student teacher relates to and views particular children. Student teachers tend to gravitate toward conversation with children who respond, use their names, and establish eye contact, and to those children who are most like themselves, making them feel "at home." They also interact with the child who gains their attention. Popular, well-liked children usually fit this description. Seeing the challenge in developing trust and open communication with each attending child, student teachers observe children who ignore the teacher's conversational overtures, change the subject, say something irrelevant, or otherwise reject them. They sometimes find approaching a small group of children or a child in solitary play works best.

Children who feel good about themselves and experience caring teachers usually find greater success in communication with newcomers.

Armstrong (1994) offers additional guidelines:

1. Build solid, trusting relationships before seeking information from children.
2. Keep conversation related to action that is strongly relevant to children's interests or is part of their everyday experience.
3. Try role-playing with manipulative toys that allow the relationship between early language and activity to flourish.
4. Use words and styles that "belong" to the children and that take into consideration their competence level.
5. Be empathetic; try to see situations from the child's point of view.
6. Probe for responses by asking questions a new way, but avoid suggesting answers.
7. Select times to talk that don't interfere with children's favorite activities.

Authenticity

Much has been written about being *real* with children and adults. This means honestly sharing your feelings without putting down or destroying feelings of competency and self-worth. The term "congruent-sending" was coined by Gordon (1972), well known for his work in human communication. His definition follows:

> Congruence refers to the similarity of what a person (the sender) is thinking or feeling inside, and what he communicates to the outside. When a person is being congruent, we experience him as "open," "direct," or "genuine." When we sense that a person's communication is incongruent, we judge him as "not ringing true," "insincere," "affected," or just plain "phony."

The resulting risk in sending real messages without skill is that we may experience rejection. Student teachers can learn to express a wide range of real feelings in a skillful way. Anger is perhaps the hardest to handle skillfully. Ginott (1972) has advice for dealing with anger:

> The realities of teaching make anger inevitable. Teachers need not apologize for their angry feelings. An effective teacher is neither a masochist nor a martyr. He does not play the role of a saint or act the part of an angel. He is aware of his human feelings and respects them. Though he cannot be patient, he is always authentic. His response is genuine. His words fit his feeling. He does not hide his annoyance. He does not pretend patience. He does not demonstrate hypocrisy by acting nice when feeling nasty.
>
> An enlightened teacher is not afraid of his anger because he has learned to express it without doing damage. He has mastered the secret of expressing anger without insult.
>
> . . . When angry, an enlightened teacher remains real. He describes what he sees, what he feels, and what he expects. He attacks the problem, not the person. He protects himself and safeguards his students by using "I" messages.

The following tips may help when you become aware of strong emotions or anger:

- Listen and nod while maintaining eye contact.
- Show acceptance.
- Make empathy statements.
- Acknowledge the person's feelings.
- Remain calm by deep breathing.
- Arrange a future specific time to discuss and negotiate the matter if this happens in a setting that is not conducive to conversation. With a child, wait until strong emotions abate and then talk it through.

It is wise to remember that not all situations, problems, or conflicts can be solved, and anger and strong emotions directed toward you may be displaced. Your function may be that of a "listening board" who suggests the conflict is best solved if the speaker confronts the problem with another.

A student teacher's idea of the perfect teacher as being always calm and cool may inhibit communicating and produce feelings of guilt. A multitude of emotions will be present during student teaching days; a daily diary or journal helps students pinpoint feelings in early stages, and written expression is often easier than oral sharing with a supervisor. Usually, pleasant feelings are the ones most easily described and orally transmitted. Recognizing the buildup of angry feelings may take a special tuning into the self. Common tension signals include:

- Shrill, harsh, or louder voice tone.
- Inability to see humor in a situation.
- Withdrawal and/or silence.
- Continual mental rehashing of an emotionally trying encounter.

Sharing feelings, including those you consider negative, may help develop a closeness to others.

"I" messages—Thomas Gordon's term for a response to a child's behavior that focuses on how the adult feels rather than on the child's character.

"I" Messages

Message sending takes practice and is only one part of a communication sequence: input or sending. A series of teacher-sent "I" messages (which communicate the sender's feelings without blaming or judging another) follow. You will probably be able to picture the incident that evoked them.

"I'm very sad that these pages in our book about horses are torn and crumpled. Book pages need to be turned with care, like this."

"I get so upset when materials I planned to use with the children disappear."

"Wait a minute. If all the student teachers take a break together, there will be only one adult in the classroom. I'm frustrated; I thought there was a clear statement about taking separate breaks."

"I'm confused about this assignment. I feel like I missed an explanation. Can we talk about it sometime today?"

"I'm feeling very insecure right now. I thought I sensed your disapproval when you asked the children to stop the activity planned for them."

One should guard against "I" messages that are destructive; they sometimes send solutions or involve blaming and judgmental phrases. These are false "I" messages:

"I feel frustrated when you behave so stupidly."

"I am angry when you don't keep your promises. Nobody will be able to trust you."

The ability to send "I" messages is a communication skill that follows recognition of feelings and an effort to communicate directly with the individuals concerned. At times, we provoke strong feelings within ourselves, and an "inner" dialogue ensues. "I" messages do not tend to build defensiveness as do "you" messages. The communication starts on the right foot.

"you" message—Thomas Gordon's term for a response to a child's behavior that focuses on the child's character (usually in negative terms) rather than on how the adult feels.

Exercising integrity during moments of choice is an important consideration. Moral dilemmas are frequently faced by student teachers who may or may not weigh decisions before responding to stimuli. It is sometimes so easy to give defensive responses during periods of growth (like student teaching). This type of response may stretch or cloud the truth.

LISTENING: THE ABILITY TO RECEIVE

We listen with our ears, of course,
But surely it is true
That eyes, the lips, and hands, and feet
can help us listen, too.

Though commonly used with children, this poem may aid student teachers' communicative listening skills. The poem is describing active listening, a term also attributed to Gordon (1972):

active listening (with adults)—the process of putting into your own words a message you received from another based on your understanding of what you thought you heard.

In recent years psychotherapists have called our attention to a new kind of listening, "active listening." More than passively attending to the message of the sender, it is a process of putting your understanding of that message to its severest of tests—namely, forcing yourself to put into your own words to the sender for verification or for subsequent correction.

March (2002) points out the need to closely attend to speakers:

Positive attention is the most valuable tool we have for enriching the quality of our relationships. Positive attention is *listening without distraction.*

Think of everyone as a person who needs attention. Then you will automatically begin to treat others with more compassion and respect.

One encounters four basic types of verbal communication (from other adults):

1. Communication, for *building relationships*
2. *Cathartic* communication, for releasing emotions and relating our troubles
3. *Informational* communication, for sharing ideas, information, and data
4. *Persuasive* communication, for reinforcing and changing attitudes or producing a desired action

People who listen interact with others more effectively and make fewer mistakes. To practice good listening, try the following tips:

- Focus on content and ideas.
- Don't prejudge or second-guess.
- Listen for feelings.
- Jot down facts when appropriate.
- Make eye contact; watch nonverbal cues.
- Avoid emotional rebuttals by keeping an open mind. Realize there are emotionally laden words.
- Give signs you're actively receiving.
- Try to identify main ideas and supportive ideas. Store key words because they'll make messages easier to remember.
- Rephrase, ask, and/or answer questions whether explicit or implied.
- There are times when one chooses not to respond to another's comment.

The active listening process is probably more difficult to learn than that of "I" message sending. Most individuals have developed listening habits that block true listening (see Figure 8–10). Lundsteen (1976) has labeled four chief listening distortions:

1. *Attitude cutoff* blocks the reception of information at the spoken source because expectation acts on selection. For example, if a student has a strong negative reaction every time he hears the word "test," he might not hear the rest of this message: "The test of any man lies in action."
2. *Motive attributing* is illustrated by the person who says of a speaker, "He is just selling me a public relations line for the establishment," and by the child who thinks, "Teachers just like to talk; they don't really expect me to listen the first time because they are going to repeat directions ten times anyway."
3. *Organizational mix-up* happens while one is trying to put someone else's message together: "Did he say 'turn left, then right, then right, then left,' or . . . ?" or "Did he say 'tired' or 'tried'?"
4. *Self-preoccupation* causes distortion because the "listener" is busy formulating his reply and never hears the message: "I'll get him for that; as soon as he stops talking, I'll make a crack about how short he is, then . . ."

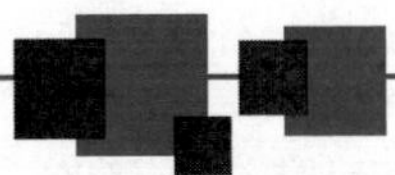

Why We Don't Hear Others

If you want to listen so you really hear what others say, make sure you're not a:

- Mind reader. You'll hear little or nothing as you think "What is this person really thinking or feeling?"
- Rehearser. Your mental tryouts for "Here's what I'll say next" tune out the speaker.
- Filterer. Some call this selective listening—hearing only what you want to hear.
- Dreamer. Drifting off during a face-to-face conversation can lead to an embarrassing "What did you say?" or "Could you repeat that?"
- Identifier. If you refer everything you hear to your experience, you probably didn't really hear what was said.
- Comparer. When you get side-tracked assessing the messenger, you're sure to miss the message.
- Derailer. Changing the subject too quickly soon tells others you're not interested in anything they have to say.
- Sparrer. You hear what's said but quickly belittle it or discount it. That puts you in the same class as the derailer.
- Placater. Agreeing with everything you hear just to be nice or to avoid conflict does not mean you're a good listener.

Source: *The Writing Lab*, Department of English, Purdue University, 1356 Heavilon Hall, West Lafayette, IN 47907.

Figure 8–10 Hearing others. From Communications Briefings, (1997) Vol. XVI, NO. IV, Alexandria, VA: Capitol Publications. Reprinted with permission from Communication Briefings.

> Preoccupation with one's own message is a frequent distortion for young listeners. Hanging onto their own thoughts during communications takes a great deal of their attention and energy. Some teachers help out by suggesting that young listeners make small, quick pictures to help cue their ideas when their turn to speak arrives. That way, they can get back to listening. Older children may jot down "shorthand" notes to help them hold onto ideas and return to the line of communication.

New active listening habits can change lives and communicating styles, giving individuals a chance to develop closeness, insight, and empathy.

> To understand accurately how another person thinks or feels from his point of view, to put yourself momentarily into his shoes, to see the world as he is seeing it—you as a listener run the risk of having your own opinions and attitudes changed (Gordon, 1972).

Many authors suggest listening is much more than hearing:

To develop new listening habits, it is necessary to make a strong effort. The effort will pay off dramatically because it provides an opportunity to know others at a deeper level. It is a chance to open a small inner door and catch a glimpse of the "authentic" self. By listening closely, a new perception of an individual can be revealed; our own thoughts about how we are going to answer are secondary.

> Before that, when I went to a party I would think anxiously "Now try hard. Be lively. Say bright things. Don't let them down." And when tired, I would drink a lot of coffee to keep this up. But now before going to a party, I just tell myself to listen with affection to anyone who talked to me, to be in their shoes when they talk; to try to know them without my mind pressing against theirs, or arguing, or changing the subject. No! My attitude is: "Tell me more. This person is showing me his soul. It is a little dry and meager and full of grinding talk just now, but presently he will begin to think, not just automatically talk. He will show his true self. Then he will be wonderfully alive . . ." (Ueland, 1941/1966).

The student teacher hopes others recognize her teaching competencies. Being anxious to display what one knows, one can focus communication on sending messages that concentrate on self rather than really listening to others. New listening skills will take conscious practicing. To gain skill in reflective listening, an exercise called "mirroring" is often used. The following examples mirror back to the child the feeling the listener received.

1. *Child, pleading*: "I don't want to eat these baked potatoes. I hate them."
   Listener: "You don't like baked potatoes."
2. *Child, pleading and forlorn:* "I don't have anything to do today. What can I do? I wish there was something to do!"
   Listener: "You're bored and lonely."
3. *Child, angry and confused:* "I hate Julie. She always cries and tries to get her way. If I don't do what she wants, she goes home."
   Listener: "You're angry and confused."
4. *Child, stubborn and indignant:* "I don't want to take a bath. I'm not even dirty. I hate baths anyway. Why do I have to take a bath every day?"
   Listener: "You don't want to take a bath."
5. *Child, crying:* "Fran won't let me play with her dolls. She's mean. Make her give me some of them to play with."
   Listener: "You're angry with Fran."
6. *Child, crying because of hurt finger:* "Ow! Ow! It hurts! Ow!"
   Listener: "It sure hurts."

Adults find mirroring and reflecting back feeling statements easier with children than adults. With use, mirroring statements feel more comfortable, and the sender, whether a child or an adult, feels he has been heard. With adults, clarifying mirroring-type *questions* seem more natural and are conducted in the following fashion:

> "Am I hearing you say you're really angry right now?"
> "Is frustration what you're feeling?"
> "You're saying you don't want to be told what to do?"

Staff Communication Tips

Harris (1995) suggests the following tips to improve staff communication:

- Beware of kicking and stroking at the same time. When we tell someone something positive, then reprimand, then end with a positive, we call that sandwiching. Some workshops teach this as a soft technique, but it does send conflicting messages.

- Whenever possible, plan the message. Think of what the message is and how, where, and when you want to send it.
- In order for communication to be effective, spend as much time listening as talking. Be attentive.
- Don't imply a choice if there is not a choice. Tentative language and manner are fine in some circumstances, but they often suggest an option that may not exist.
- Tape record an hour or so of routine, day-to-day conversations. Look for hidden agendas, soft or padded language, and other indicators that you are not sending clear messages.
- Say what you mean, mean what you say.
- Feedback is a continuous process, not just a one-time action. Learn to give and elicit feedback on a regular basis.
- Look at the person you are talking to and establish eye contact throughout the conversation.
- Sometimes, it is better to deliver a message to a group of people at once. It is, however, still important to allow for feedback and to follow other rules such as eye contact.
- If it appears that no one is listening, the problem may be exactly that. No one—including us—is listening.

Additional suggestions follow:

- Try to think of two possible ways to resolve the problem at hand before speaking to a coworker or supervisor.
- When weighing possible problem solutions, identify possible joint benefits.
- Paraphrase differing opinions to clarify ideas.
- Admit changing your mind and view it as appropriate and mature.
- Admit doubt and error. Be seen as a collaborator.

Warner (1995) notes there is not much one can do about negative or unprofessional teachers except smile, be pleasant, minimize contact, and seek out professional, positive-minded colleagues.

Copeland (1997) outlines three choices in dealing with problems important to staff members. This chapter concentrates on choice #2.

Choice #1: I am satisfied with things the way they are. I can live with what's going on, so I won't worry about it.

Choice #2: I am unhappy with my situation, and I am on a path of trying to resolve the conflict. If my first effort doesn't succeed, I will try something else.

Choice #3: I will quit my job.

THEORIES IN PROBLEM-SOLVING

In your attempts to solve problems, you will want to adopt a planned approach rather than a random one. Glickman's planned and thoughtful responses (1981) are as follows:

- *Listening:* saying nothing, perhaps nodding, being attentive, waiting for the speaker to finish.
- *Clarifying:* replying with questions intended to give a fuller understanding of the problem.
- *Encouraging:* talking about problem factors.

- *Presenting:* offering your thoughts on the situation or behavior.
- *Problem-solving:* initiating the discussion with statements aimed at exploring solutions.
- *Negotiating:* attempting to reach a settlement quickly.
- *Demonstrating:* physically showing how to act, what to do, or what to say.
- *Directing:* detailing what one must do.
- *Reinforcing:* delineating the conditions and consequences of the solution.

Freire (1993) has identified three aspects of problem-solving: naming the problem, analyzing the causes, and acting to solve the problem. In addition, Freire has identified three stages of consciousness in problem-solving: magical problem-solving, naive problem-solving, and critical problem-solving. Personalizing this theory for student teachers as it relates to problem-solving styles involves answering the following:

- Do you passively accept problems as just your luck without trying to change them?
- Do you realize problems exist, putting the cause on your own shoulders?
- Do you tend to blame the system, the process, or the situation rather than yourself or others?

Breulin (2001) urges teachers faced with a problem to ask themselves the following:

- What keeps this situation from being right?
- What is stopping the resolution of this problem? What are the obstacles?
- What is keeping me from succeeding here?

He states that tackling a small problem or a slice of a large one successfully creates a ripple effect and gives one the confidence to move forward. He notes that one may be used to assuming that one's problems are always rooted in oneself. In reality, it may stem from another person, community, or culture. He believes significant inroads in problem-solving occur when one is curious enough to keep asking questions and courageous enough to face what one learns. See Figure 8–11 for helpful and unhelpful human behaviors in conflict situations.

A PROBLEM-SOLVING PROCESS

Most problems can be faced in a sequential manner. This text suggests problem-solving in a rational manner when emotions are under control. Take some time alone to cool down or physically burn off excessive tension before you try to use it. Substituting new behaviors into your problem-solving style takes time and effort. Practice is necessary.

Sending "I" messages and active listening will avert problem buildup. However, you do have the choice of living with a problem and not working on it. This can work for short periods but usually erodes the quality of your relationship with others or with yourself. Alienation occurs in most instances, but you may prefer this course of action and be prepared for its consequences. Most often, you will choose to confront others or yourself and work toward solutions that eliminate the problem. Familiarize yourself with the following. It suits many different situations.

Step 1. Recognition of tensions, emotions, or the problem.

Step 2. Analysis. (Who and what is involved? When and where does it occur? Whose problem is it?)

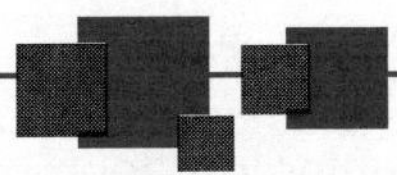

Helpful Behaviors when situations arise

- Accept conflict as part of life. Focus on the problem rather than people's personalities or personal characteristics. Gather information and facts. Seek clarity on any aspect of the situation you question.
- Discuss the problem with only those directly involved. If only one person, seek that person out at a peaceful, private time.
- Talk about the now, not the past. Address your feelings and others' feelings. Deal with common goals and future positive courses of action.
- Blow off steam or ventilate with someone not connected to work, if necessary, someone who listens with confidentiality and could help solve or sort out who, including yourself, has a problem; an honest, unbiased sounding board.

Behaviors that can increase conflict

- Make the situation personal. Concentrate on why this always happens to you. Blame it wholly on the other person. Blow it out of proportion. Search for some hidden cause for its happening to you.
- Bring up every past situation, hurt, feeling, slight, or the unwelcomed or unprofessional behavior of others involved. Exaggerate happenings and your feelings.
- Stomp off and refuse to discuss the issue.
- Get other staff or other people on your side. Get them involved with the strength of your case. Talk to anyone who will listen to you, even if they have other work responsibilities.

Figure 8–11 Conflict behaviors—helpful and otherwise

Step 3. Sending "I" messages. (Active listening and reflecting messages.)

Step 4. Discussion. (Probing; getting more data. Who owns the problem?)

Step 5. Stating both sides of the problem clearly.

Step 6. Proposing and finding possible solutions.

Step 7. Agreement to try one of these solutions. Agreement to meet again if the solution does not work.

Step 8. Consideration of willingness, time, and effort to solve the problem.

This process can be attempted but will not work if one party refuses to talk, mediate, or look for courses of action that will satisfy everyone involved. Refusing to act on solutions also hinders the process. Problem-solving is two-sided even when you are the only one involved. At Step 2, one sometimes realizes the problem belongs to another, and the best course of action is to help that person communicate with someone else. Often a problem may disappear at Step 3.

The discussion, Step 4, can include "I'm really interested in talking about it" or "Let's talk; we'll examine just what's happening to us." However, there is a tendency to blame rather than identify contributing causes. Getting stuck and not moving past Step 4 hampers resolution of the problem. Statements like "You're right; I really avoid cleaning that sink," or "I'm really bothered by interruptions during planned group times," all involve owning the problem.

Before possible solutions are mentioned, a clear statement of conflicting views, Step 5, adds clarification.

With a child: "You'd like to paint next, and I told Carlos it's his turn."

With a fellow student teacher: "You feel the way I handle Peter is increasing his shyness, and I feel it's helping him."

With a cooperating teacher: "I think my activity was suitable for the group, but you think it didn't challenge them."

With a supervisor: "You feel I tend to avoid planning outdoor activities; I think I've planned quite a few."

Your confrontation might start at Step 6. ("Let's figure out some way to make the noisy time right before nap a little calmer and quieter.") Finding alternate solutions admits there are probably a number of possibilities. "Together we'll figure a way" or "That's one way; here's another idea." A do-it-my-way attitude inhibits joint agreement. Thinking alternatives over and getting back together is helpful at times. Seeking a consultant who offers ideas can aid solving problems that participants see as hopeless.

When all parties decide to try one solution, Step 7, consideration should be given to meeting again if that particular alternative does not work. ("We'll try it this week and discuss whether it's working next Monday.")

Step 8 reinforces both sides. "We figured it out." "Thanks for taking the time to solve this." "I appreciated your efforts in effecting a solution." This process is not to be used as a panacea; rather, it contains helpful guidelines.

Classroom problems can involve any aspect of the student teaching situation (see Figure 8–12). Interpersonal conflicts will take both courage and consideration of the proper time and place to confront.

Figure 8–12 A student teacher may have to step in if a child doesn't realize he is blocking the slide.

> The teacher is sometimes afraid to confront a child who is hostile, caustic, or vengeful. Such a teacher avoids and avoids until the accumulation of feelings becomes so unbearable an explosion occurs, and the teacher loses control. Once the self is out of control, there is no possibility to bring about a positive resolution of the problem. But when the hateful, rejection emotions subside, there is always hope that the teacher can come to terms with the child and reach a depth of relatedness and mutuality (Moustakas, 1966).

Arrange to problem-solve when participants have no classroom responsibilities and where there will not be any interruptions or noninvolved observers.

Can teachers promote child problem-solving and discovery? Britz (1993) encourages teachers to articulate problems they face and discuss solutions with children. She feels children then become more aware of the significance of the problem-solving process.

Problem-solving conversations can involve individual children and small and large groups.

Negotiation Skills

It has been said we do not get what we deserve in life but what we negotiate, and that negotiation is not about fairness.

After an individual or staff conflict is apparent, one usually decides if it is worth resolving and then identifies who has the power to make a resolution decision. The goal in negotiation is to uncover a solution that contending participants feel comfortable with: in other words, win-win or get-give resolutions.

Negotiating a series of steps can aid progress and create the attitude "How are we going to work together on this?" One must clarify his position and know what is desired and what option one could consider and might settle for. Many times, options that are acceptable to both parties depend on the creative brainstorming that ensues during the negotiation process. Active listening is mandatory. Thinking about the best settings conductive to negotiating and the comfort of participants can enhance outcomes. Taking a walk together in a semisecluded area may work, or relaxed staff rooms or meeting rooms may be appropriate when groups of people are involved.

Written materials by negotiation experts suggest opposing speakers speak in tune with the other side's interests, mentioning why options offered might benefit one or both sides. Face-saving solutions are seen as important considerations.

Negotiations end with a commitment, or agreed-upon plan or a follow-up date to try again for an amicable solution.

It is easy to see that staffs with a sense of community who respect diversity and diverse opinions have an advantage in the negotiation process. Groups that believe conflict is natural and healthy may more effectively handle problems.

Unfortunately, negotiation breaks down when attitudes include an unwillingness to confront conflict or even admit it exists, or when an unwillingness to listen or accept others' ideas characterizes behavior. Delpit (1995) suggests teachers at times must learn to be vulnerable enough in their thinking to turn "upside down" to allow others' ideas to enter consciousness.

Resistance

Resistance to rules and not conforming to what is expected can be seen both in children and adults. It is usually viewed as negative behavior. Moustakas (1966) believes it is healthy:

> Resistance is a way for the child to maintain his own sense of self in the light of external pressures to manipulate and change him. It is a healthy response, an effort of the individual to sustain the integrity of the self.

Figure 8–13 Through problem-solving, we can actually understand a child at a deeper level.

Resistance and controversy can become challenges that develop our understanding and let us know others at a deeper level (see Figure 8–13). Though confrontations may frighten student teachers in early days, later they are seen as opportunities to know more about children and adults.

> The anxiety in facing an embittered, destructive child can be eliminated only in actual confrontation with the dread child because until we actually meet him, we cannot know him (Moustakas, 1966).

SUMMARY

Student teaching is a miniature slice of life and living. Problems arise and are common to all. Some situations change with time; others need extended communication to be resolved.

Growth and change are experienced sometimes easily, sometimes painfully. It is helpful to maintain a caring and sharing feeling, open communication, and a sense of humor. Time and successful experience take care of most initial difficulties. The supervisor's and cooperating teacher's role are to provide supportive assistance. Team status may evolve slowly and depend on student effort.

Skill in sending and receiving oral and written messages is a necessary skill for student teachers. The whole sharing and caring climate of the student teaching experience depends in part on communication know-how. Developing rapport with adults and children during early days helps people become relaxed and comfortable, promoting student teacher attempts to display emerging competencies.

Love and acceptance are established in a variety of ways. Authenticity in communication is deemed highly desirable and effective during student teaching. "I" messages are an integral part of effective communication skills. Skill in sending

"I" messages and active, reflective listening increase with practice and become a natural part of the student teaching experience.

Problem-solving skills are important for student teachers. There seem to be definite styles of relating to others during problem-solving situations. Students are urged to practice new techniques in negotiation. Early fears of confronting tend to disappear as communicative problem-solving becomes a way to know and understand others. In problem-solving, teachers model the skills for children; therefore, the children may also learn to use them.

HELPFUL WEB SITES

http://www.peace-ed.org

Peace Education Foundation. Offers a look at classroom-tested curricula.

http://clas:uiuc.edu

Early Childhood Research Institute. A source for those working with culturally and linguistically diverse children and families.

http://www.apa.org/

American Psychological Association. Search for violence issues.

http://www.nea.org

National Education Association. Search professional relationships.

http://ericeece.org/

ERIC Clearinghouse on Elementary and Early Childhood Education. Lists discussion groups.

http://csefel.uiuc.edu/

The Center on Social and Emotional Foundations for Early Learning. Search social and emotional outcomes and communication techniques.

SUGGESTED ACTIVITIES

A. Rate the following situations as M (major problem) or m (minor concern). Discuss the results in small groups.

1. A student teacher is placed in a class where the child of a best friend is attending. The best friend asks for daily reports.
2. Little Johnny tells a cooperating teacher that he is afraid of the student teacher.
3. Bonnie, a student teacher, finds she is susceptible to colds and infections.
4. Children do not respond to the student teacher's rule statements.
5. The student teacher has had no background experience with children of the ethnic group where placed.
6. The student teacher is used as an aide in the classroom.
7. A child's mother tells the cooperating teacher she does not like the idea of a student teacher taking over the classroom.
8. The supervisor rarely visits the classroom.
9. One of the student teacher's planned activities ends in pandemonium. Paint is all over the walls and floor, and the children are wild.
10. A student teacher has difficulty planning activities that suit the children's age and interest level.

B. List briefly three possible courses of action for the following student teacher situations. Of the three, which do you feel is the best course of action?

1. Amy, a fellow student teacher, confides in you that she objects to the way her cooperating teacher punishes children.
2. Joey, a four-year-old, says, "You're not the teacher. I don't have to do that" when you ask him to return blocks he has played with to the bookcase.
3. You have a great idea about rearranging the room and do so in the morning before the children or cooperating teacher arrive.
4. You tried very hard to encourage Qwan to complete a task, and the cooperating teacher quickly finishes the task for him to make sure he is not late for snack.
5. You cannot seem to get any feedback on your abilities as a student teacher from either the cooperating teacher or the supervisor.
6. You notice you are spending an increasing amount of time straightening, table wiping, sink cleaning, and with block area maintenance.
7. You realize you do not know any parents' first names, and half the semester is over.
8. Manuela and Colleen are student teaching in the same classroom. Manuela feels Colleen is insensitive to Mexican culture and rarely builds a sense of ethnic pride in the children.
9. Carol, a student teacher, plays the guitar and is a talented folksinger. She has not planned a classroom activity to share her talent.
10. Your supervisor gives you credit for setting up a new activity area that the children are exploring with enthusiasm; however, the cooperating teacher was the one who set up this activity. Because your supervisor has encouraged you to add new activities, you did not correct the mistake. The next day, you feel badly about taking credit but are reticent to approach your supervisor with the truth.

C. Answer the following questions: If you don't know an answer right away, think about it or ask someone close to you.

- How do I behave when I'm feeling over-stressed? (Some people get angry, others withdraw, some cry more easily, others become forgetful, and so on)
- What are some of the warning signs that tell I am about to go over the amount of stress I can handle?
- What do I do that helps relax me and release my stress?
- Are my ways of relaxing healthy for me?
- Do I have time in my life that is just for me? If yes, how often during the week?
- Do I take my own need for relaxation and time out seriously enough?
- Do I know any relaxation techniques that I can practice?
- Am I aware of how I talk to myself inside my own mind? Am I telling myself negative or hopeless things that contribute to increasing my stress level?
- Am I aware that I have a choice about how I want to deal with my own stress?

Analyzing your reactions to stress can be eye-opening.

D. Form groups of six for the following role-playing activity. Select two members to role-play; others will be observers. Switch role-playing until all group members have had two turns.

"Role-Playing in Reflecting Listening"

Directions: Analyze each of the following role-played statements or situations. Offer suggestions for active listening responses.

1. Student teacher to cooperating teacher: "Your room needs more organization."
2. Cooperating teacher to student teacher: "Mary, have you been having problems at home lately?"
3. Irritated cooperating teacher to student teacher: "John, you've been ill too often. We must be able to rely on our student teachers to be here every day."
4. Critical parent to student teacher: "My daughter needs her sweater on when she goes out of doors."
5. One student teacher to another: "Mrs. Brown, the director, only sees what I do wrong, not what I do right."
6. One student teacher to another: "You always leave the sink a mess."
7. John, a preschooler, is dumping paint on the floor.
8. Student teacher to child who is not going to the wash area: "It's time to wash hands."
9. Mary, a four-year-old, hit you because you insisted that she share a toy.
10. College supervisor to student teacher: "Filomena, I'm confused. Your assignments are always late. Weren't my directions clear?"
11. Cooperating teacher to student teacher: "When you were doing your activity, I had a difficult time not stepping in. The boys were destroying the girls' work."

E. Consider the following statements. (1) A teacher saying to a child "I liked the way you helped your friend button his coat." This is an appropriate statement. (2) Rough-and-tumble play prepares preschool boys to be successful in later competitive sports and life in general.

In a group, allow three to five minutes to agree with the first statement verbally. In the next three to five minutes, have group members disagree. Do the same with the second statement.

Follow this exercise with a discussion centered on the difficulties encountered (if any) in really listening and giving value to opinions that conflict with individual viewpoints.

F. Complete the following anonymously on a piece of paper. Collect and tally slips from a group of classmates. Discuss results. Use the following scale:

1 = Never; 2 = Infrequently; 3 = Sometimes; 4 = Often; 5 = Always.

1. I am anxious about spending too much of my time and attention with some children and consequently neglecting others. _____
2. I am not sure my behavior management techniques are appropriate. _____
3. I am not certain my planned activities are developmentally appropriate. _____
4. Unruly children cause me problems. _____
5. My lesson planning makes me doubt my ability. _____
6. I am anxious about creating a good working relationship with my cooperating teacher or other staff members. _____
7. I am anxious about having lesson plan flops. _____
8. I am anxious about creating classroom chaos when planning creative activities. _____
9. I am anxious about getting all the paperwork done in time. _____
10. I am anxious about what lesson the college supervisor will come to see. _____

11. I am anxious about having time to study in other college classes. _____
12. I am anxious about developing a portfolio. _____
13. I am anxious concerning my contact with parents. _____
14. I am anxious about working in the neighborhood where I have been assigned. _____
15. I am anxious because I am from a different culture or ethnic group than the children. _____
16. I am anxious because my cooperating teacher doesn't seem to like me. _____
17. I am anxious because of the staff friction that exists at my placement site. _____
18. I am afraid of saying the wrong thing to my supervisor. _____
19. I am anxious about being watched. _____
20. I am anxious about the cooperating teacher's assessment of my competency. _____

G. In the following situations, state as clearly as possible what you think are both sides of the problem. Then describe two alternatives that you feel might satisfy both parties of each conflict.

1. Cecelia has been assigned to student teach from 9:00 A.M. to 2:30 P.M. on Tuesdays. Her cooperating teacher, Mr. Kifer, notices she has been leaving early. Cecelia has been arriving 10 to 15 minutes early each day. Her cooperating teacher confronts Cecelia one day before she departs. "Leaving early, Cecelia?"
2. Henri, a four-year-old, has been told repeatedly by the student teacher that he must put the blocks he used back on the shelf. Henri has ignored the request continually. The student teacher requests the cooperating teacher ask Henri to replace the blocks because he does not respond to the student teacher.
3. The cooperating teacher has been silent most of the morning. The student teacher can feel tension mounting and says, "I'm really feeling uncomfortable because I sense there is something wrong." The cooperating teacher ignores the remark. At the end of work, the student discusses the situation with the supervisor.
4. Christopher, a student teacher, is fuming. "After all the work I put into the activity, she didn't even mention it," he says to Charlotte, another student teacher.
5. "I'd really like to present this new song to the children," says Robin, a student teacher. "You didn't put it in the plan book, Robin, and I have a full day planned," the cooperating teacher says. "Let's talk about it; I can see the disappointment on your face." Robin replies, "It's not disappointment. I can't see why the schedule is so inflexible." "Let's talk about that after the morning session, Robin."
6. "I sure needed your help at circle today," the cooperating teacher said. "I was in the bathroom with Anthony; he's got those pants that button at the shoulders," the student teacher answers.
7. "I'm really tired today, Mrs. Cuffaro," the student teacher answers when asked why she stayed in the housekeeping area most of the morning. Mrs. Cuffaro says, "There were lots of other children who could have used your assistance, Annette. Will you have time to talk when the children are napping?" "Sure," Annette replies.
8. Miriam, an attractive student teacher, is assigned to an on-campus laboratory school. Male friends often hang around the lobby or ask the secretary to give her messages and notes. The secretary has told Miriam this is

bothersome. Miriam tells the secretary the notes often concern getting a ride home because she does not have a car.

H. Responding and reacting. Read and score the following using a 1 to 5 scale. Then discuss with a group of classmates.

1. You are criticized for conducting a developmentally inappropriate child activity. This situation will impact you.

   For a long time 1 2 3 4 5 Quickly pass

2. You accidentally break a child's cherished sharing object. This will:

   Affect you greatly 1 2 3 4 5 You'll forgive yourself

3. A child runs and hides every time you enter the classroom. This situation will affect you:

   Not at all 1 2 3 4 5 Completely

4. You lost a valued object borrowed from your cooperating teacher. The consequences of this situation will:

   Last forever 1 2 3 4 5 Quickly pass

5. Your cooperating teacher gives you a failed rating in student teaching. The consequences of this action will:

   Last forever 1 2 3 4 5 Quickly pass

6. Your supervising instructor pointed out your many professional teaching skills. This will:

   Affect all aspects of your life: 1 2 3 4 5 Be limited to this situation

7. A parent says to you, "I'm sure you don't like my son. I see the way you treat him!" This statement will:

   Worry you greatly 1 2 3 4 5 Worry you not at all

8. You are recognized as the year's outstanding student teacher. In this situation you would feel:

   Not responsible at all 1 2 3 4 5 Completely responsible

9. The center where you are employed as a teacher is understaffed, of poor quality, and unclean. To what extent do you feel responsible for improving this situation?

   Not responsible at all 1 2 3 4 5 Completely responsible

10. Your personal and student teaching obligations are out of balance. To what extent can you influence this situation?

   Not at all 1 2 3 4 5 Completely

REVIEW

A. Briefly describe what you feel are prime areas or issues of conflict in student teaching.

B. Write a student teacher "I" message for each of the following situations:

1. Fred, your cooperating teacher, does not have his usual warm greeting and has barely spoken to you all morning.
2. Your supervisor has given you a failing grade on an assignment. You spent many hours on that assignment, and you feel like dropping the class.
3. You cried during the staff meeting when other adults suggested one of your activities with the children was a flop.
4. Another student teacher in your classroom is not living up to assigned duties, making it twice as difficult for you.
5. A child says to you, "I wish you were my mommy."
6. Your cooperating teacher has asked you not to pick up and hold a particular child. You feel the child needs special attention.

7. An irate parent says to you, "This school policy about bringing toys from home is ridiculous."
8. Your neighbor says to you, "I hear you're going to college to become a baby-sitter. How wasteful of your talents."

C. Give an example of an appropriate student teacher verbalization for each of the following:

1. Offer a personal greeting to a new child.
2. Avoid expressing shock when a child asks about genitalia seen on another child.

D. Choose the best answer to complete each statement.

1. Your cooperating teacher has informed your supervisor that you were not prepared for class on the preceding day. This is not the first time it has happened. Your supervisor seems upset because you two have already discussed this problem. In talking to your supervisor, you want to use active listening techniques in communicating. You say,
   a. "You need to explain assignment dates again, please."
   b. "She's always criticizing me; I'm really upset."
   c. "But I was prepared. I brought in two flannelboard stories and a music game!"
   d. "I can see you're disappointed and perhaps a bit angry, too."
   e. "Isn't there any way I can please the two of you?"
2. Your cooperating teacher is always stepping in and taking over in guidance situations. You have pleaded to be allowed to follow through so children will know you mean what you say. You decide to send a congruent feeling statement at a staff meeting. You say,
   a. "I'm really frustrated. You always take over."
   b. "I've had it. Can't you let me finish what I start?"
   c. "I'm confused. I want the children to know I mean what I say, but it's just not happening."
   d. "You need to step back and let me follow through with the children."
   e. "I know you're trying to help me, but I don't need your help."
3. You feel you can easily handle the whole day's program, but you haven't been given the opportunity. You say to your supervisor,
   a. "Please help me. The cooperating teacher doesn't give me enough to do."
   b. "I feel I'm competent enough to handle a whole day's program."
   c. "I'm just doing cleanup and housekeeping most of the time."
   d. "You could ask my cooperating teacher to give me more responsibility."
   e. "I'll sure be happy when I finish and have my own class."
4. Mrs. Schultz is angry and yells, "Janita wet her pants again. I don't think any of you remembered to remind her!" You respond by saying,
   a. "You're upset because you don't think we reminded Janita."
   b. "They all wet sometimes, Mrs. Schultz!"
   c. "I didn't see her wet today."
   d. "We remind all the children right before snacks."
   e. "My child wets at school also!"
5. Congruent sending and authentic sending are
   a. very different.
   b. easy skills for most adults.
   c. similar to active listening.
   d. very similar.
   e. similar to parcel post sending.

E. Create a one-day wonder.

F. Arrange the following problem-solving steps in order, based on the eight-step sequence. You may find that more than one applies to the same step.

1. Cooperating teacher: "We'll put paintings without names in this box this week and see what happens." Student teacher: "Okay."
2. Student teacher: "You feel children's artwork should always have the child's name printed in the upper left corner."
3. Cooperating teacher: "You could put names on the artwork when you're the adult in the art area."
4. Student teacher: "I feel the child's name should be put on the artwork only when the child gives permission to do so. If the children don't ask to have their names put on, they will learn the consequences when it's time to take the art home."
5. Student teacher: "I could tell each child what will happen if there is no name on her painting."
6. Cooperating teacher: "There's been quite a bottleneck when parents try to find their child's artwork at departure time. Sometimes, there are no names printed in the upper left corner."
7. Student teacher: "You would like to put each child's name on his artwork, and I think each child can learn something if I don't print his name when he does not give me permission to do so."
8. Student teacher: "I appreciate your understanding my point of view."
9. Cooperating teacher: "You could write the child's name lightly if that child said no."
10. Cooperating teacher: "I think the lesson to be learned isn't worth the commotion at closing."
11. Student teacher: "This is the way I feel about names on artwork."

G. Using Glickman's (1981) "planful" responses, identify the following statements. (Example: "Tell me more about it." *Encouraging.*)

1. "Do you mean you're feeling angry?"
2. "Just stop helping the child."
3. "The way I look at it, you've been asking for a lot of direction from the cooperating teacher."
4. "I'll put the chairs up on Tuesdays; you can do it on Thursdays."
5. "Tell her it's her turn."
6. "If you straighten the closet every day, he'll get the message and do it, too."
7. "I think I hear anxiety in your voice."
8. "Look the speaker in the eyes."
9. "There's more, isn't there?"

H. List as many possible alternative solutions as you can for the following problem.

Winona has been placed with a cooperating teacher who, in her opinion, has created a classroom environment that offers the children few play choices. She has communicated this idea to her cooperating teacher, who then asks Winona for suggestions. Winona's suggestions might include . . .

I. List four actions, behaviors, or verbalizations commonly used in conflict situations that definitely will not promote conflict resolution.

CASE SCENARIO

Setting: A morning Kindergarten class. Mrs. Kitayama is Miss Ling's cooperating teacher. To make the names easier for the students, many of whom are second language speakers of English, Mrs. Kitayama is called Mrs. K and Miss Ling is called Miss L.

The schedule starts with the children writing their names on a sheet of chart paper placed on a table near the door to the room to facilitate attendance and to encourage the children's reading and writing skills. Mrs. K always has a question for them to answer and the children place their names on a "no" or "yes" column in response. Today Miss L has written the question, "Do you like chocolate ice cream or vanilla?" She has written "Chocolate" in one column and "Vanilla" in the other.

Mrs. K questions her. "Was there a reason you asked the opening question on the attendance paper as you did?"

"Absolutely," answers Miss. L. "I've noticed that several of the students are beginning to read and I thought having "Chocolate" and "Vanilla" would be different and intriguing. I noticed that Fwasia, who generally comes early, helped those who couldn't read the words. I sometimes wonder why her parents didn't start her in school last year. Do you know why she entered late, Mrs. K?"

"Yes, I do," Mrs. K responds. "Fwasia's family speaks Farsi at home. She had a second year in preschool in order to build her English language skills. She began to read last fall and she enjoys helping those who don't read as well.

"I also want to compliment you on the choice of *Corduroy* and the art activity you designed to go with it. And you brought your own teddy bear to share. Great idea! You made the directions for the drawing of a teddy bear easy enough to follow, and you found that the children didn't have experience passing out paper.

"I honestly hadn't given thought to the children's knowing how to pass out paper. When I saw their confusion, it seemed logical to ask those at the ends of the lines to stand and pass to the rest of the children on their line. I must admit that coming from a fourth grade assignment last semester to this kindergarten has really been a learning experience.

continues . . .

. . . continued

Questions for Discussion:

1. Have you ever been in a situation where you overestimated what the students in you classroom knew?
2. What do you think about Miss. L changing the opening question routine from "yes-no" answers to "chocolate" "vanilla" choices?
3. How would you characterize the communication between Mrs. K and Miss. L?
4. What do you think you could do to facilitate the communication with your cooperating teacher if it's not really open?

REFERENCES

Armstrong, J. L. (1994, January). Mad, sad, or glad: Children speak out about child care. *Young Children, 49*(2).

Breulin, D. C. (2001, May). Be your own shrink: Small steps. *Bottom Line, 22*(6), 11–22

Brighton, C. M. (1999). Keeping good teachers: Lessons from novices. In M. Scherer (Ed.). *A better beginning: Supporting and mentoring new teachers* (pp. 197–201). Alexandria, VA: Association for Supervision and Curriculum Development.

Britz, J. (1993). *Problem solving in early childhood classrooms.* ERIC Digest, EDO-PS-93-1.

Burke, C. (1998, September 17). *Communication skills that matter.* SkillPath seminar, the Women's Conference, Boise, ID.

Canter, T. (1998). *First-class teacher: Successful strategies for new teachers.* Santa Monica, CA: Canter and Associates, Inc.

Carter, M., & Curtis, D. (1994). *Training teachers: A harvest of theory and practice.* St. Paul, MN: Redleaf Press.

Caruso, J. J., & Fawcett, M. T. (1999). *Supervision in early childhood education: A developmental perspective.* New York: Teachers College Press.

Copeland, T. (1997, January/February). *How to help your staff cope with conflict.* Child Care Information Exchange.

Danoff, J., Breitbart, V., & Barr, E. (1977). *Open for children.* New York: McGraw-Hill.

Delpit, L. (1995). *Other people's children: Cultural conflict in the classroom.* New York: The New Press.

Freeman, D. (1968). *Corduroy.* New York: Viking Press.

Freire, P. (1993). *Pedagogy of the oppressed* (20th an. ed.). New York: Continuum.

Ginott, H. (1972). I'm angry! I'm appalled! I am furious! *Teacher and child.* New York: Macmillan. Reprinted in *Today's Education Magazine*, NEA Journal (Nov. 19, 1972).

Glickman, C. D. (1981). *Developmental supervision.* Alexandria, VA: Association for Supervision and Curriculum Development.

Gordon, T. (1972). The risks of effective communication. *Parent Notebook*, a publication of Effectiveness Training Associates.

Gordon-Nourok, E. (1979). *You're a student teacher!* Sierra Madre, CA: SCAEYC.

Harris, J. (1995, July/August). Is anybody out there listening? *Child Care Information Exchange, 104.*

Hurst, B., & Reding, G. (1999b). *Keeping the light in your eyes: A guide for helping teachers discover, remember, relive, and rediscover the joy of teaching.* Scottsdale, AZ: Holcomb Hathaway.

Hutchins, P. (1968). *Rosie's walk.* New York: MacMillan.

Keirsey, D., & Bates, M. (1984). *Please understand me* (5th ed.). Del Mar, CA: Gnosology Books.

Leeds, D. (2001, September). Good things come to those who ask ... The power of questions. *Bottom Line, 22*(18), 6–8.

Lundsteen, S. W. (1976). *Children learn to communicate.* Englewood Cliffs, NJ: Prentice-Hall.

March, A. A. (2002, April). Are you listening? The simple strategy for enhancing relationships . . . Business and personal. *Bottom Line, 23*(7), 1–2

Morton, L. L., Vesco, R., Williams, N. H., & Awender, M. A. (1997). Student teacher anxieties related to class management, pedagogy, evaluation, and staff relations. *British Journal of Educational Psychology, 67.*

Moustakas, C. (1966). *The authentic teacher.* Cambridge: Howard A. Doyle.

Read, K., & Patterson, J. (1980). *The nursery school and kindergarten* (7th ed.). New York: Holt, Rinehart & Winston.

Rogers, C., & Freiberg, H. (1994). *Freedom to learn* (3rd ed.). New York: Merrill/Macmillan.

Sanders, J. (2002). Personal Interview. Boxwood Child Center, San Jose, CA.

SkillPath Seminars. (1997). *Conflict management skills for women.* Mission, KS: SkillPath Publications.

Ueland, B. (1941, November). Tell me more. *Ladies Home Journal, 58*(51), as quoted by Moustakas, C. (1966). *The Authentic Teacher.* Cambridge: Howard A. Doyle.

Warner, J. (1995). *The unauthorized TEACHER'S survival guide.* Indianapolis, IN: Park Avenue Publications.

SECTION V

The Child

CHAPTER 9

Case Studies, Analyses, and Applications

Objectives

After studying this chapter, the student should be able to:

1. Use at least three different types of observation forms: narrative (anecdotal), event sampling, and fixed interval (time sampling).
2. Analyze a child's behavior from information gathered through observation and develop an individual learning plan for the child.
3. Describe the difference between observation and conjecture.
4. Discuss the role of the school and parents in working with a child.

Guillermo was my most fascinating child. He was bilingual. His family from Guatemala was trying so hard to adjust to the United States.

—Forrest Graham

I'll be looking for a part-time job so I can go on in school. The more children I encounter the more I realize I need to know more.

—Mukema Oblatela

CASE STUDIES

As a student teacher, you may be asked to complete a child case study. The assignment requires in-depth analysis and recording of the child's achievements, development, and learning processes.

case study—an in-depth study of a child that involves several days of observation at differing times during the day and the use of several different types of observation forms.

A collection of data can involve:

- systematic observations
- work samples
- assessments and testing
- reviewing creative artwork
- videos, photographs, or tape recordings
- dictations
- anecdotal records (factual notes recording spontaneous events and happenings)
- checklists, inventories, or rating scales
- interviews with child and others
- home visits and other activities

rating scale—an assessment of specific skills or concepts that are rated on some qualitative dimension of excellence or accomplishment.

What is collected may depend on both your college instructor's assignment criteria and the purpose of the study.

Materials and data are arranged in chronological order so assessments can compare earlier with later work and happenings. If student teacher evaluation is required, records document child progress and student teacher hypothesis. Case study development can often provide a basis for planning parent-teacher conferences.

A strict code of confidentiality and anonymity concerning the child's identity is observed when student teachers collect data or share evaluations. Parents' presence in the school or classroom make confidentiality extremely important. The temptation students face in wanting to discuss their case study child with other adults has led to a few unfortunate and emotionally charged parent-school discussions.

Assignments may require a "whole child" view or narrower aspects of the child's development and/or behavior.

Most training programs assign in-depth case studies so student teachers begin to realize the benefits accrued from watching one child intently, and attempting to satisfy curiosity about the hows and whys of that one child's actions and speech. Student teachers, therefore, become researchers who reserve fast judgments, interpret carefully, hypothesize, explore many possible reasons for behavior, and begin to see child development "in the flesh."

OBSERVATION FORMS

In this chapter, we are going to go beyond our earlier description of behavior and observation in order to help you understand how to use different types of observation forms, and more importantly, how to use the information learned to develop learning plans for the observed child.

Narrative

This is one of the simplest forms to use when observing children. A narrative describes the child's behavior as it occurs. As the observer, you can sit to one side

Figure 9–1 Observation can take place inside the classroom.

of the room or yard with a small notebook (see Figure 9–1). Pick a child to observe, and simply record what you see. Your narrative might look something like this:

> Stevie, one of the new children in the room of five-year-olds at the ABC School, enters the room and hangs onto his mother's coat with his finger in his mouth. He looks unhappy as his mother says impatiently, "Let go, Stevie; you're too big to act like a baby. You know I'm in a hurry to get to work this morning." Stevie looks at another child, Hiroku, who is playing with the blocks. "Look at how nicely Hiroku is playing! Why don't you go over and play with him?"
>
> Stevie begins to cry as his mother attempts to drag him over to the block area. He whines, "Don't wanta stay today, Mama. Wanta go home!"
>
> Mrs. Thomas, the teacher, intervenes. "Mrs. Conway, could you stay awhile today? I know Stevie would like to show you the dinosaur he made yesterday. It's drying on the shelf over by the window. Stevie, why don't you show the dinosaur to your Mom?"
>
> (Mrs. Thomas really knows how to handle Stevie's reluctance to separate from his mother, doesn't she? Look at how happy he is now, showing his dinosaur to his Mom! I remember how much time he took yesterday when he made it; I didn't think he'd ever finish! But Mrs. Thomas let him take as much time as he needed to feel satisfied. I guess she knew that if he got started describing the dinosaur to his mother, he'd forget about her having to leave. I wonder why Mrs. Conway doesn't give Stevie a little extra time each day when she brings him instead of hurrying him so. She knows he hates to be left in a hurry!)
>
> After a minute or two of describing the dinosaur and its ferocity, Stevie goes to the door with his mother. "Bye, Mom. See you this afternoon." Stevie runs off. "Hiroku, let me play with some of the blocks!" "OK, Stevie. Wanta help me build a garage for the big trucks?"
>
> "Sure."
>
> Stevie and Hiroku work quickly and build a garage for three of the big trucks.
>
> Juan and Mike come in together with Mike's older brother Pat.
>
> "I'll be back at 3:30 when school gets out. Be ready, you two."
>
> "Teacher will see we're ready, Pat; you know we'll be ready," says Mike.
>
> Juan goes over to the garage Stevie and Hiroku have built. "I want the red truck," he demands. "Can't have it. We need it," protests Stevie. Juan grabs the truck. Stevie gets to his feet and shouts, "Gimme it back!" Stevie tries to grab the truck from Juan. A tug-of-war begins as both boys shake the truck between them. Hiroku says to Stevie, "Aw, let him have it. We got enough trucks anyway." Stevie lets go of the truck, sits back down on the floor, puts his finger in his mouth, and sulks.

How might this same interaction appear if you were using a different observation form? (However easy the narrative is to read, it does remove you from the classroom action while you are writing.) The narrative can be abbreviated somewhat through the use of the anecdotal record form. Figure 9–2 illustrates this narrative in anecdotal form.

Student Teacher: MB

Name of School: ABC School, Child-Care Center — Date: 16 September

Identity Key (DO NOT use real name)	Description of What Child Is Doing	Time	Comments
S. — Stevie	S. enters, clings to M.'s coat. Finger in mouth	8:03	S. looks unhappy.
M. — S.'s Mom	M., "Let go, S. You're too big to act like a baby.I'm in a hurry; you know it!"		I wish S.'s M. wouldn't do that!
T. — Teacher	Lk how nice H. plays by self!		
H. — Hiroku	Why not play w/him		
J. — Juan	S. cries.	8:05	
Mi. — Mike	T. suggests S. show M. dinosaur fr yesterday.		I wish I'd thought of that; S. is really proud of his dinosaur.
P. — Pat, Mike's brother	S. and M. to see dino.		
	S. says "Bye" to M.; goes to H., "Lemme play w/you."	8:08	
	H. says, "Let's build a garage for the trucks."		Good for H.; he always has good ideas!
* *	* * * * *	*	* * *
	J., Mi., & P. come in.	8:47	
	J. says, "I want the red truck."		
	S., "No; we need it." J. grabs the truck.	8:55	Oh oh, I better watch & see what happens.
	H. says, "Let him have it. We have enough trucks."		I love kids like H. He is so mature!

Figure 9–2 An anecdotal record form

Event Sampling Form

In contrast to the narrative and anecdotal forms, an event sampling form (see Figure 9–3) might be used. In this form, Stevie's play behaviors are being observed. In addition, the times of each observation are indicated to provide additional information. Two theorists lend themselves to a consideration of children's play behaviors in terms of an observation model. They are Parten (1932), whose play categories have been useful for many years, and Piaget (1962).

Parten divided play behaviors into the following categories: onlooking play (observing and talking, but not participating), solitary play (play without reference

event sampling—a method of observation in which the observer records a specific behavior only when it occurs.

onlooking play—according to Parten, standing to the side of a room or play yard and observing the action of others but not taking part.

solitary play—according to Parten, playing by oneself.

parallel play—according to Parten, one child playing next to another but using different materials and not interacting.

associative play—according to Parten, one child playing next to another and using the same materials, but each working independently of the other.

cooperative play—according to Parten, two children using the same materials and working on the same project.

symbolic play—according to Piaget, using materials in play for a different purpose than the usual, for example, pretending that a block is a truck.

practice play—according to Piaget, performing the same task over and over again until a sense of mastery is achieved.

games—according to Piaget, playing according to a set of rules.

to another child), parallel play (play in which two or more children may be using similar materials without personal interaction), associative play (play in which two or more children may be using the same materials but each child is doing a separate activity; for example, each child may be using blocks, building separate towers), and cooperative play (play in which there is a common goal toward which two or more children are working; for example, the children are using blocks to build one house).

Piaget suggested that there are three types of play common among preschoolers: symbolic play (play in which the objects with which the child is playing become something else; for example, blocks become a garage or a house), practice play (play in which the child continuously repeats an activity as though to master it; for example, in block play, trying over and over to build an ever taller structure without calling it a tower), and games (play in which the children follow a set of agreed-upon rules).

In looking at the anecdotal record and narrative account of Stevie's early-morning activities, it would be noted on the event sampling form that he was involved in cooperative-symbolic play with Hiroku. If, however, Stevie was followed throughout the day, observations might look more like the rest of the event sampling form in Figure 9–3.

Fixed Interval Model

Many student teachers do not have the time to sit and observe; they are, instead, actively involved in what is happening in the classroom, often teaching or supervising small groups of students. The fixed interval or time sampling model may be the observation form to use (see Figure 9–4).

Child: Stevie　　Date: 16 September

	Symbolic	Practice	Games
Onlooking:	Watching H. & J. in playhouse (9:45 A.M.)		
Solitary:	Pretending to be Superman on jungle gym (10:23 A.M.)	Putting puzzles together (8:35 A.M.) On swg. Trying to pump self (10:40 A.M.)	
Parallel:	Bldg rd for car in sandbox (3:20 P.M.)	Dumping H_2O fr 1 container to another at H_2O table (2:57 P.M.)	
Associative:		Bldg towers w/sm blks next to H. (8:30 A.M.)	
Cooperative:	Bldg garage w/lrg blks w/H. (8:12 A.M.)		Following H.'s directions for card game, "War" (2:10 P.M.)

Figure 9–3 A two-dimensional play model, combining event and time sampling

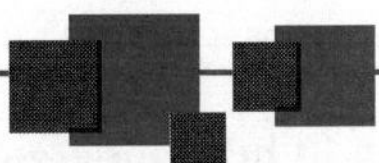

Child: Maya T = teacher St = Student; Ss = students	Grade: 3rd Date: 12 October

8:30 A.M.:	Enters classroom, places lunch box & jacket in cubby
8:30 A.M.:	Sits at desk, talks to J. (a student in her group), ignores math "sponge" activity on board
8:40 A.M.:	Still talks to J.
8:45 A.M.:	(Bell rings)
	(I was busy taking roll & lunch count; didn't note what M. was doing)
8:50 A.M.:	Talks to G. (another St. in her group)
	(Should be saying Pledge of Allegiance and completing math "sponge" activity on chalkboard)
8:55 A.M.:	(T. reminds children that 1st activity of the A.M. will begin at 9:00 & that "sponge" problems are to be placed in her "in-basket")
	Maya quickly completes problems & turns in paper
9:00 A.M.:	All Ss sitting quietly on carpet squares, choosing centers; Maya waves hand excitedly; "Writing center! Writing center!"
	T reminds her that she has been in the writing center for the past two days and that others like the writing center, too
	"Why not try the math center, Maya?" T. suggests
9:05 A.M.:	Maya pouts, "But, I want to go to the writing center"
9:10 A.M.:	Still pouting but goes to math center where tangram puzzles and pieces are arranged to stimulate problem-solving
9:15 A.M.:	M. complains, "These tangrams are too easy! Can I make some of my own?" T. says "Of course, Maya; maybe you'd like to have B. work with you?" "No!" . . . emphatically said
9:25 A.M.:	M. working very carefully
9:30 A.M.:	M. still working carefully
9:45 A.M.:	(I'm too busy; unable to check on M.)
9:50 A.M.:	M. looks intent on creating a new design
9:55 A.M.:	T. rings a bell & warns Ss they have five min to finish their center work. Reminds those who haven't that they can finish after recess
10:00 A.M.:	M. says, "I'm nearly finished with my design; may I stay in for recess and work on it?" T. suggests to M. that she should get some fresh air and exercise too. M. groans but agrees

(I have yard duty this A.M. recess and I notice that Maya is off by herself drawing in the dirt. I wonder if she's still working on her new tangram design or dreaming up a new one. As I approach her, she quickly erases what she's been working on.)

Figure 9–4 Fixed interval or time sampling model

ONLINE COMPANION

Tape Recordings

Vivian Gussin Paley (1992) often left a tape recorder running in her kindergarten classroom so she could replay the recording at a later time. She felt the replay of children's voices often helped her clarify a problem. She attempted to create specific curriculum for individual children and the total class. She believed she did not hear everything said the first time around. By replaying the recording, she had more opportunity to reflect and offer "tailor-made" activities.

Ayers (1993) suggests an educator must be part detective and part researcher, sifting the clues children leave. Collecting data, testing hypotheses, and looking at children as they really are to flush out impressions and make credible the story of their growth and development are all part of this research.

Checklists and Rating Scales

Centers and teachers often create their own developmental checklists to pinpoint children's attainments and progress. Often, these indicate whether a skill or understanding is present and at what date it was observed. Other checklist and rating forms may use a "yes" "no" or selected spot on a continuum between two extremes. They ask the observer to select an answer among a choice of answers. The focus on both a check list or rating scale can be broad or narrow. For example, if a teacher or center wishes to probe when and how many attending children select books from the classroom library center on an average day, which books are popular, and how much time each child spent with each selected book, the checklist would provide a space for children's names, time child spends with a selected book, title of book(s), a time of day, and perhaps a "yes" "no" space for handled book with care. This checklist would be useful not only for evaluating library center use but also individual child behaviors.

ANALYSIS OF OBSERVATION

As you look at your fixed-interval observations and comments on Maya in Figure 9–4, what hypotheses might you generate? Has Maya resolved the Erikson tasks appropriate for her age? Does she appear field sensitive or independent? What may be the indications of whether she is concrete operational or not?

Certainly, given the speed with which Maya finished the math "sponge" problems and her subsequent absorption in the tangram activities, it is easy to hypothesize that Maya is positively resolving the task of industry. Also, her assertion that she would like to be at the writing center and asking if she could design her own tangrams suggests successful resolution of initiative. Her ignoring the "sponge" problems until the last minute may indicate that the problems are too simple for her and that she needs an extra challenge in math, or assuming that she rushed through them unsuccessfully, an indication of some unresolved autonomy. Checking to see how well she has completed the problems will allow you to accept or reject that particular hypothesis.

Maya's desire to work alone and carefully with the tangrams, plus her wanting to create her own designs, could be indications of a field independent learning style. Observing her step-by-step analysis of the tangram puzzles might also suggest a logical sequential learning style. And her enjoyment of math challenges, as you have seen before, suggests that she may be concrete operational.

As mentioned in the observations of Stevie, the best method is to combine forms, using different ones for different purposes. Although they take the most time, the narrative and anecdotal forms provide the most information. Forms such as the two-dimensional play model are handy to use when time is limited. They also supplement the narrative forms well and provide much information relevant to their single purpose. We have used the example of play behaviors, but you might want to use social behaviors or attending behaviors.

When working with a child who is asocial, antisocial, or overly social, social behaviors become more important to observe. One such form (see Figure 9–5)

Pupil: Maya
Observer: Student Teacher
Teacher: Cooperating teacher

Date: 14 October
Times: 8:37 A.M.
8:57 A.M.
9:28 A.M.
10:09 A.M.
10:38 A.M.

8:37 A.M.: Children wating for bell

	1	2	3	4	
A			3		Activity: T. arranging papers
B			3		at her desk; most Ss working
C			3		on math "sponge" activity.
D			3		
E		3			Maya has been talking to J.;
F		3			now is looking out the window.
G		3			
H		3			
I			3		Talking to G. and J.;
J			3		G. shushes her.
K			3		
L			3		

8:57 A.M.: "Sponge" time

	1	2	3	4	
A			3		
B			3		
C			3		
D			3		
E	4				Tchr reminds
F	4				M. to finish
G	4				math "sponge"
H	3				paper.
I	3				
J	3				Maya really
K	3				works fast! I
L	3				am surprised she does as well as she does.

9:28 A.M.: 1st Center Activity Time

	1	2	3	4	
A	3				Maya wrkg on
B	3				tangrams (her choice).
C	3				
D	3				
F	3				Interesting, Maya seems
G		3			to be daydreaming.
H	3				
I	3				
J	3				I'm really pleased to
K	3				see how well Maya can
L	3				work.

10:09 A.M.: Recess

	1	2	3	4	
A		3			
B		3			
C	3				Maya is truly
E	3				engrossed—
F	3				wonder what
G	3				she's doing?
H	3				
I		3			
J		3			
K	3				I bet she's
L	3				drawing another tangram design!

10:38 A.M.: 2nd Center Activity Time

	1	2	3	4	(Maya is working on map of neighborhood w/J., G., & W.)
A	3				
B	3				
C	3				
D	3				
E	2				T. compliments group
F	2				on how well the map
G	2				is progressing
H	2				
I	3				
J	3				
K				3	Maya's angry because G. wants to use different map symbol
L				3	than she; T. waits to see if Ss can resolve own conflict.

Figure 9–5 Teacher/pupil interaction scale (TPIS)

was developed for use in the classroom and is called the Teacher/Pupil Interaction Scale (TPIS). The scale measures four types of teacher behavior and four types of student behavior on another two-dimension form. The teacher behaviors are: (1) instruction, (2) reinforcing, (3) nonattending, and (4) disapproving. The student behaviors are (1) attending, (2) scanning, (3) social, and (4) disruptive. Both teacher and student behaviors are defined as follows.

Teacher Behavior

Instruction: Makes explanation, talks to pupil, gives directions, asks questions, and so on.

Reinforcing: Dispenses appreciation, smiles, nods; makes physical contact by patting, touching; dispenses material rewards.

Nonattending or *neutrals:* Withholds attention, sits passively, attends to personal notes, works with other pupils, attends to activities that do not include the pupil being observed.

Disapproving: Criticizes, corrects, admonishes, reproves, expresses generally negative feelings, statements, and the like.

Pupil Behavior

Attending: When receiving direction or instructions, maintains eye contact or heeds direction. When performing desk work, attends to work (turns pages, uses pencil, looks at paper). When addressed by teacher, child attends.

Scanning: Looks about room; watches other children; daydreams; makes no verbal or physical contact with other children.

Social contacts: Teaches other children; talks to others; walks about room interacting with others but does not attract the general attention of the class with noise or disturbances.

Disruptive: Calls attention to self by behaviors that are audible/visible throughout the room (for example, tapping with pencil, throwing objects, shouting).

Figure 9–6 A child in solitary play would fit into number one of the four TPIS student behavior categories.

It is difficult to think that all teacher/pupil interactions could be reduced to only four actions by each. But if you use the scale, you will discover that many actions can be comfortably placed in one of the four categories (see Figure 9–6).

The real advantage of the TPIS is that the observer records interactions for only one minute at a time. Thus, it lends itself to the busy teacher who does not have the leisure to complete a narrative, anecdotal, or play model form. TPIS rating procedures are as follows:

1. The observer makes a judgment each five seconds for a one-minute sample of teacher/pupil interaction. Three five-minute blocks taken during an hour over a three-day period provide a reliable basis for judging the typical behavior of a pupil. A five-minute block consists of five one-minute samples, with a one-minute pause between each sample.
2. Pupil behavior is designated by the column in which the rating is made.
3. Each row indicates a single five-second sample.
4. The teacher behavior is designated by a number (1 through 4) and is entered in the column that describes what the pupil is doing.

Please note in Figure 9–5 that the example does not include a five-minute block of time but rather includes five one-minute samplings of behavior taken at times when the student teacher found a minute in which to record. You may find for your own purposes that taking one-minute samplings throughout the day gives you as much information as you need in order to develop a picture of what the child you are observing is like. Also, please note that we included a brief description of the action in order to help clarify the coding. Remember that the horizontal numbers at the top refer to pupil behavior; the numbers entered by the observer refer to teaching behavior.

Analyzing Observations

One reason, perhaps the main reason, for observing children is to help you, as the observer, better understand the child. This is why we used two children to illustrate the observation techniques covered in the chapter.

Stevie: What have we learned about Stevie just from observing him in action? What questions have we raised? Let us start with our opening narrative observation.

Stevie.

Stevie has difficulty separating from his mother when she brings him to school. The narrative describes typical behavior, not exceptional. If we caught Stevie on an exceptional day, we would have noted that this was not his usual behavior. We can also surmise that Stevie's mother almost seems to encourage his desire not to have her leave; in spite of reminding him that she has to leave quickly, she takes time to listen to Stevie describe his dinosaur. Stevie then seems quite happy to let his mother leave, especially because his friend Hiroku is playing with the large blocks, which Stevie enjoys. In the later interchange between Stevie and Juan, we might guess that Juan is the more assertive because he simply tells Stevie that he wants the red truck and takes it. We might also guess that Stevie does not know how to solve his problem as smoothly as Hiroku, as he enters into a tug-of-war with Juan over the truck. Hiroku, in contrast, recognizes that even if Juan takes the red truck, he and Stevie still have two trucks with which to play; arguing over the third truck is not worth it. A later indication of Hiroku's social maturity (and leadership ability) occurs in the incident of the card game. Hiroku knows how to play "War" and patiently explains the rules to Stevie. Even when Stevie loses his temper and throws the cards because he thinks Hiroku will win, Hiroku does not lose his temper but instead, quietly picks up the cards.

An analysis of Stevie's play behaviors tends to show that, except for his play with Hiroku, Stevie prefers solitary or parallel play to cooperative or associative play. He also appears to use symbolic and practice play more than play involving rules such as the card game. We might surmise that Stevie, intellectually, is not at the stage where he can understand or internalize what rules mean. Perhaps giving him some of the Piagetian tasks, measuring his ability to classify and conserve, would be of value in understanding Stevie more fully. This idea may be pursued later.

Other observations of Stevie have noted the following behaviors: during music times in the large group, Stevie typically sings loudly and off-key. The cooperating teacher has asked us to ignore him because she feels he's doing it for the attention. "Shushing" him, she feels, will only reinforce the behavior. Some of the other children are already beginning to ask him to be quiet; others are laughing at him. When this happens, Stevie giggles and sings even louder and more off-key. At times, the cooperating teacher cannot totally ignore Stevie and has told him to leave the group if he is unable to behave, a move that usually quiets the boy.

A second observed behavior causing concern occurred on the afternoon of the morning Stevie and Juan had argued over the red truck. During outdoors free play after rest time, Stevie was playing with Hiroku in the sandbox. They had been smoothing the sand and building a road for some of the small cars from the outside toy box. Juan had climbed into the sandbox and joined them when Stevie picked up a fistful of sand and threw it at Juan. Shaking his head and rubbing his eyes, Juan complained about sand in his eyes. At this point, the cooperating teacher sent Juan to the school nurse to have his eyes washed out, asked Stevie to come out of the sandbox, and took him aside to reexplain the school rules about playing in the sandbox. Indirect attempts to discover if Stevie deliberately had thrown the sand at Juan because he was still angry about the incident with the truck may prove fruitless. When asked point-blank, however, if he had thrown the sand at Juan because he was angry, Stevie is likely to answer "yes." He may not understand that his anger is related to the incident of the truck, though, because that had happened a while before.

In a conference with Stevie's mother, the cooperating teacher has learned that because she and her husband are renting a small house with only two bedrooms, Stevie and his two brothers sleep in the same room and go to bed at the same time. "After all," she says, "the boys are only four years apart in age. They go to bed between 8:00 P.M. and 9:00 P.M., depending on what's on television. Their father and I let them watch one show each evening if they've been good and if Tommy, the eight-year-old, has done his homework." When asked when the boys are awakened, she replies, "We have to be up at 6:00 A.M. so we can get breakfast and still get to work on time. And you might know that Stevie knows every trick in the world to make us get a late start!" The mother states that she believes the boys get enough sleep, especially with the nap the two younger ones receive at the after-school care center each day. (The middle boy, a first grader, comes to the center after school each day as does the older boy.)

Stevie's father works at a local foundry; his mother is a clerk-typist in a county office. Although Mr. Conway works 8:00 A.M. to 4:00 P.M. and could pick up his sons at approximately 4:45 P.M., he firmly believes that their care is his wife's responsibility. Thus, the three boys have to wait until about 5:45 P.M. when their mother can pick them up. Efforts on the part of the center staff, director, and teachers to persuade the father to attend parent/teacher/staff conferences have met with flat refusals and the statement that "raising kids is a woman's responsibility, not a man's; you speak to my wife."

The effect of the father's attitude is apparent in the behavior of the three boys, Stevie in particular. Smaller than most of the other five-year-olds at the center, Stevie tends to be slyly aggressive rather than overtly. He seems to know that in a one-to-one argument with any of the other boys in the room, he would lose. So he throws sand or blocks, trips another, or knocks over another child's block tower. "But, teacher, it was an accident," he will insist when confronted. Another effect of his father's attitude is seen in Stevie's choices for play: large blocks, trucks and cars, swings and jungle gym, tricycles, wagons, puzzles, and clay. But go in the dramatic play center? Paint at the easel? Stevie calls these activities "sissy" and refuses to play.

His attachment to Hiroku seems to be related to the fact that Hiroku is the tallest and best coordinated boy in the room. Hiroku appears to understand Stevie's need to be associated with him and cheerfully accepts Stevie's company. It is difficult for Stevie when Hiroku is absent. On those days, Stevie stays by the teacher's side or stands along the wall with his finger in mouth and just watches what is going on.

Stevie's mother has been asked about his playmates at home. "Why, with two older brothers to play with, he doesn't need anybody else!" she replies. The teacher gently points out that Stevie seems "lost" when Hiroku is absent and suggests that maybe Stevie could invite a child home to visit him on the weekend. The mother's reaction to this suggestion is as though the teacher has taken leave of her senses. "With three young ones already, you're telling me I should have another one over? What's wrong with Stevie playing with his brothers? They play real nice together, hardly ever any arguing!" The teacher realizes that one of Stevie's problems socially is the fact that he does not need to make friends in order to have someone with whom to play. The teacher also realizes that Stevie's friendship with Hiroku may be related more to the fact that Hiroku is bigger and more mature, and may remind Stevie of his next older brother. The teacher also realizes, after talking with Stevie's mother, that his parents do not share her concern with Stevie's lack of sociableness.

Finally, the teacher decides to have you, her student teacher, make several observations of Stevie. In this way, she hopes to develop a learning plan for Stevie through which she can encourage him to greater sociability.

Maya. As a result of the time sampling of Maya's behavior (see Figure 9–4), we have already discussed some of the possible hypotheses. You have noted Maya's behavior on the TPIS two days later than your original observation with the time sampling. What new information have you learned? First of all, you have checked Maya's math "sponge" activities and discovered that not only has she completed the set correctly but that she has also lined up each problem neatly and sequentially. On the second day of free-choice center activities (a three-days-per-week morning option in your cooperating teacher's classroom), it was interesting to note that Maya chose to work in the math manipulatives center to design another tangram. (You had tried to solve the one she worked on so industriously two days before and had found it difficult.) You formulate an hypothesis that Maya appears to be an advanced thinker, perhaps a potential candidate for the school's gifted-and-talented (GATE) program. As you were observing with the TPIS while supervising the map activity, you have also noticed Maya's spatial abilities. She has had no difficulty placing her home on the map in geographic relation to the school; her argument with Graciela was based, in part, on the latter's insistence that her home was located in closer proximity to the school than Maya felt it was, and in part, on Graciela's insistence that houses should be indicated on the map by a square with a roof and Maya's equal insistence that the representation did not have to look like a little house, that a square would do as well. Graciela eventually agrees with Maya and the two girls place squares on the map indicating where their respective homes are located. Later, in checking with the cooperating teacher, you discover that Maya is correct in her placement of where Graciela lives, not Graciela. You wonder if Maya will bring up the misplacement with Graciela the next day the girls choose to work on the map.

In the meantime, you ask your cooperating teacher if you may administer some of the Piagetian tasks to Maya to test your hypothesis regarding her being in the concrete operational stage. The teacher suggests that you should ask Maya's parents for permission, so you write a short letter for Maya to take home with a tear-off slip at the bottom for Mr. or Mrs. Wiesniewski to sign. The next day, permission granted, you take Maya to the nurse's office and present some of the Piagetian tasks. She finds it easy to conserve mass, length, liquid quantity, and area, and complains, "These games are kind of dumb, don't you think? Haven't you anything harder?" At age eight, you don't think she'll be able to solve the concept of displacement of water but you set out the necessary glasses and weighted, small plastic pill containers in front of her. She confidently predicts that the heavier object will displace more water and is surprised when it doesn't. She asks if she can put both objects back in the water herself and you say, "Of course." She picks up both (the pill containers are weighted unequally with heavy screws and bolts), manipulates them, looks at them, places one and then the other back in the jars of water. Much to your surprise (as she takes the objects out of the water again), she then announces, "I think this is kinda like the balls of clay. It doesn't make any difference whether they were round or sausage-shaped; they still had the same amount of clay. I think that it may not make any difference how much the pill bottles weigh; it may just be how big they are." In your mind, there is no doubt that Maya is likely gifted. You try one more task, asking Maya to project what life may be like for her when she's an adult. Here, her fertile imagination and her enjoyment of science fiction color her response.

A conference with the cooperating teacher, Mr. and Mrs. Wiesniewski, and you has resulted in the parents' decision to allow you to develop an individual learning plan for Maya at the math center to stimulate her problem-solving abilities and challenge her advanced mathematical reasoning abilities.

Mr. and Mrs. Wiesniewski also agree to allow Maya to be tested for possible placement in the school's GATE program the following year. (In the school district where you are student teaching, the GATE program is only for fourth and fifth graders. Prior to fourth grade, classroom teachers are expected to provide extra stimulation for gifted children within the regular classroom.)

Applications: Developing a Learning Plan for Stevie

Because the goal or objective for Stevie is to increase his sociability, what social behaviors have been observed? There is his social behavior toward his mother as he shows her his dinosaur, describes it, and acts out its ferocity. Next, there is his accepting Hiroku's invitation to build a garage with the large blocks, and his cooperative play with Hiroku in building towers of small blocks as well as a garage of large ones. Later, there is his cooperative play with Hiroku as they play the card game. In every case of positive social interaction recorded, Stevie was interacting only with Hiroku. In terms of other social behaviors, Stevie interacted with the class, Juan, and Hiroku in neutral or negative ways.

Also noted through the observations is the pride with which Stevie talks to his mother about his dinosaur and the care with which he paints it. The teacher thinks that perhaps having the children who made dinosaurs talk about them would be a way in which Stevie could make a positive impression on the other children.

How will the learning plan look? As with any lesson plan, a learning plan for even one child should contain five elements: (1) the name of the child for whom the plan is being developed; (2) the objective for the plan; (3) any materials or equipment necessary; (4) teacher and student activities; and (5) a time estimate and an evaluation of the plan's effectiveness (see Figure 9–7).

Because Hiroku is one of the "stars" in the room of five-year-olds, you might also plan to ask another child or two to join Stevie and Hiroku as they play with the blocks. Stevie may not want to share, but the chances are that Hiroku will. In this way, Stevie will be playing with two more children other than Hiroku. Why two more? It is easier to exclude one child from play than two children. Also, if Stevie does not want to play with anyone but Hiroku, the other two can play together parallel to Stevie and Hiroku.

Another ploy might be to ask Stevie to introduce a new child, assuming a new child enters the center. In this way, Stevie could learn to feel important to another child in much the same way Hiroku feels important in his relationship with Stevie.

Still another idea might be to ask Stevie to bring one of his favorite books from home to share during story time. The teacher would have determined, of course, that Stevie has some books at home. She may also have asked his mother if Stevie has one favorite book. Similar to this idea is the sharing of a favorite toy. However, this is not always an appropriate idea, especially if one of the children has no toy

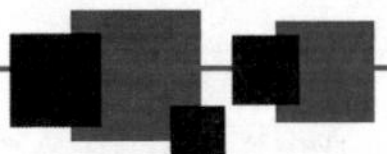

Name: Stevie — Date: 25 September

Objective: Stevie will show off his dinosaur to the other children. He will name it, describe its appearance, and pretend to be a dinosaur.

Materials and Equipment: The dinosaurs the children have made.

Procedures:

Teacher Activities	Student Activities	Time
1. During morning circle time, ask the children who made dinosaurs if they would like to share them with the others.		
2. Wait for answers.	Most children will enthusiastically say	5 min.
3. If Stevie doesn't respond, ask him directly.	"Me, I want to show mine!"	
4. Compliment Stevie on what a good dinosaur he made.		
5. Compliment another child or two.		
6. Have children get their dinosaurs.	Children go to shelf where dinosaurs	2 min.
7. Ask who wants to go first.	are drying. (Make sure they're dry first.)	
8. Unless Stevie volunteers, pick a more outgoing child to start.	After one or maybe two children share, have Stevie share.	5 min. for each child
9. If Stevie forgets, remind him that he knows the name of his dinosaur, its size, what it eats, and so on.		
10. Thank the children who shared. Remind the rest that they'll have time tomorrow.		

Evaluation:

Figure 9–7 An individual learning plan

to share; a teacher should be careful about encouraging children to bring toys from home. In addition, some children are possessive about their toys and become upset if another child plays with them. Some centers encourage the sharing of toys, but once the toy has been displayed and explained, it is put away until the child leaves for home. At other centers, if a child brings a toy, then that child is expected to share it. A breakable toy might be shown, but it would not be shared.

Let us now assume that our interventions regarding the development of Stevie's sociability have met with some success. What are the next steps? Perhaps we will no longer need to develop an individual learning plan for Stevie. It is quite possible that he will continue to make progress without any special attention. It is also possible that, having made progress in social development, we would want to turn our attention to his emotional or physical development. In order to get a clearer picture of Stevie's development, we might want to use a developmental checklist or a standard test or inventory. (A checklist can be found in the Appendix.)

Developing a Learning Plan for Maya

The easiest, least objectionable way to provide challenging math learning exercises for Maya is to devise a set of new activities for the math learning center. You will, of course, provide activities that the others in the class can succeed in and enjoy, but you will also prepare several advanced activities designed for Maya's special ability (see Figure 9–8).

OBSERVATION AND CONJECTURE

At the beginning of this chapter we listed, as an objective, the ability to describe the difference between observation and conjecture. We deliberately used both throughout the various observations.

Study the narrative in the first pages of this chapter. The observation starts with a simple description of Stevie entering the child care center one morning. As soon as we state, "He really looks unhappy," however, we are no longer simply describing; we are making an inference about how Stevie must feel based on

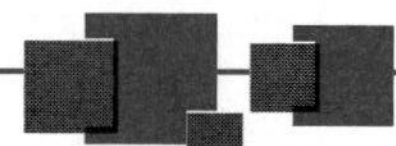

Child: Maya	Date: 17–28 October
Objective:	Maya will explore addition and subtraction of fractions using fraction tiles. After practice, she will design her own algorithms. (It is possible that Brent, Akiko, Jaynese, Tomas, and Richie are also ready for this exploration in fractions. If so, perhaps Maya can be paired with one of them and work cooperatively on designing problems for the others.)
Materials	At least four sets of fraction tiles; equipment: simple problems for student practice; direction cards.
Procedures:	
Anticipatory Set:	Announce to students that there is a new activity involving something called fractions in the math center for anyone interested to try. Ask the class as a whole if anyone knows what a fraction is. Anticipate several answers. Ask students to explain their reasoning behind any answer they might give.
Instruction:	Ask students who are willing to come to the chalkboard and write their fractions, presenting them in some pictorial way. Have other students ask any questions they may wish to ask regarding what the volunteers have drawn on the board. Readiness to learn fractions will become apparent in the answers.
Guided Practice:	Because the activities are placed at a learning center, guided practice almost becomes a form of independent practice. Students typically work in groups of two to five at the math center and assist each other in the learning process. You will also have left the tangram exercises and exercises in addition, subtraction, and multiplication with manipulatives for those students not ready for fractions.
Closure:	At the end of the two-week trial period with fractions in the math center, you will meet in a small group with those students who have been using the experiences with fractions and ask them what they think they've learned. Depending on answers, you plan to leave the center as is to allow for more independent practice for some and add some new challenges for those who are ready for them.

Figure 9–8 Individual learning plan for Maya

how he looks. We are giving an opinion about the child. Opinions based on evidence are conjectures.

On the anecdotal record form (see Figure 9–2), the column labeled "Comments" is for your conjectures or hypotheses as to why a child or another person may have done something. The column labeled "Description of What Child Is Doing" is for description only. Notice that there are no value terms used; any value words are saved for the "Comments" column.

In the fixed-interval or time sampling model (see Figure 9–4), notice that the student teacher made several value judgments ("ignores math 'sponge'," "quickly completes," "waves hand excitedly," "working very carefully") in her use of qualifying words. Her "hypothesis" is that Maya is ignoring the math sponge exercise and so is her assumption that Maya quickly completed it. How did she know Maya had completed the activity? It might have been better for the student teacher to have simply described Maya's behavior and written her conjectures or hypotheses at the bottom. The same mistake is made on the TPIS observation form (see Figure 9–5). How does the student teacher know Maya is "engrossed?" Obviously, she is again making an hypothesis or conjecture.

Applications: More about Individual Learning Plans

Although not specifically covered earlier, in preparing an individual learning plan, you must always remember the child's total environment (see Figure 9–9). Let us take a look at Maria (see Figure 9–10). Is her behavior a cause of concern? It is important to consider what is normal. Assuming that it is early in September and that Maria is a new student in the center, her behavior of watching others from a distance and playing by herself (see Figure 9–11) may not be unusual for a marginally bilingual child from a culture in which females are expected to be quiet and nonassertive. Observing quietly at first is normal behavior for many young children. If Maria had been in school for seven or eight months, she might have become more social and acquired a greater knowledge of English. (We are

bilingual—ability to use two languages.

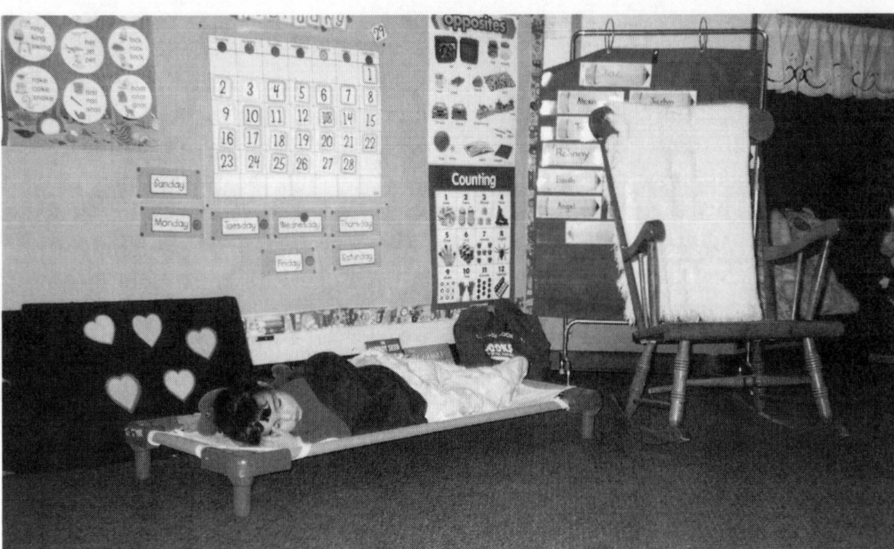

Figure 9–9 An individual plan could include provision for a longer nap.

Name of School: ______			Student Teacher: ______ Date: ______
Identity Key (do NOT use real name)	Description of What Child Is Doing	Time	Comments
M. — Maria T. — Teacher ST. — Student Teacher S. — Susie J. — Janine B. — Bobby Sv. — Stevie	M. arrives at school. Clings to mother's hand, hides behind her skirt. Thumb in mouth.	9:05	Ask T. how long M. has been coming. I bet she's new.
	M. goes over to puzzle rack, chooses a puzzle, goes to table. Dumps out, and works puzzle quickly and quietly. B. & Sv. come over to work puzzles they've chosen.	9:22	Her eye/hand coordination seems good.
	M. looks at them, says nothing, goes to easels, watches S. paint. S. asks M. if she wants to paint. M. doesn't answer.	9:30	I wonder why M. doesn't respond. Ask T. if M. has hearing problem.
	M. comes to snack table, sits down where T. indicates she should. Does not interact with other children at table.	10:15	Is M. ever a quiet child.
	M. stands outside of playhouse, watches S. & J. They don't ask her to join them.	10:47	She looks like she'd like to play.
	M. goes right to swings, knows how to pump.	10:55	Nothing wrong with her coordination.
	During Hap Palmer record M. watches others, does not follow directions.	11:17	Hearing? Maybe limited English? (She looks of Spanish background.)

Figure 9–10 Anecdotal record on Maria

Figure 9–11 When Maria is not watching others play from a distance, she is playing by herself.

assuming Maria is attending a preschool in which competence in speaking English is encouraged. Some preschools attempt to preserve the child's original language rather than to encourage the use of English.)

What does our observation of Maria suggest in regard to planning for her education? First, it suggests that we want to answer our questions: is she hard of hearing? Is Spanish her dominant language? Is she encouraged to be obedient and well-behaved at home? Let us assume that she is not hard of hearing, that Spanish is her dominant language, and that she is encouraged to be quiet and obedient at home. Now, what are our goals for Maria?

We might want to encourage Maria's interaction with Susie and Janine, two of the more outgoing children in the center (see Figure 9–12). Because Susie can easily think of something to play with another child, we might suggest that Susie ask Maria to join her in an activity. We should, however, be more cautious with Janine. We know we can pair Maria with Janine at the easels or at the puzzle table, but it might not be a good idea to pair them together at activities such as sociodramatic play unless Susie is present. Janine might be less tolerant of a child who is not familiar with the English language. In contrast, Susie might even know some Spanish, if there are a number of Spanish-speaking children at the center. You might speak to Maria in Spanish yourself. Undoubtedly your cooperating teacher does.

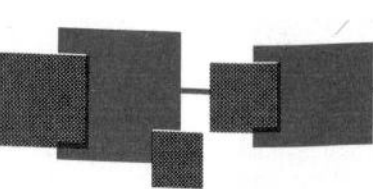

Name: Mrs. Gomes
Room: 11 Grade: 2
Subject: Integration of science, literature, language arts, reading, and math
Week: 27
Date: 2–6 May
Theme: Pets

Morning Block:

8:30 A.M.: "Sponge" activity: Writing and drawing in journals.
Sentence starts: "My pet . . ." and "If I had a pet, it would be a . . ." and "If I were a pet, I'd want to be a . . ."

8:45 A.M.: Read: first five pages of The Biggest Bear by Lynd Ward.
Ask children to predict what they think will happen next.
In cooperative learning groups, have children write and illustrate what they predict will happen on the next two pages.

9:15 A.M.: Have reporters in each group read what group has predicted. After proofreading, post completed stories on bulletin board.

9:50 A.M.: Recess.

10:00 A.M.: Brainstorming: Have children state what their pets are.
In order to include students with no pets, ask them to say what pet they would like to have or which classroom pet they like best. After the first few pets have been listed, ask children to predict which one seems to be the most popular pet among the students in classroom #11. Write down the prediction at the top of the chalkboard for future reference. As additional pets in any one category are named, keep a tally of them. Have children graph results. Ask children to look at their graphs and see how accurate their prediction of what the most popular pet was.

10:45 A.M.: Snack time. (Lunch at 12:30 P.M. seems too late for many of the children; so, during "snack time," your cooperating teacher allows students to eat a part of their lunch or to bring a snack if they're having the school-provided lunch. [A unit on nutrition has taught them to bring nutritious snacks].)

11:00 A.M.: Physical Education with PE resource teacher.

11:40 A.M.: If not completed earlier, each cooperative group will proofread and copy their story pages for posting on the bulletin board. Then groups are to choose one pet for further study. Each group should choose a different pet from any other group. Any two groups choosing the same pet will decide cooperatively which one should change. (The class has studied conflict resolution.) After choices are made, group leaders are to go to the in-class library and look for books about their pet. This is an activity that will be carried throughout the week as groups focus on the history of their pet, its foods, its size, its popularity, how it lives in the wild and how it lives in a home, and how it is raised. Students may bring in photographs of their own pets to illustrate the final reports.

(While children are working, my cooperating teacher plays soft classical music in the background. I've noticed that the children seem to enjoy it.)

Figure 9–14 Second grade lesson plan

family of five children of whom she is the oldest.) In second grade, Joelle is exhibiting the following behaviors: she frequently engages in aggressive hitting and kicking on the play yard, both before school and during recesses; in the classroom, you have seen her destroy a seat-mate's creative writing paper, throw books on the floor, and use foul language. More than once, you or your cooperating teacher have had to remind Joelle to handle the classroom pets more gently; you both know that one of the fish died because Joelle removed it from the aquarium "to see what would happen," she said.

The Student Teacher's Role

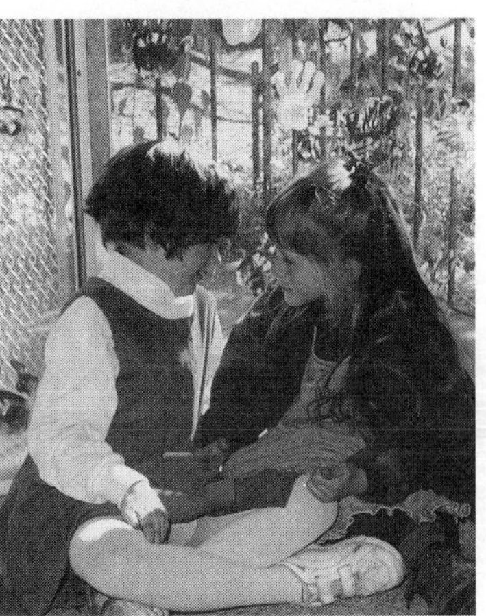

Figure 9–12 These two children are good friends, and will accept Maria and play with her.

One of the roles of a student teacher is that of an observer. During the first days of placement, the student teacher will often be given time to observe. This is an especially valuable time for both the student teacher and the cooperating teacher. Take advantage of this period. Observe several children carefully; confer with your cooperating teacher and college supervisor regarding which children to observe. After you have completed your observations, discuss them with your cooperating teacher, supervisor, and peers. It is fascinating to listen to someone else's perceptions of your observations. Often, we become emotionally involved with the children whom we observe; thus, we can receive a different perspective from those who do not know them as well, or who know them as well as does our cooperating teacher. This situation can be reversed. Many cooperating teachers know that their judgment of children can be obscured by knowledge of the children's backgrounds. A student teacher's judgment, in contrast, is not affected by this factor.

We are reminded of a time when we were new to a community and had, as one of our students in a kindergarten, a five-year-old named Tony. Not knowing Tony's background, we evaluated his behaviors based on our expectations of and experiences with five-year-olds. Tony appeared to be quite ordinary and average. His intellectual, linguistic (language), physical, social, and emotional development were appropriate for his age. He was, in many ways, typical in comparison to other five-year-olds. Later, during our first parent conference, we discovered that Tony's father was the president of a local college. If we had known that fact, it is likely we might have treated Tony as if he was an exceptional child. His physical development was perhaps more advanced; at five, he could skip well, pump himself on a swing, and was beginning to learn how to jump rope. He also had good ball-handling skills and could catch and throw competently. (Tony had ample opportunity to swing, jump rope, throw and catch a ball, and learn how to skip because he had an older brother who encouraged him to learn these skills.) We might have expected Tony's language development to be advanced; he was exposed to a sophisticated level of language every day through contact with his father and mother. Regarding social and emotional development, Tony again seemed to be average for his age; he had several friends among the boys of his own age group; he seemed to have the usual amount of curiosity and competence for boys of his age.

If we had known that Tony's father was a college president, we could have expected more from Tony than what he could deliver. What are the results of expecting more than a child can deliver? The child may stop trying to succeed. Another result is that the child may become aggressive and frustrated when asked to accomplish more than the child is able to do.

Assume that Tony is a current student of ours. Should an individual learning plan be developed for Tony? The activities offered to the other children would most likely be appropriate for Tony. Let us also assume we had a conference with his parents. From this meeting, we discovered that they have high hopes for Tony's success in school. In fact, they had placed him in a preschool to increase his "readiness" for kindergarten. They state that because Tony already knows the alphabet letters and sounds, they expect him to begin to learn how to read and want him placed in a preprimer. Because they insist that Tony also knows his numerals to 100, they also expect him to begin to learn addition and subtraction. Furthermore, they expect Tony to become more attentive, to increase his attention span. Tony's parents expressed no interest in Tony's physical learning experiences. They feel that he does not need any specific teaching in terms of physical ability; because he has a climbing structure at home, he receives all the physical exercise he needs.

In this hypothetical situation, some of Tony's parents' goals will be met through the regular curriculum. We might honestly feel that some of their other goals are more appropriate for first grade. Should we tell his parents this? Will they listen?

We can reassure Tony's parents that we share some of the same goals. We can remind them to attend the upcoming Back-to-School Night, at which time the goals and expectations of our program will be explained. We can stress to Tony's parents that helping Tony feel good about himself is as worthwhile a goal as is allowing him time to explore the different activities available in our classroom.

Figure 9–13 Working on a one-to-one basis

What is the student teacher's role in working with Tony? It could be to give him a one-to-one learning opportunity. The cooperating teacher might ask you to confirm whether or not Tony (and other children as well) recognizes the alphabet letters and sounds, and whether he understands the concept of numbers or has simply memorized his numerals from 1 to 100. As a result of your checking how much Tony and any of the other children know and remember from preschool, the cooperating teacher might decide that the parents' expectations are not appropriate. In the meantime, however, in order to let the parents feel more confident about the kindergarten program, the cooperating teacher might assign you to work with Tony on a one-to-one basis. The cooperating teacher may feel that in time, Tony's parents will realize that their expectations are unrealistic.

We have suggested thus far that the student teacher has a role in observing children who are chosen by the cooperating teacher, the supervisor, or the student teacher herself. A second role is that of working on a one-to-one basis with an individual child (see Figure 9–13). The student teacher may also be a participant in parent conferences and in-school and out-of-school activities.

parent education—programs aimed at enhancing parent-child relations and improving parenting competence.

Student teachers quite naturally are invited (and urged) to attend functions such as parent education meetings, staff conferences, parent or school-sponsored dinners, and fund-raising events. The student teacher should become a part of the life of the school or child care center.

Conferencing

The student teacher is often included in parent conferences, and defers to the cooperating teacher for the most part. Naturally, if you are asked a direct question by either the parent or teacher, you should answer. Primarily, however, your role will be that of observer rather than participant. You should remember that statements made at a parent conference are confidential. The privacy of parents and children should be respected. Do not repeat anything that was said with others except when appropriate. For example, if your cooperating teacher asks you for your opinions after a conference, you would naturally discuss them. Also, the cooperating teacher might assign you the task of reporting on the conference.

One exception to this rule of confidentiality occurs in student teaching seminars. It is appropriate to discuss your student teaching assignment with your peers and supervisor, but child and family names are confidential.

Referral Resources

Many schools and early childhood care centers have a list of local resources a student teacher may examine. Most also require parents to list their family doctor and other pertinent emergency information at the time of registration. Frequently, low-cost clinics are used for referrals. The same is true for dental care. Under PL 101-476, most preschools and centers are expected to refer suspected special needs children for testing to their local elementary school districts, and many also refer, on the request of parents, to private counseling services, educational psychologists, or psychiatrists.

Two other frequently used resources are county child care referral services and child abuse agencies. Your local telephone book will have county office listings. In California, for example, most counties have a Child Care Coordinating Council, or Four Cs as it is widely known. Four Cs is a resource for all parents and schools, centers, and family child care homes. They maintain up-to-date lists of licensed schools, centers, and family child care homes, among other resources listed. Four Cs will also assist the newcomer who wants to inquire about licensing a new family child care home. They can provide information on local resources that are not available from other sources. For example, a newcomer with a child who has a health special need may know of a national organization but not a local one. Other parents may not know of local chapters because they do not know about the national organization itself. Currently, one of the growing needs of families is after-school child care. Fortunately, many school districts operate on-site, after-school care programs. Others contract with their local parks and recreation departments or with local nonprofit organizations such as the YMCA or parent-sponsored groups. Bussing is frequently supplied for children who have to be transported from their school to another facility. Student teachers occasionally are encouraged to become after-school care workers in order to supplement their incomes.

Other referral sources are public and private social services. These services can offer a wide variety of help ranging from food stamps to foster home care to financial aid to Alcoholics Anonymous.

More Examples of Developing Individual Learning Plans

At this point, we would like to present a few other models of individual learning plans so that you can try out different forms to see which works best.

Study Figure 9–14. It is a lesson plan for second-grade science and focuses on the topic of pets. The classroom contains several pets: a rabbit, a mouse, an aquarium with tropical fish, and a terrarium with a turtle. The cooperating teacher has brought her pet parakeet for the children to observe, and at the end of the week, she is planning a "Pets' Day." Parents have been duly notified; children who wish will bring their pets into the courtyard outside the classroom. Those without pets at home have been provided with several options: using one of the classroom pets and studying it during the week of "Pets' Day" and reporting on that pet as their own; designing their own special pet and making a clay or papier-mâché model of it, specifying what it eats, when it sleeps, and so on; choosing one of the many books about pets, ordinary and unusual, and presenting an oral informational report about the pet they've chosen from the book; and so forth. Extra supervision has been elicited from among the parents who have volunteered for occasional help. And, as the student teacher assigned to the classroom, you have been asked by your cooperating teacher to design an individual plan for Joelle.

Let us assume that Joelle's mother had been suspected of child abuse when Joelle was in first grade and that the teacher had even reported one incident of suspicious bruises to Child Protective Services (CPS). After an investigation, CPS did not feel removal from the home was justified but did recommend counseling for the mother. (The father had deserted the family on the birth of Joelle's youngest sibling, and your cooperating teacher has told you that Joelle comes from a large

Learning Plans. Note in looking at Figure 9–15 that the student teacher's individual learning plan is not totally separate from her cooperating teacher's; instead, it dovetails with her's. Mrs. Gomes has asked the student teacher to design the integrated unit on pets and added her own suggestions where she has

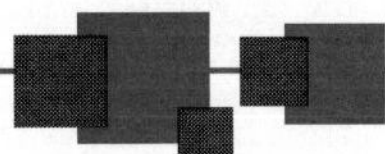

Morning Block: 8:45 A.M.–12:30 P.M.

8:30 A.M.: Greet Joelle with a smile when she enters, stay near her desk as students begin journal assignment to help her if she seems to have difficulty getting started, and to ask her questions to stimulate her thinking, if this seems necessary. Perhaps ask her if she has a pet and what it is. (I've noticed that Joelle usually arrives at school between 8:30 and 8:35 A.M. and generally settles down initially to write or draw in her journal, so my job here will be to help her with her thoughts and spelling, if she asks, which she has done in the past.)

8:45 A.M.: I'll be reading The Biggest Bear; when students are asked for ideas about what they think will happen next, I'll look to see if Joelle has her hand raised and be sure to call on her, and, I hope, compliment her response.

Work with Joelle's cooperative learning group. Look for signs of frustration on her part; remind other students in the group that there are no bad ideas. (I've noted that sometimes the others in her group don't listen to Joelle or ignore her input because they sometimes think what she says isn't of value in their eyes. A gentle reminder usually helps.)

If I sense that Joelle is getting ready to explode, I'll urge her to come with me to the back of the room where I've set up a special lesson, related to the topics of pets, she can work on. (I've brought in 25 pounds of clay for students to use in various art projects and I'll urge Joelle to punch and pound the clay to smooth out the air bubbles and make a model of her pet or an imaginary one. The punching and pounding is needed to remove the air bubbles anyway, and it should help relieve some of the anger I've seen Joelle display.)

9:50 A.M.: I'll be going out with Joelle to the play yard to try to observe what sets her off. If possible, I hope to be able to intervene before any arguments. I'm going to work with her using some of the ideas from the conflict resolution lessons or other simple ideas like counting to 10 before acting; taking a deep breath; going to another part of the play yard; talking to me; and so on. (I don't know how successful any of these may be, and I'm hopeful, too, that a reminder of some of the conflict resolution ideas she learned earlier this year may be enough to get Joelle to think before she strikes.)

10:00 A.M.: During this part of the morning, I'll be busy asking the children what kinds of pets they have and writing the categories on the chalkboard. I'll be especially alert to Joelle's participation at this point. If she does not participate and, especially if she makes any negative remarks or looks angry, my cooperative teacher is prepared to take over for me, and I'll take Joelle to the art room. (We are fortunate at our school that we have a separate room for art activities that we can not do in the regular classroom. I'm fortunate in that few classes use the art room during the mornings. But, I'll check the schedule when I come to school. If necessary, I'll switch plans and take Joelle to the art room initially and to the back of our room now.) Because I will have already determined what kind of pet Joelle either has or hasn't or what kind of pet she would really like to have, what we'll be doing in the art room is constructing a "home" for her pet with the wood scraps available there. This activity will allow Joelle to pound nails with the hammer, and again, provide her with a way to vent her anger.

10:45 A.M.: If we are still in the art room, I'll ask Joelle if she wants to return to the classroom or stay here for snack time.

11:00 A.M.: PE—Joelle rarely has difficulty during PE because she likes the activities and Mrs. Okahara.

11:40 A.M.: If necessary, accompany Joelle to counselor; otherwise repeat other steps.

Figure 9–15 Learning plan for Joelle. Topic: pets

thought it necessary. Notice that although the student teacher is to conduct the brainstorming session, Mrs. Gomes is prepared to take over should Joelle become unruly. This is a cooperative effort on the part of the two; Mrs. Gomes has assigned Joelle to the student teacher in the hope that working on a one-to-one basis with a new person and being given a choice of narrowly defined activities will demonstrate to Joelle that there are acceptable ways to show anger that do not hurt anyone.

How has Mrs. Gomes arrived at this course of action? First, she has taken into account that many children who are abused are angry and aggressive, and that schools see this aggression in fighting behavior on the play yard and destructive behaviors in the classroom. Together with the school counselor, Mrs. Gomes, the student teacher, and the principal have designed the plan for Joelle. Not every elementary school has a counselor, but this district has made an effort to reduce aggressive acts in schools with a high incidence of vandalism and acts of violence against pupils. One of the reasons behind the district's problem has been the closing of a large manufacturing plant that had employed a majority of the town's workers. Recently there have been a rise in the divorce rate, more cases of alcoholism, and an increasing number of reported child abuse incidents. This cooperative action works well with students like Joelle who have special needs but who are not, under federal definitions, "children with disabilities."

There will be times when a student teacher is asked to work one to one with a special needs or at-risk child. We will cover this in greater detail in our next chapter.

Parent Involvement. We have not discussed in detail the parents' role in the development of an individual learning plan. The best plans are those made with the parents' approval and support. Certainly, in the case of Stevie, the mother seems to care and be concerned. Although she may not see any reason to worry about Stevie's social behavior at home, she may be easily persuaded that he could be more social at school.

In Maria's case, her mother might want Maria to learn both English and Spanish. That could be her reason for placing Maria in a bilingual center. In writing an individual learning plan for Maria, then, the mother's concern that Maria retain her knowledge of Spanish while learning English must be respected.

In the example of Tony, the problem is possibly that the parents' goals are different than those of the school, at least initially. Assigning the student teacher to work with Tony on a one-to-one basis might be all that is necessary, especially because he is typical for his age.

We have provided a model of an individual plan for a possibly abused second grader, Joelle. As the oldest child of five in a dysfunctional family, she appears to need clear limits, suggestions for alternative actions, and, very likely, more attention from a CAREing adult. The clear limits are based on an analysis (using the Dreikur model) of her aggressive actions as revenge against her mother's suspected abuse that is generalized against all adults in a position of authority. Offering Joelle a choice between two alternatives helps her resolve her need to exert autonomy and recognizes her need for power or control over at least one part of her life. (We would suspect that she has very little power at home.) Not mentioned, but applicable in this example, are the logical consequences that have been arranged for antisocial behavior at this particular school: isolation or removal from the class by segregation at the front or back of the room under supervision of a student teacher, aide, or parent volunteer; removal to the art room; removal to talk to the counselor. In each example, the removal does not exclude the student from an assignment because alternatives related to the primary assignment are offered.

You should note in all of our examples that the goal of the school is parent education as well as child education. Especially in Stevie's and Tony's cases, where the parents' perceptions of the children differ with those of the school, it is important for the teacher and/or director to enable the parent to see more clearly what the child's needs are at school. This is not always easy to accomplish. Sometimes, compromises must be made. One such compromise is suggested in the example of Joelle by having the student teacher work with her on a one-to-one basis to establish rapport and provide alternative actions to channel her aggressive tendencies.

SUMMARY

In this chapter, we presented several examples of observation techniques. The simplest is the narrative, but it also requires the most time. Although it is more complicated, the Teacher/Pupil Interaction Scale (TPIS) takes little time, can be put onto a 3 x 5 index card, is inconspicuous, and can be supplemented with comments to the side describing the action being noted. Also introduced were the two-dimensional play model and a time sampling model; an anecdotal record form was reviewed. No one form is any better than any other, and student teachers are urged to use their own creativity to devise forms for their own specific uses.

We discussed the development of an individual learning plan for a child. Examples of how an individual plan dovetails with the cooperating teacher's plan were presented. In addition, we discussed the roles of the parent, school, and student teacher in developing and implementing such a plan.

HELPFUL WEB SITES

http://ericee.org

ERIC. Strategies to enhance the achievement of gifted minority children. Click on digests.

http://zerotothree.org

National Center for Infants, Toddlers, and Families. General information and publications.

http://www.apa.org/

The American Psychological Association. Search "early childhood assessment."

http://ericps.ed.uiuc.edu

National Child Care Information Center. Disseminates child care information and provides linkages.

SUGGESTED ACTIVITIES

A. Try out some of the observation forms presented. Discuss the results of data gathered in terms of effective information received.

B. Select a child, with your cooperating teacher's approval, for whom you will develop an individual learning plan. Implement the plan and evaluate its effectiveness. Use the form in Figure 9–8 or look at the example in Figure 9–14.

C. Think of one child you are currently trying to help. With a group of classmates, discuss what learning outcomes would be visible (seen in the child's behavior or performance) if you succeeded beyond your wildest dreams. List attempts (teaching strategies) that might produce the observable learning and observable changes in the child. Think about environmental factors, scheduling, teacher words or behaviors, planned child activities, and conferences with others as possible teaching strategies.

D. Read the following situations. Then read the statement made by a parent. What would you consider to be an appropriate response? Discuss your responses with your peers, cooperating teacher, and supervisor.

1. One day, Tony gets into a fight with Alfredo. As you know, Tony's father is a college president and his mother a well-educated CPA; however, Alfredo is from a single-parent family. He also belongs to an ethnic and religious minority. The fight was provoked by Alfredo who perceives Tony as stuck up. Your cooperating teacher calls both of Tony's parents and asks for a conference. Tony's mother responds immediately and says, "What's going on in your school? How come Tony got assaulted? What are you going to do about it?"

2. Joelle Farmer arrives at school one morning with bruises on her arm. (As mentioned previously, abuse had been reported when Joelle was in first grade.) You suspect that Mrs. Farmer has abused the child again, and with your cooperating teacher's permission, you walk with Joelle to the nurse's office. After her examination, the nurse confirms your suspicions and suggests that the police should be notified. "Why don't we call CPS?" you ask. The school nurse replies, "Because Joelle has been abused before and the investigation by CPS was inconclusive, and frankly, I think nothing was done and I think we might accomplish more if we call the police. You do know that only the police can remove Joelle from the custody of her mother, don't you?" Returning to Mrs. Gomes' room, you tell her what the nurse has suggested: you are not sure that you should be the person making the phone call to the police. Mrs. Gomes reassures you that she will make the call during the first recess.

   Later that morning, Mrs. Farmer storms into the classroom and screams, "Who do you think you are calling the police on me? Are you telling me I beat up my own kid?"

3. You are concerned about Mark's apparent neglect. He arrives at preschool in dirty, torn clothing. His hair would never be combed if it were not done at school; he often smells of stale urine and fecal matter. You discover that his underpants look like they have been worn for a month without having been washed. You ask the cooperating teacher if you and she can make a home visit. The mother says, "No. The mister don't want no one to come when he ain't home." You finally persuade her that it is important to talk about Mark. She reluctantly agrees. After the usual opening remarks, you ask, "Do you have a washing machine at home?" Mark's mother responds negatively, eyes you suspiciously, and asks, "What business is it of yours whether the mister and me has a washing machine?"

4. Kathy Mumford caught your attention for two reasons. First, she is always cocking her head to one side and holding it close to the paper when she draws or writes. You notice she frequently squints when she tries to read material on the chalkboard and has, more than once, copied a math "sponge" problem incorrectly. One day, she even asked you if she could switch seats with Alicia so she could see the side chalkboard more easily. You have also had to repeat directions for Kathy and have noticed that she sometimes asks her seatmate to reexplain directions to her. You do not have the services of a school nurse, so you call Kathy's mother and ask if she can come to the school for a short conference. In the meantime, you

look at Kathy's registration form and doctor's statement. The doctor has noted a slight nearsightedness but no apparent hearing problem. You suspect that Kathy has deficiencies in both, yet you hesitate to contradict Kathy's pediatrician. When Mrs. Mumford arrives, you decide to ask about Kathy's behavior at home. Mrs. Mumford admits that Kathy does sit close to the television and seems inattentive at times. "I thought Kathy might have a problem hearing but Mr. Mumford, he put an end to Kathy's not hearing. You know what he did? He sat in the kitchen while she was in the family room and whispered, 'Kathy, do you want some ice cream, honey?' Well, Kathy answered right away! Mr. Mumford and I both think Kathy just gets too involved in things. She's not deaf!"

5. Josip is one of those students who never sits still for a minute. He moves around constantly from the moment he enters the child care center until nap time, when he must be urged strongly to lie down. Nap time is agony for Josip; he twists and turns, grumbles, sighs to himself, and disturbs everyone around him. Yet when he does fall asleep, you have difficulty awakening him. Sometimes, in fact, your cooperating teacher has allowed him to continue to sleep. You think Josip may not get enough sleep at night and decide, with your cooperating teacher's approval, to ask his mother about it. "Mrs. Milutin, when does Josip go to bed?" you ask. "Sometimes he really takes a long nap at school."

   Mrs. Milutin responds, "Well, of course he sleeps at school! That is why his father and I cannot get him to sleep at home! Maybe if you do not allow Josip to sleep at school, he will sleep better at home!"

E. Read the following. Discuss with a small group of classmates while answering the questions below.

   "Today, more children than ever before come to school with addictions, diseases, and disorders such as fetal alcohol syndrome, and without having had sufficient sleep, food, or supervision at home" (Grant & Murray, 1999).

   1. Would you say this quote applies mostly to elementary school children?
   2. Have you suspected children in your placement class may have problems one could attribute to one of these factors? If so, what have you noticed?

REVIEW

A. List examples of observation techniques, and state at least one reason why each technique is effective.

B. Read the following descriptions of behavior. For each child, analyze and develop a learning plan that contains at least one general behavioral objective.

   1. Denise, a five-year-old kindergartner, is sitting on the swing. "Teacher, come push me," she demands. "Try to pump, Denise," responds the teacher. "Don't know how," Denise whines. "Push me, Susan," Denise says to a child going by on a tricycle. "Can't now. Push yourself," answers Susan. Pete comes up to the swing. "Get off and let me swing," he states. "No! My swing!" Denise cries. (Denise looks like she is going to cry.) The teacher's aide comes over and asks, "Do you want me to show you how to make the swing go?" Denise answers, "Please."
   2. The following chart was developed by Greg, a student teacher in a first-grade classroom. He was interested in Brian's attending behavior. Starting with the TPIS, he adapted it into a simpler form on which he could check

off observations as he noticed them throughout the 9:00 A.M. to 10:00 A.M. activity hour. On a 3 x 5 card, which he could hold in his palm, Greg drew a vertical line, dividing the card in half lengthwise. He then wrote "Attending" on one side, "Nonattending" on the other. (Question: How much attending behavior should the teacher expect of a six-year-old during a free-choice center activity period? Do Greg's observations appear to provide sufficient information to develop any conjectures about Brian's behavior? What hypotheses might you suggest regarding Brian's sitting under the desk behavior? Discuss the possibilities with your student teacher peers and instructor.) (See Figure 9–16.)

3. Johnny, a three-and-a-half-year-old in a morning preschool, is the subject of the third observation. The two-dimensional play model, combining event and time sampling, was used to gather data. (Question: Do three-year-olds do as much onlooking and solitary play as Johnny? Should you be concerned?) (See Figure 9–17.)

4. Jimmy is a four-year-old at a private child care center. Figure 9–18 is a time sample of his behavior during outside free play. (Question: Is Jimmy's poor gross motor coordination something about which the teacher should be concerned?)

Attending	Nonattending			
Mon.	9:05	yes (t.i.)*		
	9:16		no	(sitting
	9:27		no	under desk)
	9:40		no	
	9:48	yes (t.i.)		
Tues.	9:07		no	
	9:18		no	
	9:25	yes (t.i.)		
	9:34	yes		
	9:40		no	(sitting
	9:47		no	under the
	9:55		no	desk again)
Wed.	9:02		no	
	9:12	yes (t.i.)		
	9:20	yes (t.i.)		
	9:35		no	
	9:42		no	
	9:58		no	
Thurs.	9:05		no	
	9:15	yes (t.i.)		
	9:33	yes		
	9:48		no	(back under
	9:55		no	the desk again)
Fri.	Brian was absent			

*t.i. = teacher initiated

Figure 9–16 Attending/nonattending chart

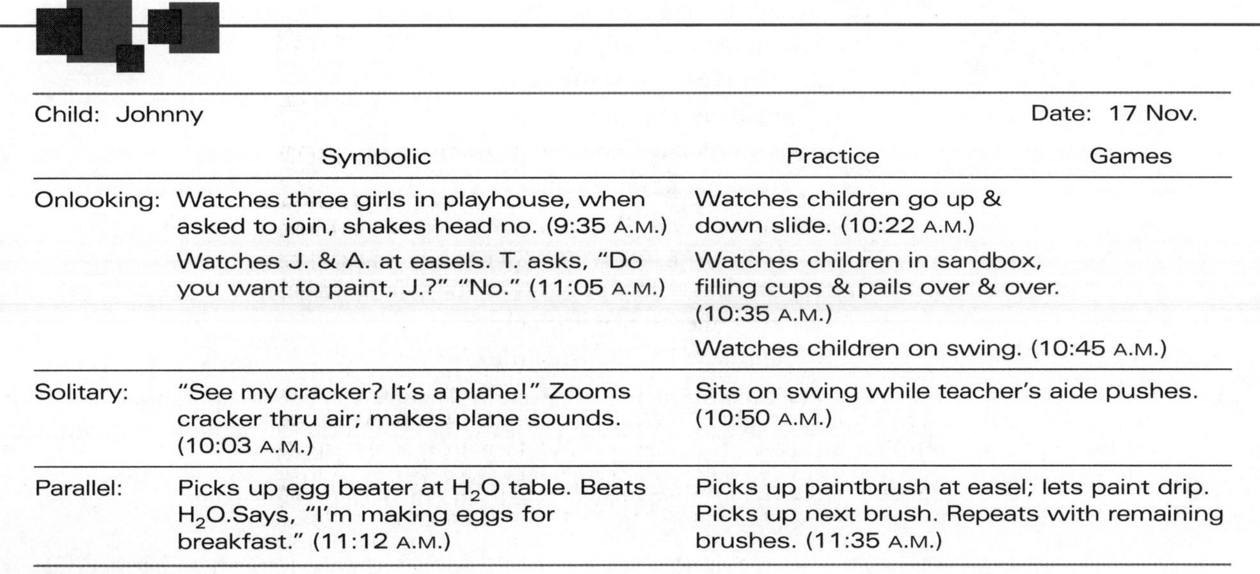

Child: Johnny   Date: 17 Nov.

	Symbolic	Practice	Games
Onlooking:	Watches three girls in playhouse, when asked to join, shakes head no. (9:35 A.M.) Watches J. & A. at easels. T. asks, "Do you want to paint, J.?" "No." (11:05 A.M.)	Watches children go up & down slide. (10:22 A.M.) Watches children in sandbox, filling cups & pails over & over. (10:35 A.M.) Watches children on swing. (10:45 A.M.)	
Solitary:	"See my cracker? It's a plane!" Zooms cracker thru air; makes plane sounds. (10:03 A.M.)	Sits on swing while teacher's aide pushes. (10:50 A.M.)	
Parallel:	Picks up egg beater at H_2O table. Beats H_2O.Says, "I'm making eggs for breakfast." (11:12 A.M.)	Picks up paintbrush at easel; lets paint drip. Picks up next brush. Repeats with remaining brushes. (11:35 A.M.)	

Figure 9–17 Observation sample

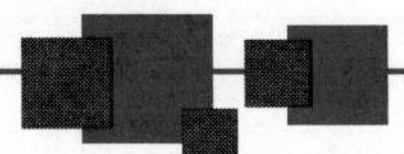

10:05 A.M.: J. runs stiffly toward two of his friends on tricycles. "Let me ride!" he shouts.

10:10 A.M.: J. is happily riding on the back of E.'s tricycle. E. has to stop to let J. climb on. J. first placed his left foot on, lifted it off, placed the same foot on again, took it off; finally he put his right foot on and then successfully put his left foot on.

10:15 A.M.: J. is still riding on the back of E.'s tricycle.

10:20 A.M.: J. and E. have switched places. J. had difficulty pedaling up the slight grade. E. pushed from behind.

10:25 A.M.: E. has suggested that he, J., and S. go to the workbench. J. picks up the hammer and a nail. He hits the nail awkwardly into a block of wood. E. says, "Hey, watch me! Hold the nail like this!"

10:30 A.M.: E. is holding J.'s hands with his, showing him how to drive the nail into the block of wood.

10:35 A.M.: J. is sitting in the sandbox, shoveling sand into a bucket. E. is still at the work bench.

10:40 A.M.: J. is putting sand into another bucket. He looks surprised when the bucket overflows. He reaches for the first bucket. S. says, "I'm using it now," and pushes a third pail toward J.

10:45 A.M.: J. and S. are smoothing down the sand, calling it a road. They go and get a couple of cars to run on their road. E. joins them, having completed his project at the workbench.

10:50 A.M.: When called to clean up for activity time, J. climbs out of the sandbox. As he does this, his foot catches on the edge and he falls down. He gives the sandbox a kick and joins the others to come inside.

Figure 9–18 Observation time sample

C. Identify each of the following statements as either inferences or observations.
 1. Juan likes to read.
 2. Susette has a new dress.
 3. Sammy is a mean boy.
 4. Kimberly has emotional problems.
 5. Janine has a smile on her face.
 6. Mikel hit Sandel on the playground.
 7. Maria had a frown on her face.
 8. Mark looks unhappy.
 9. Kathy likes to play with clay.
 10. Lupe is an affectionate little girl.

D. For each of the five children in Chapter 9, write an appropriate behavioral objective for an individual learning plan in the curriculum area indicated.
 1. Tony will be able to . . .
 (An objective related to learning the letters in his name)
 2. Joelle will be able to . . .
 (An objective related to writing a short paragraph about her pet)
 3. Maya will be able to . . .
 (An objective related to her creating at least two original tangrams)
 4. Kathy will be able to . . .
 (An objective related to classifying at least five common fruits and vegetables in the proper class)
 5. Josip will be able to . . .
 (An objective related to trying at least two or three foods that are new to him)

CASE SCENARIO

Setting: A large urban preschool and extended day child care center. Many children are from ethnically diverse families. The student teacher, Jui-Li, has been placed in a room of three-year-olds. Suzon, the cooperating teacher, and Lili, her assistant, are bilingual in at least one of the home languages in the classroom.

Jui-Li is both observing and helping. She has developed a few activities that Suzon has let her try. There is one child, Lucia, about whom Jui-Li has questions. The following conversation starts with Lili and later involves Suzon.

Jui-Li states. "I can't understand why Lucia acts so angry all the time. If I hadn't intervened this morning during circle time, she would have hit Jorge with that small block she had hidden in her hand."

"You have to keep your eyes on Lucia. I know when I haven't, she's knocked down a tower someone has built,

continues . . .

. . . continued

smashed a puzzle, and even torn a painting hung to dry. One day when I wasn't looking, she even chewed on one of the books in the reading area! You can see her teeth marks all over it; fortunately, though, it's a board book!" Lili tells Jui-Li.

After saying "Goodbye" to the last child, Suzon walks into the room and joins the conversation. Turning to Jui-Li, she asks, "You've studied child development. How might that knowledge help you in understanding Lucia's acting out behavior?"

"I guess, according to Erikson, there might be a question about whether Lucia has ever resolved the very first task of infancy. I honestly don't think she trusts anybody. And if I look at the Maslow hierarchy, I might question whether she has enough to eat. She often arrives in the same ill-fitting clothes every day and she really needs a bath! There may be a question as to whether her basic needs have been met. Do these possibilities seem reasonable?" Jui-Li inquires.

"Do you know where she lives?" asks Suzon. "Or if she has a family? Perhaps I should fill you in on some of the background, but confidentiality is a must.

Questions for Discussion:

1. What might cause a child not to have resolved Erikson's "basic trust?"
2. Why would a child destroy another child's work or try to hit an another child?
3. What hypotheses might you advance about Lucia's family?
4. Should Lucia be discussed with Jui-Li's college supervisor? Is the child's name important to a discussion?

REFERENCES

Ayers, W. (1993). *To teach: The journey of a teacher.* New York: Teachers College Press.

Grant, G., & Murray C. (1999). *Teaching in America: The slow revolution.* Cambridge, MA: Harvard University Press.

Paley, V. G. (1992). *You can't say you can't play.* Cambridge, MA: Harvard University Press.

Parten, M. B. (1932). Social participation among preschool children. *Journal of Abnormal and Social Psychology, 33.*

Piaget, J. (1962). *Play, dreams and imitation in childhood.* New York: W. W. Norton.

Ward, L. (1952). *The biggest bear*. Boston: Houghton Mifflin.

Working with Children with Special Needs

Objectives After studying this chapter, the student should be able to:

1. Define "special."
2. List at least five characteristics of "special" children.
3. State the categories of "special need" according to the Individuals with Disabilities Education Act, PL 101-476.
4. Discuss the concept of "least restrictive environment."
5. Discuss the implications of "least restrictive environment" to the teacher of an early childhood program.
6. Discuss the implications of recent special education laws for preschools, child care centers, and elementary schools.

Just when I thought I knew the characteristics of two-year-olds well, along came Gregory! He taught me to look for new ways to reach individual children.

—Danielle Tracy

I was asked to work with one of the children who had a learning disability. I really got involved in what was happening in the child's home. I became interested in the child's life.

—Deanna Miller

When I started student teaching in Ms. Hessler's first grade class, I wondered who Jessica was. She always had an aide who seemed to work only with her. She wouldn't always look at me when I spoke to her. What a surprise to learn she was supposedly autistic! I never would have guessed!

—Brianna FitzGerald

At first I had real problems understanding Eric; his speech was so full of mispronunciations. It surprised me that his classmates seemed to know exactly what he was trying to say. Before I finished student teaching, though, I too had little difficulty understanding him.

—Samantha Hope Maier

LAWS RELATING TO THE EDUCATION OF YOUNG CHILDREN WITH SPECIAL NEEDS

We know that most of you think that all children are special; we do also. However, it is important to recognize that some children have needs beyond those of the average child; some have needs that can be met only by a team of specialists working together for the welfare of the children. To meet the needs of "special" children, the federal government has passed several laws related to people with special needs (see Figure 10–1). Although the first was passed nearly forty years ago (Public Law 89-313, 1965), the primary laws that currently define how preschools, child care centers, and public schools are to serve special needs children are PL 94-142, PL 99-457, PL 101-119, and the subsequent amendments to the latter.

The Education of All Handicapped Children Act, PL 94-142

The provisions of Public Law 94-142 have been repeated, with some amendments, in most of the subsequent laws related to special education. These are:

PL 89-313	(1965)	Provided federal funds to establish early intervention programs for "children with disabilities," birth to age five. (Voluntary.)
PL 90-538	(1968)	Established the Handicapped Children's Early Education Program (HCEEP), now the Early Education Program for Children with Disabilities (EEPCD). (Voluntary initially.)
PL 91-230	(1969)	Provided funds to states for the education of "young children with disabilities." (Voluntary.)
PL 93-644	(1974)	Amended Head Start legislation and required that 10 percent of children served must be those with disabilities.
PL 94-142	(1975)	The Education for All Handicapped Children Act; discussed in detail in this chapter.
PL 98-199	(1983)	Provided grants to states to plan, develop, and implement a service delivery system for handicapped children, birth through age five. (Mandatory for states receiving federal funds.)
PL 99-457	(1986)	Again provided funds to states to plan services for children, birth through age five, as a condition to receiving further federal funds. (Essentially, then, became mandatory.) Also discussed in this chapter.
PL 101-336	(1990)	Americans with Disabilities Act: Required that individuals with disabilities, including children, have equal access to public and private services.
PL 101-476	(1990)	The Individuals with Disabilities Act (IDEA); discussed in this chapter.*
PL 102-119	(1991)	Allowed states up to two years to implement PL 101-476 (IDEA), because of differences between fiscal years of some states and federal government.

In 1994 through 2003, PL 101-476 has been evaluated and refunded. Since the passage of IDEA in 1997, the emphasis in making placements for special needs children has been on inclusion, IDEA could be seen as the Inclusion of the Disabled in Education Act (Lewis & Doorlag, 2003).

*This act has been evaluated and refunded. The act (IDEA) has emphasized the inclusion of children with special needs (Lewis & Doorlag, 2003).

Figure 10–1 Public laws related to special education for young children

- A free and appropriate public education for all special needs children. (Included are special education and related services, and the use of the term "handicapped" and the stipulation of ages five to 18 years as age limits. States with programs for children between the ages of three to five are also covered.)
- Each child identified as needing special education or related services must have an Individual Education Program (IEP) written by the multidisciplinary team working with the child and approved by the parents.
- Parents are to be involved at every step in the process from identification, assessment, educational placement, and evaluation of that placement. Furthermore, parents must agree to the assessment procedures used to identify the need for services, and approve the IEP and the evaluation.
- Each child is to be placed in the "least restrictive environment" (LRE) (see Figures 10–2, 10–3, and 10–4).
- Due process is guaranteed for every child and family. The parents have the right to sue a district if they feel that the best interests of their child are not being met.
- Any assessment of the child must be done with instruments that are nondiscriminatory in terms of race and ethnicity. Assessment must also be in the child's dominant language or in the child's preferred mode of communication (sign, for example).

Individual Education Program (IEP)—with special needs children, an individual education program that states the short-term and long-term learning objectives, how they will be accomplished and by whom, and applicable dates. It must be approved by both parents and school.

least restrictive environment—a provision of Public Law 94-142 that handicapped children be placed in a program as close as possible to a setting designed for nonhandicapped children, while being able to meet each child's special needs.

Figure 10–2 The "least restrictive environment" may be having the child sit in a special chair . . .

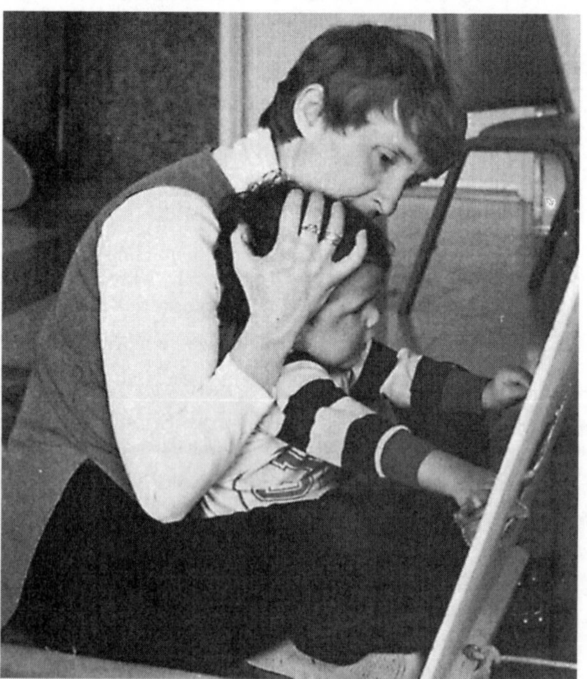

Figure 10–3 . . . or it may be having the physical therapist position the child's head while the child uses his arms . . .

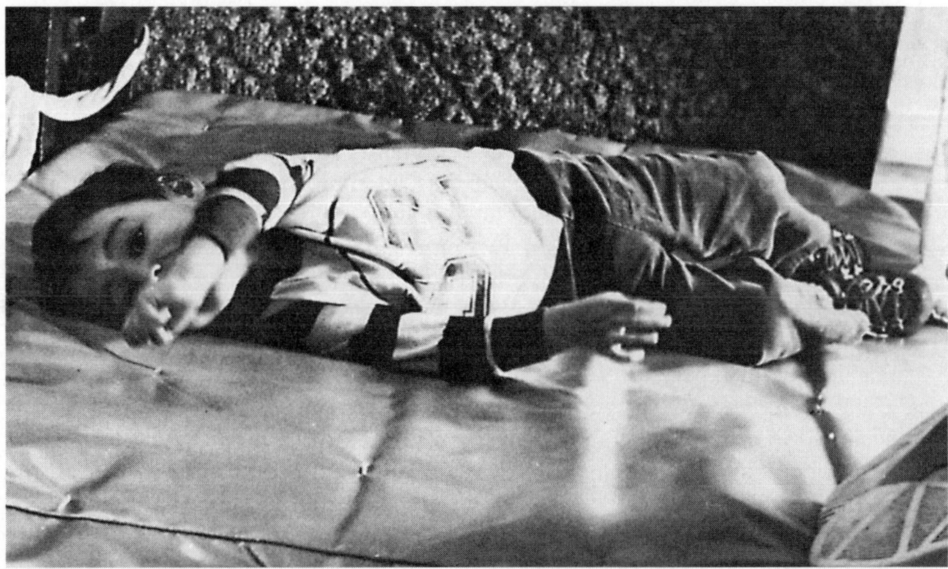

Figure 10-4 . . . or it may be letting the child roll free on a mat.

Amendments to the Education of All Handicapped Children Act, PL 99-457

These amendments include the following:

- Children between the ages of three and five years are to receive the same free services as PL 94-142 guaranteed to those between the years of five to 18, even in those states that did not originally have programs for preschoolers.
- They are to receive an Individual Family Service Plan (IFSP); the equivalent of an IEP for school-aged children) in recognition of the importance of involving the family in programs for the very young.
- State grants for programs for infants and toddlers are also to be funded so that states may develop comprehensive, coordinated, multidisciplinary, interagency programs.
- Recognizing the difficulty of being able to pinpoint specific diagnoses with the very young is the release from the requirement to label categorically. Thus, the very young child being serviced under PL 99-457 does not have to be specifically labeled, as under PL 99-142, to receive services.

Individualized Family Service Plan (IFSP)—required by the 1986 Education of the Handicapped Act Amendments for handicapped children under the age of three and their families; the IFSP, often developed by a transdisciplinary team that includes the parents, determines goals and objectives that build on the strengths of the child and family.

Both the "special" and "normal" child profit from association with each other. One private preschool has a policy to integrate "special" and "normal" children. The director allows four identified "special" children in a class of 24. Over the period of 30 years since this policy has been in effect, the school has taught mentally retarded children, children with orthopedic problems, and partially sighted, hard of hearing, emotionally disturbed, speech-impaired, and health-impaired children, as well as other children who were not as yet identified as having specific learning disabilities. With parental permission, other children can learn to help orthopedically impaired children with bathroom visits and other activities, and both children profit.

Individuals with Disabilities Education Act, PL 101-476

With the passage in 1990 of the Individuals with Disabilities Education Act (IDEA), not only were the provisions of PL 94-142 and its amendments incorporated into the new law, but the term "handicapped" became "children with disabilities." Added to the law was a provision for children whose first language or mode of communication might not be English. Two more categories of special needs were defined by PL 101-576: children with autism and children with traumatic brain injuries. Three additional services were also included: rehabilitation counseling, social work services, and spoken descriptions of on-screen video productions (DVS) that are provided over the second of two audio channels on stereo television sets.

Prior to the passage of PL 101-476, PL 101-336 (1990), known as the Americans with Disabilities Act, became law. The Americans with Disabilities Act is "major civil rights legislation that extends beyond educational issues. Specifically, it requires that individuals with disabilities have equal access and reasonable accommodations to public and private services, including equal access to enrollment in early childhood facilities" (Wolery & Wilbers, 1994).

Implications of Special Education Laws

Perhaps the major shift in providing services in recent years has been the concept of inclusion. Inclusion has led to having various kinds of special needs children, even those with severe disabilities, included in regular classrooms both at the preschool and public school level. What it means for you as a student teacher is that you may be asked by your cooperating teacher to work with a special needs child.

It is clear that the public laws include early childhood education. For this reason, you are likely to find some special needs children in your school or center.

Student Teaching with Children with Special Needs

Student teachers in two-year degree or other shorter training programs may feel inadequate because few of their academic classes touched in depth or in detail on teaching strategies, goals, specific disabilities, program modifications, and so on that would prepare them to work with children with special needs. Baccalaureate level student teachers also may not have encountered specific special education coursework. Many states now require a class on working with children with special needs for certification or licensing.

An understanding of the positive aspects of including young children with special needs in regular classrooms helps.

Advocates of inclusion usually cite the following benefits:

- All attending children, both those with and those without disabilities, make gains
- The social and play skills of children with disabilities grow and develop
- Children's sensitivity to and acceptance of disabled peers results
- The higher the quality of the child development program, the more probable individualized intervention occurs
- Severe disabilities require intensive, professional support systems

What is a student teacher to do? First, accept the disabilities you find. They may range from mild to moderate to severe. Become a team player in helping each child reach his potential. Know that your cooperating teacher may have already:

- Assessed the classroom environment and needed staff
- Developed a routine or schedule for each identified child with special needs
- Developed individual learning objectives and plans
- Made curriculum modifications or adaptions to enhance child participation, which may include
  —special equipment
  —room arrangement
  —classroom materials and adjustments
  —activity simplification
  —peer mentoring, and giving attention to child preferences and needs
- Assessed individual children's progress

Most cooperating teachers will expect student teachers to be instrumental in helping them both observe and work toward special needs children's progress, and also be aware of individual plans, modifications, adaptions necessary, and the teaching teams' efforts.

Ask for specifics on each child if you have questions. Be alert and inquisitive about child behaviors or teaching practices you find questionable. The author remembers, as a new teacher, observing a disabled preschool child who would not pull up her pants after toileting. She was capable of doing so but would not. The teacher monitoring the child's behavior would calmly but firmly say, "Just reach down. Grab your pants and pull up. "I think that you can pull up your underwear. I will wait. You can do it." The teacher repeated this periodically. The child tried an array of behaviors including pleading, crying, sulking, calling the teacher names, pulling long strings off the toilet paper rolls, looking sad, and continually flushing the toilet, but the teacher held her ground. A stranger coming into the classroom might think the teacher cruel, unfeeling, and perhaps obstinate. In the end, after a good half hour, the child pulled her pants up. The staff's intent with this child after parent consultation was to increase the child's independence and self-help skills.

Using book or Internet resources will increase your knowledge of specific special needs disabilities. You'll discover resources for parents as well as teachers. A second list of Web sites is found at the chapter's end. Most all communities have school district, local, state, and federal agencies and entities that have been created to help children with special needs and their families. Investigate. The administrator or director of your student teaching assignment school is responsible, after considerable collaboration with the teaching team and parents, to make child or parent referrals if necessary.

"SPECIAL" CHILDREN

"Special" children are as different from each other as are "normal" children, but not all "special" children are easily recognizable (see Figures 10–5 and 10–6). There are signs that can help you identify a "special" child. Does Johnny hold his head to one side constantly? Does he squint? (He may need glasses.) Does he ignore directions unless you are close to him and facing him? Is his speech unclear? (He may have a hearing problem.) Does the child have frequent bouts with *otitis media*, a middle ear infection?

Is a child not learning to talk at the same rate as her peers? (She may have a problem of language delay.) Is she still using baby talk when most of her peers have outgrown it? (She may have a speech problem.) Is she frequently out of breath?

Figure 10-5 Children can overcome physical limitations.

Figure 10-6 Not all children with special needs are easily recognizable.

Does she sneeze often? (She may have an allergy that should be properly diagnosed by a doctor.) Fortunately, most health problems are diagnosed by family doctors; your role might simply be to monitor the child's medication if the doctor asks you. Children taking medication often have to be observed to decide if the dosage is appropriate; doctors must know if the child's behavior changes in any way such as increased drowsiness or irritability.

Is the child extremely aggressive or withdrawn? (He may be emotionally disturbed.) Is the child extremely active? Does he have a short attention span? Is he easily distracted? Does he have problems with cause-and-effect relationships? Does he have difficulty in putting his thoughts into words? (He may have a learning disability.)

Is the child much slower than her peers in talking and completing cognitive work such as classifying objects? (She may be mildly developmentally delayed.) It is important to note that these characteristics are only indications of the problem, not solid evidence that the problem does exist. Only a qualified person can make the actual determination.

Do you have a child at your center who is talking in sentences at age two or two-and-a-half? Is this child larger, taller, and heavier than other children of the same age? Does this child enjoy excellent health? Does he already know the names of the primary and secondary colors? Does the child already know the letters in his name? Does this child see relationships between seemingly unrelated objects? This child may be "special" in the sense of being gifted or talented.

Working with the "Special" Child in Inclusive Settings

There are few concepts that have been as misunderstood as the term "inclusion." Nowhere in any special needs law does the word appear. As mentioned before, PL 94-142 and PL 101-476 use only the phrase "least restrictive environment." However, the LRE phrase does state that "to the maximum extent appropriate, children with disabilities, including children in public or private institutions or other care facilities, are educated with nondisabled children" (McCarthy, 1994).

inclusion—a term that has widely replaced the term "mainstreaming" and that emphasizes placement of the special needs child in the regular classroom with, perhaps, greater assistance from special education services. There is still controversy as to whether total inclusion is best for every special needs child.

As McCarthy states,

> In a fully inclusive model, students with disabilities, no matter how severe, are taught in the regular education classroom of their home school with their age and grade peers for the full day with support services provided within that classroom. . . . Whether full inclusion is appropriate for *all* children with disabilities remains the source of considerable debate.

What does this mean for you as a student teacher? Can children with special needs be integrated smoothly all day into regular programs? Does the mandate mean that you will have to work with disruptive children in a regular classroom, preschool or elementary, or a child care center? If, after you finish your teacher training, you decide to open your own family child care home or preschool, will you have to enroll children with special needs? (In a question and answer bulletin of October 1997 from the U.S. Department of Justice, Civil Rights Division, Disability Rights Section, the answer clearly is "yes.")

But whether you realize it or not, many preschools and child care centers always have had special needs children, especially those with less obvious disabilities. Many preschool and primary age children do not have obvious special needs and are enrolled before any diagnosis is completed. And, as mentioned before, some preschools have enrolled children with severe disabilities. Typically, children with less severe disabilities or those with "hidden" disabilities are frequently diagnosed in both preschools and elementary schools. How many of you may have had a vision impairment diagnosed in elementary school, a mild to moderate hearing loss, a learning disability, a scoliosis (spinal curvature), or an attention deficit? Also, many young children experience bouts of depression that go undiagnosed.

The implications for teachers and caregivers of young children involve, first of all, the need for collaboration. As Allred, Briem, and Black (1998) suggest, parents, caregivers, and teachers all need to be involved. Existing routines both at home and out-of-home settings need to be considered, as must the goals of each setting. For the greatest chance of success, all adults in the child's life should plan together for the ultimate good of the child. "Above all, team members must continually reexamine and reevaluate the child's goals to be sure they are functional and realistic for the particular child, family, and . . . environment" (Allred, Briem, & Black, 1998).

In agreement with Allred, Briem, and Black, Stafford and Green (1996) propose that teachers look at their instructional methods to see how these might be adjusted and/or changed to meet the needs of special needs students. Furthermore, they suggest that the children themselves be involved in any implementation of integration (they used the concept of "friends helping friends" approach), that inclusion be planned carefully, and that teachers need to model appropriate behavior. In addition, any appropriate behaviors, such as positive interaction with children with special needs on the part of other children, should be praised. Finally, cooperative learning activities have proven to be most successful in integration. Stafford and Green caution, however, that successful integration or inclusion requires support from the administration and related support personnel, and from the families of the special needs children.

Schoen and her associates Auen and Arvanitis (1997) looked at the inclusion of children with special needs in three settings: a public school, a preschool class, and a for-profit child care center. The authors' conclusion is as follows:

> Not only was the integration plan enriching for the children and the parents, it was a fulfilling experience for all the professionals involved. . . . [T]he integration program was about children learning about others and, in turn, learning about themselves.

If you have the opportunity to work and teach in an inclusive setting, you may also find it a fulfilling experience, and in the process, learn more about yourselves.

In general, working with the "special" child is not much different than working with the "normal" child. Your cooperating teacher will, in most instances, give you clues for teaching a "special" child.

Speech-Impaired Children

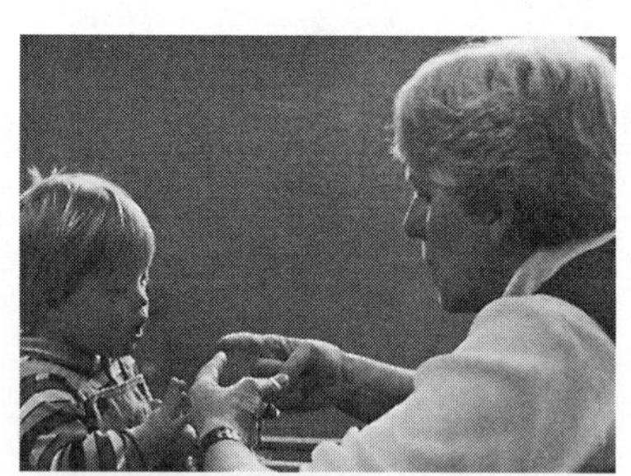

Figure 10–7 It is common to work one to one with a child with specal needs.

The child with a speech or language impairment may need one-to-one tutoring (see Figure 10–7). An early indication of a hearing impairment is lack of language skills or unclear speech. If you suspect a child has a hearing loss, you should discuss your perceptions with your cooperating teacher. She may suggest to the parent that the hearing be checked. If the child is experiencing language delay, it may be because the parent has not spent much time talking to the child. Indeed, some children speak in what sounds like "television language." You should provide these children with opportunities to use verbal language. You may need to name objects for them and provide them with descriptive adjectives. You may play several language activities with these children such as feelie-box games and guessing games in which they describe and use language.

Mentally Impaired Children

The mentally impaired child may need no special attention beyond your being attuned to activities that may be frustrating. Your teacher may ask you to assist the child in certain activities known to be more difficult. For example, during a fingerplay, you may be asked to hold the child on your lap and to manipulate the child's fingers. The mentally impaired child might also need some extra help in language; slow language development is often a characteristic.

Mildly mentally impaired children often integrate well into the preschool setting. They often have good social development, and their physical development may be almost normal. Their language may be simpler than that of peers, but they often make their needs known through body language. They may not be able to do some of the cognitive tasks well, but they can derive as much pleasure from painting, role-playing, and playing with clay, blocks, and trucks as any other child. Knowing that this child is less able cognitively than some of the other children, you can work with activities the child *can* do successfully and reduce the amount of stress associated with goals that are too high.

Children with Orthopedic and/or Health Disabilities

There are many different types of physical disabilities and health problems. In working with children who have orthopedic and/or health disabilities, the only difficulty you may encounter is whether or not your setting is wheelchair accessible and whether or not you need to be more attentive to health problems on unhealthy air days. Asthma and allergies are the most common health problems of young children, and these children are more sensitive to smog and seasonal pollens than are others.

Your cooperating teacher may want you to help a child in a wheelchair go to the bathroom or may ask you to assist a child with leg braces reset the braces as he sits at or rises from a table or the floor.

Some other specific strategies include:

- acquainting yourself with any special equipment needed by the child
- being alert to medication the child may be taking
- remembering to tell your cooperating teacher about any changes in the child's behavior you may have noticed that she may have missed
- being aware of the fact that a chronically ill child may be absent frequently and that close contact must be kept among parents, the school, and specialists

Children with Hearing Disabilities

Children with hearing disabilities may wear hearing aids, or if profoundly disabled, use sign language. These children will vary in their competencies just as "normal" children do. Their language may be somewhat delayed, and your cooperating teacher may ask you to work with them on language games. You are not expected to learn sign, but you may find it helpful to learn a few simple signs from the sign language specialist who should be assisting in the classroom.

Strategies for working with a hearing-disabled child include:

- speaking directly to him using normal, well-articulated speech and normal gestures
- seating the child where she can see you if you are reading a story, doing a finger play, or another visual activity
- encouraging others to include the hearing-impaired child in their activities
- encouraging the other children to follow your examples above
- being alert to the need for your cooperating teacher to change the batteries on a child's hearing aid if the child seems confused or is rubbing her ears, or using any other signal that shows she is not hearing. (Your cooperating teacher or the specialist may show you how to do this to save their attention and time.)

In one case involving a child who was hard of hearing, all of the children learned sign language in order to communicate better with the child. In fact, the children learned sign language faster than the teacher!

Visually Impaired Children

As with hearing impairments, visual problems vary widely. These children frequently have been in regular classrooms for years. Remember our asking earlier how many of you were first diagnosed by a teacher as possibly needing glasses?

Among the strategies to use are:

- being alert to the child who may not see well and who may be holding books close to his face, placing his head close to the picture he is drawing, or complaining of headaches or nausea after trying to concentrate on a visual work activity
- remembering that the partially sighted and/or blind child needs to have a room where furniture and equipment are kept in predictable arrangements. If you ask if you can bring in a newly designed center, be sure to orient the visually impaired child to its placement and how to use the activity
- setting the television to a channel that provides a verbal description of what is happening for the viewer with a visual disability.

Commercial and public television programs sometimes are closed captioned (CC) for the hearing impaired and/or employ descriptive video service (DVS) for the visually impaired.

Behavior Disorders

There is probably no area more controversial than that involving behavioral difficulties. Many teachers may think a child is emotionally disturbed but do not know how to approach a parent. The term "behavior disorders" is more commonly used now to indicate children who have problems of behavior but who may not, in terms of a psychiatric definition, be truly "emotionally disturbed." Often, when you see a young child with behavior problems, you are likely to see a family with problems. The term "dysfunctional" is sometimes used to describe families with problems that affect their children. To many parents, even the suggestion of a behavior problem with their child brings about a defensive reaction such as, "Are you telling me I'm a bad parent? That I don't know how to raise my own child?" Teachers and administrators attempt to avoid value-laden terms that may arouse a defensive reaction in parents, and instead, will substitute terminology such as "acts out," "has no friends," "daydreams," "fights," or "tries to hide in the back of the room." We have to understand how difficult it is for a parent to accept the possibility that something may be "wrong" with the child. If the parents have no idea that the child is not perfectly "normal," it becomes extremely difficult to convince them that there may be a problem.

Facing the possibility that their child may not be perfect, some parents actually grieve for the lost image of what their child was to have been. They grieve in much the same way they would grieve if the child had died. They become angry and accuse us of prejudice, of not really knowing their child. Some parents verbally attack our skills and suggested diagnosis; others deny that anything is wrong. Most go through a period in which they blame themselves for causing the child's problems. In some instances, we may feel that they are indeed responsible for the problems of the child, and we must be careful not to prejudge.

The child with a behavior disorder may or may not present a problem in the classroom. In one example, a behavior-disordered (depressive) child was placed in a regular preschool. The children quickly learned to tolerate temper tantrums and screaming. To a visiting stranger, they would explain, "Don't worry about Richie. He just needs to be alone now." In many ways, the children were more tolerant than some of the parents.

Certainly, the child who shows aggression presents a challenge and must be watched closely. For this reason, it is not uncommon for the teacher to assign an aide or student teacher to work on a one-to-one basis with the child to try to control the child's outbursts. Holding the child on your lap, allowing the child to hit a heavy chair cushion instead of a child or adult, removing a child to the back of a classroom or "benching" on the play yard, allowing the child to punch clay or pound nails into scrap wood instead of hurting another person, having the child bite on a leather strap or chew a wad of sugarless bubblegum when she feels like biting, or having the child run around the playground when she feels like exploding are all good techniques. Remember that behavior modification works well with children who are behavior disordered.

You should be aware that as the withdrawn, depressed child becomes better, he is likely to become aggressive. This is known as the pendulum effect. When a depressed child reaches this stage and begins to act out, some parents become angry and fearful; they stop therapy, not understanding that the child must release the pent-up anger. They do not understand that it will take time for the child to learn how to deal with anger in socially acceptable ways. We can reassure the parent that this phase is normal for the child. We can also be alert for signs that the child needs to be alone to stomp, yell, throw, and hit without hurting anyone. In some schools, the child may be directed to go to another room where the child can throw Nerf balls, pound on clay, or hit a weighted clown doll. In others, there may be a time-out corner where the child will be told to stay until she feels ready to rejoin the group. Whatever the technique used, you may be asked to remain with the child for safety purposes. At the same time, you can acknowledge the child's anger and suggest ways in which the child can channel it in a positive direction.

The Learning Disabled Child

The child suspected of having learning disabilities presents a challenge. Although some parents are willing to accept a diagnosis of possible learning disabilities, others are not. What is a learning disability? According to PL 94–142, a "specific learning disability

> . . . means a disorder in one or more of the basic psychological processes involved in understanding or in using language, spoken or written, which may manifest itself in an imperfect ability to listen, think, speak, read, write, spell, or do mathematical calculations (Federal Register, 1977, 300.5).

learning disability—a condition thought to be associated with neurological dysfunction and characterized by difficulty in mastering a skill such as reading or numerical calculation

School districts commonly define a learning disability in terms of a child's actual achievement in relation to the achievement of his age peers. The unfortunate result of this practice has been postponing the identification of a student until he is two or more years behind age peers, a practice that has meant, in too many cases, three and even four years of failure for the child. The damage to the child's self-esteem can be almost irreparable. Another commonly used definition is that a learning disability is reflected as a significant discrepancy between the child's potential ability and his actual achievement in learning to read, write, or figure. The curriculum areas of reading, language arts, and mathematics are most typically involved.

Does this mean that a preschooler does not have a learning disability? Many preschool teachers, parents, and educational psychologists who are capable diagnosticians would disagree.

What are some of the characteristics you might see in a preschooler that could signal the possibility of a learning disability? Typically, you see a child who appears immature; who frequently has difficulties with language, both receptive and expressive; who acts impulsively; and who may seem to be "hyperactive." (Be careful about calling a child hyperactive, though; be aware that high energy does not necessarily mean hyperactive.)

Ask yourself the following questions:

- Does the child in your preschool have difficulty using language?
- Does he use unreferenced pronouns because he can't remember what the object's name is?
- Is this the child who cannot think of more than one word to describe an object in a feelie box or repeats a word a playmate has just used instead of coming up with her own?
- Does this child display poor coordination for her age?
- Does the child have difficulty following simple requests?
- Does he dislike changes in the routines of the preschool?
- Does the four-year-old child prefer interacting with the three-year-olds more than with the children her own age?
- Is the four-year-old child unable to tell what letter you've drawn on his back, indicating difficulty transferring from a tactile to a visual image?
- Do you have to remind this child constantly of the rules from day to day?

None of these characteristics by itself would be symptomatic of a possible learning disability; taken together and being seen daily might be cause for suggesting a more formal evaluation by a qualified expert in learning disabilities. In the meantime, the child's parents may ask your cooperating teacher if she can arrange for some one-on-one learning for their child. In turn, the cooperating teacher may ask them to attend a conference involving everyone who works with the child to develop an individual learning plan that will involve them all (see Figure 10–8). (See the Appendix for checklists to use to determine modality strengths and weaknesses, and a sample individual learning plan.)

Dyslexia

Many children with a specific learning disability have a condition known as dyslexia, a problem "manifested by difficulty in learning to read, write, or spell, despite conventional instruction, adequate intelligence, and socio-cultural opportunity" (Orton Dyslexia Society, 1988). As a student teacher, you may be asked to work one-to-one with a dyslexic student, allowing the student to have extra time to finish a written assignment, for example, or having the student present an oral report instead of a written one. You may be asked to write a story the student dictates.

Interventions used by Wadlington, Jacob, and Bailey (1996) involve helping dyslexic students with organizational and study skills, which, of course, are of value to all the students. They also advocate using a multisensory approach to reading tasks, allowing for extra time and providing audiotaped books for students to use together with the standard readers. In spelling, they concentrate on having students learn phonetically regular words before introducing any that are phonetically irregular. They accept handwriting that is not perfect as long as it is

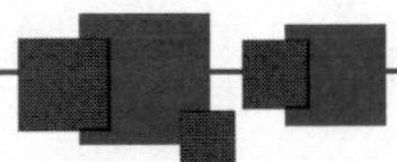

SCHOOL: ABC Preschool STUDENT'S NAME: Tommy C.A.: 43 DATE: 14 Oct

LONG-RANGE GOAL: Tommy will expand his vocabulary both at school and at home.

FUNCTIONAL DESCRIPTION OF THE PROBLEM: Tommy speaks in telegraphic sentences; his language is frequently unintelligible, which has led to interpersonal problems with peers. Assessments by School District DEF shows that Tommy is developmentally normal on all criteria except language. His pediatrician's report shows no difficulty with hearing but a severe case of pneumonia when Tommy was 8 mo., followed by a relapse at 9 mo. Tommy's mother admits overprotecting him and worrying about his frequent bouts with upper respiratory infections. Tommy's attention span appears short relative to peers at ABC Preschool.

BEHAVIORAL STRENGTHS: Tommy is agile and well coordinated.

SHORT-TERM OBJECTIVES	INTERVENTION ACTIVITIES AND MATERIALS	PERSON(S) RESPONSIBLE
(Section 3153, Title V Regulations) (Specify time, specific behavior, evaluation conditions & criteria)		
1. Tommy will use 3–4 word sentences when talking in the classroom. (6 mo.)	ST or aide will model speaking in complete sentences & ask child to repeat model; "Feelie Box" will be used on 1:1	Teacher, with assistance of ST or aide
4. Tommy will retell stories using complete sentences of 3–4 words (8 mo.)	Mother or father will read to boy each evening before bed, model complete sentence construction & have him repeat or construct his own sentences	Parents
6. Tommy will practice using sentences under guidance of District DEF's speech therapist. Word lotto games, etc., will also be used. (6 mo.)	Peabody Early Experiences Kit	Speech & language therapist
9. Mr. & Mrs. Fabian will be offered an opportunity to participate in LDA (Learning Disabilities Association) support group & to receive counseling. (on-going)	District DEF psychologist gives parents information regarding County LDA support group; may ask LDA to call parents	DEF School Dist. psychologist

CRITERION MEASURE without modeling or prompting. Tommy will be speaking in 3–4 word complete sentences.

Reviewed: ____________________ ____________________

____________________ Speech Therapist

____

Teacher

____

Revision(s) Recommended: School Psychologist

____________________ Date: ____________________

(Parent 1) (Parent 2)

Figure 10-8 Part of an individualized family services plan

legible. Extra time is allowed for all language arts activities and for test-taking. You might want to talk to your cooperating teacher about some of these ideas if he has not already done so.

Attention Deficit Disorder (ADD)

attention deficit disorder (ADD)—attention deficit disorder. It causes children to have difficulty in sustaining attention in the classroom and in concentrating on an assigned task for any length of time.

attention deficit with hyperactivity disorder (ADHD)—attention deficit with hyperactivity disorder. Like ADD, it causes attention problems as well as an inability to sit still and concentrate for very long. Children with ADHD are said to "bounce off the walls."

One category in special education often seen in child care and schools today is attention deficit disorder (ADD) and attention deficit with hyperactivity disorder (ADHD). The *Diagnostic and Statistical Manual of Mental Disorders* (DSM-IV, American Psychiatric Association, 1994), recognizes three kinds of attention disorders: the previously mentioned ADD and ADHD plus a third, an unspecified attention disorder. As with learning disabilities, there are some who believe ADD and ADHD are simply labels for children whose temperament runs at a faster rate than "normal" (Armstrong,1996; Reid, Maag, & Vasa, 1994; Smelter, Rasch, Fleming, Nazos, & Baranowski, 1996).

Children with ADD typically have difficulty concentrating for prolonged periods of time, some even for five or 10 minutes. For some of these children, taking a stimulant drug such as Ritalin, Dexadrine, or Cylert appears to help. For others, especially those allergic to drug therapy, specifically designed computer games appear to help.

If you have children with ADD in your center or classroom, one proven way to work with them is to keep them busy. Allowing them the freedom to move from one center to another is another way. However, a room with many choices may be difficult for ADD children; in many ways, they need less stimulation rather than more. You may have to suggest gently to the child that he choose one of two options. "I notice no one is painting at one of the easels, and I also notice that your friend Jean Pierre is the only child playing with the blocks. Why don't you paint a picture or join Jean Pierre?" Your room may have a sheltered corner or area where these children may go when overstimulated.

Hogan (1997) stresses that "like all children, children with ADHD need love, acceptance, discipline, and the freedom to grow and learn." To that end, she suggests that teachers first learn as much as they can about ADD and ADHD. Then, they can set attention goals for their students. Hogan states that there may be a need to modify assignments and to tailor academic materials to individual learning styles and abilities. The need to be flexible is paramount (for example, allow a student to lie on the floor to read or let a second student "hide" under the teacher's desk). If an assignment is completed, why does a student need to sit at a desk for the entire time? In fact, in one L-shaped third-grade classroom where one of your co-authors had a student teacher, there was a study carrel over in the side room where any student could go. Although originally planned for the ADD and ADHD students assigned to the room, many of the so-called normal students would move to the study carrel where they found it easier to concentrate.

An article in *US News and World Report* told of a new procedure to aid in the diagnosis of ADHD (Fischer, 2000). The diagnostic test, developed by psychiatrists at McLean Hospital in Massachusetts, utilizes an infrared tracking device to measure minute movements of children as they attempt a 15-minute, essentially boring test. The test consists of having the child press the space bar on a computer keyboard every time she perceives a star appearing. The test has proven valid in a correct diagnosis for six of 11 boys who took it. (The other five had been misdiagnosed.)

A new brain-imaging test, T2 Relaxometry, is believed to help researchers devise new treatment procedures for children not helped by psychoactive drugs like Ritalin. Martin Teicher, director of the Developmental Biopsychiatry Research

Program at McLean, developed the test. He states, "All types of disorders, from anxiety to manic-depression to conduct disorders are now mistaken for ADHD . . . and everyone suffers for that diagnostic sloppiness" (Fischer, 2000).

Of concern to many parents, teachers, and others is what has been called the overprescription to younger and younger children of psychoactive drugs, Ritalin and Prozac in particular. Some educators believe that too many preschool children are being placed on these drugs when the effects of long-term use on the very young are not known.

The Gifted Child

Teachers are considering new ways to think about and observe gifted children. Very young children, culturally and linguistically diverse children, and economically disadvantaged children may escape detection, particularly if standardized assessments are used. Smutny (2001) urges educators to consider factors fundamental to a "fair assessment" of children's abilities. These follow:

gifted children—children who perform significantly above average in intellectual and creative areas.

- *Look for giftedness in more domains than the academic* (for exaample, creative imagination, wit, improvisation, kinesthetic abilities, and hands-on problem-solving). Become aware of your own ideas about what giftedness looks like or what behaviors indicate high potential. Don't assume that gifted children are early readers or even high achievers. Don't assume that an athletic child with little interest in academics or a bilingual student struggling with English is unlikely to be gifted.
- *Look beyond "good" or "bad" behavior.* Consider the role that good behavior plays in your or your school's assessment of a child's ability. Do teacher-pleasers get more opportunity as a reward for their good behavior? While problem behavior needs to be addressed, some gifted kids act up because of frustration or boredom.
- *Create activities that demand higher level thinking and creative solutions.* It is obvious that a child who needs hands-on activities to process information and analyze problems will not show these abilities if no such activities occur in the classroom. Be willing to incorporate different learning styles and materials so that more young students can demonstrate their strengths.
- *Allow students to express their ideas in different ways.* For example, a child from another culture may have a novel solution to a problem, but may express this better through diagrams and drawings than verbal or written expression. Offer young students a variety of ways to show what they are learning.
- *Ask children about their work.* Do not assume that you know what a student is trying to do or whether or not it works. It may be that their ideas are more interesting or sophisticated than their abilities to express them. Uneven development is common in young children and cultural differences may enhance this phenomenon.

When assessing the behavior of young children, teachers need to be sensitive to differences in learning style, development, and cultural background that influence the way they process information and respond to activities in the classroom (Smutny, 2001).

Non-English Proficient Children

Children of immigrant and newly arrived families are increasingly represented in classrooms. Their numbers are expected to grow dramatically during the next decade and include Hispanics, Asians, Pacific Islanders, and others.

Student teachers may face the immediate task of communicating acceptance and respect to children with varying degrees of standard English proficiency. No single description fits these children. They are widely diverse. Teachers strive to decrease children's feelings of alienation and isolation, if it exists (Thonis, 1990). Many of these children have backgrounds and cultural understandings that can be tapped as classroom resources.

Student teachers need to become familiar with the specific planning and program(s) for students who do not understand and/or speak English. Planning is based on the following assessments:

- How proficient is the child in the language of the home?
- Can the child understand and speak English?
- Is the child's language and speech appropriate for his age?
- What degree of comfort or discomfort is present at school?
- What experiences are developmentally appropriate for this child?

Children Born to Mothers Who Were Substance Abusers

Children born to mothers who were or are substance abusers are often born addicted to the drugs the mother was abusing, and may appear to be hyperactive, to be learning disabled, or to have an attention deficit. Caregivers working with these children have noted that they often overreact to stimuli; thus, they need environments that contain fewer, rather than more, curriculum possibilities and fewer children with whom to interact.

As infants, these children may need constant care. They are frequently born prematurely and have to spend their first weeks, and even months, in pediatric intensive care units in a hospital. After release from the hospital, caregivers may still need to use pediatric monitors with these infants when they sleep because sudden infant death syndrome (SIDS) has more frequently been observed with them. These infants have also been difficult to console when crying. They appear to have difficulty in adjusting to change. Swaddling the infants has been shown effective.

On entry into preschool and school, these children still become overstimulated. They may strike out at anyone—child or adult—physically near them, and their behavior may be unpredictable. Obviously, this leads to difficulties in establishing friendships with the other children. Children born to substance-abusing mothers have been shown to work better in small groups and in rooms with minimal stimuli. For more information, you may want to contact your local children's hospital or large-city school district. School districts in many cities such as Los Angeles, New York, and Chicago have suggestions for how to work more effectively with these children. Don't be afraid to contact them.

WORKING WITH CHILDREN WITH SPECIAL NEEDS

Among the several techniques proven effective with the learning disabled and other special needs children are:

- *Structure.* A well-planned classroom. Classroom rules are posted for older children and repeated often to younger ones so they understand the limits.
- *Consistency of discipline* by the teacher.

- *Behavior modification.*
- *CARE.* Be congruent, acceptant, reliable, and empathetic. It works with all children, especially those with special needs.
- *Alternate quiet and active activities.* Provide for enough physical exercise to tire the active child; allow the child enough freedom to move around often. Do not expect the child to sit still unless you are there.
- *Love.* One parent and educator, Thomas Armstrong (1996) questions whether ADD and ADHD exist or whether children so labeled simply need CAREing and love. Armstrong decried the tendency of parents and teachers to ask medical doctors to place the seemingly inattentive, overactive child on stimulants or drug therapy. He advocates instead that we use diet, physical exercise, relaxation exercises, and proven educational techniques such as those previously mentioned. We urge you to do the same.

Vulnerable Children

Which children are considered "vulnerable?" Initially, these were children who had a parent or parents who were alcoholic, were substance abusers, or who had psychiatric problems. Children who lived in poverty conditions (inadequate housing, inadequate clothing, insufficient food for their needs, and so on) are also considered vulnerable. Weissbourd (1996) lists the attributes of teachers who work with vulnerable children in Figure 10–9. These attributes, in fact, could apply to characteristics needed by any and all teachers.

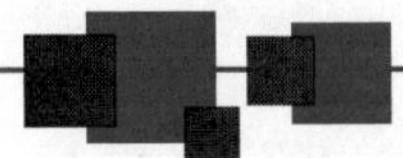

Attributes of Effective Teachers Working with Vulnerable Children

1. Effective teachers operationalize high expectations for every child.
2. Effective teachers attribute failure to aspects of a child or classroom that can be positively influenced, rather than to intractable aspects of a child, family, or community.
3. Effective teachers provide every student with the elements from which real and durable self-esteem is built, including specific, tangible skills and achievements, progressively increased responsibilities, and opportunities to give to others.
4. Effective teachers view children as having complex constellations of strengths and weaknesses and communicate this understanding to parents.
5. Effective teachers work to develop children's adaptive capacities, their ability to manage disappointment and conflict.
6. Effective teachers pick up on the quiet troubles that undermine children in school, such as mild hunger or wearing the same clothes day after day and respond aggressively to these problems.
7. Effective teachers view the classroom and school as a complex culture and system and seek to understand the difficulties of a child in terms of the interactions between a particular child and a particular culture and system.
8. Effective teachers engage parents proactively and have the skills to work with parents when a child is in crisis.
9. Effective teachers are self-observing and are responsive to feedback and ideas from both other school staff and children—they see children as active partners in their education.
10. Effective teachers know when to respond to a child's problem themselves and when a child needs to see another professional who has specialized training.
11. Effective teachers innovate, take risks, and reshape their activities based on close attention to results.

Figure 10-9 Attributes of effective teachers working with vulnerable children. From *The Vulnerable Child* by Richard Weissbourd. Copyright 1996 by Richard Weissbourd. Reprinted by permission of Perseus Books Publishers, a member of Perseus Books, L.L.C.

At-Risk Children

at-risk children—because of adverse environmental factors, for instance, poverty or low birth weight, children considered at risk for developmental delay and/or for doing poorly in school.

Today, we can look at a broader definition of vulnerable children and include any child living in an environment that is not optimal for the child's positive growth. Look again at the attributes listed in Figure 10–9. If you can internalize them, you will have no difficulty with at-risk children or any others!

Children Who "Fall through the Cracks"

Many children you are likely to see in your rooms may have some characteristics of a child with special needs but on such a mild basis that they do not qualify under the law for any supportive help. Others may be "special" because of a recent traumatic incident in their lives, the loss of a beloved grandparent, for example, or a sibling with cancer. Or they may have witnessed an accident that caused injury or death to someone, whether that person was known to them or not. Our best advice: remember that all children are unique and that all, at one time or another in their lives, are likely to be special and to need your love and care (see Figure 10–10).

One descriptive resource that provides profiles of nine special needs children, told from the perspectives of teachers, parents, and children themselves, is *Children with Special Needs: Lessons for Early Childhood Professionals*, by Kostelnik, et al. (2002).

Working with Parents of Special Needs Children

Research (Chinn, Winn, & Walters, 1985) has shown that parents of special needs children go through a process similar to the grief reactions described by Kubler-Ross in *On Death and Dying* (1969). In interactions with parents, you may

Figure 10–10 A wheelchair-bound child has access to sand play with this specially designed equipment.

see a father denying that his son has a problem while the mother is blaming herself and is wracked with guilt. Also, parents often project feelings of blame on the preschool, center, or elementary school. One reason for the high divorce rate among parents of special needs children is that two parents are seldom at the same step in the grief process at the same time, a fact that obviously leads to dissension at home.

In cases where the child has a clear disability, diagnosed by a medical doctor at an early age, parents have to adjust and do learn to accept the child and any concomitant problems earlier than parents of a child who has what are often called "invisible handicaps:" learning disabilities, mild retardation, and behavior disorders. What this means to teachers of both preschools and elementary schools is that they may have to be especially sensitive to what stage of grieving the parents may be in. Working with these parents may require all of a teacher's communication skills, and a teacher still may not be successful in persuading parents that their child needs "special" attention. (This is one reason why elementary schools may assign a child, whose family is "income eligible," to work with the Chapter 1 teacher or another child to receive help from a reading specialist, student teacher, aide, or volunteer. [Chapter 1 of PL 95-581, the Education Consolidation Act of 1981, provides federal funds for compensatory education of children from low-income families.])

Commonly Used Tests

Retardation is easily measured with any well-known standard intelligence test. Despite the fact that intelligence testing (often called IQ testing for Intelligence Quotient, a figure based on the standard deviation of the norm group and 100 as the mean or average) has come under fire over the past 20 to 30 years, its use is still widespread. As a tool in understanding the child's intellectual development in regard to predicting possible success in school, the IQ test provides valuable information. Combined with other measures of a child's development (such as the checklist previously referred to and found in the Appendix), the IQ test can provide a differential picture of the child's school-related abilities. One major drawback to the **Stanford-Binet Intelligence Scale** is its verbal emphasis. The *Wechsler Intelligence Scale for Children (WISC-III)* and the *Wechsler Preschool/Primary Intelligence Scale-Revised* attempt to provide both verbal and performance measures of intelligence. However, both of these tests may discriminate against a child from a racial and/or cultural minority. Even though both have been translated into other languages, there is still the question of appropriateness. For most preschools, a developmental checklist provides as good or better information than an IQ test. The major advantage to the IQ test, of course, is in its use in diagnosing mental retardation. It seldom, however, provides clues regarding how to work with the child who is diagnosed as retarded.

Stanford-Binet intelligence scale—a widely used test that yields an intelligence quotient (IQ).

If we use a developmental checklist (see the Appendix) which relies on our observation of the child, we can develop a learning plan based on what we see. Noting that a three-year-old child can walk upstairs alternating the feet, but walks downstairs one foot at a time, we might have the child hold our hand at first. Then, we can have the child hold onto a railing. Finally, we can urge the child to try without any support. If we note that a child is still speaking two-word sentences, we can provide for more language experiences on a one-to-one basis. In every case, we should not urge the child to accomplish tasks that are not appropriate to her developmental level. The child who cannot gallop will not learn to skip, but perhaps the child is ready to learn how to slide one foot after the other sideways.

Head Start has developed a screening and assessment process (see Figure 10–11) that occurs throughout the program year on a periodic schedule rather than only on the child's entrance into a Head Start program. This allows analysis and, hopefully, reassurance that the child is on track for achieving the expected developmental outcomes envisioned through staff and families' use of an individualized education program (IEP). The process is called Early and Periodic Screen, Diagnosis, and Treatment program (EPSDT) (O'Brien, 2001).

The Individual Family Services Plan

You should note that Figure 10–8 represents only selected items that might be listed on Tommy Fabian's IFSP. (Remember, at the elementary school level, the IFSP becomes, as required by law, an IEP.) As stipulated in PL 99-457, a multidisciplinary approach is taken, one that involves the preschool, the local school district, and a local community resource group. The student teacher, under the direction of the cooperating teacher, has an important role in modeling language and in listening to responses; the school district speech therapist and psychologist each have their roles in working both with Tommy and with the family. Finally, a community organization, the local county chapter of the Learning Disability Association (LDA), has been enlisted for family support. (It is important to remember that having a special needs child has shown that parents often experience feelings of disbelief, anger, and helplessness; a support group can be invaluable in alleviating these feelings.)

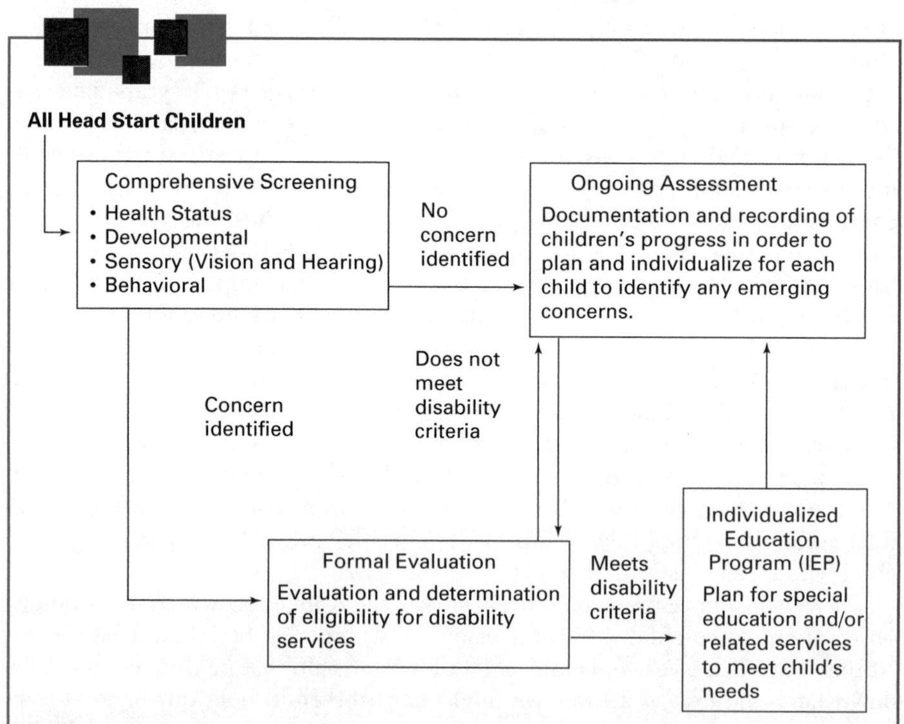

Figure 10–11 The screening and assessment process. From O'Brien, J. (2001, April). *How screening and assessment practices support quality disabilities services in Head Start.* Head Start Bulletin (70) 20–23. Courtesy of Head Start: National Head Start Bulletin.

SUMMARY

In this brief introduction to the "special" child, we presented an overview of current thinking regarding the integration of the child with special needs into the regular classroom. We attempted to show that, in many instances, the child with special needs can do very well in the regular room. Such integration has almost always been successful. Of course, there can be awkward moments initially, but other children often prove more tolerant than adults in accepting the "special" child. Children with special needs are no different than any other child; if you meet them with kindness and CARE, they will reciprocate.

We presented an overview of the public laws and listed some of their major provisions. We discussed the term "least restrictive environment" and emphasized that what is least restrictive for one child may not be for another.

We have presented a sample of short-term objectives from an Individual Family Services Plan (IFSP) for a family with a preschool child who may have a possible learning disability. We have also explained why working with families who have special needs children can present difficulties.

Finally, we offered some practical suggestions for working with the "special" child. We tend to agree that these techniques seem appropriate for all children. Methods that work well with one population are often applicable to another.

HELPFUL WEB SITES

http://cpmcnet.columbia.edu

National Center for Children in Poverty. Offers a newsletter promoting prevention of poverty.

http://www.ncbe.gwu.edu

National Clearinghouse for Bilingual Education. Language education information.

http://www.naeyc.org

National Association for the Education of Young Children. Read NAEYC's position statement on school readiness.

http://ericec.org

ERIC Clearinghouse on Disabilities and Gifted Education. Behavioral disorders and learning disabilities can be researched.

http://www.cec.sped.org

Council for Exceptional Children. Provides information to teachers, administrators, and others concerned with the education of gifted children and those with special needs.

Additional Web Sites For Student Teachers Working with Children with Special Needs

http://www.nichy.org

National Information Center for Children and Youth with Disabilities (NICHCY). Online free publications; case studies; and information on visual impairments, hearing impairments, cerebral palsy, mental retardation, and assessing programs for infant/toddlers.

http://www.kidstogether.org/

Kids Get Together. A clearinghouse with links. Learn about language disabilities.

http://www.aamr.org
American Association for Mental Retardation. Fact sheets available.

http://www.autism-society.org/
Autism Society of America. Causes and types of autism.

http://www.lekotek.org/
National Lekotek Center. Focus on children with special needs. Click on Information Resources.

http://tiger.coe.missouri.edu/
Center for Innovation in Education (CISE). Search cultural and linguistic diversity. An IDEA Guide is available.

http://www.ncela.gwu.edu/
The National Clearinghouse for English Language. Acquisition and Language Instruction (NCELA). Information on education of linguistically and culturally diverse learners.

http://www.fpg.unc.edu
FGP Child Development Institute. Click publications dealing with disabilities.

http://www.BehaviorAdvisor.Com/
Behavior Management Advice. Understanding and managing behavior.

http://www.ericec.org
CEC maintains a library and database on research in special and gifted education, and provides information on legislation.

http://www.aspensys.com/
Ask ERIC (Educational Resources Information Center).

http://www.easter-seals.org
Easter Seals.

http://www.modimes.org
March of Dimes.

http://www.chadd.org
Specific to children with special needs. The title tells exactly what you might find at the Web site. CHADD (Children and Adults with Attention Deficit Hyperactivity Disorder).

http://ldanatl/.org
Learning Disabilities Association of America (LDA).

http://interdys.org
The Orton Dyslexia Society (now the International Dyslexia Association (IDA).

SUGGESTED ACTIVITIES

A. Visit a preschool or elementary school that has children with special needs in attendance. Spend at least one morning watching the "special" children, taking notes as you observe. What similarities and/or differences do you find between the "special" children and the "other" children? Discuss your answers with your peers and supervisor.

B. Visit a preschool for "special" children or a special education class in an elementary school. Again, take notes on your observations. In what ways is this "special" class different from or similar to the regular classroom? Discuss your answers with your peers and supervisor.

C. Visit a residential center for children with special needs. Discuss your observations with your peers and supervisor.

REVIEW

A. Write your own definition of "special."

B. List five characteristics of a child with special needs.

C. Read the following descriptions of behavior. Identify the child in each situation as possibly "special." Discuss your answers with your peers and supervisor.

1. Ladan is a new child in your room of four-year-olds. Her mother says that the family speaks English in the home; however, you have doubts. In the classroom, Ladan seems to be more of a spectator than a participant. You note that when playing "Simon Says," Ladan does not appear to know what to do but copies her neighbor.
2. Richie is an abused two-year-old who has recently been placed in a foster home. He enters preschool every morning like a small whirlwind, running around the room, kicking at block structures other children have built, knocking over puzzles others are making, and screaming at the top of his lungs.
3. Even though Kosuke has been in your kindergarten class for nearly the entire year, his behavior has not changed noticeably from the first day. He still clings to his mother's hand when she brings him to school, and he cries for three to five minutes after she leaves. He has only one friend in the room, and efforts to persuade him to play or work with another child are met with tears.
4. Elena, a pretty, dark-haired seven-year-old in your after-school child care center, complains every day she comes in about her headaches and her queasy stomach. You wondered if she was coming down with the flu (it had been going around), but Elena has no fever and the complaints are a chronic occurrence.
5. Jorge is a student in a bilingual first grade but seldom talks in either Spanish or in English. When he does speak, he usually speaks so softly that only the students next to him can hear. When you urge him to speak up, Jorge often lowers his head and says nothing. He does appear to understand when given directions but you are concerned about his non-communicative behavior. When his mother is questioned, she's not concerned because Jorge's older brother Carlos had displayed similar behavior when he had first entered school.

CASE SCENARIO

Setting: A first-grade classroom in a public school. Matt is the newly assigned student teacher. Mrs. Levinson is his cooperating teacher, and Dr.Canalas, the university supervisor. After his first week in the room, Dr. Canalas and Mrs. Levinson meet after school with Matt.

"Well, Matt, how do you like the class?" asks Mrs. Levinson.

Matt answers, "The children sure are little! And what is happening with Carl? He's constantly moving: tapping his foot, rapping his fingers, sharpening his pencil, asking to go to the boy's room. I've noticed he has difficulty writing; his handwriting is almost illegible and he moves awkwardly at recess."

"You've observed some of the same behaviors we have," Mrs. Levinson states. "Dr. Canalas, what have you noticed? You've only come once but I know you're pretty observant. Any hypotheses?"

"I'd like Matt to tell us what he thinks might be behind Carl's behavior. Matt, what hypotheses might you suggest?" Dr. Canalas turns toward Matt.

"Well, I've only been here a week but I can't help but think Carl might be hyperactive. In fact, could he be ADHD? Then again, could he be somewhat slow intellectually? I don't think he has a problem hearing, but I'd want that checked, too. Do you think I'm on the right track?" Matt asks.

Questions for Discussion:

1. Does Matt seem to understand what might be causing Carl's behavior in the classroom?
2. What are some of the symptoms of a child who has ADHD?
3. Are there other background factors that might cause the same observed behavior displayed by Carl?
4. In a week's time, does a student teacher really have the time to observe an individual child sufficiently? What might you say to your cooperating teacher and college supervisor if you were put in Matt's situation?

REFERENCES

Allred, K. W., Briem, R., & Black, S. J. (1998, September). Collaboratively addressing the needs of young children with disabilities. *Young Children, 53*(5).

American Psychiatric Association. (1994). *Diagnostic and statistical manual of mental disorders* (4th ed.). Washington, DC: Author

Armstrong, T. (1996, February). ADD: Does it really exist? *Phi Delta Kappan, 77*(6).

Chinn, P. C., Winn, J., & Walters, R. H. (1985). *Two-way talking with parents of special children: A process of positive communication.* St. Louis, MO: C. V. Mosby.

Federal Register. (1977). PL 94-142, 300.5.

Fischer, J. S. (April 10, 2000). Taking a picture of a mind gone awhirl: New imaging method bolsters ADHD diagnosis. *US News and World Report, 128*(14).

Hogan, D. (1997, Spring). ADHD: A travel guide to success. *Childhood Education, 73*(3).

Kostelnik, M. J., Onaga, E., Rohde, B., & Whiren, A. (2002). *Children with special needs: Lessons for early childhood professionals.* New York: Teachers College Press.

Kubler-Ross, E. (1969). *On death and dying.* New York: Macmillan.

Lewis, R. B., & Doorlag, D. H. (2003). *Teaching special students in general education classrooms* (6th ed.). Upper Saddle River, NJ: Merrill/Prentice Hall.

McCarthy, M. M. (1994, November). Inclusion and the law: Recent judicial developments. Research Bulletin, a publication of the Center for Evaluation, Development and Research, *Phi Delta Kappan, 13.*

National Association for the Education of Young Children. (n.d.). Understanding the Americans with Disabilities Act: Information for early childhood progams. [Brochure]. Washington, DC: Author.

O'Brien, J. (2001, April). How screening and assessment practices support quality disabilities services in Head Start. *Head Start Bulletin*, (70), 20–23.

Orton Dyslexia Society. (1988). *Definition. Perspectives.* Baltimore: Author.

Reid, R., Maag, J., & Vasa, S. (1994). Attention deficit hyperactivity disorder as a disability category: A critique. *Exceptional Children, 60*(3).

Schoen, T. M., Auen, J., & Arvanitis, M. (1997, January). Children blossom in a special and general education integration program—A private child care center and a public school collaborate. *Young Children, 52*(2).

Smelter, R. W., Rasch, B. W., Fleming, J., Nazos, P., & Baranowski, S. (1996, February). Is attention deficit disorder becoming a desired diagnosis? *Phi Delta Kappan, 77*(6).

Smutney, J. F. (2001, Winter). Identifying young gifted disadvantaged children in the K-3 classroom. *Gifted Education Communicator, 32*(4), 35–36.

Stafford, S. H., & Green, V. P. (1996, Spring). Preschool integration: Strategies for teachers. *Childhood Education, 72*(4).

Terman, L. M., & Merrill, M. A. (1985). *Stanford-Binet scale* (4th ed.). Chicago: Riverside

Thonis, E. W. (1990, February/March). Teaching English as a second language. *Reading Today,* IRA, 7(4).

U.S. Department of Justice, Civil Rights Division, Disability Rights Section. (1997, October). *Commonly asked questions about child care centers and the Americans with Disabilities Act.* Washington, DC: Author.

Wadlington, E., Jacob, S., & Bailey, S. (1996, Fall). Teaching students with dyslexia in the regular classroom. *Childhood Education, 73*(1).

Wechsler, D. (1991). *Manual for the Wechsler intelligence scale for children (WISC-III)* (3rd ed.). San Antonio, TX: Psychological Corporation.

Wechsler, D. (1989). *Manual for the Wechsler preschool and primary scale of intelligence-revised (WPPSI-R).* San Antonio, TX: Psychological Corporation.

Weissbourd, R. (1996). *The vulnerable child. Reading,* MA: Addison-Wesley.

Wolery, M., & Wilbers, J. S. (Eds.). (1994). *Including children with special needs in early childhood programs.* Washington, DC: National Association for the Education of Young Children.

SECTION VI

Parents

CHAPTER 11

The Changing American Family

Objectives

After studying this chapter, the student should be able to:

1. List a minimum of five factors influencing families in the United States today.
2. Discuss five or six of the major changes seen in families today.
3. List at least five ways in which parents can serve as volunteers.
4. State a minimum of five precautions to remember when working with parents.
5. Design a plan for parent participation in any school or center in which the student hopes to be employed.

At my first PTA meeting, I remember being apprehensive and then astounded at the tremendous diversity of parents and other relatives in attendance. We looked like a mini-UN conference!

—Karen Sarafian

Many young children lead complicated lives. When they talk about their dad, their stepdad, their mother's boyfriend, their father's girlfriend, and so on, they don't bat an eye. And Mondays, after some children have been with their weekend parent, some have adjustment problems or are overly tired.

—Clarisa Ho

THE AMERICAN FAMILY IN THE NEW MILLENNIUM

child abuse—any action or inaction that harms a child or puts that child at risk.

As the 21st century begins, the family configurations in the United States continue to change. Witness the following facts.

- The estimated number of **child abuse** and neglect cases reported in the United States in 1997 was over two million (National Center on Child Abuse and Neglect, 1997).
- Roughly 5 percent of children in the United States from birth to age five have a disability (U.S. Bureau of the Census, 2001).
- In 1999, almost half (48 percent) of all children born to women ages 21 to 24 of all races and ethnicities were born out of wedlock (Will, 2002).
- In California, more than half of the state's newborns are Latinos. Based on birth rates, Latinos will comprise the *majority* of children entering California kindergartens in the fall of 2006 (Richardson & Fields, 2003).
- Two-thirds of the states spent more than 10 times as much on corrections and prisons as on child care and early education programs (Children's Defense Fund, 1997).
- As reported by the Associated Press (1998), more unmarried mothers were choosing to remain single, a rise of 18 percent since the 1930s.
- The number of single-parent fathers, though only 3.4 percent of the total, had risen from less than 1 percent a decade earlier (Children's Defense Fund).
- By 2000, the majority of children in the schools were expected to be children of minorities. (In California, this was already true in the year 1989–1990.)
- 21 Key Facts About American Children

3 in 5	preschoolers have mothers in the labor force.
2 in 5	preschoolers eligible for Head Start do not participate in the program.
1 in 3	is born to unmarried parents.
1 in 3	will be poor at some point in childhood.
1 in 3	is behind a year or more in school.
1 in 4	lives with only one parent.
1 in 5	is born to a mother who did not graduate from high school.
1 in 5	children under three is poor now.
1 in 6	is born to a mother who did not receive prenatal care in the first three moths of pregnancy.
1 in 7	children eligible for federal child care assistance through the Child Care and Development Block Grant receives it.
1 in 8	has no health insurance.
1 in 8	never graduates high school.
1 in 8	is born to a teenage mother.
1 in 8	lives in a family receiving food stamps.
1 in 12	has a disability.
1 in 13	was born with a low birthweight.
1 in 16	lives in *extreme* poverty.
1 in 24	lives with neither parent.
1 in 60	sees their parent divorce in any year.
1 in 141	will die before his first birthday.
1 in 1,056	will be killed by firearms before age 20.

From Children's Defense Fund (2002). *The State of Children in America's Union: A 2002 Action Guide to Leave No Child Behind.* Washington, DC: Author.

Two additional factors that need mentioning here are the amount of technology apparent in young children's lives and recently immigrated families. Computer use and cell phone use have changed the way family members communicate, and video games are frequently the way they entertain themselves. Immigrant families, particularly those from Latin America and Asia, have impacted schools and social service departments in a number of the nation's coastal and border areas. The American family is simply more culturally diverse.

What do all these facts and figures say to you as student teachers? First, you need to be sensitive to the needs of the children in your care or in your classroom. Not all will come from a two-parent home where both mother and father are the biological parents. Many more will come from a two-parent home where only one of the parents is the biological one. You can expect more children in your room to have only one parent, who will usually be the mother but sometimes will be the father. You will need to be especially sensitive about planning Mother's Day, Father's Day, and even Grandparent's Day activities.

Lewis (1996) relates her experience with a child in a child care center that was planning a Mother's Day breakfast. The boy was crying because he had no mother at home; he lived with his aunt. When the teacher reassured him that he could invite his aunt to the breakfast, he sobbed, "But she's not my mother." What might the child care center have done to have avoided this trauma for the child?

Another incident one of your authors experienced involved a puzzled child living with her single father. In an activity in which a group of children were putting together creative Mother's Day cards, Marlin (a girl) asked if her card could say "Happy Mother's Day, Daddy."

CHANGES MANDATED BY THE NEW WELFARE LAW

The Children's Defense Fund (1997) report on *The State of America's Children: Yearbook 1997* analyzed the welfare reform law of 1996 and its impact on families.

- First, the former guarantee of cash assistance to families with children was ended, and a block grant to the states was created that had no assurances of help to poor children.
- Aid to Families with Dependent Children (AFDC) became a new program called Temporary Assistance to Needy Families (TANF).
- States required families to work while receiving cash assistance through TANF and shortened the time limit suggested by the federal government.
- Some states imposed a five-year lifetime limit on TANF aid and others made the lifetime limit shorter. Some shortened the time limit to 48 months; others limited aid to 24 months with extensions possible. (You may want to check what your state allows.)
- TANF gave states a huge amount of discretion in how to use their block grant funds. Almost all national standards were eliminated.
- A second major change made large budget cuts in the food stamp program, in the children's part of the Supplementary Security Income (SSI) program, and in other programs such as the Summer Food Service Program, the Title XX Social Services Block Grant, and Medicaid.
- A third radical change, denial of public benefits to legal immigrants, was fortunately corrected.

Has the New Welfare Reform Act Helped?

TANF has been reported to help many who previously had received AFDC. Reports from several states, including Oregon and California, have been generally more positive than negative. Welfare rolls have been reduced across the country.

On the positive side, women who were interviewed stated that becoming educated and being given job training had improved their self-esteem. One woman specifically mentioned that she now felt she was a better role model for her children. Another talked about how she never thought she could pass her high school equivalency exam, much less earn a college degree. She now has a bachelor's degree and is working at a local high-tech company as a research associate.

On the negative side are reports of people who have been unable to benefit from job training and who, if working, are employed at low-level, minimum-wage jobs that provide no benefits such as medical and dental insurance. Still others have been unable to acquire enough skills, and many have significant mental problems that prevent them from profiting from job training. Some who originally found employment are no longer employed; others find that the job they have is a long one-and-a-half to two-hour bus trip from where they live and have become discouraged and overstressed. According to Curiel (1999), welfare reform has been particularly hurtful to children of immigrants. Reform has created a two-tier system for many immigrant families. Services are available for children born in the United States but not available to those born in a foreign country.

Changes such as these stress many families, and we, as teachers and caregivers, must be sensitive to the stress that the families of the children in our care and classrooms feel. We also need to be aware of our own stress levels; we are not going to be effective in conferencing with a stressed parent if we cannot effectively manage our own stress. And to help the children in our care achieve their full potential, we must keep lines of communication with parents open; we must try to establish some kind of rapport so that we, as teachers, form a partnership with the parents to better help the children. We need always to remember that the parents are their children's first teachers, and in many ways, their best teachers.

Wingert (2000) suggests welfare reform has pushed a million preschoolers into mostly low-quality child care and some of these children are showing evidence of developmental delay. She points out that researchers from two universities interviewed a thousand mothers who then rated their children's care. The homes of relatives and baby-sitters were rated to be of lower quality than child care centers by their parents. Many mothers said they could not find or afford better alternatives.

EARLY CHILDHOOD EDUCATION IN THE 20TH CENTURY

For the most part, throughout the first half of the 20th century, the education of young children was an opportunity available only to those who could afford it, primarily the middle and upper middle classes. It was also available in college communities and suburban cities. During World War II, one exception to this pattern emerged. Child care centers such as the Kaiser Centers, located near war-related industries, operated 24 hours each day, provided medical care for the sick child, gave a hot meal that could be taken home with the parent after a long day at the shipyard, and offered other services such as counseling. After the war, the centers closed.

With the advent of Head Start and the concept of compensatory education, the federal government entered the field of early childhood education; that influence is still felt today. Legislators passed the Economic Opportunity Act of 1964 and the Elementary and Secondary Education Act of 1965, which funded "early intervention" programs; many still exist today (Goodlad, 1984). Written into these acts were provisos for active parent participation. Parents from poverty backgrounds with little or no education were presumed to be knowledgeable. In particular, they were knowledgeable about their children and community. No longer would an upper middle class "do-gooder," usually white, come into a minority neighborhood and tell parents how to raise and educate their children. It was a major step forward to where we are today, with Parent Advisory Committees and parent volunteers.

Where are we today? Throughout the 1970s, 1980s, and 1990s, there was a growing trend to full-time child care. As inflation problems hit more families, more mothers joined the workforce. This created a need for extended child care, which led many former nursery schools to offer after-school care. It also led to franchised operations such as Kindercare. The number of children being cared for in licensed care grew steadily. Currently, approximately 38 percent of the children in child care are cared for in a center; nearly 33 percent are cared for by relatives; 21 percent are cared for in **family child care homes**, 6 percent are cared for by an unrelated caregiver in the child's home, and the remaining 2 percent are cared for in a variety of other ways. Parent priorities in selecting child care overwhelmingly concern attention to children's safety, amount and quality of care, providers' communication to parents about their child, and cleanliness followed by concerns about individualized attention, staff warmth, discipline, caregiver experience, parent's ability to drop in unannounced, food service, and appropriate adult-to-child ratios.

family child care homes—child care for young children located in a private, licensed home.

The 1990s saw a gradual increase in the number of employers providing or sponsoring child care services, particularly those who employ a large number of women. Some employers have established their own child care centers. Others have provided vouchers for employees with children, which are redeemable at certain child care centers in the community. Some employers have arranged for a home computer, connected to the employee's computer at work, to allow a mother with very young children to work at home. This has been especially beneficial for nursing mothers and their babies.

Demographers do not expect a decline in the working parent's need for child care. Predictions based on birth rate suggest "In 2005, the number of children 5 and under is projected to be 20 million and will start a slow, steady growth rate for the next 25 years" (Allen, 1998) (see Figure 11–1).

Changing Children

Not only do we see changes in the American family, we also see changes in children. Among those cited by Chandler (1996) are:

- children with limited attention spans but who do not have attention deficit disorder (ADD), or who are not learning disabled and who run the risk of being misidentified
- more children, at ever younger ages, experimenting with drugs, cigarettes, and sex
- more children placed on psychotropic drugs such as Ritalin and Prozac, at younger and younger ages
- more suicides among children
- more violence

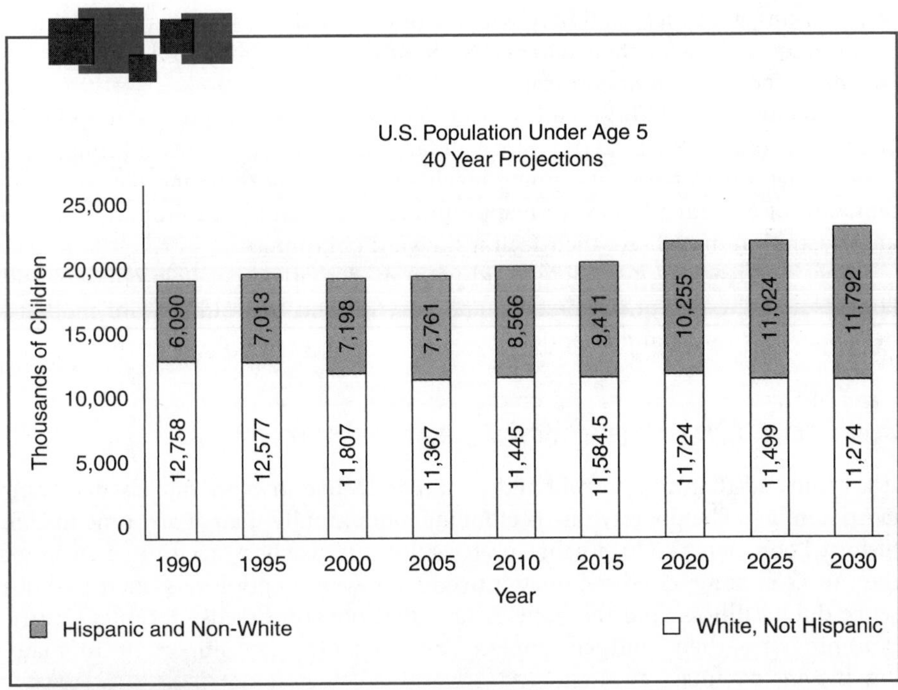

Figure 11–1 Trends in demand for center-based child care and early education. Reprinted with permission from *Child Care Information Exchange*. P.O. Box 3249, Redmond, WA 98073, (800) 221-2864.

- more parents who have abdicated their responsibilities as parents where the child becomes the parent in choosing what will be served for dinner or where the family will go on vacation
- children who are seemingly more sophisticated but who are, in reality, less shielded from adult concerns such as sexually transmitted diseases and AIDS, child abuse, child abduction, and so forth
- children who, as a result of being made aware of adult concerns, have lost a part of their childhood, as Elkind, author of *The Hurried Child*, would suggest

Chandler's greatest concern is that the lack of nurturance and protection by the parents will lead to the development of what she terms "hollow men and women, [who] lacking a conscience . . . are likely to act more violently and destructively." What can you do? It becomes ever more important for you, as future teachers, to provide the nurturance and protection some of your children need.

The Children's Defense Fund (2002) suggests the national economic recession that began in 2001 has adversely affected young children:

> It has undone much of the employment gains for parents in 1995–2000 that helped to reduce child poverty during those prosperous years. The number of children with an unemployed parent jumped by 1.2 million (41 percent) between the end of 2000 and 2001.

Daily crime and violence, and the less than adequate health care that exists in some inner cities, can sap a family's hope of ever attaining economic security. Young children touched by despair and anger display the resultant behaviors in school settings.

Working with these children, who are often called "at risk," may mean interacting frequently with their parents. Screening children's day-to-day health has become a very important concern.

In many cases of abuse and neglect, family stress is the precipitating factor (Marotz, Cross, & Rush, 2001). Since all families experience stressful times, it is family reactions to stress, its coping mechanisms or lack of them, that is important. Out-of-control adults with inappropriate and often out-of-proportion anger and frustration may direct their feelings toward children.

Sensitive teaching techniques and program activities that help children and families adapt, cope, problem-solve, and survive, and that aid upward mobility, need staff discussion and attention.

Are the Children You Teach Hungry?

It is estimated that millions of children under 18 live in economically disadvantaged families. The poverty rate is climbing more rapidly than at any time in U.S. history. Poor diets produce behavioral results, and teachers need to be aware of the causes of some children's inattentiveness, lower energy levels, increased absence due to illness, and the hopelessness that poverty breeds. A center's nutrition program, then, and cleanliness have become very important to many low-income parents.

On the other end of the scale are America's overweight youngsters. The percentage of obese children in the United States has skyrocketed to 25 percent (Sutterby & Frost, 2002).

Rarely are parents' child care fees addressed in early childhood teacher training programs. Student teachers need to understand parents' fees can be a hardship for some families. Many families will not qualify for subsidized care in public programs. Parents near but just above low-income qualifying levels are particularly impacted. Wronge (2001) reviewed California child care costs and found child care one of the largest family expenditures, with full-time toddler care costing more than 50 percent of fair market rent for a two-bedroom apartment in almost every California county. The San Francisco Bay area is among the most expensive with toddler care costing over $600 a month.

The Importance of Fathers

Another sobering statistic comes from a U.S. News & World Report study of why fathers are important, titled "Honor Thy Children." Shapiro and Schrof (1995) state that two of every five children in the United States do not live with their biological father. They and their associates raised several issues such as whether or not marriage and parenting skills can be taught, how children can reconnect to noncustodial fathers, whether divorces should be more difficult to obtain, and in what ways fathers can be supportive. The study pointed out the part that fathers play in the raising of their children. Shapiro and Schrof open with the sentence, "Dad is destiny," and continue with "More than virtually any other factor, a biological father's presence in the family will determine a child's success and happiness. Rich or poor, white or black, the children of divorce and those born outside marriage, struggle through life at a measurable disadvantage, according to a growing chorus of social thinkers." Material from research in the field is presented to reinforce their claim of disadvantage. The opening article in the U.S. News study concludes with a quote from David Blankenhorn, author of *Fatherless America: Confronting Our Most Urgent Social Problem*, and founder of the New York–based

Institute for American Values, "being a loving father and a good husband is the best part of being a man."

PARENTS AS VOLUNTEERS

As student teachers, you will be directly involved with any parent volunteers in your cooperating teacher's room. It is important to maintain a cordial and collegial relationship with any of them. You are, after all, a professional, and you should always remember that. Your cooperating teacher has the responsibility of supervising a student teacher, paid teacher aides, *and* parent volunteers in the classroom. As time passes, you may be asked to do some partial or full supervision of aides and volunteers under your cooperating teacher's direction. Observing how your cooperating teacher interacts and instructs aides and volunteers is a prudent move. A conversation about your interaction with aides and volunteers usually takes place early in your placement. If you feel awkward, discuss your supervisory responsibilities early in your placement. Some cooperating teachers expect student teachers to watch and direct aides or volunteers who need specific, step-by-step directions for certain classroom tasks.

In many ways, the well-educated, middle- or upper middle-class parent has often been involved at the preschool level, in cooperative schools, and child development centers associated with universities. These same parents often carried their interest and involvement in their children's education into the elementary school as volunteers. Prior to World War II, few married women worked, and there were few single parents. Because of the Depression during the 1930s, there were no paid aides in most elementary schools. Teachers who wanted to individualize programs often asked parents for help. Others felt parents did not belong in the classroom, although they were welcome at PTA/PTO meetings and at school fund-raising events. Volunteers have been part of Head Start since 1965 (Wallach, 2001). It was hoped classroom experience might improve parenting skill and lead to future parental employment in Head Start. Today's Head Start parents and community volunteers continue to provide paid and unpaid support for classrooms, yard activities, transportation, center upkeep, and serve as bilingual and special needs resources.

PTA/PTO—Parent-Teacher Association/Parent-Teacher Organization.

teacher-pupil ratio—the number of qualified teachers per attending children in a given classroom. Usually mandated by a state's licensing law, or adopted by another administrative or legislative body.

The compensatory education programs brought a new focus on the parent (Brewer, 1992). The findings of many studies on class size and the effects of the teacher-pupil ratio on learning are in favor of smaller classes. A review of 59 studies revealed that lowering the teacher-pupil ratio led to better results on cognitive measures and favorable effects on both teachers and students in terms of higher morale, more positive attitudes, self concepts, and the like (Smith & Glass, 1990). One of the easiest ways to lower the teacher-pupil ratio is through the use of parent volunteers (see Figure 11–2).

Figure 11–2 Parent volunteers reduce the number of children per adult in a classroom.

With young children, many states limit the child-adult ratio for preschool to 15:1 for four-year-olds, 12:1 for three-year-olds, and as low as 3:1 for infants. Unfortunately, in public elementary schools, classes in the primary grades (grades one through three) are often as large as 31:1 or even higher, and are dependent on the teachers' contract with the local school board. One kindergarten where we placed a student teacher had 33 students in the classroom with only one teacher and one part-time aide. On the other hand, most professionals believe smaller class size in both preschools and elementary schools promotes a higher quality of education. A concerted effort to obtain smaller class size in public elementary schools was apparent in many states during the late 1990s. California legislators mandated and funded a ratio of 20 children to one teacher in kindergarten through third grade. Unfortunately, current budget cuts in California have affected the legislation.

It is presumed that the younger the child, the more the child needs adult attention. Although the concept of using parent volunteers works in theory, in practice there are many limitations. In many households, both parents are working and do not have the time to volunteer; others, particularly low-income and/or minority parents, may not feel welcome or needed, or feel that they have no skills or knowledge of value to share. Wallach (2001) points out the welfare reform law of 1996 has made it more difficult for early childhood programs to recruit volunteers. Publically assisted parents must work or go to school.

What is a teacher to do when federal and state mandates require parent participation? As always, there is less of a problem with the nonworking parent. There may be many reasons why the parent does not work, and you need to be sensitive to them. One parent may not work because there is a baby at home and no one with whom the baby can be left. Another may be disabled or have problems with mobility.

parent-teacher conference—a one on one interaction between the teacher and the child's parent(s).

In most communities in past years, the administration of school programs was left to the professionals: the principal and teachers in a public school, and the director in a preschool. Most of these professionals were middle class, often white. They perceived their role as one of informing parents about their children's behaviors, especially learning behaviors. Thus, parent-teacher conferences were held at regular intervals. During these conferences, teachers told parents what their children had been doing on various measures of learning and classroom behavior. The professionals sometimes felt that the parent did not know how to parent; they sometimes looked down on the parent whose English was different and whose clothing was old, torn, and unstylish. Parent-teacher organizations were usually led by middle-class, nonworking mothers. Lower-class parents tended to be ignored if they attended. Soon they stopped coming, and unkind teachers and other parents would say, "Well, what can you expect of parents with no background in school who speak broken English? They just don't care." Fortunately, federal compensatory education programs demanded parent participation. It is recognized that almost all parents love and care for their children and want what is best for them. Of course, there are those to whom children are a nuisance, but this is a phenomenon found across all social classes. There are neglectful upper-class parents, as well as uncaring middle- and lower-class families.

It is time to change our definition of parent volunteer work. Traditionally, teachers, both in preschool and elementary school settings, have looked at parent volunteers as extra hands in the classroom. But with nearly 62 percent of all women with children six and under working (and that figure jumps to over 70 percent when mothers of five- to 18-year-olds are included), we need to look at parent volunteerism in a different way. Are we realistic when we expect parents to be able to assist in the classroom? In what other ways can we involve parents? How can we attract the busy career-oriented parent, the overworked single parent, the homemaker with three small children, or the undereducated teen parent? What expectations should we have regarding their possible involvement?

In what ways can parents in different early childhood programs involve themselves or live up to a center's expectation? They:

- provide insights, background material, and perspectives that help facilitate individualized learning and program planning
- serve as supportive users of child care services by attending meetings, participating in projects, and receiving school information pertinent to their child's growth and development or to the school's viability

- teach their children and reinforce school learning and experiences
- volunteer and provide classroom assistance and materials
- consult with teachers (centers) serving as collaborators and advisors
- work as paid classroom aides, providing unique talents and social and cultural continuity for attending children
- participate in the center's decision-making process
- financially support the center's continued operation and existence, thereby providing jobs for workers
- vote for measures that provide support and upgrade early childhood education for America's children and families

HOW TO MOTIVATE PARENTS TO VOLUNTEER

As student teachers, you are not expected to recruit or motivate any parent to volunteer. On the other hand, if your cooperating teacher notices that you have established a warm relationship with one parent in particular, he may suggest that you speak to this parent about volunteering to do something for the class, whether it be baking some cupcakes for an upcoming class party or bringing in some old magazines for children to use in collages. Most of the time, of course, you will not be involved except perhaps in working together with a parent volunteer in the classroom or on a class trip.

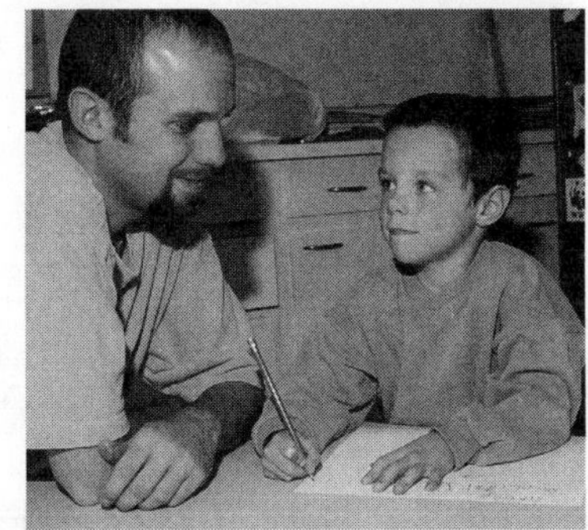

Figure 11–3 Parent volunteers often help with instruction.

One might say that anything a parent does of her own free will to be of some service to the teacher is being a volunteer (see Figures 11–3 and 11–4). Parents have been baking cookies for classroom parties for years. They have also sewn beanbags, mixed homemade clay, and brought in old toys for a toy share-in. Parents have built climbing structures and dramatic play equipment, put up fences, installed swings, and cleaned yards and rooms. Many of these activities have been done at home or on the parents' free time (see Figure 11–5). These are volunteer activities.

Preschools tend to maintain close contact with parents, and, to a certain extent, the same procedures are used by elementary schools. Both send newsletters

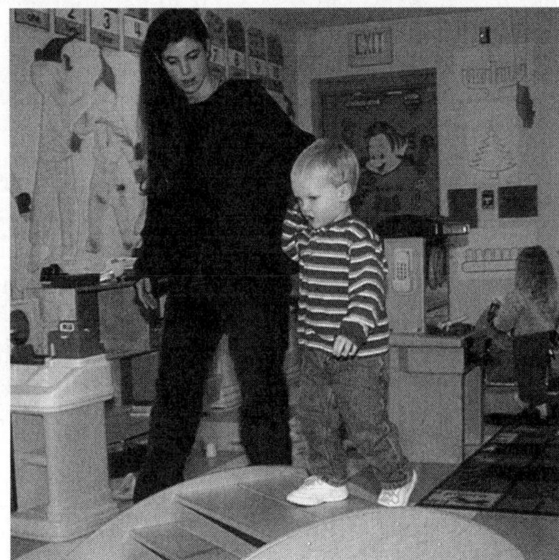

Figure 11–4 There are so many classroom tasks for volunteers.

Figure 11–5 This father enjoys volunteering at the school on his day off.

home to parents; typically, both hold parent conferences (generally scheduled at least twice during the year); teachers in both settings regularly telephone parents (too often, unfortunately, to report a problem with the child rather than to report a successful incident); both frequently have fund-raisers planned and implemented by a PTA/PTO/Parent Advisory Committee. The formal nature of many of these forms of communication may be one reason some principals advocate informal contact with parents.

> One elementary school principal we know insists that all teachers, including student teachers assigned to her school, telephone the parents of every student in their respective classes at least once a month. During the opening week of school, teachers send home a notice with their students that lists times when they will be free to make or receive calls and asks parents to indicate what times will best suit their busy schedules. These hours generally include at least one lunch hour and one after school period of two hours.
>
> Some teachers who live locally also may indicate hours available in the early evening. The result has been overwhelmingly positive. One parent states, "I used to dread hearing from Robert's teacher; I knew it had to be about something bad he'd done. Now, I hear about the good things he's done and it makes the not-so-good things seem a lot better!" (A thank you to Suzon Kornblum, principal at Walters School, Fremont, CA, for sharing this anecdote.)

Regardless of how we may feel that parents do not want to be bothered, they do want to keep in close touch with their children's teachers and do not look on a phone call or a short conference as a "bother." No parent likes to be called only when something goes wrong; regularly scheduled conferences, other than when they are formally required for biannual reporting, help build rapport and a sense of teamwork between parent and teacher.

Working parents often can help more than teachers assume they can; many wait to be called and are disappointed when they are not. One reason parents stated that they would like to be *invited* to volunteer is that they may not feel like they can make a regular commitment to the classroom but that they can and would like to be invited to help out occasionally. Other parents are simply more reserved or may feel that they have little to offer, and are, therefore, reluctant to volunteer unless asked. Teachers may mistake reticence as a "no" when the parent may be expecting the teacher to say, "Would you be able to . . . ?"

Special events, as we might remember from our own school days, are a sure winner and draw a large number of parents into the school. When the weather permits, one family child care home provider plans Saturday family picnics for the parents of the children in her care; she also plans birthday and holiday parties. As a result, she has a waiting list of neighborhood working parents who would like to have their infants, toddlers, or preschoolers in her home care.

One elementary school principal starts the year with a barbecue for the families of all the children attending his school and underwrites the cost of the hot dogs himself; the PTA provides the buns, condiments, baked beans, soft drinks, and ice cream bars. Parents are asked only to bring themselves and all of their children, regardless of age. This principal has managed to turn around a school with many dissatisfied parents, much dissension among the different ethnic groups in attendance, and too much vandalism.

Other highlights of the school year include Saturday morning as well as evening PTA meetings to accommodate the schools' parent population, composed largely of two working parents or working single parents. Child care is always provided, and there is a potluck lunch on Saturdays. A major highlight (and fundraiser) of the year in the spring is the annual International Day festival, when parents from the different ethnic groups provide foods, and there are folksinging and dancing performances by their children.

Throughout the year, different classrooms sponsor programs for the parents; a bulletin board in the entry hall of the school is reserved for the student of the week, with an appropriate certificate awarded every Friday. The parents of the child are invited to attend the award ceremony, and many parents arrange their work hours so they can. The student of the week plans his bulletin board; the child's school and family pictures may be displayed; there are drawings of favorite toys, TV shows, foods, posting of best papers, and so on.

Before the end of the school year, every child in attendance receives a schoolwide award of some kind for creative writing effort, top math grade in her classroom, best drawing or painting, best craft project, grade-level science fair awards, and so forth. Knowing that not every student can be a schoolwide student of the week, several teachers have a classroom student of the week. One kindergarten teacher has the other children draw a picture of their student-of-the-week classmate; the pictures are then posted on the bulletin board together with the student-of-the-week's own picture and school picture. Teachers of older students often have classmates write an essay about their student-of-the-week peer.

Some of the special occasions include a schoolwide science fair with grade-level prizes awarded (incidentally, every participant receives at least an "honorable mention" ribbon); a schoolwide arts-and-crafts fair, again with grade-level awards and the added benefit to the children of an opportunity to sell their creations should they choose; the publication of a school creative writing book, in which every child has a self-chosen best effort (drawing, painting, essay, poem, myth, and so on) bound and placed on display in the school library. Books from previous years are fitted with pockets and check-out cards, and are among the more popular items carried in the library. Special occasions are limited only by the imagination of the teachers, parents, directors, and/or principals planning them.

The question remains, though, how do you persuade nonparticipating parents that they are needed? Most, if not all, preschools, centers, and elementary schools have parent handbooks that provide basic information about the school or center for parents; many also have staff handbooks available for teachers and student teachers that provide helpful hints. They often include communication strategies and specific techniques and activities useful in working with parents.

One way to encourage a parent to participate is to speak to the parent about your expectations for his involvement at the time the child is registered. Some centers and schools provide parents with a list of activities in which they may participate; the parent is asked to check those activities she feels comfortable doing. The teacher then calls on the parent when needed and invites the parent to help.

The home visit can lead to better rapport between the parent and school. It is possible for a discerning teacher to note special talents on a home visit (hand-sewn curtains or drapes; potted plants; newly painted walls that the parents did themselves; cooking abilities). The teacher can follow up by requesting that the parent use the talent on a school project (see Figure 11–6). Parents who protest that they have no skills may think the teacher means teaching skills and may not realize that wielding a paintbrush can sometimes be of more value. Gardening skills are also frequently overlooked. Parents may not realize how much care goes into maintaining the landscape of a center and may be delighted to spend an afternoon digging the ground for a garden the children will be planting during the next week. A teacher might want to sprout beans and peas and then transfer them

home visit—a one-on-one interaction between the teacher and the parent(s) in the child's home.

Figure 11-6 A creative bulletin board depicting family pictures

into a vegetable garden, allowing the children to weed and water the beans and peas, watch them grow, and finally pick, cook, and eat the fruits of their labor.

McCracken (1995) recommends the following:

- People's names are pronounced and spelled correctly (ask if you're not sure)
- Family members are welcome as active participants in the group's activities (taking children's dictation; sharing family stories, treasures, or recipes)
- Continuity between home and group is valued (staff communicate in children's home languages, information is exchanged regularly)
- Differences with family members or among staff are resolved gracefully (using the same conflict resolution techniques we facilitate with children)
- We bring the community into our class-room (volunteers, hands-on demonstrations, acknowledgment of donations of materials such as lumber or books)
- Children reach out into the community (frequent field trips; walks around the neighborhood; getting to know people, buildings)

Many teachers today keep in touch with parents and students by e-mail. Some post assignments, due dates, upcoming events, requests for help, and so on. Parents and students can e-mail the teacher with comments and questions. E-mail provides a two-way communication device to keep information and concerns flowing.

To build strong partnerships with parents, Rosenthal and Sawyers (1996) advocate building on parents' strengths. They believe that we professionals have too long looked at some families as being dysfunctional and overlooked the strengths those families might have. Too long have we considered some parents incapable of being our allies and as only needing to be tolerated. If we enter into a relationship with any parent with such a bias, it prevents us from looking at what this parent may be able to contribute. Rosenthal and Sawyers strongly believe that schools must become "family-friendly" through such activities as potluck meals in the classroom, parent tutoring programs with their own children, adult literacy programs, and informal meetings with the principal.

Workman and Gage (1997) agree and advise using a Family Strengths Model approach to parent involvement at the preschool. They "believe that if early childhood professionals were to define parent involvement in a different, broader context, focusing on issues of partnership rather than participation or attendance, their view would be altered significantly."

The Family Strengths Model is an integrated process that includes "emotional support, joint problem solving, and concrete assistance" (Workman & Gage, 1997). Workman and Gage's program uses a Family Development Plan to clarify preschool and parent goals. It is written together with the parent(s), teachers, and director. It focuses on ways the parent and school can work as partners in the overall development of the child.

Among the suggestions Kelley-Laine (1998) mentions is the need, among other goals, to identify parents' agendas in order to make the best use of their energy and resources. Kelly et al. (1998) mention the need for such seemingly obvious things as an attractive physical school appearance. Located in an inner-city, high-poverty, crime-ridden metropolitan area, Kelly and her associates found that providing parents with "A Place to Hang Our Hats," a room of their own where parents can meet and talk, sit in comfortable chairs, read from a selection of parent-oriented materials, helps parents feel more "at home." The parents' room also provides a safe place for parents, students, and teachers to meet informally as well as formally. If your school has an empty room, why not think about redecorating it and turning it into a parents' room?

Powell (1998), addressing Head Start parents and the mandate for their participation, cautions that the new welfare reform may reduce the opportunity for parent participation because parents are involved in job training and work responsibilities.

Fege (1997) looks at the possibility that there will be parental rights legislation that would allow parents to have the right to "direct the upbringing and education of their children" and "to direct and control the upbringing, education, values, and discipline of their children." These phrases are from actual proposed laws in two of 26 states. Neither law passed. But even the U.S. Congress has been considering laws related to parents' rights. Fege states that such laws are not necessary, and instead, have proved highly divisive in the states that have proposed them. He suggests, instead, that schools should look at such legislation as a wake-up call to provide for greater parental input on issues that concern them.

Cultural Consistency

What is apparent today in most early childhood classrooms are visual signs, implemented programs, and staff behaviors aimed at providing children and parent volunteers with a degree of cultural consistency between home and school. Individual family cultures and beliefs are respected. Educators believe in the ability of parents to make good parental decisions. Parents are the true experts concerning their own children. Professional early childhood staff members function as supportive partners, realizing there may be stages in each family's development. They are not only child educators and advocates but also parent educators, family advocates, and supportive family resources.

Teachers consistently share information about children's center learnings and experiences, and guide parents by alerting them to children's progress in attaining developmental milestones. In this way, a continuity between home and school is maintained.

Studies of Parent Participation

A friend who is a kindergarten teacher in a private church-sponsored school visits the home of every incoming child during the late summer. She always brings a simple toy to entertain the child and to make the child feel important. With the child busily occupied, the parents then feel more relaxed, rapport is easily established, and requests for help are met with a more positive frame of mind. This teacher usually has between one-fourth and one-third of her parents unable to help out during the school day due to work or school commitments. The remaining parents are expected to donate at least one morning or afternoon each week to the program. Even knowing that they are expected to assist once each week, many parents are relatively inactive. Of 20 parents, this teacher knows she will be fortunate if four or five assist regularly. More likely than not, assistance will be limited to out-of-school kinds of assistance (baking cookies, making bean bags) rather than in-school assistance (D. Hessler, personal communication, October 1995).

Figure 11–7 Two parents enjoying their school's appreciation lunch for volunteers.

Teachers who work with parent volunteers value the parents and their labor (see Figure 11–7). A teacher of an ungraded primary class in a suburban school district knows that her classroom cannot function without the assistance of parent volunteers. Because her class is an optional one within the structure of a traditional elementary school, one expectation of all parents, choosing this setting for their children, is active parent involvement in the classroom. In the same district, there is one entire elementary school operating without standard age-level grades. Again, the expectation of parents who choose this school is their active classroom involvement (G. A. Peters, personal communication, April 1988).

Comer (1998) relates the story of how one school in New Haven, Connecticut, went from having children scoring at the bottom of the achievement tests every year to having the top scores in the district. How was this accomplished? One key was the active involvement of parents in making curriculum decisions cooperatively with teachers. Another key was providing these basically low-income, often stressed families with an array of social services and empowering them as knowledgeable teachers of their own children. A third key was the retraining of the teaching staff, including the transfer of teachers unable to accept change.

Generally, there are advantages for everyone involved in parent participation programs. Teachers have the additional resource of the volunteer's time, energy, and talent; parents have the satisfaction of knowing that they are making an active contribution to their children's learning; and children feel that their parents care more, so they achieve more in school.

Tom Kerr (1993), editor of *Early Childhood News*, suggests the following strategies for promoting parent involvement in Head Start:

1. Inform parents about performance standards . . . guide and review with them throughout the planning and participation stages to ensure that standards are being met.
2. Reinforce the shared decision-making responsibilities of staff, administrators, board members, and parents through substantive training of staff and parents on their roles and responsibilities.
3. Emphasize and demonstrate the Head Start program's philosophy about parent involvement, including the importance of the partnership concept in preservice and in-service staff training.

Parent Handbooks

It was recommended in earlier chapters that student teachers familiarize themselves with parent handbooks. Not only do they provide valuable information about a center's or school's mission, philosophy, and program goals, but also acquaint student teachers to expectations concerning parents' involvement in school activities and services including volunteering, home visits, parent conferencing, and center meetings. Child health, guidance, and confidentiality policies are usually spelled out, along with particulars concerning administering child medications.

Teacher Attributes

Comer and Poussaint (1992) note the following teacher attributes positively influence teacher-parent relationships:

- warmth
- openness
- sensitivity
- flexibility
- reliability
- accessibility

From parents' perspectives, these teacher characteristics are desirable: trust, warmth, closeness, positive self-image, effective classroom management, child-centeredness, positive discipline, nurturance, and effective teaching skills (Swick, 1992).

Strategies

Swick (1992) describes strategies he believes have proven valuable in the promotion of strong parent-school partnerships:

> The degree to which strategies are related to the needs and interests of parents and to the unique situations of schools and teachers influences the level of success. Home visits, conferences, parent centers, telecommunication, involvement in the classroom, participatory decision-making, parent and adult education programs, home learning activities, and family-school networking are some of the many strategies that have effectively engaged parents and teachers in supportive and collaborative roles.

Parents Seeking Advice

Many parents of young children are seeking additional child-rearing advice, especially about disciplining, toilet training, sleep issues, crying and *how to help their children learn.* The Commonwealth Fund Study of Parents with Young Children surveyed 2,017 parents of children one to three years of age and noted, despite the extensive sources of child-rearing information available, parents wanted to know additional ways to help and encourage child learning. In fact, it topped the list of parental requests (McLearn, Davis, Schoen, & Parker, 1998). Figure 11–8 displays percentages of parent interactions in selected probed activities.

Although parental desire to increase their child's learning ability was present, the study concluded:

> Mothers and fathers do not report engaging in important activities with their children on a regular basis. For example, fewer than one in five parents in this study read or looked at a book with their child more than once a day; only slightly more than one-third sang or played music more than once a day; and almost one-third of parents did not even play with their child more than once a day.

Activity	Not at All	Once or Twice a Week	Several Times a Week	About Once a Day	More Than Once a Day
Read a book or look at a picture book	16	23	21	20	19
Sing or play music	8	13	20	23	36
Play	1	1	14	15	69
Hug and cuddle	•••	1	10	6	83

Data are percent distribution.

Figure 11-8 Parent activities with child. From McLearn, K. T., Davis, K., Schoen, C., and Parker, S. (1998, March). *Listening to parents: A national study of parents with young children.* New York: The Commonwealth Fund. Reprinted with permission from The Commonwealth Fund.

Parents are busy, to be sure, and there just does not seem to be enough time to do even more, especially if the importance of these activities in the child's development is undervalued.

In 2001, Lally, Lerner, and Lurie-Hurvitz reviewed a landmark national study attempting to gauge adult and parent knowledge of child development. They suggest that while American adults and parents are well informed about many areas of child development, significant gaps exist, including the following:

- an understanding of the depth of a baby's emotional life and how deeply babies are affected by their daily interaction with caregivers and their environments
- parent theories on spoiling and spanking
- parents' expectations of young children's behavior or actions at different ages
- an understanding of possible choices of activities to promote development

Can early childhood educators emphasize the importance of these and other parental activities in young children's development? They can when their training has included depth in child development and early childhood education coursework, and their goals include assisting parents to raise sufficiently healthy, happy, motivated, and confident children able to succeed in early childhood and beyond.

Grandparents

Expect to see some children's grandparents working in classrooms or at drop off and exit times. A range of social problems including divorce, teenage childbirth, economics, single parenthood, drugs, addiction, and unemployment have catapulted many grandparents into an involved role in their grandchildren's lives (K. S. Berger, 2001). In 1998, 6.7 percent of children in the United States were living exclusively with grandparents. For 34 percent, their single-parent offspring also lived in the same household (E.H. Berger, 2004).

Other nonresident grandparents actively participate in the daily lives of their grandchildren. A diversity of grandparent-grandchild relationships exists, depending on the family's ethnic and cultural background.

Immigrant grandparents, especially Mexican-American and Asian-American, tend to encourage traditional cultural values, beliefs, language, and customs, and promote pride in the family's heritage.

Family Support Structure

NAEYC (1998) indicates the ethical responsibilities to families (see Figure 11–9). Child centers are becoming increasingly important as supportive parent partners in young children's care and education (see Figure 11–10). Student teachers can expect to become teachers who will be more involved in parents' needs and lives than past generations of care providers.

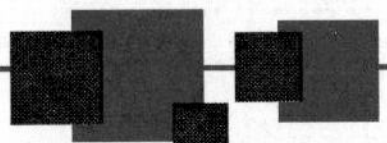

Families are of primary importance in children's development. (The term family may include others, besides parents, who are responsibly involved with the child.) Because the family and the early childhood practitioner have a common interest in the child's welfare, we acknowledge a primary responsibility to bring about collaboration between the home and school in ways that enhance the child's development.

Ideals:

I-2.1—To develop relationships of mutual trust with families we serve.

I-2.2—To acknowledge and build upon strengths and competencies as we support families in their task of nurturing children.

I-2.3—To respect the dignity of each family and its culture, language, customs, and beliefs.

I-2.4—To respect families' childrearing values and their right to make decisions for their children.

I-2.5—To interpret each child's progress to parents within the framework of a developmental perspective and to help families understand and appreciate the value of developmentally appropriate early childhood practices.

I-2.6—To help family members improve their understanding of their children and to enhance their skills as parents.

I-2.7—To participate in building support networks for families by providing them with opportunities to interact with program staff, other families, community resources, and professional services.

Principles:

P-2.1—We shall not deny family members access to their child's classroom or program setting.

P-2.2—We shall inform families of program philosophy, policies, and personnel qualifications, and explain why we teach as we do—which should be in accordance with out ethical responsibilities to children.

P-2.3—We shall inform families of and, when appropriate, involve them in policy decisions.

P-2.4—We shall involve families in significant decisions affecting their child.

P-2.5—We shall inform the family of accidents involving their child, of risks such as exposures to contagious disease that may result in infection, and of occurrences that might result in emotional stress.

P-2.6—To improve the quality of early childhood care and education, we shall cooperate with qualified child development researchers. Families shall be fully informed of any proposed research projects involving their children and shall have the opportunity to give or withhold consent without penalty. We shall not permit or participate in research that could in any way hinder the education, development, or well-being of children.

continues

Figure 11-9 Ethical responsibilities to families. From *Code of Ethical Conduct and Statement of Commitment: Guidelines for Responsible Behavior in Early Childhood Education*, 1998. Reprinted with permission from the National Association for the Education of Young Children.

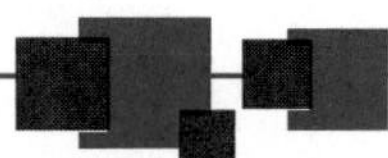

P-2.7— We shall not engage in or support exploitation of families. We shall not use our relationship with a family for private advantage or personal gain, or enter into relationships with family members that might impair our effectiveness in working with children.

P-2.8— We shall develop written policies for the protection of confidentiality and the disclosure of children's records. These policy documents shall be made available to all program personnel and families. Disclosure of children's records beyond family members, program personnel, and consultants having an obligation of confidentiality shall require familial consent (except in cases of abuse or neglect).

P-2.9— We shall maintain confidentiality and shall respect the family's right to privacy, refraining from disclosure of confidential information and intrusion into family life. However, when we have reason to believe that a child's welfare is at risk, it is permissible to share confidential information with agencies and individuals who may be able to intervene in the child's interest.

P-2.10— In cases where family members are in conflict, we shall work openly, sharing our observations of the child, to help all parties involved make informed decisions. We shall refrain from becoming an advocate for one party.

P-2.11— We shall be familiar with and appropriately use community resources and professional services that support families. After a referral has been made, we shall follow up to ensure that services have been appropriately provided.

Figure 11-9 (continued)

Parent Outreach

Many families have multiple, complicated needs, and child care programs generally are not funded to address them. Groginsky, Robison, and Smith (1999) note:

> Families with young children face unprecedented levels of stress, including community violence and crime, domestic violence, child abuse and neglect, teenage pregnancy, health threats such as HIV/AIDS, lack of adequate nutrition and health care, family conflict, and divorce. For many young children, biological and environmental factors pose danger to their development.

State legislative bodies are encouraging linkages among state programs and services, and also are promoting comprehensive initiatives that integrate family resource services (Groginsky, Robison, & Smith, 1999). State prekindergarten programs, innovative preschool funding approaches, and coordination with existing Head Start programs have happened in a number of states that recognize the severity of family problems that create at-risk children.

Prekindergarten centers with the funds necessary to support such activities are expanding parent services and supportive assistance programs.

A number of activities and questions should be considered in developing an early childhood parent outreach plan.

1. Gather information about families in the community.
   a. What are their needs?
   b. Are parents willing to attend meetings?
2. Collect the following data:
   a. Is parental discipline strict, too easy, or moderate?
   b. How is (are) guidance technique(s) affecting young children?

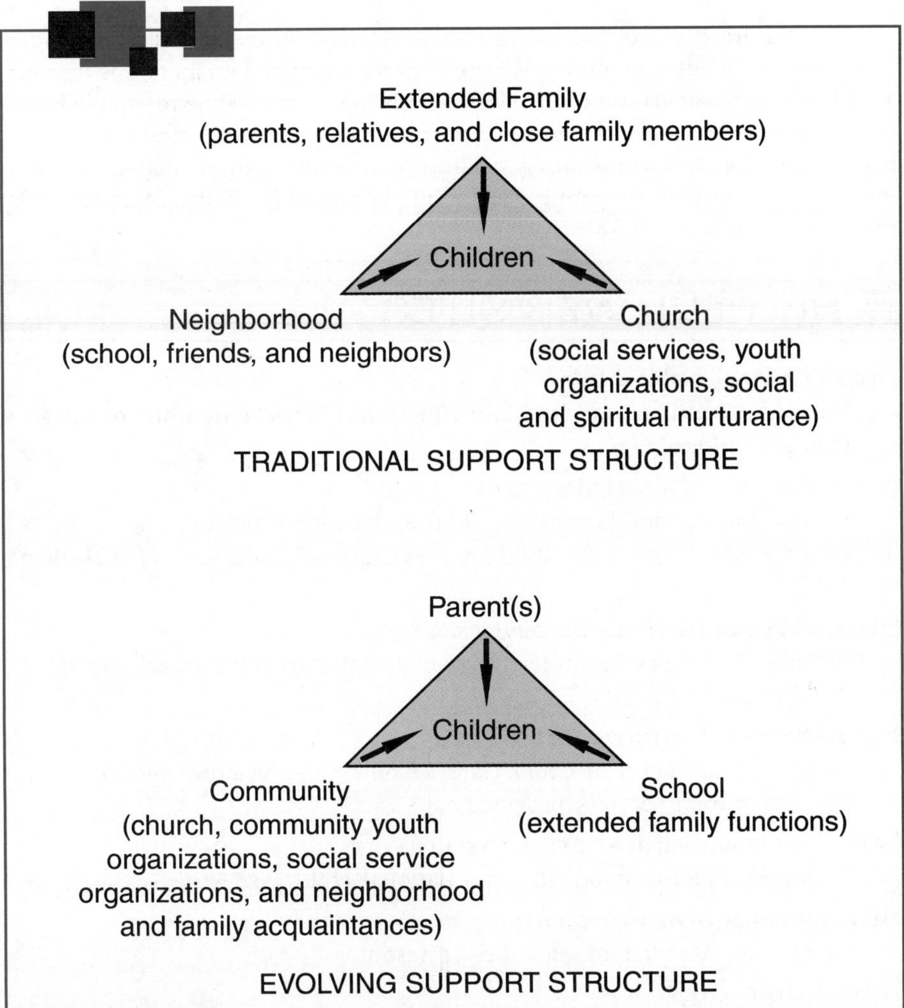

Figure 11–10 Changing support structures for children and families. Reprinted with permission from the National Association for the Education of Young Children.

c. What are family communication styles?
d. Do children with antisocial behaviors exist?
e. Is substance abuse prevalent in the community?
f. What is causing parent stress? Poverty? Isolation? Crime? Unemployment? Lack of resources? Other factors?

Remember the ideas previously mentioned by Rosenthal and Sawyers (1996), Workman and Gage (1997), and Kelley-Laine (1998) as you and your cooperating teacher consider planning a parent outreach program.

SUMMARY

Parent participation is a many-faceted phenomenon. Volunteering includes assisting in the classroom as well as baking cookies for snack time, helping build climbing structures, attending parent education meetings, sewing beanbags, and many more activities.

The historical use of parents as volunteers was discussed and some studies on the use of parents as volunteers were reviewed. Remember, do not be discouraged if parent participation in the classroom is low. It takes time to establish rapport with parents, especially those from different cultures. Remember that the keys to success are establishing good lines of communication; shared decision-making, together with cooperative planning of curriculum; and acceptance of the parent. Show that you CARE.

HELPFUL WEB SITES

http://www.calib.com/

National Clearinghouse on Child Abuse and Neglect Information. Readings and information.

http://www.childstats.gov/

Federal Interagency Forum on Child and Family Statistics. Search for a report entitled America's Children: Key National Indicators of Well-Being 2002.

http://www.familiesandwork.org

Families and Work Institute. Curricular materials for teachers can be downloaded.

http://www.naccrra.net

National Association of Child Care Resource and Referral Agencies. Research parent services provided.

http://www.childrensdefense.org

Children's Defense Fund. Reviews national child care issues.

http://childcareaware.org

Child Care Aware. Links families to resources.

http://npin.org/

NPIN: National Parent Information Center. Family information.

SUGGESTED ACTIVITIES

A. Visit three or four different types of preschools or elementary schools. These might include a publicly supported child care center, a proprietary preschool and/or child center, an adult education-sponsored preschool, the early childhood center associated with your college or university, a public elementary school, and a private and/or parochial elementary school. Talk with the teachers, directors, or principals about how they involve parents. Discuss your findings with your peers and supervisor.

B. With your cooperating teacher, develop a list of activities for volunteers for use in your own classroom.

C. Role-play the following situations.

1. Parent feels children "caught" in doctor play with suggestive overtones should have their school enrollment terminated.
2. Parent group asks teacher to increase academic instruction with children.
3. Father requests teachers to encourage a child bitten by another to bite the attacker.
4. Parent requests nail-biting child be punished at school.

REVIEW

A. List five different ways in which parents can serve as volunteers.

B. Name five precautions to keep in mind when working with parents.

C. Design a plan for a parent education meeting. What are your objectives? What materials or equipment will you need? Describe the procedures. Discuss your plan with your cooperating teacher, peers, and supervisor. Implement the plan and evaluate its effectiveness.

CASE SCENARIO

Setting: Suzanne, the daughter of an elementary school teacher, was enrolled in a small (18-child) private preschool in a suburban neighborhood. Suzanne, an older four-year-old, had attended for over a year.

Suzanne enjoyed activities, particularly music and art, and books were a favorite choice. She often was found in the book loft with pals pretending to read, and laughing and pointing to illustrations. Able to read a few words, she delighted in sharing these with her teachers. Active in the play yard, she was a sought-after playmate, easily enticing others with her creative play games. Suzanne's mother asked for a conference and described a troubling behavior Suzanne had displayed at home. Suzanne had been stung by a bee a few months earlier, and since had, at times, become hysterical, screaming "It's on me! Get it off!" while flailing and flapping her arms as if to remove a bee.

The staff developed a plan of action contingent on an episode at school. Teachers would remain calm and protect Suzanne and others from harm or distress by gently moving Suzanne to a quiet area if possible. When Suzanne quieted, staff would calmly say something like "I don't see any bees on you, Suzanne. There are no bees flying around you" or something similar.

Fortunately, Suzanne was alone with a student teacher when she became highly agitated, trying to slap imaginary bees from herself. The student teacher waited, showing no excitement, and acted as a calm observer. As Suzanne quieted, the student teacher said, "There really aren't any bees. This is a game, isn't it?" Suzanne answered, "My mother thinks there are bees." Suzanne then walked off to play with others.

continues . . .

. . . continued

Questions for Discussion:

1. Do you feel the staff and student teacher listened seriously to the parent's concern?
2. What next step(s) should the staff undertake?
3. How would you describe the student teacher's handling of Suzanne?
4. What might have happened if the student teacher had not had prior knowledge of Suzanne's behavior at home?

REFERENCES

Allen, D. (1998, September/October). Trends in demand for center-based child care and early education. *Child Care Information Exchange, 123.*

Associated Press. (1998, August 31). Census shows families in transition. *Statesman Journal.*

Berger, E. H. (2004). Parents as partners in education: Families and schools working together (6th ed.). Upper Saddle River, NJ: Pearson/Merrill Prentice Hall.

Berger, K. S. (2001). *The developing person through the life span.* New York: Worth Publishers.

Blankenhorn, D. (1995). *Fatherless America: Confronting our most urgent social problem.* New York: Basic Books.

Brewer, J. A. (1992). *Early childhood education: Preschool through primary grades.* Boston: Allyn & Bacon.

Chandler, L. A. (1996, Annual Theme). Changing children in a changing society. *Childhood Education, 72*(5).

Children's Defense Fund. (2002). *The state of children in America's union: A 2002 action guide to leave no child behind.* Washington, DC: Author.

Children's Defense Fund. (1997). *The state of America's children: Yearbook 1997.* Washington, DC: Author.

Comer, J. (1998, November). Educating poor minority children. *Scientific American, 259*(11).

Comer, J. P., & Poussaint, A. F. (1992). *Raising black children: Questions and answers for parents and teachers.* New York: NAL-Dutton.

Curiel, J. (1999, June 24). Welfare reform hurts immigrants' children, new research shows. *San Francisco Chronicle.*

Elkind, D. (1981). *The hurried child.* Cambridge, MA: Perseus Books.

Fege, A. F. (1997, November). Parental rights: Yes! Parental rights legislation: No! *Educational Leadership, 55*(3).

Goodlad, J. (1984). *A place called school: Prospects for the future.* New York: McGraw-Hill.

Groginsky, S., Robison, S., & Smith, S. (1999). *Making child care better: State initiatives.* Washington, DC: National Conference of State Legislatures.

Kelley-Laine, K. (1998, International Focus Issue). Parents as partners in schooling: The current state of affairs. *Childhood Education, 74*(6).

Kelly, P. A., Brown, S., Butler, A., Gittens, P., Taylor, C., & Zeller, P. (1998, September). A place to hang their hats. *Educational Leadership, 56*(1).

Kerr, T. (Ed.). (1993, November/December). *Promoting parent involvement in Head Start. Early Childhood News, 7*(1), 16–20.

Lally, J. R., Lerner, C., & Lurie-Hurvitz, E. (2001, March). National survey reveals gaps in public's and parent's knowledge about early childhood development. *Young Children, 56*(2), 49–51.

Lewis, E. G. (1996, March). What mother? What father? *Young Children, 51*(3).

McCracken, J. (1995, July/August). Image-building: A hands-on developmental process. *Child Care Information Exchange, 104.*

McLearn, K., Davis, K., Schoen, C., & Parker, S. (1998). Listening to parents: A national survey of parents with young children. New York: The Commonwealth Fund.

Marotz, L. R., Cross, M. Z., & Rush, J. M. (2001). *Health, safety and nutrition for the young child.* Clifton Park, NY: Thomson Delmar Learning.

National Association for the Education of Young Children. (1998). Code of Ethical Conduct and Statement of Commitment: Guidelines for responsible behavior in early childhood education.

National Center on Child Abuse and Neglect. (1997). *Child maltreatment 1995: Report from the states to the National Center on Child Abuse and Neglect.* Washington, DC: Government Printing Office.

Powell, D. (1998, September). Reweaving parents into the fabric of early childhood programs. *Young Children, 53*(6).

Richardson, L., & Fields, R. (2003, February 6). More than half of the state's newborns are Latinos. *San Jose Mercury News,* 15A.

Rosenthal, D. M., & Sawyers, J. Y. (1996, Summer). Building successful home/school partnerships: Strategies for parent support and involvement. *Childhood Education, 72*(4).

Shapiro, J. P., & Schrof, J. M. (With Tharp, M., & Friedman, D.). (1995, February 27). Honor thy children. *U.S. News & World Report, 118*(8).

Smith, M. L., & Glass, G. V. (1990, Winter). Meta-analysis of research on class size and its relationship to attitudes and instruction. *American Educational Research Journal, 27.*

Sutterby, J. A., & Frost, J. L. (2002, May). Making playgrounds fit for children and children fit on playgrounds. *Young Children, 57*(3), 36–41.

Swick, K. J. (1992). *Teacher-parent partnerships.* ERIC Digest, EDO-PS-92-12.

U. S. Bureau of the Census. (1997). Washington, DC: Author

U. S. Bureau of the Census. (2001). Americans with disabilities: Current population reports. Table 5. Washington, DC: Government Printing Office.

Wallach, L. B. (2001, September). Volunteers in Head Start: How to strengthen your program. *Young Children, 56*(5), 24–28.

Will, G. F. (2002, January 7). Schools can't fix family failings. *San Jose Mercury News,* 7B.

Wingert, P. (2000, February 14). A child-care warning. *Newsweek, 65.*

Workman, S. H., & Gage, J. A. (1997, May). Family-school partnerships: A family strength approach. *Young Children, 52*(4).

Wronge, Y. S. (2001, November 28). Child care still top problem for area families, study says. *San Jose Mercury News,* 19A.

CHAPTER 12

Parents and Student Teachers

Objectives

After studying this chapter, the student should be able to:

1. Name at least five techniques to use when interacting with parents.
2. Watch a videotape, or listen to an audiotape, of a parent-teacher conference and analyze the interaction according to a theory of communication such as the Johari model.
3. Participate in a mock parent-teacher conference, role-playing both parent and teacher.
4. Make a home visit with the cooperating teacher, write a report on the results of the home visit, and discuss it with peers, cooperating teacher, and supervisor.
5. Discuss possible parent misunderstanding of the student teacher's role and responsibilities.

What an education! It was impossible to ignore how individual parents separated from their children each day. Some kids got a farewell kiss and hug, others seemed shoved into the room.

—Bing Anza Bohtua

Deliver me from parent conferences! It's like walking on eggs blindfolded, and talking with someone who expects you to be an expert on a subject (their child) that they know a hundred times better than you do.

—Shyree Torsham

I was placed at a parent cooperative preschool for student teaching. The play yard had the most creative and innovative play materials and structures. I learned what compulsory father involvement could achieve, and marveled at the Saturday father work crew's hard work. It was a terrifically maintained facility.

—Nana Ghukar

The politics of some parent advisory group members confused many issues. My cooperating teacher and the school's director were models of professionalism. They seemed to be able to soothe differing factions with ease. This part of student teaching reminded me of something I remembered from previous classes. The school really was a microcosm of our diverse American society.

—Rae Jean Wittsby

INTERACTING WITH PARENTS

Most interactions with parents are informal (see Figure 12–1). The most frequent interaction occurs when parents bring and pick up their children from the center or school. The parents will say something to the teacher or smile and nod. These constitute interactions. When we have noted that children have done something commendable during the day, we will often mention it briefly to the parents when the children are picked up. Likewise, if we think there has been a problem, we often take a few minutes to explain what has happened. Communications such as these are typical of the informal kind. Internet communication is increasingly used for home-school messages, parent feedback, and parent resource information.

More formal communications consist of scheduled parent-teacher conferences and home visits. During a parent-teacher conference, a teacher might discuss the developing friendship between two children (see Figure 12–2). In each case, the parents will have prior notice about the conference or home visit. They can then plan ahead. If the meeting is to take place at school, the parents can anticipate questions they may need to ask. Some parents may tell what they think we want to hear rather than the truth.

Kyle and McIntyre (2000) believe that to educate effectively, teachers must reach out to students' families in ways not traditionally imagined, and bridge the ever-widening gap between home and school so that children realize they are known, cared about, and expected to achieve. Research suggests one of the keys to successful teaching is creating personal connections with children inside and outside of school (Epstein, 1998).

Figure 12–1 Informal communications often occur at arrival times.

Figure 12–2 The development of friendships may be discussed at parent-teacher conferences.

THE IMPORTANCE OF PARENT-TEACHER PARTNERSHIPS

Although educators agree parent-teacher relationships are important, preservice teachers and student teachers may have received little training or experience working with parents. Brand (1996) points out teachers are the most influential link in home-school collaboration. Communication seems the biggest barrier Epstein (1986) notes. Without providing teachers with strategies and techniques, partnerships may not happen.

While teachers may feel completely at home with children and fellow teachers, Winkleman (1999) suggests that collaborating with parents can be a frightening and sometimes difficult challenge.

Winkleman surveyed student teachers who soon would become new elementary school teachers. He found their anxieties about parents centered in four general areas:

1. Defending curriculum and teaching practices
2. Involving families in their child's education
3. Deciding how much family participation they really wanted in their classroom
4. Communicating about children's problems and weaknesses

Parent surveys and interviews with parent program volunteers can gather information that assesses the need for improved relationships. Most parents want to be informed about their child's program and progress at school, and what happens there. Parents are eager to know how to support their child's growing skills, knowledge, and ability. Validating and celebrating what parents do for children and what teachers provide help partnerships thrive.

There are a vast number of levels of parent involvement that aid center goal realization. All sorts of parent-teacher discussion groups, workshops, socials, volunteer projects, work parties, and so on are possible. Many schools now alert parents during their child's enrollment to the parent's expected level of participation in school activities. With changing family life patterns, teachers may feel it is becoming harder and harder to involve the many diverse and work-consumed families of enrolled children.

Student teachers can observe their cooperating teacher's care of teacher-parent relationships, noting the effectiveness of communications and actions.

First impressions of a child care facility form as parents park, enter, and observe lobby areas. The upkeep and maintenance of the school, grounds, and equipment catch parents' eyes. Sounds and smells are noted. The people and conversations encountered, and staff manner and demeanor create distinct impressions. Parent phone inquiries also allow callers to assess the warmth, knowledge, and careful attention to detail provided by the answering staff member. Each center is felt to have a unique personality as judged by each new parent.

Most cooperating teachers will introduce student teachers to parents and other volunteers and professionals visiting the classroom. If you are in a position of meeting a parent for the first time and your cooperating teacher is otherwise occupied and unable to introduce you, remember above all that you are a professional and maintain a professional demeanor.

New student teachers are encouraged to observe staff and parent exchanges. As the student teacher becomes acquainted and skilled, some cooperating teachers may feel parent contact can be handled by the student. It is wise to discuss this point with your cooperating teacher and college supervisor. Helping parents feel at ease is an art.

Parent Boards, Committees, and Councils

Parents may serve on advisory committees, boards, or councils, and have active administrative involvement including teacher hiring and dismissal. They may exercise budgetary control and assume legal responsibilities. Each center differs uniquely with greater parent involvement mandated in publicly funded programs. Church associated, parent cooperative, and nonprofit programs also frequently use parent advisors. Profit-making centers, on the other hand, rarely seek or depend on parental input in administrative decisions.

Establishing a Professional Image and Rapport

Parents' interactions with student teachers differ widely. Many classrooms and schools design program features to create as much parent involvement as possible. Others may have somewhat limited parental contacts that consist mainly of "dropping off" and "picking up" conversations, and of formal evaluation-consultant parent conferences, as was earlier mentioned. In either situation, the student teacher's professionalism is displayed by the student's actions, appearance, and demeanor. Student teachers' friendly, supportive attitude, and conversational skill help parents seeking clarification concerning the student teacher's apprenticeship. It's best to explain your position as a "learner" and a fledgling novice hopeful of working toward ever greater classroom responsibility and competencies.

In working with other staff, student teachers may wish to make positive comments. Most people know when praise is deserved, and can easily recognize the difference between superficial "stroking" and sincere encouragement, appreciation, and praise (Caruso & Fawcett, 1999). Pointing out specific actions helps; for example, "You moved next to Alfaro at circle and that calmed him. I didn't have to stop reading. That helped, thank you."

Parental Understanding of the Cooperating Teacher's Role

Cooperating teachers may have orally or in print communicated to enrolled children's parents their role as a mentor, guide, collaborator, and consultant in the student teacher's placement. The visits of college supervisors may also have been a topic of discussion. Their aim is to give parents a clear picture of a student teacher's role and responsibilities, and of the cooperating teacher's role as a work supervisor. Parental fears concerning the student teacher's handling of children's behavior, the degree of confidentiality expected, and the student teacher's possible lack of experience, besides other parent concerns, can be allayed through open discussion if fears exist. Most parents see student teachers as a classroom asset able to offer their children additional attention and educational opportunity.

Daily Classroom Interactions with Staffing Adults and Parent Volunteers

In many classrooms, outside observers may have difficulty distinguishing differences in roles among teachers, teaching aides, volunteers, and student teachers. Each may possess uniquely individual skills and style. A hierarchy of responsibility may not be readily apparent. The student teacher will understand that the cooperating teacher has ultimate responsibility, and directs and supervises children, the planned program, and classroom adults. No easy task in most busy classrooms!

Pitfalls

Unfortunately, some parents may view student teachers as experts to be quizzed on child development issues, their child's intelligence, talents, educational progress, and so on. This may feel complimentary, but student teachers should refer all such queries to their cooperating teachers. Unfortunate is the student teacher who is placed in a program where political or conflicting issues have developed. The role of fence sitter or a cooperating teacher's defender is a difficult one. Our advice is to direct parent complaints or criticisms to the person or persons involved, and to broach the matter quickly with the cooperating teacher and college supervisor.

Student teachers in campus laboratory schools may have children's parents as classmates and friends. Parents can view student teachers as inside information resources. Student teachers may need to guard their comments closely, avoid gossip, and emphasize the confidentiality expected of them. It can be a difficult situation when the child of one's best friend is now part of a student teacher's child group. The authors' advice is again to direct the friend to the cooperating teacher if questions exist.

Children's Separation from Parents

Student teachers will observe daily how individual children enter and separate from their parents or adult caregiver at arrival. Separating from parents can be painful, even though preschool is exciting and challenging (Stone, 1987). Some children need time to adjust and readjust to group care, and experience separation anxiety. Student teachers are often asked to aid entering children by providing attentive, patient support and comfort.

separation anxiety—emotional difficulty experienced by some young children when leaving their parents or other primary caregivers.

If the child permits, holding the child is suggested. Words that help could be, "You want your mom, but she needs to go to work. After nap time, she'll come to get you. Let's go see what Lorie and Ebert are making at the center table."

Be prepared to stay near, hold, or comfort a crying child when a parent needs to leave after staying for an additional time to help the child with the transition. Short periods of parent absence are lengthened, and with teacher coaching, assurance, and parent firmness, most children adjust.

Stone (1987) mentions a teacher technique that aids some children with separation anxiety. "You're having a pretty hard time. Would it help if I wrote a note from you to your father? Tell me what to write in your note."

Problems with Reunion at Pickup Time

Many systems and ideas have been used to make parent pickup time easier for children, teachers, and parents. Teacher messages and the relating of anecdotes to individual parents often quickly take place at this time. Because cooperating teachers have the ultimate responsibility in a classroom, student teachers may respond to parent inquiries but also should refer the parent to the regular teaching staff. Children's belongings, including projects and artwork, are collected beforehand. Children are made ready to be picked up, and at times, are partially or fully dressed for outdoors. Teachers usually step in to help parents with dawdling or obstinate child behavior. Stone (1987) suggests friendly casual teacher actions, looks, and good-byes, and conveying limited "child-concerned" information in a brief conversation. If more detailed information about the child is necessary for a parent, a note or follow-up telephone call to arrange a conference is in order.

The teacher's goal is to have a smooth transition with established routines. Schools adopt a variety of procedures to make departure times successful and as stress-free as possible.

MODELS OF COMMUNICATION

One communication model compares the process of communication to a telephone call in which there is a caller who is sending a message through a specific channel—the telephone—to a receiver, who has to decode the message (Berlo, 1960). Whether the message is understood depends on five variables: the communication skills and the attitudes of both the receiver and sender, their knowledge, the social system to which each belongs, and their cultures (see Figure 12–3). Any differences between the sender and receiver on any of the variables can lead to misunderstandings.

Let us study a hypothetical situation involving Hernán, a student in your full-day, bilingual kindergarten; his mother, Mrs. Camacho; and Mrs. Garcia, the teacher. Mrs. Garcia thinks that Hernán is not getting enough sleep and telephones Mrs. Camacho to ask if she can come for a brief conference when she picks up her children. Mrs. Camacho reluctantly agrees. Before the teacher and mother meet, they may already be processing information.

Mrs. Garcia's inner thoughts are as follows:

> Hernán always looks tired when his mother brings him to school every morning. During our rest time, he often falls asleep. Not many of the other five-year-olds do. For most of them, in fact, rest time is "squirm" time. It seems that we hardly even begin to turn on the music on the tape recorder before Hernán falls sound asleep. I've also noticed that Hernán is hard to awaken when rest time is over; I think he'd like to sleep for a longer period of time than we give him. I bet he doesn't get enough sleep at home. I think I'll talk to his mother about it.

After making an appointment with Mrs. Camacho for that evening, Mrs. Garcia may begin plans on how to approach the subject of Hernán's sleep schedule. Her ideas may be as follows:

> I've always believed that the best approach in working with parents is first to let them know that I have the welfare of their child

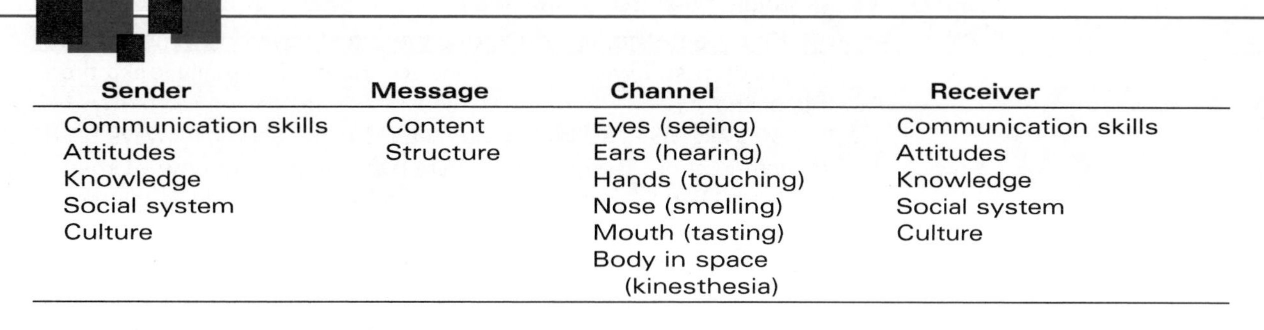

Sender	Message	Channel	Receiver
Communication skills	Content	Eyes (seeing)	Communication skills
Attitudes	Structure	Ears (hearing)	Attitudes
Knowledge		Hands (touching)	Knowledge
Social system		Nose (smelling)	Social system
Culture		Mouth (tasting)	Culture
		Body in space (kinesthesia)	

Figure 12-3 Variables in a communication model

on my mind. I think I'll start by stating how much I enjoy having Hernán attend school. Then, let me see, should I come right out and ask how much sleep he gets? Maybe it would sound better if I ask when he goes to bed and when he gets up. If I don't think he's getting enough sleep, I can ask Hernán's mother how much sleep she thinks Hernán should get. Wait a minute, maybe I can ask her how much sleep her other children, Tomás and Roberto, used to get when they were five. No, I think asking when Hernán goes to bed and gets up is a better approach. Mrs. Camacho seems like a knowledgeable and caring mother. Certainly, Hernán arrives clean and well dressed every day.

In the meantime, Hernán's mother may be thinking along these lines:

Now why would Hernán's teacher want to talk about Hernán? I thought I filled her in on everything she needed to know when I enrolled him. Maybe he's been acting up at school. Maybe he got into a fight with Dave. Goodness knows he talks about beating up Dave if he keeps teasing him. Maybe it's finally happened. Carlos (Hernán's father) would surely be proud of Hernán for a change. He's always telling the boy to stop being such a sissy and letting Roberto or Tomás stick up for him! Maybe she wants me to bake something for school or take a day off work to help out. She knows I can't afford to take any more time off.

Perhaps a different approach would have been to ask the question over the telephone. Indeed, many teachers would do exactly this. Why bother a busy parent with a conference if the information can be handled on the telephone? Other teachers, however, prefer to ask any sensitive questions face to face in order to watch reactions. (Because many schools ask parents to fill out extensive questionnaires, some parents could feel that, through questioning of this type, their word is being doubted.)

Let us now proceed with the actual interaction between the two parties.

Teacher: Mrs. Camacho, please come into my office where it'll be quieter. Boys, why don't you find something to play with? Hernán, why don't you show Tomás where things are around the room? Roberto, I bet you remember where to find toys, don't you? (The boys go off to play, and Mrs. Camacho and Mrs. Garcia go into the office. Mrs. Garcia asks Mrs. Camacho if she would like a cup of coffee. Mrs. Camacho accepts.)

Mrs. Camacho, as you know, we are always concerned about the children and want what's best for them. (She really looks tired this evening.)

Mother: (What's Mrs. Garcia mean? I know she has always been concerned about the children in her class. I remember how worried she was when Roberto had the flu two years ago, and I've told her more than once how happy I was that Hernán was placed in her class.) Yes, I remember how you called me when Roberto was so ill.

Teacher: Well, I've noticed that Hernán seems to sleep heavily during rest. Does he take a rest on weekends? (That's as good a start as I can think of. Start with an observation; ask the parent if she has noted similar behavior at home. That's worked before.)

Mother: (I wonder what she's angling for?) Let's see. I think Hernán always takes a rest on the weekend. I like the boys to keep pretty much the same schedules as during the week, you know.

Teacher: What time does Hernán go to bed? Is it the same time as on weekdays? (I might as well simply ask her.)

Mother: We put the boys to bed between 8:00 P.M. and 9:00 P.M. weekdays, and we like to do the same on weekends so Mr. Camacho and I can get to a late movie or dinner once in a while. (What does she want? She *knows* what time the boys go to bed.)

Teacher: Do the boys get up at the same time on the weekend? (There, maybe that will get at what I'm trying to say. I'd lay odds that they sleep longer in the morning on the weekends.)

Mother: Tomás is usually up before Mr. Camacho and me. He likes to go into the living room and watch television Saturday mornings. When Mr. Camacho and I get up, all three boys are usually glued to the television.

Teacher: What time would that be?

Mother: About 9:00 A.M. usually. You see, Saturdays are the only days we get to sleep in, and we know the boys will be fine watching television. Also, their grandmother is usually up around 8:00 a.m., and she keeps an eye on the boys, especially if they go in the yard to play.

Teacher: Is Hernán ever asleep when you get up?

Mother: Once in a while but not usually. If we let the boys watch television Friday evening until 9:00, Hernán is usually still asleep after Mr. Camacho and I get up Saturday. Why are you asking me these questions about sleep and bedtimes? (I wonder what she wants to know.)

Teacher: I've wondered whether Hernán slept more on the weekend than during the week. You see, as I said before, I've noticed that he really falls sound asleep during rest time. You know, some children need more sleep than others. Have you noticed any difference with the three boys? (Maybe this will give her an idea that Hernán may need more sleep than the others. I hope so.)

Mother: Let me think. When Tomás was little, he didn't used to sleep too much. I remember it really annoyed me when I was carrying Roberto that Tomás didn't want to take a nap! And he wasn't even two yet! Roberto, though, was taking a nap even after he came home from kindergarten. I remember being glad kindergarten was just a half-day program then. (Mrs. Garcia nods.) Roberto always needed more sleep than Tomás. That Tomás is like a live wire, always sparking!

Teacher: What about Hernán?

Mother: Hernán always seemed more like Tomás when he was little. But lately he seems more like Roberto. He and Roberto are real close, you know, always playing together. Tomás has his own friends now, especially since he's on the soccer team. Say, why don't you ask Tomás when Hernán gets up Saturday mornings? (Mrs. Camacho's voice trails off.) I think you're wondering if having all three boys go to bed at the same time is right for Hernán. Is Hernán getting enough rest?

Teacher: Exactly. What do you think?

At this point, we are going to analyze the interaction according to the model in Figure 12–3. Let us look first at our sender, Mrs. Garcia. What do her communication skills seem like? What appears to be her attitude toward Mrs. Camacho? On what is she basing her knowledge of the situation? From what kind of social system does Mrs. Garcia come? What is her cultural background? What about Hernán's mother? What is her cultural background? First, we might suggest that Mrs. Garcia's communication skills are reasonably sharp. She starts with an observation of Hernán and asks Mrs. Camacho to confirm or deny similar behavior on weekends. Then Mrs. Garcia attempts to bring Mrs. Camacho to the same conclusion by asking if she had noted any differences between one boy and another. Eventually, because her communication skills are reasonably sharp, Mrs. Camacho realizes what Mrs. Garcia is asking and asks the question herself.

Second, in studying the interaction, we might surmise that Mrs. Garcia and Mrs. Camacho have smooth lines of communication between them. (You will note your cooperating teacher easily deals with parents who are known from previous experiences. You will also note, as a general rule, that the more a teacher deals with parents, the greater that teacher's skill.)

Next, what can we guess about Mrs. Garcia's social system and culture? Her social system is her school and her family; her culture may be seen as Hispanic-American middle class. Mrs. Camacho's social system appears to be bureaucratic at work (she is a clerk at a county office). Given Mr. Camacho's occupation at a foundry, we might surmise that the Camachos are from the Hispanic American working class. Although Mrs. Garcia and Mrs. Camacho are both Hispanic, we do not know if they are from the same Hispanic cultural group. It is possible that one is from a Puerto Rican background and the other from a Mexican one. The differences in their social class may contribute to their differing views. A home visit might confirm many of our surmises. If we make further inquiries, we might discover that Mrs. Camacho has had some advanced secretarial training at a local community college and that she attended a communications workshop for county employees who deal with the public.

Let us now look at the message. What was its content? How was it treated? What structure did it take? Simply, the content involved describing Hernán's rest time behavior at school to his mother. Mrs. Garcia was reporting to Mrs. Camacho. The structure involved verbal input, watching nonverbal input closely. It also involved asking questions in order to persuade Mrs. Camacho to see that Hernán might need more sleep. Part of the structure was also concerned with arranging the factors in a particular order. First, Mrs. Garcia directed the boys to entertain themselves and suggested to Hernán that he show his oldest brother the location of toys and equipment. In this way, Mrs. Garcia gave Hernán a job to do that would make him feel more competent and give him the opportunity to direct his bossy, oldest brother. Then Mrs. Garcia spoke directly to the second-oldest boy, telling him that he would know where things were and, indirectly, rewarding him for his good memory.

Next, Mrs. Garcia arranged for a quiet and private conference. (In a case such as this, Mrs. Garcia probably would have asked her aide to take charge in the room.) Knowing that Mrs. Camacho would enjoy a cup of coffee, Mrs. Garcia offered her some. (Having something to drink and/or eat helps establish rapport. It also helps a tired parent relax.) In addition, Mrs. Garcia did not sit behind her desk but, instead, sat on a chair next to Mrs. Camacho.

kinesthetic sense—information from the body's system that provides knowledge about the body, its parts, and its movement; involves the "feel" of movement without reference to visual or verbal cues.

What channels of communication were used during the interaction? Most obviously were the ears for hearing and the eyes for seeing. Because Mrs. Garcia offered a cup of coffee to Mrs. Camacho, the mouth or sense of taste would have been involved also. It is difficult not to involve the sense of touch and the kinesthetic sense. Shaking hands involves touch; walking, sitting down, and holding a mug of coffee all involve the kinesthetic sense. It is through these messages from our senses that we interpret the stimuli that form our world. Under many circumstances, each person involved may have separate interpretations of the same set of stimuli; this is where misunderstandings develop. In our multicultural, multiracial culture, we are, perhaps, prone to misunderstandings that can arise from different interpretations of the same data.

Look at Figure 12–3. Let us assume that Mrs. Garcia is a well-educated (master's degree in early childhood education), articulate, middle-class Hispanic woman. Let us further assume that she was raised by educated religious parents. Mrs. Garcia's values will reflect her upbringing. Strict but warm-hearted, she believes in practicing her religion every day. She attempts to see the good in everyone. Even when she disagrees with someone, she tries to see his point. A believer in family, Mrs. Garcia also defers to Mr. Garcia in personal family matters.

What would happen if Hernán's mother was a poorly educated single parent who had just arrived in this country? Her reaction to Mrs. Garcia might be very different than what was previously described. First, using Figure 12–3, there would be a difference on each of the variables or characteristics listed under Sender and Receiver. These differences in communication skills, knowledge, social system, and culture could make it extremely difficult for Mrs. Garcia to communicate with Mrs. Camacho.

Even less obvious differences can block understanding. One such block was suggested in the first description of Hernán's parents. Mr. Camacho was described as a foundry worker. As a result, the boys had to remain at the school an hour longer than necessary because he would not pick them up. It was further suggested that Mr. Camacho was proud of his oldest boy, Tomás, because of his size and athletic ability and less proud of Hernán who was small for his age. We might also assume a difference in the way in which Mrs. Garcia and Mrs. Camacho view Hernán. For example, Mrs. Garcia might see a sensitive, quiet little boy who needs a lot of loving care. Mrs. Camacho might see Hernán as a "sissy" who was afraid to stand up for his own rights. Mrs. Garcia might try to educate the parents to make them change their attitude about what characteristics a boy or man should have. In doing so, it is likely that she might fail. This is because attitudes are resistant to change. Mrs. Garcia might have more success helping Hernán feel better about himself in terms of activities at school. Mrs. Garcia should interfere in the family matter only if she perceives that Mrs. Camacho has some doubts about her husband's views. Even then, Mrs. Garcia should proceed carefully. Changing family attitudes is risky. Regardless of how we might feel about how a father treats his son, it is important to remember that the child has to learn to live with the parent's attitude.

The Johari Model

Let us now consider a second model of communication: the Johari model, which was named after its two originators, Joseph Luft and Harry Ingham. The Johari model is presented in Figure 12–4. In the model, there are four "windows." The upper left corner window is "open;" in other words, what is presented to another person is known both to the other person and to ourselves. The upper right corner is the "blind" window. This window represents those aspects of ourselves that are evident to others but not to ourselves. The lower left corner is the "hidden" window. In any interpersonal exchange, there may be aspects of ourselves that we may want to hide from another person. The last window, on the bottom right side, is "unknown." There are aspects about a person both unknown to that person as well as to any observer.

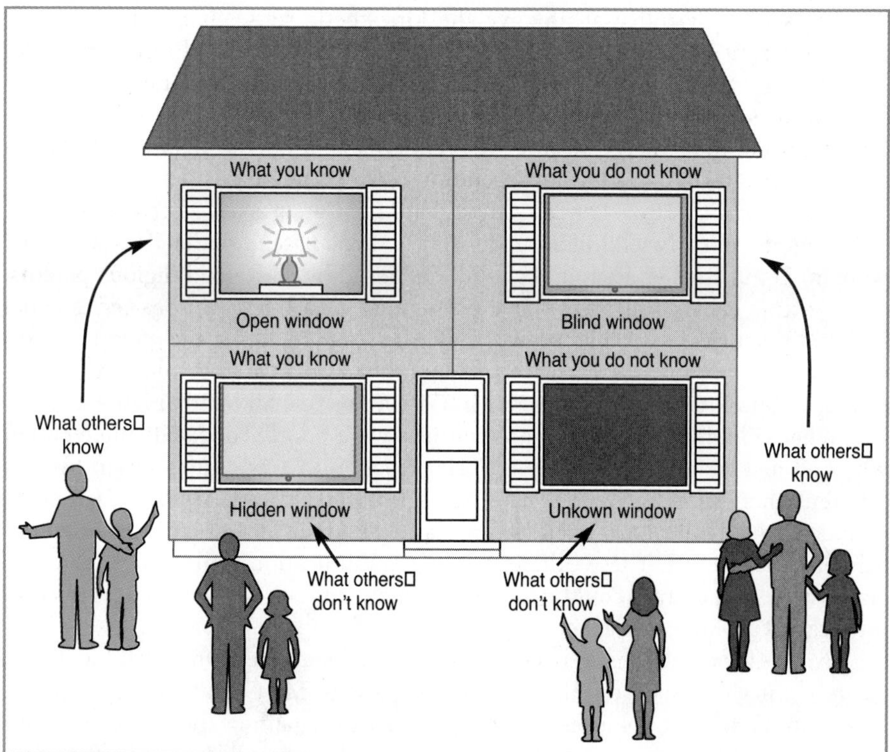

Figure 12–4 Adapted from Joseph Luft, *Of Human Interaction*, Palo Alto, CA: National Press Books. The Johari Model.

Let us use the example of the interaction between Mrs. Garcia and Mrs. Camacho to illustrate how the Johari window might look. Before the conference, Mrs. Camacho might keep the "open" part of her window fairly small. Mrs. Garcia, in contrast, may have a larger "open" window and keep her "hidden" window larger, at least initially. As the two women begin to feel more comfortable, the "open" windows of each will widen, and Mrs. Garcia's "hidden" window will become smaller. Mrs. Camacho's "blind" window may become smaller as she begins to realize that Hernán may need more sleep, something that she had not thought about before.

The Johari model can be adjusted to increase or decrease various parts according to the situation. For example, as a person grows older, she will often learn more about the self; that person's "blind" and "unknown" windows may grow smaller. In a new social situation in which one feels uncomfortable, one's "open" window might be quite small. With a best friend, however, this "open" window might be very large.

Nonverbal Communication

We have suggested that nonverbal communication often tells more than verbal communication about how someone feels. In the previous example, the teacher noted that Mrs. Camacho seemed tired. Was there any evidence for this? Most likely, it was based on nonverbal communication. Study Figure 12–5. You will note that nonverbal communication involves body talk such as gestures, facial expression, eye expression, stance, and large body muscles. Motions such as a wave of the hand, a shrug of the shoulders, a smile, standing erect, or slumping

	Specific Physical Expression					
Message sent through body talk	Gesture	Facial expression	Eye expression	Large body muscles	Stance or posture	Comments

	Specific Vocal Expression				
Message sent vocally	Tone	Pitch	Rate	Loudness	Comments

Figure 12-5 Nonverbal interaction sheet

all send messages. Actions like pushing one's chair closer or away from another and learning forward or back also seem to send messages.

Just as nonverbal communications give clues, so does verbal communication. The tone, pitch, rate, and loudness of a person's voice send messages. When a person is excited, the pitch of the voice will rise, and the rate of speech will increase. Excitement causes a person to speak louder. Anger often makes a person speak louder and quicker, but the pitch may become lower and the tone hard. As mentioned in Chapter 8, we should strive to be "active listeners." We should listen to hidden messages, not just to words.

The observation that Mrs. Camacho looks tired is based on her knit eyebrows, turned-down corners of the mouth, slumping shoulders, quiet voice, and slow rate of speech. She may use no words to indicate her fatigue. In fact, listening only to her words does not give us any clue as to how she feels. This is based totally on nonverbal clues and our active listening.

Conferencing: Communication Techniques

In two-year college training programs, student teachers may be invited to sit in on parent conferences or home visits playing the role of an observer. They may be asked to study child behaviors or actions, but conclusions are confidential and discussed only with cooperating teachers. Four- and five-year college training programs may or may not offer student teachers opportunities to conduct parent conferences and home visits.

In order to grasp fully the different methods of communication, it is a good idea to role-play situations. You should take turns with your peers role-playing parents and teachers. Try this: on a 3 x 5 card, write a communication problem you have observed at your center or school. Place all the cards in a box. Pair off with another student teacher and pick a problem from the box. Discuss and decide how you both would resolve the problem. Present your results to the class. Your peers should use the models of communication to analyze the action of the conference being role-played. You and your partner should use the same form so that you can discuss how you both see the action. You will find this exercise interesting. It will be helpful to be aware of some specific communication techniques that work in conjunction with the models of communication.

The following are suggestions for planning and conducting teacher-parent conferences:

- In working with parents, the first rule is to put them at ease. Seat the parents comfortably. Offer something to eat or drink, especially if the conference is at the end of a workday.
- Try to begin the conference in a positive manner. Even if you need to report a child's negative behavior or ask the parent a difficult question, always start on a positive note. Comment on the child's good behaviors or actions before stating what the child does incorrectly.
- Try to elicit from the parent a description of the child's behavior in school. (This is especially appropriate in a setting such as a parent-cooperative or child development center.) (See Figure 12–6.) If the parent has not seen the child in action at school, ask about the child's observed behavior at home or in other social settings such as church, if appropriate. This will enable you to study the degree of parental perceptivity regarding the child's behavior.
- Be specific when describing the child's behavior. Avoid generalities. Use descriptive, preferably written, accounts taken over a period of at least three consecutive days, with several samplings per day.
- Keep samples of the child's work in a folder with the child's name and with the date indicating when the sampling was taken. Actual samples of work can speak louder and more eloquently than words.
- Avoid comparisons with other children. Each child is unique. Most develop in idiosyncratic ways that make comparisons unfair. (If the comparison must

idiosyncratic—a characteristic peculiar to an individual.

Figure 12-6 Many centers encourage parents to spend a day at school and then consult with staff.

be done for a valid reason, do this carefully and only with your cooperating teacher's permission.)

- When you have to present some negative behavior, *avoid*, as much as possible, making any evaluation about the goodness or badness of the child and/or the parent.
- Remember your attitude is important. You can choose to CARE.
- Keep any conference "on focus." Remember that most parents are busy; their time is valuable. Do not waste it. Discuss whatever is supposed to be discussed. Do not stray off course.
- Be cheerful, friendly, and tactful.
- Act cordially; remember your manners, even if the parents forget theirs. Remember that it takes two to argue.
- Be honest; avoid euphemisms. Do not say "Tony is certainly a creative child!" when you really mean "Boy! Can Tony ever find ways to bother me!"
- Be business-like, even with a parent who may be a friend. In this situation, you are the professional, not the friend.
- Know your facts and the program so well that you never feel defensive discussing it.
- Be enthusiastic, even if you are tired and feeling down.
- Do not discuss another child unless it is appropriate.
- Do not make judgments before you have had the opportunity to see all the evidence.
- Do not betray confidences. A child will often tell you something that should not be repeated or something about the parents, which is best overlooked. If, however, you think the disclosure is important to the child's welfare, discuss with your cooperating teacher and/or college supervisor. Rely on their recommendations.
- Observe the parents' body language. It will often tell you more about how they are really feeling than the words they say.

In the rest of this chapter, we will present some ground rules for home visits as well as some ideas for parent involvement in the school.

PLANNING THE HOME VISIT

Some schools have a policy that the family of each enrolled child must be visited at least once during the school year. Other schools, both public and private, have a policy that teachers should visit the families of every enrolled child during the latter part of the summer prior to the opening of school. If you are student teaching in a school where home visits are an accepted feature, planning a home visit usually involves no more than choosing, with your cooperating teacher, which home to visit. Many times, the cooperating teacher may ask you to visit the home of a child with whom you are having difficulty establishing rapport. Other times, you may be asked to visit the home of a child with whom you have had little interaction. You may be asked to visit the home of a child who needs more attention than another.

In planning a home visit, Wellhousen (1996) believes that teachers (and student teachers) should familiarize themselves with the neighborhoods in which the home visit will take place. Hildebrand (1993) states, "A home visit is the single most effective act that can be performed for developing harmonious relationships between child and teacher."

Wellhousen (1996) emphasizes that the home visit provides you with much information. You can learn:

- about the child (interests, fears, attitude toward school, eating and sleeping habits, sources of cognitive stimulation)
- about the parent (attitudes toward school, discipline techniques, educational background, perception of parent and teacher roles)
- about the family (lifestyle, roles of family members, sibling relationships, preferred leisure activities)

Successful home visits have brief agendas, but are flexible and responsive to issues the families might raise (Kyle & McIntyre, 2000). Questions a teacher prepares beforehand help guide discussions. Questions can probe child interests, favorite activities, how the child learns best, interactions with other children out of school, what the child talks about having done at school, or other features of the child's school and home life.

Your first step is to contact the parents and let them know you would like to make a home visit. Because most parents will ask why, it is a good idea to discuss the reason for the visit with your cooperating teacher prior to telephoning or speaking to the parents. In many cases, your response may be simply that you would like to get to know the child better. Other times, the cooperating teacher will suggest you tell the parents that your cooperating teacher recommended your visiting the home. If the school requires home visits, the parents may be more hospitable than those from a center without such a policy.

Another point that should be made concerns planning home visits at homes of parents from different ethnic or social groups. Parents may be suspicious of your motive in wanting to visit, especially at a school or center without a home visitation policy. In this situation, you should defer to the wishes of your cooperating teacher, and allow the cooperating teacher to make the choice and the initial contact with the parents. In some cases, you will accompany the cooperating teacher rather than make a solo visit.

Regarding the question of home visits, in most cases it is best to ask the parents when they bring or pick up their child. It helps to watch nonverbal cues in planning how you will ask. (Obviously, if the parents seem tired, cross, and/or hurried, you should wait. It is better to ask when the parents are in a good mood and when they have the time to talk for a few minutes.) Naturally, the longer you are at a center, the better some parents will begin to know you. With one of these parents, you may feel quite comfortable about planning the home visit over the telephone. Your cooperating teacher may even encourage a telephone contact so that you can gain experience making such calls.

Let us assume that you and your cooperating teacher have discussed which child's home that you and your cooperating teacher are to visit. Your cooperating teacher will speak to the parents, preferably in person. She waits until the parent comes to pick up the child and seems unrushed. At this point, she could ask if there is a convenient time for the two of you to visit the child at home. The mother will most likely ask why; your cooperating teacher may say, "We'd like to get to know Sandy better."

Mrs. Campbell, Sandy's mother, may or may not bring up some obstacles. She may work in a 9:00 A.M. to 5:00 P.M. job so that, unless you could plan the visit on the weekend, it would not be convenient for her. (Of course, home visits can be planned at any time, including weekends, evenings, and even holidays.) Your cooperating teacher may suggest an evening or a coming holiday. Naturally, some parents do not work; therefore, they may have more time during the day in which to plan a visit. (Sandy Campbell comes from an economically disadvantaged family and receives a free lunch. She often arrives at school in clean, but too large clothing, and appears wan and undersized. You feel a home visit might provide you with an opportunity to know the child's background, and thus the child, better.)

After setting the time and day for the home visit, you may want to talk again with your cooperating teacher. What is the purpose of the home visit? Most commonly, it provides you with the opportunity to become better acquainted with the child. What should you look for? In addition to seeing how the child behaves at home, you are interested in watching the interactions that take place between the child and others in the home: parents, siblings, other relatives, and/or friends. Logically, too, you will want to note what kind of a home it is. A loving, child-developing relationship may be observed in homes differing widely in economic circumstances.

Now the two of you are ready for the home visit. You both have talked to Mrs. Campbell, and she has suggested that a week from Saturday at 2:00 P.M. would be best for her. Because you live in a large, urban community, you have to plan on a trip across town. You both estimate that it will take about one-half hour to make the trip and allow an extra 15 minutes in case you get lost.

THE HOME VISIT

You arrive at the Campbells' apartment a few minutes early. You both decide to look around before you go into the apartment. The Campbells live in a lower-income area. The streets are dirty and littered with paper, broken bottles, and empty soda and beer cans. There is little grass in front of the apartment house; the yard is generally unkempt and weedy. The apartment house, like the others on the street, is built in motel fashion. It is badly in need of paint, and you easily can see that local teenagers have used the walls for graffiti. There are at least two abandoned cars on the street. One has no tires and its windows are smashed; the other is resting on its rims and is severely dented as though it had been hit in an accident and never repaired. Further down the street, a group of youths are playing soccer in the street. Some of them appear to belong to an ethnic minority. A radio or record player is blaring from one of the apartments; a baby is heard crying.

You get out of the car, lock it, and look at the mailboxes to see which apartment is the Campbells'. They live in apartment 2E. You begin to make your way through the cluttered hallway and almost trip over a small, grubby child riding a rickety, old tricycle. "Who ya lookin' for?" she demands. You tell her you are going to visit the Campbells. The little girl responds negatively. "Oh them! They're sure stuck up. Why dya want to see them?" You walk past the child, who keeps pestering you with questions. When she sees that you have no intention of answering, she rides off.

You walk up the stairs to the second floor, noting the chipped paint and shaky railings. You go past the apartments with the blaring radio and the crying child, arriving finally at 2E. You ring the bell. Sandy answers. She is spotlessly clean and wearing what appears to be her Sunday dress. She greets you shyly, ducking her head. You enter a sparsely furnished but immaculate apartment. The television is on; Sandy goes into the kitchen and announces your arrival. Mrs. Campbell enters and asks you to sit. She has just made some tea and offers you some. You thank her and accept. She leaves and returns quickly with four steaming mugs, one each for you and your cooperating teacher, one for herself, and a small one for Sandy.

Before your cooperating teacher can ask anything, Mrs. Campbell hesitantly and nervously says, "I want to apologize for making you come all this way on a

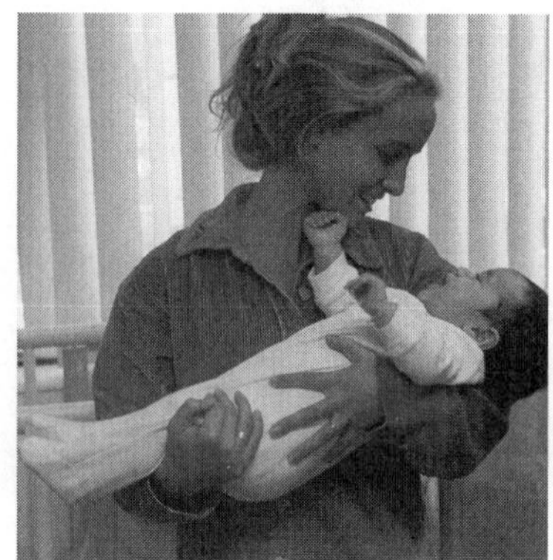

Figure 12–7 Home visits often help a teacher understand parent relationships with siblings not yet old enough to attend preschool.

Saturday, but I dare not ask for time off from work. And I did think your wanting to visit us was such a nice thing. It's good for Sandy to see you're interested in her like that." Your cooperating teacher murmurs something about wanting to get to know Mrs. Campbell better as well (see Figure 12–7). Mrs. Campbell suggests to Sandy that she show you some of her books. "I think books are so important. Sandy and I go to the library every two weeks, and she picks out six books to bring home to read. You know I read to her every night, don't you?"

You wonder if Sandy and Mrs. Campbell live by themselves or if there are any others who share the apartment. You then remember that Mrs. Campbell listed two parents on Sandy's school enrollment form. "Is Mr. Campbell at work?" your cooperating teacher asks. Mrs. Campbell sighs. "I only wish he were!" she says. Sandy announces, "Daddy's at the races. He thinks Sandy's Dream is going to win today. He told me my name would bring him good luck." Mrs. Campbell admonishes Sandy. "Now, you be quiet, Sandy. Miss Julie doesn't care about what Daddy's doing." Mrs. Campbell smiles slightly and shrugs her shoulders. "Mr. Campbell has been out of work lately and has been going to the races to pass the time." Without thinking, the teacher asks what Mr. Campbell does for a living. "He's a heavy equipment operator; you know, he operates those big road-grading machines they use to build highways. Only, there hasn't been much work lately, and Mr. Campbell doesn't like to take jobs away from home. It makes it real hard on Sandy and me, though, because there's only my salary to live on. You know, we used to have our own home in suburbia, but we had to give it up in order to pay our bills after John lost his last job."

You remember that Mrs. Campbell listed her job as billing clerk for a large corporation with headquarters in your area. You get the impression that Mrs. Campbell is trying very hard to maintain her small apartment the same way she kept her former home.

A shout from the apartment next door can be heard. "You'll have to ignore the Browns," Mrs. Campbell says. "They always fight when he's had too much to drink." Angry voices can be heard screaming at each other.

Sandy disappears and returns with a dilapidated rag doll in her arms. "Want to see Andrea?" she asks, thrusting the doll under your nose. (Sandy pronounces it like An-Dray-a.) "Sandy, don't bother Miss Julie when we're talking," admonishes Mrs. Campbell. "That's okay, Mrs. Campbell." You pick up the doll and look closely at it, smiling at Sandy. "Sandy, I think you love your doll very much, don't you?" Sandy enthusiastically nods her head. Mrs. Campbell gives her a quick look and shake of her head. Sandy goes over to her mother, sits down on the rug, and plays with her doll.

The cooperating teacher and Mrs. Campbell continue the conversation for another 15 or 20 minutes. You wonder if Mr. Campbell will come home from the racetrack before you leave, and you decide that Mrs. Campbell chose this time for you to come, knowing that Mr. Campbell would not be there. It makes you wonder about their relationship. Mrs. Campbell has offered no information about Mr. Campbell other than to answer the teacher's question about his work. You sense some underlying feelings of anger and despair, but also feel that it is none of your business.

You both soon rise to leave and thank Mrs. Campbell and Sandy for their hospitality. You and your teacher hand Sandy your mugs. She turns to her mother and asks if she can walk you to your car. Mrs. Campbell replies, "Okay, Sandy, but come right back upstairs. I don't want you playing with those no-good riffraff downstairs." She turns to your cooperating teacher and explains that the children who live below are "real rough and use language I don't approve of so I don't let Sandy play with them." "They swear," Sandy volunteers, "and use words my

Momma and Daddy won't let me repeat." Mrs. Campbell glances quickly at the teacher.

"It's not so bad now, but I worry about when Sandy grows a little older. It won't be easy keeping her away from them when they all get into school together. "Her face brightens a little. "But maybe we'll be able to move from here by then. We're trying to save so we can move across Main Street." You understand what she means. The houses and apartments across Main Street are cleaner and better kept; most people own their own homes.

Reflections on the Home Visit

After returning to your own home, you jot down your impressions of the visit with Mrs. Campbell and Sandy. Your first impression is that they seem out of place in the neighborhood. Mrs. Campbell obviously attempts to keep the apartment clean. Sandy is always clean and wears clean clothes to school. At the age of four, she already knows to wash her hands when she goes to the bathroom; you have not had to remind her as you have the other children. You also noted that Sandy eats slowly and uses good manners, reflecting good training at home.

Your second impression is that Mrs. Campbell is under great strain where Mr. Campbell is concerned. You understand why Sandy is such a quiet child. Mrs. Campbell is a quiet woman who is training Sandy to be a quiet child at home. You also understand why Sandy rarely mentions her father. It is obvious that Mrs. Campbell disapproves of her husband spending time at the races. You suspect that Mr. and Mrs. Campbell have probably had many arguments about this matter, especially because their finances seem somewhat precarious. You may have also surmised that the couple has had many arguments about Mr. Campbell's unemployment. These disagreements may be another reason why Sandy is quiet and subdued. Sandy may blame herself for the difficulties her parents express between themselves. You begin to realize why Sandy needs emotional support before trying something new and requires much praise when accomplishing something that is fairly simple. In addition, Sandy's desire to please her mother is carried into her relationship with adults at school; she is always seeking adult approval. "Is this the way you want it done?" or "Can you help me?"

As you relate your impressions to your cooperating teacher, you have another thought. Not only did the Campbells seem out of place in the neighborhood, but you suspect that Mrs. Campbell has no friends among her neighbors. You wonder to whom she would turn when and if she ever needed help. The cooperating teacher suggests that Mrs. Campbell might receive support from the pastor at her church. She had listed a church affiliation on the questionnaire that she completed when she enrolled Sandy. You and your cooperating teacher agree that Mrs. Campbell probably attends church regularly. Certainly, Sandy has talked enough about Sunday school to confirm this possibility. You are slightly relieved to think that Mrs. Campbell is not quite as isolated as you had thought.

OTHER HOME-SCHOOL INTERACTIONS

At this point, we have talked only about two types of home and school interactions: the parent conference (formal and informal) and the home visit. There are many other types of interactions as well (see Figure 12–8).

A center may conduct regular parent education programs. Some preschools, especially those associated with adult education classes on child development, include parent education as a mandatory part of their program. Other preschools

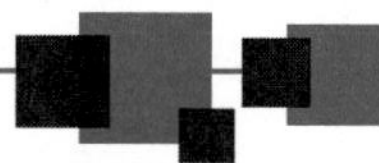

Kindergarten News

October 24

Language Arts: Reviewing M, F, R, S, N, T, and learning the short sound of the vowel a.

Working on colors, especially purple.

Math: Continue counting, sorting, and patterning, and working with the numbers 2 and 3.

Social Studies: This week is Red Ribbon Week when we talk about keeping our bodies healthy and saying no to drugs.

Science: The sense of touch and taste.

Music: We will be studying the opera Lucia Di Lammermoor.

Art: Halloween art.

P.E.: Working with balls.

We will have a Halloween Party Friday morning. There is a 12:00 dismissal. We will be making a costume, so do not send one.

Progress reports will be given out Friday. Attached to this newsletter is your scheduled time for a conference, either Friday afternoon or sometime Monday. If the time scheduled doesn't work out for you, please let me know and we can reschedule.

Next Tuesday, Nov. 2, we will be privileged to have the San Francisco Opera Guild come to our school and perform a preview of Lucia Di Lammermoor.

Regards.
M. Andreozzi

Figure 12–8 Example of a parochial school teacher's newsletter to parents

send home checklists of possible topics for parents in planning parent education meetings. Topics may range from discipline and related problems to specific areas of the curriculum to planning for emergencies. Kieff and Wellhousen (2000) caution about making assumptions associated with planning parent meetings such as assuming family members:

- can read advanced take-home announcements
- are available for time(s) scheduled
- have transportation
- can understand English
- can bring foods, snacks, and so on
- are children's biological parents
- have circumstances, lifestyles, and cultures that are the same as the teaching staff
- will communicate the barriers they face in attending school meetings

These authors have designed family involvement planning worksheets (see Figures 12–9 and 12–10).

Most elementary schools have regularly scheduled PTA/PTO meetings. Typically, the September meeting is called Back-to-School night and offers an explanation by each teacher of the class curriculum. Generally, teachers arrange displays of the children's work on bulletin boards and explain curriculum goals for the year. Many teachers have parent sign-up sheets posted for parent volunteer help, and all teachers attempt to establish rapport with their respective parent groups. Student teachers are traditionally introduced at this time also.

Family Involvement Planning Worksheet

Name of activity/event ________________________

Proposed date and time ________________________

Location ________________________

Targeted participants ________________________

Consider the descriptors below to identify family-related factors that could create barriers, and prevent or limit the participation of families. After identifying possible barriers, adapt the activity or event to incude all families.

Family structures

Consider who are the primary caregivers for the children. Consider the presence of younger and older siblings living at home.

- ❑ divorced parents
- ❑ single parent
- ❑ grandparent(s)
- ❑ blended family
- ❑ split families
- ❑ foster parents
- ❑ legal guardian
- ❑ widowed parent
- ❑ same-sex parents
- ❑ family member with disability
- ❑ teen parents
- ❑ other________________

Possible barriers include

Family lifestyles

Consider the daily challenges or routines affecting the children and each family.

- ❑ income level
- ❑ employment hours and time of day, number of jobs
- ❑ risks or dangers involved in work
- ❑ travel distance
- ❑ migrant status
- ❑ unemployment
- ❑ caring for an elderly or a disabiled family member
- ❑ latch-key child care
- ❑ transporation
- ❑ reading ability
- ❑ number of family members or siblings
- ❑ incarcerated parent
- ❑ community
- ❑ education level
- ❑ housing
- ❑ access to telephone
- ❑ resources
- ❑ other________________

possible barriers include ________________________

Family cultures

Consider the cultural aspects of each family. Avoid stereotypes.

- ❑ religious backgrounds
- ❑ holiday celebrations
- ❑ dietary restrictions
- ❑ views on child-rearing
- ❑ languages
- ❑ nonverbal communication styles
  - eye contact
  - gestures
  - touching
  - proximity during conversations
- ❑ other________________

Possible barriers include ________________________

How the activity or event can be adapted to include all families represented in the class or school ________________________

Figure 12–9 Family involvement planning worksheet. Reprinted with permission from the National Association for the Education of Young Children.

Common Barriers and Possible Modifications Checklist

Barriers	❑ Modifications
Time	❑ breakfast meetings ❑ weekend events ❑ one event scheduled over a number of days ❑ open invitations
Transportation	❑ school bus or van ❑ car pool arranged by teacher or parent volunteer ❑ buddy system among families
Child care	❑ school-provided child care ❑ chid care provided by parent organization ❑ buddy system among families
Decorations/ celebrations	❑ artwork created by children in the art center ❑ artwork generated during a theme/project study
Curriculum	❑ opportunities for children to make multiple gifts and cards, and to pick their recipients ❑ family members share expertise and culture ❑ bias-free curriculum
Food	❑ multiple menus available ❑ buffets ❑ picnics
Printed material	❑ translate copies ❑ make audiotapes ❑ make telephone calls ❑ use voice mail or e-mail
Special guest	❑ guest not specified by role ❑ a pal or friend ❑ open invitations to extended family members or a noncustodial parent
Expense	❑ support provided by community businesses underwriting the event or materials needed
Misunderstanding the role as parent volunteer in the classroom	❑ volunteer training sessions ❑ specific routines created ❑ recorded or printed instructions
Misunderstanding the parental role in home-extension learning activities	❑ specific routines created for home-extension learning activities ❑ parent workshops to explain activities ❑ demonstration tapes ❑ demonstrations during home visits
Discomfort in school situations	❑ alternative home visits or neighborhood meetings ❑ buddy systems among families ❑ small-group meetings

Figure 12–10 Common barriers and possible modifications checklist. Reprinted with permission from the National Association for the Education of Young Children.

Another form of home-school interaction consists of formal and informal written communications. Most public school districts and private schools send newsletters home to parents. These typically include a calendar of upcoming district and school events, and articles for parents on specific parts of the curriculum, ideas for parents to implement at home, and so on. These may be written by the superintendent and/or headmaster/director or by curriculum specialists and consultants. Sometimes, individual teachers prepare newsletters to send to parents or for students to take home to their parents. They frequently include news about topics that had been taught in the class that week, articles written and illustrated by the children themselves, requests for toys and/or books, requests for volunteers for an upcoming field trip, and so on. Newsletters frequently include curriculum items for parents to try at home (especially arts and crafts), recipes for snacks, and a question/answer column for parents. They may also contain a swap column or notices of toys to exchange. There may even be a column written by the parents. Some centers and most school newsletters advertise parent education/PTA/PTO meetings.

In many elementary schools, e-mail goes back and forth regularly. Some schools also maintain "chat rooms" that parents, students, teachers, and the public can access. It is wise for teachers to review what research suggests concerning parents' influence on their children's school achievement. It is generally accepted that family income, culture, ethnicity, or parents' levels of education does not accurately predict child achievement. What is predictive? According to Henderson and Berla (1994), the parents' realization that (1) they are an important educational resource and (2) they are willing to involve themselves in both their children's schooling and community matters. Understanding this helps teachers appreciate and promote parents' efforts.

Parent Education Meetings

The following ideas are suggested by Foster (1994):

- Plan together with parents and include the children (they have ideas, too); you may want a committee of parents, a teacher, and perhaps the children of one or two of the parents to do the planning
- Assess parent needs and interests
- If the school, center, or child care facility is not close to where parents live, ask them for help in locating an alternative meeting place
- If you have parents who do not have cars or do not drive, the meeting place should be accessible by public transportation, or arrange for carpools with those parents who do have cars and drive
- During the meeting, arrange for child care and activities for the children; then parents do not have to worry about who will care for or keep their children busily occupied
- Plan refreshments and activities for the parents
- Plan for a meeting that will last no more than an hour or one hour 15 minutes
- Open with a short introduction
- Decide whether a presentation will be a lecture, a video, a panel discussion, or something else
- Keep in mind the parents' abilities to process English if it is not their primary language
- If this is the first meeting of the year, think about having an icebreaker so that parents can get to know each other
- Remember that people talk more frequently in small groups, so you might want to plan a short presentation, followed by small group discussion, and ending with sharing from each small group
- Parents enjoy handouts or activities that involve making something they can take home
- Always be sure to thank the parents for coming and have fliers with information about the next meeting—topic, date, and time—available to hand out

A Poll of Elementary School Children's Parents' Opinions

The focus of the 30th annual Phi Delta Kappa/Gallup Poll on the public's attitudes toward the public schools (Rose & Gallup, 1998) was on public funding of private and church-related schools. The gap between the parents who favor (44 percent) and the parents who oppose (50 percent) has narrowed considerably over the past five years. In 1993, only 24 percent of parents polled were in favor in comparison to 74 percent who were opposed. A related question was asked about whether those polled would favor allowing parents to send their school-age children to any public, private, or parochial school of their choice with the government paying part or all of the tuition. Fifty-one percent were in favor of the idea with 45 percent opposed, a reversal of the results on the 1996 poll.

Groups most likely to favor were nonwhites (68 percent) and young people (18- to 29-year-olds) (63 percent). Most likely to oppose were those in the 50 to 64 age range (56 percent) and those living in rural areas (58 percent).

Because of fears that public funding of private and parochial schools would encourage families with financial means to move out of the public systems, a question was asked about whether or not those in favor of public funding for private schools would send their children to a public or private school. Fifty-one percent would keep their children in the public school they were now attending. Of the 46 percent who would move their children, 22 percent said they would choose a private school, 17 percent a parochial school, and 6 percent another public school. These results suggest that 57 percent of the parents polled would keep their children in a public school.

Of the problems perceived in the public schools, violence was listed first by 20 percent of the public school parents but by only 10 percent of the nonpublic school parents. Discipline problems were listed by 29 percent of the nonpublic school parents, clearly their number one concern, but by only 9 percent of the public school parents, a drop from 12 percent the previous year. Use of drugs was the second concern of public school parents (12 percent) but was a concern of only 8 percent of the nonpublic school parents. Their number two concern was overcrowded schools (22 percent). Funding (lack of financial support) was the number three concern of the public school parents but was a distant number five concern by only 2 percent of the nonpublic school parents.

Other findings of the poll are equally interesting: a majority of all parents polled favored an amendment to the Constitution that would allow prayers in the public schools.

An overwhelming percentage of parents praised as effective such communication techniques as open houses (89 percent), newsletters (87 percent), open hearings (85 percent), neighborhood discussion groups (81 percent), public school hotlines (77 percent), televised board meetings (74 percent), and Internet chat rooms set up by the local school (63 percent).

When asked about placing immigrant children who do not know English, parents clearly were divided: approximately one-third favored placing them in English-only classes with minimum tutoring help, another nearly one-third favored teaching them in their home language, and the last one-third suggested the children should learn English prior to instruction in a regular class.

When asked whether or not they thought the public schools were better or worse than they were when the parents were in school, the public school parents were almost split fifty-fifty. Forty-nine percent felt the public schools today were better; 43 percent said they were worse; 6 percent stated that there was no difference. Nonpublic school parents predictably said that the public schools were worse by 55 percent; 38 percent felt they were better. Only 3 percent believed there was no difference. (For more information, you may want to read the results for yourselves. They are printed in the September 1998 issue of the *Phi Delta Kappan.*)

Precautions

Obviously, a survey of parents whose children are enrolled in your center or school will be of more value than a national survey. You will never truly know what activities the parents perceive as being important unless you ask.

If you belong to a racial or ethnic group that is different from that of the parents, you will need to be especially sensitive to the cultural differences. Even social class differences among people of the same racial and ethnic group can lead to communication blocks. Differences in education promote problems also. You need to know whether the parents can read and understand English well enough to answer the survey.

If you have several non- or limited English-speaking (NES or LES) parents, you may want to have another person translate the survey, either orally or in writing, so that the NES or LES parents can provide input. If you know of even one parent who has difficulty reading English, you can discuss the questions on your survey in an informal interview, asking the questions orally. With LES and NES parents, it is sometimes of value to ask the parents to spend some time in the room with their child. Then you can ask the child to explain to the parents what is happening in the room. Children, especially preschoolers, acquire a second language much more easily than adults, and they make good teachers for their parents. This is particularly true in centers where there is warmth and respect for everyone.

When there are obvious social class differences, it is important to realize that some parents may not be active in school activities because they do not believe they are wanted or educated enough. This can result in the parents feeling that they are not respected by the teacher, director, or student teacher. This feeling can become more bitter if the teacher belongs to a different race or ethnic group. As you begin to work with minority families, you will need to develop insight into the problems that may be unique to them.

Single-parent families are also prone to stress, some created by the myths surrounding the stereotype of the minority or single parent. It is a myth, for example, that the child from a single-parent family will have emotional problems. The truth may be that had the parent remained married to an abusive other parent, the child might have been disturbed. Likewise, it is a myth that the single parent lacks interest in the school's activities. Because most single parents are women, and women tend to have lower-paying jobs with less personal freedom, they may not be able to participate in the school program. Be very careful not to interpret this as a lack of interest. The truth may be that single parents cannot take time off from work to be more active. The single parent may compensate by talking with the child every evening and sending notes when questions arise. The single parent may not have time to bake cookies for a party but may be willing to buy napkins. Another single parent may not have time to be a classroom volunteer but may be able to arrange her work time to chaperone a field trip.

Be aware that single parents may need a support group, especially if they have no family members living close by. If you have several children from single-parent families, you might even want to plan a parent education meeting devoted to their needs. At one Head Start center, the number one request by parents who were asked about preferences for the program's parent education meeting was the topic of "stress and the single parent" (A. Cutteridge, personal communication, November 1990).

Be sensitive, especially if you are in an infant/toddler center; understand that the parent may feel guilty leaving his child every day to go to work. Even parents of older children can feel this way, as can parents from families in which both parents work. Remember that whereas some mothers work, not because they want to but because they have to, others, mostly professionals, choose to work because they enjoy their jobs.

Unfortunately, many families cannot exist without the income from two working parents. Be sensitive to ways in which they can involve themselves in the life of the center without taking away from their limited time. Parent education meetings are fine, but not if a parent of limited income has to hire a baby-sitter. Knowing this, your cooperating teacher or director may make arrangements for children to be cared for on site. Many families may not have a car and must rely on public transportation. Find out when buses travel and what routes are available. Make sure the meetings end on time so a parent does not miss the bus.

Remember that parent education, however important it may seem to you, may not be as valuable to every parent. Many will choose to attend when the topic presented meets their needs and be absent when it does not. Others may find it too hectic to try to attend a meeting held in the evening. They may reason that there is not enough time after getting out of work, picking up the children, arriving home, fixing dinner, and eating.

There will always be one parent on whom you can rely, regardless of the circumstances. Do not take advantage of this. Some parents cannot say "no."

Parent-Teacher Dilemmas

The NAEYC revised statement on developmentally appropriate practice recommends preschool program goals be developed in collaboration with families (Bredekamp & Copple, 1997). This focus on collaboration with families changes older ideas that emphasized early childhood educators as supportive assistants, rescuers, or compensators of families with less than ideal home environments. Educators realize a typical class of school children displays ethnic, racial, and cultural diversity. Collaboration affords educators insights that can strengthen home-school involvement and parent-teacher bonds, and that can increase understanding of the plight of enrolled families.

collaboration—a desire or need to create or discover something new, while thinking and working with others. It is a process of joint decision-making. It involves discussion, different views and perspectives, shared goals, building new shared understandings, and perhaps the creation or new outlook or course of action.

Powell (1998) notes the movement toward a more inclusive role of parents in early childhood programs appears to depend partly on parent and staff confidence in each other. He points out that parent-teacher agreement on *caregiving* or *teaching practices*, *perceived staff competence in relating to young children* and *open communication* are important to the quality of parent-staff relationships.

At a time when early childhood experts are urging teachers to implement more informal, open-ended, child-initiated curriculums, teachers face an increased demand for basic skill, academic instruction for preschool children. Stipek, Rosenblatt, and Di Rocco (1994) believe teachers have two choices for dealing with parental pressure: they can give in, or they can try to educate parents. Stipek et al. recommend the second choice. Because parents and teachers have fundamentally the same goals for young children, the task of educating parents about developmentally appropriate practice may be easier than it would seem.

Parents Seeking Help

Because of the increasing focus on literacy, brain growth, development during early childhood, and ordinary child-rearing concerns, questions will be directed to early childhood personnel. Many parents seek direct help concerning what home activities they can provide (see Figure 12–11). Greenberg (1998) offers a listing of practical home activities in Figure 12–12.

Early childhood educators may hesitate. They may not realize that many parents may not have the confidence in their ability to help children. Powell (1998) suggests parents can become very active and resourceful in promoting their child's "educability" when given the skills and opportunity to be involved in school activities.

Your student teaching assignments and experiences may involve a higher level of school-parent interaction than in previous years as colleges and training programs give greater emphasis to parent involvement. Competencies in this area of teaching are increasingly important as teachers assume a leadership role in reaching out to involve families and other community members in the life of the school or center.

Figure 12–11 This classroom maintains a book bag/suggested home activities bag near the exit door for parent convenience.

Teachers brainstorming with parents during meetings dedicated to this topic often come up with language- and literacy-promoting activities that adults and their preschool children can engage in *together* at home or school, whether they be in English, a different home language, or both. Suggestions include

- talk with your children, no matter how young, about what you're doing
- look and listen when your child talks to you
- respond promptly and in a friendly way to baby noises, baby talk, and preschool chitchat
- clip and study coupons
- write shopping lists
- discuss and fetch familiar items off the supermarket shelf
- read ingredients on food products before purchasing or using them
- discuss recipes, ingredients, utensils, and the process of preparing food and setting the table
- read the writing on cereal boxes, soup cans, and so forth
- write or read words on birthday cakes
- write and read personal-reminder notes
- write and read phone and other messages to family members and post near the phone, on the fridge, on a bulletin-board message center
- read dates and printed information, plus handwritten reminders, on the calendar
- read the mail, giving children the junk mail to read
- enjoy browsing through catalogs that arrive in the mail
- talk on the phone and encourage your child to talk on the phone
- read manufacturers' labels and laundering instructions on children's clothing
- read aloud instructions for assembling play equipment
- read aloud sewing patterns
- have lots of books in the home—get them from the library, inexpensive children's book clubs (Scholastic, for example), yard sales and fund-raisers, used book sales, and bookstore sales
- save a space at the kitchen table where the child can keep the cook company and draw or write
- read magazines, newspapers, and books in the child's presence
- write letters (business, personal correspondence)

continues

Figure 12–12 Language-and-literacy promoting activities that adults and their young children can engage in together. From Greenberg, P. (1998, September). Warmly and calmly teaching young children to read, write and spell: Thoughts about the first four of twelve well-known principles. Part 2. *Young Children, 53*(5). Reprinted with permission from the National Association for the Education of Young Children.

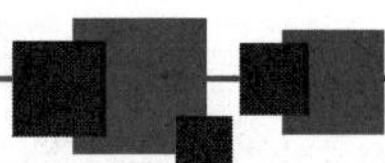

- write postcards to the child when out of town
- send birthday, anniversary, and graduation cards, often with personally added notes
- hang large sheets of newsprint or butcher paper on a wall or easel and encourage drawing and scribbling
- answer questions such as what does p-o-p-c-o-r-n spell?
- refrain from correcting the child when he baby talks, scribble writes, or guesses spelling
- reduce the child's worry if she says, "I don't know *how* to write/read;" respond, "It's wonderful the way you're learning!"
- appreciate the child's experimentation and practice when he spontaneously practices the letters in his name or pretends to write script
- subscribe to a children's magazine such as *Spider, Cricket, Ranger Rick*, or *Highlights*, and read it with the child
- get library cards for yourself and your child; go to the library together every few weeks
- sing together
- play cards and board games (read directions, discuss rules and what's happening) such as
  - — Candyland —Old Maid
  - — Go Fish —Monopoly
  - — Hearts —checkers
  - — War —jigsaw puzzles
- read appropriate picture books several times a day
- tape yourself reading stories and encourage the child to play them at will
- watch a sensible amount of appropriate TV or videos together and discuss both the programs and ads
- tell anecdotes and little stories from parents' or teachers' childhood or *their* parents' or grandparents' lives
- play outdoor games together and throw a ball, softball
- swim, picnic, hike, camp, sled, fish, garden, fly kites, fix bikes or cars, chatting while sharing these enjoyable experiences
- pick up litter, read the print on the packaging
- read the names, letters, and numbers on athletes' shirts
- read the sayings on people's T-shirts and sweatshirts
- play the alphabet game while driving in town or on interstates
- read bumper stickers and billboards
- read street signs, store logos, maps, road signs, and highway markers to or with the child
- read license plate numbers, state names, and messages such as "You have a friend in Pennsylvania"
- read the words on banners and flags
- write the names of flowers and vegetables on sticks to put in the garden as they are planted
- advertise and make signs for a yard or garage sale

Figure 12–12 (continued)

SUMMARY

In this chapter, we discussed interactions between parents and student teachers and between parents and teachers. We have presented you with three models of communication, both verbal and nonverbal. Finally, we presented a list of some specific techniques to use when interacting with parents.

Always remember that most parent-teacher communication is informal in nature. Therefore, it is important to remember that the impression you make in informal interactions may often set the stage for how a parent views and accepts you.

We have detailed a home visit as seen from the student teacher's perspective. We included illustrations not only of the physical description of the parents' home but also of the feelings experienced by the student teacher. We also discussed other home and school interactions, from the informal and formal interview to the newsletter and parent education meeting. Finally, we have cautioned you to be aware of cultural, familial differences, pointing out that these exist even within what appears to be a single culture.

Awareness of the parents' communities can be obtained through procedures as simple as a drive through the neighborhood or as complex as a formal written survey for parents to answer. Such knowledge will make you more sensitive to the parents and help you communicate with them. The parents will then be more interested in what is going on at the school and will be more willing to become active in its support.

HELPFUL WEB SITES

http://www.fape.org

Families and Communities—Families and Advocates Partnership for Education (FAPE). Has public information concerning coordinated efforts.

http://www.nncc.org/

National Network for Child Care. Search for children's developmental milestones.

http://www.npin.org/

National Parent Information Network. Select information concerning the process of parenting and family involvement.

http://www.asha.org/

American Speech-Language-Hearing Association. Parent activities to stimulate language growth are offered.

SUGGESTED ACTIVITIES

A. If your school has videotape equipment, role-play a difficult parent conference in which you play the teacher attempting to talk to a mother about her physically aggressive child and she refuses to believe you. Observe yourself during playback. Using Figure 12–5, notice your nonverbal communications. Analyze your verbal communication, using either Figure 12–3 or 12–4. Discuss your analysis with your peers, supervisor, and/or cooperating teacher.

B. Observe the arrival of children and parents at a local preschool program. Who greets them? How are separation difficulties managed? How are teachers building school-home relationships? Would you change any school procedures? If so, why?

C. With your cooperating teacher's permission, interview some of the parents at your center. What kinds of support systems do they appear to have? What type of activity at the center do they enjoy or do they prefer not to participate? Why?

D. Check the mode of transportation used by the parents at your center. Do most of them have their own cars? Do many of them use public transportation? Do some of them walk? What are the implications for parent education meetings regarding the most common mode of transportation? Discuss this with your peers, cooperating teacher, and supervisor.

E. How are local schools in your community helping to assimilate newly arrived immigrants into the system? What kinds of specialized materials are being used, if any? What kinds of specialized services are offered? Discuss your findings with your peers and supervisor.

F. Interview a single parent. Find out some of the advantages and the disadvantages of raising a child alone. What support system does the parent need? What are some of the resources they use? Have they been satisfied with the services?

G. With a group of four classmates, discuss how a teacher might demonstrate sensitivity toward the following parents:
   - single parent who had child while in high school
   - low-income parent
   - grandparent raising daughter's child
   - foreign-born parent
   - parent whose child wears designer clothes to school
   - nonliterate parent
   - newly divorced parent
   - non-English speaking parent
   - parent employed as school's cook
   - Asian parent who works as a classroom volunteer
   - Hispanic parent who is a migrant worker
   - out-of-work, welfare parent

H. Role play the following parent-teacher confrontational exchanges. In groups of six peers, select one member to role-play the teacher and another the parent. Discuss scenarios, then share with the total training group.
   1. Mrs. G. decides to have her class of three-year-olds celebrate Martin Luther King Jr.'s birthday. Mr. L. complains emphasizing this is beyond his child's understanding.
   2. Miss R., Joshua's mom, feels his teacher takes far too many field trips with the children.
   3. Mrs. T. tells her child's teacher that in six months, her child hasn't learned one new thing.
   4. Mrs. S., a parent, says "Don't ever call me at home!" with considerable anger in her voice.
   5. Mr. N., a teacher, asks Mardell's mother to find objects at home beginning with the letter B. She glares at him and says, "I'm paying you to educate my daughter. Preschool homework is ridiculous."
   6. A parent volunteer, Mrs. P., says, "After watching Raoul today, I can see he is bored in your classroom.

J. Read the following. Then discuss with a group of peers how the reading relates to you, a student teacher. Share your group's ideas with the total training group.

> Perhaps the greatest challenge of our generation is to be role models for the children of 2010 by demonstrating through our actions as well as words that an inclusive democracy is viable in our communities, workplaces, and nation. This will often require that we grow by reaching out beyond our social enclave to listen, talk, and cooperate with people who are different (Washington & Andrews, 1998).

K. Examine Figure 12–13. In speaking to the child's parent, what might be one of the parent's concerns besides the fact he has no paint apron on?

REVIEW

A. Using the Johari model, draw how you might appear in the following:
   1. How you appear to your best friend.
   2. How a young child might appear to his parent.
   3. Anyone in a new environment.
   4. An older person facing a new situation.
   5. A student on the first day of class.
   6. Someone who is unsure of herself.
   7. A teacher who unexpectedly is asked by the principal to come into his office.
   8. Your reaction when the director of your placement center comes into your room unexpectedly.
   9. How you may appear to your students on the last day of class.
   10. How you may appear to a group of peers whom you know well and respect.

Figure 12–13 Seeing individuality.

B. Rate your knowledge and effectiveness in parent-teacher working relationships using the following rating scale: 1 = Knowledgeable; 2 = Somewhat knowledgeable; 3 = Little knowledge; 4 = No knowledge.
   1. I am able to conduct professional conferences and interviews with parents. ________
   2. I could design and develop and adequate parent education and involvement program for an early childhood center. ________
   3. I feel comfortable in planning and conducting parent meetings and workshops. ________
   4. I possess the ability to successfully involve parents in classroom activities. ________
   5. I am aware of a wide range of parent-involvement possibilities and strategies. ________
   6. I possess professional communication skills and abilities useful in parent contacts. ________
   7. I can develop positive relationships with the parents of attending children. ________
   8. I understand the importance of school-home partnerships concerned with children's growth and education. ________

C. Read the following dialogue, then complete the activity that follows.

   Setting: It is early in the year. This is Susie's first experience in preschool. An only child of older parents, Susie always comes to school in clean dresses with ruffles and lace trim. Susie is average in size for her four years. She is attractive and has dark hair and dark eyes. A rather dominant child, Susie has excellent language skills, which she uses to boss other children. Because of this behavior, Susie has come into conflict with Janice, a small, wiry child who has been attending the preschool since she was three. Janice is very assertive and clearly resents Susie. Susie does not like Janice. Their mutual dislike has led to a clothing pulling incident. As a result, the ruffle on Susie's dress was partially torn off, and Janice's shirt collar was ripped. As the student teacher, you became involved because the incident erupted on the playground when you were in charge. Mrs. Brown, your cooperating teacher, has contacted both mothers and arranged to see each parent separately. She has asked you to talk to Mrs. Smith, Janice's mother, while she talks to Mrs. Jones, Susie's mother. She explains further that Mrs. Smith is rather proud of Janice's assertiveness and understands that it sometimes leads Janice into altercations with the other children. You have met Mrs. Smith before and have sat in on at least one parent conference with her. You feel comfortable explaining what happened. (Some training programs advise cooperating teachers that student teachers are not qualified to hold individual conferences with parents.)

Student teacher (ST): Mrs. Smith, it is good to see you again. Wouldn't you like to come into the office? I think there may be a cup of coffee left in the pot. (You greet Mrs. Smith with a smile. You remember that she likes a cup of coffee after work, and had two cups during the last conference. You pour a cup of coffee for Mrs. Smith and a cup of tea for yourself. You sit in the chair at right angles to her.)

Mrs. Smith (MS): Thank you. You know how much I enjoy my coffee, don't you? Now, what's happened? I know you wouldn't ask me here without a reason.

ST: Well, today, when the children were outside for free play, Janice and Susie had an argument. (You say this with a shrug of your shoulders and a slightly nervous smile.)

MS: I've been wondering when that would happen. You know, Janice often tells me how much she hates Susie! (She says this looking directly at you. You begin to feel uncomfortable and look away.) What happened exactly?

ST: Well, Janice and Susie got into a clothes-pulling fight. Unfortunately, Janice's shirt collar was torn, and the ruffle on Susie's dress was ripped. (You look at the floor as you say this, feeling uncomfortable about not having intervened before the fight erupted.)

MS: You know, Janice's shirt was new. I should have known better than to let her wear it to school. (She laughs.) You know, I sometimes think Janice is more like a boy than a girl! That's why I let her wear pants all the time. Fortunately, a torn shirt is easy to mend, but I hate mending! I never did figure why Susie always has a dress on; it must really hamper her play. (She looks sharply at you.) Hey, it's okay. These things happen from time to time. I know Janice well enough to know that she's bound to get into a fight once in a while. She's just like her older brother. In fact, I think he's the one she admires most!

Identify the following statements as either true or false. If the validity of any statement cannot be determined due to lack of information, identify it as such.

1. Mrs. Smith seems to be more comfortable than the student teacher.
2. The student teacher's approach to the conference was effective.
3. The student teacher watched Mrs. Smith's body language.
4. Mrs. Smith understands the situation well.

5. This was probably one of the student teacher's first conferences alone without the support of the cooperating teacher.
6. According to the model in Figure 12–3, both Mrs. Smith and the student teacher appear to have equally refined communication skills.
7. According to the model in Figure 12–3, the student teacher and Mrs. Smith are most likely from the same culture.
8. According to the model in Figure 12–4, Mrs. Smith reveals a larger "open" window than the student teacher.
9. Based on the model in Figure 12–4, the student teacher most likely has a larger "blind" window than Mrs. Smith.
10. The student teacher appears to have a larger "hidden" window than Mrs. Smith.

D. Name five suggestions for planning a parent-teacher conference.

E. Using one of the communication models presented, analyze the home visit reported in this chapter. Ask the following questions of yourself.
1. Were the communication skills of the student teacher and Mrs. Campbell equally sharp?
2. Did the student teacher and Mrs. Campbell seem to have similar attitudes? Did they have similar values? Is it likely that they came from similar cultural backgrounds?
3. Using the Johari model, describe the communication skills of the student teacher and Mrs. Campbell.

F. Read the following statements. Determine whether they are effective communication statements or blocks to effective communication. If any statement is neither, identify it as such.
1. *To parent who picks up child late:* "Mrs. Jones, you know you're supposed to pick up Susan before 6:00 P.M."
2. *Quietly, and on a one to one with a parent about an upcoming parent education meeting:* "We've followed up on your request, and at Tuesday's meeting, one of the county social workers will talk about applying for food stamps and TANF. We hope you'll be able to attend."
3. *To parent bringing child to center in the morning:* "Why don't you go with Randy to the science corner? He has something to show you. Randy, show your Dad what you found yesterday."
4. *To parent with limited skills in English:* "Mrs. Paliwal, we hope you'll be able to stay today so you can see the kinds of things we do here at ABC School. You know, we think it's important for the parent to become involved in the school's activities, and Anil seems so shy. I think he might feel better if you could stay with him for a few minutes. How about it?"
5. *On the telephone to parent whose child has been involved in a fight at school:* "Mr. Smith, we're hoping you might stop by early this evening to pick Steve up. We know how busy you are, but we're busy, too, and Steve needs you."
6. *To a mother volunteer who is berating a child other than hers:* "You know we never raise our voices."
7. *To a parent reading a story to her own child during free play:* "Mrs. Smith, would you please watch the children at the waterplay table?
8. *To harried parent who arrives with crying child later than usual; mother is late for work and is blaming the child. To child:* "Jimmy, I know you like to play

with clay; why don't you go over to the clay table and ask Miss Susan what she is doing?"

9. *On the telephone to parent whose daughter wet her pants and has no dry ones at school:* "Mrs. Carter, Kathy wet her pants this morning. I hope you won't mind that we put her into a spare pair we had on hand. Tomorrow, you can bring an extra pair so if Kathy has another accident, she'll have her own clothes to wear."
10. *Across the playground to a parent pushing her own child on a swing:* "Mrs. Koster, come over here please. Mary knows how to pump herself. Don't baby her."

CASE SCENARIO

Setting: A community college laboratory school.

Mark, a four-year-old, had been enrolled in the Child Development Center attached to an older community college in a large metropolitan city since age three.

Observing Mark was a joyful experience for those enrolled as early childhood majors who chose him as a subject of study. He was energetic, with his own pack of special buddies who were willing to investigate or participate in any classroom or outdoor adventure. Physically strong, of average height, and well coordinated, he possessed obvious good health. Mark was often described as a sweet dynamo, quick to offer his ideas in classroom discussions. Mark was also the kind of child his teachers described as progressing above average in all developmental areas.

His single mother, a community college sophomore, expected to transfer to a local university in the fall. She often picked up Mark's older elementary school aged brother first so both came into the center at pickup time. Mark would excitedly show his brother his school projects or demonstrate how he could maneuver a new piece of outdoor equipment. It was easy to see that Mark idolized his brother, and a close relationship was apparent with his mom. His professionally employed father had custody on some weekends but never attended school functions. Mark talked, at times, about enjoyed camping trips and ball games with dad.

Without warning, Mark's behavior changed. He appeared sleepy, withdrawn, uninterested in the activities around him. He sat in one spot for long periods and sought to be alone in the play yard. His friends approached him but he would either not talk or say he didn't want to play when they offered ideas. The staff alerted Mark's mom to his "not a

continues . . .

. . . continued

good day" and suggested monitoring his health.

Teachers had talked to Mark, asking if he felt sick, but he'd indicated he didn't hurt anywhere. The staff's plan was to record Mark's behavior the next day and engage him by delicately probing and offering as much close, physical contact as he seemed to accept.

A meeting with Mark's mother was set as soon as possible. His behavior led teachers to suspect depression. When the meeting took place, Mark's mother immediately broke down and was extremely distraught. She explained Mark's father, who had remarried about six month's earlier, had begun a suit for full custody of Mark's older brother but not for Mark. The father thought that Mark was the result of a relationship Mark's mother had while they were legally separated.

Questions for Discussion:

1. Was the center's handling of Mark's changed behavior appropriate?
2. Is documenting Mark's daily behavior important? Why?
3. Is parent-center communication working effectively? If yes, what brings you to that conclusion? If no, explain.

REFERENCES

Berlo, D. K. (1960). *The process of communication.* New York: Holt, Rinehart & Winston.

Brand, S. (1996, January). Making parent involvement a reality: Helping teachers develop partnerships with parents. *Young Children, 51*(2).

Bredekamp, S., & Copple, C. (Eds.). (1997). *Developmentally appropriate practice in early childhood programs* (rev. ed.). Washington, DC: National Association for the Education of Young Children.

Caruso, J. J., & Fawcett, M. T. (1999). *Supervision in early childhood education: A developmental perspective.* New York: Teachers College Press.

Epstein, J. (1998). *School and family partnerships: Preparing educators and improving schools.* Boulder, CO: Westview Press.

Epstein, J. (1986). Parent's reaction to teacher practices of parent involvement. *Elementary School Journal, 86.*

Foster, S. M. (1994, November). Successful parent meetings. *Young Children, 50*(1).

Greenberg, P. (1998, September). Warmly and calmly teaching young children to read, write and spell: Thoughts about the first four of twelve well-known principles, Part 2. *Young Children, 53*(5).

Henderson, A. T., & Berla, N. (1994). *A new generation of evidence: The family is critical to student achievement.* Columbia, MD: National Committee of Citizens in Education.

Hildebrand, V. (1993). *Management of child development centers.* New York: Macmillan.

Kieff, J., & Wellhousen, K. (2000, May). Planning family involvement in early childhood programs. *Young Children, 55*(3), 18–25.

Kyle, D., & McIntyre, E. (2000, October). Family visits benefit teachers and families—and students most of all. *Practitioner Brief #1.* Santa Cruz, CA: Center for Research on Education, Diversity and Excellence, University of California Brochure.

Morris, V., Taylor, S., Knight, J., & Wasson, R. (1996). Preparing teachers to reach out to families and communities. *Action in Teacher Education, XVIII*(1).

Powell, D. R. (1998, September). Reweaving parents into the fabric of early childhood programs. *Young Children, 53*(6).

Rose, L. C., & Gallup, A. M. (1998, September). The 30th annual Phi Delta Kappa/Gallup Poll of the public's attitudes toward the public schools. *Phi Delta Kappan, 80*(1).

Stipek, D., Rosenblatt, L., & Di Rocco, L. (1994, March). Making parents your allies. *Young Children, 49*(3).

Stone, J. G. (1987). *Teacher-parent relationships.* Washington, DC: National Association for the Education of Young Children.

Washington, V., & Andrews, J. D. (Eds.). (1998). *Children of 2010.* Washington, DC: National Association for the Education of Young Children.

Wellhousen, K. (1996, November). Be it ever so humble: Developing a study of homes for today's diverse society. *Young Children, 52*(1).

Winkleman, P. H. (1999). Family involvement in education: The apprehensions of student teachers. In M. S. Ammon (Ed.). *Joining hands: Preparing teachers to make meaningful home-school connections* (pp. 79–100). Sacramento, CA: California Department of Education, California Commission on Teacher Credentialing.

SECTION VII

Professional Concerns

CHAPTER 13

Quality Programs

Objectives

After studying this chapter, the student should be able to:

1. List 10 factors of a quality program.
2. Describe the different types of quality programs.
3. Discuss the relationship between a program's philosophy and its quality.
4. Discuss the importance of the teacher and director in a quality program.
5. List six of the areas evaluated under NAEYC accreditation criteria.
6. Discuss the process of self-evaluation and its relationship to the accreditation process.

I'll never forget the time I watched my cooperating teacher's enthusiasm at reading group time. She looked as if she enjoyed the story as much as the group of children. At recess I asked if it was a new reading series. She told me the book had been used for three years at her grade level. I marveled at her ability to make reading the story new, alive, and interesting to yet another group of children.

—Marie Ota

My cooperating teacher and I became good friends. We still see one another at district meetings. I was privileged to have apprenticed under such an excellent model.

—Rich Bacon

In looking at the concept of quality, what comes to your mind? High quality always suggests something that goes beyond the ordinary. In a program for young children, then, quality suggests that it exceeds minimal standards. We might also want to include the fact that a high-quality program, in general, seeks to employ well-trained teachers who more than meet the minimal education requirements of their respective states, and usually pays a higher salary and offers more benefits than programs of lesser quality.

Whitebook (1995) points out that high-quality centers are those that meet standards higher than the minimum ones set by the state. They are also the programs "that have access to extra resources beyond parent fees." In one quality, nonprofit, parent-participation preschool with which we are familiar, the director has a master's degree in early childhood education (ECE), and every teacher but one with a master's has a bachelor's degree in ECE, child development, or a related field. (The state of California requires only 12 semester units in ECE to teach in a nonpublic program.)

Child development researchers have identified continuity of care from consistent, sensitive, well-trained, and well-compensated caregivers as a key ingredient of good quality care (Groginsky, Robison, & Smith, 1999).

MEETING CHILDREN'S NEEDS

Among the factors to consider regarding the quality of an early childhood program is whether the program meets each child's developmental needs. There must be an awareness of and attention to the needs of the children.

What are the needs of children during their early years? Accepting the validity of theories discussed in previous chapters, we know that their needs are to self-actualize, to know and understand, and to develop aesthetically. Children need to trust the significant people in their environment, resolve the questions of autonomy and initiative, and learn to become industrious.

Implications According to Maslow's and Erikson's Theories

Let us briefly return to the theories of Maslow and Erikson. What are the implications for a quality program in regard to these theories? The first factor would be an environment in which the child's physical safety was considered. Quality programs have the physical environment arranged so that the children can explore without encountering physical dangers such as electric cords, tables with sharp edges, unprotected electric outlets that children could poke at, and so on. In a quality program, the physical environment has been childproofed.

Figure 13–1 Courtesy of Iowa State University Child Development Laboratory School (outdoor play)

The second factor is attention to the child's need for psychological safety. Essentially, a quality program should provide for predictability, decision opportunities, and reasonable limits. Predictability teaches the rudiments to learning about time and safety. With predictability comes the safety of knowing that certain activities will happen at certain times such as snack time, group time, indoor and outdoor play, and the like (see Figures 13–1 and 13–2).

Children have little control over their lives, and in our modern industrial society, they have little opportunity to contribute to the family welfare. If, however, they have freedom of choice within the limits set, they can and do exert control over this part of their lives and thus learn how to make decisions. They also learn to accept the consequences of their decisions. Limits allow the child the safety of knowing what behaviors are acceptable and not acceptable. Limits teach the child the

Figure 13–2 Shade covers over outdoor play structures are necessary in this location. Courtesy of Tulsa Community College, West Campus.

concept of right versus wrong and help the child develop inner control over behavior.

Figure 13–3 Investigating equipment is part of the fun.

A third factor is attention to belongingness and love needs. A quality program will provide for these. All children need to feel that they are a part of a social group; a preschool, child care center, classroom, and family can provide the sense of group identity that is so important for the young child's positive growth.

Esteem needs are met in a quality program. Care is taken by all staff members to ensure that the children's self-concepts are enhanced. Look to see how the workers in a program relate to the children. Do they CARE? Do they take time to listen to the children? Do they compliment children when they have accomplished some goal? Do they make a conscious effort to bolster the children's self-esteem?

Are self-actualization needs met? Quality programs have enough equipment and materials with which the children can interact (see Figure 13–3). Are there enough art materials, books, and cut-and-paste opportunities? Is there a climbing apparatus? Are there tricycles and swings enough so that no child has to wait too long? Are there enough puzzles? Are they challenging? Is the dramatic play center well furnished? Are there enough props to stimulate sociodramatic play? Are there both large and small blocks? Is there a water table, a sand area, a terrarium, an aquarium, a magnifying glass? Are there enough small manipulatives? Are the play areas and yard clean and well kept? Do the children look happy?

Balanced Program

A quality program will have a balanced curriculum: language, motor activities, arts and crafts, story time, music, creative movement, counting opportunities, matching pictures, colors, shapes, science opportunities; none of these is neglected in a quality program. Because of its importance, language will be emphasized in curricular areas in a quality program. Look at and listen how language is used and encouraged. It is during the preschool years of two-and-a-half to five that the child makes the most progress in language. Having a vocabulary of maybe only 300 words at two-and-a-half years, the preschool child will expand this to perhaps 3,000 by age five. In receptive vocabulary, the 800 known by the two-and-a-half-year-old will grow to nearly 10,000 by age five. At the same time, the child is learning the syntax rules of the language: present, past, and future tenses; the use of the negative form, the interrogatory form, and the conditional. All of this language ability is, for the most part, acquired without formal teaching. A quality program, however, recognizes this growth of language in the young child and provides opportunities for the child to hear language being used in proper context, to listen to models of language, and to practice growing language competencies. In addition, a quality program affords many opportunities for language enrichment (see Figure 13–4).

syntax—involves the grammatical rules that govern the structure of sentences.

A quality program will have a quiet corner or private space for the children so that any child can be alone when necessary or desired. Children, especially those who spend long hours in a center every day, need time and space to be alone. Some children live in homes that afford them little or no privacy.

Personnel and Philosophies

Perhaps the most important factor in quality programs is the personality of the teacher and director, essentially the physical, mental, emotional, and social characteristics. Is this a person who really *likes* children? Does this person appear to be upbeat? Are there "laugh lines" in the corners of the eyes? Does this person smile when talking? Does there appear to be a mutual respect between this person and the children? When talking to the children, does this person stoop or kneel in order to be at their level? Is this person *with* the children or *over* the children? Is this a person trained in child development? A warm, loving, knowledgeable teacher and director can make almost any program—public or private—a quality one, given the space and materials with which to work.

The second most important factor is the underlying philosophy of the program, the basic principles by which the program is guided. Are there stated objectives? Is there a written statement of philosophy? Is the curriculum based on a knowledge

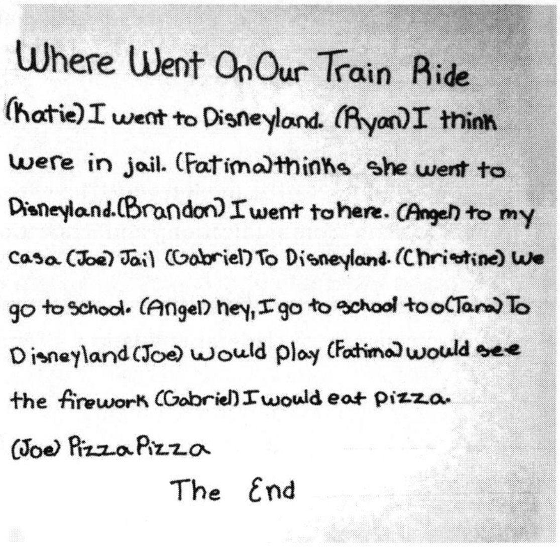

Where Went On Our Train Ride
(Katie) I went to Disneyland. (Ryan) I think were in jail. (Fatima) thinks she went to Disneyland. (Brandon) I went to here. (Angel) to my casa (Joe) Jail (Gabriel) To Disneyland. (Christine) We go to school. (Angel) hey, I go to school too (Tara) To Disneyland (Joe) would play (Fatima) would see the firework (Gabriel) I would eat pizza. (Joe) Pizza Pizza
The End

Figure 13–4 A wall chart with each child's contribution promotes language use and understanding.

of child development principles? Are there printed materials describing the program in terms of what the teacher and director want for the children? Or is this a program with no statement of purpose, no written goals, no clear curriculum? Worse yet, is this a program that assumes that you know all you need to know about the program on the basis of its label (for example, Montessori, Christian)?

Beware of any program that uses a name and has no written philosophy or goals. Beware, also, of a program where stated goals are not congruent with child development principles. Watch out for the program whose philosophy does not stress respect and love for each child. Beware of any program in which helping children acquire strong self-concepts is not listed as a goal. Be wary of a program in which one part of the curriculum is overemphasized at the expense of the others. A cognitive curriculum is fine if attention is also given to the child's social, emotional, and physical growth needs as well.

self-concepts—perceptions and feelings children may have about themselves, gathered largely from how the important people in their world respond to them.

Be wary of a program with teachers who stress boys' activities as different from girls' activities. Be wary of teachers who seem to have different expectations of boys and girls.

STANDARDS OF QUALITY PROGRAMS

A review of nationally recognized standards for early childhood group facilities developed by early childhood professional organizations and city, state, and public government agencies usually includes the following:

1. Ample space indoors and outdoors (a minimum of 35 square feet per child indoors and 100 square feet of space per child outdoors).
2. Safe, sanitary, and health-protective environments monitored and inspected by professional health agencies.
3. A planned child health curriculum component.
4. Programs and routines designed and conducted in accord with developmental levels and needs of attending children (see Figure 13–5).
5. Developmentally appropriate equipment and play materials in adequate and sufficient supply for the age and number of enrolled young children (see Figure 13–6).
6. Planned programs of instruction promoting children's intellectual, social, emotional, physical, and creative development.
7. Language and literacy promotion through varied and integrated activities.
8. Parent and community involvement, communication, and education center components.
9. Trained staff-child ratios that allow optimum child growth and opportunity.
10. Programs exceed minimum licensing or federal-regulating agency standards.
11. Continual observation of children's progress and development.
12. Use of community resources and participation in community efforts to upgrade and improve services to children and families.
13. Attainment of accreditation or recognition of high-quality care program provisions by recognized professional evaluators.

Figure 13–5 A K-2 daily schedule.

Turner (2002a) describes the essential elements of quality identified by New Mexico's Comprehensive Professional Development System in Early Care, Education and Family Support in the following:

> We defined an essential element of quality as a statement that defines a goal of practice, which has a base of legitimacy or validity

Figure 13–6 Each classroom is unique.

based on scientific data, or when this evidence is lacking, representing the widely-agreed upon, state-of-the-art, high quality level of practice. Viewed this way, essential elements of quality are not static, rather they are revised and improved as the knowledge base increases and as new scientific findings become available.

The NAEYC is widely recognized for its leadership role in standards development and center accreditation (see Figure 13–7). Standards vary somewhat between organizations and agencies, but in studying the above list, it is easy to see that, although not specifically stated, Maslow's hierarchy of needs is considered. Erikson's developmental tasks have been considered as well. NAEYC's list, however, goes beyond simply relating conditions to developmental theory. It also introduces the importance of looking at minimum standards as set by governmental authorities, suggesting that a good program exceeds such minimal standards. For example, federal or state standards may suggest that a ratio of 12 children (two- and three-year-olds) to one adult is sufficient. A quality program may have eight to 10 children for every adult.

Although a school cannot become licensed without meeting minimum standards regarding indoor and outdoor space, there are programs that average the number of children throughout the day and exceed the minimum recommended number during hours of prime use. For example, a center may be licensed for 28 children and have as few as 10 present at 8:00 A.M. and eight at 5:45 P.M.; yet, they may have as many as 34 present between 10:00 A.M. and 3:00 P.M. The total number of children present throughout the day may be averaged so that a parent may never be aware of the overcrowding at midday. Some centers will employ a nutrition aide at lunchtime to assist in meal preparation. Although this person may never work with the children, she may be counted as an adult when figuring the ratio of children to adults. Many parents are unaware of these types of practices, none of which would be present in a quality program.

Figure 13–7 Programs often display their licenses, awards, and accreditation certificates if they have received them.

TYPES OF QUALITY PROGRAMS

parent cooperatives—programs staffed by one professional teacher and a rotating staff of parents.

It is important to recognize that there are many different types of early childhood programs; each one may be of quality (see Figure 13–8). There are, for example, child care centers; state-funded child care programs; Head Start and Montessori programs; parent-cooperatives; and private, nonprofit, and profit-making preschools and primary schools. In each of these, a student teacher or parent can find good programs, mediocre programs, and, unfortunately, poor programs.

Programs reflect the underlying philosophy of their director, head teacher, or proprietor. It takes time to interview and observe carefully to determine quality. One may discover, on close observation, that children have no freedom of choice as to what toys they will play with, that they are, instead, assigned toys. It is also easy to be deceived by a glib promotional director, head teacher, or proprietor. Smooth talk and right answers do not make a quality program. Look carefully when presented with a persuasive director. Is this person putting into action policies that are in the interest of the children?

We are reminded of a private center in which there are many toys and materials for the children to play with. There is also a lot of space both indoors and outdoors. Yet it is not a quality center and does not run a quality program. Why? Unfortunately, the owner has little or no background in early childhood education, and in an effort to keep down costs, employs two teachers who meet only minimum state standards for licensing. These teachers are underpaid; consequently, there is a high rate of turnover. The owner also brings her own child to the center and has difficulty relating to any child who does not play well with her's.

There is no easy answer to "policing" poor or mediocre programs. The center in the preceding example is the only one in a lower middle-class neighborhood. There are many single parents in this neighborhood. In families with two parents, usually both parents work. Due to transportation difficulties and a lack of room in and eligibility for the community's well-known quality centers, this center is the only one available for many children.

WHO DECIDES THE QUALITY OF A PROGRAM?

As we suggested, the director has a responsibility regarding the quality of a program. Indirectly, parents also have a say in a program's quality. Obviously, there

Figure 13–8 One usually cannot judge quality from a school's exterior.

would be no program without clients (parents). Thus, if a client buys an inferior service (education), he has the choice to stop using it. The solution is, however, not always so simple. Parents may not have many options in terms of the immediate neighborhood. This may be compounded by the parents' lack of knowledge; they may judge a program by its external appearance (for example, its cleanliness, personal perceptions of the director's competence).

Quality is also dependent on the type of program. For example, in a program sponsored by a public school district, quality is determined not only by a director or teacher but also by government regulations, by the principal in whose school the program is located, and, ultimately, by the local board of education and its policies.

A public program must adhere to prescribed standards. However, in most public schools, ultimate quality depends on the teacher and the supervising principal. In a private program, quality may depend on several people. In a proprietary preschool, quality is related to the personality and training of the proprietor. Is this person a loving, caring human being? Does this person have formal training in early childhood education, or does she hire people who are loving and caring and have formal training? In any proprietary school, you will find the same range of quality as in a public program.

Who determines quality in a Montessori program, for example? Does the name, Montessori, promise that all its programs will have the same standards, the same quality? In the United States, there are two main approaches to Montessori education, both of which are called Montessori schools. One branch is the schools that are under the sponsorship of the Associatione Montessori Internationale (AMI), with headquarters in Switzerland and headed by Maria Montessori's son. AMI schools adhere very closely to Maria Montessori's original curriculum. Its teachers are trained in the philosophy, with the didactic (teaching) materials designed by Dr. Montessori herself. In AMI schools, you will generally find the same Montessori equipment used, regardless of where the school is located. You will also find that the teachers have basically the same training in philosophy and methodology. Still, there will be differences in quality. Just as in the public schools or in the proprietary centers, quality will depend, to a large extent, on the teacher's personality. Does the teacher really *like* children? Does that person CARE? Are the children happy? Look carefully.

didactic—often applied to teaching materials, indicating a built-in intent to provide specific instruction.

Montessori equipment—early childhood learning materials derived from and part of the Montessori approach.

The other type of Montessori program is sponsored by the American Montessori Society (AMS), whose headquarters are in New York State. AMS schools are less like the original Montessori schools in that, although they use the didactic materials developed by Dr. Montessori, they make use of modern trends toward a greater emphasis on gross motor and social development. AMS programs vary widely; the personalities of the directors and teachers are the important factors.

Another determining factor is who or what organization sponsors the school. Many churches sponsor schools and child care programs. In this case, quality depends not only on the personality of the director and teachers but also on the philosophy of the sponsoring church. Church-sponsored schools can also be excellent, mediocre, and poor. The teachers or child care workers always make the difference.

Studies of Quality

The *Cost, Quality and Child Outcomes in Child Care Centers study* (National Center for the Early Childhood Work Force, 1995) is described as a landmark study linking data on program costs and quality to child outcomes. Four hundred randomly selected centers in California, Colorado, Connecticut, and North Carolina were assessed. Half the centers were nonprofit and half profit-making.

The following study conclusions were highlighted by researchers:

- Child care at most centers in the United States is poor to mediocre.
- Children's cognitive and social development are positively related to the quality of their child care experience across all levels of maternal education, child gender, and ethnicity.
- Consistent with previous research, the quality of child care is related to specific variables:

  —staff-child ratios
  —staff education
  —administrators' prior experience
  —teacher wages
  —teacher education
  —specialized training
- States with more stringent licensing standards have fewer poor-quality centers. Centers that comply with additional standards beyond those required for licensing provide higher quality services.
- Centers provide higher than average, overall quality when they have access to extra resources that are used to improve quality.
- Center child care, even mediocre-quality care, is costly to provide.
- Good-quality services cost more than those of mediocre quality but not a lot more.
- Center enrollment affects costs.

Bryant, Maxwell, and Burchinal (1999) listed the following findings from a study involving 508 children in North Carolina's Smart Start:

> Overall, only 14 percent of the preschool classes in 1994 were providing good quality care. In 1996, 25 percent of the preschool classes were providing it.

Wiechel (2001) describes Smart Start's quality improvement efforts:

> North Carolina's Smart Start is a comprehensive public/private initiative to help children enter school healthy and ready to succeed. The North Carolina Partnership for Children provides state-level leadership for the initiative, sets statewide benchmarks for young children and families, and makes grants to county or multi-county collaboratives. These collaboratives assess community early childhood needs and design comprehensive plans to improve and integrate services.

Most professionals agree with NAEYC's National Institute for Early Childhood Professional Development that "the most important determinant of the quality of children's experiences are the adults who are responsible for children's care and education" (NAEYC, 1994). Alter (1997) describes additional factors impacting child care quality:

> The statistics are horrifying. Average pay for child-care workers: $12,000, with turnover greater than every occupation except gas-station attendants. Average training: none. Average portion of a low-income parent's wage that goes for this often inadequate care: 25 percent.

Working with experts, Kagan and his co-authors developed five guiding principles as the basis for implementing adequate compensation:

1. Early childhood teachers require training and professional competence.
2. Teachers with comparable qualifications and experience should receive the same salary and benefits, whether teaching in a public elementary school or in early childhood education.
3. Staff compensation should vary by qualifications and by degree of responsibility.
4. Staff should have a range of formal qualifications, with a portion of center teachers and family child care teachers holding bachelor's degrees and administrators holding advanced degrees.
5. Entry-level positions should be maintained so that preservice qualifications do not become a barrier to individuals from low socioeconomic backgrounds or minority groups seeking to enter the field (Kagan, et al., 2002).

They also note the many experts they consulted in developing their recommended principles what many early childhood professionals have advocated for decades: that early childhood staff should earn wages linked to those earned by public elementary school teachers, with salaries varying depending on the locale, experience, degrees, levels of training, work responsibilities, and professional behavior and skill. Health, retirement, and vacation benefits should also be provided to all staff positions.

Vobejda (1997) believes concerned early childhood professionals feel a crisis exists in hiring and retraining quality child care employees. With the draw of higher wages in other fields, an exodus of workers exists; consequently, the job applicant pool is often filled with people who lack qualifications and training, and who sometimes possess limited reading, writing, and verbal English fluency. Whitebook (1997) notes half of the country's 3 million child-care workers were likely to quit their jobs and head for higher pay during 1997.

Research has repeatedly confirmed that a key to quality and the prevention of harm in child care lies in the training and qualifications of the people who work with young children (Whitebook, Howes, & Phillips, 1989).

Cost, Quality and Child Outcomes in Child Care Centers (National Center for the Early Childhood Work Force, 1995) reinforces what was found in the national child care study in that overall quality of care in center-based child care programs is poor to mediocre (Whitebook, Phillips, & Howes, 1993).

Many factors contribute to poor quality including strong price competition in the marketplace, lack of consumer demand for quality, poor licensing standards, staff-child ratios, staff education, administrator experience, and center revenue and resources, to name but a few.

As mentioned, several of the programs reviewed in the Cost, Quality and Child Outcomes (CQ&O) study (National Center for the Early Childhood Work Force, 1995) proved to be only poor to mediocre. Those for infants and toddlers were poor enough to raise concern (Cryer & Phillipsen, 1997). But not all were negative, although the negatives were highlighted in the national media. One promising finding about the CQ&O Study Team programs (25 of 390 preschool classrooms; 14 of 222 infant/toddler classrooms) was that those accredited by the NAEYC consistently received higher scores on the Early Childhood Environment Rating Scale (ECERS) and the Infant/Toddler Environment Rating Scale (ITERS) (Cryer & Phillipsen, 1997). As accreditation becomes more popular, we are likely to find more quality programs.

The ECERS is a 37-item scale with seven categories: space and furnishings, personal care routines, language-reasoning, activities (fine motor, art, music/movement, blocks, and the like), interaction (supervision of gross motor activities, for example), program structure, and parents and staff. It currently has been revised and tested for reliability and validity (Clifford, 1998). The revised scale has 43 items; attention to cultural diversity and the inclusion of special needs children are now subsumed within the seven categories rather than being considered separately as before. The ITERS is currently undergoing revision. It includes 35 items, including adult personal area, meals/snacks, personal grooming, furnishings for relaxation, art, dramatic play, space to be alone, and others.

Greenberg and Springen (2000) report that an ongoing study on early child care by the National Institute of Child Health and Human Development found children in high-quality, center-based care outperformed children in other kinds of high-quality care (for example, family child care homes, relatives, and so on) in language development and cognitive skills like problem-solving and reasoning. They also tended to have fewer behavioral problems.

Most experts and researchers believe high-quality programs have a recommended adult-child ratio, a relatively small group size, age-appropriate activities, a safe environment, and access to comprehensive services as needed such as health and nutrition and parent involvement.

Head Start Family and Experiences Survey (FACES) is a longitudinal study of a nationally representative sample of Head Start programs. Its purpose is to examine the overall quality and outcomes of Head Start using specific Program Performance Measures (see Figure 13–9) (Tarullo & Doan, 1999). In 1997 and 1998, children and families in 40 national Head Start programs were observed and assessed by teachers and parents in the areas of emergent literacy, numeracy, general cognitive skills, gross and fine motor skills, social behavior and attitudes, positive learning attitudes, emotional well-being, and physical health. Classrooms were assessed on scheduling, the early learning environment, and teacher behavior. Tarullo and Doan (1999) have reviewed preliminary findings in the following:

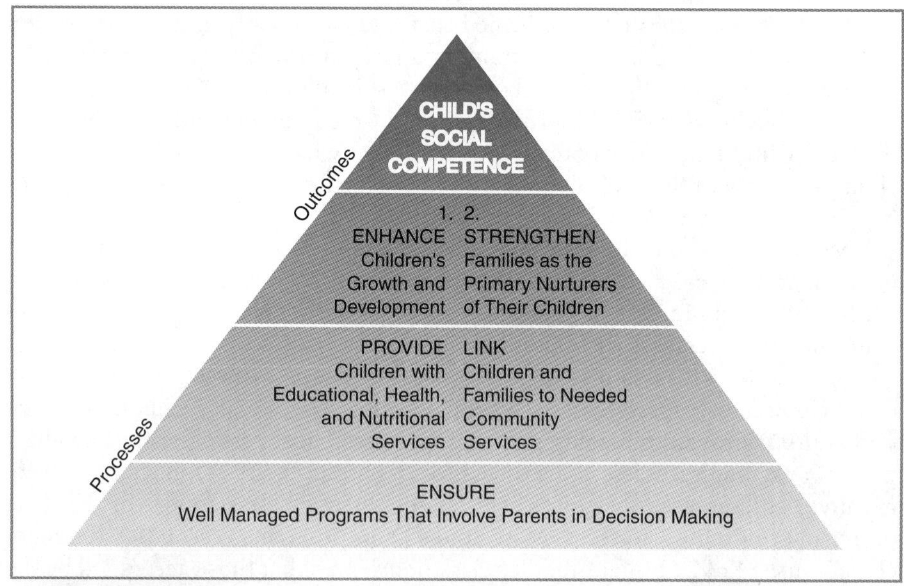

Figure 13–9 Quality ratings in preschool and infant classrooms. From Cost, quality, and child outcomes in child care centers. (1995, May). *Young Children, 50*(4). Reprinted with permission from the National Association for the Education of Young Children, NAEYC, (c) 1995.

> Research has consistently linked aspects of classroom quality such as low child-adult ratio, small group size, responsiveness of teacher-child interaction, and richness of learning environments to better child outcomes. For the first time, using a national sample, FACES tests the same linkages in Head Start. Preliminary data show that the higher the quality of a Head Start classroom, the more likely that children will show higher levels of skills, and over time, display greater gains in developmental outcomes.

Additional study data is available at the Head Start Bureau Web page at www.acf.dhhs.gov/.

Prekindergarten teachers with the highest levels of education are found in public school prekindergartens. Those with lowest levels are teaching in for-profit centers (Morgan, et al., 1993).

The Quality 2000 Initiative

The Quality 2000: Advancing Early Care and Education Initiative (hereafter referred to as the Initiative) proposes that its "primary goal . . . is that by the year 2010, high quality early care and education programs will be available and accessible to all children from birth to age five whose parents choose to enroll them" (Kagan & Neuman, 1997).

The recommendations made by the people involved in writing the Initiative are not simple: each is comprehensive and broad; each is a vision of what might be. Each includes several examples of strategies, which, if followed, are designed to achieve the goal of the recommendation.

Recommendation one concerns program quality:

> Imagine a time when we expect and support quality in all family child care and center-based programs . . . allowing staff flexibility in using state-of-the-art strategies, technologies, and resources creatively and cost effectively.

Possible strategies are:

- Promote cultural sensitivity and cultural pluralism.
- Encourage pedagogical inventiveness in family child care and centers.
- Focus on improving the overall organizational climate.
- Increase the number of accredited programs.
- Link programs to networks, supportive services, or other community resources (Kagan & Neuman, 1997).

Recommendation two concerns children:

> Imagine a time when clear results and expectations are specified and used to guide individual planning for all three- and four-year-old children, based on all domains of development (social/emotional, physical/motor, cognitive, language) and approaches to learning.

Some of its strategies are:

- Identify appropriate results.
- Develop appropriate strategies and instruments.
- Share results effectively, ensuring safeguards for children (Kagan & Neuman, 1997).

Recommendation three involves the parents and family; four, staff credentialing; five, staff training and preparation; six, program licensing; seven, funding and financing; and eight, governance structures. We will consider more details about staff credentialing and training and preparation in Chapter 14.

Financing, however, is worth a quick look here. Whitebook (1995) writes, "Higher quality centers [in the CQ&O study] were also those whose teachers had completed more education . . . and were paid higher wages and had less turnover." Certainly, recommendation seven would concur. As Kagan and Neuman (1997) state, "Adequate funding is essential to ensuring that all children have access to quality early care and education services . . ."

Legislative Efforts

Early childhood researchers know it is not enough to identify problems that contribute to lower-quality programs; they also must advocate realistic solutions that change national polices (Epstein, 1999). Groginsky, Robison, and Smith (1999) cite ways past and present day state legislators and policymakers have upgraded their programs:

> State legislators and other policymakers have addressed this concern (poor to mediocre child care) by focusing on improving child care quality in a variety of ways. A base measurement of quality levels is state regulation, which includes licensing standards for child-to-staff ratios, professional qualifications and physical space, among others. These standards represent a minimum level of health and safety for a child. In recent years, state decision makers have gone *beyond regulations* to make child care experiences better for young children. Four key ways that legislatures are moving in this direction include:

- Ensuring an effective workforce through training, education and career development
- Establishing program quality standards
- Improving reimbursement policies to advance good quality and access
- Developing comprehensive services for young children

How have states financed legislative and other state efforts to improve quality? Stoney (2001) believes by thinking "outside the box:"

- Arkansas enacted a new surcharge on beer to be earmarked for child care.
- Maine, Kansas, and Kentucky have earmarked tobacco settlement funds.
- Georgia created a lottery and set aside a portion of the proceeds for prekindergarten.
- Missouri earmarked a portion of the Gaming Commission Fund.
- Colorado has an innovative child care contributions tax credit, as well as a voluntary income tax check-off to raise money for child care quality.
- Oregon is considering a new tax credit to spur business investment in child care.
- Rhode Island taps into health care funds to help pay the cost of health insurance for child care providers.
- Connecticut makes tax-exempt bonds available to help finance facilities, then uses funds from the Temporary Assistance for Needy Families (TANF) program to underwrite a portion of the debt.

- New York, Washington, Boston, and other local governments have used criminal justice funds to help create child care centers in court buildings.
- Local 1199, the National Health and Human Services Employees Union, raises nearly $9 million each year for child care subsidies through collective bargaining agreements with employers in New York.
- Indiana's Dekko Foundation is building child care endowment funds in six counties.

Many studies have associated good quality child care with positive outcomes for children including better language, cognitive and social skills, fewer behavioral problems, and stronger mother-child relationships (Groginsky, Robison, & Smith, 1999). The High/Scope Perry Preschool project found low-income children's attendance in a good early education program led to children's greater academic success, better adult job achievement, and half as many arrests in later life (Schweinhart, Barnes, & Weikart, 1993).

The True Cost of Quality Child Care

Family budgets are strained in many households because of child care costs. If child care fees were increased and parents assumed the true costs for quality care, experts estimate the cost for parents would be as much as $8,500 per year (Vobejda, 1997), leaving little left for other family living expenses. Political platforms often include promises to enhance child care quality and access, but child care advocates do not expect an infusion of federal, state, or private monies in amounts necessary to alleviate the present U.S. situation.

Research has just begun to undercover the "true costs" of operating a quality early childhood program. Hidden costs have been borne by early childhood workers through foregone wages and benefits. The Cost, Quality and Child Outcomes Study team (Helburn, 1995), after studying 401 child care centers, estimates that 25 percent of the full cost of care and education of enrolled children was covered by some form of subsidy, primarily through low staff wages, but also building, rent, or occupancy aid, volunteers, donated goods, and in-kind contributions.

Conclusions cited in the Cost, Quality and Child Outcomes in Child Care Centers public report (Helburn 1995) estimated as much as 19 percent of the center's full costs were borne by workers who earned less than comparable workers with similar educational backgrounds.

ACCREDITATION AND ITS RELATIONSHIP TO QUALITY

For many years, schools (usually high schools, although both elementary and middle schools or junior highs have been involved), colleges, and universities have undergone periodic accreditation procedures by the Accrediting Commission for Schools (2000), hereafter referred to as the Commission. The Commission divides the United States into several regions that each have separate commissioners who use the same criteria to evaluate programs.

Over the past five years, the Commission has worked intensively with an advisory group composed of representatives from the Western Association to revise the accreditation process for the region. Input was solicited from schools, colleges and universities, and took into account current thinking and research about

accreditation—"the granting of approval to an institution of learning by an official review board after the school has met specific requirements." (The American Heritage Dictionary, 2nd College Edition. (1982). Boston, MA: Houghton Mifflin.)

teaching and learning. The result has been to shift the focus of accreditation from the previously used list of factors to a focus on student outcomes. The new *Focus on Learning* (2000) specifies four categories of criteria by which schools will be assessed. These are:

1. Organization for Student Learning
2. Curriculum and Instruction
3. Support for Student Personal and Academic Growth
4. Resource Management and Development

The new focus was developed to ensure that the "critical elements of school change were integral to the *Focus on Learning* design" and include the following specific features:

- Clarification of the school's purpose and expected schoolwide learning results for all students.
- The involvement of the school community in self-directed problem-solving.
- The opportunity for the following:
  —analysis of the actual program for students
  —meaningful dialogue
  —collaboration and shared decision-making
- The use of high-quality criteria to analyze the program for students.
- The development of a schoolwide action plan to support desired learning results.
- The opportunity for an outside perspective regarding the proposed changes through the Visiting Committee's dialogue and findings.
- The monitoring of progress in meeting or redefining goals and actions through accreditation reviews and reports.

It is obvious that the new criteria place an emphasis on change so a school can better serve its students, parents, and community.

Visiting Committee members undergo training each year to ensure that they are up to date on any changes involved in the accreditation process and to provide members with additional practice regarding the application of the criteria prior to the visitation. Committee members include teachers, administrators, college/university faculty, students (if appropriate), and community representatives such as school board members and/or representatives of business and industry. There are generally five or six members on any one Visiting Committee. After the visitation, a written report is forwarded to the Commission with the accreditation recommendation. The commissioners meet, usually in the late spring, read all of the Visiting Committee reports, and vote either to approve or amend the Visiting Committee's recommendations. Accreditation terms are generally for six years (maximum), three, one, or to deny.

Because many elementary and middle schools do not go through regional accreditation by the Commission, several states have instituted their own version of accreditation, commonly referred to as program quality review (PQR). In California and some other states, for example, the state board of education requires that all schools in the state undergo periodic PQRs. These involve a self-study, as does accreditation by the Commission, and review by a team of evaluators. Included on the review team are teachers, administrators, and state board of education representatives who have all received training in how to conduct a PQR. The reviewers prepare a report for the state superintendent of instruction and the state board of education members who have the final authority to accept the report, ask that the school undergo further review, or reject the report. Reviews are conducted every three years, so it is a continuing process.

NAEYC Accreditation

The NAEYC, concerned with how to ensure quality programs for young children, especially as they relate to developmentally appropriate practices, established the National Academy of Early Childhood Programs to administer accreditation procedures in 1985. These involved some of the same steps used by the Accrediting Commission for Schools. Any program wishing to be accredited writes NAEYC and requests that it be placed on the calendar for an accreditation visit. Once the date of the visit is confirmed, the program conducts a self-study, involving formal reports by the administrator, the staff, and parents. The result is a program description that includes a center or school profile, the results of classroom observations (both the teacher and the director complete this), and the results of the administrator report that ties together the results of the ratings of the program by staff and parents. Areas evaluated are:

1. Interactions among staff and children
2. Curriculum
3. Staff-parent interaction
4. Staff qualification and development
5. Administration
6. Staffing
7. Physical environment
8. Health and safety
9. Nutrition and food service
10. Evaluation (Bredekamp, 1987)

After completion of the self-study and its subsequent reception at NAEYC, a trained validator visits the center or school to verify the self-study much in the same manner as the Visiting Committee or the PQR reviewers. The validator's report is then read by at least three commissioners who make the final accreditation decision. As the process becomes better known, as more and more programs implement developmentally appropriate practices, and especially as parents begin to demand accredited programs for their children, the number of approved programs should rise. There were 8,192 NAEYC-accredited early childhood programs serving more than 720,000 young children in 2002 (NAEYC, 2002).

Does accreditation assure quality? In many ways, yes. The self-study alerts teachers, directors, principals, and others involved in the process to any areas of needed improvement, especially those impinging directly on standards required for accreditation. Often, then, when visiting committees, reviewers, or validators arrive, changes have already been instituted to improve an area likely to cause concern. One principal difference, though, between the accreditation by the Accrediting Commission and that of the program quality review or National Academy is the point on philosophy. Where the Commission accredits on how closely, among other factors listed, the curriculum goals match school philosophy, PQR reviewers are interested in how closely elementary school curriculum goals and objectives match those set forth in state curriculum guides, and National Academy validators observe to see how closely preschool/child care centers/preschool-primary school goals and objectives match the standards of the National Academy. Thus, emphasis shifts from school to state to national standards.

In an attempt to answer the question why, with soaring investment in early care and education and with so many accredited centers, does quality remain low, Kagan, et al. (2002) suggest:

> The answer is twofold. Most important, the resources to do the job are simply inadequate.
>
> and
>
> While inadequate resources are absolutely the first and major problem, they are not the only issue. *How resources are spent* is also important.

State lawmakers have turned their attention toward accreditation by promoting voluntary accreditation. The National Conference of State Legislatures publication, *Making Child Care Better: State Initiatives*, notes accreditation legislation in some states often includes language that is broad enough for programs to acquire accreditation by a range of organizations, but other states specify NAEYC accreditation (Groginsky, Robison, & Smith, 1999).

A number of states have chosen to develop differential subsidy rates to more closely match the cost of providing accredited care and improve quality, and to increase parent availability of accredited programs (Warman, 1998). Warman has identified 10 states (Florida, Minnesota, New Mexico, South Carolina, Vermont, Wisconsin, New Jersey, Kentucky, Mississippi, and Connecticut) with higher subsidy rates for accredited care, and two other states (Arizona and Oklahoma) with unfunded systems to pay accredited programs' higher rates. Some states (Arizona, Connecticut, Texas, Wisconsin, and the District of Columbia) provide minigrants, training, technical assistance, and bonuses to help individual programs achieve accreditation (Warman, 1998).

Sixteen states are promoting child care quality by setting reimbursement rates that reward caregivers for higher quality (Report on Preschool Programs, 1998). To receive the highest rates, centers must have been accredited by the NAEYC or another recognized entity.

A highly trained teaching staff is the strongest predictor of program quality along with the levels of staff compensation. Teacher and administrator turnover is a problem and a staffing crisis exists in most areas of the country. *La Ristra*, New Mexico's publication, concludes that ignoring the factors that contribute to lack of quality is a poor course of action:

> An acute problem left unattended eventually becomes status quo, yet is not less in need of urgent action. So it is with the child care staffing crisis. For three decades advocates and researchers have sounded warnings that without massive sustained effort to improve child care employment, turnover will continue unabated and children, families and caregivers will suffer the consequences.
>
> and
>
> At the heart of the crisis lie the insufficient resources to attract and retain a workforce able to sustain developmentally appropriate environments for children (Turner, 2002b).

Whitebook and Sakai (2002) point out centers receiving intensive support including on-site technical assistance from an early childhood professional, custom-designed training for staff and directors, funds to cover release time for staff participating in training, and an ongoing facilitated support group for directors achieved accreditation at more than twice the rate of centers receiving moderate support or seeking accreditation independently, and at nearly 10 times the rate of centers with only limited support.

THE COMER PROJECT FOR CHANGE IN EDUCATION

Dr. James P. Comer's work in the public schools of New Haven, Connecticut, shows us that change can take years (Goldberg, 1997). The original School Development Project started in the 1968–1969 school year with two elementary schools in low-income, predominantly African American areas. Test scores were 19 months below grade level and did not reach grade level until 1979. By 1984, scores were 12 months above grade level. What had happened?

Learning obstacles were identified and remedied. The project focused on what might be called the ecology of the total school: children, parents, administrators, custodial staff, and the community in which the school was located. Changes were made: schools were painted and cleaned; staff became a part of the decision-making process; teachers were retrained and/or transferred; and so were administrators.

Today, the Comer Project for Change in Education is now operating in more than 600 schools in 82 school districts in 26 states. The results continue to be good, but experience has taught those involved that change, although slow, "can yield to good will and hard work" (Goldberg, 1997). Goldberg quotes Comer as saying, "I have maintained a steady focus on child development and the importance of considering that. This is what I have tried to bring to education." We wish there were more people like Dr. Comer!

MENTORING PROGRAMS

The more experienced worker tutoring and serving as an example to the new worker has always been a way of training. Mentoring programs have emerged as one of the most promising ways to stabilize and support the child care workforce in order to guarantee more reliable and high-quality care for young children (National Center for the Early Childhood Work Force, 1995a). Some states including Arkansas, California, Florida, Maine, Maryland, Minnesota, Montana, Ohio, Rhode Island, South Dakota, Utah, West Virginia, and Wisconsin operate mentoring and apprenticeship programs for early childhood teachers (Groginsky, Robison, & Smith, 1999).

The National Center for the Early Childhood Work Force (1995a) describes the **mentoring** effort:

mentoring—guidance by an experienced and trusted teacher who is frequently paired with a new inexperienced teacher or aide, and who assists the new teacher with ideas and advice.

> Throughout the country, mentoring programs have emerged as one of the most promising strategies to retain experienced teachers and providers and thereby guarantee more reliable, high quality care for young children. Experienced teachers and providers participate in programs designed to give them the skills necessary to teach other adults how to care for and educate infants and young children. Upon taking on the role of mentor teacher, most teachers and providers receive additional compensation for training protégés; gain new respect from their co-workers and parents and renew their own commitment to working with children in the classroom or home. As dozens of programs develop, the need to share information grows.

The Early Childhood Mentoring Alliance, a newly emerging group, intends to provide a forum for sharing information and providing technical assistance. The Alliance is supported by a consortium of foundations.

Teacher Support Programs for Public School Teachers

Beginning and newly credentialed elementary school teachers are finding many public school districts are not letting them "sink or swim" their first teaching year. Many districts realize teacher quality is the single most important factor in improving student achievement (Haycock, 1998). These districts are investing in and designing teacher-induction programs that focus on supportive assistance. American schools expect to hire more than 2 million teachers in the next decade (Moir, Gless, & Baron, 1999).

California's Beginning Teacher Support and Assessment (BTSA) program is a statewide initiative jointly administered by the California Department of Education and the California Commission on Teacher Credentialing. This program allots $3,000 for each beginning teacher and some local districts augment with additional funding. Funds are being used a number of ways including onsite collaboration, classroom supplies, aids, technical assistance, and so on.

Most new teachers see themselves as agents of change, and are inspired and committed to the idea that they will make a difference in children's educational lives. Teacher-induction programs hope to sustain and nurture that idealism.

SUMMARY

In this chapter, we attempted to provide guidelines by which you can evaluate the quality of an early childhood education program. We have suggested that a quality program is one that takes into consideration the developmental needs of the children and that exceeds, rather than meets, minimum standards for state licensing. We have also suggested that quality programs may be found in many different settings ranging from federally funded programs to parent-cooperatives and proprietary profit-making centers.

We also presented a review of the accreditation processes sponsored by the Accrediting Commission for Schools and by the California State Board of Education's Program Quality Review, because these apply to the provision of quality elementary school programs. NAEYC's National Academy of Early Childhood Programs and its accreditation process was briefly explained as was its impact on quality programs for children from birth through age eight. (Most accredited programs are for children from birth through age five, the public schools not applying for accreditation through NAEYC but, instead, undergoing program quality review or some other form of state accreditation.)

Quality programs depend on you as student teachers. You need to strive to preserve and improve programs when you enter the field. Quality programs can exist only if quality people fight for them.

HELPFUL WEB SITES

http://www.naeyc.org

National Association for the Education of Young Children. Proceed to Academy destination for NAEYC accreditation information.

http://www.ecs.org/

Education Commission of the States. Readings on state funding, teacher qualifications, program standards, legislation, and other early childhood issues.

http://www.fpg.unc.edu/
Frank Porter Graham Child Care Center, University of North Carolina. Readings on quality care.

http://www.ed.gov/
National Institute on Early Childhood Development. Search research and child care categories.

http://headstartinfo.org
Head Start. General information and publications.

http://www.ericeece.org/
ERIC. Search text of *Five Perspectives on Quality in Early Childhood Programs*.

http://www.mcrel.org/
Mid-Continent Research for Education and Learning (MCREL). The mission of this group is to make a difference in the quality of education.

SUGGESTED ACTIVITIES

A. Visit at least three of these different types of early childhood programs: a Montessori school, a Head Start program, an NAEYC accredited program, a proprietary child care center, and/or a public school kindergarten, first, second, or third grade classroom. Evaluate them on the 13 factors of a good program from NAEYC, or look at the Accrediting Commission for Schools criteria. Interview the teachers and/or the principal of the school you visit and ask them about their self-study. Are the programs of equally good quality? Why or why not?

B. Summarize your evaluations of the programs you choose to observe. Discuss your ideas with your peers and supervisor.

C. Discuss the following quote in a small group. Report your group's reactions.

> I'm offended by women who claim to recognize that the poor quality of much of child care is a national scandal but are so badly organized that for a decade many states have actually had to return federal child-care money to Washington because no one persuaded their lame legislatures to match it (Alter, 1997).

REVIEW

A. List 10 features of a quality early childhood program.

B. Read each of the following descriptions of different early childhood programs. Decide whether each paragraph is describing a quality program, a mediocre program, or a poor program. If you do not have sufficient data to make a decision, indicate this. Discuss your answers and opinions with peers and your college supervisor.

1. This private preschool/child care center is located in a former public school. Each morning, the director greets every child as they enter. Each child has a wide choice of activities. Clay containers are placed on one table; crayon boxes and paper on another; scissors, old magazines, and scraps of construction paper are on a third, with sheets of blank

paper and glue sticks. Some children prefer to go to the block area, the book corner, or dramatic play corner. The outside play area beckons those who wish to climb, ride, swing, or play at the water table or in the sandbox.

The director has a degree in early childhood education, as does the only paid aide. Parents are seen often; both fathers and mothers stay with their children for a few minutes. The director speaks to each parent and sends home a monthly newsletter to inform parents of special activities and to solicit help for special projects. (For example, both the indoor and outdoor climbing structures were built by parents.)

The director carefully interviews every prospective family who wishes to place their children in the center. The director insists on at least one visit by both parents and the child before final acceptance. Prospective parents receive a written statement of philosophy and curriculum. During these meetings, the director has been known to state, "I expect parents to interview me as carefully as I interview them."

2. This after-school program is sponsored by a franchised nonprofit organization. The director of the program has an AA degree in early childhood education. Certified teachers or CDA holders work with the children (ages five to nine). In addition, there are many volunteers recruited from a local community college and high school. The program is located in empty classrooms in four elementary schools and in the nonprofit organization's main facility.

   Because the latter facility does not meet state standards, children are asked to join the organization. As a result, the organization is exempt from having to meet standards. For example, although there is ample outside play area at the school sites, there is none at the main facility site. This after-school program has a written statement of purpose and goals, a conceptual outline covering such items as safety, self-image, adult role models, a stimulating environment, and so on; a parent advisory group; and a daily schedule listing curriculum factors. The adult-to-child ratio is listed as 15:1 but has been known to exceed 25:1 when volunteers have been absent.

   The program schedules free time for the first 30 minutes so that the children can unwind from their school day. This is followed by snack time, activity time (arts and crafts, gymnastics, swimming, field trips, and the like), cleanup time, and free time during which quiet activities such as games, reading, homework, and drawing can be done.

3. This Montessori program (AMS) is located in the parish hall of a church. The director is a breezy, enthusiastic woman whose wealthy father sponsored her investment in the school. She received some training at the American Montessori Schools Center in New York, but she does not hold any degree. Her school has the usual Montessori equipment, and children can be seen quietly engaged in a variety of the typical self-directed activities: fitting shapes into a board, placing cylinders of various sizes into the appropriate holes, washing dolls' clothes on the washboard, sweeping the walk, and so on. One boy intrigues the observer; he is busy peeling carrots with a peeler and is very intent.

   The director spends much time talking on the phone with friends; most of the instruction is left to the aides. She recently attended a self-improvement seminar and is anxious for her employees to do the same. She is not willing, however, to pay their way. The turnover among her employees is high; she pays an aide only minimum wage.

The children in the program appear subdued and do not display much spontaneity. At least one parent has removed a child from the program because the director ridiculed the child's obesity.

4. This first-grade program is located in a large public elementary school of approximately 900 students in kindergarten through fifth grade. Having been opened only four years ago, the school is almost new. The primary wing contains 12 classrooms. Each room is carpeted and has regular and clerestory windows that allow for a maximum of natural light to be suffused throughout the room. Each room also has a side area with linoleum floor that contains a sink, water fountain, storage closets, a small refrigerator, and a round table suitable for six to eight students and an aide or parent volunteer. This area also contains a two-sided easel. Children sit in groups of two to four at individual desks arranged in small groups.

   The first grade teacher has a guinea pig in a cage on a shelf labeled "Discovery Center." Located on the shelf are books containing pictures of guinea pigs, some requiring little or no reading, others requiring more. A chart depicting the amount of food and water used by Rafael (the name voted on by the class) each day is maintained by the children assigned on a rotating basis to Rafael's care. A bulletin board by the entry door has a graph completed by the children of drawings of their favorite foods. Another graph posted on the wall contains pictures drawn by the children illustrating the different ways they come to school.

   On your visit, some children are busy working with a parent volunteer at the side table on a story she is assisting them in writing. Two other children are taking care of Rafael. A student teacher has grouped six more children in a small circle at the back of the room near the teacher's desk and is doing some one-to-one correspondence exercises with them. The cooperating teacher has assigned different groups math exercises using the Math Their Way manipulatives and is circulating around the room responding to questions and posing her own questions to check on student understanding.

C. Discuss mentoring as it relates to a program's possible quality.

D. How would you describe the quality of our nation's child care? Cite sources.

CASE SCENARIO

Setting: Mrs. Rush, director of Little Pals Preschool is interviewing Ms. Corlone, mother of three-year-old Bree. The mother is assessing the school for the possible enrollment of her daughter.

"Here's our brochure, Ms. Corlone. We have an excellent program. You are quite lucky because we actually will have one opening next week. Please follow me, I'm sure you would like to see our classrooms."

continues . . .

. . . continued

As they approach a classroom door, Ms. Corlone notices that the school's interior is freshly painted and spotlessly clean. As they enter the classroom, Ms. Corlone notes the room of four-year-olds is quiet and tidy. All the children are seated, working on what looks to be dittoed paper. Mrs. Rush whispers that the children all know their ABCs and can count to 50. Mrs. Rush approaches the teacher who is applying smiley face stickers on children's papers, and introduces her. Many elaborate pieces of child art decorate the walls, along with alphabet letters, word charts, and crayoned pages of coloring books. A world globe and a collection of library books are available. A computer and televison set sits along one wall. The center of the room features a large, colorful round rug that Mrs. Rush says is used for group instruction. Mrs. Rush enthusiastically describes extra lessons in dance that take place one day a week. These lessons are available if parents so choose.

Mrs. Rush shows Ms. Corlone the play yard. It is full of expensive, commercially designed large climbing structures, swinging bridges, and slides. It looks like an elaborate, well-tended city park.

Before Ms. Corlone leaves, Mrs. Rush asks if she has any questions. She says "no" and leaves after thanking Mrs. Rush for the tour and her time.

Questions for Discussion:

1. Pretend you are Bree. What questions would you have liked your mother to ask?
2. Would this type of school impress a parent favorably? Why?
3. What reservations would you have concerning the quality of Little Pals Preschool?

REFERENCES

Accrediting Commission for Schools, Western Association for Schools and Colleges (WASC). (2000). *Focus on Learning*. Burlingame, CA: Author.

Alter, J. (1997, November 3). Making child care macho. *Newsweek*.

Bredekamp, S. (Ed.). (1987). *Guide to accreditation by the national academy of early childhood programs*. Washington, DC: National Association for the Education of Young Children.

Bryant, D. M., Maxwell, K. L., & Burchinal, M. (1999). Effects of a community initiative on the quality of child care. *Early Childhood Research Quarterly, 14*, 449–464.

Clifford, R. M. (1998, November 20). *Measuring quality in preschool settings: The development of the revised early childhood environment rating scale*. Paper presented at the National Association for the Education of Young Children Conference, Toronto, Canada.

Cost, Quality and Child Outcomes Study Team. (1995). *Cost, quality, and child outcomes in child care centers.* Denver: Department of Economics, University of Colorado at Denver.

Cryer, D., & Phillipsen, L. (1997, July). A close-up look at child care program strengths and weaknesses. *Young Children, 52*(5).

Epstein, A. S. (1999). Pathways to quality in Head Start, public school, and private nonprofit early childhood programs. *Journal of Research in Childhood Education, 13*(2), 101–119.

Goldberg, M. F. (1997, March). Maintaining a focus on child development: An interview with Dr. James P. Comer. *Phi Delta Kappan, 78*(7).

Greenberg, S. H., & Springen, K. (2000, October 16). Back to day care. *Newsweek,* 61–62.

Groginsky, S., Robison, S., & Smith, S. (1999). *Making child care better: State initiatives.* Washington, DC: National Conference of State Legislatures.

Haycock, K. (1998, Summer). Good teaching matters: How well-qualified teachers can close the gap. *Thinking K-16,* 3(2), 1–2.

Helburn, S. (Ed.). (1995). *Cost, quality and child outcomes in child care.* Center for Research in Economics and Social Policy, Department of Economics, University of Colorado.

Kagan, S. L., & Neuman, M. J. (1997, September). Highlights of the quality 2000 initiative: Not by chance. *Young Children, 52*(6).

Kagan, S. L., Brandon, R. N., Ripple, C. H. , Maher, E. J., & Joesch, J. M. (2002, May). Supporting quality early childhood care and education. *Young Children, 57*(3), 58-65.

Moir, E., Gless, J., & Baron, W. (1999). A support program with heart: The Santa Cruz project. In M. Scherer (Ed.). *A better beginning: Supporting and mentoring new teachers* (pp. 106–113). Alexandria, VA: Association for Supervision and Curriculum Development.

Morgan, G., Azer, S., Costley, J., Genser, A., Goodman, I., Lombardi, J., & McGrimsey, B. (1993). *Making a career of it: The state of the states report on career development in early care and education.* Boston: The Center for Career Development in Early Care and Education at Wheelock College.

National Association for the Education of Young Children (NAEYC). (2002). Our mission. *Young Children, 57*(6), 98–99.

National Association for the Education of Young Children. (1994, March). Professional development. *Young Children, 49*(3).

National Center for the Early Childhood Work Force. (1995, January). Mentoring programs: An emerging child care career path. *Compensation Initiatives Bulletin, 1*(3).

National Center for the Early Childhood Work Force. (1995). *Cost, quality, and child outcomes in child care centers.* Washington, DC: Author.

No author. (1998, August 19). Sixteen states use tiered rates to promote child care quality. *Report on Preschool Programs, 30*(17).

Schweinhart, L. J., Barnes, H. V., & Weikart, D. P. (1993). *Significant benefits: The High/Scope Perry preschool study through age 27.* Ypsilanti, MI: High/Scope Press.

Tarullo, L. B., & Doan, H. M. (1999, March). Linking Head Start quality to child outcomes: The FACES study. *Head Start Bulletin, 65,* 18–19.

Turner, P. (2002a). Best practices. In P. Turner (Ed.). *La Ristra: New Mexico's comprehensive professional development system in early care, education, and family support* (pp. 77–82). Santa Fe, NM: Office of Child Development, Youth and Families Department.

Turner, P. (Ed.). (2002b). *La Ristra: New Mexico's comprehensive professional development system in early care, education, and family support.* Santa Fe, NM: Office of Child Development, Youth and Families Department.

Vobejda, B. (1997, October 22). Employee shortage at day-care to be addressed. *The Idaho Statesman.*

Warman, B. (1998, September). Trends in state accreditation policies. *Young Children, 53*(5).

Whitebook, M. (1995, May). What's good for child care teachers is good for our country's children. *Young Children, 50*(4).

Whitebook, M. (1997, October 22). Employee shortage at day-care to be addressed. *The Idaho Statesman.*

Whitebook, M., Howes, C., & Phillips, D. (1989). *Who cares? Child care teachers and the quality of care in America. The national child care staffing study.* Washington, DC: National Center for the Early Childhood Work Force.

Whitebook, M., Phillips, D., & Howes, C. (1993). *The national child care staffing study revisited.* Oakland, CA: Child Care Employee Project.

Whitebook, M., & Sakai, L. (2002, November). Readers write. *Young Children, 57*(6), 7.

Wiechel, J. (2001, Summer). Eliminating the "non-system" of governance. *State Education Leader, 19*(2), 13–15.

CHAPTER 14

Professional Commitment and Growth

Objectives

After studying this chapter, the student should be able to:

1. Define professionalism.
2. Explain the importance of acquiring a sense of professional commitment.
3. List four different activities that promote individual professional growth.
4. Name two early childhood professional associations and describe the benefits of membership in each.

My family and friends complained that I didn't have time for them when I was in student teaching practicum. And I didn't! I barely kept up and turned assignments in late at times.

—Bill Jackson

My most memorable experience in student teaching has been the kindness, help, and cooperation that I received. So much praise and encouragement made it easier.

—Carole Mehors

My dream is to have a school of my own among evergreen trees in a small mountain town. I'll call the school "Tiny Piney" or "Evergreen Academy" or such.

—Nomsa Ncube

I was convinced my cooperating teacher didn't like me! Our teaching styles seemed so different. Her attitude toward teaching made me wonder why she'd kept at it so long. Things got better. She had big problems in her personal life which she struggled to keep out of her classroom manner. It was then that I caught glimpses of her teaching strengths.

—Carrie Lee Foulkes

Professionals—individuals engaged in occupations considered learned endeavors such as law, medicine, or as in this text, education.

As a student teacher, you are already considered a professional. Professionals are those individuals whose work is predominantly nonroutine and intellectual in character. They make constant decisions that call for a substantial degree of discretion and judgment. Accept the fact that an early childhood educator is in a profession requiring lifelong learning (White, 2000). Professional status is gained through a display and application of professionally recognized teaching skills and techniques. Admittedly, some of your skills are new, emerging, and wobbly, whereas others are definitely observable. You are currently being measured against standards established by those in the same profession.

DEFINITIONS

Professionalism is the ability to plan knowledgeably and competently to make a sustained difference: to diagnose and analyze situations, to select the most appropriate interventions, to apply them skillfully, and to describe why they were selected (VanderVen, 1988). As early as 1925, in attempting to define professionalism for the business community, Follet stated, "Profession connotes for most people a foundation of science and a motive of service [that must] rest on the basis of a proved body of knowledge [and be] . . . used in the service of others" (Fox & Urwick, 1982). Although there is no question that early childhood educators are involved in the service of others, there are questions about education and the "body of knowledge." Most would agree that child development is one block of the proven body of knowledge; however, when states allow the licensing of child care workers with no more than six semester units of coursework or less, does this constitute a "foundation of science?" One answer to this question has been the NAEYC's development of an early childhood career lattice. The key elements listed in "A Conceptual Framework for Early Childhood Professional Development" (NAEYC, 1994) are those which, if achieved, are all a part of what professionalism encompasses. But more of this later when we discuss professional development. One mark of the professional is that professionals are always learning, always seeking to be better at what they do, always growing in knowledge and ability to perform their jobs.

career lattice—recognizes that the early childhood profession is made up of individuals with varied backgrounds; a lattice allows for both horizontal and vertical movement among positions, with accompanying levels of education, experience, responsibility, and pay.

CONCERNS IN THE PROFESSION

Your teaching day includes tasks that on the surface, appear custodial in nature such as helping at cleanup time, supervising the children as they wash their hands, serving them snacks, and encouraging them to rest. Each is a learning time for children, and your professional skill is at work. Helping a child who is struggling to slip on a sweater is done in a professional way and is an opportunity to help the child become more independent.

Professional status, everyone agrees, is a problem for this career field. Societies award status to trained, educated individuals who provide valuable services to society. People can easily tick off on one hand high-status professions and possibly what they consider middle-status professions. Early childhood workers will not be among them.

What are the possible reasons this career field has not obtained the recognition and status it deserves? There are no simple answers but rather many conjectures by many writers. Included among those frequently cited reasons are the following:

- A blurred image between parenting and paid child care providers in the public's mind.

- Public attitudes that almost anyone can watch children.
- Public perceptions including child care as requiring little or no specific knowledge, education, or skill.
- Caregivers' attitudes toward themselves, particularly feelings of personal or collective lack of power.
- Lack of early childhood teacher self-esteem or assertiveness.
- A public perception of child care workers providing a dedicated service rather than a service for personal gain.
- A lack of societal concern for children by the clients of the early childhood professional.
- The turnover rate of prekindergarten teachers as opposed to the lifelong careers of other recognized professionals.
- Lack of a professional culture that includes values, norms, terminology, agreement, and symbols common to members of the profession.
- An unclear or controversial body of theoretical knowledge, and specialized technique(s) that serve as the basis for work actions, advice giving, or planned child activities.
- Less than well-known and publicly recognized professional associations, societies, and standard monitoring groups.
- A body of recognized professional child care teacher attributes or common standards by which individuals could be measured or licensed.
- Lack of the career groups' collective political clout.
- Lack of employee bargaining power in work situations.
- Low or minimal entry-level requirements or qualifications.
- The historical origins of child care work.
- General public attitudes concerning the failure of educational systems.
- Lack of state uniformity in educational requirements for beginning early childhood teachers.

Primary-level professionals may find the last two items applicable to their situation also, and a general concern about the quality of primary school education, together with the lack of uniformity from one state to another.

In addition, primary-level professionals may discover:

- A lack of respect for public education and the feeling that public education has failed.
- A feeling that the teacher unions (the National Education Association and the American Federation of Teachers) are too powerful politically and protect teachers who should be fired.
- A lack of understanding by parents, and often by principals, regarding what constitutes "developmentally appropriate practice."

Grant and Murray (1999) report a hopeful trend:

> Recent Gallup Polls show some upward change in the American public's evaluation of teaching as a career: two-thirds of parents said they would like to see a child of theirs become a teacher and 73 percent of all respondents said they would encourage "the brightest person you know" to become a teacher.

Many early childhood staffers' reticence to accept themselves as professionals may be partly responsible for low salaries and job classifications that equate prekindergarten teacher's work with attendants, custodians, and domestics. The "baby-sitter" image in the public's view has been difficult to escape. Advocacy training is now a recommended part of preservice training.

A teacher's pride in the profession is justified. After student teaching, you will know that the job of an early childhood teacher is demanding, challenging, complex, necessitates constant decisions, and can be physically and emotionally taxing, as well as being highly satisfying and rewarding.

The early childhood teaching profession should attract and hold the best candidates our society has to offer who work with our society's most prized resource and hope for the future: children and families.

PROFESSIONAL BEHAVIOR AND COMMITMENT

Professionalism entails understanding both children and yourself, plus dilligence. Some of the demands that "pros" make on themselves and their behaviors are:

1. Being a professional requires that you give full measure of devotion to the job.
2. Being a professional means you don't need rules to make yourself act like a professional.
3. Professionals accept responsibilities assigned to them with as much grace as they can muster and then work in a positive way to change those duties that deter their teaching.
4. A professional joins with others in professional organizations that exchange research and ideas on how children learn and institute action to benefit all children.
5. A professional understands, is aware of prejudices, and makes a concerted effort to get rid of them.
6. A professional treats children as people with feelings.
7. A professional speaks up for the child when the child needs somebody to speak out in the child's behalf.
8. A professional is an educator who is informed about modern trends in education.

Other behaviors that mark you as a professional range from those that seems obvious to those that are subtle. As a professional, you will:

- be punctual
- notify your center or school, in advance if possible, when you must be absent
- be prepared
- dress appropriately
- maintain confidentiality and avoid gossiping about either the children or your peers
- maintain positive health habits (e.g., cleanliness in personal hygiene, modeling positive eating habits, demonstrating ways to deal with stressful situations positively, and so on)
- become an advocate for children and early childhood workers

Student teachers may spend long hours both in and out of their classrooms, and may feel that they are barely hanging on. This feeling can continue through the first year on the job. Vukelich and Wrenn (1999) describe a new teacher's inner thoughts. They quote from a journal written by one of the graduates of their elementary teacher education program:

> [I have chosen the] most complex job in the world. . . . How will I possibly remember everything I have learned? . . . There were all the curriculum areas to know. Then there was knowing the children I would teach—their learning styles, environments, personalities, disabilities, gifts, intelligences. The list was endless!

Even though this young woman had received what she felt had been a "superb education," her first year of teaching proved to be daunting. She wrote, "[I] probably cried enough to fill an oversized Jacuzzi tub" and "put in a tremendous number of hours." As with many first-year teachers, she was concerned with simply trying to survive.

Katz (1972) has proposed that teachers go through three stages of professional development. During the first year, they focus on *survival* in much the same way our young woman above did. During the next two or three to five years, they begin to *consolidate* what they know and begin to feel like they finally know what they are doing. Finally, they reach the *maturity* level and feel that they truly are professionals.

Caruso (2000) identifies six phases for both student teachers (ST), and their cooperating teachers (CT) in student teacher placement classrooms:

Phase #1—anticipation/excitement (CT) and anxiety/euphoria (ST).

Phase #2—confusion/clarity. Both (ST) and (CT).

Phase #3—on stage/backstage (CT) and competence/inadequacy (ST).

Phase #4—letting go/hanging on (CT) and new awareness/renewed doubts (ST).

Phase #5—coteacher/solo teacher (CT) and more confidence/greater adequacy (ST).

Phase #6—loss/relief (CT).

During Phase #6, Caruso believes cooperating teachers may experience the following:

- a period of reflection
- pride in their student teacher
- satisfaction with their mentoring and supervision
- a sense of loss
- reward for their student teacher's success
- feelings of gratitude and relief
- feelings about being on their own again
- concerned if their student teacher did not succeed
- a possible questioning of their suitability as a cooperating teacher
- a need to consult with other cooperating teachers
- a need to plan to do things differently next time
- questioning whether to accept or not accept another student teacher

And student teachers in Phase #6 may experience the following:

- separation difficulty
- guilt about not accomplishing to the extent they hoped
- loss

- anxiety as they return to campus, apply for jobs, or reassess their career goals
- a great sense of accomplishment
- pride in success or disappointment if not successful
- reflection, which Caruso sees as probably the most important aspect of the final phase (Caruso, 2000)

Look back to Caruso's six phases. Where would you place yourself?

In looking at elementary school teachers, one study stated that it took a new teacher three years of teaching at the same grade level to begin to feel competent about what he was doing. The implication, then, for a principal is not to reassign a new teacher to another grade level for at least three years and to recognize that some others may need a longer exposure at the one grade level before they feel comfortable about what they are doing.

Anxieties stem from a desire to become a professional while at the same time questioning one's stamina, endurance, and capability to do so. Your commitment to the profession will be nourished by the supportive adults that surround you in your student teaching experience.

Severe tests to a student teacher's professional commitment may happen if a placement site models attitudes that downgrade the value and worth of the profession. When negative behavior is present in the teachers (at any given facility), it is not unusual to see new teachers taking the same negative attitudes as staff who have been there awhile (Moore, 1998). A good grasp on professional conduct and commitment helps the student teacher sort out less than professional behavior. Improved and continued high standards in the profession depend on the newly trained professionals' enthusiasm, idealism, knowledge, and skills, and the experienced professionals' leadership. Newly trained professionals can strengthen the field through their identification with practicing, committed professionals.

Advocacy

Advocacy takes time, energy, and knowledge. It involves everyday contact with people. Student teachers may have a desire to become involved but lack the knowledge of how to begin.

One way to involve yourself in advocacy is to list 10 issues you feel are the most pressing. Then select the one issue that moves you most strongly. Student teaching commitments may make advocacy at this time near to impossible! These paragraphs strive to make you aware of the need for future advocacy. In your daily contacts with other adults, particularly family and friends, you will be instrumental in their developing opinions of child care and early childhood education. You are, right now, a representative of the profession. What you say and do may influence others' priorities and voting behavior.

One of your 10 issues might have been that young children in child care need well-trained early childhood educators. Why? Because research supports the idea that better trained early childhood teachers provide higher quality care. A second issue you might have considered is that early childhood workers deserve better pay and adequate benefits. Well-paid professionals tend to stay in the profession rather than leave for better jobs. This curbs staff turnover, which erodes the quality of child care services.

Advocacy is a skill! Besides everyday public contact opportunities, and letter writing, many professionals join in group efforts that involve contacting and influencing legislators through local, state, and federal efforts such as demonstrations, celebrations similar to the Week of the Young Child, and other public activities that support the welfare of young children and their families. Children cannot advocate on their own behalf for improvements in their lives; they need others willing to do so.

Because advocacy means being aware of legislation, the legislative process, and individuals and groups who support child care issues (see Figure 14–1), a first step is identifying groups or individuals who monitor and help author legislation. Moore (1998) points out that our society does not support the efforts of teachers working with young children, as is the case in some other countries.

PROFESSIONAL GROWTH AND DEVELOPMENT

Early childhood teaching offers each professional a lifelong learning challenge. The goal of professional growth includes the unfolding of potentials and achieving greater self-actualization. True self-actualization leads to an increasing sense of responsibility and a deepening desire to serve humanity.

Maslow (1971) has described the conflict individuals face as they struggle toward increasing excellence.

> Every human being has both sets of forces within him. One set clings to safety and defensiveness out of fear, tending to regress

ADVOCACY GROUPS

ABC (Alliance for Better Child Care), 122 C Street, NW, Suite 400, Washington, DC 20001. Focuses on increased support for child care.

ACT (Action for Children's Television), 20 University Road, Cambridge, MA 02138. Focuses on children's improved television programming.

American Bar Association, 1800 M Street, NW, Suite 200, South, Washington, DC 20036. Focuses on child protection and child welfare issues.

Association of Child Advocates, P.O. Box 5873, Cleveland, OH 44101-0873. Focuses on a national association of state advocacy groups, information, and technical assistance resources; offers a national conference.

CCAC (Child Care Action Campaign), 330 Seventh Avenue, 17th Floor, New York, NY 10032. Actively promotes child and child care workers issues.

Center for Career Development in Early Care and Education, Wheelock College, 200 The Riverway, Boston, MA 02215. Supports advocacy efforts.

Center for Public Advocacy Research, 12 W. 37th Street, New York, NY 10018. Focuses on research and policy.

Children's Defense Fund, 25 E Street, NW, Washington, DC 20001. Monitors federal legislation and policy.

Children's Foundation, 725 15th Street, NW, Suite 505, Washington, DC 20005-2109. Focuses on improved quality of children's lives.

The Center for the Child Care Work Force, 733 15th Street, NW, Suite 1037, Washington, DC 20005. Focuses on collation of facts and figures related to child care workers and advocates for improved salaries and working conditions.

Figure 14–1 Advocacy groups and resources

> backward, hanging on to the past . . . afraid to grow away from primitive communication with mother uterus and breast, afraid to take chances, afraid to jeopardize what he already has, afraid of independence, freedom and separateness. The other set of forces impels him forward toward wholeness of Self and uniqueness of Self, toward full functioning of all his capacities, toward confidence in the face of the external world at the same time he can accept his deepest, real, unconscious Self.

When your future job includes promotional, material, or rewarding incentives, it may add impetus. Your attitude toward your professionalism will give a high priority to activities that contribute to your skill development.

As a professional, you will actively pursue growth. Maslow (1971) describes the struggle and possible outcomes of your pursuit.

> Therefore we can consider the process of healthy growth to be a never ending series of free choice situations, confronting each individual at every point throughout his life, in which he must choose between the delights of safety and growth, dependence and independence, regression and progression, immaturity and maturity.

Your efforts to grow professionally will become part of your life's pattern. You will experience the "tugs and pulls" of finding the time and energy to follow your commitment.

Professional Growth Plans

Many public agencies and school districts develop written professional growth plans for their employees knowing that staff's development efforts impact the quality of services. Research has repeatedly emphasized that the educational background of staff members is a critical component of high-quality child care and staff turnover (Honig & Hirallal, 1998; Burchinal, et al., 2000).

The majority of early childhood educators, especially those in the private sectors, will plan individual courses of action to attain professional growth. They may not have the inducements such as stipends, release time, transportation provisions, or salary schedules that reward their efforts as do some public employees.

A California program, The Child Development Corps, provides a professional development stipend ($500 to 600 per year) to child care teachers, directors, and home-based providers meeting certain education and training qualifications who commit to continuing their professional development and have provided service prior to the receipt of the stipend (Whitebook & Eichberg, 2002). See Figure 14–2 for other public policy.

Kagan and associates (2002) have listed experts' recommendations for building professional development systems to promote a nationally qualified workforce:

- Training and credentialing should be ongoing so that preservice formal education requirements do not constitute a barrier to people from low socioeconomic backgrounds and immigrant teachers seeking to enter the field.
- All staff should participate yearly in ongoing professional development activities.
- The costs of professional development should be fully subsidized for low-wage staff including paying the costs of substitutes. As their salaries increase, staff will share in the costs of professional development as do elementary school teachers.
- The costs of expanding and maintaining the institutions that provide the training must be included in the estimates.

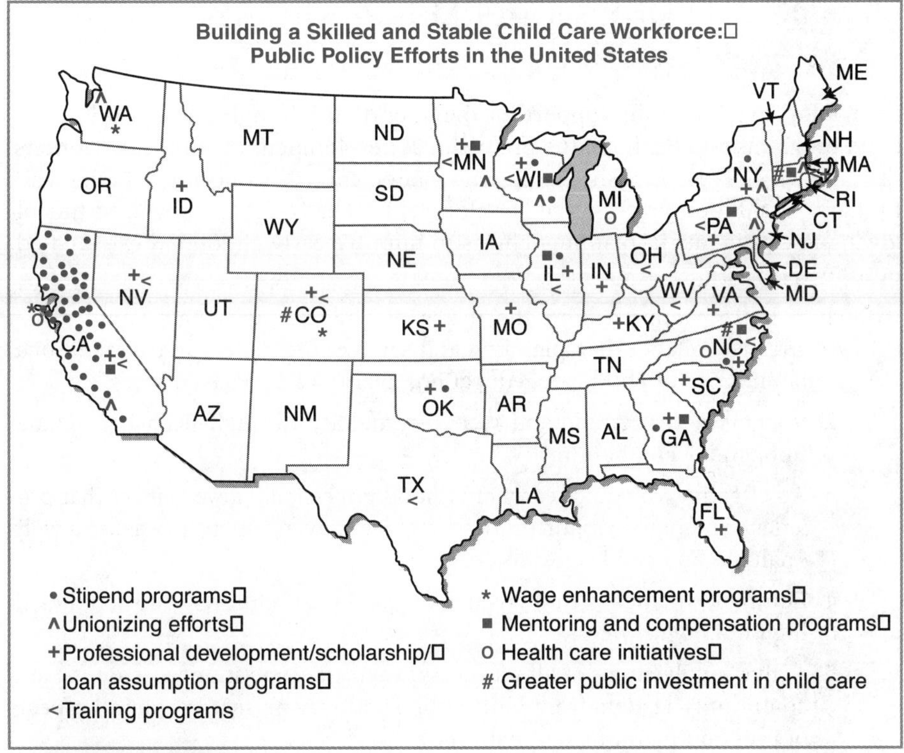

Figure 14–2 Reprinted with permission from the National Association for the Education of Young Children.

Individual Learning Cycles

Just as you have watched children take enormous steps in learning one day and just mark time another, your professional growth may not be constant and steady. Harrison (1978) observed the phenomenon of "risk and retreat" in self-directed learning.

> The learning cycle is our name for the natural process of advance and retreat in learning. We observed early in our experiments with self-directed learning that individuals would move out and take personal risks and then would move back to reflect and integrate the experience.

Such "risk and retreat" relates to what Piaget described as the process of equilibration. You, as a learner, assimilate new material first as an accommodation with past learning (the risk); then, the assimilation becomes "play" (the retreat). But such a retreat is important to the process of equilibration as you seek to establish an equilibrium between old and new learning.

Reflection or standing still at times may give ideas time to hatch. Being aware of your own creative thinking can make you more aware of this creative process in children.

Many other factors will influence the ebb and flow of your future growth as a teacher. The energy-draining nature of teaching's demanding work can sometimes dampen enthusiasm for future growth, as can the attitudes of those with whom you work. You may periodically need contacts with other professionals to rekindle your commitment.

NAEYC's Professional Development Position Statement

In an effort to gain public support for the importance of high-quality early childhood programs and facilitate the professional development of child care workers, the NAEYC (1994) published a position statement, "A Conceptual Framework for Early Childhood Professional Development." The NAEYC recognized the following key elements in planning efforts to improve early childhood care and education systems:

1. A holistic approach to the needs of children and their families that stresses collaborative planning and service integration across traditional boundaries of child care, education, health, and social services.
2. Systems that promote and recognize quality through licensing, regulation, and accreditation.
3. An effective system of early childhood *professional development* that provides meaningful opportunities for career advancement to ensure a well-qualified and stable workforce.
4. Equitable financing that ensures access for all children and families to high-quality services.
5. Active involvement of all players—providers, practitioners, parents, and community leaders from both public and private sectors—in all aspects of program planning and delivery.

Working with a number of other groups, the NAEYC's National Institute for Early Childhood Professional Development fosters the development of a comprehensive, articulated system of professional development for *all* individuals in *all* early childhood settings. The NAEYC framework includes various components and uses the symbol lattice to communicate combining diversity and uniqueness (Johnson & McCracken, 1994). Both vertical and horizontal strands of the lattice system are interconnected in the model, which connects additional preparation and training to increased responsibility and compensation.

Defining characteristics of early childhood professionals, the NAEYC (1994) identified a specialized body of knowledge and competencies that set early childhood professionals apart from other professionals. They:

- demonstrate an understanding of *child development* and apply this knowledge in practice
- *observe and assess children's behavior* in planning and individualized teaching practices and curriculum
- establish and maintain *a safe and healthy environment* for children
- *plan and implement [a] developmentally appropriate curriculum* that advances all areas of children's learning and development, including social, emotional, intellectual, and physical competence (see Figure 14–3)
- establish supportive relationships with children and implement developmentally appropriate techniques of *guidance and group management*
- establish and maintain positive and productive *relationships with families*
- support the development and learning of individual children, recognizing that children are best understood in the context of *family, culture, and society*
- demonstrate an understanding of the early childhood profession and make a commitment to *professionalism*

Figure 14–3 Being able to assist young children's computer skills is an evolving teacher competency.

Professional early childhood workers must incorporate these ideas into the daily responsibility to establish and maintain productive relationships with colleagues, work effectively as members of an instructional team, communicate effectively with parents and other family members, and communicate effectively with other professionals and agencies concerned with children and families in the larger community to support children's development, learning, and well-being.

Levels of Training

Figure 14–4 displays NAEYC's identified levels of professional development.

This is designed to reflect a continuum of professional development. The levels identify levels of preparation programs for which standards have been established nationally.

Early Childhood Professional Level VI
Successful completion of a Ph.D. or Ed.D. in a program conforming to NAEYC guidelines; OR
Successful demonstration of the knowledge, performance, and dispositions expected as outcomes of a doctoral degree program conforming to NAEYC guidelines.

Early Childhood Professional Level V
Successful completion of a master's degree in a program conforming to NAEYC guidelines; OR
Successful demonstration of the knowledge, performance, and dispositions expected as outcomes of a master's degree program conforming to NAEYC guidelines.

Early Childhood Professional Level VI
Successful completion of a baccalaureate degree from a program conforming to NAEYC guidelines; OR
State certification meeting NAEYC/ATE certification guidelines; OR
Successful completion of a baccalaureate degree in another field with more than thirty professional units in early childhood development/education including 300 hours of supervised teaching experience, including 150 hours each for two of the following three age groups: infants and toddlers, three- to five-year-olds, or the primary grades; OR
Successful demonstration of the knowledge, performance, and dispositions expected as outcomes of a baccalaureate degree program conforming to NAEYC guidelines.

Early Childhood Professional Level III
Successful completion of an associate degree from a program conforming to NAEYC guidelines; OR
Successful completion of an associate degree in a related field, plus thirty units of professional studies in early childhood development/education including 300 hours of supervised teaching experience in an early childhood program; OR
Successful demonstration of the knowledge, performance, and dispositions expected as outcomes of an associate degree program conforming to NAEYC guidelines.

continues

Figure 14–4 Definitions of early childhood professional categories. From Professional development. (1994, March). *Young Children, 49*(3). Reprinted with permission from the National Association for the Education of Young Children.

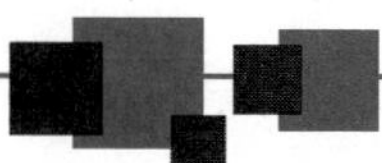

Early Childhood Professional Level II
II. A. Successful completion of the CDA Professional Preparation Program OR completion of a systematic, comprehensive training program that prepares an individual to successfully acquire the CDA Credential through direct assessment.

II. B. Successful completion of a one-year early childhood certification program.

Early Childhood Professional Level I
Individuals who are employed in an early childhood professional role working under supervision or with support (e.g., linkages with provider association or network or enrollment in supervised practicum) and participating in training designed to lead to the assessment of individual competencies or acquisition of a degree.

Figure 14–4 (continued)

The following principles of the professional development process were gathered from NAEYC's (1994) review of available research:

1. Professional development is an ongoing process.
2. Professional development experiences are most effective when grounded in a sound theoretical and philosophical base and structured as a coherent and systematic program.
3. Professional development experiences are most successful when they respond to an individual's background, experiences, and current context of her role.
4. Effective professional development opportunities are structured to promote clear linkages between theory and practice.
5. Providers of effective professional development experiences have an appropriate knowledge and experience base.
6. Effective professional development experiences use an active, hands-on approach and stress an interactive approach that encourages students to learn from one another.
7. Effective professional development experiences contribute to positive self-esteem by acknowledging the skills and resources brought to the training process as opposed to creating feelings of self-doubt or inadequacy by immediately calling into question an individual's current practice.
8. Effective professional development experiences provide opportunities for application and reflection, and allow for individuals to be observed and receive feedback on what has been learned.
9. Students and professionals should be involved in the planning and design of their professional development program.

Figure 14–5 is an example of a career ladder that is found in a number of states. Each state's specific definition of what constitutes completion of each level may differ widely.

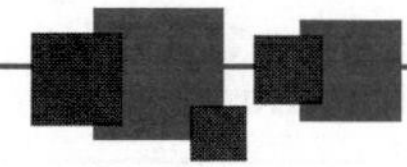

Career Ladder Citing Certificates, Credentials, and Degrees

Doctorate

Master's Degree

Bachelor's Degree in Early Childhood/Child Development**

Associate Degree in Early Childhood Education**

A certficate* awarded after a number of college credits are accumulated in an approved associate degree program.

Completion of a Child Development Associate (CDA) credential at an institution of higher education that articulates into a certificate program or an associate degree program.

Certificate of completion of an entry level early childhood training course with specified hour or unit credit.

*Certification in some states may be undertaken by state departments, associations, training agencies, or private entities.
**Degree granting institutions have different department names such as Family Studies, Human Services, and so on.

Figure 14–5 Career ladder citing certificates, credentials, and degrees

Most large centers have career ladders or lattices which show up, down, and lateral job positions; necessary qualifications; and an organizational chart. Salary schedules also may be available.

New Standards and Compensation

The rising demand for high-quality child care, new standards, and stiffer educational staff qualifications has not caused increased salaries, benefits, or improved working conditions (see Figure 14–6). Bright spots occur in some areas of the child care field including Head Start, military child care, and in states initiating or instituting state funded prekindergarten programs or universal Pre-K programs. There is still a long way to go before equitable compensation becomes a reality for most early childhood workers. What exactly does exist? In 1998,Whitebook, Howes, and Phillips reported the national average annual salary was $12,500 a year for child care center workers.

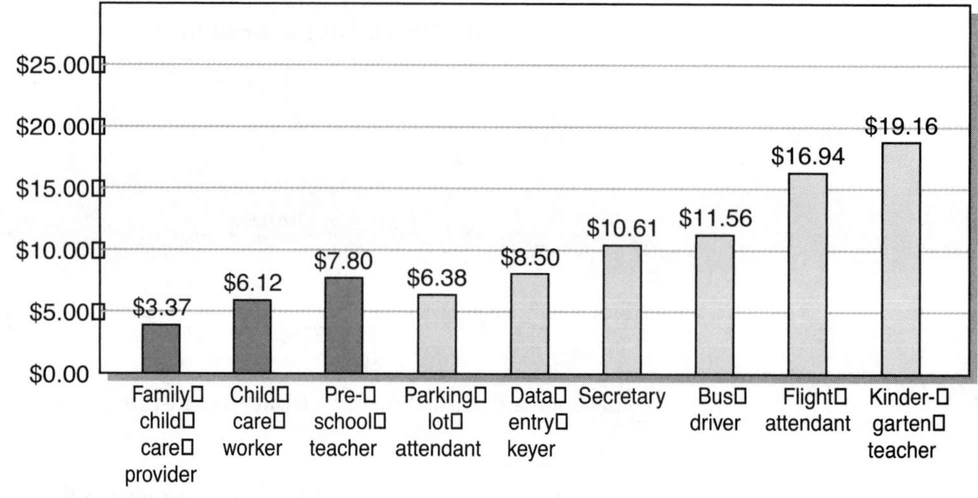

Figure 14–6 Child care work force earnings in perspective: A comparison of median hourly wages between child care jobs and other occupations.

Whitebook and Eichberg (2002) give the career field hope for salary improvement in the following:

> . . . in the last three years, driven in part by a robust economy and a shortage of trained workers, many states—among them California, Illinois, New York, North Carolina, Rhode Island, Washington, and Wisconsin—have initiated or expanded publicly funded programs focused on building a more skilled and stable child care workforce. Initiatives are also being developed in Connecticut, Georgia, Idaho, Kansas, Missouri, Oklahoma, and Pennsylvania. In some states, local governmental entities are establishing programs.

A study funded by the Pew Charitable Trusts reveals preschool and child care teachers reported earning an average of $19,610 a year in 1999 with the national range from $15,140 in Alabama to $23,750 in Minnesota (Hagel, 2002).

PROFESSIONAL GROWTH OPPORTUNITIES

At times, when the enthusiasm for teaching seems to dwindle, teachers need to pursue other courses of action to refresh their excitement and eagerness to learn and grow. Early childhood teachers have a wide range of alternative routes to professional growth. For example:

- Additional credit coursework and advanced degrees
- Apprenticing and exchanging teachers
- Independent study
- Visitation and travel
- Professional group membership
- Mentoring by other professionals
- Workshops, meetings, and skill and study sessions (see Figure 14–7)

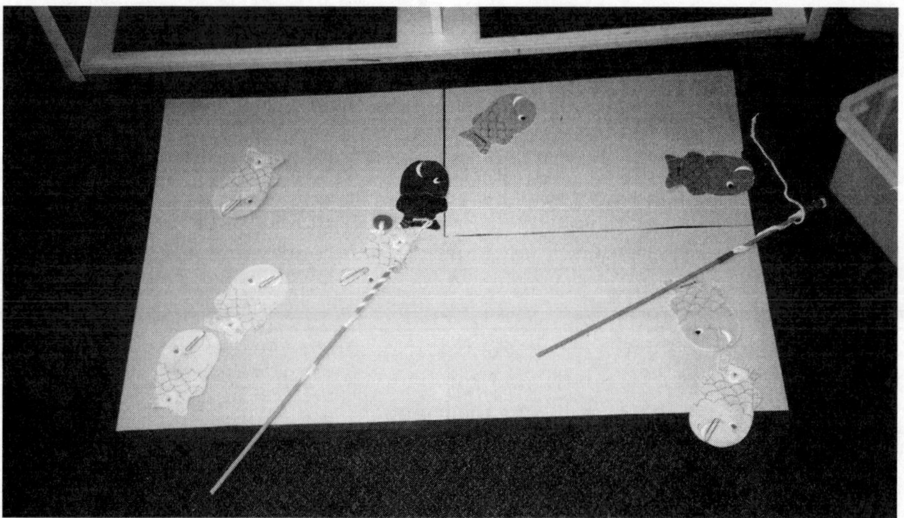

Figure 14–7 Game-making workshops are popular with early childhood educators.

- Other training programs and projects
- Inservice training
- Conference attendance

Administrative Planning for Staff's Professional Growth

After reviewing their former student's journal, Vukelich and Wrenn (1999) propose the following tenets of quality professional development.

Professional development should:

- Focus on a single subject
- Focus on participants' needs
- Be ongoing and sustained
- Engage participants in the pursuit of answers to genuine questions, problems, and curiosities
- Provide for participants' meaningful engagement
- Help participants develop collegial relationships
- Encourage participants to reflect on their teaching.

Vukelich and Wrenn (1999) caution administrators and others who plan for the professional development of their teachers to avoid the one-day, one-shot, "this is good for everyone" approach. Those who feel the information is valid need far more than one day to change teaching behaviors. An introduction should be followed by opportunities to practice, mentoring by a teacher knowledgeable in the new practice, critiques of attempts to implement the new ideas, and further practice.

A one-day, one-shot approach does not produce change in any teacher whose needs the approach does not meet (Sykes, 1996). Under those conditions, the presentation is usually ignored, and the teacher considers that his time has been wasted. Your authors know only too well how one-day shots on material in which they already have a background or in which they are not interested are considered time wasters.

New Approaches to Professional Development

To consider what they call a "new vision," Sparks and Hirsh (1997) suggest that a paradigm shift is necessary. Traditional ways of conducting staff development denies the very ways in which teachers want their students to learn: activities that engage, experiences that actively involve, and problems that require solutions. Sitting passively in a classroom before or after a busy workday encourages boredom and sleepiness. Sparks and Hirsh see a need to teach teachers in much the same ways in which they want their students to learn. That requires active learning, opportunities for small-group discussion, and working toward solutions of real problems.

Smith (1996) would concur. She recognizes that the same principles that are behind quality programs for children should also lie behind programs for professional development. The implications for professional development programs are logical.

- If, indeed, all development begins with social interaction, any professional development program must allow for social interaction.
- If learning drives development, opportunities for teachers to learn must be offered and must suit individual learning styles.
- If close interpersonal relationships enhance learning, teachers must be given the opportunity to establish such relationships.
- We must always remember that the goals of development are culturally determined.
- Just as children need to have an active role in constructing their own unique understandings within the cultural context, so do teachers.

If one of the goals of professional development is to persuade teachers to unlock their creativity and to try new practices, Sykes (1996) suggests that an entire school (or child care center) be involved in any projected changes. From the principal (director), to the teachers, to lunchroom personnel, to the janitor: all should work on changes to improve the environment and learning programs for the students (children).

Hoerr (1996) cites collegiality as a new way to define instructional leadership. The principal or director needs to work with teachers to share leadership responsibilities. But, as Hoerr cautions, the fact that most teachers spend 80 to 90 percent of their day in the classroom leaves little time to develop collegial relationships with a principal or director.

In addition, few teachers are trained to help peers grow professionally and are frequently reluctant to see themselves as "teachers of teachers." Some, however creative they may be, do not see themselves as having any ideas worth sharing.

Hoerr (1996) provides the following suggestions for principals and directors:

- *Time is our most precious resource.* Teachers and administrators must be able to meet frequently enough and for sufficiently long periods to discuss educational philosophies and share ideas.
- *An invitation is better than a command.* Change is best viewed as a series of concentric circles, starting small and expanding. An administrator may start with a small nucleus of interested teachers willing to take the risk to look at their roles differently. Their enthusiasm then becomes contagious and spreads to their peers.

- *Power shared is power multiplied.* Why should teachers not be empowered to handle the part of the budget dealing with materials and resources for their classrooms? One of your authors remembers when, just hired for a new teaching job, she was told she had a budget of $2,000 to spend on materials for her classroom. What a wonderful experience that was!
- *We practice what we value.* When a director or other administrator delegates responsibility, teachers feel most collegial.
- *Focus on an important issue.* One way to discover what teachers feel are the important issues is simply to ask, preferably by completion of an anonymous checklist of probable issues. Another way is to plan a series of weekly meetings around an article or book that all have read and to have a teacher chair the meeting.

But, as Darling-Hammond (1996) states in the title of her article, "What Matters Most: A Competent Teacher for Every Child," teachers must recognize that they are learners first and that learning is a lifelong process. When you graduate and receive your credential or license, you have just started on a road to competency, one that will continue throughout life: your own professional development.

Additional Coursework

Credit and noncredit college coursework leads to advanced skill and degrees. Coursework frequently results in on-the-job application of ideas, spreading enthusiasm throughout a preschool center. Local college career placement centers and/or counseling centers provide a review of college catalogs and bulletins. Coursework descriptions and particulars can be examined for all colleges. Additional college services often include career guidance, financial aid information, college housing particulars, job placement boards, and tutoring assistance.

Articulation Agreements

Examine the transferability of community college credit coursework and degrees to baccalaureate degree programs at degree-granting institutions. If articulation agreements exist, usually both institutions have had representatives meet and tailor coursework so a smooth transition is possible. Credits can be accepted as elective units or as equivalent units. Since institutions differ, it is prudent to consult college counselors and early childhood department chairpersons at both institutions. Local centers and agency groups have increased their efforts to coordinate their staff's training needs with colleges, and in some cases, have funded their workers' college attendance and offered facilities for onsite classes.

Many Head Start staff members needed to obtain academic degrees by 2003. This was mandated by the reauthorization of the Head Start Act in 1998. Head Start also has provided leadership in encouraging articulation agreements (Stam, 2002; Ball, 2002).

Distance Learning

A number of colleges offer distance learning opportunities offered online, on television, by satellite, by correspondence, and a few by conference call. Questions to ask if one is interested follow:

- What are the qualifications of the sponsoring institution?
- Are instructors credentialed?
- Is the institution accredited?
- Is financial assistance available?

- Is it a degree-awarding program? Will credits awarded satisfy degree requirements at other colleges?
- What skills should one have? Computer skills? Other?
- Is what is offered geared for independent study or are there opportunities to interact with peers?
- What resources does a student need? Computer? Cable television? Satellite access? Software and hardware? Other?
- Are reading materials covered in enrollment costs?
- Are any student support systems in place? Local facilitators? Tutoring? Technical assistance?
- How and when can one contact the instructor (Nealy-Shane, 2002)?

software—the "instructions" that direct a computer to perform an activity, usually stored on a disk or directly in the computer. Many such programs are available for young children.

Computer Expertise

Many colleges are now insisting students display computer literacy and skill before graduation. Teacher training programs—already full of requirements and electives—have been slow to institute coursework. Most student teachers in two-year community college programs pursue an independent course of study to acquire computer expertise. Many public libraries have developed computer centers where Internet access and help are available. The increasing computer skills preschoolers exhibit surprize most early childhood teachers. Commercial early childhood program software is abundant and entering young children's lives at a amazing rate.

Child comments on favorite computer characters leave the uninitiated teacher at a loss for a pertinent response. Young children seem to be progressing in computer skills as fast or faster than some of their preschool teachers.

The teacher with computer literacy is able to guide child use and discovery. The computer then becomes a valuable child and adult learning aid, and an indispensable adult communication, recording, and researching tool.

computer literacy—familiarity with and knowledge about computers.

Teacher Certification

National certification as an "Early Childhood Generalist" is awarded by the National Board for Professional Teaching Standards (NBPTS). It is voluntary and requires fees. Applicants who successfully meet rigorous standards become certified and join a distinguished group of 3,800 others (Guiding & Hyson, 2002). The professional advantages of completing the process and pursuing this credential might be advanced teaching skills, upward mobility, and the ability to become a leader in the field.

Each state has developed some state policy concerning teacher certification and credentialing. There is a definite lack of commonality. The most prevalent pattern of certification (six states) authorizes certificate holders to teach children from three to eight years of age.

The best place to consult when trying to determine what credentials, certificates, permits, and licenses exist for workers in early childhood programs in a particular state is that state's department of education. It's best to secure requirements in writing. Often, teacher qualification requirements change, depending on funding sources. Publicly supported centers usually have higher and stricter standards requiring the completion of additional education and experience.

Unfortunately, many states do not require beginning early childhood teachers to have successfully completed college-level coursework before entering the career field. This is changing rapidly as parents demand trained caregivers and quality programs.

At the elementary school level, a master's degree is required for permanent certification in most states, and 56 percent of public school teachers hold master's degrees, up from 27 percent in 1971 (Grant & Murray, 1999).

Apprenticing, Demonstrating, and Exchanging Teaching

You may know a teacher with whom you would like to study and whose direction and tutelage could be growth-producing. Volunteering in this teacher's classroom offers opportunities for closer examination of techniques. It may be possible to earn college credit through enrolling in a cooperative work experience program or independent study course; check with your local college.

In a demonstration-teaching arrangement, you watch and discuss methods with practicing teachers (see Figure 14–8). Hearing explanations and asking questions give insight into different ways to accomplish teaching goals. Most professionals will provide this type of short-term arrangement.

Figure 14–8 Study sessions promote teacher growth.

Exchanging teachers within a school is sometimes considered growth-producing. New partnerships stimulate new blends of techniques. Many schools permit a shifting of staff members, enabling gifted and talented teachers to share their ideas. Cross-matching and lively discussions act as healthy catalysts.

Mentoring

Mentoring programs are an established and increasingly available vehicle to enhance staff professional development and retention. Mentoring for teachers offers an approach to teacher training within the context of the teaching environment and emphasizes excellence daily practice. Merrill (2002) notes mentoring programs differ, and range from infomal buddy system arrangements to structured meetings with a trained mentor who may be a fellow employee or a mentor provided through a partnership with another local program or agency. Many mentors have received training in mentoring skills, adult development, observation, and communication. Funding may be provided for both the mentor and mentee. Most mentors are chosen for their expertise and are considered master teachers. Increased collaboration in the mentoring process often leads to sharing ideas, reflective thinking, research and implementation, enthusiasm, and improved overall program quality. In other words, it is a dynamic professional growth opportunity for both participants.

The percentage of teachers who experience mentoring in their first year of teaching has tripled in the past 20 years, and 48 percent of mentored teachers report they benefitted (Grant & Murray, 1999).

Internships

Internships are employed positions for a designated period of time. Teacher interns work under the direction of experienced practitioners and assume a variety of teaching responsibilities. Grant and Murray (1999) recommend:

> Internships are just as important for teachers as for medical doctors. Neither the craft of healing nor that of teaching can be learned at the highest levels without such forms of induction into the profession. Teachers also need more substantial, intellectually challenging opportunities for professional growth throughout their careers, like those architects and professors now enjoy, such as sabbaticals and opportunities for research and learning new techniques.

Association for Childhood Education International (ACEI)—professional organization that focuses on issues of children from infancy to early adolescence, including those involving international and intercultural concerns.

Independent Study

Self-planned study allows one to choose the subject, sequence, depth, and breadth of professional growth. Your home library will grow yearly, funds permitting! You will spend much time reading books and other materials. These resources will be a tribute to your professional commitment. Professional journals and magazines provide research articles and practical suggestions. A brief list of periodicals follows:

- *Young Children* (bimonthly publication of the NAEYC)
- *Childhood Education* (published quarterly by the Association for Childhood Education International, plus an annual theme issue and an international issue)
- *American Education Research Journal*
- *The Black Child Advocate* (quarterly newsletter) (see Figure 14–9)

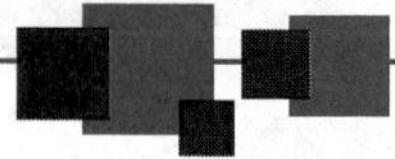

ACEI (Association for Childhood Education International) 11501 Georgia Avenue, Suite 315, Wheaton, MD 20902. Interested in high standards and professional practices. Journal, books, and informational materials publisher.

AMS (American Montessori Society, Inc.), 175 Fifth Avenue, New York, NY 10010. An organization that focuses on Maria Montessori's approach to early learning, which emphasizes providing children with purposeful work in an environment prepared with self-educative, manipulative learning devices for language, math, science, practical life, and so on.

CDA (Council for Early Childhood Professional Recognition), 1341 G Street, NW, Washington, DC 20005-3105. Offers a national credential to successful candidates after assessment of competencies. A newsletter and educational resources are also available.

CEC (Council for Exceptional Children)/DEC (Division for Early Childhood), 1920 Association Drive, Reston, VA 20091. An organization of teachers, school administrators, and teacher educators focusing on the concerns of children who are gifted; retarded; are visually, auditorily, or physically disabled; or who have behavioral disorders, learning disabilities, or speech defects.

CWLA (Child Welfare League of America), 440 First Steet, NW, Suite 310, Washington, DC 20001. Devoted to assisting deprived, neglected, and abused children. Publishes informational material.

NAEYC (National Association for the Education of Young Children), 1509 16th Street, NW, Washington, DC 20036. Association of early childhood professionals interested in quality education. Publishes books, a journal, and a wide range of teacher and parent materials.

National Black Child Development Institute, 1023 15th Street, NW, Suite 600, Washington, DC 20005. Publishes *The Black Child Advocate* and *Child Health Talk.*

Society for Research in Child Development, 100 N. Carolina Avenue, SE, Suite 1, Washington, DC 20063.

OCD (Office of Child Development, U.S. Department of Health and Human Services), PO Box 1182, Washington, DC 20013. Responsible for long-range planning and development of concepts in children's and parent's programs and legislation affecting children.

PCPI (Parent Cooperative Preschools International), 9111 Alton Parkway., Silver Spring, MD 20910. An organization of individuals and groups interested in promoting the exchange of resources and information among persons involved in cooperative nursery schools, kindergartens, and other parent-sponsored preschool groups.

ERIC/ECE (Educational Resources Information Center, Early Childhood Education), 805 West Pennsylvania Avenue, Urbana, IL 61801. Collects and catalogs material of interest to early childhood educators.

Figure 14–9 Professional groups, resources, organizations, and associations

- *Day Care and Early Education*
- *Child Care Quarterly*
- *Child Health Talk* (quarterly publication)
- *Learning*
- *Child Study Journal*

Organization and association newsletters carry timely information of interest.

A starting point for independent study may be the bibliographies and book titles you collected during your training.

Visitation and Travel

Other teachers' classrooms will always be a valuable resource and study possibility. Observing other classrooms offers good ideas, clever solutions, and provocative discoveries. It is amazing how many early childhood programs extend professional courtesy to visiting early childhood contemporaries if approached. Travelers, contacting administrators and directors beforehand, often are able to tour facilities, interview staff, and observe program activities. A written letter of introduction from a supervisor to include in a request-to-visit letter and your e-mail address is a good idea. For tax purposes, keep records of a visit, including notes on conversations, photographs, happenings, and ideas that might help your professional growth. Professional groups' conferences often schedule tours of local outstanding programs.

Almost every country in the world has group child care, and you have probably developed a list of programs in your own community you would like to observe. The professional courtesy of allowing observers is widespread. Directors and staff members frequently provide guided tours that include explanations and discussions of goals, program components, and teaching philosophies.

Professional Group Membership

You will find professional early childhood group membership to be one of the best ways to locate skill development opportunities. A common goal of professional associations and organizations is to provide educational services and resources to members (see Figure 14–9).

Association publications are generally reasonably priced and current. Publication listings are available on request from main office headquarters.

There are special student membership rates, and joining a local affiliate or branch group during student teaching is highly recommended. Association newsletters will keep you informed of activities and developments of interest to professionals.

The advantages of local professional membership are numerous. Workshops, study sessions, and conferences provide favorable circumstances for professional development. There are opportunities to meet other professionals, discuss views and concerns, and jointly solve problems. The talents of early childhood experts are tapped for the benefit of all the members.

A fascinating and exhilarating experience awaits the student teacher on first attending a national conference. There will be so much to see and sample, so many inspiring ideas, materials, and equipment to examine; a virtual overdose of stimuli that wholesomely feeds your attempt to grow.

NAEYC sponsors a yearly springtime public celebration called The Week of the Young Child. The celebration promotes a public awareness. Working together, communities can make children's early years count. During the week, professionals reach out to people, families, community, business leaders, and policymakers who can be instrumental in improving opportunities for young children and those who work with them. Events honor all who provide services, supportive assistance, and education to children and families.

Workshops, Meetings, and Skill and Study Sessions

Workshops, skill sessions, and meetings are smaller versions of state and national conferences. Diverse and varied, they cover topics related to early childhood. Practical how-to's, theoretical presentations, and advocacy meetings are popular.

Identification with the spirit of professionalism, which can be defined as striving for excellence, motivates many of the attending participants. Most communities schedule many professional growth meetings each year and encourage student teacher attendance.

Inservice Training

Inservice training sessions are designed to suit the training needs of a particular group of teachers and/or caregivers. They are arranged by sponsoring agencies or employers. Typically, consultants and specialists lead, guide, plan, and present skill development sessions and/or assessments of program components. There is usually no fee and attendance is mandatory. Often, staffs decided the nature and scope of the inservice training, and paid substitutes free staff members from child supervision duties.

PARENTS' ATTITUDES TOWARD PROFESSIONALISM

Early childhood teachers may make many assumptions concerning how attending children's parents view their work. It is important to assess parents' attitudes and perceptions, and plan strategies that encourage acceptance of early childhood educators as professionals.

SUMMARY

Student teachers strive for recognition of their professional skills and try to achieve standards established by those in the same profession. Pride in the early childhood profession grows as student teachers realize the dedication and skills of others already teaching. The important contribution the profession makes to children, families, and society cannot be overrated. The commitment to update continually and gain additional skills begins in training and continues for a lifetime. Each professional teacher is responsible for his own unique growth planning schedule.

Many activity choices leading to advanced skills are available and most professionals engage in a wide variety. Additional coursework and training, professional group membership, conference and workshop attendance, inservice training, visitation, and exchange teaching lead to the learning and discovering of new techniques. Social interactions in educative settings reinforce individual teachers' commitment to professionalism.

With all the choices that are possible, keep in mind the precaution cited by Sykes (1996) about "one-shot, one-day" wonders. Success as a professional is always a lifelong process.

HELPFUL WEB SITES

http://www.hsbbs.org
: Head Start. Offers a calendar of events for Head Start and other early childhood conferences, meetings, and activities.

http://www.acf.hhs.gov/
: Independent study of summaries of Head Start research.

http://www.naeyc.org/
: NAEYC. Lists what the professional organization offers.

http://www.ecs.org
: Education Commission of the States. Investigate education or early childhood issues.

http://www.ftj.com
: Forrest T. Jones & Co., Inc. Information concerning NAEYC's insurance for early childhood workers.

http://www.eclu.uc.edu
: University of Cincinnati. Distance degree learning particulars.

http://www.acei.org
: Association for Childhood Education International. Find out what this professional association offers.

http://www.cudenver.edu/
: Colorado Early Childhood Professional Credential Office. Check out Colorado's five credential levels.

http://www.nipdc.org
: New Jersey Professional Development Center for Early Care and Education. Click on "Professional Standards and Articulation."

http://www.ccw.org
: The Center for the Child Care Workforce. Provides updates of proposed, newly funded, and existing child care compensation efforts.

http://www.nlci.org
: National Latino Children's Institute. A clearinghouse and resource center site concentrating on Latino children's issues.

SUGGESTED ACTIVITIES

A. Join a professional organization.

B. Read three articles in an issue of *Young Children* and discuss with your peers.

C. In groups of four to six, develop a chart that lists factors that promote professionalism and those that impede professionalism in early childhood teachers.

D. Rate each statement based on the following scale. Discuss your results with the class.

strongly agree	mildly agree	cannot decide	mildly disagree	strongly disagree
1	2	3	4	5

1. Being professional includes proper makeup and clothing at work.
2. It is unprofessional to keep using the same techniques over and over.
3. Professional commitment is more important than professional growth.
4. Professional growth can involve coursework that does not pertain to children and/or families.
5. A teacher can grow professionally by studying children in the classroom.
6. Professional association fees are so expensive that student teachers can rarely afford to join.
7. One of the real causes for the lack of status of early childhood teachers is their own attitudes toward professional growth.
8. It is difficult to feel like a professional when salaries are so low.
9. Most teachers who pursue professional skills receive little recognition for their efforts.
10. You can learn all you need to know about handling children's behavior by watching a master teacher.
11. Sweatpants, T-shirts, and tennis shoes are very comfortable, but they are not very professional looking (Franquet, 1997).
12. The community should see child care as not just a social service but as an income-generating, job-creating industry that is vital to the economic infrastructure of any city (Petersen, 2002).
13. We need to let our students see that we are learning with them, that learning takes place everywhere, that learning is forever. Teachers are in the business of igniting excitement in their students. One way is by creating opportunities for our own learning. If we are not involved in the process ourselves, our own light is dimmed (Hurst & Reding, 1999).

E. Investigate groups in your community that schedule skill sessions, workshops, or meetings offering growth opportunities to early childhood teachers. Report your findings to the class.

REVIEW

A. Name four benefits of professional group membership.

B. Match items in Column I with those in Column II.

I	II
1. rate of teacher growth	a. pulling ideas together
2. commitment	b. code of ethics
3. standards	c. advances and retreats
4. consolidation	d. depends on individual's activities
5. learning cycle	e. ranges from high to low
6. professionals	f. constant intellectual decisions
7. apprenticing	g. expert advice
8. visitation	h. onsite training
9. workshops	i. studying with another
10. inservice training	j. professional courtesy

C. Select the answer that best completes each statement.

1. The person most responsible for a particular teacher's professional growth is:
   a. the employer.
   b. the parent.
   c. the child.
   d. the teacher.
   e. None of these.
2. Of the following entries, the one that is a well-known early childhood professional magazine is:
   a. *The Whole Child.*
   b. *Child and Learning.*
   c. *Young Children.*
   d. *Helping the Child.*
   e. *The Professional Growth Journal.*

D. Describe attitudes that motivate teachers to spend time at weekend workshops.

E. Complete the following statement: Lifelong learning is typical of the professional teacher who . . .

F. In the following paragraphs, make note of all statements that indicate questionable professionalism.

I made an appointment to observe a class in a community school. As I arrived, the director nodded and indicated that I was to enter a classroom labeled "The Three's Room." The teacher and aide looked at me, then quickly looked away. I sat quietly near the wall. The teacher approached, demanding, "Who sent you in here?" "The director," I answered. She went back to the aide and whispered to him briefly. The teacher began a conversation with Mrs. Brown, who just arrived. She mentioned that her daughter, Molly, refused to eat lunch and kicked a hole in a cot at naptime. "I told you I'd tell your mother," the teacher said to Molly, who was standing at her mother's side.

Time for outside play was announced. The teacher and aide left the room for the play area. One or two children failed to follow the group outside. I wasn't sure if I could leave them inside so I stood in the doorway and looked out. The children must have headed out the other door to the director's office while I took note of the play equipment.

The aide approached. "Looking for a job?" he asked. "I could work afternoons," I answered. "Well, the person who teaches four-year-olds is quitting," he offered. "It's an easy job. You just watch them after naptime until their parents come." "Thanks for telling me about it," I said.

I left the yard to return to the director's office. She was on the phone with a parent and motioned me to sit in a chair opposite her desk. She was describing the school's academic program to the parent, and winked at me when she told the parent every child learned the alphabet, shapes, and colors, besides reading a number of words. She hung up the phone and said to me, "Sometimes they're hard to sell." I thanked the director for allowing me to observe. She acknowledged this and asked, "Did you notice the teacher or aide leaving the children unsupervised?

I've been too busy to watch them, but we've had a couple of complaints." "No," I lied, not wanting to become involved. Hoping to change the subject, I asked, "Do you have any openings for a teacher in the afternoon hours?" Because I needed money badly, a part-time job would be welcome. "We will have a position available starting the first week of October," she answered. The director then proceeded to describe job duties. They ranged from planning the program to mopping the floors at the end of the day. I told her I needed time to think over the offer. The director insisted she needed to know immediately, so I accepted.

CASE SCENARIO

Setting: A Head Start program in a large urban city. The Director, Mr. Roberts, is talking to the Assistant Director for Professional Development, Mr. Toy.

"Now that our teachers must be working toward a BA degree, what steps have you taken?" inquires Mr. Roberts.

"The City College is very willing to help those teachers and aides who want to take coursework for their AA. They even are willing to come to our facility for class offerings," responds Mr. Toy. "On the other hand, State University is more reluctant. Their Extension Division can offer some courses, but ultimately, students may have to go on campus. It is possible, though, that they could set up our conference room as a distance learning center; that's the direction I'm encouraging."

"Does State University offer any courses on-line?" Mr. Roberts asks.

"Only for lower division undergraduate courses," answers Mr. Toy, "and obviously, although a good idea for self-motivated students, these courses are more expensive than those offered at City College. I'm not sure how many of our teachers and aides have computer access either, or whether they would want to take a course on-line. Perhaps we should survey our staff and ask for their preferences?"

"A good idea," enthuses Mr. Roberts.

Questions for Discussion:

1. Should Mr. Roberts and Mr. Toy have discussed articulation ageements?
2. If you had an opportunity to take a course on-line, would you be interested in doing so?
3. Have you already taken an on-line course? What was your reaction to it? Were you satisfied with your learning? Why or why not?

REFERENCES

Ball, R. A. (2002). Strategies for building partnerships with academic institutions. *The Head Start Bulletin, 72,* 3–4.

Burchinal, M. R., Roberts, J. E., Riggins, R., Zeisel, S. A., Neebe, E., & Bryant, D. (2000). Relating quality of center-based child care to early cognitive and language development longitudinally. *Child Development, 71*(2), 339–357

Caruso, J. J. (2000, January). Cooperating teacher and student teacher phases of development. *Young Children, 55*(1), 75–81.

Darling-Hammond, L. (1996, November). What matters most: A competent teacher for every child. *Phi Delta Kappan, 78*(3).

Fox, E. M., & Urwick, L. (1982). *Dynamic administration: The collected papers of Mary Parker Follet.* New York: Hippocrene Books.

Franquet, M. (1997, July). R-E-S-P-E-C-T: Can I have some? Please! *Young Children, 52*(2).

Grant, C., & Murray, C. (1999). *Teaching in America: The slow revolution.* Cambridge, MA: Harvard University Press.

Guiding, R., & Hyson, M. (2002, September). National Board certification: The next professional step? *Young Children, 57*(5), 60–61.

Hagel, J. (2002, January 8). Study finds preschools short on standards, teacher pay. *San Jose Mercury News,* 6A.

Harrison, R. (1978). *Self-directed learning. Human growth games.* Beverly Hills, CA: Sage Publications.

Hoerr, T. R. (1996, January). Collegiality: A new way to define instructional leadership. *Phi Delta Kappan, 77*(5).

Honig, A. S., & Hirallal, A. (1998). Which counts more for excellence in childcare staff—Years of service, education level or ECE coursework? *Early Child Development and Care, V*(145), 32–46.

Hurst, B., & Reding, G. (1999). *Keeping the light in your eyes: A guide for helping teachers discover, remember, relive and rediscover the joy of teaching.* Scottsdale, AZ: Holcomb Hathaway.

Johnson, J., & McCracken, J. B. (Eds.). (1994). *The early childhood career lattice: Perspectives on professional development.* Washington, DC: National Association for the Education of Young Children.

Kagan, S. L., Brandon, R. N., Ripple, C.H., Maher, E. J., & Joesch, J. M. (2002, May). Supporting quality early childhood care and education. *Young Children, 57*(3), 58–65.

Katz, L. (1972, February). Developmental stages of preschool teachers. *The Elementary School Journal.*

Maslow, A. (1971). Defense and growth. From R. H. Anderson, & H. G. Shane. *As the twig is bent.* Boston: Houghton Mifflin.

Merrill, S. (2002). Mentoring in Head Start programs. *The Head Start Bulletin, 72,* 32–33.

Moore, M. (1998, May/June). Improving the performance of child care workers: A serious dilemma. *Journal of Early Education and Family Review, 5*(5).

National Association for the Education of Young Children. (1994, March). NAEYC position statement: A conceptual framework for early childhood professional development. *Young Children, 49*(3).

Nealy-Shane, D. (2002). Choosing a distance education program. *The Head Start Bulletin, 72,* 25.

Petersen, D. (Quoted in Corcoran, K.). (2002, November 12). Report: Child care is cog in economy. *San Jose Mercury News,* 1–2B.

Smith, A. B. (1996, International Focus Issue). Quality programs that care and educate. *Childhood Education, 72*(6).

Sparks, D., & Hirsh, S. (1997). A new vision for staff development. Alexandria, VA: Association for Supervision and Curriculum Development.

Stam, B. R. (2002). Achieving associate degrees: Working with community colleges and Head Start staff. *The Head Start Bulletin, 72*, 5.

Sykes, G. (1996, March). Reform *of* and *as* professional development. *Phi Delta Kappan, 77*(7).

VanderVen, K. (1988). Pathways to professionalism. In B. Spodek, O. Saracho, & D. Peters (Eds.). *Professionalism and the early childhood educator.* New York: Columbia University Press.

Vukelich, C., & Wrenn, L. C. (1999, Spring). Quality professional development: What do we think we know? *Childhood Education, 75*(3).

White, A. T. (2000, March). "My morale has fallen and it can't get up!" *Education Digest, 15*(7), 61–63.

Whitebook, M., Howes, C., & Phillips, D. (1998). *Worthy work, unlivable wages: The national child care staffing study 1988–1997.* Washington, DC: Center for the Child Care Workforce.

Whitebook, M., & Eichberg, A. (2002, May). Defining policies to improve child-care workforce compensation. *Young Children, 57*(3), 66–72.

Trends and Issues

Objectives **After studying this chapter, the student should be able to:**

1. Discuss one trend and its influence on planning children's programs.
2. Write a brief statement describing the nation's current public policy decisions and young children's care.
3. Choose an issue, and with a peer, present the salient facts concerning the issue.

I'll be advocating for children and myself as long as I teach. I couldn't believe my cooperating teacher was so concerned about children's rights, laws, and working conditions. I was just trying to become a really good teacher. She's so aware of factors influencing quality care and works in her free time with professional groups and projects. That's dedication!

—Dale Wildeagle

I think I can say I'm an eclectic student teacher. I grab the best of what I see and it's incorporated into my teaching style. There's also some original, unique, me included.

—Ann Ng

My cooperating teacher is a baseball buff. You wouldn't believe how he uses baseball-related material to teach children math and science.

—Shirley Booker-Maddux

Any consideration of the trends and issues existing in our field must be selective. It is probable that a trend in which you are deeply interested has been mentioned briefly or even been omitted, and that an issue about which you feel strongly also has been neglected. Included in this chapter are the trends and issues we think have primacy. As a consequence, then, you may wish to focus on those that are important to you.

TRENDS

When we look at current trends, the purposes of education also come to mind. We could do well to remember what is etched on John Dewey's memorial stone at the University of Vermont. In part, it reads:

> Ours is the responsibility of conserving, transmitting, rectifying, and expanding the heritage of values we have received that those who come after us may receive it more solid and secure, more widely accessible, and more generously shared than we have received it (Beane, 1998).

But what is happening to Dewey's dream for education in the United States? How many of us can agree on what our common values are? Has education become more accessible and more generously shared?

Some of the current trends in early childhood education and in education in general, follow. (You may wish to refer to some of the facts listed about families in Chapter 11.)

- The move toward the privatization of public education through public school support of charter schools funded by private sources such as the Edison schools (Chubb, 1998; Guthrie, 1998; Zollers & Ramanathan, 1998).
- The charter school movement within the public sector (Goenner, 1996; Nathan, 1996; Wells & Research Associates, 1998).
- The low wages in child care have resulted in an annual turnover rate of more than 30 percent for child care teachers, compared to a 14 percent turnover rate for public school teachers whose average salary is $39,385.00 per year (NAEYC, 2000).
- The average salary of a child care worker is only $15,430 a year, less than yearly salaries of funeral attendants, bellhops, and garbage collectors (Children's Defense Fund, 2001).
- The Census Bureau tells us that during a typical week, 14 million young children, or three-fourths of all children under age five, are in some form of regular child care arrangement (Lombardi, 2001).
- Full-day care easily costs $4,000 to $10,000 per year, at least as much as college tuition at a public university (Children's Defense Fund, 2001).
- U. S. public schools will need 2.2 million new teachers before 2010 (Marx, 2001).
- In the early part of the 21st century, minorities will comprise 40 percent of American students but just 5 percent of U. S. teachers (Marx, 2001).
- In the past five years, the number of unionized child care facilities in the public and private sectors has risen from a handful to a few thousand in several states including Washington, Ohio, and Pennsylvania. Most unionized child care workers are employed by public facilities including Head Start (Haynes, 2001).

- About 850,000 of the nation's 50 million children are home-schooled (Toppo, 2001; Ramirez, 1998).
- Thirteen percent of employers now provide full or partial funding for employees' costs for backup child care for their preschoolers, sick care, or emergency child care, up from 5 percent in 1993 (Jackson, 1999).
- More than one-half of community college students are first-generation students: that is, neither of their parents attended college (Philippe, 1997).
- It is estimated that one-quarter of all children three to nine years old have parents who were born outside of the United States (Gadsden & Ray, 2002).
- Real wages for most child care teaching staff have remained stagnant over the past decade (Center for the Child Care Workforce, 1998).
- Family violence or abuse, whether physical, emotional, or verbal, is the most direct form of violence that children experience. The risk of family violence is increased substantially when other risk factors such as emotionally abusive relationships, substance abuse, or stressors associated with poverty are present in their lives (Bonds, 2002).
- According to an ongoing study on early child care by the National Institute of Child Health and Human Development, children in high-quality, center-based care outperform children in other kinds of high-quality care in language development and cognitive skills like problem-solving and reasoning (Greenberg & Springen, 2000).
- The percentage of children in organized care facilities rose 32 percent in 1997 according to the National Survey of America's Families (Greenberg & Springen, 2000).
- State spending on pre-K programs has expanded by nearly $1 billion since 1991 (Greenberg & Springen, 2000).
- The Head Start Act (1998) requires that by September, 2003 at least half of all Head Start teachers in center-based programs have an associate, bachelor's, or an advanced degree in early childhood education or a related field degree, plus experience (Nealy-Shane, 2002).
- The need to prepare an estimated 2 million teachers over the next 10 years (Association for Supervision and Curriculum Development, 1999).
- Transforming schools into learning communities (Bush & Wilson, 1997; Felner, Kasak, Mulhall, & Flowers, 1997).
- School-age programs before and after elementary school attendance.

We will not discuss all of these trends; we have chosen to expand only on those that are more salient.

Few specialists argue with facts indicating the continued need for child care for working parents.

The following situations, promoted by present national child care policies, are attracting public attention:

- The lack of quality care for infants and toddlers within the financial reach of single-parent workers.
- Middle-income (and higher) parents are supporting child care for low-income parents through taxes. Public programs have higher teacher qualifications and better teacher-child ratios. Parents desire quality for their own children, and find few private centers with ratios and teacher qualifications equal to publicly funded centers.
- Many parents want a center with a strong education component. Some state licensing laws for private centers mandate only child custodial safety. Publicly

funded centers have developmental child programs, but most taxpaying parents find their children ineligible for services.

These issues of national or family responsibility, child and family rights, and existing inequity will affect every early childhood educator.

There is hope, because our country is moving closer to establishing a national policy regarding early childhood education and child care. Expanded federal funding for programs and services is expected during the new millennium. Efforts to improve quality and affordability have become political issues, as are child care administrative entities, training of staff and providers, standards, and standard enforcement. More and more action groups and politicians are voicing their opinions and positions. Two-parent and single-parent working families are no longer viewed as the exception but rather the norm. Proposed solutions to concerns over our children's educational achievements compared to children in other industrialized nations, and housing, school dropout rates, teen pregnancy, poverty, and other national problems, urge the provision of quality education. The U.S. teen pregnancy rate seems less of a problem and recorded a 20-year low in 1995. Teens are using contraceptives or abstaining ("Report: Teen pregnancy," 1998).

There are indications that the quality of care and early education for young children is declining. Although the educational level of staff has improved, ratios and group sizes appear to be getting worse. Numerous programs do not meet their own state standards for group size and staff-to-child ratios, especially in programs for infants and toddlers. Compensation remains low, and not surprisingly, staff turnover is high (Shore, 1997).

Child Poverty

The following figures concerning child poverty are gleaned from U.S. General Accounting Office (1993) and U.S. Department of Commerce (1993) statistics:

- Not only were preschool children poorer than the rest of the population in 1990; they also became poorer between 1980 and 1990, a trend that continued through 1999.
- 12.1 million children–one in six–live in poverty.
- From 1979 to 1999—the number of poor children rose by 17 percent.
- An American child today is more likely to be poor than 20 or 30 years ago.
- Three out of four poor children (78 percent) live in families where someone worked in 1999.
- In 1999, more than 3.6 million children lived in families either paying at least half their income on rent or living in severely substandard housing.
- Food stamps are reaching fewer children. Fewer than 72 children received food stamps for every 100 poor children in 1999, down from 88 children per hundred in 1996.
- Unequal incomes help explain why so many children remain poor in an era of unprecedented prosperity (Children's Defense Fund, 2001).

Child Abuse

Although not directly related to poverty, child abuse can be one of the consequences. Other causes are thought to be the current loss of jobs due to "downsizing," as it has been called; the concomitant problem of new jobs being in the service sector, and consequently, less well paying than the job downsized;

the need for two incomes to support families financially and the often related stress placed on these families; and substance abuse in families such as alcoholism. Most likely, there are other causes for child abuse; we have simply listed some of the more obvious.

All states require teachers to report suspected cases of child abuse. Berliner (1993) explains:

> Each state's child abuse reporting law defines child abuse, designates mandated reporters, describes standards and procedures for making a report, and establishes the consequences for failure to report.
>
> Abuse law entails:
>
> - sexual abuse (adult-child sexual contact)
> - physical abuse (intentional injury)
> - failure to provide a child's basic needs (neglect)
> - emotional abuse

Teachers and child care providers are specified as mandated reporters in state law; consequently, penalties exist for nonreporters. Most states provide immunity from liability to all "good-faith child abuse reporters," not only mandated reporters. Approximately 12 states have enacted provisions for civil or criminal penalties for malicious reports of child abuse. A reasonable suspicion of child abuse is a valid reason for reporting.

To whom do you report? Child protective services (CPS) and law enforcement agencies are the two most common agencies receiving reports and investigating them. Generally, if the suspicion of abuse is not life threatening, CPS is the agency called. If, however, the child seems in immediate danger, a law enforcement agency is usually notified because only they can legally remove a child from the custody of the parent(s).

One caveat here: child care professionals and teachers need to be aware of the cultural values and ethnic differences in families of attending children. Newly arrived families may not be aware of abuse law and may continue to use corporal punishment or other harsh disciplinary practices, or even health practices deemed appropriate in their country of origin.

> On a warm, sunny day in mid-October, Eugenia, a newly enrolled Filipina child in the first grade classroom where you are student teaching, comes to school one morning with a heavy wool scarf wrapped around her neck. During the morning, you note that she appears uncomfortable, but all efforts to persuade her to remove the scarf are unsuccessful. After lunch, as the classroom becomes even warmer and Eugenia is sweating visibly, she finally takes off the heavy wool scarf. Immediately you notice large round welts on her neck and suspect child abuse. Your cooperating teacher also notices the welts, goes to the office, and notifies CPS.
>
> Before the end of the school day, a social worker from CPS arrives and removes Eugenia from the classroom to talk to her. Unfortunately, the child's English is not well developed. When the mother arrives at school to pick up Eugenia and walk home with her, the social worker informs her that she is reluctant to allow the child to go. The mother, who speaks only Tagalog, cannot understand what is happening; Eugenia is unable to explain what is happening either. A police officer is called, but she also cannot

speak Tagalog. At this point, the school secretary intervenes and suggests calling in a classroom aide who speaks both Tagalog and English fluently.

When the aide speaks to the mother and questions her about the welts on Eugenia's neck, she translates, "Eugenia's mother simply was doing what she has always done in the Philippines when one of her children has awakened with a complaint about a sore throat. She took a large coin, probably a quarter, judging from the size of the welts, heated it, and rubbed Eugenia's neck with it, producing the welts you see. Then the scarf is wrapped around the neck to hold in the heat. The practice is common among rural, relatively uneducated people in certain parts of the Philippines."

State and Local Funding Decisions

As federal taxes are returned to states, decisions concerning amounts to be allocated to young children's programs and services will be made at state and local levels. Young children's needs will compete with other social and welfare needs. Professionals are fearful, and they worry about cutbacks in existing publicly funded operations. As taxpayers, they may support decreasing federal administrative costs although they also support increased federal funding for ensuring and expanding child program quality.

Universal and State Prekindergarten Programs

One of the most exciting and encouraging happenings in early childhood education is state legislation and funding for prekindergarten programs. Thirty-seven states have initiated prekindergarten programs that are educationally focused on helping children enter kindergarten ready to learn (Groginsky, Robison, & Smith, 1999). Although state programs vary in length of day, number of children served, and what is addressed, many programs include attention to children's nutrition, health, dental, and mental health needs, and include parent involvement components. Commonly, programs target preschoolers from low income families. Georgia and Oklahoma have established programs for all four-year-olds, if their parents so choose.

Georgia's governor, Zell Miller, states:

> It is time that America determines to make the most out of this critical time in a child's life. If our children are going to compete in a global market, we must make them global thinkers. It is incumbent to do everything we can—as soon as we can—to prepare them to learn and to function in a world no longer limited by state or national boundaries (Early Developments, 2000).

Groginsky, Robison, and Smith (1999) point out state investment in programs range from $1 million annually to more than $200 million, but seven states limit their prekindergarten funding to public schools. Other states seek existing entities such as Head Start, child care agencies, and community-based organizations, or form contractual arrangements with public schools. State prekindergarten programs have a variety of names, which include school readiness, community partnerships, learning readiness, and early childhood assistance programs.

What will all this mean to student teachers just entering the field? More job opportunities, better compensation (in some cases the same pay as public school teachers), higher standards regarding teacher qualifications and training, a chance for increased benefits, stipends for future training, more specialized job titles, a new public image, and a hope that with all the state and federal interest in quality care, the inequities that exist for early childhood educators will finally disappear.

Standards in Teacher Preparation

Increasingly stringent standards regulating all facets of child care, including teacher preparation, are a reality. Present federal legislation mandates higher state standards for some states in an attempt to increase the overall quality of prekindergarten child care.

Child care teaching staffs with training when compared to other women in the labor force have attained higher levels of formal education. Most teachers view learning as a lifelong pursuit. Saturday, summer, and evening study is commonplace, and many colleges offer a continuous array of growth opportunities and updating opportunities.

As Whitebook, Howes, and Phillips (1989) point out:

> The education and work environment of child care teachers are essential determinants of the quality of care. Teaching staff provide more *sensitive* and *appropriate care giving* if they completed more years of formal education, received early childhood training at the college level. . . .

Increased legislative interest in public elementary school teacher testing is apparent. Whitmire (1998) notes:

> A teacher quality bill that is expected to clear Congress shortly would require teachers' colleges to reveal data about pass-fail rates of its graduates on state certification tests.

Colleges with teacher preparation programs will, if legislation passes and is signed by the president, have to disclose numbers of teacher candidates passing state certification tests. Many see this legislation as an important step in improving the quality of teaching in America's public schools. The legislation also includes provisions allowing school districts to offer signing bonuses to qualified teachers willing to work in high-poverty areas.

A joint effort between NAEYC and ACCESS (American Associate Degree Early Childhood Educators) has led to a voluntary system for approving professional preparation programs in associate degree-granting institutions.

The approval system is based on the childhood profession's agreed-upon standards for the preparation of early childhood professionals. Community colleges will be able to apply beginning in the year 2004. Guidelines were developed by NAEYC and endorsed by the Association of Teacher Educators (ATE) and the Division of Early Childhood of the Council for Exceptional Children (DEC/CEC). The program approval system has promoted articulation of early childhood training college credit hours (units) between associate institutions and baccalaureate institutions with both following a common set of accepted national standards.

A variety of prekindergarten standards are used in state Pre-K programs including Head Start performance standards, NAEYC's Developmentally Appropriate Practice Standards, newly adopted state standards, or other standards. The state of

Illinois is working toward a "seamless education system" from prekindergarten to postsecondary education by linking, coordinating, and supporting quality standards. A newly formed Governor's Task Force on Universal Access to Preschool in Illinois will focus specifically on creating a five-year blueprint for achieving the goal of quality early childhood education opportunities for all three- to five-year-olds (Loucks, 2001).

President Bush's State of the Union Address (January 2002), emphasized the need to prepare children to read and succeed in school, and proposed a new early childhood initiative: Good Start, Grow Smart. The initiative promotes a stronger federal-state partnership and asks states to develop quality criteria for early childhood education including voluntary guidelines on prereading and language skills that align with public elementary school standards.

A growing number of lawmakers have authorized higher reimbursement payments for child care centers and family child care homes who meet national accreditation standards, stricter licensing standards, or other quality of care standards (Groginsky, Robison, & Smith, 1999).

Shortage of Trained Teachers

The Association for Supervision and Curriculum Development (ASCD, 1999) estimates that there will be a shortage of two million teachers over the next 10 years in the kindergarten through grade 12 public schools. At the same time, ASCD projects an increase of nearly three million more students than are currently enrolled. What has happened?

Teachers who entered the field during the baby boom years are now retiring. Others, especially those in urban areas, have become disillusioned and have left teaching. Still others, especially in the shortage areas of math and science, never take teaching jobs; private industry and other businesses pay substantially more than teaching.

What is known about America's practicing teachers? According to Grant and Murray (1999), teachers are:

- happier and more satisfied than they have been in decades
- better trained and doing a better job that most people believe
- overwhelmingly female and white; consequently, teachers of color are underrepresented
- on an average, age 43
- at high school level, predominately female rather than male
- from families with fathers considered to be professional, semiprofessional, managers, or self-employed rather than working-class or farm families as was the case previously
- reporting they feel connected and engaged in meaningful work

Three-fourths of all teachers are married and have children.

To meet what is already a shortage in many districts, some encourage paraprofessionals to acquire their teaching credential, and some districts help with financing and adjusted work hours. Other districts have attracted retiring military personnel, especially those trained in one of the sciences or in math.

But these districts also have standards for the people they recruit. Many are minorities; many already have some units toward their bachelor's degree. The Pathways to Teaching Careers Program of Norfolk State University, Virginia, requires that prospective candidates have 75 credits toward graduation, be interested in working in an area of high need (for example, early childhood education, special education, math, and science), have a minimum 2.5 grade point average, and be committed to work in an urban area. The Teacher Opportunity Program, sponsored by the University of Louisville, Kentucky, is somewhat similar, but it also recruits prospective candidates from other career fields. A common theme of the various programs recruiting future teachers, especially those from ethnic and racial minorities, is to look to the local communities to find candidates.

Other programs involved in recruiting and training teachers are Teach for America (http://www.teachforamerica.org or 1-800-832-1230), Troops to Teachers (http://voled or 1-800-231-6242), Recruiting New Teachers (http://www.rnt.org or 617-489-6000), and Pathways to Teaching Careers (http://www.dewittwallace.org/ or 212-251-9800). At the high school level, Phi Delta Kappa sponsors the Future Educators of America (FEA) clubs. Like the Future Teachers of America clubs, FEA sponsors an annual summer camp and has a scholarship program (http://www.pdkintl.org/ or 1-800-766-1156).

Reacting to the need of many school districts to increase both teacher quality and teacher quantity, Congress enacted legislation allotting $1.2 billion in the 1999 federal budget for school districts to hire and train teachers (Specht, 1998).

Brennan (1998) points out that projections of the demographic composition of America's teaching force indicate a serious problem regarding the minority representation among teachers. In public schools across the nation, Brennan suggests a significant and widening disparity between the percentage of students from ethnic minority groups, most notably African Americans and Hispanics, and the percentage of teachers representing these groups. The U.S. teaching force is expected to be largely white and female (92 percent) while the United States experiences a growing minority child population in the new millenium (Howey & Zimpher, 1991).

Charter Schools

When we look at the growing number of charter schools, it is important to remember that although many are funded by the public school district in which they are located, others are funded privately by businesses and corporations. Minnesota was the first state to establish a charter school in 1991, followed by California. In 1996, however, Michigan had the most charter schools proportionally in operation (Goenner, 1996).

Currently, there are several management companies operating an estimated 770 schools in the United States. The Edison Project of New York has perhaps received the most publicity, but then the company was created by media entrepreneur Chris Whittle. Whittle is the sponsor of Channel One, which has brought child-oriented news and commercials into the classrooms that subscribe to the service (Guthrie, 1998).

As of the fall of 1998, there were 51 Edison Project partnerships throughout the country: six in California and four in the San Francisco Bay area alone. Founder and chairman of the Gap clothing stores, Don Fisher, made an initial pledge of $25 million to help improve the public schools in San Francisco if they would agree to be taken over and managed as charter schools by the Edison Project. Philadelphia transferred 42 failing city schools to private operators including Edison Schools Incorporated and two universities (*San Jose Mercury News*, 2002).

This has created a great deal of controversy among teachers' unions, the city of San Francisco, and child advocate Margaret Brodkin. She thinks "it's 'an outrage' when education officials hand over public schools, financed by tax dollars, to for-profit companies" (Guthrie, 1998). Superintendent Bill Rojas disagrees. He welcomes Fisher's support and has accepted support from Charles Schwab as well. (Schwab, having been a student with a learning disability, initially financed Gateway High School, designed specifically for students with learning disabilities.)

Edison Elementary School in San Francisco has newly painted walls, polished floors, and clean windows. Each classroom has new furniture, computers, phones, books and clocks, and the children wear uniforms. Teachers are paid $2,300 more a year than in other San Francisco public schools, but they work a longer day and a longer school year (Guthrie, 1998).

There is no tuition charged; students who attend Edison School are recruited from throughout the district. They represent a cross-section of the school population with the exception proportionally of Asian Americans. The white population is 5.8 percent, African American is 38.4, Latinos comprise 40 percent, and 16 percent are Asian and/or Pacific Islander (Guthrie, 1998).

Edison Project schools have not been in operation for a long enough period of time in San Francisco to see how student achievement will compare to the other schools in the district. Fisher is convinced, however, and has pledged $1.3 million to transition 15 more schools to the Edison Project model.

Evaluation of Charter Schools. Zollers and Ramanathan (1998) completed a study of charter schools in Massachusetts and found to their dismay that special needs students were routinely discouraged from entering or were eased out. "Each of the original for-profits has a substantially lower percentage of students with disabilities than its local district." They also discovered that "substantial numbers of students with disabilities, mostly those with complicated disabilities and expensive needs, have left the for-profits and returned to their local districts."

In 1998, Zollers and Ramanathan conducted a nationwide survey on charter schools and the enrollment of students with disabilities, and "found that many charter founders were concerned that special education would bankrupt their schools." Zollers and Ramanathan counter this argument by pointing out that the for-profit schools are the richest in the state.

Wells and her research associates (1998) from the University of California, Los Angeles, studied 17 charter schools in 10 different school districts in California and had some of the same reservations as did Zollers and Ramanathan. Among their findings were the following:

- There was little evidence that the charter schools were more accountable for student outcomes.
- The charter schools were not necessarily more efficient.
- Students left in the public schools had parents who were least involved in their children's education.
- Students with behavior problems tended to remain in the public schools. This finding supports that of Zollers and Ramanathan in Massachusetts.
- Communication between the charter schools and the public schools in their respective districts was poor.
- Fewer students from ethnic and racial minorities were enrolled.

Wells and her research associates (1998) concluded:

> Unless charter schools begin living up to some of the assumptions that have so far propelled them, it is time to reassess this magic bullet of school reform. And this time we need to ask hard questions about equity and equal opportunities.

Finn, Manno, and Vanourek (2000) attempted to evaluate charter schools and found most charter schools are "positive." They reviewed other charter school studies and report outcomes are not always good. They believe charter schools enroll federal lunch-program eligible children, those with disabiities, and limited English-speaking children in like proportion to those served by regular schools, but charter schools enroll a higher percentage of minority youngsters. They also note academic and behavioral standards are high, and some children will be "counseled out," suspended, or expelled.

Parent Choice. One of the touted benefits of charter schools is the fact that they offer parents a choice. Other choices for parents include vouchers. As Wagner (1996) states, "We all want more choices . . . [and] there is a great deal of hype about school choice." He points out one fantasy, as he calls it, associated with the concept of choice: greater choice of schools will create better schools. But the reality Wagner sees in the Cambridge, Massachusetts, schools is quite different. Giving parents choices of which of 13 K–8 schools they would like to send their children has meant that "several of the schools enjoy good reputations . . . [but] are oversubscribed. Parents do not often get their first choice of school." Regrettably, Wagner writes, "The majority of the thirteen schools seem virtually interchangeable and are mediocre."

Miner (1998) states that her opposition to vouchers stems from her experiences as a reporter for the *Milwaukee Journal*. She had attempted to report on a parent meeting taking place at one of the schools of choice. However, she was unable to attend it; the meeting was only for parents and reporters were barred by lawyers.

Milwaukee began offering vouchers to parents in 1990; initially, the program was limited to low-income children at a handful of nonreligious schools. The program has now expanded to as many as 15,000 children also attending private and religious schools. Miner states that Cleveland has a similar program. The issue, then, is the classic one of separation of church and state. Ultimately, Miner believes the U.S. Supreme Court will decide.

Miner's concerns are as follows: under Milwaukee's voucher program, participating schools:

- Do not have to obey the state's open meetings and records laws
- Do not have to hire certified teachers, or even require a college degree
- Do not have to release information on employee wages or benefits
- Do not have to administer the statewide tests required of the public schools
- Do not have to publicly release data such as test scores, attendance figures, or suspension and drop-out rates

The only requirement is a "financial and performance evaluation audit" of the entire voucher program to be submitted to the legislature in the year 2000 (Miner, 1998).

Ramirez (1998) suggests that the rationale behind the push for vouchers is driven by the theory that "public schools will become market-driven; they will become more efficient and run like a business." But he feels that there is little data to support the contention.

Public school alternatives already include intra- and interdistrict choice, magnet schools, the existing array of private and parochial schools, and now charter schools. Even with all these choices, parents still may, and do, choose to home-school their children.

Ramirez (1998) concludes that:

> Ultimately vouchers are about politics, not improving education. . . . The economic theory of open-market competition

as a justification for vouchers and the solution to an ailing education system is voodoo economics.

Your authors' advice: visit a charter school or a magnet school; talk to the teachers, parents, and students; talk to parents about vouchers; talk to another parent who home-schools. Use the criteria developed by the NAEYC to determine for yourself whether you think these options provide a better education than does a local school.

Growing Private Investment in Preschool Programs

Americans place child care among the top five services the federal government should provide.

Private enterprise has scrutinized child care as a potentially lucrative industry. Chains of preschools grow ever larger.

A number of child care businesses in the United States are expanding and testing the waters outside U.S. borders. KinderCare has opened a center in England and plans an additional 40 to 50 centers there (Neugebauer, 1995). La Petite Academy, the nation's second largest child care chain, operates four centers in Tokyo. Bright Horizons Children's Centers, one of the nation's largest operator of centers for employees, has also been involved in Japanese child care development. Asian and South American countries are seen as future sites for the child care business investment.

Interactions between child care communities and businesses are increasing. Neugebauer (1995) points out that doing business in foreign lands sounds exotic and exciting; increasingly, systems, products, and support will flow freely across national boundaries.

Studies of Father Involvement

The Early Head Start Research and Education Project is among the first to explore the involvement of low-income fathers in their children's lives (Raikes & Tarullo, 1999). The study investigated what influenced a father's participation in a center's activities and what factors contributed to an enjoyment of fathering. A study strand funded by the Ford Foundation focuses on different strategies programs used and the program's effectiveness.

Early study findings include the following. Centers have:

- Increased efforts to hire men in various staffing capacities
- Identified one staff member whose responsibility includes promoting father involvement
- Attempted to employ a variety of father-involvement strategies including men's support groups, increasing language program material addressing both parents, using male role models, surveying fathers, changing schedules for the convenience of working fathers, including fathers in home visits, involving male staff in male volunteer recruitment, and focusing on family relationships as well as traditional mother-child interactions

Conversations with fathers noted by study investigators cite fathers determination to "be there" for their infants and toddlers and to assume financial responsibility. Fathers stated they believed mothers wanted them to be active, physical caregivers. Fathers mentioned dealing with ill or crying children has caused frustration. Rough and tumble play, cuddling, and tickling were described by fathers as their primary mode of play. Although fathers felt few fatherhood support systems or role models were available, they also confessed they are reluctant to accept help.

School-age Programs

Before- and after-school child care programs are a viable and growing phenomenon. They developed during the mid- and late 1970s and blossomed in the 1980s and 1990s. The demand has grown in proportion to the number of employed mothers both from two-parent and one-parent households. It has also grown in proportion to the numbers of mothers of preschool children in some kind of child care. School-age child care is seen as a regular program designed for children ages five to 12 during the times when school is not in session and parents are at their employment before school, after school, and on school holidays. Neugebauer (1998) states that school-age care is the fastest growing segment of child care and possibly the least visible. He estimates (based on a parent survey) that 80 percent of working parents seek some form of school-age care (see Figure 15–1).

Bussing is frequently supplied for children who have to be transported from their elementary school to another facility. Student teachers occasionally are given student teaching placements in school-age care programs.

After-school programs are specifically designed for kindergartners through fifth graders after they have completed their academic day. Many children who are older than fifth graders are involved in extracurricular activities that finish later in the day, closer to the time a parent would return home from work, or are seen as able to fend for themselves. Many primary children who are not enrolled in school-age programs return to empty houses with their keys around their necks to do chores and homework. These latchkey children, as they are called, may also care for younger siblings. An estimated two to six million school-age children are left at home without adult supervision before and after school, and there seems no end to the pressing and increasing need for quality school-age programs.

latchkey children—school-aged children who, after school, return to an empty home because their parents are at work.

Figure 15–1 Working parents continue to need school-age child care programs for their children.

Quality in School-Age Programs

Because there are many organizations caring for school-aged children, there are issues related to quality. The principal issue is whether or not the program meets state licensing standards. Your college supervisor may want to apprise you of your own state's regulations and recommendations for quality school-age child care.

Some programs encourage and even demand that children in their care join their organization. The organization may be exempt from meeting state standards. It may only have to meet the organization's own standards. One program, for example, did not have child-sized toilets in its bathrooms at its main building. Parents did not complain because they were happy to have their children cared for by an organization they trusted.

Researchers have begun to identify factors that contribute to the quality of after-school programming. When:

- Child-adult ratios are higher and teachers less educated, some staff interact more negatively with children
- Programs offer a wider variety of activities and more flexible programing, staff interactions are more positive
- Staff turnover is high, it impacts program quality
- Child-adult ratios were lower and programming more flexible, staff appeared warmer, more sensitive, and supportive
- Children spent less time waiting and less time watching television; more time was spent interacting positively with staff
- Staff possessed higher levels of education, they were more likely to use positive behavior management strategies; and the staff of nonprofit programs seemed more positive, warmer, used more positive behavior management, used less television, and were able to keep children occupied (Vandell & Su, 1999)

Growing evidence shows after-school programs can have significant academic and social benefits, particularly when programs supplement material learned during the regular school day with skills training and recreational activities (Harvard Education Letter, 2002).

Movement toward establishing standards for school-age programs has been prompted by various professional associations and groups.

ISSUES

There are many issues we could have chosen to present. Some have already been covered. We have, therefore, chosen to introduce only a few of the major issues here:

- The anti-bias curriculum
- Violence prevention and kindness curricululm
- Computer use with young children
- Family child care
- Family support and resource centers
- Security concerns
- Adequate compensation

Anti-bias Curriculum

As lifestyles change and demographers point out projected higher birth rates for some culturally diverse and newly arrived populations, increased interest in bias-free child activity planning for all children has occurred in early childhood programs. A nonsexist and nonracist child curriculum continues to be important, along with increased sensitivity to possible biased opinions or visual models presented in instruction and instructional media.

Single-parent families, seniors, children of color, children and adults with disabilities, one-child families, and minority ethnic families appear with increasing frequency in children's books and commercial instructional materials as publishers have become responsive to early childhood educators.

Carter and Curtis (1994), influenced by the anti-bias curriculum work of Derman-Sparks and the ABC Task Force (1989), have identified current assumptions that serve as the basis for decision-making in their early childhood teacher training. They feel, as they continue their growth as teacher trainers, that these assumptions could change or be modified. Carter and Curtis (1994) assume the following:

1. Everybody has a culture; culture is learned and includes, but goes beyond, ethnicity.
2. The dominant culture of power in this country has been shaped by European American male perspectives and interests.
3. Bias comes in many forms; invisibility and lack of cultural relevancy are as detrimental as stereotyping.
4. Antibias practices require that we recognize European American cultural dominance and learn how its assumptions become a bias when applied universally. We must learn new attitudes, information, and behaviors as we unlearn acquired biases.
5. To be inclusive and genuinely multicultural requires that we make a place for those historically left out, misrepresented, or disenfranchised. Given the stakes, this will likely stir up emotions and conflict that we must learn to work with.
6. Adults come to programs and workshops with a complex web of influences from backgrounds that must be untangled as they learn and unlearn across diversity.
7. As adults come to deeper understandings about themselves and working with diversity, these understandings will influence their work with children, going beyond tokenism to counter biases and be culturally sensitive.

Which of these assumptions are new to you and may change your values? Did any assumption reinforce a value you already had? Could these assumptions affect your work with adults and children of varied backgrounds? How?

VIOLENCE PREVENTION AND KINDNESS CURRICULUM

Early childhood activity planning that promotes kindness and nonviolent problem-solving is increasing and being created by a growing number of teachers. Child activities that emphasize love, empathy, gentleness, respect, friendship, responsibility, self-control, and conflict resolution are valued. Rice (1996) writes:

> During the last thirty years, our educational system has shied away from teaching right and wrong because of a view that doing so

would restrict personal freedom. Unfortunately, this lack of emphasis on basic values coupled with the stressing of rights over responsibilities has helped produce a less kind and less gentle society.

A quality program strives as a first step to ensure children feel safe and loved. Teachers model a "peace-loving" nature, conflict resolution techniques, an ability to calm themselves, and an ability to solve problems reasonably in their daily interactions. They prevent children from becoming victims of violence in their classroom. Although anger is a normal feeling, teachers believe children can learn to manage it and understand there are "okay" and "not okay" ways to express it. When problems arise, young children with adult support can be encouraged to think of more than one solution and can grow more adept as they age. The key is for children to stop and think, and choose a nonviolent, safe, and fair course of action.

Levin (2003) suggests that there are many ways wherein teachers can build what she calls "a peaceable classroom." She includes standard ideas such as teaching conflict resolution and an appreciation of a class' diversity, but also stresses building a sense of safety and community.

Computers and Young Children

Figure 15-2 Some young children are well acquainted with computers.

There has been much interest in computers and early childhood packaged software development. More and more, children are actually using computers rather than merely observing them. As Alexander (2001) points out, while school districts are spending huge sums on training adults to speak the language of computers, young children are growing up computer literate (see Figure 15–2). Companies are creating effects on color television screens with voice prompts, musical sounds, and clever picture forms, and have developed simple keyboards. As screen happenings are shared and discussed, child interest and motivation increase.

Contrary to popular beliefs that children would become isolated, sitting in their separate cubicles and working at a keyboard, this has not been the case. Walk into any center with computers and observe. You frequently will find two or even three children playing and/or working with any given program as the following observes:

On a recent visit to a private kindergarten program with computers, both in the classroom and in a computer lab, we observed Kimberly, sitting with her friend Christina, at the classroom computer, excitedly telling her friend about the program they were exploring, "Grandma and Me."

"My grandma and I went to the beach, too," Christina interjected, "but there weren't many other people there that day because it was foggy and cold."

"That's not part of the story, Christina," admonished Kimberly, "Look at what happens next."

The two girls sat at the computer for about 25 minutes, Kimberly "reading" the story to Christina who had not used this particular program before. Christina kept interrupting with her own story of her visit to the beach with her own grandma. Eventually, Kimberly seemed to realize Christina's need to tell about her trip to the beach and ignored the fact that it was different than the program they were using. She even suggested that perhaps Christina could "write" about her trip to the beach with her grandma when they went to the computer lab.

> On a later visit to the computer lab, both girls were absorbed in using the "KidPix" program. Christina kept telling Kimberly how she used the "Flying Colors" program when she visited her grandma and how it differed from what they were trying to do with "KidPix."

In preschool classrooms, computer use is designed as a social experience. Children help one another and take turns with teacher help and supervision if problems arise.

Haugland (2000), an advocate for early childhood computer use, suggests that when used effectively, computers make an excellent learning tool, imparting to children knowledge and skills far beyond expectations. She believes *how* they are used to be more important than *if* they are used.

> Computers clearly have a powerful influence on children, and thus how we use them is especially important. To integrate computers and maximize children's learning, four steps are critical: selecting developmental software, selecting developmental websites, integrating these resources into the curriculum, and selecting computers to support these learning experiences.

Should we worry that the future will be a single child working at a single computer? The answer is a resounding no! In most elementary school primary grades, children work in twos and even threes at the computer. Children accept correction from the computer more easily than they do from the teacher; thus, the computer becomes a tool for reinforcing mathematics concepts, for example, and for science problem-solving as well as for word processing and classroom desktop publishing (Kearsley, Hunger, & Furlong, 1992).

NAEYC has established guidelines for using technology in the classroom. Alexander (2001) reports recent studies indicate technology has a positive impact on children's learning and contributes to improved performance. In Pennsylvania, a state Cyberstart program is attempting to connect the state's child care centers to the Internet. Taylor (2000) suggests more that 60 percent of all new jobs require some technology skills, and "computer literacy" is as critical today as "literacy" was to their parents and grandparents. She believes recent studies show a "digital divide" between races and classes in America continues to grow.

Family Child Care Homes

A merger of interests is evolving between in-home and in-center staffers. Networking has provided additional contacts. Professional early childhood conferences and college coursework are offered specifically to attract family home educators and to probe mutual concerns. Another factor that has helped is the number of early childhood graduates with AA degrees who have opted to establish child care homes of their own. Often, financial rewards for family home educators surpass those of private proprietary in-center teachers.

Some states are adding education and training requirements for family home care providers. California, for example, requires that all family home care providers must have training in health, safety, and nutrition; first aid; and cardiopulmonary resuscitation (CPR) (including CPR for infants and young children). Family child care providers are also expected to obtain 15 hours of in-service training each year. Typically, these hours are met by attendance at local conferences sponsored by such groups as NAEYC and Association for Childhood Education International (ACEI) affiliates. Local resource and referral agencies also arrange for training, as does the Red Cross.

A shortage exists for infant and toddler care as more and more mothers of very young children enter or remain in the workforce. The trend appears to be toward regulation by states and the stipulation for some kind of training. The National Association of Family Child Care and NAEYC do accredit family care homes of those providers choosing to undergo the process. Perhaps as more providers choose to become accredited, parents will be more comfortable in their choice of a family child care home for their infants and toddlers, as well as for their older children.

If you are interested in the criteria and process involved in accrediting family child care providers, you should contact the National Association of Family Child Care in Washington, DC. Their telephone numbers are 1-800-359-3817 (for information) and 1-817-831-5095 (to become accredited).

FAMILY SUPPORT AND RESOURCE CENTERS

Family support programs differ uniquely and can offer family support services including child care, parent education, literacy tutoring, screening, information and referral, counseling, crisis intervention, and other features. Many programs focus on families with young children. Family support has the goal of helping families cope with the stresses of daily life. They offer new information about child development, reduce parents' isolation, and provide links to other existing social services and supports (Groginsky, Robison, & Smith, 1999). Twenty-five states maintain statewide comprehensive family support or parent education programs, and six states have appropriated funds for the development and expansion of home visiting programs and family resource centers.

Vermont's neighborhood parent-child centers include child care along with a wide range of other services. These parent-child centers are closely coordinated with the Success By Six Initiative, a statewide effort to ensure Vermont's children are ready for school. West Virginia's Starting Points Family Resource Centers also provide a comprehensive array of family support services.

Early childhood educators are bound to be affected by states' efforts to coordinate child care with other public family support services.

Security Concerns

After the terrible tragedy in Oklahoma City's child care center on April 19, 1995, security has become a real concern. The Child Care Information Exchange ("Is your center secure?" 1995) encourages centers to conduct security audits. The following questions are suggested for audits:

1. Do you have specific procedures in place for responding to all likely emergencies (natural disasters, fires, accidents)?
2. Do you have a written procedure for evacuating your center that staff and children can implement on "autopilot?"
3. Do you have an off-site location where children can be kept until parents can pick them up if your building cannot be reinhabited after an evacuation? Are parents aware of this arrangement?
4. Do you have a plan for notifying parents when you have to evacuate your building and leave all records behind?
5. Do you have supplies readily available to provide for staff and children's needs when you evacuate your building on short notice or when you

must remain with children in your building for an indefinite time in an emergency?

6. If you had to account for every child in your center, what would you do to determine that 100 percent were present? If you used this procedure today, would you be able to account for each child? Would this procedure be effective if you had to evacuate under stressful conditions?
7. Do you have sound procedures in place for continually accounting for all children on field trips?
8. Do you have regular maintenance procedures established and followed for center vehicles? Are vehicle drivers carefully screened? Are they trained to handle emergency situations?
9. Is access to the center controlled in a consistent and sensible way?
10. What procedures do you have to limit visitor access to child-occupied areas of the center? Are there facility features that help secure the perimeter of the building and that notify personnel when security has been breached?
11. Are parents dropping off and picking up children in any possible danger? Are staff coming to and leaving work in any danger? What are your strategies for ensuring their safety?
12. Do you have procedures for dealing with an adult who is under the influence of drugs or alcohol when he arrives to pick up a child?
13. Do you have procedures to ensure that children are released only to adults specifically authorized to pick them up? (Some programs are requiring photo IDs of anyone authorized to pick up the child.)
14. Do you have procedures to provide assurance that incidents of abuse cannot occur at your center?
15. Do you have rigorous screening practices to assure that only qualified staff are employed by the center?
16. Do you have procedures for immediately responding to accusations of abuse?
17. Before undertaking a corporate/government management contract, are you adequately evaluating the risks per the location of the facility, the type of business being conducted by the corporate sponsor, and other uses of the building?
18. Does your program have an aggressive policy to ensure that children wear seat belts?
19. Are parents or staff smoking around children? How does your program inform adults about the risks secondhand smoke poses to young children and about the negative role modeled by smokers?
20. Does your center have routines established for preventing the spread of communicable disease? More importantly, are these rigidly adhered to?
21. Does your area have child care for sick children? Parents should be given the name(s) of any facility or family care home that specializes in caring for sick children, including infants and toddlers. As more and more mothers of young children enter the workforce, centers or homes specializing in sick child care are on the increase. These are frequently staffed with licensed vocational/ practical nurses (LVNs/LPNs) or registered nurses (RNs), and usually have a pediatrician on call for emergencies.

Although these suggestions are aimed at preschool and child care center directors and teachers, they are, in many ways, applicable to elementary schools, public and private. In these days of child abduction by noncustodial parents and strangers, many schools have implemented controlled access to children, requiring visitors to sign in and out at the office, community aides questioning those in the halls whom they do not recognize. In some schools that have experienced violence, requiring students, teachers, and visitors to pass through a metal detector is not uncommon. Companies such as KinderView and ParentWatch have developed Internet video access services that allow parents to watch their child and the school's program during the school day for a monthly subscriber fee.

Adequate Compensation

Dating back to the earliest days of the NAEYC, a concern about salaries and working conditions existed. This organization, over 90,000 members strong, launched its quality, compensation, and affordability activities in 1987. In 1990, NAEYC's Full Cost of Quality Campaign attempted to inform both the profession and the public concerning the real and true cost of quality programs.

Quote from a first year teacher:

> I am upset because I found a center I love and a program that is truly child-centered. The children learn so much and are happy. I would hate to give up my happiness as a teacher just because the wages are too low to support myself (Lebo & Rajotte, 1998).

Quote from a director with 14 years experience:

> The worst thing that I face is the starting salaries. I think that it is so hard to go by our pay scale when I'm looking for new staff. I just can't hire someone good for $6.00 per hour. The truth is that if you stick to the wages of the current scales, you end up sacrificing quality (Lebo & Rajotte, 1998).

Although compensation for early childhood educators is still inadequate and inequitable for many practitioners, there are some bright spots on the horizon. Legislators in at least four states—Texas, Arkansas, California, and New Hampshire—have considered different strategies to improve wages (Groginsky, Robison, & Smith, 1999). Some states are developing career development initiatives and policies that simultaneously address weak compensation and levels of training.

The nine northeastern states in the United States appear the most active in pursuing increased compensation strategies with all states in this area initiating indirect programs to improve early childhood wages or benefits (Twombly, Montilla, & De Vita, 2001).

In North Carolina, TEACH, a component of its statewide Smart Start Initiative, rewards participants incrementally as they complete a predetermined amount of education leading to a credential or degree. The state of Washington approved a $4 million fund to increase wages for early childhood educators who achieve a two-year degree. A growing number of other states are dispensing funds through contractual relationships, and have authorized higher reimbursement rates to accredited programs or those meeting stricter standards (Groginsky, Robison, & Smith, 1999).

Although some state and national happenings look promising, Kagan and associates (2002) paint a depressing picture of early childhood compensation:

> Today's reality is that even with increased commitments to early care and education from the federal government and states, qual-

ity remains embarrassingly poor, staff salaries are inadequate, and high-quality care is not affordable for most parents despite increasing subsidies.

Worthy Wage Campaign. The National Center for the Early Childhood Work Force, (renamed The Center for the Child Care Work Force), a policy, advocacy, and research organization, initiated the Worthy Wage Campaign in 1991. Any child care worker or interested individual can become a campaign member. Many early childhood professionals and leaders have urged advocacy for worthy wages.

The Worthy Wage Campaign is calling for a minimum average wage of $10.00 an hour and comprehensive health care benefits.

Morgan et al. (1994) reflect the feeling of most workers in the following: "Increased knowledge and skills in early care and education should be rewarded with increased responsibility, compensation, and status. . . . Licensed individuals as well as child care centers."

SUMMARY

Most of society's economic, social, political, and technological trends affect families and young children. Knowledge of trends is crucial to effective teaching, program planning, and supportive relationships with parents. Changes occur that can enhance children's opportunities and potentials, have neutral effects, or create inequities or unfavorable development.

As you already know, books have been written on many of the above trends and issues; our intent was to whet your interests and present brief overviews, together with a few examples, of the differing trends and issues as we see them.

HELPFUL WEB SITES

http://www.actagainstviolence.org

ACT Against Violence Project. Learn about a public service advertising campaign that supports adults and children working against violence.

http://childrenandcomputers.com

Children and Computers. Provides descriptions of publishers and prices of developmental software.

http://www.esrnational.org

Educators for Social Responsibility.

http://www.home-ed-magazine.com

Home Education. Information about home-schooled issues.

http://www.ibm.com/

KidSmart-IBM. A multimedia guide to computers and early learning is available online, and answers questions regarding computer use to support learning.

http://www.nccp.org/

The National Center for Children in Poverty. Search for a publication titled *Ready to enter: What research tells policymakers about strategies to promote social and emotional school readiness among three-and four-year-old children.*

http://www.whitehouse.gov/

United States Government. Information on the Bush administration's Early Childhood Initiative and search for early childhood education policy goals.

http://www.ojp.usdoj.gov

U.S. Department of Justice. Statistics about incarcerated parents and their children

http://nieer.org

National Institute for Early Education Research. Research, working papers, newsletter, events, and information.

http://www.childtrendsdatabank.org

Child Trends DataBank. National trends concerning child and family health, social and emotional development, and a wide range of information pertaining to early childhood.

SUGGESTED ACTIVITIES

A. Make a list of current issues in early childhood teaching. In groups of three to five, arrange them in order of their importance for young children's education and welfare in the United States. Share and compare results with the whole group.

B. Read an article on a trend or issue in early childhood education (ECE), ECE teaching, or ECE programs. Use the *Current Index to Journals in Education*, ERIC, or some other resource to locate one. On a separate sheet, provide the following information to review the article.
   - Title of article
   - Author(s)
   - Journal or publication's name
   - Date of publication
   - Page numbers
   - General findings of the study or article (number of subjects, ages, testing device or procedure, results), key ideas, points, or conclusions
   - Your reactions

C. With a small peer group, discuss the inherent advantages that could be possible if your state department of education was responsible for the certification and/or licensing of all teachers, educators, and child care practitioners working with infants, toddlers, and preschoolers. Think about training standards, required coursework, ease in transferring units from two-year training programs and colleges to four-year programs, status, working conditions, compensation, child care quality, and so on. Any disadvantages? List your group's ideas and share with the total group.

D. With a team of four classmates, investigate your state funding of preschool programs with block grant monies or state funds. Try to obtain the following:
   - Who administers funds for state-sponsored preschools?
   - Are programs licensed? Accredited?
   - What are teacher qualifications?
   - Are reimbursement rates different if preschools are accredited or judged to be of excellent quality?
   - Do written guidelines exist for state preschool programs?
   - Is state public money given to private profit-making schools for child care?

- What are the qualifications necessary for parents who wish to enroll a child? Do parents pay fees?
- Are state or federal funds used to enhance teacher compensation or benefits?

Report your findings to the total group.

E. Research the ERIC Clearinghouse on Elementary and Early Childhood Education's Web site at http://ericeece.org. ERIC is a nationwide system funded by the National Institute of Education. ERIC contains a vast storehouse of information on all aspects of early childhood education. Print out one article of interest to you. Report your findings to your training group.

REVIEW

A. List five current debatable trends and/or issues in early childhood education.

B. Describe briefly what you feel is public policy on child care in the United States.

C. Choose the answer that best completes each statement.

1. The real issue in increasing public schools' sponsorship of preschool programs is:
   a. the mediocrity of public education.
   b. our private enterprise system.
   c. lack of parent pressure for programs.
   d. quality care as a public priority.
   e. all of these.
2. Child care teachers' compensation is:
   a. equal to other workers with similar education and experience.
   b. about $6 to $7 per hour in many states.
   c. probably the cause of high turnover of staff.
   d. increasing with increased public funding.
   e. b and c.
3. There appears to be a(an) _________ of trained early childhood teachers.
   a. oversupply in certain geographic areas
   b. exodus
   c. shortage
   d. good supply in certain geographic areas
   e. all the above.
4. The training standards for early childhood teachers and public elementary school teachers can be described as:
   a. becoming increasingly demanding for one group but remaining static for the other.
   b. similar.
   c. staying relatively stable.
   d. increasingly stringent for both groups.

D. List four subjects on which much education-related research is currently focused.

CASE SCENARIO

Setting: A student teacher in a second grade classroom.

The student teacher in Ms. Ng's second-grade classroom remained late one afternoon to read the children's journals. At 5:30 P.M., the student teacher, while leaving school, notices an older child (fourth or fifth grade) sitting on the front steps of the school crying. The school is locked and all staff has departed.

"What's wrong?" she inquires.

"I missed the school bus and no one's come to pick me up," responds the child.

"Did you ask the secretary to call your parents?" she asks.

"She said no one answered at home and my dad's work phone was answered by his voice mail, so she left a message that I needed to be picked up but he hasn't come!" the child responds.

"Do you want me to wait with you?" the student teacher says.

"Please. I'd feel so much better. It's beginning to get dark and I'm afraid."

After waiting more than an hour, the student teacher suggests driving the child home.

"My mom and dad are divorced and I live with my dad; we don't know where my mom is," the child offers.

On the way to the child's home, a car without lights hits the student teacher's car. Both the child and the student teacher are shaken up, and the driver's side of the car is damaged.

Questions for Discussion:

1. Would you have handled the situation the same way? Why or why not?
2. Have you been prepared through college or other training classes to act professionally if this had happened to you?
3. Are there other good alternatives to driving the child home?

REFERENCES

Alexander, P. (2001, Summer). Young children bridge the digital divide. *State Education Leader, 19*(2), 7–8.

Association for Supervision and Curriculum Development. (1999, January). Preparing two million: How districts and states attract and retain teachers. *Education Update, 41*(1).

Beane, J. A. (1998, October). Reclaiming a democratic purpose for education. *Educational Leadership, 56*(2).

Berliner, L. (1993, August). Identifying and reporting suspected child abuse and neglect. *Topics in Language Disorders, 13*(4).

Brennan, S. (1998, Summer). Increasing minority representation in the teaching profession through alternative certification: A case study. *The Teacher Educator, 34*(1).

Bonds, T. (2002). The effects of violence on mental health. *Head Start Bulletin,* (73), 29–33.

Bush, G. W. (2002). State of the union address. Washington, DC.

Bush, J., & Wilson, C. S. (1997, October). Linking schools with youth and family centers. *Educational Leadership, 55*(2).

Carter, M., & Curtis, D. (1994). *Training teachers: A harvest of theory and practice.* St. Paul, MN: Redleaf Press.,

Center for the Child Care Workforce. (1998). *Working together for kids: Parent action guide.* Washington, DC: Author.

Children's Defense Fund. (2001). *2001 State of America's Children.* Washington, DC: Author.

Chubb, J. E. (1998, November). Edison scores again in Boston. *Phi Delta Kappan, 80*(3).

Derman-Sparks, L., & The ABC Task Force. (1989). *Anti-bias curriculum: Tools for empowering young children.* Washington, DC: National Association for the Education of Young Children.

Early Developments. (2000, Spring). NCEDL news. *Early Developments, 4*(1), 14–16.

Felner, R. D., Kasak, D., Mulhall, P., & Flowers, N. (1997, March). The project on high performance learning communities: Applying the land-grant model to school reform. *Phi Delta Kappan, 78*(7).

Finn, C. E., Manno, B. V., & Vanourek, G. (2000). *Charter schools in action: Renewing public education.* Princeton, NJ: Princeton University Press.

Gadsden, V., & Ray, A. (2002, November). Engaging fathers: Issues and considerations for early childhood educators. *Young Children, 57*(6), 32–43.

Goenner, J. N. (1996, September). Charter schools: The revitalization of public education. *Phi Delta Kappan, 78*(1).

Grant, G., & Murray, C. (1999). *Teaching in America: The slow revolution.* Cambridge, MA: Harvard University Press.

Greenberg, S. H., & Springen, K. (2000, October 16). Back to day care. *Newsweek,* 61–62.

Groginsky, S., Robison, S., & Smith, S. (1999). *Making child care better: State initiatives.* Washington, DC: National Conference of State Legislatures.

Guthrie, J. (1998, October 18). The fisher king. *San Francisco Examiner.*

Harvard Education Letter. (2002, November 19). Schools supplement curricula with afterschool programs. Author.

Haugland, S. W. (2000, January). Early childhood classrooms in the 21st century: Using computers to maximize learning. *Young Children, 55*(1), 12–18.

Haynes, V. D. (2001, April 16). Unions swiftly recruit child-care workers. *San Jose Mercury News,* 1PC.

Howey, K., & Zimpher, N. (Eds.). (1991). *Restructuring the education of teachers: Report of the Commission on the Education of Teachers into the 21st century.* Reston, VA: Association of Teacher Educators.

Is your center secure? (1995, July/August). *Child Care Information Exchange,* 104.

Jackson, M. (1999, September 23). Employers fund backup day-care. *Idaho Statesman,* 1D.

Kagan, S. L., Brandon, R. N., Ripple, C. H, Maker, E. J., & Joesch, J. M. (2002, May). Supporting quality early childhood care and education. *Young Children, 58*(3), 58–65.

Kearsley, G., Hunter, B., & Furlong, M. (1992). *We teach with technology: New visions for education.* Wilsonville, OR: Franklin, Beedle & Associates.

KinderCare on *Business Week* Top 1000 list. (1987 July). *Child Care Information Exchange, 56.*

Lebo, D., & Rajotte, V. (1998). *Stories from the field: From rocking the cradle to rocking the boat.* Silver Spring, MD: Montgomery Child Care Association.

Levin, D. E. (2003). *Teaching young children in violent times: Building a peaceable classroom* (2nd ed.). Cambridge, MA: Educators for Social Responsibility and Washington, DC: National Association for the Education of Young Children.

Lombardi, J. (2001, January). It's time to redesign child care to create 21st century early education. *Young Children, 56*(3), 74–77.

Loucks, H. E. (2001, Summer). From thought to action: Illinois P-16 partnership for educational excellence. *State Education Leader, 19*(2), 13–14.

Marx, G. (2001, May). 10 trends for tomorrow's kids. *Education Digest, 66*(9), 5–10.

Miller, Z. (2000). Quote in NCEDL news. *Early Developments, 4*(1), 14–16.

Miner, B. (1998, October). Why I don't vouch for vouchers. *Educational Leadership, 56*(2).

Morgan, G., Azer, S. L., Costley, J. B., Elliott, K., Genser, A., Goodman, I. F., & McGrimsey, B. (1994, March). Mediocre care: Double jeopardy for black children. *Young Children, 49*(3), 80–83.

Nathan, J. (1996, September). Possibilities, problems, and progress: Early lessons from the charter movement. *Phi Delta Kappan, 78*(1).

National Association for the Education of Young Children. (2000, May). Promising strategies for increasing compensation. *Young Children, 55*(3), 58–59.

Nealy-Shane, D. (2002). Choosing a distance education program. *Head Start Bulletin, 72*, 25.

Neugebauer, R. (1995, July/August). Child care and the global economy. *Child Care Information Exchange, 104.*

Neugebauer, R. (1998, September/October). Who's who in school-age care. Child *Care Information Exchange.*

Philippe, K. A. (1997). *National profile of community colleges: Trends and statistics 1997–1998.* Washington, DC: American Association of Community Colleges.

Raikes, H. H., & Tarullo, L. B. (1999, March). Early Head Start Research and Evaluation Project. *Head Start Bulletin*, 65, 20–22.

Ramirez, A. (1998, October). Vouchers and voodoo economics. *Educational Leadership, 56*(2).

Report: Teen pregnancy rate at 20-year low in U.S. (1998, October 16). *The Idaho Statesman.*

Rice, J. A. (1996). *The kindness curriculum: Introducing children to loving values.* St. Paul, MN: Redleaf Press.

San Jose Mercury News. (2002, April 18). 42 failing Philadelphia schools to be privatized. *San Jose Mercury News*, 5A.

Shore, R. (1997). *Rethinking the brain.* New York: Families and Work Institute.

Specht, J. (1998, October 16). Congress waits for vote today on budget deal. *The Idaho Statesman.*

Taylor, H. (2000, February). Technology: A key to the future. *Head Start Bulletin*, 66,1.

Toppo, G. (2001, August 4). Study finds 850,000 American children are homeschooled. *The Idaho Statesman*, 5 Main.

Twombly, E. C., Montilla, M. D., & De Vita, C. J. (2001). *State initiatives to increase compensation for child care workers.* New York: The Urban Institute.

U.S. Department of Commerce, Bureau of the Census. (1993). *Poverty in the United States: 1992.* Current population reports, series P60-185.

U.S. General Accounting Office. (1993). Poor preschool-aged children: Numbers increase but most not in preschool. GAO/HRD-93-111BR.

Vandell, D. L., & Su, H. (1999, November). Child care and school-age children. *Young Children, 54*(6), 62–71.

Wells, A. S., & Research Associates. (1998, December). Charter school reform in California: Does it meet expectations? *Phi Delta Kappan, 80*(4).

Whitebook, M. (1995). *Salary improvements in Head Start: Lessons for the early care and education field.* Washington, DC: Center for the Child Care Workforce.

Whitebook, M., Howes, C., & Phillips, D. (1989). *Who cares? Child care teachers and quality of care in America.* Berkeley, CA: CCEP.

Whitmire, R. (1998, September 30). Congress demanding higher teacher quality. *The Idaho Statesman.*

Zollers, N. J., & Ramanathan, A. K. (1998, December). For-profit charter schools and students with disabilities: The sordid side of the business of schooling. *Phi Delta Kappan, 80*(4).

SECTION VIII

Infant/Toddler Placements

CHAPTER 16

Student Teaching with Infants and Toddlers

Objectives **After studying this chapter, the student should be able to:**

1. List at least three characteristics of a quality infant/toddler center.
2. Discuss two of the findings in the research on child care for infants and toddlers.
3. Describe the general regulations of an infant center (including health concerns).
4. Cite techniques for approaching and working with children.
5. Describe caregiving as a teaching activity.
6. Identify activities for infants and toddlers.

I asked to be placed in an infant/toddler center. Student teaching there pointed out caregiver skills I hadn't dreamed of. Thank heavens I've a strong back. That's really necessary!

—Michaela Grossman

Wash your hands, wash your hands, then, do it again. I think the staff said that hundreds of times!

—Pat Booth

One of my friends said I'd never want children of my own if I worked at a toddler program. Wrong! It made me want children of my own even more.

—Briana DeLong

So you have the opportunity to student teach in an infant/toddler center! And what a learning experience you will have!

STANDARDS

Most infants and toddlers today are cared for by relatives or in family child care homes. Many parents feel, rightly or wrongly, that the infant thrives better in an environment most like the home. Family child care homes are popular. State licensing in California mandates low adult-infant and adult-toddler ratios. The NAEYC has been urging a ratio of 1:4 as a national standard. A quality center may deliberately choose to keep its ratio 1:3.

One of the reasons for the lack of national standards lies in the belief that all young children, especially infants and toddlers, belong at home with their mothers. This attitude, however, does not reflect what is happening in the workplace. The fastest growing group of new workers is women with children under the age of six.

CHARACTERISTICS OF A QUALITY INFANT/TODDLER CENTER

As with quality characteristics of a preschool/child care center, some of the same are quality indicators of an infant/toddler center. A study by the National Institute of Child Health and Human Development (NICHD, 1996) highlighted the following as critical to the provision of sensitive, warm, responsive care:

- A low caregiver-to-infant/toddler ratio was the number one indicator of quality. The closer the ratio came to 1:1, the higher the quality. Thus, high-quality care was frequently found in home settings with relatives and sitters (including fathers and grandmothers).
- A smaller group size provided for higher quality care.
- Caregivers who were less authoritarian were more likely to provide positive interactions with infants.
- A safe, uncluttered physical environment with age-appropriate materials was the fourth sign of quality.

Reinsberg (1995) supports these findings. She lists security as being the most important factor so that infants can develop a sense of trust. To accomplish this, "Primary caregivers and other consistent staff are the single most important factor." At Reinsberg's college center, student teachers were assigned for longer periods of time to provide for greater consistency and to reduce the infant/toddler-caregiver ratio to 2:1 on most days.

To respond to the NICHD finding about group size, the center kept the group size in the infant/toddler room lower than the number for which it was licensed. To guarantee greater safety for rapidly growing infants, a partition was installed to separate the very young infants from the older, more mobile ones.

Believing that the room was becoming overstimulating and noisy, Reinsberg, her teachers, and students stopped holding casual conversations with each other and began to listen more for the sounds the infants and toddlers were making. They soon discovered that the infants and toddlers were more relaxed in the quieter setting.

Diapering routines were changed to become more responsive to the needs of the children themselves. Rather than adhering to a strict schedule, caregivers

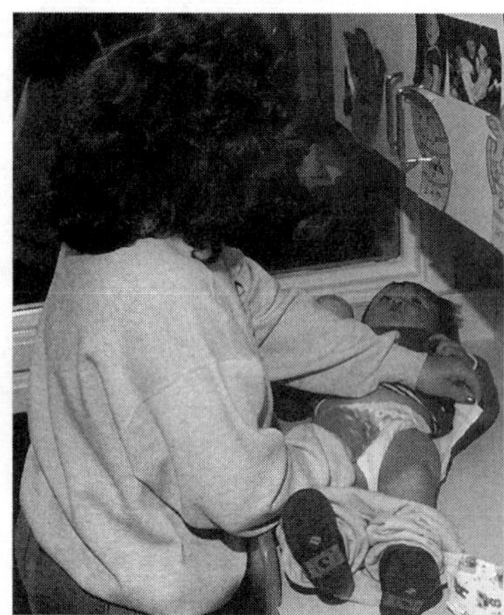

Figure 16–1 The curriculum in an infant center includes changing diapers.

began to wait until they noticed an infant appeared uncomfortable or that a toddler was ready to change. Then, adhering to the principles outlined by Madga Gerber, caregivers slowed down the process of changing diapers. They talked to the child about what they were doing and involved the child in the process. The same process was followed in feeding the infants and toddlers (see Figure 16–1).

Speaking softly to the infants and toddlers, student teachers found themselves more "in tune" with them. The student teachers also began to anticipate when an infant was hungry or when he was sleepy.

Reinsberg (1995) highlights the need for close communication with parents and the need to reevaluate what they do at the center to assure continuing quality care. Several centers chart feeding times and amounts, and also sleeping and diapering times in a notebook that goes home with the parent every day. The parent then enters the feeding, sleeping, and diapering times in the same notebook and brings it back to the center each day. What procedures does your center use?

Greenberg (1996) lists the following as characteristics needed by an infant/toddler center:

- Kind, leisurely physical and emotional care from one primary caregiver comes first!
- Parents should be encouraged to stay and play as much as they can. (This may be one reason for the growing number of businesses with child care facilities on site or located near by.)
- A baby is emotionally a part of her parents, just as she recently was physically a part of them.
- When a baby is without a parent, she's without a piece of herself.
- It's important to take time to provide the emotional support a baby needs.
- Babies separated from their beloveds for many hours may become depressed. The goal [of an infant/toddler caregiver] is for each baby to have a happy day.

Quality Family Child Care

In a family child care home of one of our former students, three large, sunny rooms in the bottom level of a split-level house serve for her family child care. A fourth room, the downstairs bathroom, houses the changing table and potty chairs for the preschoolers in care. A door from the room used by the preschoolers opens to a large fenced backyard with a climbing structure and covered sandbox. In the infant room, a large playpen serves to separate the older, crawling babies from the very small ones.

Our former student and her daughter are licensed for a total of 12 infants, toddlers, and preschoolers. However, although she could take more infants, she will only enroll two, and no more than four toddlers, together with six preschoolers. Of the two infants for whom she cares, one is more mobile than the other and is allowed to roam safely in the carpeted room. A mirror is attached to the wall at floor level; infants thoroughly enjoy looking at themselves. Electrical outlets are covered; no electrical cords are evident. A rocking chair is in one corner of the room. A bookshelf loaded with appropriate toys for the crawler to reach is along the wall. A second bookshelf contains small board books with brightly colored pictures and minimal stories.

The four toddlers have a second room, separated from the infant room by a gate, with toys more appropriate for their ages on one shelf, books on another shelf, blocks on a third, cars, trucks, trains, puzzles, and other stimulating toys lined on other shelves, all within reach of the toddlers and preschoolers (see Figure 16–2). A small table with four chairs is along the window wall. A soft couch is on the opposite one. The walls are brightly painted with Pooh characters, complements of a friend who is a commercial painter.

Preschoolers share a third room, separated from the toddler room by a low partition that allows caregivers to easily monitor activities.

Attachment Issues in Infant/Toddler Care

Over the past 20 or so years, there have been many studies of attachment. One of the crucial issues in infant/toddler care is whether the children involved would establish bonds with their working parents. Studies have shown that infants do bond with their parents, and in centers where they are consistently assigned to one caregiver for extended periods of time, infants will establish secondary bonds with that caregiver. This is why in some infant/toddler centers, a caregiver will move with the child from the infant to the toddler room.

attachment—the child's bond with a teacher established over time in personal interactions.

As Raikes (1996) writes,

> The essence of the attachment paradigm is that infants form affectional bonds with their caregivers and that these affectional bonds create a sense of trust, secure base, and positive expectation in the infants.

In other words, infants with securely attached bonds to parents and caregiver will be able to resolve the Erikson task of learning to trust.

Special Issues of Infant/Toddler Care

Separation from Parents.

As Daniel (1998) writes, mothers historically stayed home, and those who worked were frequently considered negatively. Many women themselves approach the use of child care with feelings of guilt, even though family finances may dictate that they work. Add to this society's condemnation of working mothers (especially those with infants), parents' concerns about how to find a caregiver they can trust, and a quality care setting.

Daniel (1998) stresses some of the points previously mentioned:

- Good infant and toddler programs assign a primary caregiver to each child. (In the family child care home cited before, the mother had the primary care of a newly enrolled infant of two months. When the child was nine months and crawling, she enrolled a second very young infant of six weeks. Her daughter, however, had the primary care of the new infant; the mother retained the primary care of the older one.)
- Caregivers should have formal and informal communication with parents about the details of the child's day in order to help form viable program-parent partnerships. (A notebook—mentioned before, with notations of feeding and sleeping times and diaper changes—that goes back and forth between caregiver and parent is certainly one way of maintaining formal contact. As the infant grows, notations can include such features as turning over, sitting up, walking, and so on. Taking a few minutes of time to talk when the infant is brought or picked up allows for informal communication.)
- Low staff turnover is essential to building emotional trust between caregiver and infant and between caregiver and parent.

Figure 16–2 Simple yet inviting shelf arrangements suit toddlers.

Infant/Toddler Child Care and Identity Formation

If, as Greenberg (1996) states, a baby is emotionally a part of his parents just as he was physically a part prior to birth, how does an infant/toddler center deal with the infant's or toddler's developing sense of being separate from the parent, his sense of identity? Lally (1995) decries the lack of research on the impact of child care on the infant's identity formation. He cites some of the early studies that showed how infants look to their mothers and/or caregivers for signals about what to do. Some of the lessons learned become incorporated into the child's sense of self. The child learns, for example:

identity formation—the way in which a young child separates from his parents, and establishes his own character traits and personality.

- what to fear
- which behaviors are seen as appropriate
- how messages are received and acted upon
- how to successfully get needs met by others
- what emotions and intensity of emotions can be safely expressed
- how interesting the child is (Lally, 1995)

Lally agrees in his implications for infant/toddler care with the quality indicators mentioned by Greenberg (1996), Reinsberg (1995), and the NICHD study (1996). He also cautions against intellectual stimulation and suggests that being responsive to infants and toddlers, allowing them to make their own choices about what toys they want to play with (see Figure 16–3) and what books or puzzles they want, is more valuable to their optimal development.

Infants and Toddlers with Special Needs

Sexton, Snyder, Sharpton, and Stricklin (1993) wrote a position paper for the Association for Childhood Education International (ACEI) concerning the inclusion

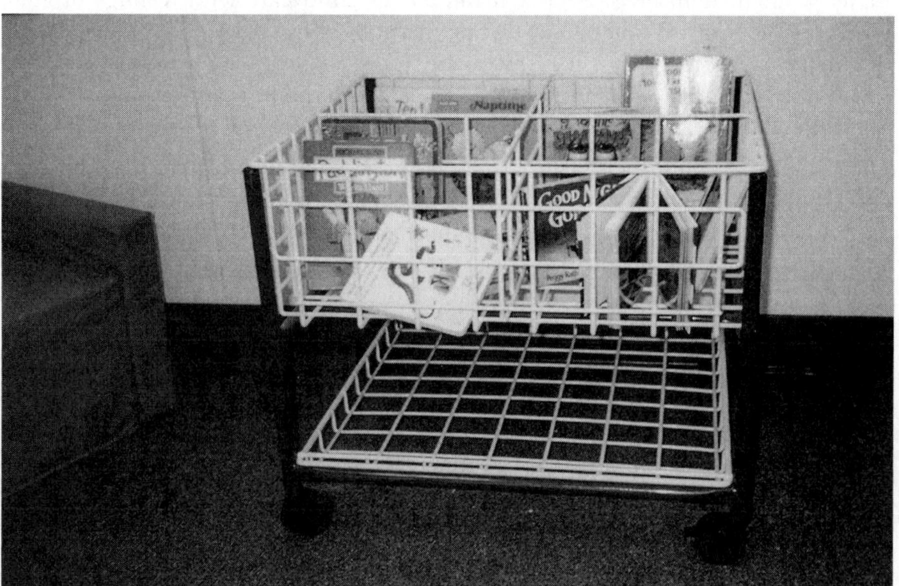

Figure 16–3 Books may be placed on a rolling cart in toddler centers.

of infants and toddlers with special needs into regular programs. The authors mention the following sobering facts and figures, gleaned from a variety of sources:

- Each year, some 425,000 newborns will manifest a disability within the first four years of life.
- Some 350,000 to 375,000 newborns each year have been exposed prenatally to drugs, including alcohol.
- Each year, approximately 412,000 infants are born prematurely.
- Human immunodeficiency virus (HIV) has become the greatest infectious cause of pediatric mental retardation in the United States. In October 1992, the Centers for Disease Control reported 3,426 cases of acquired immunodeficiency syndrome (AIDS) among children under the age of 13 and estimated that several times as many children are infected with HIV (Sexton, et al., 1993).
- An estimated 3,000,000 to 4,000,000 Americans are homeless, and the estimated number of homeless children on any given night is anywhere from as low as 68,000 to as high as 500,000 (Sexton, et al., 1993).

Sexton and his co-authors then reaffirm:

- the effectiveness of early intervention
- the mandate of the law that special needs children be included with their nondisabled peers
- the need for families to have access to services like quality care, education, and special intervention:
- the fact that increasingly diverse populations of infants and toddlers present great challenges to child care and educational systems
- the need for action to support child care and education in meeting the challenges of diversity and inclusion
- the need to validate the quality of infant/toddler programs and that these should support full inclusion
- the necessity for child care, health care, and education to be integrated, and for individualized care and education be provided to all infants/toddlers and their families
- to this end, the need for collaboration among the different fields of early childhood mentioned above
- the right for all infants/toddlers and family members to child care, education, and intervention to be delivered by trained personnel with appropriate certification or licenses and who are adequately compensated (Sexton, et al., 1993)

Infants Born to Teenage Parents

DeJong and Cottrell (1999) state that child care programs for children born to teenage parents must have some extra features not found in most infant/toddler care settings. They believe that the major goals of programs for these "special" parents must be to assist them as follows:

- to stay in school to earn a high school diploma or its equivalent
- to continue their postsecondary education
- to improve their parenting skills
- to reduce repeat pregnancies
- to deliver normal birth-weight babies of at least 5.5 pounds

STUDENT TEACHING WITH INFANTS AND TODDLERS

An infant/toddler center is an entirely new world, one that is completely different from the preschool environment. Every infant/toddler center is operated a little differently. However, most centers have similar regulations regarding children's health, caregivers' health, feeding, and diaper-changing procedures. A student teacher should request a staff handbook. Read it before you go to the center. Be prepared to ask questions about anything you do not understand. Babies need consistency, and it is important that you are able to fit into the center routines as quickly as possible. Most important, relax and enjoy the children!

APPROACHING AND WORKING WITH CHILDREN

When working with infants and toddlers, remember that every child is an individual. Even tiny infants have preferences. They may like to sleep on their backs or sides rather than stomachs; they may like to be burped on the shoulder rather than on your knees. When you are caring for a child, take a minute to try and find out what some of their preferences may be.

When working with children of this age, remember:

- Your size may be frightening to a child.
- Keep confidential material to yourself. Medical, financial, personal, and family information is privileged information that helps you understand the child more completely.

Working with Infants

Children need to hear your voice, so *talk to them*. They need the social contact that only another person can provide. Hearing language is also the way children learn to talk. Be sure you use clear, simple language. *Speak softly*. Voice tone and volume greatly affect the children. If you speak in a loud, excited voice, the children are very likely to become loud and excited in response.

Encourage anticipation by telling the children what you are going to do. Say "Now we are going to change your diaper." They will respond and cooperate when you let them know what to expect.

Try to be at *eye level with the children*. Sitting or kneeling on the floor brings you closer to their line of vision. *Make eye contact*. When bottle-feeding, playing, diapering, and the like, look directly at the children. Meet and hold their gaze when talking to them. You like to have people look at you; babies undoubtedly feel the same way.

Move slowly around infants. Young children do everything in slow motion. They often get upset and overstimulated when adults run around them excitedly. Young infants need time to understand the changes that are happening. Be affectionate and warm but *do not hover*. Be ready to hug, hold, and comfort when they need it, but let them be free to explore. Young children need to be able to move around and experience their environment. They need to find their own solutions to problems whenever they can. Let the children experiment with toys and invent uses. Intervene only when they are likely to get hurt, are obviously in distress, or are too frustrated to cope. Becoming independent, competent, and self-sufficient is hard work; children need loving, secure adults and a safe place to begin the process.

Encourage the babies to help you in caregiving. You need to dress them, change them, and feed them. However, they will help if you let them. Recognize their attempts to participate and encourage them. It does not take much longer, and the rewards are many times greater.

There has been an increased use of signing with infants as a result of current attention to infants' and toddlers' communication and prereading skills. Early childhood infant educators are much more aware of infants' attempts to communicate with nonverbal hand, arm, facial, eye, and body movements or expressions. Almost all adults realize arms extended upward means "I want to be picked up" and most adults watch children's eyes to find out what has attracted attention. Skilled caregivers working in infant centers may understand each infant's unique and individual signing attempts, then imitate and pair the child's signs with simple words or phases such as "bottle" or "ball, you want the ball." This gives infants the idea that they are indeed communicating, for their signs elicit caregiver actions. Researchers believe this signing interaction does not inhibit but rather enhances the infants' and toddlers' eventual use of words (Lapinski, 1996). Acredolo and Goodwyn (2000) state successful baby signing stimulates brain development, particularly in areas involving language, memory, and concept development.

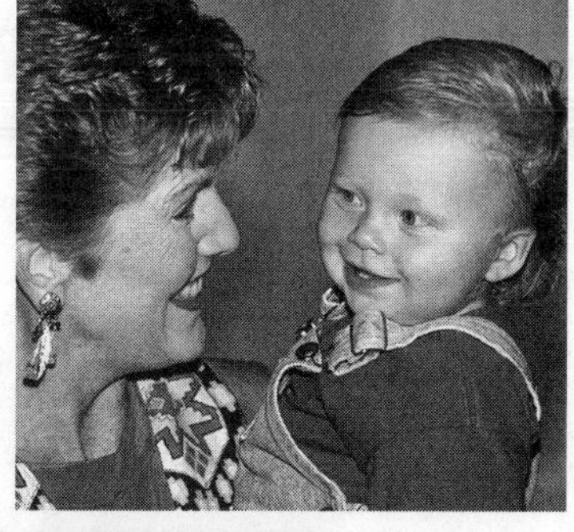

Figure 16–4 This toddler sees himself as a separate individual.

Working with Toddlers

Toddlers are a very special group. They are just beginning to understand that they are people (see Figure 16–4). They are seeing themselves as separate from their parents for the first time. They are compelled to explore and understand their environment (see Figure 16–5). They must assert themselves as individuals. If you can recognize their need to be individuals without feeling personal insecurity, you will have made a giant step in dealing effectively with them.

Toddlers, more so than infants, will challenge your authority. They may test you until they can feel secure in your response. You will need to call on all your reserves of strength, firmness, patience, and love to deal with them. They are loving, affectionate, giving, sharing, joyful, spontaneous people; take pleasure in them.

You may find some of the following ideas helpful when you are working with toddlers. Read the suggestions, and think about them. Try to put them into practice.

Make *positive statements*. Say "Feet belong on the floor." When children hear the words "don't" and "no" constantly, they begin to ignore them.

Give choices only when you intend to honor them. If Johnny's mother said that her son must wear his jacket when playing outside, do not ask John, "Do you want your jacket?" Instead, say "Your mom wants you to wear a jacket today." If you give a choice and the toddler says "no," you are already in a conflict you could have avoided.

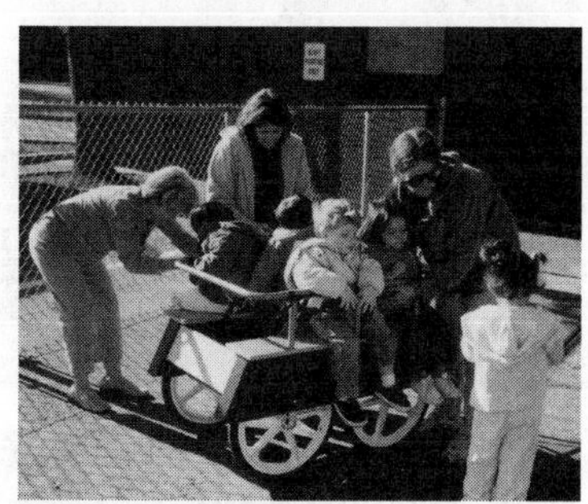

Figure 16–5 Going on a long walk may require special equipment, and lots of teacher help.

Avoid problems by *being alert*. Watch for signs that a child may be getting too frustrated to handle a situation or that a fight over a toy is about to start.

Use distraction whenever possible. If you see two children insisting on the same toy, see if the children can work it out themselves. If not, try to interest one of them in something else. You might point out a toy just like it or remind them of another enjoyable activity.

If an argument does erupt, *avoid taking sides*. Help both children understand how the other child feels. *Encourage the use of words* to handle situations. Encourage the children to name things, to express happiness, sorrow, excitement, and other emotions. *Let the children talk.* Correct grammar and pronunciation will come later. Practicing verbal expression is the most important thing.

Act on your own suggestions. If you say, "Time to clean up. Start putting the toys away," the children are more likely to follow your suggestions if they are accompanied by actions.

Make *alternative suggestions* if some children continually ignore safety rules or disturb others: suggest an alternate activity the child likes; suggest taking turns; suggest cooperation; or remove the child from the activity. Be firm but calm. *Do not take the children's reactions personally.* You may hear "I don't like you!" Say, "I know you are angry. It's okay to be angry." Toddlers respect fairness and desperately want limits they can depend on.

Do not make promises you cannot keep. Just say you will have to ask if you do not know. Toddlers understand that.

GENERAL RULES AND REGULATIONS

The physical setting and philosophy of a center will determine how various routines are carried out (see Figure 16–6). Centers usually have specific rules and routines regarding health and safety, medications, emergencies, feeding, diapering, and naps.

Health and Safety

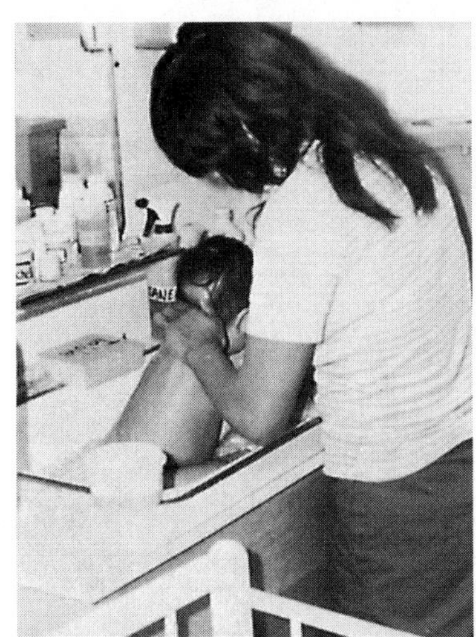

Figure 16–6 Bathing routines require safe surroundings.

- Smoking is not allowed in infant/toddler centers.
- Coffee, tea, and other beverages should only be consumed in staff areas.
- Never leave a child unattended on a changing table or in a high chair.
- Do not leave children unattended inside or outside. They can easily injure themselves.
- Ill infants should not be in the center. Infants who have bad colds, fevers, or contagious diseases are usually cared for at home.
- If you are ill, you should not be in the center. You will not be efficient if you are not feeling well. In addition, your illness may spread to the children. If you contract a contagious illness, notify the center immediately.
- Wash your hands. The most important health measure you can take is to wash your hands before and after diapering or cleaning noses and before feeding a child.
- Watch for signs that a child may not feel well. Some symptoms are digging at or pulling ears, listlessness, glassy eyes, diarrhea, and limping.
- Parents should be given the name(s) of any facility or child care home that specializes in caring for sick children, including infants and toddlers.

Medication

Normally, only a regular staff person will be allowed to give medication. You should be aware of medication schedules for the children. You might need to remind the staff when medications are due.

You also need to be aware of the effects medications may have on the children. They may become sleepy, agitated, or show allergic symptoms. You must be alert to changes that occur when medicine is given and be able to communicate these to the staff.

Emergencies

- *Stay calm.*
- Speak calmly and quietly to the child.
- Alert the staff that an emergency has occurred. They should be able to administer the appropriate first aid measures until the child can see a physician.
- Help calm the other children. They will respond to the situation the same way you do. If you are agitated and upset, they will respond to your feelings; likewise, if you remain calm, they usually will also.

Feeding

- *Wash your hands.*
- Read the child's chart to see what kind of food and/or formula to give and how much. (Remember: Do not feed a child from a baby food jar; use a dish (see Figure 16–7). Saliva, which contains bacteria, will get in the jar and spoil the remaining food.
- Gather all the things you need for feeding: bib, washcloth, spoons, sponges, and so on. It may be helpful to bring one spoon for you to feed the child and a spoon for the infant to "help."
- Tell the infant what you are going to do. Let the infant anticipate being fed.
- Settle the child comfortably. You may want to make sure the child has a clean, dry diaper before feeding so she will be more comfortable and attentive.
- The child will let you know when more food is desired. When the child opens the mouth, respond by feeding.
- Talk to the child. Eating is a time to enjoy pleasant conversation and socialization, and young children like being talked to. You can talk about the food, its texture, color, temperature, and taste. Eye contact is important.
- Encourage the child to help feed himself. It is a little messier, but it means more independence later.
- If they refuse to take the last ounce of a bottle or the last little bit of solid food, do not push it. Children know when they are not hungry.
- Be sure to burp bottle-fed children when they need it. You may want to check with the child's caregiver for any special instructions.
- When the baby is finished, wash the face and hands. Again, tell the baby you are going to do this. Encourage the child to take part in this activity. Be gentle with the washcloth.
- Take off the bib and put the baby down to play.
- Clean up. Be sure to wipe off the high chair, the tray, the table, and the floor. Put dishes and bottles in the sink.
- Record what and how the child ate.

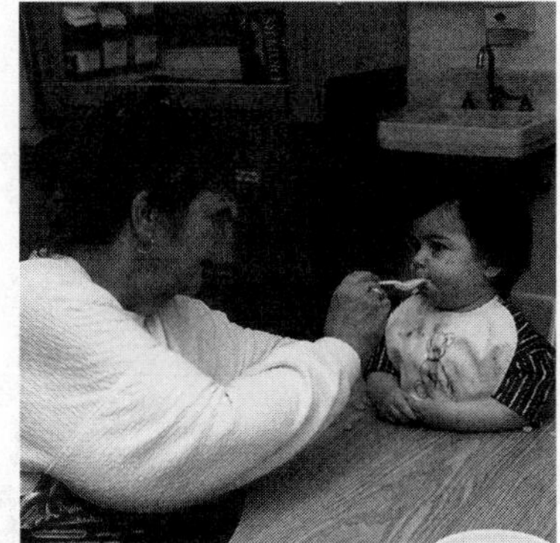

Figure 16–7 Children at this infant/toddler center are fed from dishes, not from jars.

Diapering

- Gather everything you need to change the baby: diapers, clean clothes, baby wipes, medicated ointment (if needed), and anything else that may be required.
- Tell the child what you are going to do. Set the child on the diaper table.

- Keep one hand on the child at all times.
- Take off the wet diaper and clean the child thoroughly with a warm, wet cloth. Apply any ointment according to the parent's instructions.
- Talk to the child about the process. Talk about being wet, dry, and clean. Describe the process of dressing and undressing; you can talk about the baby's clothes and body parts. Involve the baby in the process. Ask the child to lift the legs or give you an arm to put through the sleeve. (Note: How diapers are changed also gives children messages about their sexuality. If you are relaxed and casual about changing them and washing their genital area, children get the message that they are okay.)
- Put the child in a safe place. Dispose of the diaper and soiled clothes according to the directions you are given.
- Clean the changing table. Use germicidal solution.
- Wash your hands. Clean changing tables and clean hands will help prevent the spread of disease.
- Record the diaper change. Be sure to note bowel movements. Make note of diarrhea, constipation, diaper rash, unusually strong urine odor, or anything else that seems out of the ordinary.

Toilet Learning

Toilet learning is too frequently treated with embarrassment in parenting books, and meager research has been done on the topic. Many parents and caretakers do not understand that although bladder and bowel control is a skill, it may not be taught; it is learned.

Infants begin life with automatic emptying of the bladder and bowel. Bladder capacity is so small that wetting may occur every hour or so. Automatic emptying is triggered by the filling of the bladder or bowel that sets off rhythmic contractions over which the infant has no control.

It is not until the nervous system matures during the first year or two that infants and toddlers show awareness of the sensations of a full bladder or bowel. What behaviors would alert you to this?

- A look of concentration while all activity stops.
- Crossing the legs.
- Fidgeting.
- Holding onto the crotch with one or both hands.
- Less frequent wetting.
- Regularity you can count on.
- A keener awareness of body functions.
- A sudden dislike of things messy.
- A more sensitive sniffer.
- Use of the appropriate vocabulary.
- Improving communication abilities.
- Some self-dressing skills.
- An interest in the habits of others (Eisenberg & Murkoff, 1995).

Conscious holding of urine is helped by a gradually increasing bladder capacity. By the second year, capacity has usually doubled, and the frequency of wetting is about every two or three hours. Emptying is still automatic and dependent on a full bladder or bowel. When parents or caregivers boast that toddlers at 14, 18, or 21 months are toilet trained, be aware that this is more often an indication that the parents/caregivers recognize the signs of the impending need and place the child on a potty chair than it is an indication that the child is toilet trained.

In some world cultures, parents support their infants in toilet use at very young ages. This is accomplished "through close observation, physical contact, emotional support, mutual trust, and reading non-verbal cues" (Baba, 2003). When parents place their infants in an infant care center or family child care home, their expectations may be that caregivers will continue to support the infants' toilet use. This can lead to misunderstandings if caregivers and parents have different perceptions about the time for toilet learning. Caregivers should be sensitive to the point of view of parents and try to honor their requests. At the same time, caregivers must be honest about their own needs and time restrictions. Open communication between caregivers and parents is essential!

By three years, most children have learned to resist the emptying of their bowels until it suits them. At this age also, most children have learned to hold urine for a considerable time when the bladder is full. This holding ability requires conscious control of the perineal muscles, used in the same way as is the bowel sphincter. At this age, however, accidents often occur because children do not have total control over urine release. This becomes so obvious when the child who has just been taken to the toilet and not urinated goes back to play and immediately wets.

During the fourth year, most children have acquired conscious control over both bowel and bladder muscles. But it is important to remember that full control is not completely accomplished until about six years of age when starting the urine stream from a partially full bladder becomes possible.

Learning bladder and bowel control is far from simple. Think of what children must learn:

- to remove and replace pants
- eventually to flush the toilet
- to use toilet tissue
- to wash their hands upon completion

In spite of these complexities, most children acquire toileting skills with a minimum of help.

When Should Toilet Learning Begin?

The answer to this is to recognize that toilet learning will be most successful when the children show clear signs of recognizing bladder or bowel tension. These signs vary from child to child; you will be able to recognize them after they have occurred several times just before the child has wet or had a bowel movement. Look for any of the following signs mentioned earlier: stopping what she is doing and looking as if she is concentrating; crossing his legs as if trying to prevent himself from wetting; beginning to fidget, pulling at you; making sounds or using baby words such as "wee-wee;" and/or putting her hands on her crotch as if she could feel she is about to empty her bladder.

How Do You Handle Accidents?

The number one rule is to remember that accidents are inevitable. Treat accidents matter-of-factly. Wash your hands. Change the child's pants and clean up without

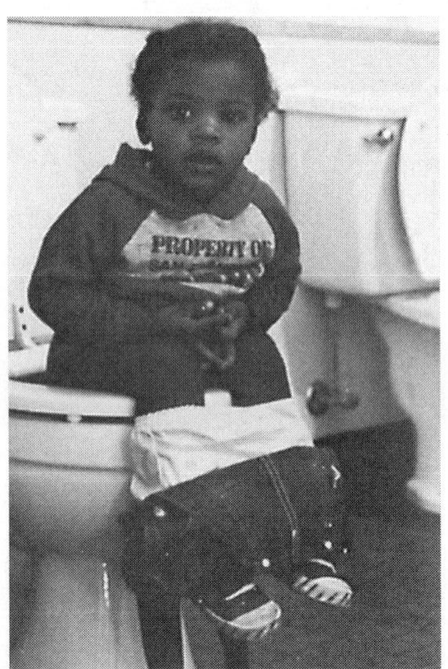

Figure 16–8 Learning to use the toilet

irritation. Wash your hands again; disinfect the changing table if it was used. If you have missed the child's cue and not moved fast enough to help the child urinate or defecate, compliment the child on his ability to try to get your attention. Recognize that some accidents may be your fault, not the child's.

Many people will give you advice about toilet learning. Your cooperating teacher may follow a routine of taking toddlers to a potty chair at regular intervals. Even if you know that most toddlers do not acquire complete control until four to six years of age, you can go along with the center's policy; regular toileting helps those toddlers with regular rhythmicity acquire control at an earlier age than those with an irregular rhythmicity (see Figure 16–8). If a parent complains that her child was "toilet trained" before she placed him in the child care center and is angry because your cooperating teacher has asked her to bring in diapers, let the cooperating teacher handle the problem. If the parent tries to involve you, defer to center policy. Be patient with those parents who keep their child in diapers at age three. Perhaps, as busy, working parents, they find it easier than to try to learn the subtle cues the child may be providing. Or, they may not know what cues to look for.

One Final Word

Most children learn by example. As one two-year-old learns to use the toilet independently, she becomes a role model for other children. In a family-type center with a mixture of ages, older children provide the role models for the younger ones. Parents also become role models for their children at home. Treat toilet learning like the natural process it is and do not worry about the three-year-old who still is having daily accidents.

Check for problems such as constipation, diarrhea, painful urination, and so on. Check for any dietary-related difficulties: a diet low in fluids and fiber will often provide cues to problems with constipation. Above all, relax and don't make a big deal about toileting; all children will learn eventually, with or without formal teaching!

Biting

Next to toilet learning, probably no other behavior causes as many difficulties for teachers and caregivers than does biting. Carothers (1990) states that biting occurs most frequently "when children are one to two years of age" and feel that it is related to the child's social development. Biting by three-year-olds is generally related to a specific stressor in the child's life.

General guidelines include:

- Remembering that biting, for the biter, is very effective. To persuade the child to give up the habit involves teaching the child new behaviors.
- Aggression occurs most often because the toddler is unable to espress wants, needs, or feelings in words.
- Making a determination of what situations lead to the child's biting. Intervening and suggesting to the child that she can use her words will help. Actually saying what you think the child is thinking also works, especially with a child who does not have many words in his expressive vocabulary.
- Redirection and distraction can be very effective with toddlers.
- When biting occurs, give a firm, clear message that the behavior is not acceptable. Use the same words with each occasion: "No biting, John," or "Biting is not allowed, Mary."

- Remove the biter to a short time-out after the incident.
- Console the child who was bitten.
- If the biting appears to be related to teething, offer the child a teething ring or a soft, pliable plastic toy to chew.
- Deal with biting immediately. Asking a parent to talk about biting at home is ineffectual. Toddlers cannot remember carry-over instructions.
- Remember that toddlers need a lot of time and repetition to learn new behaviors. You may want to keep a record of how many times a day the biting occurs and at what times of day.
- Ask for the parent's help to reinforce substitute behaviors for biting when at home.

What should you tell parents? In a student teaching assignment, defer to your cooperating teacher; she will know what to do. Carothers (1990) presents the following ideas:

- As briefly as possible, tell the parents of the child who was bitten what happened. Do not tell the parent the name of the biter.

  In one case, a family child care provider had two toddlers, a boy and a girl, who always seemed at odds with each other. The girl had resorted to biting more than once. But one day when the boy went home with bite marks on his arm and his mother inquired about what had happened, she was surprised to learn that he had bitten himself! She was sure that the little girl was at fault. Instead, her son had become frustrated with trying to complete a puzzle, and when he could not force the last piece into place, bit himself.

- Ask the parents of the biter if he has bitten another child when at home. It is important to determine whether the behavior occurs only in the child care setting or if it also appears at home.
- Enlist their help in eliminating the behavior. Suggest to the parents to teach the child to use her words. Teach the parents to use the same expressions that are used at the center. Consistency is the key.

When dealing with conflict betweeen toddlers, Da Ros and Kovach (1998) suggest that, before intervening, caregivers look at what is happening in the process (see Figure 16–9). Given toddlers' immature social development, Da Ros and Kovach feel that conflict is inevitable with toddlers and that the caregivers' approaches to resolve conflict may, in actuality, exacerbate the problem. By taking time to assess where the toddlers are in the process of the conflict, caregivers will understand better how to react. Can the caregiver prevent what conflict might erupt? Once conflict has appeared, what intervention strategies work best?

Da Ros and Kovach (1998) suggest the following strategies:

- Remain at the children's eye level.
- Watch and wait before interceding.
- Use "I" messages.
- Move closer to the conflict.
- Use language that tells the toddler what you see happening.
- Prevent injury by interceding quickly with both children when necessary.
- Provide just enough help to allow toddlers to solve their own dilemmas.
- Be available to comfort each child (squat down, remain at the child's level, have your arms open).

Process of Conflict

	Potential Conflict	Emerging Conflict	Engaging Conflict	Struggling Conflict	(Disengaging) Resolving Conflict
Toddler Behavior	Aggressive acting Child in close proximity to other children	Two toddlers in opposition over object Dissipate/escalate	Toddlers fully involved Engage in physical contact Not at maximum level	Emotionally invested in process (crying, yelling) Actively engaged in physical contact Tug-of-war Climatic Stakes are high	Win, lose, or draw Emotional process is diffusing Anticipate Disengaging
Caregiver Strategies	Keenly observe More proximal	Assess at child's eye level Analyze Remain neutral Nonjudgmental	Watching and waiting Keep safe Allow natural consequences Remain neutral, attentive, focused	"I" messages; use singular pronouns Verbalize what is happening (sportscasting) Prevent hurting Available to each Keep own emotions in check Model gentleness	Provide help for them to problem-solve Available to each Do not leave scene until a toddler leaves Model gentleness Verbalize affect, emotions
			Level of Intrusiveness		
	Least intrusive		**Moderate**		**Interactive**

Figure 16–9 Strategies for caregivers to use when toddlers come into conflict with each other. Reprinted by permission of D. A. DaRos and B. A. Kaach, and ACEI. Copyright© 2001 by ACEI.

- Stay at the spot until the toddler disengages from the scene.
- Verbalize what you see happening.
- Model gentleness to the aggressor.
- Offer yourself, instead of objects, for comfort (for example, your lap) if a child appears to want comfort.
- Continue to verbalize what you see going on by using active, reflective listening.

Do not try to "fix" the problem or overreact; and above all, do not expect a toddler to respond in adult ways.

Nap Time

Young children may vary considerably in their nap times. You must be alert to signs of sleepiness in order to prevent a young child from becoming overtired. Toddlers usually learn very quickly to adjust to the nap schedule of the program. Watch for yawning, rubbing of eyes, pulling of hair, thumb-sucking, and disinterest in toys or people.

All these are signs that a young child may be ready for a nap. Before putting the child down, quickly check his schedule. Make sure the child is dry and is not due to be fed soon. You may want to feed a child a little ahead of schedule if the child is sleepy. Make sure you have a clean crib and blanket. Also, check to see if the child has any special toy to sleep with.

If you are helping a child who is new to the center, the child may be reluctant to take a nap. This is because the child is in a strange place that is full of strangers.

Check to see if the child prefers to sleep on the back, side, or stomach. Most infants are placed on their backs or sides to sleep as a precaution against sudden infant death syndrome (SIDS). If the parent assures you that the infant prefers sleeping on his stomach, be sure that no pillow or too soft a cover is used, or a stuffed toy with which the infant accidentally could be smothered. Many older infants and toddlers enjoy sleeping on their stomachs.

Sudden infant death syndrome (SIDS)—sudden infant death syndrome, where death of an infant occurs generally during the first three months of life and for which there is no known cause.

You may find it helpful to sing softly, rub the back gently, or rock in order to help the child settle down to sleep. Dimming the center's lights may help calm the child. Many times, all the excitement of the center and the other children make it difficult for babies to sleep. Be patient but firm.

Do not feel you failed if you do not get instant success. Ask the staff for suggestions. Infant center staffs are usually more than willing to answer questions, listen to concerns, or offer suggestions.

CAREGIVING AS A TEACHING ACTIVITY

Consider the following curriculum areas, usually included in the preschool program: motor, cognitive, language, social, sensory, self-esteem, and mathematics. All these areas are encountered during routine caregiving activities (see Figure 16–10).

Think about the routines when you change a diaper:

■ You talk to the child, telling what is going to happen. The child is developing a sense of sequential events.	language mathematics social
■ You take off the child's diaper and let the legs move freely. The child feels the air on the body.	motor sensory

Figure 16–10 Music is another toddler curriculum area.

■ You tell the child that the diaper is wet or contains a bowel movement.	cognitive sensory
■ You wash the child with a washcloth or wipe. You apply diaper rash medication if necessary. You talk about how this feels.	sensory language cognitive
■ You put a new diaper on the child and then, possibly, clothes. The new diaper is dry and feels more comfortable.	sensory language cognitive
■ You talk about what is happening, encouraging the infant to help you by lifting the legs, putting out an arm, and so on.	language motor social
■ The infant is now more comfortable and probably happier. You have had an opportunity for a special one-to-one experience with the child. For a few minutes of a busy morning, the infant has your complete attention.	self-esteem sensory social
What about feeding?	
■ You know it is time to give a bottle or feed a child. You tell the child you are going to prepare the food. You are again helping the child develop a sense of sequence of time.	mathematics language social
■ The young infant may be just starting to eat and learning to eat from a spoon; the older infant may be using fingers or learning to use a spoon. How special you feel when you succeed.	motor language self-esteem
■ You sit with the child or a small group of children while they eat lunch. You talk about what they are eating, about how	social language cognitive

it tastes, ts texture, and color. A child who does not like peas may be encouraged to try three peas or two pieces of the carrots.	sensory mathematics
■ The bottle-fed child or slightly older infant has your total attention. You talk to the child. You make eye contact while feeding the infant, holding the child close and safe.	self-esteem language sensory
■ After the child has eaten, you wash the face and hands with a warm, wet cloth. First, the right hand; then, left. The older child may be able to help you.	sensory language cognitive motor

Diapering and feeding are just two examples of the many routines that happen in an infant center. Think of how many things are happening to a child during these routines. Think about what else is happening. What other messages is the infant receiving? Think about bathing and dressing to go outside. What about nap time? What kinds of things could you do that would make nap time smoother and be a more complete experience for each child?

A CURRICULUM FOR INFANTS AND TODDLERS

Another question often raised by people who are unfamiliar with infants and toddlers is "What do you mean when you say you 'teach' infants and toddlers?" Many people, including parents, misunderstand just how much their children learn during their first years of life. Even those who do know may feel that all the children do is play.

For a thorough treatment of what can be considered a developmentally appropriate curriculum for infants and toddlers, see Bredekamp's (1987) *Developmentally Appropriate Practice*. Educators and student teachers may find Lally's developmental stages helpful. He considers children from birth through eight months as being in the stage of "the early months," eight- to 18-month-olds as "crawlers and walkers," 18-month-olds to three-year-olds as "toddlers and two-year-olds."

Lowman and Ruhmann (1998) alert practitioners to the idea that toddler environments should not be "scaled-down" versions of preschoolers' classrooms. Classrooms described as being saturated with sensorimotor activities are more developmentally appropriate. Lowman and Ruhmann recommend a simplified arrangement with four activity areas:

1. Large motor zone.
2. Dramatic-play zone.
3. Messy zone.
4. A quiet zone.

"Multi-S environments," a term coined by Lowman and Ruhmann, include simplicity, seclusion, softness, sensory features, stimulation, stability, safety, and sanitation.

ACTIVITIES IN THE INFANT/TODDLER CENTER

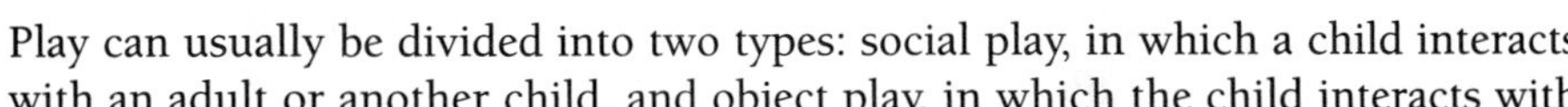

Play can usually be divided into two types: social play, in which a child interacts with an adult or another child, and object play, in which the child interacts with an object or toy. Children of all ages engage in both types of play and the following guidelines are true for any child.

Effective Social Play

- Activities for infants are not preschool activities that are "geared down." Infants are a specific age group who need specific activities.
- Play *with* the children, not *to* them. Try to interact, not entertain. The adult can initiate the activity but should wait for the child to respond.
- Involve different ways of communicating in your social interactions: looking, touching, holding, laughing, talking, rocking, singing, and laughing. Give infants a lot of different social responses to learn.
- Be sensitive to infants' signals. If they are interested, they will laugh, coo, look, smile, and reach. If tired or disinterested, they may fuss, turn away, or fall asleep.
- *Talk* to the infant. Children learn speech from the moment they are born. The more language they hear, the more they will learn. Name actions, objects, and people.
- Offer new ways of doing things. Demonstrate how something works. Encourage persistence. Do not direct children as to the "right" way to use a toy; let them explore and experiment. (Obviously, if some danger is involved, use your judgment and intervene when necessary.)
- Be sensitive to variations initiated by the child and be ready to respond to them.

A child can use play materials either alone or with an adult. Adults should use judgment in the choice of materials presented to each age group. A toy that a two-month-old might enjoy might not be appropriate for a nine-month-old. When offering materials to the children, remember:

- Toys and materials should encourage action. Materials should not just entertain but elicit some action.
- Toys should respond to the child's action. When the child pushes or pulls a toy, the toy should react. The ability to control parts of one's world, to learn cause and effect, is an important part of learning at this early age.
- Materials should be versatile. The more ways a toy can be used, the better it is.
- Whenever possible, toys should provide more than one kind of sensory output. For example, a clear rattle lets the child see, as well as hear, the action.

Play and playthings are an important part of the environment. Do not believe that constant stimulation is the aim. Even very young infants need time to be alone and to get away from it all. It is important to be sensitive to the infant's cues about feelings to help avoid overstimulation and distress.

The following are some activity ideas for infants (one to 12 months old). Remember that some activities are appropriate for many ages.

- Change the infant's position for a different view.
- Use bells, rattles, and spoons to make noise.
- Exercise the infant's arms and legs.
- Rub the infant's body with different textured materials.
- Put large, clear pictures at eye level for the infant to look at.
- Imitate the sounds the infant makes.

- Record the children's sounds and play them back.
- Put toys slightly out of reach to encourage rolling over and reaching.
- Take the babies outside on warm days. Let them feel the grass and see trees and plants.
- Call the children by name.
- Play peekaboo with the children.
- Hide toys and encourage the children to look for them.
- Attach a string to toys and show the children how to pull them. (Caution: Do not leave the child unattended with the string; they may get entangled.)
- Make puppets for the children to look at and hold.
- Let the children play with safe unbreakable mirrors.
- Play games and sing, using parts of the body. Make up songs about feet, hands, noses, and so on.
- Show children how to bang two toys together.
- Let the child feed herself. Give peas, diced cooked carrots, or small pieces of fruit to practice with.
- Play patty-cake, "row-row-row your boat." Encourage the children to finish the songs for you.
- Listen for airplanes, trucks, cars, dogs, and the like outside, and call the children's attention to them.
- Roll a ball to the child and encourage the child to roll it back.
- Play hide-and-seek.
- Play music for the children; encourage them to clap along.
- Have hats for the children to wear. Let them see themselves in the mirror.
- Read to the children. Point out the pictures; encourage the child to point to them.
- Let the children play with different textures.
- Put toys upside down and sideways. See how the children respond to the changes.
- Play pretending games.
- Show the children how to stack blocks.
- Make obstacle courses for the children to crawl over, around, and through.
- Let them play with measuring cups and spoons in water, sand, or cornmeal.
- Play "follow the leader."
- Make an incline for the children to roll objects down.
- Have the children set the table with plastic cups and dishes.
- Hide a clock or toy under a towel and see if one of the children can find it.
- Have purses and bags for the children to carry things in.
- Give the children puppets to play with. Watch how they use them.
- Let the children fingerpaint with nontoxic paint.
- Let them go barefoot in the sand and grass so they can feel the textures.
- Use old-fashioned clothespins for the children to put around the rim of a coffee can or plastic container. (Make sure that any sharp edges are filed down.)
- Encourage the children to help put their toys away.
- Let them practice opening containers (e.g., plastic margarine bowls). Put a toy in the container to encourage them to open it.

- Make toys for the children; be inventive! Let your imagination go. Remember that the toys should have no sharp edges and should be too large to fit in the mouth.

Infant activities grow gradually more and more complex as the children mature. Usually, by 12 to 14 months, the child is walking and beginning to talk. An infant of this age is quite accomplished mentally. The infant understands that objects are separate and detached. The infant rotates, reverses, and stacks things, and places them in and removes them from containers in order to further consider their separateness.

Projects for toddlers can be more complex in response to their increased mental and physical abilities. Small group activities can usually be tried with some success. When planning activities for and working with toddlers, remember that the activities should be kept as simple as possible. In addition, plan ahead. Anything that can go wrong will. Bring everything needed to start and finish the project.

Following are some ideas you might want to try with the toddlers. Watch the children, and see what you can think they might enjoy.

- *Easel painting* (one-color paint; use soap to help it come out of clothes).
- Have *waterplay*. Use measuring cups for pouring.
- *Coloring*. Use a limited number of large-size crayons and a large sheet of paper. For a change, try covering the whole table with paper.
- *Collage*. Try using starch and tissue paper with paintbrushes.
- *Fingerpainting*. For a change, try yogurt or pudding. (Be sensitive to the feelings of those parents who don't want their children to "play" with food.)
- *Paint on cloth* pinned to the easel. It makes a great gift for parents.
- *Music*. Use drums, rhythm sticks, clapping games, simple exercises to music.
  —Be aware of recent findings about music perhaps helping the brain to make connections and thus enhancing the child's ability to learn. Honig (1995) suggests that singing simple melodies is very soothing to babies; use the nonsense syllables they use; do not be afraid to use a simple tune like "Twinkle, twinkle, little star." "Happy birthday to you" will work, too.
  —Do not worry if you do not have a beautiful voice. Babies love all rhythmic, musical sounds. You do not even have to be able to carry a tune! The infants will not care!
  —Use a tape recorder or CD player to play music softy in the background as infants and toddlers play.
  —Use music to announce transitions. Sing, "Now we're going out to play" to the tune of "Mary had a little lamb" and repeat it each time you go out to play. Soon you will find the children singing along with you (Honig, 1995).
- *Flannelboard stories*. Keep them short and graphic.
- *Bubble blowing*. This should be done sitting down. Emphasize blowing through a straw. Use a cup with water and soap. Collect *all* straws; they can be dangerous if a child falls on them. Note: A small slit cut near the top of the straw prevents a child sucking up soapy water.
- *Gluing*. Use torn paper, tissue, magazine pictures, and the like. Avoid small beans, peas, and so on that could be swallowed or put up noses.
- *Modeling dough*, made with salt, flour, and nontoxic color.
- *Hand and footprints*.
- *Body tracings*.
- *Paint a large cardboard box*; cut shapes in the sides. Children can climb through the sides after they paint it.

- *Go on a sock walk.* Plant the seeds collected on a wet sponge. (More suitable for older toddlers.)
- *Do simple shape rubbings.* (More suitable for older toddlers.)
- *Make simple roll-out cookies* or use frozen dough for the children to roll out and cut with cookie cutters.

CHILD'S PHYSICAL ENVIRONMENT*

As a student teacher, the new adult at your placement site, you will need to study both indoor and outdoor space. Try to answer the following:

- Are there as many play spaces at any one time as there are children enrolled in the program?
- Are the outdoor spaces safe?
- Are climbing structures high enough to challenge the children but low enough and cushioned underneath so falls will not hurt or injure any child?
- Are there enough wheeled vehicles for the number of children who want to ride them?
- Is there a "road" for the wheeled vehicles to follow? Are traffic rules made clear and enforced?
- If there is a sandbox, is there a cover?
- Are water tables set away from major play areas but close to the water supply?
- If a splashing pool is used, is it located near the water supply and sufficiently far from the rest of the play area to prevent children from being splashed who do not want to be wet? Is the pool drained at night and stored?
- Are there outside and inside water fountains? Are these at child height?
- If cups or plastic glasses are used, are they disposable or personalized to minimize the spread of germs?
- Are there child-sized toilets or potty chairs? Are they easily accessible to children learning to use the toilet? Are they out of the way of crawlers? Are they disinfected frequently and always after bowel movements?
- Is there a sink for washing hands by the diaper changing table? Is there a sink in the staff bathroom area for washing hands after toileting?
- Do staff wash their hands before preparing food?
- Are children directed to wash their hands before eating?

Infant and Toddler Language Development

It is never too early to read to children. Just the sound of the voice, the lilting quality of speech, and the caregiver's proximity ultimately aids in language acquisition. Initially, one may just point to pictures and name objects for the child(ren). Later, explanations can be expanded and feedback requested from the children. Although it is never too early to read, it is important to gauge reading level and length of time spent on one activity, according to how the children respond. Ability to concentrate varies dramatically among children. However, it is true that very young children generally have very short attention spans. The ability to focus on a given object or activity increases dramatically in the first three years. Studies show that the "observing" child is participating and learning even while not actively involved in the current activity.

**This part of Chapter 16 was contributed by Kathy Kelley, Director, Campus Child Care Center and instructor in early childhood education, Chabot College, Hayward, California.*

Heavy cardboard books, designed for small hands, are easily handled, excellent manipulatives, and a wonderful way for children to have their first experiences with "reading." Simple board books with brightly colored pictures and a simple, repetitive story line are best. *Brown Bear, Brown Bear What Do You See?*, *Goodnight Moon*, *The Very Hungry Caterpillar*, and *The Three Little Kittens* are all good books for babies and toddlers. Parents and your local children's librarian can point you to others, especially newly published ones or books on special topics. Kupetz and Green (1997) suggest the following guidelines:

- Read to a young child when you are in the mood to do so.
- Choose a book that is not only appropriate for the child but is also one you like.
- Remember that timing is important. A fussy baby or a busily playing toddler will not be interested in a book at that moment.
- Establish a special reading time.
- Position the child so that pictures can be seen easily. Many children enjoy sitting on a lap or cuddling next to you in an easy chair.
- Allow the child to help you, and do not worry if they turn more than one page at a time or want to start in the middle of a favorite book. One toddler, whom we both know, wanted the same book read every day literally for weeks until he had committed it to memory!
- Point to and identify things in the pictures as you read.
- React positively to the child's attempts to name objects, turn pages, and verbalize.
- Use your voice as a tool; vary pitch, speed, rhythm, even loudness. Do remember, though, that a quiet voice is often best.
- Be responsive to the children; listen to their comments.

One surefire activity of interest to children of any age is music. Simply singing can create great excitement and provides tremendous opportunities for learning. Whereas speech is unpredictable, music uses words that are the same with every repetition (even with possible minor variations). Children more easily learn the words to songs within the pattern of melody, rhythm, and rhyme, thereby enhancing their language development. Kurkjian (1990) uses a broad musical repertoire to facilitate English-language learning in her (mostly) limited English-proficient kindergarten class. According to Kurkjian, a daily ritual use of children's songs, with substitution of words, accomplishes the English teaching in this setting.

The use of concrete "props" at music time reinforces learning. There are hundreds of songs incorporating body parts and including movement components that bring forth peals of delight from the children. In the context of music, even the shy child is more readily drawn out and more willingly participates.

AWARENESS OF YOUR OWN NEEDS AS A CAREGIVER

We have taken the preponderance of this chapter to discuss elements of caregiving essential to the optimal development of very young children. Doubtless, in reading of and thinking about all these elements, you have wondered if and why children ever turn out all right. How can any caregiver provide enough, yet not too much, essential nurturance for good outcomes? Amidst wondering all this, you might wonder "What about me as the provider? How can I take care of myself?"

The child care profession is notorious for low wages, long hours, and difficult assignments. Historically, providers have received little respect, few benefits, and not much money.

Although everyone talks about children representing the future, children can be the first losers in times of economic hardship. Although the importance of the early years are widely acknowledged, we see poor allocation of resources to early childhood endeavors.

Fortunately, in recent years, more effort has gone into the area of early childhood development, the provision of child care, and the education of our children in the early years. Also fortunately, the profession of early childhood education is increasingly espoused by informed, educated, and intelligent providers. It is essential that we view ourselves as professionals, that we present ourselves to the world as professionals, and that we expect to be accepted as equals in a world of professionals. In order to accomplish this, we must first learn to value ourselves.

In your relationships with parents and coworkers, believe in your professional status and behave accordingly. Making yourself knowledgeable, keeping yourself interested, treating your infant charges and their parents as well as your coworkers sensitively and ethically will reap great rewards for you in how all these people respond to you in turn. Continue to educate yourself not only by participating in classes and reading but by remaining open to the different experiences of the different families in your center, the individual children, and the other staff members. A willingness to be aware of different needs and different capabilities in those around you is a hallmark of professionalism.

In the course of each day, as well as in a global sense, we as caregivers must learn also to take care of ourselves. Just as the infants must be given opportunities to balance activity with periods of rest, the providers must have opportunities to make choices in their activities, locations, and levels of stimulation. There are countless activities that potentially enhance any given domain of development. As the caregiver, select the one you can enjoy for that day. Children understand that the needs of their caregivers vary. They can (to a limited extent) moderate their levels of noise, activity, and curiosity if they understand that these conflict with the needs of their caregiver.

Perhaps most importantly, take your responsibilities seriously, but do not take responsibility for those elements of your job that you cannot change. Most every child care center has dysfunctional families in attendance. Every center has its own challenges internally. Part of being a professional is the recognition of these challenges, the willingness to work to resolve what is in your power to change, and the ability to accept those aspects that are not changeable.

Consistent Care

For the babies themselves, consistent and responsive care is more complicated. If possible, infants should have the same caregiver for most of their time in child care. If it is absolutely necessary to have multiple caretakers, the child should be well acquainted with any secondary caregivers before her primary caregiver leaves. Any person(s) involved with a group of children should have a thorough familiarity with the facility, its policies, and any program components.

Regular, routine care is essential for infants. Routines provide comfort and security for children, especially the very young. Learning and positive growth experiences are only possible when stress is at a minimum, and routine reduces stress for children. This does not mean that we should avoid novelty entirely! However, novel situations should occur in a context of predictability.

One of the most essential predictable elements must be that caregivers respond to the needs of the infants. Most early childhood experts agree that it is impossible to "spoil" a child before six months to a year of age (Bowlby, 1982; Elkind & Weiner, 1978; Spock & Rothenburg, 1992; White, 1975). White does "not believe you can spoil a baby in the first seven months of life." In fact, he strongly suggests, "you respond to your baby's crying in a natural way." Elkind and Weiner (1978) cite research studies indicating "that parents who respond to their infants' cries are likely to provide conditions of warmth and nurturance that will stop the crying, enable their children to feel secure, and make them less likely to cry or demand unreasonable attention in the future." They go on to contrast the children of unresponsive parents, who tend to fuss and cry a great deal later on. "Babies whose cries are heard and responded to promptly and with loving care tend to become relatively undemanding, easily satisfied, and well-behaved infants." Bowlby (1982) talks about spoiling in relation to attachment. He states,

> . . . no harm comes to [the child] when [the mother] gives him as much of her presence and attention as he seems to want. Thus, in regard to mothering—as to food—a young child seems to be so made that, if from the first he is permitted to decide, he can satisfactorily regulate his own "intake."

To echo these experts, a caregiver should respond promptly to calls for attention, attempt to discover the cause of discomfort or need, and if there is no serious problem, comfort the child. Only if she clearly cannot make an effective intervention after trying the above should she allow a young infant to "cry it out" (White, 1975).

For older children, too, responsiveness can only assist in nurturing a positive developmental outcome. The basic sense of trust comes out of having one's needs taken seriously and having them responded to appropriately. Not only will responsive care create trust for the caregiver, but also the child will feel valued and validated, resulting in a positive sense of self-esteem. Elkind, in a 1989 conference in Sacramento on "The Hurried Child," pointed out that the best way to prepare a child to face hardship is to provide a loving, nurturing environment in which she can develop self-esteem and trust in her caregivers.

Positive nurturance has even been found to affect physical growth. Caplan and Caplan (1979) note:

> All children need the security of knowing that they are satisfactory, that they are loved and valued (without any reservations). Interest, attention, praise, comfort, assurance—none of these slows down the growth process, and of themselves, none will spoil a child.

Responsive care does not apply only to the crying infant. It is equally important for the exploring, curious, learning child. Thus, responsiveness also applies to awareness of developmental level; current level of functioning; and knowledge of appropriate tasks, objects, and expectations for given ages.

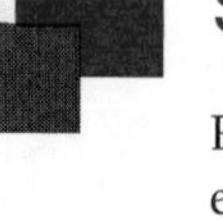

SAFETY

Probably the first element parents look for in a care situation is safety. Every parent and provider has heard countless times of the importance of childproofing their space. Gerber (1971) advocates total noninterference with infants' exploration whenever possible, and this is possible, she says, only by providing a totally safe, childproof environment geared to the developmental levels of the children.

Among the essential considerations in childproofing are:

- Dangerous objects are not present or are locked up; these objects include sharp or breakable items, chemicals (drugs, cleansers, cosmetics), plastic bags, balloons, or other items that can cause suffocation. Furniture is sturdy, and bookcases are fastened to the wall so that the children learning to walk will not pull them down on themselves when using them for support or when attempting to climb them.
- Electrical sockets are plugged with childproof inserts; electrical appliances cannot be pulled down or turned on by children.
- Heaters are safe to walk on or touch, or are covered with a safety grate.
- Windows and doors are latched with childproof latches.
- The facility is clean and well maintained; rugs are fastened down and regularly vacuumed.
- Staff do not drink coffee or other hot liquids that can spill on children or that children can consume.
- Staff are vigilant about activities of children rather than conversing among themselves.
- Caregivers are aware of health hazards and infectious diseases, and take routine steps to minimize the spread of illness. It is an undervalued health fact that merely washing hands each time a diaper is changed or a nose wiped can cut illness (or exposure to illness) by over 75 percent. Regularly wiping door knobs, washing toys, and minimizing the use of baby bottles in the play area can likewise cut illness for both providers and children.
- Awareness of contagious illnesses and their symptoms must also be exercised by staff, with rigid guidelines for attendance by children exhibiting those symptoms.
- Lists of toxic plants should be readily available, particularly if the center has either indoor or outdoor plants within children's reach.
- Lists of parent emergency numbers, paramedics, and poison control centers should be posted in locations readily available and known to staff. Emergency treatment consent forms must be on file for each child, with guidelines about parental preferences.
- Lists of child allergies (if any) and medical conditions should also be readily available and visible to staff.
- Food service should take into consideration potential spoilage of dairy products if left unrefrigerated or if mixed with even miniscule amounts of saliva.

SUMMARY

In this chapter, we discussed why there is a need for quality infant and toddler care. We also mentioned some of the characteristics of quality programs. The research tends to reveal more positive outcomes of early care, especially regarding later social adjustment, and cognitive and language development.

Infant and toddler center routines and procedures depend on the philosophy and physical setting. Every center has guidelines for the caregivers' behaviors. Knowing guidelines and fitting quickly into center practice are prime student teacher goals.

Learning takes place during each child's encounter with a caregiver. Caregivers can develop many skills for the child's benefit. Many action activities and experiences planned for this age group incorporate reciprocal responses from adults and play objects. The roots of independence and verbal ability develop as do individual preferences.

HELPFUL WEB SITES

http://www.acf.hhs.gov/
U.S. Department of Health and Human Resources. Search for information on Early Head Start.

http://www.zerotothree.org
Zero to Three. Investigate their journal and other publications

http://www.naeyc.org
National Association for the Education of Young Children. Select infant and toddler readings.

http://www.whitehouse.gov/
The White House. Learn about "Good Start, Grow Smart:" The Bush Administration Early Childhood Initiative.

http://www.nccic.org
National Child Care Information Center. Find the on-line library.

SUGGESTED ACTIVITIES

A. If you have not worked in or done student teaching in an infant/toddler center, visit one for one hour. List all staff behaviors that protect children's health or safety. Report your findings to the group.

B. Research, through local licensing agencies, the number of infant/toddler programs that were licensed in the past year in your community.

C. In groups of three to four, discuss infant/toddler care for teenage parents. Decide what type of care would best suit the teenage parents in your community. Report your ideas to the class.

REVIEW

A. List three characteristics of a quality infant/toddler center.

B. Describe expected student teacher behavior during emergencies.

C. List ways a caregiver could promote learning when bathing a 15-month-old child.

D. List possible signals that indicate a child is tired.

E. Select the answer that best completes each statement.

1. The factor that may best limit the spread of infection is:
   a. periodic caregiver screening.
   b. change of room temperature.
   c. hand-washing.
   d. the use of clean sponges.
   e. the use of spray disinfectants.
2. When feeding a young child:
   a. watch for signals that indicate the child is full.
   b. make sure the child finishes a small serving.

c. he is expected to try a little of everything.
d. eat along with the child.
e. all of these.

3. Telling infants that it is time to change their diapers is:
a. ridiculous and silly.
b. difficult.
c. not important.
d. important.
e. important, but you should use baby talk.

4. An important part of student teachers' work in an infant and toddler center is:
a. recording care specifics and asking when in doubt.
b. watching first, rather than pitching right in.
c. to let the regular staff do most of the talking.
d. to move quickly and efficiently.
e. telling parents how their children are acting.

5. If an infant or toddler is using a toy incorrectly:
a. show the proper usage.
b. show you can do it correctly.
c. leave the child alone if it is not dangerous.
d. talk about the right way to use it.
e. all of these.

CASE SCENARIO

Setting: A family child care home. The caregiver, Robin, and her husband, Tom, recently bought a new split-level home so that the lower level could be devoted to her child care. Downstairs, there are two reasonably large rooms, a bathroom, and an ample storage area under the stairs for a lot of the children's toys.

The smaller of the two rooms is the infant room. Currently, Robin has seven children in her care: two babies, a one-month-old girl, a four-month-old boy, two four-year-old girls, and one five-year-old boy, Gordon, who attends an afternoon kindergarten program.

The infant room is furnished with a crib, a play pen, a carpeted area for crawling, a wind-up swing, and a mirror placed low on the wall so infants can see themselves. The room for older children is well furnished with a low table and chairs for crafts, puzzles, snacks, and so on. There is a low couch perfect for Robin to sit on for reading to the older children when the infants are sleeping. Robin has decorated the walls with the letters of the alphabet and the numbers from one to 10. She also had a local artist paint a mural of teddy bears playing on the wall by the couch. The window wall is

continues . . .

. . . continued

opposite with built-in shelves below for puzzles, small cars, and other play objects.

Outside, Robin has a large grassy fenced area with a climbing structure, a swing set, and a paved area for wheeled toys such as tricycles, wagons, and large trucks. Tom has built a playhouse and a cave-like structure, in which the children enjoy.

Gordon's mother has asked Robin whether or not she'll be able to take care of her expected baby after she's born.

"I'm really hoping you'll be able to take the new baby after it's born. Any chance one of your current children won't be here next fall? You've been so good with Gordon and I know how good you'd be with my new baby."

"I'm not sure," Robin answers, "but Gordon will be in first grade next year so he'll not be here until after school.

"The doctor says that the baby is due some time in December. Hey, did you decide to follow through on applying for accreditation?" Gordon mother queries.

"I don't think it's worth the effort for me." replies Robin. I'm always fully enrolled . For me, taking all that time and completing all that paperwork is almost too overwhelming to even think about!"

Questions for Discussion:

1. Would you want to place your own baby or toddler in Robin's family child care home?
2. Does Robin's family child care program seem like a quality one? (Check the criteria listed in this chapter to guide your response.)
3. What are your state's licensing recommendations concerning adult-child ratios in family day homes?

REFERENCES

Acredolo, L., & Goodwyn, S. (2000). *Baby minds: Brain-building games your baby will love to play.* New York: Bantam Books.

Baba, S. (Spring 2003). Diversity corner: Toilet learning in different cultures. *SMAEYC Newslink*, Newletter published by the San Mateo Association for the Education of Young Children, 2.

Bowlby, J. (1982). *Attachment and loss, 1* (2nd ed.). New York: Basic Books.

Bredekamp, S. (Ed.). (1987). *Developmentally appropriate practice in early childhood programs serving children from birth through age 8.* Washington, DC: National Association for the Education of Young Children.

Caplan, F., & Caplan, T. (1979). *Second twelve months of life.* New York: Putnam.

Carothers, L. (1990). *When young children bite—for teachers and day care workers.* Project Enlightenment handout. Wake County Public School System, Raleigh, NC.

Daniel, J. E. (1998, November). A modern mother's place is wherever her children are: Facilitating infant and toddler mothers' transitions in child care. *Young Children, 53*(6).

Da Ros, D. A., & Kovach, B. A. (1998, Fall). Assisting toddlers and caregivers during conflict resolutions: Interactions that promote socialization. *Childhood Education, 75*(1).

DeJong, L., & Cottrell, B. H. (1999, January). Designing infant child care programs to meet the needs of children born to teenage parents. *Young Children, 54*(1).

Eisenberg, A., & Murkoff, H. E. (1995, March). What to expect: Is it potty time? *Parenting.*

Elkind, D., & Weiner, B. (1978). *Development of the child.* New York: John Wiley.

Gerber, M. (1971). *Resources for infant educators.* Los Angeles: Resources for Infant Educators.

Greenberg, P. (1996, May). Do you take care of babies? *Young Children, 51*(4).

Honig, A. S. (1995, July). Singing with infants and toddlers. *Young Children, 50*(5).

Kupetz, B. N., & Green, E. J. (1997, January). Sharing books with infants and toddlers: Facing the challenges. *Young Children, 52*(2).

Kurkjian, J. (1990, March 17). Music for the young child. California Music Educators Association Conference, Oakland, CA.

Lally, J. R. (1995, November). The impact of child care policies and practices on infant/toddler identity formation. *Young Children, 51*(1).

Lapinski, S. (1996, May). Signs of intelligence. *Child, 11*(4), 46–51.

Lowman, L., & Ruhmann, L. (1998, May). Simply sensational spaces: A multi-S approach to toddler environments. *Young Children, 53*(3).

National Institute of Child Health and Human Development. (1996). Characteristics of infant child care: Factors contributing to positive caregiving. *Early Childhood Research Quarterly, 11*(3).

Raikes, H. (1996, July). A secure base for babies: Applying attachment concepts to the infant care setting. *Young Children, 51*(5).

Reinsberg, J. (1995, September). Reflections on quality infant care. *Young Children, 50*(6).

Sexton, D., Snyder, P., Sharpton, W. R., & Stricklin, S. (1993, Annual Theme Issue). Infants and toddlers with special needs and their families. *Childhood Education, 69*(5).

Spock, B., & Rothenburg, M. (1992). *Baby and child care.* New York: Dutton.

White, B. (1975). *The first three years of life.* Englewood Cliffs, NJ: Prentice-Hall.

EPILOGUE

You may be somewhat exhausted and exhilarated at this point. Finishing a student teaching training program is a tremendous accomplishment, a validation of sorts. Congratulations! Best wishes for your continued success.

The deep feelings you have experienced, the emotional highs, and perhaps lows encountered in student teaching, will remain memorable. You will look back and see your student teaching as a time of growth.

The career field needs your energy, ideas, dedication, and enthusiasm. Children await the unique teacher you have become.

APPENDIX

INTRODUCTION

The materials in the Appendix complement the materials in the chapters listed, but are auxiliary. Instructors and/or students may choose or omit as they wish.

Chapter 1

SUMMARY OF PORTFOLIO ISSUES AND QUESTIONS

The characteristics of a useful portfolio are:

A clear purpose
—To demonstrate progress toward applying competencies
—To facilitate student growth and reflection
—A supporting document for articulation purposes

Integration between course- and fieldwork
—Both processes and product are documented
—Student selected examples of applied theory
—Shows growth over time in the knowledge base

Multiple sources of information
—Attestations from instructors, supervisors, parents, and children may include evaluations
—Artifacts from courses and field experiences
—Reproductions including photographs, videos, audio tapes

Authenticity (direct link between instruction and evidence)
—A road map through the portfolio with the basis for the organization defined
—Captions describing each document, its context, and the reason for including it
—Course syllabi including objectives and transcripts

Dynamic Assessment, capturing growth and change over time
—Reproduction from each practicum, fieldwork, and student teaching experience
—Selected papers over the course of study
—Attestations

Student Ownership
—Personal statement
—Philosophy of education for young children
—Selection, with guidance, of style of organizing the portfolio as well as of the items to be included

Multiple purposes (student growth and reflection, assessment and evaluation, and program evaluation)
—Identify student strengths and weaknesses for setting goals with advisor support
—Facilitate peer support and feedback in regular portfolio sessions
—Feedback to instructors on the efficacy of instruction in a given course and in a program as a whole, particularly in the area of applying theoretical knowledge
—Tangible evidence of degree of mastery of the competencies for purposes of articulation/transfer to more advanced study; reduce needless repetition of materials
—Show degree of understanding of and experience with special needs, multicultural, and bilingual populations

From Turner, P. (Ed.). (2002). *La Ristra: New Mexico's comprehensive professional development system in early care, education, and family support.* Santa Fe, NM: Children, Youth and Families Department, State of New Mexico. Reprinted with permission.

Chapter 3

CRITERION-REFERENCED INSTRUMENT

Field-Based Assessment Competencies

The 10 areas include:

1. Child Development Principles
2. Program Planning and Curriculum Development
3. Program Implementation and Classroom Management
4. Program Administration
5. Family and Community Relations
6. Cultural Pluralism
7. Children with Exceptional Needs
8. Assessment of Children
9. Evaluation of Program Effectiveness
10. Professional Behavior

I. Child Development Principles

1) Demonstrates knowledge of various theories of development and current research that are responsive to the needs of the total child.
2) Demonstrates knowledge of children from conception through age eight, with the exception that the candidate will demonstrate more in-depth knowledge about the particular age of the children in the program.
3) Demonstrates knowledge of physical development and the forces that influence it.
4) Demonstrates knowledge of social-emotional development and the forces that influence it, including the effect of family, school, society, and culture.
5) Demonstrates knowledge of personal development and the forces that influence it.
6) Demonstrates knowledge of cognitive development, including language development and creativity, and the forces that influence it.
7) Demonstrates knowledge of the significance and influence of play behavior on the child's growth and development.

II. Program Planning and Curriculum Development
Knowledge

1) Demonstrates knowledge of child development principles in planning programs.
2) Demonstrates knowledge of factors to consider in planning an appropriate environment, indoor and outdoor, which enhances the development of children.

Application

1) Implements a curriculum based on child development principles, including the areas of (a) Large/Small Motor Activities; (b) Language Arts; (c) Science and Math; (d) Creative Arts; (e) Social Sciences; and (f) Personal Development.
2) Demonstrates the ability to work as an effective member of a team in program planning.
3) Helps provide an indoor/outdoor environment that meets the needs of young children.
4) Selects and utilizes alternate teaching techniques and curriculum materials in certain situations that would stimulate and encourage active child participation.
5) Demonstrates the ability to interpret and use collected data in planning curriculum to meet the individual needs of the child.

III. Program Implementation and Classroom Management

Knowledge

1) Demonstrates knowledge of appropriate teaching techniques in the learning environment.
2) Demonstrates knowledge of how to facilitate effective child-adult relationships.
3) Demonstrates knowledge of play as an appropriate teaching technique.
4) Recognizes the unique contributions of staff.

Application

1) Provides children opportunities for making choices in learning, problem solving, and creative activities, whenever appropriate.
2) Utilizes play as an appropriate teaching technique.
3) Plans daily schedules that include a rhythm of physical and intellectual activities.
4) Utilizes positive suggestions in adult-child and staff relations.
5) Recognizes the importance of setting limits for children appropriate to their developmental level.
6) Models teacher behavior in accordance with expectations set for the children.

IV. Program Administration

Knowledge

1) Where applicable, discusses ways in which the candidate works with a governing board.
2) Can discuss philosophy of education for young children.
3) Has knowledge of licensing regulations and guidelines.
4) Has knowledge of revenue sources and conceptualization of budget priorities related to fiscal planning.

Application

1) Implements the regulations and guidelines regarding child development program operations (e.g., health, safety, and nutrition of the teacher and children; teacher-student ratios).
2) Maintains an effective record-keeping system that includes information on required reports, child and family, and any other necessary information.
3) Utilizes an adequate handbook regarding personnel management.
4) Demonstrates ability to provide guidance and direction to coworker.
5) Coordinates staff training and development programs.
6) Recommends and participates in selection and ordering of appropriate equipment and materials within the framework of the budget.
7) Develops a suggested budget for the program in one or all areas, and assists the senior staff in establishing budget priorities.

V. Family and Community Relations

Knowledge

1) Demonstrates an understanding of the social, multicultural, and linguistically relevant patterns and parenting styles of families.

Application

1) Provides for communication with parents and community, and utilizes applicable community resources.
2) Encourages parent participation and provides opportunities for parent involvement.
3) Provides for assessment of parent needs and makes arrangements for appropriate parent education and/or utilization of available resources.

4) Provides for continuity between the child's home and school experience.
5) Utilizes a wide variety of community resources that could contribute to an effective program.
6) Provides guidance to parents regarding effective ways to meet the developmental needs of children.
7) Establishes and maintains effective channels of communication with parents, including conferencing and visitation.

VI. Cultural Pluralism

Knowledge

1) Has knowledge of cultural background and needs of target populations.
2) Discusses multicultural implications for the program with staff, parents, and community members.

Application

1) Demonstrates ability to relate to parents and children from a variety of social, cultural, ethnic, and racial backgrounds.
2) Demonstrates ability to develop in the classroom an atmosphere of interest and respect for each other's culture.
3) Provides opportunities in the classroom to help children value the similarities and differences in their cultural backgrounds.
4) Demonstrates ability to design classroom activities and materials that enable children to learn about each other's cultures.
5) Makes provisions for communicating with parents and children who have limited knowledge of English.

VII. Children with Exceptional Needs

Knowledge

1) Demonstrates knowledge of the unique needs of the exceptional child.
2) Has knowledge of various forms of handicapping conditions that have an impact on child behavior.
3) Has knowledge of the sources of information regarding the legal rights of parents of exceptional children.
4) Can discuss how to implement an Individualized Educational Plan (IEP) when the need arises. (This may be demonstrated if an exceptional child is enrolled in the program.)

Application

1) Demonstrates the ability to develop a classroom atmosphere of understanding, consideration, and respect for the handicapped children integrated into the program.
2) Provides effective and appropriate methods of mainstreaming children with special needs.
3) Demonstrates teaching techniques that reflect understanding of the child with special needs.
4) Provides facilities and curriculum materials appropriate to the child with special needs.
5) Demonstrates the ability to work with the support services available for special needs children and their families in the program.

VIII. Assessment of Children

Knowledge

1) Demonstrates knowledge of appropriate instruments and assessment techniques for infants and children, and the sources from which they may be obtained.
2) Recognizes the effect of the ethnic, linguistic, and cultural backgrounds of the children on test performance and the limitations of most currently available assessment instruments.

Application

1) Utilizes long-range and short-range assessment methods.
2) Utilizes appropriate instruments and assessment techniques for infants and children.
3) Demonstrates the ability to evaluate and report a child's progress in terms of stated objectives and philosophy.
4) Demonstrates the ability to observe objectively and record information accurately.
5) Makes an effort, whenever possible, to utilize assessment instruments and techniques that are not culturally biased.

IX. Evaluation of Program Effectiveness

Knowledge

1) Demonstrates knowledge of the purposes, principles, and practices of program evaluation with emphasis on the importance of evaluating programs for young children.

2) Demonstrates knowledge of the significant areas to be considered in program evaluation (e.g., curriculum, child motivation, peer relationships, teacher-child relationships, etc.).

Application

1) Demonstrates the ability to analyze and evaluate all program elements and the effectiveness in meeting the children's developmental needs.
2) Demonstrates the ability to evaluate the effectiveness of the program with parents.
3) Utilizes effective program evaluation techniques for both long-range and short-range evaluation.
4) Utilizes evaluation results to continually improve the program if needed and to adapt to changing needs.

X. Professional Behavior

Knowledge

1) Has knowledge of the professional standards and behavior of an early childhood teacher.
2) Understands the significance and role of professional ethics in student-teacher interactions, teacher-teacher interactions; and parent-teacher-community interactions.
3) Maintains knowledge of current information in the field of early childhood/child development education relevant to one's own professional needs.

Application

1) Continues to grow and develop professionally through coursework and continued experience.
2) Understands and performs the teaching role with professional standards and demeanor.
3) Maintains professional ethics, including but not limited to keeping the confidentiality of the child and family.
4) Demonstrates ability to work as a member of a team.
5) Demonstrates personal qualities resulting in effective functioning as a teacher of young children.
6) Uses self-evaluation on a regular basis.

Chapter 4

WHAT ARE THE PREFERRED LEARNING MODALITIES OF YOUR STUDENTS?
(Appropriate for use in elementary grades)

Test for Three Types of Learners

How do you determine whether a student is a visual, auditory, or kinesthetic learner? To give the test, you need:

1. A group of not more than 15 students because it is difficult to observe more than that number of students at one time.
2. A list of the students' names that you can mark as you observe their reactions.

V—Visual learner
A—Auditory learner
K—Kinesthetic learner

Reactions to watch for:

Visual learners will usually close their eyes or look at the ceiling as they try to recall a visual picture.

Auditory learners will move their lips or whisper as they try to memorize.

Kinesthetic learners will use their fingers to count off items or write in the air.

The student with a photographic mind will repeat things exactly in the order they are given and will be disturbed if someone changes the order.

Giving the Test

Start by telling your students that you are going to see what kind of learners they are: visual, auditory, or kinesthetic.

This test consists of pretending that the students are going to the store to get some items for you. First you will WRITE the list on the board, allowing students to watch you, but *they must not copy it*. Next, you will give them the list ORALLY; you will not write it and *neither must they*. Then you will dictate the list orally to them, and *they will write it down*.

Note: Most predominant characteristic used is a symptom. One specific test or tests where student has the highest recall is a reinforcement of his native way of learning. However, the symptoms are the prime indication.

First Presentation

1. Write the following list on the board while the students are watching. Do not let them write:

   toothpaste soap
   Kleenex comb
   stationery

   Note: For younger students, use the following list:

   pencil ice cream stamps
   toy paper

2. Allow students to view the list for approximately one minute while you observe their reactions and mark the symptoms after the students' names.
3. Erase the list.
4. Ask, "Who would like to repeat the items for me?"
5. Observe that the visual learners will wave their hands enthusiastically.
6. Call on them to recite ORALLY, one at a time. Note that after a few students have recited, a few more timid hands will go up. These usually are auditory learners who have learned the list, not from seeing it, but from hearing the list from other students.
7. As you notice a student's symptoms, mark V, A, or K after her name.

Second Presentation

1. Dictate the following list orally (no writing by either teacher or students). Repeat the dictation a second time, pausing for a moment after each item.

   folder paper rubber bands
   talcum powder nail file
   nail file or popcorn
   cough drops eraser
   shaving cream Band-Aids

2. Observe that the visual learners will close their eyes to try to see the items. The auditory learners will whisper each item as you dictate it. The kinesthetic learners will use their hands to mark off the number of items or will write the words in the air.
3. Ask, "Who would like to repeat the list?"
4. The auditory learners will be the most eager to respond, although other students will try to repeat the items you have dictated.
5. Make the appropriate notations of V, A, or K after the students' names as you observe their reactions.

Third Presentation

1. Tell the students to have pencil and paper ready to write the following list as you dictate it orally. Tell them you will not count spelling. In fact, spell any words as you dictate if you see the spelling creates a problem.

   lipstick pen
   Band-Aids soap
   razor blades or candy
   cough syrup comb
   fountain pen string

2. After you have finished dictating the list, tell the students to turn their papers over and rewrite the list. Then ask them to look at the one they have written from your dictation.
3. When they have finished rewriting the list, tell them to take another piece of paper and *write the list from memory*.

4. After they have finished, check to see which students have been able to repeat the list wholly or in part.
5. Notice that students who were unsuccessful in either the first or second presentation of the test are frequently the first ones to finish. The test may be repeated, using numbers. Most students have a different form of recall for numbers than they have for words.

Evaluation of the Test

1. A teacher will have a better understanding of the individual differences of the students.
2. The teacher can encourage the students to find their natural way of learning. "Join it—don't fight it."
3. Although all three types of learning should be developed, a student should use his natural way to learn when he is under pressure of studying for tests, and the like.

The *visual learner* should realize that while he learns fast, he can forget equally as fast. To strengthen his recall, it is good to develop the practice of writing and outlining the subject.

The *auditory learner* will benefit by use of a tape recorder. The more she hears a subject, the more recall is possible.

The *kinesthetic learner* must write to recall material learned. Outlining material is a very effective method of strengthening recall.

A photographic mind is like a polaroid camera; the picture develops fast and can fade equally as fast unless the emulsion is placed on the picture. In the learning process, the emulsion is to *write* as well as *look*. The photographic mind will often have a real problem in abstract thinking, especially in math. Seeing the picture in association with the abstraction often assists a student of this type.

Usually, a person has more than one way to learn. He may be, perhaps highly visual, fairly kinesthetic, not auditory, or any other combination. However, all three types of learning should be developed as far as possible in each student. An audio learner should try to visualize what she hears. A visual learner should try to be more attentive in lecture programs or language laboratory work. A kinesthetic learner should try to listen and to visualize, but all three need to write.

How can a teacher cover all three types of learners in one group? By presenting material in the three ways of learning.

Visual: Ability to *hear* and *write* what is *seen*.

Auditory: Ability to *recognize visually* and *write* what is *heard*.

Kinesthetic: Ability to *hear* and *visualize* what is *written*.

The Auditory Learner

1. His attention to visual tasks may be poor.
2. He seems bored or restless during silent filmstrips.
3. He attends more to sound than to the screen during films.
4. He may have poor handwriting.
5. His drawing or other artwork is poor.
6. Work copied from the board may often turn out badly.
7. He may have reversals or inversions in writing, or he may leave out whole words or parts of words.
8. He might prefer word games, riddles, and noisy or active toys and games to more visually oriented games like checkers, other board games, or puzzles.
9. He may rub his eyes or show other signs of eye problems, or complain that his eyes bother him.
10. He may do poorly on written spelling, but he may be a better speller in spelling bees.
11. He may not remember much of what he has read, and he does better on material discussed in class.
12. He may read below grade level, or below the level expected for his general ability.
13. His comprehension is probably better on oral reading than on silent reading.
14. His math errors may show consistent patterns, inattention to signs, or confusion of similar numerals.
15. He may do poorly on map activities.
16. He may not seem to observe things others comment on.
17. He may do poorly on sight words and flashcard drills.
18. He may be poor at visual word attack so that he confuses words that look similar.

19. He may do poorly on matching activities, but given the chance, will sort through a stack of photocopies for the clearest copy.
20. He probably dislikes seat work activities.
21. He may often skip words or even whole lines in reading and uses his finger as a pointer whenever possible.
22. He may enjoy memory work.
23. He may be a mumbler.
24. He may have trouble identifying "how many" without counting.
25. He seems brighter than his IQ test scores or achievement scores would lead you to believe.
26. His papers are probably poorly organized; often, he writes the answers in the wrong blank on workbook pages, or can't find where the answers go.
27. He may seem lost on material requiring a separate answer sheet.
28. He has trouble locating words in the dictionary or index and has trouble telling time.

The Visual Learner

1. She may seem to ignore verbal directions.
2. Questions or instructions must often be repeated, frequently in different words.
3. She may frequently have a "blank" expression on her face, or may seem to daydream during classes that are primarily verbal.
4. She may substitute gestures for words, or may seem, by her gestures, to be literally groping for a word.
5. She may have poor speech, in terms of either low vocabulary, poor flexibility of vocal patterns, or articulation.
6. She may watch the teacher's lips closely and may be distressed when she cannot see her face such as when she is talking while writing on the blackboard or discussing a filmstrip in a darkened room.
7. She often looks to see what everyone else is doing before following instructions.
8. She may play the TV, tape, or record player too loudly.
9. She may say "What?" or "Huh?" often.
10. She seems to misunderstand often.
11. She often speaks too loudly, though she may dislike speaking before the group or listening to others.
12. She prefers the "show" aspects of "show-and-tell" and she prefers filmstrips to tapes.
13. She may have trouble discriminating similar words or sounds that she hears. "Bill," "bell," "bull," and "ball" may all sound the same to her, and she certainly cannot discriminate "pin" from "pen."
14. She may do poorly in phonics-based activities.
15. She often can't remember information given verbally.
16. She may describe things in terms of visual stimuli and omit auditory descriptive material.
17. She prefers visual games such as board games, or active games and toys to those that involve listening or speaking.
18. Her speech may be inappropriate for her age or she may not have learned the language patterns of her home (even if the home patterns are not standard American English).
19. She may have trouble associating sounds and objects.
20. She may substitute words similar in sound or meaning for one another.
21. She seems to know few words' synonyms commonly known by children at her age or ability level.
22. She may "get lost" in role verbalizations, even the alphabet, rote counting, or memorizing her times tables.
23. She may not enjoy music as much as she enjoys artwork.
24. She may have a speech defect; if so, it is probably an articulation problem.
25. She may respond less rapidly than her peers to unusual sounds: a far-off siren, an audio source, or a musical instrument in a nearby classroom.

Motor Control

Definition: ability to control the motor or physical movement made in response to a visual, auditory, or tactile stimulus.

Fine motor control: the ability to coordinate fine motor muscles such as those required in eye-hand tasks, coloring, drawing, printing, writing, and so on.

Gross motor control: the development and awareness of large muscle activity. Most common areas of development are:

1. rolling
2. sitting
3. crawling
4. walking
5. running
6. throwing
7. jumping
8. skipping
9. dancing
10. self-identification
11. muscular strength

Resource for help: *Remediation of Learning Disabilities* by Robert E. Valett

Attention

Definition: the ability to attend to or heed the situation in which one is currently *involved.*
Characteristics of the child with an attention disability:

1. Easily distracted by noise.
2. Hyperactive— "can't sit still."
3. Gets overly excited when there is a change in daily routine.
4. Has difficulty making transitions from one activity to another.
5. Goes from one activity to another when there is "free choice."
6. Doesn't complete work.
7. Is more upset by physiological distress than other children (hunger, physical discomfort).

Directionality and Spatial Relations

Definition: the ability to know right from left, up from down, forward from backward, and directional orientation.
Characteristics of the child with directionality and spatial relations disabilities:

1. Does not know left from right.
2. May have difficulty copying.
3. Has difficulty mastering concepts dependent on correct sequence: reading, writing, mathematics (place value), geography (maps), and so on.
4. Lack of uniformity in writing and spacing.
5. Letters may be placed haphazardly on paper.
6. Shows reversals and incorrect sequencing of letters in reading and spelling.
7. May get lost easily; may often appear disoriented.
8. May not know location of parts of his body; may have difficulty putting on clothes or drawing figures accurately.

Verbal Expression

Definition: the ability to understand words, to express oneself verbally, and to articulate words clearly.
Characteristics of the child with a verbal expression disability:

1. Shy, seldom talks in class.
2. Tends to respond with one-word answers.
3. Cannot tell what has happened in a story he has just read.
4. When the child talks, he expresses few ideas.

Conceptual Skills

Definition: the ability to acquire and utilize general information from education and experience.
Characteristics of the child with conceptual skills disabilities:

1. Is unable to use concepts involving time.
2. Cannot sort pictures into categories, such as farm animals, machinery, and plants.
3. Cannot easily classify objects verbally (e.g., name all the animals you can).
4. Is unable to use concepts relating to feelings and emotional reactions of people.
5. Cannot easily determine similarities and differences existing between objects (e.g., How are a pig and a cow alike? How are they different?).

Behavior

Characteristics of the child with behavioral disabilities:

1. Aggressive, irritable, then remorseful.
2. Impulsive—lacks self-control, touches and handles things.
3. Withdraws—on the outskirts of activities.
4. Easily excitable, overreacts.
5. Erratic behavior; quick changes of emotional response.
6. Hyperactive.
7. Hypoactive.
8. Short attention span compared to peers.
9. Easily distracted by noise, color, movement, activity, detail.
10. Cannot complete work independently.
11. Inappropriate or extreme laughter, tears, anger.
12. Defensiveness: denies responsibility, argumentative about obligations, rules; overreacts to demands for compliance.
13. Shows frequent frustration, irritation, reducing ability to cope with daily tasks.
14. Requires more than usual amount of individual help and attention in order to learn.
15. Attention jumps from one thought to another.
16. Repeats verbally when no longer appropriate (perseverates).

Chapter 6

BEHAVIOR MODIFICATION

In terms of behavior modification, it is important to be objective. The term has acquired a negative connotation that is unfounded. Everyone uses behavior modification, whether it is recognized or not, from turning off the lights when children are to be quiet to planning and implementing a behavior modification plan. In any plan, there are seven steps.

1. Keep a log of observations on the child. Really look at what the child is doing. Do this at least five times a day, for at least three days in a row (see Figure AP–1).
2. Read your observations; look for patterns. Is this child predictable? Does he usually have a temper tantrum around 9:30 A.M.? Does the child often fight with another in late afternoon?
3. Look for the reinforcers of the behavior noted in your observations. Does the child misbehave in order to get attention from the adults in the room? Do friends admire the behavior?
4. Decide on a schedule of reinforcement after finding the current reinforcer.

5. Implement the new reinforcement schedule. Give it time. Many teachers fail to use a reinforcement plan for a long enough period of time. Try a minimum of two weeks to two or three months. (Behavior that has taken two or three years to develop will not change in one or two days.)
6. Keep a second log of observations. On the basis of your study of the initial observations, analyze this second series and note whether your reinforcement schedule has worked.
7. Stop your planned reinforcement schedule. See if the child goes back to the former pattern of behavior. If so, go back to the second step and start over.

Look at the second and third steps. You have completed your observations, and now you need to find the reinforcers of the observed behavior. The behavior must bring some kind of reward to the child. As the teacher, your job is to discover what the reward is.

Many student teachers fail to understand the nature of the child's reward system. You look at what an adult perceives as negative behavior (hitting another child, for example), and you may decide to institute a schedule of reinforcement or a behavior modification plan without taking that first step: understanding why the child hits.

Study Step 4, planning a reinforcement schedule. Look at the child in the sample log in Figure AP–1. Assume that the description of behavior is typical of Maria's everyday behavior.

Student Teacher: ____________________

Name of School: ________________________________ Date: ____________________

Identity Key (do NOT use real name)	Description of What Child is Doing	Time	Comments
M. – Maria T. – Teacher	M. arrives at school. Clings to mother's hand, hides behind her skirt. Thumb in mouth.	9:05	Ask T. how long M. has been coming. I bet she's new.
ST. – Student Teacher J. – Janine S. – Susie	M. goes over to puzzle rack, chooses a puzzle, goes to table. Dumps out, and works puzzle quickly and quietly. B. & Sv. come over to work puzzles they've chosen.	9:22	Her eye/hand coordination seems good.
B. – Bobby Sv. – Stevie	M. looks at them, says nothing, goes to easels, watches S. paint. S. asks M. if she wants to paint. M. doesn't answer.	9:30	I wonder why M. doesn't respond. Ask T. if M. has hearing problem.
	M. comes to snack table, sits down where T. indicates she should. Does not interact withother children at table.	10:15	Is M. ever a quiet child!
	M. stands outside of playhouse, watches S. & J. They don't ask her to join them.	10:47	She looks like she'd like to play.
	M. goes to swings, knows how to pump.	10:55	Nothing wrong with her coordination.
	During Hap Palmer record M. watches others, does not follow directions.	11:17	Hearing? Maybe limited English? (She looks of Spanish background.)

Figure AP–1 Anecdotal record form

In your analysis of the log, what do you see? Three questions have been raised: Is Maria fairly new to the school? Does she have a hearing problem? Is she bilingual or does she have limited understanding of English? The answers to these questions come during the discussion of observations. Yes, Maria is new to the school. This is only her second week. No, she does not have a hearing problem but she is bilingual. In fact, the cooperating teacher suspects that Maria may be less bilingual than her mother claims. What has reinforced Maria's behavior? First, she is unfamiliar with English. Second, her cultural background is different. Girls of Hispanic background are often expected to be quiet, helpful around the house, and obedient to their elders. Certainly, this explains Maria's behavior because she willingly helps with cleanup. What are appropriate goals for Maria? Assume that you and your cooperating teacher decide that the most appropriate goal is to help Maria feel more comfortable in the room and that adult approval is the most logical reinforcer to use. Your reinforcement schedule might start by greeting Maria at the door every day when she arrives. Smile at her and say, "Buenas dias Maria. It's nice to see you today." Take her by the hand and go with her to a different activity each day. (If Maria seems uncomfortable changing activities so often, stay with the activities she enjoys at first.) Introduce her to the other children at the activity she chooses. Take advantage of the fact that Susie is one of the more mature, self-confident children in the room, and quietly ask her to include Maria in some of her activities. Instead of allowing Maria to watch Susie paint, go to Maria with her painting smock, put it on her, and suggest that she try the activity. When she does pick up the brush and experiment with painting, compliment her action.

Do not worry about Maria's lack of knowledge of the English language. When Maria hesitates, use pointing and naming to help her. Accept the fact that Maria may always be a shy child; do not push her to be outgoing if that is not her nature.

Continue these activities each day. After a few weeks, make another set of observations. (You may not need this step; you may already see the difference.) Still, it is good practice to do the second observation just to check on your feelings. It is more than likely that Maria is already greeting you with a smile as she enters, and that she is beginning to play with Susie and some of the other more outgoing children.

Do you believe that changing Maria's behavior was easy? A more difficult example could have been chosen. However, cases like Maria's are common, and many children enjoy a period of watching and listening before joining in activities. You should become aware of these common problems in order to become sensitive about your potential power in the classroom. The word "power" is deliberately being used because, next to the parents or primary caretakers, you, as teacher, are the second most important person in the child's life. You have a tremendous potential for influencing the child.

Aggression is defined here as any intentional behavior that results in physical or mental injury to any person or animal, or in damage to or destruction of property. Aggressive actions can be accidental actions, in which there is no intentionality; instrumental actions, in which the child deliberately employs aggression in pursuit of a goal; or hostile actions, in which the child acts to cause harm to another person.

Assertion is defined here as behavior through which a child maintains and defends his or her own rights and concerns. Assertive behavior reflects the child's developing competence and autonomous functioning and represents an important form of developmental progress. Assertiveness also affords the young child a healthy form of self-defense against becoming the victim of the aggressions of others.

Cooperation is defined here as any activity that involves the willing interdependence of two or more children. It should be distinguished from compliance, which may represent obedience to rules or authority, rather than intentional cooperation. When children willingly collaborate in using materials, for example, their interactions are usually quite different than when they are told to "share."

From Jewett, J. (1992). *Aggression and cooperation: Helping young children develop constructive strategies.* ERIC Digest, EDO-PS-92-10.

Chapter 9

DEVELOPMENTAL CHECKLIST

Name: ______________________ Birth date: ______________

	Present	Date Observed
I. Infants		
3 mo. Motor Development		
Neck muscles support head steadily		
Moves arms/legs vigorously		
May move arm/leg on one side together		
On stomach, holds chest/head erect 10 seconds		
When picked up, brings body up compactly		
May bat at objects		
Reaches with both arms		
Perceptual Development		
Follows slowly moving object w/eyes and head from one side of body to other		
Looks at fingers individually		
Stops sucking to listen		
Visually seeks source of sound by turning head and neck		
Hands usually held open		
Social Development		
Smiles easily and spontaneously		
Gurgles and coos in response to being spoken to		
Responds to familiar faces with smile		
Protests when left by mother		
Cries differentially when hungry, wet, cross		
Cognitive Development		
Begins to show memory; waits for expected reward like feeding		
Begins to recognize family members and others close to her		
Explores own face, eyes, mouth with hand		
Responds to stimulation with whole body		
6 mo. Motor Development		
Rolls from back to stomach		
Turns and twists in all directions		
Gets up on hands and knees, rocks		
Creeps on stomach; may go forward and backward		
Balances well when sitting, leans forward		
Sits in chair and bounces		
Grasps dangling object		
May sit unsupported for 30 minutes		
Rolls from back to stomach		
Perceptual Development		
Holds one block, reaches for second, looks at a third		
Reaches to grab dropped object		
Coos, hums, stops crying in response to music		

		Present	Date Observed
	Likes to play with food		
	Displays interest in finger-feeding self		
	Has strong taste preferences		
	Rotates wrist to turn and manipulate objects		
	Often reaches with one arm instead of both		
	Sleeps through the night		
	Social Development		
	Prefers play with people		
	Babbles and becomes excited during active play		
	Babbles more in response to female voices		
	Vocalizes pleasure/displeasure		
	Gurgles when spoken to		
	Tries to imitate facial expressions		
	Turns in response to name		
	Smiles at mirror image		
	Disturbed by strangers		
	Cognitive Development		
	Remains alert two hours at a time		
	Inspects objects for a long time		
	Eyes direct hand for reaching		
	Likes to look at objects upside down and create change of perspective		
	May compare two objects		
	Has abrupt mood changes; primary emotions: pleasure, complaint, temper		
9 mo.	Motor Development		
	Crawls with one hand full		
	Turns while crawling		
	May crawl upstairs		
	Sits well		
	Gets self into sitting position easily		
	Pulls to standing		
	May "cruise" along furniture		
	Social Development		
	Eager for approval		
	Begins to evaluate people's moods		
	Imitates play		
	Enjoys peekaboo		
	Chooses toy for play		
	Sensitive to other children; may cry if they cry		
	May fight for disputed toy		
	Imitates cough, tongue clicks		
	Cognitive Development		
	Uncovers toy he has seen hidden		
	Anticipates reward		
	Follows simple directions		
	Shows symbolic thinking/role-play		
	May say "dada" and/or "mama"		
	Grows bored with same stimuli		

	Present	Date Observed
II. Toddlers		
12 mo. Motor Development		
Can stand, cruise, may walk		
Pivots body 90 degrees when standing		
If walking, probably prefers crawling		
May add stopping, waving, backing, carrying toys to walking		
Climbs up and down stairs, holding hand		
May climb out of crib or playpen		
Gets to standing by flexing knees, pushing from squat position		
Lowers self to sitting position with ease		
Makes swimming motions in bath		
Wants to self-feed		
May undress self		
Perceptual Development		
Reaches accurately for object as she looks away		
Puts things back together as well as takes them apart		
Builds tower of two to three blocks after demonstration		
Uses hammer and pegboard		
Likely to put one or two objects in mouth and grasp a third		
Cares for doll, teddy bear—feeding, cuddling, bathing		
Enjoys water play in bath or sink		
Social Development		
Expresses many emotions		
Recognizes emotions in others		
Gives affection to people		
Shows interest in what adults do		
May demand more help than needed because it's easier		
May refuse new foods		
Resists napping, may have tantrums		
Fears strange people, places		
Reacts sharply to separation from mother		
Distinguishes self from others		
Cognitive Development		
Perceives objects as detached and separate to be used in play		
Unwraps toys		
Finds hidden object, remembers where it last was		
Remembers events		
Groups a few objects by shape and color		
Identifies animals in picture books		
Responds to directions		
Understands much of what is said to him		
Experiments with spatial relationships: heights, distances		
Stops when "no" is said		
Points to named body part		
18 mo. Motor Development		
Walks well, seldom falls		
Sits self in small chair		
Walks up/down stairs one step at time holding hand of adult or rail		

		Present	Date Observed
	Enjoys push toys		
	Likes to push furniture		
	Enjoys pull toys		
	Enjoys riding toys to propel with feet on ground		
	Strings large beads with shoelace		
	Takes off shoes and socks		
	Swings rhythmically in time to music		
	Follows one- or two-step directions		
	Perceptual Development		
	Demonstrates good eye-hand coordination with small manipulatives		
	Will look at picture book briefly, turns pages but not one at a time		
	Enjoys small objects she can manipulate		
	Social Development		
	Makes distinction between "mine" and "yours"		
	Makes social contact with other children		
	Smiles and looks at others		
	May begin to indicate what he wants by talking, pointing, grunting, body language		
	Cognitive Development		
	Plays with blocks, can build tower of two to three blocks without model		
	Can sort by colors, shapes (if exposed)		
	Remembers where she put a toy even if the next day		
III. Two-Year-Olds			
	Gross Motor		
2.0 yrs.	Runs well without falling		
	Kicks ball without overbalancing		
	Stairs: goes up/down alone two feet per step		
	Jumps from first step, one foot leading		
	Stops when running to change direction		
	Propels self on wheeled toy with feet on floor		
	Catches large ball by body trapping		
	Jumps eight inches to 14 inches		
2.6 yrs.	Walks several steps tiptoe		
	Walks several steps backwards		
	Walks upstairs alternating feet		
	Stands on balance beam without assistance		
	Throws objects and tracks visually		
	Bounces ball, catches with both hands		
	Bends at waist to pick up object from floor		
	Jumps over string two inches to eight inches high		
	Fine Motor		
2.0 yrs.	Turns knob on TV, toys		
	Turns door knobs, opens door		
	Builds three- to five-block tower		
	Holds pencil in fist		
	Scribbles, stays on paper		
	Puts ring on stick		

		Present	Date Observed
	Strings one-inch beads		
	Puts small objects into container		
	Paints with whole arm movement		
	Folds paper in half		
2.6 yrs.	Removes jar lids		
	Builds seven- to nine-block tower		
	Completes simple inset puzzle		
	Traces circle		
	Paints with wrist action		
	Uses spoon without spilling		
	Holds glass, cup with one hand		
	Makes small cuts in paper with scissors		
	Places six pegs in pegboard		
Language and Speech			
Receptive:			
	Understands most commonly used nouns and verbs		
	Responds to two-part command		
	Enjoys simple storybooks		
	Points to common objects when they are named		
	Understands functions of objects (e.g., cup-drink)		
	Understands 200 to 400 words		
Expressive:			
	Verbalizes own actions		
	Uses two- to three-word phrases		
	Asks what and where questions		
	Makes negative statements		
	Labels action in pictures		
	Approximately 50-word vocabulary (two years.)		
	Answers questions		
Speech Sounds:			
	Substitutes some consonant sounds (e.g., *w* for *r*, *d* for *th*)		
	Articulates all consonants with few deviations, *p*, *b*, *m*, *w*, *h*, *k*, *g*, *n*, *t*, *d*		
Psychosocial Skills			
	Sees self as separate person		
	Conscious of possessions—"mine"		
	Shy with strangers		
	Knows gender identity		
	Watches others, may join in play		
	Begins to use dramatic play		
	Helps put things away		
	Participates in small-group activity (sings, claps, dances)		
	Says "no" frequently, obeys when asked		
	Understands and stays away from common dangers		
Cognitive Skills			
	Responds to three-part command		
	Selects and looks at picture books		
	Given three items, can associate which two go together		

		Present	Date Observed
	Recognizes self in mirror		
	Uses toys symbolically		
	Imitates adult actions in dramatic play		
	Self-Help Skills		
	Can undress self		
	Can partially dress self		
	Gains mastery over toilet needs		
	Can drink from fountain		
	Washes/dries hands with assistance		
IV. Three-Year-Olds			
	Gross Motor		
3.0 yrs.	Runs smoothly		
	Stairs: walks down, alternating feet		
	Climbs ladder on play equipment		
	Throws tennis ball three feet		
	Pedals tricycle		
	One or two hops on dominant foot		
	Can make sharp turns while running		
	Balances briefly on dominant foot		
3.6 yrs.	Stands on either foot briefly		
	Hops on either foot		
	Jumps over objects—six inches		
	Pedals tricycle around corners		
	Walks forward on balance beam several steps		
	Fine Motor		
3.0 yrs.	Uses one hand consistently in most activities		
	Strings 1/2-inch beads		
	Traces horizontal/vertical lines		
	Copies/imitates circles		
	Cuts six-inch paper into two pieces		
	Makes cakes/ropes of clay		
3.6 yrs.	Winds up toy		
	Completes five- to seven-piece inset puzzle		
	Sorts dissimilar objects		
	Makes ball with clay		
	Language and Speech		
Receptive:			
	Understands size and time concepts		
	Enjoys being read to		
	Understands "if, then, and because" concepts		
	Carries out two to four related directions		
	Understands 800 words		
	Responds to questions		
Expressive:			
	Gives full name		
	Knows sex and can state girl or boy		
	Uses three- to four-word phrases		
	Uses /-*s* on nouns to indicate plurals		

		Present	Date Observed
	Uses /-*ed* on verbs to indicate past tense		
	Repeats simple songs, fingerplays		
	Speech is 70 percent to 80 percent intelligible		
	Vocabulary of over 500 words		
	Speech Sounds:		
	f, *y*, *z*, *ng*, *wh*		
	Psychosocial Skills		
	Joins in interactive games		
	Shares toys		
	Takes turns (with assistance)		
	Enjoys sociodramatic play		
	Cognitive Skills		
	Matches six colors		
	Names one color		
	Counts two blocks		
	Counts by rote to 10		
	Matches pictures		
	Classifies objects by physical attributes, one class at a time (e.g., color, shape, size)		
	Stacks blocks or rings in order of size		
	Knows age		
	Asks questions for information (why and how)		
	Can "picture read" a story book		
	Self-Help Skills		
	Pours well from small pitcher		
	Spreads soft butter with knife		
	Buttons and unbuttons large buttons		
	Blows nose when reminded		
	Uses toilet independently		
V. Four-Year-Olds			
	Gross Motor		
4.0 yrs.	Stairs: walks down, alternating feet, holding rail		
	Stands on dominant foot five seconds		
	Gallops		
	Jumps 10 consecutive times		
	Walks sideways on balance beam		
	Catches beanbag thrown from a distance of three feet		
	Throws two beanbags into wastebasket, underhand, from distance of three feet		
	Hops on preferred foot distance of one yard		
4.6 yrs.	Walks forward on line, heel-toe, two yards		
	Stands on either foot for five seconds		
	Walks upstairs holding object in one hand without holding the rail		
	Walks to rhythm		
	Attempts to keep time to simple music with hand instruments		
	Turns somersault (forward roll)		
	Fine Motor		
4.0 yrs.	Builds 10- to 12-block tower		

		Present	Date Observed
	Completes three- to five-piece puzzle, not inset		
	Draws person with arms, legs, eyes, nose, mouth		
	Copies a cross		
	Imitates a square		
	Cuts a triangle		
	Creases paper with fingers		
	Cuts on continuous line		
4.6 yrs.	Completes six- to 10-piece puzzle, not inset		
	Grasps pencil correctly		
	Copies a few capital letters		
	Copies triangle		
	May copy square		
	Cuts curved lines and circles with 1/4-inch accuracy		
Language and Speech			
Receptive:			
	Follows three unrelated commands		
	Understands sequencing		
	Understands comparatives: big, bigger, biggest		
	Understands approximately 1,500 words		
Expressive:			
	Has mastery of inflection (can change volume and rate)		
	Uses sentences with five or more words		
	Uses adjectives, adverbs, conjunctions in complex sentences		
	Speech about 90 percent to 95 percent intelligible		
Speech Sounds:			
	s, *sh*, *r*, *ch*		
Psychosocial Skills			
	Plays and interacts with others		
	Dramatic play is closer to reality with attention paid to time and space		
	Plays dress-up		
	Shows interest in sex differences		
	Plays cooperatively		
	May have imaginary playmates		
	Shows humor by silly words and rhymes		
	Tells stories, fabricates, rationalizes		
	Goes on errands outside home		
Cognitive Skills			
	Points to and names four colors		
	Draws, names, and describes picture		
	Counts three or four objects with correct pointing		
	Distinguishes between day and night		
	Can finish opposite analogies (brother = boy; sister = girl)		
	Names a penny in response to "What is this?"		
	Tells which of two is bigger, slower, heavier		
	Increased concepts of time; can talk about yesterday, last week, today, and tomorrow		
	Cuts easy food with knife		
	Laces shoes (does not tie)		

		Present	Date Observed
	Buttons front buttons		
	Washes and dries face without help		
	Brushes teeth without help		
	Toilets self, manages clothes by self		
VI. Five-Year-Olds			
	Gross Motor		
5.0 yrs.	Stands on dominant foot 10 seconds		
	Walks backward toe to heel six steps		
	Walks downstairs carrying object without holding rail		
	Skips		
	Jumps three feet		
	Hops on dominant foot two yards		
	Walks backward on balance beam		
	Catches ball with two hands		
	Rides small bike with training wheels		
5.6 yrs.	Stands on either foot 10 seconds		
	Walks backward two yards		
	Jumps rope		
	Gallops, jumps, runs in rhythm to music		
	Roller skates		
	Rides bicycle without training wheels		
	Fine Motor		
5.0 yrs.	Opens and closes large safety pin		
	Sews through holes in sewing card		
	Opens lock with key		
	Completes twenty- to twenty-five-piece puzzle, not inset		
	Draws person with head, trunk, legs, arms,hands, eyes, nose, mouth, hair, ears, fingers		
	Colors within lines		
	Cuts cardboard and cloth		
5.6 yrs.	Builds Tinkertoy structure		
	Copies first name		
	Copies rectangle		
	Copies triangle		
	Prints numerals 1 to 5		
	Handedness well-established		
	Pastes and glues appropriately		
	Cuts out paper dolls, pictures from magazine		
	Language and Speech		
Receptive:			
	Demonstrates preacademic skills such as following directions and listening		
Expressive:			
	Few differences between child's use of language and adults'		
	Can take turns in conversation		
	May have some difficulty with noun-verb agreement and irregular past tenses		
	Communicates well with family, friends, and strangers		
Speech Sounds:			
	Can correctly articulate most simple consonants and many digraphs		

	Present	Date Observed
Psychosocial Skills		
Chooses own friends		
Plays simple table games		
Plays competitive games		
Engages in sociodramatic play with peers, involving group decisions, role assignment, fair play		
Respects others' property		
Respects others' feelings		
Cognitive Skills		
Retells story from book with reasonable accuracy		
Names some letters and numbers		
Uses time concepts of yesterday and tomorrow accurately		
Begins to relate clock time to daily schedule		
Uses classroom tools such as scissors and paints meaningfully		
Draws recognizable pictures		
Orders a set of objects from smallest to largest		
Understands why things happen		
Classifies objects according to major characteristics (e.g., apples and bananas can both be eaten)		
Self-Help Skills		
Dresses self completely		
Ties bow		
Brushes teeth unassisted		
Crosses street safely		
Dries self after bathing		
Brushes hair		
Ties shoes without assistance		
VII. Six-Year-Olds		
Walks with ease		
Runs easily, turns corners smoothly		
Gallops		
Skips		
Jumps rope well		
Throws overhand, shifts weight from back to front foot		
Walks length of balance beam:		
forward		
backward		
sideways		
Rides bicycle		
Uses all playground equipment:		
swings self		
uses merry-go-round		
climbs dinosaur climber		
swings by arms across ladder		
Writes name, address, phone number		
Reads *I Can Read* books		
Can count to 100		
Can retell story after having read it		
Understands concept of numbers 1–10		

	Present	Date Observed
Understands concept of one more, one less		
Can complete simple arithmetic problems (addition and subtraction)		
Can write simple story		
Can illustrate story appropriately		
Plays cooperatively with others		
Stands up for self		
VIII. Seven-Year-Olds		
Performs all gross motor skills well except for mature overhand ball throwing		
Knows when to lead and follow		
Knows what he does well		
Knows when to ask for help		
Can draw diamond		
Draws house with straight chimney		
Enjoys card games such as Rummy, Crazy 8's, Hearts, Old Maid		
Enjoys organized sports activities such as kickball, soccer, baseball, track, swimming		
Enjoys reading		
Enjoys games such as checkers, Parcheesi		
Willing to tackle new problems		
Eats well-balanced diet		
Solid peer relations		
Is responsible		
Writes legibly		
Can articulate most speech sounds without distortion or substitution		
IX. Eight-Year-Olds		
Able to use mature overhand ball throw		
If given opportunity for practice, can perform all gross motor skills well, including the mature overhand ball throw		
Enjoys organized sports activities, may want to play on a team		
Is developing a sense of industry, an "I can do" attitude		
Knows what she can do well and when she needs help		
Enjoys reading		
Enjoys games with rules		
Is able to master pronunciation of all phonemes and most graphemes of the English language		
Enjoys word-play games such as puns and double entendre		
Has solid peer relationships		
Is able to assume responsibility for own actions		
Willing to try out new activities		
X. Nine-Year-Olds		
In addition to characteristics of eight-year-olds, nine-year-olds are usually solidly in the Piagetian stage of concrete operations. As such, they: Can master all arithmetic operations		
Understand concepts of reversibility		
Can think logically if provided with concrete situations and/or manipulatives		
Are able to conserve mass, length, area, weight, among other operations		
Can form classification hierarchies		
Are able to transfer learning from one situation to another		

	Present	Date Observed
Physically, some nine-year-olds, especially girls, may be entering a growth spurt characterized by rapid long-bone growth		
Some early development of secondary sex characteristics also possible		
Language develpment sees: Understanding of negatively worded questions such as "The only factor *not* in the sequence of events . . ." "Which one of the following is *not* . . ." and double-pronoun referrents such as "She baked her the birthday cake." "He accidentally hit him with the ball."		
Socially, nine-year-olds: Enjoy the company of their peers		
Often group into informal "clubs"		

Chapter 10

Individual Learning Plan for Alan

1. Activity title: Watching a Live Bird
2. Curriculum area: Science and language arts (vocabulary)
3. Materials needed: Live bird in cage. Table or counter for cage.
4. Location and setup of activity: Birdcage with parakeet will be set up in corner of room where two counters come together. This will keep cage safer than if placed on a table, and the counter is at eye level for children so they can see easily.
5. Number of children and adults: Alan and student teacher.
6. Preparation: Talk about pets with Alan. (Ask him what pet he has. I know he has a dog and two cats.) Ask him if he knows what a bird is. Tell him I am going to have a surprise for him.
7. Specific behavioral objective: Alan will watch the parakeet for at least three minutes. He will be able to call the bird a parakeet and say its name, Ernie. (Long-range objective could be to have Alan feed the bird and give him water.)
8. Developmental skills necessary for success: Willingness to watch and listen quietly.
9. Procedure: When Alan comes to school Tuesday, greet him at door; remind him about the surprise you promised. Take his hand; lead him to corner where birdcage is sitting. Ask Alan if he knows what is in the cage. Anticipate that he will know "bird." Tell him that this bird is called a parakeet and that the bird's name is Ernie. Ask him to repeat "parakeet" and "Ernie." Ask him what color Ernie is. Anticipate that he knows the color green. If he doesn't say green, remind him that Ernie is green. See what else is green and remind Alan that he knows what color green is: green like the grass, for example, or green like Tony's shirt.
10. Discussion: Covered under Step 9, "Procedure."
11. Apply: Later in the day, ask Alan what kind of bird Ernie is. Ask him Ernie's name. (I anticipate that Alan will be intrigued with the bird and that he will want to come back over and over to watch Ernie, if only for a minute or two. Each time, I will name the type of bird and repeat Ernie's name. I think Alan will know both "parakeet" and "Ernie" before he goes home.)
12. Cleanup: Not necessary. I will keep the birdcage cleaned.
13. Terminating statement: Probably not necessary. Otherwise, I'll remind Alan that Ernie is a parakeet and suggest that he might want to see a book about birds (I've brought several in) or play the lotto game.
14. Transition: See #13.
15. Evaluation—Activity, Teacher, Child: I am hoping, of course, that this will be a great success for all the children but especially for Alan. I'll write the evaluation after Ernie is brought in.

GLOSSARY

A

accommodation—according to Jean Piaget, one form of adaptation, which takes place when an existing concept is modified or a new concept is formed to incorporate new information or a new experience.

accreditation—"the granting of approval to an institution of learning by an official review board after the school has met specific requirements." (The American Heritage Dictionary, 2nd College Edition. (1982). Boston, MA: Houghton Mifflin.)

active listening (with adults)—the process of putting into your own words a message you received from another based on your understanding of what you thought you heard.

active listening (with children)—Thomas Gordon's term for the technique of reflecting back to children what they have said as a way to help them find their own solutions to problems.

affective—caused by or expressing emotion or feeling.

aggression—behavior deliberately intended to hurt others.

allergies—physiological reactions to environmental or food substances that can affect or alter behavior.

anecdotal records—methods of observation involving written "word pictures" of an event or behavior usually; short accounts of incidents or events of an interesting nature.

anxiety—a general sense of uneasiness that cannot be traced to a specific cause.

assertive discipline—a form of behavior management used primarily in elementary schools. The consequences of behavior are clearly stated, understood by children, and consistently applied.

assessment—the act of appraising, judging or evaluating another's efforts, performance, or actions.

assimilation—according to Jean Piaget, one form of adaptation, which takes place when the person tries to make new information or a new experience fit into an existing concept.

assistant teacher—also called aide, helper, auxiliary teacher, associate teacher, or small group leader; works under the guidance of the head teacher in providing a quality program.

Association for Childhood Education International (ACEI)—professional organization that focuses on issues of children from infancy to early adolescence, including those involving international and intercultural concerns.

associative play—according to Parten, one child playing next to another and using the same materials, but each working independently of the other.

at-risk children—because of adverse environmental factors, for instance, poverty or low birth weight, children considered at risk for developmental delay and/or for doing poorly in school.

attachment—the child's bond with a teacher established over time in personal interactions.

attention deficit disorder (ADD)—It causes children to have difficulty in sustaining attention in the classroom and in concentrating on an assigned task for any length of time.

attention deficit with hyperactivity disorder (ADHD)— Like ADD, it causes attention problems as well as an inability to sit still and concentrate for very long. Children with ADHD are said to "bounce off the walls."

authoritative—substantiated, supported, and accepted by most professionals in the field of early childhood education or having an air of authority.

authoritarian—requiring obedience and exercising control over others.

autonomy—the second stage of development described by Erik Erikson, occurring during the second year of life, in which toddlers assert their growing motor, language, and cognitive abilities by trying to become more independent.

B

balanced curriculum—a curriculum that takes into consideration and reflects a broad spectrum of cognitive, physical, socioemotional, linguistic, and creative development opportunities for young children. It attempts to neither slight nor sacrifice one developmental area for another.

behavior management—behavioral approach to guidance holding that the child's behavior is under the control of the environment, which includes space, objects, and people.

behavior modification—the systematic application of principles of reinforcement to modify behavior.

behaviorism—a theoretical viewpoint, espoused by theorists such as B. F. Skinner, who believe that behavior is shaped by environmental forces, specifically in response to reward and punishment.

biases—particular tendencies or inclinations, especially ones that prevent impartial consideration; prejudices.

bibliotherapy—the use of books that deal with emotionally sensitive topics in a developmentally appropriate way to help children gain accurate information and learn coping strategies.

bilingual—ability to use two languages.

C

career lattice—recognizes that the early childhood profession is made up of individuals with varied backgrounds; a lattice allows for both horizontal and vertical movement among positions, with accompanying levels of education, experience, responsibility, and pay.

case study—an in-depth study of a child that involves several days of observation at differing times during the day and the use of several different types of observation forms.

certification—the process by which an entity, agency, or association grants professional recognition to an individual who has met certain predetermined qualifications specified by that agency or association.

checklist—a method of evaluating children or teachers that consists of a list of behaviors, skills, concepts, or attributes that the observer checks off as a child or teacher is observed to have mastered the item.

child abuse—any action or inaction that harms a child or puts that child at risk.

Child Development Associate (CDA)—an early childhood teacher who has been assessed and successfully proven competent through the national CDA credentialling program.

classifications—according to Piaget, the child's ability to arrange similar and dissimilar objects into complex hierarchies.

classroom management—consists of supervising, planning, and directing classroom activities and the room environment. It also involves making time length decisions, providing appropriate direction, and guiding child behavior to enable children to live and work effectively with others.

clinical supervision—a process of teacher assessment that generally includes a pre-conference, observation, and a post-conference whose goal is to determine whether the teacher or student teacher has followed through with the focus discussed in the preconference.

code of ethics—agreed-upon professional standards that guide behavior and facilitate decision making in working situations.

cognitive—the process of mental development, concerned more with how children learn than with the content of what they know.

cognitive developmental theory—the theory formulated by Jean Piaget that focuses on how children's intelligence and thinking abilities emerge through distinct stages.

collaboration—a desire or need to create or discover something new, while thinking and working with others. It is a process of joint decision making. It involves: discussion, different views and perspectives, shared goals, building new shared understandings, and perhaps the creation of a new outlook or course of action.

communication—giving or receiving information, signals and/or messages.

competencies—the knowledge and skills desirable in education professionals working in various staffing positions in early childhood care.

computer literacy—familiarity with and knowledge about computers.

concrete operational stage—Piaget's period covering the elementary school years.

confidentiality—requirement that results of evaluations and assessments be shared with only the parents and appropriate school personnel.

conflict resolution—promoting child-child, or child-adult problem solving through verbal interactions, negotiation, compromise, and use of acceptable physical tactics. It may include teacher support and assistance.

congruent—refers to the similarity of what a person (the sender) is thinking and feeling, and what that person communicates; behaving/acting in a state of agreement with or reflection of inner feelings and/or values.

conservation—ability to recognize that objects remain the same in amount despite perceptual changes, usually acquired during the period of concrete operations.

constructivist theory—a theory, such as that of Jean Piaget, based on the belief that children construct knowledge for themselves rather than having it conveyed to them by some external source.

cooperative play—according to Parten, two children using the same materials and working on the same project.

cultural background—the context of one's life experience as shaped by membership in groups based on ethnicity, race, socio-economic status, gender, exceptionalities, language, religion, sexual orientation, and geographical location.

curriculum—an overall master plan of an early childhood instructional program reflecting the schools' philosophy. Consistent with a school's mission statement and goals.

D

developmentally appropriate instruction—educational practice that reflects the importance of meaningful and contextually relevant experiences for children that are based on a knowledge of attending children, their social and cultural context, and how children develop and learn.

Developmentally Appropriate Practice in Early Childhood Programs (DAP)—guidelines developed by the National Association for the Education of Young Children as a response to the growing trend toward more formal, academic instruction of young children. The primary position of the guidelines is that programs designed for young children should be based on what is known about young children's development. DAP also reflects a clear commitment regarding the rights of young children to respectful and supportive learning environments and to education preparing them for participation in a free and democratic society.

didactic—often applied to teaching materials, indicating a built-in intent to provide specific instruction.

discipline—generally considered a response to children's misbehavior.

discovery areas or centers—classroom areas specifically designed and equipped for child exploration, discovery, play, creativity or another educational opportunity.

dispositions—the values, commitments, and professional ethics that influence behaviors toward students, families, colleagues, and communities and affect children's learning, motivation, and development as well as the educator's own professional growth.

distance learning—a formal educational process in which the major portion of the instruction occurs when the learner and the instructor are not usually in the same place at the same time.

diversity—differences among groups of people and individuals based on ethnicity, race, socioeconomic status, gender, exceptionalities, language, religion, sexual orientation, geographic area or any other characteristic

early childhood practitioner—a specifically trained professional who works with children from infancy to age eight. May also be called a teacher or educator.

eclectic—describing an approach in which various desirable features from different theories or methods are selected; drawing elements from different sources.

emergent curriculum—planning based upon the daily lives of children with specific attention given to changing interests and needs.

emergent model—a program of instruction, based on child, parent, teacher, or community interests or concerns, in which there is a logical sequence of study using interconnected activities and experiences.

empowering—helping parents and children gain a sense of control over events in their lives.

equilibriation—according to Jean Piaget, the state of balance each person seeks between existing mental structures and new experiences.

ethics—a set of moral principles or values that serves as the basis for conscientious, sound, professional decision-making or judgments.

event sampling—a method of observation in which the observer records a specific behavior only when it occurs.

family child care homes—child care for young children located in a private, licensed home.

feedback—information given and deemed to be a true and accurate account of what happened. May be evaluated as positive, negative, or otherwise by the informant or listener.

field independent—a child who works independent of distractions in the surrounding environment; a child who is self-motivated and self-monitoring.

field sensitive—a child who needs encouragement from the teacher and peers for motivation, who does not trust himself, and who looks for reassurance from others.

flexible—willing to yield, modify, or adapt; change or create in a positive, productive manner.

formal operational stage—Piaget's period covering adolescence.

Formative evaluation—ongoing assessment to ensure that planned activities and methods accomplish what the teacher intended.

games—according to Piaget, playing according to a set of rules.

generalist—a person whose knowledge, aptitudes, and skills are applied to a field (occupation) as a whole.

gifted children—children who perform significantly above average in intellectual. creative, and other performance areas.

goals—overall, general overviews of what children are expected to gain from the program.

group times—also called circle or story times; time blocks during the day when all of the children and teachers join together in a common activity.

guidance—ongoing process of directing children's behavior based on the types of adults children are expected to become.

home visit—a one-on-one interaction between the teacher and the parent(s) of the child that takes place in the child's home.

I

"I" messages—Thomas Gordon's term for a response to a child's behavior that focuses on how the adult feels rather than on the child's character.

ideals—representing ones opinion of exemplary or desirable behavior.

identity formation—the way in which a young child separates from his parents and establishes his or her own character traits and personality.

idiosyncratic—a characteristic peculiar to an individual.

Indiviual Education Program (IEP)—with special needs children, an individual education program that states the short-term and long-term learning objectives, how they will be accomplished and by whom, and applicable dates. It must be approved by both parents and school.

ignoring—a principle of behavior management that involves removing all reinforcement for a given behavior to eliminate that behavior.

inclusion—a term that has widely replaced the term "mainstreaming" and that emphasizes placement of the special needs child in the regular classroom with, perhaps, greater assistance from special education services. There is still controversy as to whether total inclusion is best for every special needs child.

Individualized Family Service Plan (IFSP)—required by the 1986 Education of the Handicapped Act Amendments for handicapped children under the age of three and their families; the IFSP, often developed by a transdisciplinary team that includes the parents, determines goals and objectives that build on the strengths of the child and family.

industry—the fourth stage of development described by Erik Erikson, starting at the end of the preschool years and lasting until puberty, in which the child focuses on development of competence.

initiative—the desire to do something by oneself. Identified as a developmental stage by Erik Erikson.

integrated curriculum—a curriculum in which concurrent learning is possible by focusing on more than one ability, developmental skill, or subject matter area at the same time in the same activity. It is believed to promote children's problem solving and aid the children's ability to see relationships among a variety of ideas or events.

interactionists—those who adhere to the theory that language develops through a combination of inborn factors and environmental influences.

instructional objectives—aims or goals, usually set for an individual child, that describe in very specific and observable terms what the child is expected to master.

journal—a written and/or pictorial or audio record of experiences, occurrences, observations, feelings, questions, work actions, reflective thoughts and other happenings during student teaching.

kindergarten—German word, literally meaning "garden for children," coined by Friedrich Froebel for his program for young children.

kinesthetic sense—information from the body's system that provides knowledge about the body, its parts, and its movement; involves the "feel" of movement without reference to visual or verbal cues.

L

latchkey children—school-aged children who, after school, return to an empty home because their parents are at work.

learning centers—also called activity or interest areas; where materials and equipment are combined around common activities (for instance, art, science, or language art).

learning disability—a condition thought to be associated with neurological dysfunction and characterized by difficulty in mastering a skill such as reading or numerical calculation.

least restrictive environment—a provision of Public Law 94-142 that handicapped children be placed in a program as close as possible to a setting designed for nonhandicapped children, while being able to meet each child's special needs.

lesson plans—the working documents from which the daily program is run, specifying directions for activities.

licensing—state regulations and rules for defined child care and child education programs enacted by state law.

licensure—the official recognition by a state agency that an individual or program has met certain qualifications specified by the state and is, therefore, approved to practice in an occupation as a professional or lawfully operate a program.

logical consequences—Rudolf Dreikurs' technique of specific outcomes that follow certain behaviors and are mutually agreed upon by teacher and children or students.

manipulatives—toys and materials that require the use of the fingers and hands, for instance, puzzles, beads, and pegboards.

Maslow's Hierarchy of Needs—a theorical position which attempts to identify human needs and motivations. It describes the consequences of need fulfillment and the consequences of unmet needs on growth.

materials—the smaller, often expendable items used in early childhood programs that are replaced and replenished frequently.

mediation—a process through which a third party assists the disputants in finding a mutually acceptable solution. In mediation, the role of the third party is to assist disputants in considering or exploring all areas in

mentoring—guidance by an experienced and trusted teacher who is frequently paired with a new and inexperienced teacher or aide, and who assists the new teacher with ideas and advice.

mission—a goal or goals an individual or group sets out to perform or accomplish.

modeling—in social learning theory, the process of imitating a model.

Montessori equipment—early childhood learning materials derived from and part of the Montessori approach.

morality—characterized by words such as right, ought to be, just and fair.

narrative—an account of events, experiences, or the like seen through one's own eyes or those of another.

National Association for the Education of Young Children (NAEYC)—largest American early childhood professional organization, which deals with issues of children from birth to age eight and those who work with young children.

nativist—one who adheres to the theory that children are born with biological dispositions for learning that unfold or mature in a natural way and with little outside direction.

negotiation—direct talk among the parties of a conflict, conducted with the goal of achieving a resolution.

nurturist—one who adheres to the theory that the minds of children are blank or unformed and need educational input or direct instruction in order to develop and "output" knowledge and appropriate behavior. Knowledge is felt to be received through the senses from outside the individual.

objectives—aims; specific interpretations of general goals, providing a practical and directive tool for day-to-day program planning.

observable behavior—actions that can be seen rather than those that are inferred.

observation—the process of learning that comes from watching, noting the behavior of, and imitating models.

one-day wonders—preplanned and often prepackaged collections of materials that student teachers can easily set up or use on the spur of the moment to engage young children.

onlooking play—according to Parten, standing to the side of a room or play yard and observing the action of others but not taking part.

parallel play—according to Parten, one child playing next to another but using different materials and not interacting.

parent-cooperatives—programs staffed by one professional teacher and a rotating staff of parents

parent education—programs aimed at enhancing parent-child relations and improving parenting competence.

parent-teacher conference—a one-on-one interaction between the teacher and the child's parent(s).

pathogen—any disease-producing agent such as a virus, bacterium or other micro-organism.

performance-based program—a professional preparation program that systematically gathers, analyzes, and uses data for self-improvement and advisement of adults or children.

practice play—according to Piaget, performing the same task over and over again until a sense of mastery is achieved.

preoperational stage—Piaget's period covering the preschool years.

privileged information—facts or data possessed by an individual of a special group granted access to knowledge through their employment as educators.

professional—individual engaged in an occupation considered a learned profession such as law or medicine. In this text, the field of education.

professional portfolio—a representative collection of your student teacher accomplishments.

project approach—an instructional method that encourages children to investigate a topic. It can be undertaken by a small group, whole class, or an individual child. A key feature of a project is using research to find answers to questions.

psychosocial theory—the branch of psychology founded by Erik Erikson, in which development is described in terms of eight stages that span childhood and adulthood, each offering opportunities for personality growth and development.

PTA/PTO—Initials given to a Parent-Teacher Association or Parent-Teacher Organization.

rating scale—an assessment of specific skills or concepts that are rated on some qualitative dimension of excellence or accomplishment.

reciprocity—a policy between states (or other entities) by which advantages and privileges (credentials, training, certification) are granted (or accepted) by both states.

reflective assessment—a thoughtful evaluation process which analyzes all aspects of early childhood teachers competence and professionalism. Conducted to increase growth of skills and abilities.

reflective teaching—a serious effort to thoughtfully question teaching practices, perceptions, actions, feelings, values, cultural biases, and other features associated with the care and education of young children.

reinforcement—in behavioral theory, any response that follows a behavior that encourages repetition of that behavior

reliability—a measure or a test indicating that the test is stable and consistent, to ensure that changes in score are due to the child, not the test.

role model—a person whose behavior is imitated by others.

scaffolding—a teaching technique helpful in promoting language, understanding, and child solutions, that may include supportive and responsive teacher conversation and actions following child-initiated behavior.

schedule—a planned series of happenings for a specific time period, to accommodate needs and goals.

self-concepts—perceptions and feelings children may have about themselves, gathered largely from how the important people in their world respond to them.

self-control—restraint exercised over one's own impulses, emotions, or desires.

self-esteem—children's evaluation of their worth in positive or negative terms.

sensorimotor stage—Piaget's period covering infancy.

separation anxiety—emotional difficulty experienced by some young children when leaving their mothers or other care providers.

signing—also called signaling; refers to infant and toddler nonverbal communication attempts such as pointing, rubbing eyes, or other hand and body movements and actions that send a message to caregivers.

skill-based model—refers to a curriculum model that identifies specific physical, social, or intellectual knowledge, skills, goals, or objectives, and then plans learning activities that promote the attainment of expected child behavior, information, or action.

skills—the ability to use content, professional, and pedagogical knowledge effectively and readily in diverse teaching situations to promote child learning.

software—the "instructions" that direct a computer to perform an activity, usually stored on a disk or directly in the computer; many such programs are available for young children.

solitary play—according to Parten, playing by oneself.

specific behavioral objectives—clearly describes observable behavior, the situation in which it will occur, and the exact outcome or the criteria of successful performance.

staff development—a term that can be applied to all experiences that aid staff in improving their work with children, families, or others.

Stanford-Binet Intelligence Scale—a widely used test that yields an intelligence quotient (IQ).

stereotype—a simplified conception or image of a person or group based on race, ethnicity, religion, gender or sexual orientation.

stress—internal or external demand on a person's ability to adapt.

sudden infant death syndrome (SIDS)—where death of an infant occurs generally during the first three months of life and for which there is no known cause.

summative evaluation—an assessment that follows a specific lesson or unit to evaluate whether the children have met the teacher's or district's objectives.

symbolic play—according to Piaget, using materials in play for a different purpose than the usual, for example, pretending that a block is a truck.

symbolic representation—the ability acquired by young children to use mental images to stand for something else.

syntax—involves the grammatical rules that govern the structure of sentences.

T

teacher-dominion (directed) instruction—educational practice that is characterized by teacher-dominated lessons or activities that the teacher decides are necessary for child growth or learning, as opposed to child discovery experiences or methods.

teacher-pupil ratio—the number of children supervised by each teacher in charge.

team teaching—an approach that involves coteaching in which status and responsibility are equal rather than having a pyramid structure of authority, with one person in charge and others subordinate.

temperaments—children's inborn characteristics such as regularity, adaptability, and other dispositions that affect behavior.

tenure—status granted to an employee indicating that the position is permanent.

terminating statements—an ending summary or recap of what has been discovered, discussed, experienced, enjoyed, and so on, after a learning activity.

thematic teaching and instruction—a theme approach to child program planning including theme identification, environmental needs, activities, presentation, and evaluation, usually designed for a selected period of study. It can encompass a wide range of curriculum areas including art, music, mathematics, language, science, motor, social and other development opportunities.

theme approach—a popular child program planning approach that involves a course of study with identified child activities focused on one subject, idea, or skill such as butterflies, friendship, biking, or a picture book.

time out—a brief social isolation and temporary suspension of usual activity used at times, by some educators to decrease young children's undesirable behavior.

time sampling—a quantitative measure or count of how often a specific behavior occurs within a given amount of time.

transition statement—planned verbalization that moves young children from one activity to another.

trust—the first stage of development described by Erik Erikson, occurring during infancy, in which the child's needs should be met consistently and predictably.

values—what an individual or group of individuals believe to be intrinsically worthwhile or desirable, and are prized for themselves such as beauty, honesty, justice, respect for others and /or the environment and so on.

work sampling system—Samuel Meisel's alternative method of gathering reliable information about young children, using a combination of observations, checklists, portfolios, and summary reports.

"you" message—Thomas Gordon's term for a response to a child's behavior that focuses on the child's character (usually in negative terms) rather than on how the adult feels.

zone of proximal development (ZPD)—in Vygotsky's theory, this zone represents tasks a child cannot yet do by herself but that she can accomplish with the support of an older child or adult.

INDEX

Note: page numbers followed by f denote figures

D